The Female Eunuch

The Obstacle Race: The Fortunes of Women Painters
and Their Work

Sex and Destiny: The Politics of Human Fertility

Shakespeare

The Madwoman's Underclothes: Essays and
Occasional Writings, 1968–85

Kissing the Rod: An Anthology of Seventeenth-
Century Women's Verse (ed., with S. Hastings,
J. Medoff, M. Sansone)

Daddy, We Hardly Knew You

The Uncollected Verse of Aphra Behn (ed.)

The Change: Women, Ageing and the Menopause

The Collected Works of Katherine Philips, the Matchless Orinda, Vol. III: The Translations (ed., with
R. Little)

SLIP-SHOD SIBYLS

RECOGNITION, REJECTION AND THE WOMAN POET

GERMAINE GREER

VIKING

VIKING

Published by the Penguin Group
Penguin Books Ltd, 27 Wrights Lane, London w8 5tz, England
Penguin Books USA Inc., 375 Hudson Street, New York, New York 10014, USA
Penguin Books Australia Ltd, Ringwood, Victoria, Australia
Penguin Books Canada Ltd, 10 Alcorn Avenue, Toronto, Ontario, Canada m4v 3b2
Penguin Books (NZ) Ltd, 182–190 Wairau Road, Auckland 10, New Zealand

Penguin Books Ltd, Registered Offices: Harmondsworth, Middlesex, England

First published 1995
1 3 5 7 9 10 8 6 4 2
First edition

Copyright © Germaine Greer, 1995
The moral right of the author has been asserted

Set in 11/13·75 pt Monotype Bembo
Set by Datix International Limited, Bungay, Suffolk
Printed in Great Britain by Clays Ltd, St Ives plc

A CIP catalogue record for this book is available from the British Library

ISBN 0–670–84914–6

In memoriam

M. C. BRADBROOK
1909–1993

CONTENTS

ACKNOWLEDGEMENTS

The author wishes to thank Carol Horne, Catherine Blyth, Susan Hastings, Dr Jes Medoff, Mary Ann O'Donnell, John Kerrigan, Dr Jonathan Scott, James Raven, Dr Helen Small, Hannah Fink, Jeremy Maule, Dr Peter Beal, the late Robert Latham, Professor Janet Todd, Robin Myers, Dr Peter Adamson, Jean Gooder, Dr Mary Beard, Dr Ruth Little, Tom Morris, Dr Peter Cochrane, John Byrne, Dr Paul McHugh, Lisa Barboni, her erstwhile colleagues at the University of Tulsa, the staff of Cambridge University Library, of Newnham College Library, of the Library of the Classics Faculty, University of Cambridge, of the Biblioteca Marciana in Venice, and those struggling on at the British Library in these dark days, and, for their patience and perseverance under pressure, Judith Flanders and Peter Carson of Penguin Books.

For permission to reprint copyright extracts, the following copyright holders are gratefully acknowledged: for Robin Hyde, to Derek Challis and Oxford University Press; for Ingrid Jonker, to the Ingrid Jonker Trust; for Christine de Pisan, to Persea Books, Inc., New York; for Kathleen Raine, to the author; for Sara Teasdale, to Scribner, a division of Simon & Schuster, Inc. (Macmillan & Company); for Anne Sexton, to Sterling Lord Litcristin; for Marina Tsvetaeva, to Rogers, Coleridge and White, and Elaine Feinstein; and for Anna Wickham, to Random House UK Ltd.

Every effort has been made to trace or contact all rights holders. The publishers will be glad to make good any omissions brought to their attention.

PROLOGUE

The women who enjoyed fame as poets before the twentieth century form a curious group. They dared greatly, so greatly that we might wonder if they had delusions of grandeur. When an unschooled, almost unlettered female begins to express herself in verse, she delivers herself up to the best and the worst of which the masculine literary establishment is capable. She may be humoured, she may excite genuine wonder and admiration, she will certainly be exploited. If it were true that poetic females could not find publishers, no poetry by women would have survived and there would be no head-scratching about which women's work to include in academic curricula because there would have been no work to study. The dilemma of the student of poetry who is also passionately interested in women is that she has to find value in a mass of work that she knows to be inferior. If women had struggled fruitlessly to find publishers and to call the fact of their existence to the attention of the cultural establishment, they would have partaken of the common lot of all groups without connections among the élite, and it would not be at all easy to determine the extent to which their difficulties in finding recognition had been directly caused by the fact of their sex. The fact of their sex certainly prevented middle-class women from acquiring the same kind of education as was available to men of the same class, but the usefulness of that education to the poet is far from obvious. No male poet becomes great by merely following the rules. If we ask ourselves why we have no female Blake, for example, we will have to probe deeper, beyond questions of literacy or privilege or patronage or support or even recognition. Homer and Milton were blind; can we claim that being female is a worse handicap than being blind?

Rooms of one's own and adequate payment for work done are inaccessible to all the poor and the miseducated and the born-without-clout. Even in our own days of multifarious and competitive publishing, it is a far from simple matter to find a constructive reader for novels and poems by unknowns. It is far too great a strain upon credulous optimism to believe that what does get published and reviewed is the right part of the iceberg. It might be tempting for a woman sending off her poems to publisher after publisher to ascribe her failure to the chauvinism of male editors. There are certainly chauvinistic editors, who announce that what they are looking at is not poetry because it does not resemble their own poetry and the poetry of their friends, who half-consciously protect their own clique or 'school', but there are female chauvinist editors as well. Just how much of what poetry publishers print these days will be read fifty years from now is an impenetrable mystery.

Nowadays a poet is expected to have an individual voice. There are no rules which she can find security in obeying, no bag of tricks that she is expected to master. She has however to ask herself the one question that concerned Emily Dickinson: whether her poems live. There is no way of knowing whether they do or not until they have outlived the moment and the fashion that prevailed when they were born and their connection with the poet as a living figure on the literary scene. Poetry is now a special-interest area, not as big as food, not as small as ice-dancing, maybe about the size of ballroom dancing. The practitioners of poetry probably outnumber the readers of poetry; in the United States the number of people registered for tax purposes as poets is more than a hundred times the number of the average print run of a book of poems. Hundreds of poems turn up in my mailbag every year, many written by people who have read little or nothing of other poets' work. This is the background against which women have finally emerged as poets rather than poetesses. Shulamith Firestone said that when women and gays took over any field of human activity it was a sign that it no longer counted. As long as it counted, the male establishment kept marauding minorities out. Teachers of English literature have to go on believing that poetry is the highest form of human expression and that the text is worth all the sacrifices made for it, but there is another view that says no text, however incandescent, is worth a single human life. Many of the people who destroyed their own lives and cannibalized other people's because they believed that they had a gift were quite wrong. The doors of perception that they imagined that they were struggling through were a cynical fiction. The ideology of alcohol and inspiration, of drug-induced hallucination as vision, was mere sales talk.

It is not poetry but advertising that is the literary form of the late twentieth century. The most successful poem of my generation was probably

> Eat a
> Extra
> Egg a
> Day

and written by a woman. This is a poem that required neither grant nor lottery to finance its publication, a poem that not only earned its own living but with the energy packed into its sixteen characters generated a vast amount of commercial activity. To understand whether it was 'Art' or not, we would have to look at its full manifestation in film, video, billboard, print and radio. Then too we would understand 'text as magic'.

A teacher of poetry, rather, of the reading of poetry, is not allowed to say that she considers her specialty to be on a par with ballroom dancing. Faith in poetry as the acme of human creative expression is an absolute requirement of any who choose to study it; the person who comes to the conclusion that poets have been given too much honour in the recent past had better keep it to herself. In large measure it is women who have deified the poet; it was women who fainted when Byron came into a room, who looked for signs of superhumanity in the brow of Wordsworth and grieved over the world-woe engraved in Tennyson's cheeks. The more women adored poetry, the less able they were to write it. From being more or less practical and external, the obstacles in the path of the woman who wanted to write songs for others to sing became progressively internalized. It is less crucial for women to work out how men did this to women than it is to assess the extent to which women did this to themselves.

We can know nothing of the women who would have written poetry if they had been taught to write. We do know that for hundreds of years women put their children to sleep with lullabies that nobody thought to write down. Those lullabies were almost certainly traditional, but each mother would have invented her own verses so that she could relate her song to the experiences of her child's day. The pattern of such female creative activity is that everybody does it, some do it better than others but nobody expects credit for it. People did not queue around the block to hear Joan Warblewell put her babies to sleep. Sufficient unto the day were her compositions; she did not think to inflict her outworn and by then incomprehensible songs on her great-grandchildren's great-grand-children, still less to insist that her successors sing them exactly as she made them up. Women had their poetry, and it was probably rather like the 'ballad-thinking' that Wordsworth wanted so much to revive. Interestingly, one of the few poems Dorothy Wordsworth put her name to is a lullaby, or perhaps an epitaph for the lullaby.

> The days are cold, the nights are long,
> The north wind sings a doleful song;
> Then hush again upon my breast;
> All merry things are now at rest,
>   Save thee, my pretty Love! [etc.]

The fewer the women who could read and write, the less they feared to compete with men in making poetry and the less men feared their making it. It may seem paradoxical to argue that women poets of the Renaissance were more likely to write good poetry than women of later eras when we know that they were less likely to live to adulthood and to survive repeated pregnancy and childbirth; nevertheless, it is true. Neither Marie de France in the twelfth century nor the Countess of Pembroke at the end of the sixteenth was perplexed by any sense of inappropriateness in the fact that she wrote verse, or embarrassment at the thought that anyone would read it; both were sophisticated artificers who set themselves problems and worked to resolve them without the archness and self-consciousness of a later generation. The difference was twofold: it derived both from the way they and their contemporaries thought about women and from the way they thought about poetry.

My exploration of some of the problems presented by the woman poet begins with the notion of inspiration that underlies the distinction that is often made between poetry (the real thing) and mere verse. Anyone may versify, and the results may be interesting and entertain-ing, but only the poet can utter poetry. The correlative used for the condition in which the poet eclipsed the versifier was the image of the poet in mystic union with the muse who entered him, as it were, fertilizing his imagination and making possible the development of the living poem. Such a schema presupposes male poet and female fecundator, in symmetrical opposition to the physical pairing of female gestatrix and male fecundator. There is no obvious reason why it should, for the Muses were themselves active artificers and did not merely activate others, but there is no question, not only that poet is always male and muse always female when this account of inspiration is given, but that conscious efforts to weaken this gender-specificity seem to be ineffectual. If women themselves internalize such a notion of inspiration, and it is hard to see how they could avoid it, especially if they do not understand that it is merely a device and used ironically as often as not, there is no way that they can make sense of their own activity. Either they must impersonate the muse herself or impersonate the male poet. Impersonation of the muse leads to carelessness disguised as rhapsody; impersonation of the male leads to bombast and literature about literature. There is much to be said for ditching the whole schema and relocating creative effort in the individual personality but, again, women have special problems in demanding the kind of attention that the male creative artist assumes as his right.

One way of crawling out from under the oppressive poet–muse construct is to see oneself as a creature of a different kind, not a poet but a poet-ess. The poetess accepts that she must display characteristics associated with femininity, such as delicacy, modesty, charm, domesticity, hypersensitivity and piety, as well as the filial, sororal and maternal affections. What the poetess does not aspire to is the revelation of gut truths of womanhood, or any negative feelings of rage, contempt, protest, despair or disbelief. The excesses of poetesshood include astonishingly equable though at the same time sentimental poems on all kinds of death, including lingering descriptions of the deaths of infants and small children in which there is never a hint of the agony of child loss which in truth drove some women mad. Here is Mehetabel Wright, all of whose children miscarried or died in early infancy, from lead poisoning she thought, her loathed husband being a plumber:

> Drooping sweetness! verdant Flower!
> Blooming, withering in an hour!

Ere thy gentle breast sustains
Latest, fiercest, mortal pains,
Hear a suppliant! Let me be
Partner in thy destiny!

Exclamation points hang about the lines like bobbins on pillow lace, but they are not enough to confer energy. The imagination is on hold, or the word 'verdant' would have been rejected; apostrophizing the infant as if it had power over life and death seems verily bizarre. The poetess typically presents a sanitized version of herself; she and her poetry are deodorized, depilated and submissive. The successful poetess emerges as one of the architects of femininity; she is encouraged to set forth the feminine ideal and she is rewarded for doing so. The poetess is seldom aware that the distinguishing characteristic of poetry is ambiguity; sometimes beneath the oily surface of a poetess's work the reader can discern the swell of troubled waters, a suggestion of bitterness so densely encoded that we cannot be sure that the poetess recognized it herself.

As poetesses have constructed femininity in their own censorship of their works, they have also contributed to the construction of masculinity by writing in a masculine voice of the affairs of men. In explaining this novel hypothesis I have spent perhaps too much time in describing what English culture was like when masculinity as we understand it was only a phase of maleness and the area of intersexual overlap in emotional and sexual affairs very much greater. This was also the greatest age of English poetry, and an age when women – or rather ladies – could write with much less self-consciousness and much greater honesty than they were able to do in any subsequent era before our own.

Any general discussion of women poets has to engage with the problem of Sappho. It is first necessary to explain that there is virtually no text. All estimations of the nature of Sappho's achievement have more to do with the politics of contemporary poetry than anything that was actually going on 2,600 years ago. It seems that Sappho was a professional poet much as the Muses were, who produced works for ceremonial occasions and perhaps performed them too. A persistent tendency to construe all known fragments, most of which are corrupt, as relating to the poet's life rather than the lives of her invented personae, has resulted in confusion about her sexual orientation, her love objects and whether she actually jumped off the Leucadian rock for love of a mythical figure. The chief source of information about her is the Ovidian monologue called the *Epistula Sapphus* which avails itself of some documentary information that has only recently come to light and may be in part historical but is in no sense authentic. All kinds of commentators have manipulated the Sappho figure in wildly contrasting ways. Women who love poetry are left with the sad conviction that a great woman poet lived and worked on Lesbos but all we have left of her is a footprint in the sand. The rest is disingenuous speculation.

Scholars who struggle to get women poets admitted to the 'canon', as the corpus of poets studied by undergraduates is generally known, have been stymied in the past by a lack of reliable texts. A great deal of work is being done, without sufficient support, to establish texts for the most important women poets. If we ask ourselves whether the texts as we have them actually represent what our poet wrote, we are obliged to answer that we simply do not know. In the case of Emily Dickinson, the world was happy to have a highly edited text, which had been completely repunctuated, until a body of scholars produced an edition based on the poet's autograph, which transformed our understanding of how Dickinson wrote and how she should be read. If we try to use the same procedures of bibliograhical and textual investigation on poets like Katherine Philips, the 'Matchless Orinda', the texts that we have begin to fall apart in our hands. For most women poets we do not have copies of works in their own hand-writing, let alone examples of work in progress, with corrections and emendations. For Aphra Behn, a figure of overriding importance, we have not a single literary text of her own hand. We cannot establish her actual authorship of any poem or play. The Sappho problem continues to afflict us here, because the figures of these important women interest us more than what they wrote, and we tend to present them as kindred spirits without knowing whether they were or not. Scholarly ethics require that we try a great deal harder to get at the truth about them. Only when we understand their circumstances can we arrive at a correct assessment of their achievement.

Most views of the life of Aphra Behn have been triumphalist. She has been seen as the intimate friend of the greatest wits and beauties of her age, hobnobbing with dukes and royal mistresses, when we do not know if she had a gown to go out in, or whether she sat like many a male hack in her nightgown frantically making up the sheets so that the bookseller would give her just enough money to pay her landlord, get her clothes out of pawn and stave off debtors' prison for another week or two. The reality of most professional writers' lives is unremitting, solitary work and, at least in the last years of her life, Aphra Behn was no exception. If my investigation of the relationship between Thomas Killigrew's *Thomaso* and Behn's most successful play, *The Rover*, is on the right track, Behn was working as an amanuensis and hired hack as early as the 1650s. She may have been doing other things as well. She may have had a protector or a series of protectors. Other women who worked 'in garret high' had gentlemen callers. Scrivening may have been a family business and there may have been more than one 'Madam Behn', Anne, Astraea, Aphra or whoever.

Anne Wharton is a case of a woman poet who was falsely represented to the world as a pious and demure poetess when she was a female libertine and a devoted follower of her half-uncle, the poet Rochester. It has taken ten years of hard work to trace the poet through the maze of Chancery actions which are the principal documentation of her life and to assemble a corpus of work that at present amounts to one verse play and twenty-four poems. Anne Finch, Countess of Winchilsea, was also misrepresented by Wordsworth, who valued her principally because he saw her as a harbinger for himself. Wordsworth not only selected passages from her work, but tinkered with what he selected in order to divorce her from her social context and present her as a pre-Romantic. Wharton's works are about to appear in a new critical edition; Finch, whose work has been published in two halves, eighty years apart, awaits an editor.

The works of Letitia Elizabeth Landon are so voluminous that no publisher would today invest the enormous amount that it would cost to reprint them, especially in view of the limited readership that they would be likely to attract. Her literary journalism alone would fill many volumes, if an editor could be sure which of hundreds of unsigned reviews were by her. There would be some point in tracing out the literary factionalism of her day in order to find out whom L. E. L. offended and who was likely to have initiated the whispering campaign that became a shout. Hers is the most obvious case of a young and attractive woman being seduced into a kind of exhibition-ism for which conventional society would exact a lingering and relentless punishment. There are others, perhaps many others. L. E. L.'s champions have in the past defended her from the imputations of immorality, and their support has been ineffective, because the gossip was published and never refuted. A late twentieth-century approach should probably admit the indiscretion and at the same time diagnose the masculine dynamic that built and destroyed the phenomenon of L. E. L.

Christina Rossetti is at present the most studied of the Victorian women poets; inevitably perhaps, more attention has been given to the how than the what of her poetry. While deploring the kind of attention that is more concerned with the person of the poet than the poetry, especially when the poetry is treated as autobiography, it is important to distinguish Rossetti's sham utterances from her real poetry, the poetess from the woman poet. What is offered here is the beginning of an analysis of Rossetti's relationship with her brother, who, like so many other men in the history of women's poetry, came between the poet and her work. She was a far better poet than he, but she never corrected his work. When he made suggestions about hers, she followed them. Women poets have always suffered male interference, often gladly, as perhaps in the case of Rossetti. Whether a father encouraged or banned versifying, he affected his daughter's work. If she wrote to please him she perpetrated one kind of falsehood; if she wrote to defy him she perpetrated another. The man who corrected a woman's work clearly falsified it, if only by presenting it as more literate than it was, or more conventional. Most often the men who came between women poets and their work were other poets, whose work so impressed the women that, at the same time that they imitated it, they denied themselves any possibility of equalling, let alone eclipsing it.

The other-directedness of the woman poet explains the constant presence on the literary scene ever since the days of Queen Anne of a small group of females who enjoyed the most dazzling literary prestige during their lifetimes only to be extinguished utterly as far as posterity was concerned. The phenomenon has been repeated several times in the twentieth century. In 1972 Professor Helen Gardner dropped from *The New Oxford Book of English Verse* nearly all the women who had appeared in the *The Oxford Book of English Verse* as revised by Sir Arthur Quiller-Couch in 1939, namely Katherine Philips, Grisell Baillie, Jane Elliot, Isobel Pagan, Anna Laetitia Barbauld, Fanny Greville, Lady Anne Lindsay, Joanna Baillie, Mary

Lamb, Carolina, Lady Nairne, Felicia Hemans, Caroline Norton, Jean Ingelow, Emily Lawless, Dora Sigerson, Margaret L. Woods, Agnes Mary Frances Duclaux, Mary Elizabeth Coleridge, May Probyn, Katherine Tynan Hinkson and Frances Bannerman. Aphra Behn, Emily Brontë, Elizabeth Barrett Browning, Christina Rossetti and Alice Meynell survived the cull and were joined by new arrivals Edith Sitwell, Kathleen Raine, Anne Ridler and Stevie Smith. Nowadays the work of Ridler and Raine is unlikely to be reprinted even in anthologies of women's work, though both are still living, and Sitwell's status as an innovator has been challenged.

It would be invidious to suggest that Professor Gardner eliminated so many women from the official repository of the nation's poetic heritage because she is anti-feminist. 'Q' could perhaps have been less offended if one had accused him of including work by May Probyn or Frances Bannerman because he was chivalrous, and therein lies the most insidious aspect of the attitude of the male cultural establishment to its gaggle of women, because it is not unbecoming for a gentleman to lie to a lady. Such lying is called compliment. Sir Arthur Quiller-Couch had reason to be wary of the suffragists among his readership, and in the case of choosing between poems that were initially much of a muchness, tended to select the poem by a woman rather than another. The presence of Lady Nairne, Lady Baillie, Isobel Pagan and Jane Elliot is explained by the importance that 'Q' gave to the Scottish ballad revival; Professor Gardner gives it far less importance and therefore drops them all. Both 'Q' and Professor Gardner claim that they have chosen the poems as far as possible on the grounds of excellence alone; in neither case would the anthologist claim to be establishing an absolute criterion, for both admitted that the pressure of contemporary critical standards and tastes must be yielded to.

What these wide differences in critical standards may represent is another variation of the flying-pig syndrome, for Professor Gardner and 'Q' do not tend to disagree anywhere near as much about the great bulk of inclusions. Of the male poets included by 'Q', Professor Gardner retains most; the major differences are accountable in view of her decision to include more satiric and didactic poetry, to exclude American poets, and by the tendency of all anthologizers to include a new and wide selection from the recent past. The exclusion of twenty-one out of the twenty-five women poets represented in the old *Oxford Book* represents the honest exercise of a cultivated critical faculty – although it should be pointed out that Professor Gardner shared the Oxbridge background of Raine and Ridler and may have unconsciously overvalued their work on that account. What is obvious is that by·including his twenty-five women, Sir Arthur Quiller-Couch was applying a double aesthetic standard almost as damaging in its insidious operation as the double moral standard.

The flying-pig or dancing-dog syndrome is the chain of misunderstanding and misrepresentation that is set off by the assumption that a woman active in the arts is performing some arduous and unnatural contortion of her personality. Dr Johnson explained that women preachers are like dogs walking on their hind legs; we are so surprised to find it being done at all that we do not expect it to be done well. Many of the women who dared to write verse were astonished at their own daring and as expectant of applause as the dancing dog. They were also as likely to crash as the flying pig. The longer they were kept aloft by the wonder of the public, the more shattering the eventual crash. The admiration of the public was not usually insincere, but it was clearly based in sexist assumptions; when the nine days were past, and the wonder faded, the sexist assumptions were all that remained. Systematic overestimation of an artist's work may have a worse effect upon her achievement in the long run than unimaginative carping would have. A writer's critical poise is delicately balanced: her own estimation of the degree to which she has realized her intention can be overborne by the opinions of others, especially if she is deeply impressed by the achievements and prestige of those who are flattering her. Creative women, happening upon literary celebrity without any supporting knowledge of the poetic tradition, can hardly be expected to take the extravagant praises of eminent men with equanimity. The struggle to write and publish is arduous for anybody; women who undertake it in isolation must have a strong conviction about their native ability to undertake it. Instant and exaggerated recognition can predictably cut short their progress towards excellence.

How Sir Walter Scott could have addressed these lines to Joanna Baillie is all but incomprehensible.

> That Avon's swans, while rang the grove
> With Montfort's hate and Basil's love, –
> Awakening at the inspired strain,
> Deemed their own Shakespeare lived again.

Whatever the swans may think of Mrs Baillie, human beings have been content not to read her plays once in 150 years, while Shakespeare has been read and played millions, perhaps hundreds of millions, of times. Scott can hardly have meant what he said, for it is impossible to mean an absurdity, but the swans' judgement was repeated by near contemporaries in no spirit of irony. To Rowton's massive rhetorical question –

> Have we not a Byron in Miss Landon, a Cowper in the Countess of Winchilsea, a Spenser in Mrs Tighe, a Goldsmith in Mrs Grant, a Johnson in Hannah More, a Wycherly in Mrs Centlivre, a Collins in Mrs Radcliffe, a Coleridge in Mrs Browning, a Wordsworth in Mary Howitt, a Scott (and more) in Mrs Baillie?

– the answer is no. There is no making sense of this kind of thing, no point in asking Rowton what point he could see in naming a set of female simulacra for an arbitrarily selected group of male poets. L. E. L. knew, none better, that she was not a Byron; the Countess of Winchilsea shared only depressive disorder with Cowper. Anne Grant, crippled widow of the Vicar of Laggan in Inverness-shire, supported herself by the proceeds of the publication of her poem *The Highlanders* in 1802, which not only displayed 'simple pathos' but, according to Rowton, was as 'warm, unaffected and homely' as Goldsmith's *Deserted Village*, written in the same metre forty years earlier. Mary Tighe plagiarized Keats rather than Spenser. What Rowton is really saying is that male poets accomplished what these women did and did it earlier; the women are all, with the exception of the Countess of Winchilsea, being ranked as followers, which also means that they lagged behind.

Rowton is simply careless; he has not paused to think whether Hannah More could ever be mistaken for Johnson, which she certainly could not, let alone whether she should. He is actually both puffing his own book, *The Female Poets of Great Britain*, and displaying his own chivalry. It was not chivalry however that prompted him to include samples of the work of Caroline Symonds, who died at the age of eleven and on whose tomb is inscribed a sonnet of her own, called 'The Blighted Rosebud'.

> Scarce had thy velvet lips imbibed the dew,
>   And nature hailed thee, infant queen of May,
>   Scarce saw thy opening bloom the sun's broad ray,
> And on the air its tender fragrance threw,
> When the north wind enamoured of thee grew,
>   And from his chilling kiss, thy charms decay, [etc.]

By including this, Rowton made clear that he really thought of all the rest as a freak-show. Professor Gardner could hardly have given an adequate idea of her assessment of the achievement of Kathleen Raine, Anne Ridler and Stevie Smith if she had included them shoulder to shoulder with the minor female poets in the earlier *Oxford Book*. Her exclusion of so much feminine poetry was in fact a more feminist act, for she has made clear that as a woman she will apply no other criterion to the work of women than the highest.

The title of this book is provocative and deliberately so. It is taken from *The Dunciad*, Book III, where it was applied to the muse of the King of Dunces, the mad poetical Sibyl who will transport him in imagination to the banks of Lethe, where the souls of the dull are dipped in oblivion.

> A slip-shod Sibyl led his steps along,
> In lofty madness meditating song,
> Her tresses staring from poetic dreams,
> And never washed, but in Castalia's streams.

The term is weighted with all the contempt expressed by literary men for literary women who took themselves seriously, who risked ridicule, exploitation and calumny because they thought they had something to say, and the contempt likewise meted out to the women who fooled around with poetry, who did not try hard enough or fell for the fiction that poetry can come easily. The more we know about the women who wrote poetry in English before 1900, the more we must realize that it is not a question of women poets having been ignored or obscured but of women's poetry remaining unwritten because women were disabled and deflected by the great tradition itself, while a select band of arbitrarily chosen token women, all young, beautiful and virtuous, were rewarded for their failures. Second-rate, dishonest, fake poetry is worse than no poetry at all. To insist on equal representation or positive discrimination so that She-poetry appears on syllabuses in our schools and universities is to continue the system of false accounting that produced the double standard in the first place. This not to say that we should not work at reclaiming women's work but simply that we should be aware that we are more likely to find heroines than poets. To award them the bays without pausing to consider whether they really were victors is to misunderstand both the desperateness of their struggles and the continuing dilemma of the woman who loves both women and poetry.

{ 1 }

THE MUSE

All civilizations distinguish between the realms of male and female and all allow areas of overlap, of non-sex-differentiated activity. Twentieth-century European culture inherited a notion of gender difference wider and more rigorously contrasting than any previous civilization had professed. Robert Graves expressed the twentieth-century paradigm succinctly in 'Man does, woman is'.

> Woman with her forests, moons, flowers, waters,
> And watchful fingers:
> We claim no magic comparable to hers –
> At best poets; at worst, sorcerers.

Graves's notion of the feminine is anything but novel. The earliest expression of such an extreme position can be found in the culminating vision of Goethe's *Faust*. Liszt repeated it with fitting sublimity in the 'Chorus Mysticus' for tenor and male choir that forms the climactic conclusion of his Faust Symphony of 1854:

> Alles vergängliche
> Ist nur ein Vergleichnis;
> Das Unzulängliche,
> Hier wird's Ereignis;
> Das Unbeschreibliche,
> Hier ist's getan;
> Das Ewig-Weibliche
> Zieht uns hinan.*

---

* These word-by-word translations are for the assistance of readers with a smattering of the language in question so that they can get the sound plus the sense of the lines. They are not

And in the 'Morning-Dream Interpretation Melody' with which Walther von Stolzing wins the prize in *Die Meistersinger*, Wagner presented his version of the praise of the *Ewig-Weibliche*. In giving his own account of the artist-personality, Freud, though unseduced by notions of the artist's *Übermenschlichkeit*, attempted to explain what appeared to his Viennese contemporaries to be obvious rather than to question the basic premise of the masculinity of the artist, when he described an artist as one who is beset by 'clamorous instinctual needs' for 'honour, power, riches and the love of women'.

The rhetoric of the eternal feminine is the obverse of the reality of the actual female. To endow women with angelic status (which doesn't exist) is to deny them human status (which does) and makes a nonsense of the individual woman's struggle for achievement. It is the purest irresponsibility to argue that a woman may be infantile, greedy, stupid, cruel, totally incapable of even reading or understanding the poetry that she inspires, and yet inspire great work and achieve undying fame, because her function is unconscious, instinctual, impersonal. Such a notion would justify woman's most idiotic behaviour by her femaleness, by an unthinking acquiescence to some atavistic rhythm which would have her eat her new-born children or cheat at cards.

> O why judge Myrrhina
> As though she were a man?
> She obeys a dark wisdom
> (As Eve did before her)
> Which never can fail . . .

Eve's dark wisdom is what is supposed to have destroyed the

---

meant to be readable. A readable translation of a poem is a new poem, usually a bad one. Square brackets indicate words added to help the English-speaking reader.

> All [that is] transitory
> Is but a semblance;
> The unsatisfactory
> Becomes our circumstance;
> The indescribable
> Here is accomplished;
> The eternal-feminine
> Draws us upward!

garden of Eden and brought suffering, death and hard labour into the world. For Robert Graves women represent a wisdom beyond intelligence, a sort of *Rassensinn*, concerned with the bloody verities of survival rather than pernickety questions of good and evil. The female represents the knowledge of the libido, which the male cannot penetrate by means of his conscious or his ego or still less his superego. The female evades his systems of classification and mocks him with the partiality of his understanding, fascinating him while she appals.

> The function of poetry is religious invocation of the Muse; its use is the experience of mixed exaltation and horror that her presence excites.

It is simply untrue that all, or even most, or even much, poetry invokes the muse. By this assertion, Graves relegates occasional poetry, satiric poetry and a good deal more besides to the second division of mere verse. Most poetry that mentions the muse does so ironically. Yet so much is true, that poetry stands in a special relation to the unsynthesized manifold, differing from prose not only by virtue of its rhythm but by virtue of its ambiguity, its mysteriousness, its incantatory function. Poetry exists partly to undermine the certainties of an accepted intellectual system, by opening a fissure of awareness at which the reality of the unconquered world may enter, disrupting mental filing systems and making it possible to understand creatively, and thereby extend and modify, what is. The poet makes; poetry does not explain. It is the function of prose to explain. Graves calls the conscious intellectual faculty, out of which poetry must be produced, masculine, and the unconscious realm of inexplicables, feminine. In doing so he is merely illustrating the sexual polarity that our culture has developed, a polarity that insists upon an extraordinary and mostly improper contrast between the spheres, attributes and capacities of male and female. Graves cannot be blamed for inventing such an oppressive ontology, although he could justly be charged with having an utterly uncritical and self-indulgent attitude towards it.

The concepts of male and female which Graves is using are signposts to elements in the topography of the poet's own mind and have no relevance whatever to women as whole people. The White Goddess represents no more nor less than the side of the poet's psyche that he has come to regard with exaltation and horror, the passive, mysterious swamp of the unconscious where none of the devices of classification or ordering by which man seeks to control the external world really applies. Elizabeth Sacks has pointed out that the popularity of the male-pregnancy metaphor in Renaissance accounts of the genesis of the work of art might correspond to 'womb-envy', affording 'an essential outlet for unconscious or repressed feminine elements in the masculine psyche'. If this is so, Robert Graves, by externalizing these elements as a White Goddess who dwells implacable in a distinct and mysterious realm of her own, creates of himself a fragile and unstable hypermasculine creature, a one-dimensional man. By confusing gender with selfhood he imprisons himself in a condition replete with anxiety.

As long as the female is unprovided with the male tools for controlling the universe, she may be ignorant, passive, emotional and instinctual, and furnish a handy metaphor for the pre-verbal spring of poetry. As soon as she is equipped to reason and articulate and seeks to participate in the activity of giving a conscious form to her experience, Graves has no option but to call her masculine. He is simply being consistent. If man does and woman is, then she who does is man. Again, such a position is merely traditional; every woman who has ever written two or three lines of sense has been complimented upon having a masculine intellect.

Though Graves traces the ancestry of his own notion of the muse in *The Greek Myths*, he demonstrates little insight into how his own exaggerated idea of the almighty muse could have developed out of the 'triple Goddess in her orgiastic aspect', who became the three mountain-goddesses who taught Hermes to divine the future by dancing pebbles in water and tripled again to become the nine Muses impanelled by Apollo to adjudicate between his own and Marsyas's playing of the flute. The Muses collected the limbs of dismembered Orpheus and buried them at the foot of Mount Olympus. The Muses sang more sweetly than the Sirens, whose wing-feathers were plundered to make them crowns, at the weddings of Cadmus and Harmony, Peleus and Thetis and the funeral of Achilles. The Muses taught Aristaeus the arts of healing and prophecy and the Sphinx the riddle which Oedipus eventually answered. The Muses stabled Pegasus, who made the spring of Hippocrene for them by striking the earth with his hoof. As teachers, performers and critics, the Muses were experts. In them doing and being would appear to be fused; though they may be direct descendants of the White Goddess, they traffic, not in 'dark wisdom', but in intelligence and expertise. The classic concept of the muse enables the female poet; the twentieth-century distortion of the classic scheme silences her.

The castration of the muse was effected when poets began to explain the conception of the work of art as the consequence of spiritual intercourse between the poet and his personal muse. The act of inspiring or 'breathing into' is a penetrative act; the female muse enacts a male function upon the receptive poet, who thus quickened goes on to utter the idea in physical form. Given classical ignorance of the existence of the ovum and belief that male seed was sufficient for impregnation, the role played by the muse as the begetter of poetry was more important than the poet's female functions of gestation and parturition. The title of 'muse' would therefore be far more flattering than the title of 'poet' – if only poet and muse were not aspects of the same person. Almost as soon as Homer had invoked the muse in serious fashion, poets began to use the convention mock-modestly, apologizing for their personal muses as lazy, slip-shod, barren or unlettered. The next stage in the castration of the muse was when the grand and distant divinity enthroned on Parnassus dwindled into the poet's love object. At first, when love was seen as the force that ruled all creation and the beloved as the emissary of divine love made flesh, it transcended gender. The Petrarchan version of platonic love furnished a convention in which women could function as poets without appearing to de-sex themselves or to masquerade as muses. As might be expected, Graves has little truck with such ideas, and is forced to jettison an intellectual system that has sustained European poetry for six hundred years.

> ... what is called Platonic love, the philosopher's escape from the power of the Goddess into intellectual homosexuality, was really Socratic love ... ideal homosexuality was a far more serious moral aberrancy – it was the male intellect trying to make itself self-sufficient.

Poetry is, of course, a matter of intellect; though the matter may be provided by the unconscious, the form must be forged and appre-hended by the conscious. Neither conscious nor unconscious is actually gendered, but Graves's anxiety forces him arbitrarily to gender both in order to identify himself as masculine. Neither Dante nor Petrarch suffered from this kind of anxiety. The sex of the platonic beloved was unimportant, except in so far as the lover had to deal harshly with his own reprobate desire to despoil the object of his love, struggling perpetually to transmute a mere appetite into something rarer and more deserving. Platonic love is eternal, and can have nothing to do with the periodicity of sexual desire. It must be disinterested so can admit no alloy of fear or hate, no 'expense of spirit'. In the struggle to achieve perfect love lies all the drama of Petrarch's *Canzoniere*; under the dazzle of Petrarch's ideal we can discern the murk of unconsciousness, all the more terrifying for being placed in such contrast. The white hart bends her soft eyes upon the hunter panting after her on the other side of the brook, turning aside the fell intent which would have defiled and destroyed her. Where Graves has to rouse the monster of savagery, Petrarch is aware of it already awake and alert, stalking a world in which physical strength and courage were crucial to survival.

The more chaotic and cruel the world, the more important it was to assert that it was ruled by love; love, as the force that was manifest in every natural process and every human act, was God. All love, of parents for children, of men for women or other men, of brothers, provided it was virtuous, was a manifestation of the empowering love of God. Nowhere in the Petrarchan tradition that ruled European poetry for more than three hundred years can we find anything that positively excludes the possibility that the poet is a woman or that the muse-beloved that she invokes is male; the sex of the beloved is irrelevant. In the pre-Petrarchan tradition, women did indeed pen love-poems; the names and some of the work of twenty Occitanian ladies who wrote very direct love poetry in the twelfth century have come down to us. Christine de Pisan wrote courtly love poems in the personae of both male and female, lover and beloved, endowing the male beloved with the transcendental attributes of every beloved:

> Bien doy louer Amours de ses bienfaits,
> Qui m'a donné ami si très parfait,
> Qu'en trestous lieux chacon loe ses fais
> Et sa beauté, sa grace et tout son fait,

Qu'il n'a en lui ne blasme ne meffait;
Dieu l'a partfaict en valour et en grace,
N'on ne pourroit mieulx vouloir par souhait;
Certes c'est cil qui tous les autres passe.*

Nevertheless, Graves might argue, as the love object, regardless of its biological sex, is rendered passive by the aggressive and conquista-dorial act of making a poem, it is feminized. In our world of gross sexual polarity no adult heterosexual man would feel comfortable about being praised in such terms by a woman. Literature students often object that the Petrarchan sonnet is anti-feminist, that the lady is an aesthetic construct, an unknown, and the sum of the poetry the exaltation and display of the poet's own intellect. This would be equally true if Petrarch had been a woman or if Laura had been a man. When love is platonic, the sex of the object of the love is immaterial. Conversely sexual relations may be had with the love object without nullifying the platonic nature of the sacramental love. A wife may address a husband whose relationship with her is a figure of God's relationship with His creation using the whole panoply of Petrarchan conceits. When the poet Ercole Strozzi was murdered shortly after his marriage with Barbara Torelli, she inscribed her love and grief in a sonnet:

Spenta è d'Amor la face, il dardo è rotto,
e l'arco e la faretra e ogni sua possa,
poiché ha morte crudel la pianta scossa,
a la cui ombra cheta io dormía sotto.

Deh, perché non poss'io la breve fossa
seco entrar dove hallo il destino condotto,
colui che a pena cinque giorni e otto
Amor legò pria della gran percossa?

* [It is] well [I] must praise Love for his kindnesses
Who has given me a friend so very perfect,
That in absolutely every place each praises his deeds
And his beauty, his grace and all his actions,
That he has not in him either blame nor misdeed
God has made him perfect in valour and in grace,
Nor one could better want by wishing;
Certain it is that he all the others surpasses.

Vorrei col foco mio quel freddo ghiaccio
intepidire, e rimpastar col pianto
la polve e ravvivarla a nuova vita;

e vorrei poscia, baldanzosa e ardita
mostrarlo a lui che ruppe il caro laccio,
e dirgli:– Amor, mostro crudel, può tanto.*

By prompting her to speak in this formal fashion, love and grief together empower the poet to project herself muse-like as the animator of her husband's ashes. In that she quickens the inert the poet's role is masculine, but the grief is wifely. Strozzi was the tree she slept beneath, now burned to ash as if by lightning; by warming the ashes with the fire of her love and moistening them with her tears, she would refashion him and breathe life into him. The image recalls God's creation of Adam, but it also suggests the housewifely activity of bread-making. Torelli's defiance of death by asserting the power of love also invokes the idea of fecundity. This sonnet, often anthologized, is so finished and its massive themes so cunningly balanced in the seamless Petrarchan idiom, that it cannot be a first attempt, but no other poems by Torelli have been identified.

It is rare for a woman poet to be at ease moving between masculine and feminine, aggressive and passive postures, especially when the subject matter is love. The Petrarchan mode, born as it was out of devotional and troubadour poetry, seems to have provided a unique vehicle for those few Renaissance women whose level of literacy was equal to writing verse. As Burckhardt says in an otherwise much too

---

* Extinguished is of Love the brand, the arrow is broken,
  and the bow and the quiver and each his might,
  because has cruel death the tree shaken
  in whose shade quiet I slept below.

  Ah, why cannot I the narrow pit
  with-him enter where has-him destiny led,
  he who barely five days and eight
  Love bound before the great shock?

  [I] would with fire mine that cold ice
  warm, and reknead with tears
  the dust and revive-it to new life;

  and would then, daring and valiant,
  show-him to him who broke the dear bond,
  and tell-him; – Love, monster cruel, can do so-much.

sanguine account of the female component of *Civilisation in the Renaissance*, 'if she were a poet, some powerful utterance of feeling, rather than the confidences of the novel or diary, were looked for . . .'

In emphasizing the comprehensiveness of the individual personality, Renaissance philosophers could build a way out of both biology and sexual politics. All human potentialities were present in all people, and became manifest according to the demands made upon them and the opportunities open to them. These circumstances are not to be explained as a result of women's contribution to the economies of the Italian city states or illustrated from the behaviour of either the merchant élites, who kept their womenfolk in seclusion, or the mass of the people, who relied on women's contribution as unpaid family labourers. The difference lies not in the treatment of women but in the Renaissance attitude to gender which does not seek to characterize femaleness itself as excluding women from intellectual activity. The kind of praise of great women and the excellence of their contribution to all the arts that they had the opportunity to study that Ariosto expresses in the *Orlando Furioso* was a Renaissance convention that died out when the notion of feminine accomplishment displaced the ideal of the woman of learning. Nevertheless it should be clearly understood that most cultures and most families never gave their women the opportunity to study any arts or sciences at all, the production and rearing of children having a far higher priority than any intellectual contribution, however distinguished. We need not be surprised, therefore, to find a high proportion of widows among the women who wrote Petrarchist poetry in the Renaissance.

Vittoria Colonna became a poet after the death of her husband in 1525. There was never any suggestion that her sonneteering was peculiar or conflicted in any way with her womanliness or her virtue. On the contrary, Colonna was held in high esteem by scholars like Valdes and Ochino; Michelangelo addressed sonnets and madrigals to her; the Emperor Charles V visited her house. Colonna celebrates her husband in much the same way that Dante celebrates Beatrice, as her leading light, her guide, her instructor. His influence on her life is as the influence of the sun in nature and God in creation. The kind of condescension that is evident in the treatment of the 'Matchless Orinda' by her male contemporaries is simply unthinkable in the face of Colonna's *gravitas*. It was not Colonna's rank that silenced any tendency to impertinence; the Duchess of Newcastle's higher rank did not protect her from ridicule. Not only was English society of the Restoration more provincial, more philistine, more snobbish and more sexist than Rome in the time of Michelangelo; the Duchess herself had virtually no education, and no acquaintance with anything like the intelligentsia that welcomed Colonna as an equal. To be sure, Colonna received her share of frigid hyperbolic compliment but it was the genuine medium of exchange, and not the kind of counterfeit in which Orrery was to pay Katherine Philips.

Colonna's contemporary Veronica Gambara is best known for her sonnet celebrating her husband's eyes:

> Occhi lucenti e belli,
> com'esser può che in un medesmo istante
> nascan da voi sí nove forme e tante?
> Lieti, mesti, superbi, umili, alteri
> vi mostrate in un punto, onde di speme
> e di timor m'empiete,
> e tanti effetti dolci, acerbi e fieri
> nel core arso per voi vengono insieme
> ad ognor che volete.
> Or poi che voi mia vita e morte sete
> occhi felici, occhi beati e cari,
> siate sempre sereni, allegri e chiari.*

Gambara's confidence in writing about her husband is not simply a matter of the scope afforded by the Petrarchan convention. When her husband died in 1518, she took over the government of Correggio. Twenty years later, when she had to drive back the forces of the condottiere Galeotto della Pico della Mirandola, she took command

---

* Eyes shining and lovely
  how be can [it] be that in a selfsame instant
  are born from you such new forms and so many?
  Gay, lowering, haughty, lowly, lofty
  [you] yourselves show at one instant, thus with hope
  and with fear [you] me fill,
  and so many effects, sweet, bitter and proud
  in the heart aflame for you come all at once
  at any time that [you] wish.
  Now because you my life and death are,
  eyes happy, eyes blessed and dear,
  be always calm, joyous and clear.

of the army. Neither the assumption of authority nor the exercise of military power was seen to unsex her. As a woman she wrote, as a woman she ruled and as a woman she fought. It might be argued that the relative fluidity of female roles was typical of Italy rather than the sixteenth century; the speeches of Elizabeth I could be taken to imply that less tolerance of female authority was to be expected in England than in France or Italy in the same epoch. Some would argue that gender distinctions in Protestant Europe are still wider and deeper than they are in the south. Actual restriction of the sphere of women's activities indicates fear of what they can do rather than a conviction that they can do nothing, and a narrower gender gap than permissiveness implies. English women have always been famous in Europe for their degree of relative freedom, but then English women have always been encouraged to regard themselves as passionless. Conversely, if women are never allowed to write poetry, there is no point in convincing them that they cannot. If they never acquire enough education to write anything, there is no need to undermine their attempts by fake praise. It is only when women begin to make inroads on the male preserve that sophisticated strategies of devaluation begin to be employed.

Though neither Colonna nor Gambara was belittled for writing about a beloved man, their Venetian contemporary Gaspara Stampa, *virtuosa* and courtesan, was not so fortunate, perhaps because, in celebrating her unrequited love for Collaltino de Collalto, she takes the conceits to lengths that suggest idolatrous obsession. After the death of Stampa's father in 1531, her mother opened their house in Venice as a *ridotto*. The principal attractions were the widow's learned and beautiful daughters, Gaspara and Cassandra, both of whom could sing and play as well as any in Venice. Parabosco wrote sonnets to Gaspara; Sansovino dedicated his *Ragionamento d'Amore* to her; she corresponded with Alamanni. The most distinguished literati of Venice, by 1540 the established centre of Italian literary publishing and criticism, frequented the Stampa salon, where the highest standards of dress, behaviour and conversation were observed, under the tutelage of Sperone Speroni and Giovanni della Casa. Stampa was at the pinnacle of her profession as *virtuosa* and *cortigiana onesta* when disaster struck. She fell in love. The man she fell in love with had everything, birth, looks, riches, taste and culture: 'In all his ways and in his every deed there emanate love, grace and learning.'

> Chi vuol conoscer, donne, il mio signore,
> miri un signor di vago e dolce aspetto,
> giovane d'anni e vecchio d'intelletto,
> imagin de la gloria e del valore:
>
> di pelo biondo, e di vivo colore,
> di persona alta e spazioso petto,
> e finalmente in ogni opra perfetto,
> fuor ch'un poco (oimè lassa) empio in amore.*

There was never any question of marriage; Collalto appears to have entered into some kind of intimacy and then to have withdrawn, at first as the demands of his military career dictated and then totally. In 1549 Stampa collected some of her *Rime* for presentation to Collalto, prefaced by a letter, '*Allo illustre mio signore*', expressing the hope that seeing her sonnets gathered together would persuade him to have pity on her. The presentation of poems as documents illustrating an actual relationship marks a departure from the spirit of the Petrarchist canon, the more striking in view of Stampa's replication of the Petrarchan form, vocabulary and conventions. The editor of the posthumous publication of her *Rime* in 1554 is supposed to have been her sister. It may well have been she or the publisher who decided to include the letter and possibly even composed it, as an aid to merchandising the publication. From such beginnings it was inevitable that Stampa would become a heroine of other people's fictions: in the nineteenth century a series of spurious letters traced the course of the *Unhappy Love of Gaspara Stampa*; poems and plays were composed on the theme of her abused innocence. Then less sentimental research revealed the likelihood of her having been a professional entertainer and the Venetian equivalent of a high-class call girl.

---

* Who would know, ladies, my lord,
　　picture a gentleman of sweet and lovely aspect,
　　young in years and old in intellect,
　　image of glory and of worth;

　　of hair blond, and of lively colouring,
　　of person tall and broad [of] chest,
　　and finally in every work perfect,
　　except a little (ay me weary) impious in love.

It was the woman and not the poet who enchanted critics and artists alike. Stampa personified a myth, whether it was that of the appassionata, the betrayed virgin, the sinner redeemed by love or the emancipated woman.

Even Croce treated the *Rime* as a biographical source. The accretion of so much masculine fantasy around the figure of the poet has affected the status of her work, which is nowhere seriously studied. The claim made for Stampa by Fiora Bassanese at the end of her full-length study of the poet is not exaggerated:

> This tale of love is not a mere love story in verse. It is the depiction of a universal motif in literature and of a moving force in human life: Love. For this reason it continues to attract an audience. It elicits not only the rational and intellectual reactions of the literary scholar, but also the emotional response of the ordinary reader. It is poetry for the heart and the mind, just as Gaspara Stampa is a poet for all times.

Stampa applies the attributes of the divine but cruel beloved to Collalto, presenting him as her sole inspiration, her male muse:

> . . . voi movete lo stil, l'arte, l'ingegno,
> sensi, spiriti, pensier, voglie, alma e core.
>   Se da me nasce cosa buona,
> è vostra, non è mia: voi mi guidate,
> a voi si deve il pregio e la corona.*

In presenting herself as a humble artisan inspired to excel her native powers by the miraculous influence of the muse/beloved, Stampa follows the example of the Petrarchisti. Like them she is aware that it is she who is conferring everlasting fame upon her beloved, whose museship is a poetic fiction, a compliment that only she, the creative artist, can bestow. She differs from male sonneteers of her generation

---

* you inspire the style, the skill, the wit,
    senses, spirits, thoughts, wishes, soul and heart.
        If from me is-born [a] thing goodly,
    [it] is yours, not (is) mine: you me direct,
    To you owe themselves the esteem and the crown.

in the directness and force of her diction as well as the peculiar resonance taken on by the Petrarchan themes of enforced passivity and humble resignation when the speaker is a female who can follow no other course of action.

Northern European society has no equivalent for the high-ranking courtesans of the south, who were not primarily purveyors of sexual services. Mediterranean ladies of good family being segregated, visitors of rank could not be entertained in their houses and resorted instead to the luxurious palazzi run by the courtesans for their protectors. There the visitors saw the most elegant furnishings, the finest paintings, ate and drank the finest food and wine. The courtesans were trained to exercise taste in all aspects of refined living and therefore were expected to be expert in all the arts of love, including music and poetry. Sexual favours could be negotiated but they were not included in the services on offer. Gallantry was the medium of exchange; the courtesans demanded a high standard of both compliment and *double entendre*. Stampa committed the solecism of becoming obsessed with one gentleman and compounded its catastrophic effects by remaining obsessed with him long after he had become bored with her.

Veronica Franco, another of the first rank of courtesans, in whose house Henri III of France stayed in 1574, preserved a degree of professional detachment in her *Terze Rime*. Though she passions and plains in the accepted fashion, there is a distinct sense that her muse, none other than Apollo himself, stands for a variety of almost interchangeable incumbents. As much as with any male poet, the point of the exercise is the display of her virtuosity, wit and taste. Her elder contemporary Tullia d'Aragona, like most courtesans a courtesan's daughter, who claimed the cardinal of Aragon for her father, turned poet when her career as a high-ranking courtesan was declining. In 1547 her *Rime* were published, and as a consequence the dukes of Florence exempted her from the wearing of the yellow veil that distinguished ladies of the profession. She had been the muse/beloved of Girolamo Muzio and of Bernardo Tasso; in 1547 she made the transition to poet.

When Laura Terracina received platonical love poems from Lodovico Domenichi, Marcantonio Passero and Luigi Tansillo, she could not reply in the persona of a mythical beloved, but as a poet and therefore in kind. She showed her poetic ingenuity by returning the compliment. Compliments were what the poems were, and compliments are primarily displays of the complimenter's own powers, exercised for rather than about the recipient, though what they display may have no more relevance to the recipient's actual character than any idealized representation can be called upon to do. Terracina received pretty presents from her friends and she laboured to give them ones as pretty in exchange. The language was that of frigid, dazzling hyperbole, but no one was so churlish as to object that the poems did not fit. Terracina freely acknowledged Marcantonio Passero as her muse, probably because he encouraged her in her literary activities. He for his part gracefully accepted the compliment.

The only English counterpart of the female sonneteers of the Italian Renaissance is Lady Mary Wroth. She was neither grieving widow nor courtesan but, like her uncle Sir Philip Sidney, the victim of an unhappy adulterous passion. At the age of seventeen she was married to Sir Robert Wroth, but the man she loved was her cousin, William Herbert, Earl of Pembroke, who returned her love sufficiently to sire two children, born after she was widowed in 1614, and ultimately rejected her. Lady Mary's intellectual formation seems to have been the consequence of her familiarity with the intellectual circle at Wilton, ruled by Herbert's poet-mother, Mary, Countess of Pembroke. Unlike her aunt's, Lady Mary's literary activities caused scandal, partly because she was thought to have burlesqued the private lives of her peers in her imitation of Sidney's *Arcadia*, entitled *The Countess of Montgomery's Urania*, partly because of her own circumstances and partly because, unlike the work of other respectable poets of noble birth, hers was printed in her lifetime.

> Thus hast thou made thy self a lying wonder –
>   Fools and their baubles seldom part asunder.
> Work o' th' works, leave idle books alone,
>   For wiser and worthier women have writ none.

Lord Denny, the author of these lines, considered himself abused by Lady Mary. His words were quoted half a century later by the Duchess of Newcastle, who came in for much more of this kind of thing. Jonson, who otherwise had deep reservations about women as poets, complimented Lady Mary in generous and seemly fashion.

I that have been a lover, and could show it,
   Though not in these, in rhythms not wholly dumb,
   Since I exscribe your Sonnets, am become
A better lover, and much better Poet.

Lady Mary remains a rarity; her Petrarchan sonnet sequence is the only one in English to be addressed by a woman to a man. As such it has many points of similarity with the *Rime* of Gaspara Stampa. Though Wroth gives far less attention to the lovability of her unkind lover, within the strict confinement of the sonnet form the conventions of the remorseless cruelty of the beloved and the lover's helplessness in the face of it are forced to coil and recoil upon themselves, making repeated and antithetical use of a limited range of reference and assortment of visual emblems, so that they build to utterances of an emotional intensity far beyond the melodic resolutions of classic Petrarchism. Wroth struggles to keep her agonized and unfed love from turning into hatred; often the sonnets begin in flaring bitterness only to overthrow the demons of rancour at the volta and arrive at a new statement of emotional potency in the closing couplet. Constancy is the vaunt of the female poet, the proof of her emotional muscle, and has been so for so long that it may constitute an essential characteristic of the genus. In the middle of the twelfth century the Countess of Dia wrote:

A chantar m'er de so qu'ieu non volria,
tant me rancur de lui cui sui ama,
car l'am mais que nuilla ren que sia;
vas lui no.m val merces ni cortesia,
ni ma bettaz ni mos pretz ni mos sens,
c'atressi.m sui enganad' e trahia
com degr' esser, s'ieu fos desavinens.

D'aisso.m conort car anc non fi faillenssa,
amics, vas vos per nuilla captenenssa,
anz vos am mais non fetz Seguis Valenssa;
e platz me mout quez d'amar vos venssa,
lo mieus amics, car etz lo plus valens . . .*

---

* To sing I have of what I would not want:
  such my rancour toward the one I love,
  because [I] him love more than any thing whatever.

By the mid-seventeenth century, even in feminist France changes in taste and sensibility ruled out both the celebration of a feminized male love object and the vociferation of female passion. The Comtesse de la Suze announced in her elegies that she was dying for love of 'belle' or 'cruelle Iris' and 'belle & sage Daphné' rather than Damon or Strephon. This is less likely to indicate that the Countess was celebrating homoeroticism than that she was simply practising the art of love poetry for its own sake, much as a woman might write a song for a bass baritone. Aphra Behn dared to address love poems to male objects, but she was well aware that she was creating a frisson by doing so. More often she too adopted a male voice and a male point of view.

By 1679 Rochester's Artemiza could declare that being asked to write a letter in verse was as unsexing as being told to 'ride astride and fight'. The statement is exaggerated for comic effect, but the suggestion that the chasm between male and female spheres was widening corresponds to the development of an ideal of feminine education that was to exclude women from all serious intellectual activity. A new category, 'feminine accomplishment', was in the process of being added to the old dichotomy of ignorant or learned. Poetry was coming to be considered a verbal display of sexual potency as inappropriate for the female as crowing would be for a hen. If women who give in to the itch to versify are seen to de-sex themselves, another and particularly corrosive anxiety is added to the terrors of exposing one's intellectual operations to general scrutiny. The silencing of the female poet-lover was the literary concomitant of her castration by the denial of her independent libido. The rhetoric of musedom was an important instrument in the embarrassing of the verbalizing female. As objects of unremitting male scrutiny women are forced to be ruinously self-conscious. The professional female poet confronting this state of affairs had little

---

For him nought avails mercy nor courtesy
nor my beauty, my virtues nor my wits,
so that I am deceived and betrayed
as should be if I were despicable.

Thence myself [I] console because even so not [I] do no injury
[my] love, toward you on no account whatever,
on-the-contrary you [I] love more than did Seguis Valenssa;
and [it] pleases me much that in loving you [I] surpass
the best [of] lovers, because [he] was the most deserving

option but to capitulate to the crying up of her physical charms, and
to allow what she did to take second place in the popular imagination
to what she was. The evil effects of such self-projection, both on her
integrity as an artist and her reputation among her peers, can hardly
be exaggerated. Contemptuous gallantry has an effect even more
insidious for being internalized. Being female she could not conceive
by a female-inspiring entity, nor could she foist the kinds of functions
upon male love objects that her male contemporaries did upon
unwitting females. The act of inspiration being seen paradoxically as
passive, the notion of muse strenuously resists masculinization. The
only creative process open to the female artist would seem to be some
kind of imaginative cloning. Some such dynamic would explain the
curious fact that the female poet's subject-matter seems in some
limiting and stifling way to be herself. Whereas the male poet might
be thought to be projecting a separate entity (the work) the female
poet is invariably seen to be projecting herself in an unavoidably
immodest way.

Aware of this dynamic, Anne Bradstreet claimed that her intention
was not to show her skill or to 'set forth' herself, 'but the glory of
God'. When in 1650 her poems were brought to England by her
brother-in-law, John Woodbridge, he chose to entitle her book *The
Tenth Muse, lately Sprung up in America*. In his commendatory poem
Woodbridge argued

> That for a woman's work 'tis very rare;
> And if the nine vouchsafe the tenth a place,
> I think they rightly may yield you that grace.

The gallant fiction, that the Muses had indeed begun to express
themselves directly upon earth without the medium of a poet crafts-
man, concealed a contempt for all other women practitioners of the
art, a contempt so elaborated by Woodbridge that one is obliged to
wonder how many other women poets there can have been in New
England in the 1640s. (However many there were, they cannot have
been more inept than Woodbridge.)

> If women, I with women may compare,
> Your works are solid, others weak as air;
> Some books of women I have heard of late,

Perused some, so witless, intricate,
So void of sense and truth, as if to err
Were only wished (acting above their sphere)
And all to get, what (silly souls) they lack,
Esteem to be the wisest of the pack;
Though (for your sake) to some this be permitted,
To print, yet wish I many better witted;
Their vanity make this to be enquired,
If women are with wit and sense inspired: . . .

The phoenix-like singleness of the female muse/poet is stressed by another of Bradstreet's eulogists:

Now I believe tradition, which doth call
The Muses, Virtues, Graces, females all;
Only they are not nine, eleven nor three;
Our auth'ress proves them but one unity.

Almost the same conceit was used by Thomas Creech in the commendatory poem he contributed to Aphra Behn's *Poems on Several Occasions* in 1684:

To speak of thee no Muse will I invoke,
Thou only canst inspire what should be spoke;
For all their wealth the Nine have given to thee,
Thy rich and flowing stream has left them dry: . . .

Bradstreet's highly sophisticated and free treatment of the muse device casts a satiric light on the determination of her male mentors to hail her as a supernumerary inhabitant among the nine on Parnassus. So far from claiming divinity, she laments that hers is a 'foolish, broken, blemished Muse'. In her 'Elegy upon . . . Sir Philip Sidney' Bradstreet characterizes Sidney as the darling of the Muses and enters into an elaborate conceit of her own travailed relationship with them:

But now into such lab'rinths I am led,
With endless turns the way I find not out,
How to persist my Muses is more in doubt;

> Which makes me now with Sylvester confess,
> But Sidney's Muse can sing his worthiness.
> The Muses' aid I craved; they had no will
> To give to their detractor any quill;
> With high disdain, they said they gave no more,
> Since Sidney had exhausted all their store.
> They took from me the scribbling pen I had,
> (I to be eased of such a task was glad)
> Then to revenge this wrong, themselves engage,
> And drove me from Parnassus in a rage.

Time and again she suggests slyly that the nine Muses are fonder of men than virgin goddesses should be. In her poem 'In Honour of Du Bartas' she develops another long conceit in which her personal muse is seen as a child struck speechless by 'all the glorious sights his eyes have had':

> My muse unto a child I may compare,
> Who sees the riches of some famous fair,
> He feeds his eyes, but understanding lacks
> To comprehend the worth of all these knacks . . .

Instead of commandeering the pastoral scenes and machines of Parnassus, she domesticates her muse, using the device to illuminate the world and preoccupations of a mother. In a better-known poem, 'The Author to the Book', Bradstreet uses the commonplace of literary product as child, in this case an 'ill-formed', limping, ragged creature 'unfit for light':

> If for thy father asked, say thou hadst none;
> And as for thy mother, she alas is poor,
> Which caused her thus to send thee out of door.

Publication is not seen here as giving birth, but rather as turning the child out of doors to beg on the strength of its imperfections. In her later meditative and religious poetry, Bradstreet gave up the fiction of museship altogether.

Katherine Philips, who was also called the tenth Muse, thereby unseating Bradstreet from her perch on Parnassus, had little truck with the mechanics of musedom, representing herself only in more formal poems in the guise of an 'artless' 'trembling' muse that could manage only 'blushing' tributes in 'To . . . the Duchess of York', and as an 'obscurer Muse, upon her knees' in 'To the Queen, on her arrival at Portsmouth'. Generally she preferred to refer to her pen and her self rather than her muse, claiming in one poem that she was, as it were, muse-free, because 'Sorrow is no muse'. Indeed, the directness of Katherine Philips's speech is one of the sources of its strength. Few female poets before or since have been so free of self-consciousness.

In the commendatory poem that he contributed to the first printing of Philips's translation of Corneille's *Pompey* in 1662, the Earl of Orrery stated the intrinsic absurdity of the woman poet's situation in which what's inspired (namely the active poet) is eclipsed by what inspires her (namely the passive muse).

> In me it does not the least trouble breed,
> That your fair sex does ours in verse exceed,
> Since every poet this great truth does prove,
> Nothing so much inspires a muse as love;
> Thence has your sex the best poetic fires
> For what's inspired must yield to what inspires,
> And as our sex resigns to yours the due,
> So all of your bright sex must yield to you.

Such verse hardly warrants close reading, though the obstetric connections of 'trouble' (travail) and 'breed' add to the reader's general unease. Such praise addressed to a woman who had no pretensions to beauty or amorous conquest is mere gallantry, totally unconnected, even at odds, with critical judgement. As Philips was only too glad if any gentleman, let alone Lord Orrery himself, deigned to correct her verse, and the present manuscript evidence suggests that *Pompey*, for which this poem was originally written, was substantially rewritten by another hand, there is scant likelihood that Orrery really thought that Philips's work presented any threat to the masculine literary establishment. The strategy that he adopts, offering praise of the beauty and effortless accomplishment of one woman poet in terms so hyperbolic as to be clearly incredible and, having subtly ridiculed her, adding the corollary that no other woman is worth consideration, actually relegates all women to passivity and silence. Though the poet's muse is understood to be a fiction, here it is the female poet who is rendered imaginary. The corollary, that all women but the 'Matchless Orinda' are worthless, is the sting that has always lain in the tail of arguments like Orrery's. Abraham Cowley, faced with the inescapable duty of celebrating a woman poet much against his own gynophobic inclination, takes the composition-gestation parallel to grotesque lengths. He tells Philips that she should rejoice in the sight of her printed work as Cybele rejoices in the sight of the gods her sons:

> And in their birth thou no one touch dost find,
>   Of th' ancient curse to woman-kind,
>   Thou bringst not forth with pain,
> It neither travail is, nor labour of the brain.
> So easily they from thee come,
>   And there is so much room
> In th' unexhausted and unfathomed Womb,
>   That like the Holland Countess, thou mayst bear
> A child for ev'ry day of all the fertile year.

The poetic pregnancy motif is a pleasing paradox when applied to the male poet; its resonances when applied to the sex that regularly risked its life and health in actual childbirth can be unnerving. Even Bradstreet raises uncomfortable associations with the unsupported mother giving birth to a deformed bastard on the parish, in her admonition to her book. Cowley uses the fable of the Countess of Henneberg, who as a result of a beggarwoman's curse gave birth to 365 children on Good Friday, 1277, to represent Katherine Philips as a monster of fecundity. It is probable that Cowley and the cannier of his readers also knew that neither the Countess nor any of her brood survived. Though Philips, who had borne two children, one of whom lived only a few months, might well have shuddered at the implication that her poems were as malformed and sickly as the Countess's progeny, Cowley's poem appeared in every publication of her work.

It took a lady who assumed the name 'Philo-Philippa' and invoked Orinda as her muse to strike a more appropriate non-obstetric note, but even she is obliged to attribute museship in an odd version of the argument that woman is what others do:

If souls no sexes have, as 'tis confest
'Tis not the he or she makes poems best;
Nor can one call these verses feminine,
Be the sense vigorous and masculine.
'Tis true, Apollo sits as judge of wit,
But the nine female learned troop are it.

Forty years later Sara Fyge took this argument rather further:

There's ten celestial females govern wit,
And but two gods that dare pretend to it.

As the poet's inspiration the muse/beloved had to be not only dazzlingly virtuous but dazzlingly beautiful. Virtually all the encomia of the female poet praise her for her own beauty as well as or sometimes instead of the beauty of her work. The commendatory poems offered to Aphra Behn for her *Poems on Several Occasions with a Voyage to the Island of Love* in 1684 all prate about her beauty, which had so far faded by 1676 that she was told in a satiric poem that if she claimed conquests as a justification for receiving the bays at the hand of Apollo, she was pleading a dozen years too late. Nevertheless the gallant younger men who supplied commendatory poems in 1684 were all too eager to claim that 'Her face's beauty's copied in her style', and admonish nymphs to pray to Pan 'To make you sing, and make you look like her', and to praise her for 'Such bright eyes, and such a tuneful pen', 'A brain so glorious and a face so fair' etc. Four years later Behn wrote of this kind of praise in 'To Damon. To Inquire of him if he could tell me by the Style, who writ me a Copy of Verses, that came to me in an unknown hand':

The verse was smooth, the thought was fine,
The fancy new, the wit divine,
But filled with praises of my face and eyes,
My verse, and all those usual flatteries
To me as common as the air;
Nor could my vanity procure my care.
All which things of course are writ
And less to show esteem than wit.

Though Behn understood that falsehood is the essence of compliment and was unlikely in middle age to have her head turned by the encomiasts who rehearsed 'the wonders of her face' more enthusiastically than the achievements of her verse, the fatuousness of the gallantry must have seemed in some sense mocking or belittling to a writer who worked as hard as she. To be told that her 'pen sheds flames as dangerous as her eyes' is also to be told that her pen can accomplish no more than her eyes.

Anne Killigrew, Dryden's 'youngest virgin-daughter of the skies', was vowed by the publisher after her death at the age of twenty-five or so to have been 'A grace for beauty and a muse for wit'. Katherine Philips seems to have paid no heed to the allegations of bodily beauty, but Anne Killigrew, who was a painter as well as a poet, appears, at least in her self-portrait (crowned with laurel), to have capitulated to some extent. In her poetry however she makes no claim to musedom for herself but, in her earliest unfinished poem, 'Alexandreis', implores 'a pitying muse to inspire her frozen style', addressing her as 'the queen of verse' and 'coy goddess'. The notion of the muse as a goddess external to and far above herself reappears in her most often quoted poem, 'Upon the Saying that my Verses were made by another':

> Next Heaven my vows to thee (O sacred *Muse!*)
> I offered up, nor didst thou them refuse.
>   O queen of verse, said I, if thou'lt inspire,
> And warm my soul with thy poetic fire,
> No love of gold shall share with thee my heart,
> Or yet ambition in my breast have part,
> More rich, more noble I will ever hold
> The Muses' laurel, than a crown of gold.
> An undivided sacrifice I'll lay
> Upon thine altar, soul and body pay;
> Thou shalt my pleasure, my employment be,
> My all I'll make a holocaust to thee.

Though the invocation to the muse is a commonplace, Killigrew's treatment, in which she represents herself as a burnt offering on the altar of the goddess, implies something more self-immolatory than is normal. Her eschewal of all ambition is the oddest aspect of this extravagant devotion of her entire life as a vestal to the goddess of poetry, especially as she continues in the next strophe of her ode to reveal that the success of her poetic endeavours had in fact brought her fame and glory. In 'To My Lord Colrane' she represents hers as a slothful muse awakened only by Cleanor's praise, which the 'Severe Goddess' approved to the point of taking too much pride in it. In choosing the Pindaric form for 'The Discontent', she takes an admonitory tone with the muse:

> Here take no care, take no care, my Muse,
>> Nor ought of art or labour use:
>> But let thy lines rude and unpolished go,
> Nor equal be their feet, nor num'rous let them flow.

In this case it is the poet who puts words in the mouth of the muse, telling her to 'pronounce aloud, there's nothing good'. In 'On the Soft and Gentle Motions of Eudora' she instructs 'Divine Thalia' herself to play appropriately upon her lute to express something more musical than music. Killigrew understood the idea that love inspired all poetry and wrote a poem, 'Love the Soul of Poetry', to illustrate the fact:

> And thus Alexis does prove love to be,
> As the world's soul, the soul of poetry.

When she came to write an actual love poem, 'The Complaint of a Lover', however, she appears to have assumed a male persona, passioning for 'Rosalinda', though it should be remembered that her posthumous editor may well have altered her original in the interests of propriety.

More impudent women did not shrink from taking the personae of the 'nine female learned troop' upon themselves. When John Dryden died in 1700 six women – Delarivier Manley, Catherine Trotter, Mary Pix, Sara Fyge, Susannah Carroll and Lady Sarah Piers – wrote elegies to him in the persons of the nine Muses. Dryden's protégée, Elizabeth Thomas, whom he called by her request Corinna (after the poet Corinna of Tanagra rather than the Corinna of Ovid and Rochester, one hopes), assumes the muse as her own *Doppelgänger*, communing with her as if she were herself.

> Some generous painter now assist my pen,
> And help me draw the most despised of men:
> Or else, O Muse! do thou that charge supply,
> Thou that art injured too as well as I;
> Revenge thyself, with satire arm thy quill,
> Display the men, yet own a justice still.

The muse's quill is clearly Thomas's quill. What follows are fourteen couplets by Thomas, and then

> Enough, O Muse! thou has described him right,
> Th' emetic's strong, I sicken at the sight . . .

Four lines later, the poet changes her mind and gives the hapless muse fresh orders:

> Yet stay, proceed and paint his awkward bow,
> And if thou hast forgot, I'll tell thee how:
> Set one leg forward, draw the other back,
> Nor let the lump a booby wallow lack;
> His head bend downward with an obsequious quake,
> Then quickly raise it, with a spaniel shake.
> His honours thus performed, a speech begin
> May show th' obliging principles within:
> Thy memory to his sense I now confine,
> His be the substance, but th' expression thine.

Pillorying a fop is only one of the things that Thomas is doing in this poem; she is also shaking out the rhetoric of museship by treating her own muse as the cheapest kind of amanuensis. Perhaps this poem should be taken as evidence of the kind of services that female amanuenses performed for an employer who demanded a degree of creative control. Thomas is nowadays known to history through Sir Walter Scott's dictum that 'her person as well as her writings were dedicated to the service of the public', a statement for which he had no evidence whatsoever. Her wretched life story is a condensation of all the ills that waited upon a woman who had no option but to try to make a living by her pen in the Grub Street of the 1720s.

The Scots poet Jean Adams gave instructions to her muse a half-century later:

> Come hither to the hedge, and see
> The walks that are assigned to thee:
> All the bounds of virtue shine,
> All the plain of wisdom's thine,
> All the flowers of harmless wit
> Thou mayest pull, if thou think'st fit,
> In the fair field of history.
> All the plants of piety
> Thou mayest freely thence transplant –
> But have a care of whining cant.

The poem's irony derives from the fact that it follows the structure of the kind of admonition addressed to a young lady who had permission to make use of the gardens of her neighbours among the gentry. The tenor of the instructions appears to be tending towards the prescription of insipidity that was becoming usual in homilies addressed to young women, until Adams brings us up short by the last line.

Something like Thomas's disabused attitude underlay Martha Sansom's impersonation of the Muse Clio for her poetic correspondence with William Bond and her subsequent adoption of the sobriquet in all her literary pursuits. Though she began it as a joke, it was later held against her. Mary Leapor, a member of the servant class, noticed one important characteristic of the muse-poet, as she was accepted by publishers and literary patrons alike: in middle age she would have to leave off her poetic activities:

> The sprightly Nine must leave me then,
> This trembling hand resign its pen:
> No matron ever sweetly sung,
> Apollo only courts the young.

One of the most striking aspects of women's poetry of the eighteenth century is that nearly all of it is written in youth, sometimes in extreme youth. Versifying for women comes under the heading of 'youthful indiscretion'. Many who were poets in youth gave up writing altogether; others turned to writing of a less conspicuous variety. At the age of fifty, Henrietta, Lady Luxborough provides evidence of the kinds of second thoughts that afflicted the women who 'lisped in numbers':

> You bid my muse not cease to sing,
> You bid my ink not cease to flow,
> Then say it shall be ever spring . . .

Among the anxieties that beset her was the realization of her lack of education.

> Untrained beside in verse-like art.
> How shall my pen express my heart?
>
> In vain I call th' harmonious Nine,
>   In vain implore Apollo's aid;
> Obdurate, they refuse a line,
>   While spleen and care my rest invade . . .
>
> Better by far in lonesome den
>   To sleep unheard-of than to glow
> With treacherous wildfire of the brain,
> Th' intoxicated poet's bane.

Though the ladies of the eighteenth century presented themselves as attended by domesticated muses, they were also aware of the idea of inspiration as possession. As verse became less and less a medium for social intercourse and the cult of the bard began to take hold of the imagination of writers and readers alike, women were increasingly alienated from active participation, with the exception of those unfortunate individuals who were seduced by the notion that, being female like the muses, they were actually inspiration and could utter poetry spontaneously, virtually extempore. As Clara Reeve, who became a successful novelist in middle age, confessed:

> What though, while yet an infant young,
> The numbers trembled on my tongue;
> As youth advanced, I dared aspire,
> And trembling struck the heavenly lyre;
> What by my talents have I gained?

> By those I love to be disdained,
> By some despised, by others feared,
> Envied by fools, by witlings jeered.

The Muses were no longer mere amanuenses but had resumed their association with mountains and daemonic possession. Mary Darwall, who had begun publishing verse at the age of twenty-one, undeterred by her utter lack of education, at the age of forty-two responded to her husband's exhortation that she write some verses with an exhortation to the Muses:

> Ye Muses, aid me to explore
> The shadowy grots and mountains hoar,
> While ye your tuneful influence shed,
> And twine with bays your poet's head.
>
> Erato hears my invocation, –
> My bosom glows with inspiration, –
> Instant the fairy scenes appear,
> Pierian sounds salute my ear: –

Until, that is, her baby cries, 'And each poetic fancy flies'. Though Anna Laetitia Barbauld still felt able, in 1797, to summon a domestic muse, 'In slipshod measure loosely prattling on', to help her give a mock heroic account of wash-day in blank verse, the Muses had retreated to the realms of visionary experience. In 1790 Joanna Baillie, who had as little education as Mary Darwall and hardly knew who the Muses historically might be, had the temerity to follow them there –

> Ye are the spirits who reside
> In earth and air and ocean wide,
> In hissing flood and crackling fire,
> In horror dread and tumult dire,
> In stilly calm and stormy wind,
> And rule the answering changes in the human mind.
>
> High on the tempest-beaten hill,
> Your misty shapes ye shift at will,
> The wild fantastic clouds ye form.
> Your voice is in the midnight storm,

> Whilst, in the dark and lonely hour,
> Oft starts the boldest heart, and owns your secret power.

— only to retreat when it came to the point:

> Ye mighty spirits of the song,
> To whom the poet's prayers belong,
> My lowly bosom to inspire,
> And kindle with your sacred fire,
> Your wild obscuring heights to brave,
> Is boon, alas! too great for me to crave.

Despite this pusillanimity, Miss Baillie was declared by all the best minds of her generation to be the greatest dramatist since Shakespeare, who was understood at the time to have attained sublimity with as little education as she. She was particularly appreciated by her contemporaries because she gave herself none of the airs of a literary lady.

By the 1790s the word 'muse' was being used oftener as a verb than as a noun. Baillie's confused notion of the Muses as *genii loci* of some mysterious kind at least had the virtue that it encouraged no identification of herself with the forces of inspiration. Other women poets who, like Baillie, were unable to correct their work, having no knowledge of the rudiments of grammar or prosody, let alone of classical literature, had little choice but to accept the role of muse or visionary improvvisatrice.

The American poet Lydia Jane Pierson breaks new ground in characterizing her muse as a wayward daughter:

> Born of the sunlight and the dew
>   That met amongst the flowers,
> That on the river margin grew,
>   Beneath the willow bowers . . .
>
> The only nurse she ever knew
>   Was Nature, free, and wild, –
> Such was her birth, and so she grew
>   A moody, wayward child . . .
>
> Full oft I chid the wayward child,
>   Her wandrings to restrain;

And sought her airy limbs to bind
　　With prudence worldly chain . . .

While streaming from the Eternal Lyre
　　Like distant echoes came
A strain that wrapped her soul in fire,
　　And thrilled her trembling frame.
She sprang away – that wayward child,
　　The harp! the harp! she cried;
And still she climbs and warbles wild
　　Along the mountain side.

Such inanity signalled the death-knell of a great convention. It was not long before heterosexual women poets realized that they would have to make of inspiration a masculine penetration, and poetry the result of fecundation by it, Laura Riding's 'never-begotten perfect son / Who never can be born'. They have the mythic precedent of Dionysus, the god beloved of ecstatic but chaste women, who so possessed them that their feet flew over frozen rocks and their breasts tore through thorns without a scratch, a god whose effect produces the true poetic frenzy, the fire that animates the clay. The most unforgettable statement of that female convention is probably Kathleen Raine's 'Invocation' to a muse every bit as ruthless and tireless and frustrating as any manifestation of Graves's goddess.

There is a poem on the way,
there is a poem all around me,
the poem is in the near future,
the poem is in the upper air
above the foggy atmosphere
it hovers, a spirit
that I would make incarnate.
Let my body sweat
let snakes torment my breast
my eyes be blind, ears deaf, hands distraught
mouth parched, uterus cut out,
belly slashed, back lashed,
tongue slivered into thongs of leather
rain stones inserted in my breasts,
head severed,

> if only the lips may speak,
> if only the god will come.

Yearning like the Sibyl to be possessed by Apollo provides a perfect analogue to the idea of inspiration; Graves could not even object that it does not have its roots in archetypal prehistoric experience. Phallus worship is at least as old as the cult of the vagina. Raine is prepared to be not only de-sexed but disembowelled, destroyed if this voice may only make itself heard. There can be no question about the aggressive femaleness of her poet's persona; it is stressed into literalness. The most unnerving thing about it, besides the strangeness of poetry as a monstrous, murdering birth, is the femaleness of the final self-disintegration.

Mary Webb relates the matter more directly to personal love, identifying, as poets often do, her inspiration and her beloved within her poem.

> Why did you with strong fingers fling aside
> The gates of possibility and say
> With vital voice the words I dream today?
> Before, I was not much unsatisfied:
> But since a god has touched me and departed,
> I run through every temple broken-hearted.

The poem is not good. It clatters with sentimental prosiness and notions of the vaguest (like 'vital voice'); nevertheless the poet is thinking quite easily in this new way, of poetry as a man to be wooed and won or lost by her.

In an important study Mary K. DeShazer has traced the struggles of Louise Bogan, H. D., May Sarton, Adrienne Rich and Audre Lorde to establish their own rationale of inspiration and resolve the contradictions inherent for women in the traditional schema. It is the more astonishing then to encounter a publication that is required reading for many students of English at the University of Bristol which sets out, without a flicker of self-mockery, the old rotten schema of archetypic male maker, 'Our Hero', producing poetry by intercourse with a totally inhuman and sickeningly feminine muse. He encounters the muse in Section 14.

When, Lo! a heavenly spirit appeared before Our Hero's wearied eyes, a spirit seen in and by a blinding light. She stepped – or seemed to step – from the pool or from the fountain. She bore – or seemèd to bear – a golden lyre with silver strings in her lovely hands. She wore – or seemed to wear – a wondrous hieroglyphic robe, rippling in the air with loose pride, a robe which was adorned with all the colours and all the shapes that nature or fancy can create.

Like much of the rhythmic prose produced by pretentious but ill-educated women, this is mannered nonsense. The more astonishing it is then that such stuff has been sweated over by two male academics. Though 'the Muse of Poetry' – for such she is – or seems to be – is given to addressing Our Hero as 'my child', she also hails him as 'a great begetter' and produces his sons as proof. In Section 19, 'Failed, Forgotten and Lesser Poets', great poetry voices his concern at finding women so poorly represented in the innermost circle of poets. The M. of P. explains that Our Hero can be incarnate in women, but happens not to have been because of 'male contempt', 'the obligations of maternity' and 'the malignancies of patriarchies', but it's not really a problem because

even while inhabiting a male body, women will be the subject of your compositions and women will be (at least) half your audience. A poet endeavouring to speak for all mankind must inhabit (in reality or imagination) the souls of both men and women. And yet the fact remains. Few female shades wait near the centre.

Only people for whom words like 'soul' have less than no meaning could set their names to such tosh. There never was a poet who spoke for all mankind, with or without its female component, or even thought he did. It would have occurred to neither Homer nor Shakespeare that he was not for an age but for all time. In Section 62, the Muse having finished Our Hero's lessons in elementary prosody, she addresses him thus:

You, my Poet, my blessed Hope, my New Creation, my Only Joy, have learned some few of my Arts with (almost) all the

Aptitude for which I longed. You shall now learn those secret and hidden mysteries without which no mortal man can be a poet. Night draws on apace. Now the lily folds all her sweetness up and slips into the bosom of the pool. So fold thyself, my dearest, slip into my bosom and be lost in me.

Students reading this should receive marks for correctly identifying cliché, pleonasm and preciosity, as well as the misquotation of Tennyson. Worse is to come.

The Goddess enwrapped her Poet as the woodbine enrings the barky fingers of the elm or the honeysuckle entwines the oak, and led him to her bower, blushing like the morn.

Not even Sappho makes it into the parade of poets, otherwise known as the 'Lords of Highest Song', that the Muse of Poetry puts on for Our Hero; current feminist literary theory exists merely to be refuted in a glancing aside. Though *The Story of Poetry* is nonsensically told in this case, the schema that it sets out still persists in the one place where it can do most damage, in the minds of women poets. In the words of Carolyn Kizer:

> We who must act as handmaidens
> To our own goddess, turn too fast,
> Trip on our hems, to glimpse the muse
> Gliding below her lake or sea,
> Are left, long-staring after her,
> Narcissists by necessity . . .

Sylvia Plath saw the Muses as wicked fairy godmothers who disempowered her, countermanded her incantations and paralysed her when she would be dancing.

> Mother you sent me to piano lessons . . .
> I learned, I learned, I learned elsewhere
> From muses unhired by you, dear mother.

The argument of this chapter is contained in this octave; the traditional schema of inspiration rather than enabling the woman poet, paralyses her. The more she models herself on the tradition, the more aware she is of the way it is supposed to work, the less able she will be to find her voice. She has to reject the whole package of enculturation represented by the dismal-headed godmothers, though it should involve rejecting the person who taught her to speak in the first place, who was also the first agent of her conditioning to muteness, her mother (her self). The ultimate outcome was terrible, but the poetry is there, not only alive thirty years after her death, but gathering momentum. The name 'poet' comes from the Greek word to make. Plath *made* it.

POET, POETASTER, POETESS

A. Alvarez wrote of Sylvia Plath's achievement in *The Colossus*: 'She steers clear of feminine charm, deliciousness, gentility, supersensitivity and the act of being a poetess. She simply writes good poetry.' No one could say that Plath does not write as a woman, but it is equally clear that, in confronting the endocrinological events in women's lives and her experiences in sex, pregnancy and childbirth, she steps outside what is permitted the 'poetess', who is required, as Alvarez hints, to put on an act.

'Poet' is a fine word. Maker, imitator of God, a word with a leap in it, an insolent caper in the face of dogma. Poet is also a sexless word, or a male word. Elizabeth Barrett Browning defined poets as

> . . . The only truth-tellers now left to God,
> The only speakers of essential truth,
> Opposed to relative, comparative,
> And temporal truths . . .
>
> The only teachers who instruct mankind
> From just a shadow on a charnel-wall
> To find man's veritable stature out
> Erect, sublime . . .
>
> O delight
> And triumph of the poet, who would say
> A man's mere 'yes', a woman's common 'no',
> A little human hope of that or this,
> And says the word so that it burns you through
> With a special revelation, shakes the heart
> Of all the men and women in the world . . .

To pin a tail to the word 'poet', as in 'poetaster', 'poeticule', 'poetling', is to anchor it to earth, to condemn it to less than best. The poetess's stride is encumbered by a train of esses. There are even worse names. Spenser, like Rolland and Peacham and the Duchess of Newcastle herself, shuts woman poets into a steel stomacher and panniers by calling them 'poetresses' and only poor Aphra Behn is worse crushed by the unenviable addition of yet another sneering syllable, for she is the original 'poetastress'. All the endings are diminutive; the longer the word, the less poet there is in it. The number of true poets is and must remain small; in this select and self-purging establishment, poetesses are relentlessly relegated to the below-stairs or the nursery of poetry. This was not always the case: Sappho was called 'the Poetess' as Homer was called 'the Poet'. Provided both were equal in the general estimation, the title can have been nothing but honour. Feminists have to decide whether to drag the name of poetess up to equal estimation or to abandon the distinction as essentially slighting. If we are to judge our inheritance of She-poetry against the background of the whole poetic tradition, we might never again read the work of a female poet. There are, after all, only so many days allotted the female span and so many duties alike allotted as to crowd poetry out of it altogether.

As Mary, Lady Chudleigh wrote in 1700 in her essay 'Of Knowledge':

When I look abroad into the world, and take a survey of the rational nature, it grieves me to see what a vast disproportion there is as to intellectual endowments between the men and us. 'Tis a mortifying prospect to see them exalted to such a towering height, raised so infinitely above the generality of our sex. Some few indeed we may view with them, may shine bright in the firmament of Knowledge, but what are they to the surrounding splendours, to the multitude of lights? They are lost in the glorious crowd, and cannot be retrieved without a narrow inspection, an attentive view . . .

Lady Chudleigh's most eminent personality trait was common sense. She knew that each decade produced its treatise on learned women and that each treatise named the same women, and that none of their works was known. As the only language she could read was English, so the chief source of authority for her male contemporaries was unavailable to her, which alone would be sufficient reason for presenting her work only to women: 'I am not so vain as to believe anything of mine deserves the notice of men . . .'

The limitations of her education were not her only handicaps; isolated at her husband's country seat of Ashton in Devonshire, she had 'lived almost wholly to herself, . . . had but seldom had the opportunity of conversing with ingenious company, which', she remembered, 'Dryden, in the preface of his Miscellany, thinks to be necessary toward the gaining a fineness of style'. We can only marvel that, so discouraged, blunt Lady Chudleigh toiled away without praise or criticism at two volumes of poems and a volume of essays that were published, as well as 'two Operas, a Masque, a version of some of Lucian's Dialogues, satirical reflection upon Saqualio and etcetera' that were not. Most of her works were recorded as preserved 'in the family'; nowadays manuscripts of hers can be seen in the Houghton Library at Harvard and the Huntington, but most of her dogged labours have left no trace. Considering how she laboured to push her stone uphill, should Lady Chudleigh be denied her name of 'poetess'? Evidence of Lady Chudleigh's oppression can be seen in every line she wrote, which means perhaps that we should make a heroine of her rather than a poet. She may inspire a genuine woman poet yet, if her voice can be heard in all its inadequacy, alive and angry, and if she can be heard asking woman 'to put in for a share, to enter her claims, and not permit the men any longer to monopolise the perfections of the mind, to ingross the goods of the understanding'. She would not have women 'suffer themselves to be willingly dispossessed of their reason, and shut out of the commonwealth of learning'. Neither would she have them 'to be so far imposed on, as to be made to believe, that they are incapable of great attainments . . .'

Lady Chudleigh's painful awareness of her exclusion from the world of men did not, as far as we can tell, affect the women poets of the sixteenth century. As we have seen neither prevailing notions of gender nor of poetry acted to exclude women, or, rather, ladies, from participation in literary activity. A queen is not likely to ask permission from her subjects before she expresses herself in verse; Elizabeth I and Elizabeth, Queen of Bohemia both wrote verse; Mary, Countess of Pembroke, Elizabeth, Viscountess Falkland and Lady Mary Wroth did not apologize for their verse, or hold it beneath men's contempt.

The first sign of a sea change in attitudes to women's intellectual activity is possibly the publication of Joseph Swetnam's *Arraignment of Women* in 1617. Rachel Speght, 'Ester Sowernam' and 'Constantia Munda' all replied with defences of women, but a double intellectual standard had been raised, and is not lowered yet. Mary Oxlie of Morpeth, writing to Drummond of Hawthornden in the 1620s, apologized for her presumption:

> I never rested on the Muses' bed,
> Nor dipt my Quill in the Thessalian Fountain,
> My rustic Muse was rudely fostered,
> And flies too low to reach the double mountain.
>
> Then do not sparks with your bright suns compare,
> Perfection in a woman's work is rare . . .

Oxlie's use of would-be classical devices rather makes her point for her. There is no classical reference to the bed of the Muses, nor to an appropriate spring in Thessaly.

The daughters and the second wife of the Duke of Newcastle all wrote poetry without apology, but with a difference. Jane Cavendish, dedicating to her absent father the masque she wrote with her sister in 1645 or so, begs him to protect her modesty:

> My Lord, it is your absence makes each see
> For want of you what I'm reduced to be.
> Captive or shepherdess's life
> Gives envy leave to make no strife,
> So what becomes me better then
> But to be your daughter in your pen?
> If you're now pleased, I care not what
> Becomes of me, or what's my lot.
> Now if you like, I then do know
> I am a wit, but pray whisper't low.

Jane's stepmother, Margaret Cavendish, Duchess of Newcastle, openly avowed a consuming thirst for fame. She did not even demand that her reputation be given her by the discerning . . .

If my writing please the readers, though not the learned, it will satisfy me; for I had rather be praised in this by the most although not by the best. For all my desire is fame and fame is nothing but a great noise and noise lives most in a multitude . . .

Virginia Woolf has painted a rather fanciful picture of the Duchess living in retirement, surrounded by a bevy of ladies to whom she dictated tirelessly day and night. Certainly she exploited advantages which other women lacked to allow herself to free-associate in metre, laying bare a wild and heterogeneous fancy that has been contemptuously and inaccurately compared by one gentleman to an overturned workbox. The Duchess was blessed with an extraordinarily concrete visual imagination and a power of concentration on her object that was not even sought after by her contemporaries. In her armoury of imagery human bodies are kitchens, boiling, basting, frying and stewing away in filth and steamy heat, and human beings are bisques or custards, according to their temperament. Within this frame of homely reference beats a great heart, begging that even if 'we are inferior to men, let us shew ourselves a degree above beasts; and not eat and drink and sleep away our time as they do . . .' The great lady dashed about her great house, packing books off to the press before she had time to re-read them and discover that one of her dictated sentences was twelve pages long. The result was that even people who found her interesting and sympathetic decided that she was mad. Pepys was fascinated by her eccentric costume and disturbed to see '100 boys and girls running looking upon her' but, when he read her life of her husband, he decided that she was 'a mad, conceited, ridiculous woman and he an ass to suffer her to write what she writes to him and of him'. Dorothy Temple too decided that she was 'a little distracted'. For her part the Duchess admitted that reason and she had parted company. In 'The Poetress's Hasty Resolution' published in 1653 she explains:

I writ so fast I thought, if I lived long,
A pyramid of fame to build thereon.
Reason, observing which way I was bent,
Did stay my hand and asked me what I meant.
'Will you', said she, 'Thus waste your time in vain
'On that which in the world small praise shall gain?

'For shame! Leave off,' said she, 'The printer spare.
He'll lose by your ill poetry, I fear.'

The Duchess's stately impudence was never emulated, even by the
women poets of her own family. Her husband's granddaughter wrote
to her mother, the Countess of Bridgewater:

> Madam, I dedicate these lines to you,
> To whom, I do confess, volumes are due,
> Hoping your wonted goodness will excuse
> The errors of an infant female muse.
> 'Mongst ladies let Newcastle wear the bays,
> I only sue for pardon, not for praise.

The claim that one has written verse in order simply to ask pardon
for its inadequacies is absurd; such a contradictory posture must
necessarily trip the poet up. She must either court blame for a success
or praise for a failure. In the seventeenth century the great ladies who
confessed to an itch for rhyming were careful to present the product
of their labour in an offhand manner, although they may have taken
great pains with it. Gentlemen who penned verses had also to affect to
set no store by them; publication, even in manuscript but above all in
print, brought about loss of caste, in that intimate feelings were made
common. The ladies whose thoughts became public were in worse
trouble, for their writings exposed their ignorance and their self-
delusion. Many a lady when she arrived at the age of discretion burnt
the evidence of her youthful folly; more, perhaps much more,
women's poetry perished in the grate than has come down to us. As
Hester Wyat explained:

> What makes me write, my dearest friend, you ask,
> For our sex always thought too great a task?
> I grant you this, yet 'tis no ill-spent time,
> And my thoughts natur'ly fall into rhyme.
> Rude and unpolished from the pen they flow.
> Learning the wit and judgment must improve,
> Refine the verse, and tender passion move.

The pretext that the poem has been written only to respond to a demand from her who must be obeyed also requires that the poet accept whatever the addressee may choose to do with it.

> No guilty blush my cheeks dyes to impart
> These lines, my friend, chaste as the author's heart,
> Happy if they can answer your desire,
> Though they in flames bright as your eyes expire.

In this case the poem survived, as no other of Hester Wyat's has. Her anxiety about the possibility of an imputation of unchastity possibly dates this poem after the change in taste and morality that signalled the end of the permissive reign of Charles II, when caricature and lampoon were heaped upon the women who

> To the whole town their naked thoughts expose
> And tempt applause at once in verse and prose.

Loss of reputation was a catastrophe with irreversible consequences. Katherine Philips anxiously refuted any insinuation that she had immodestly undressed her mind in public, by quoting Sir Edward Dering's epilogue to *Pompey*:

> No bolder thought can tax
> These rhymes of blemish to the blushing sex,
> As chaste the lines, as harmless is the Sense,
> As the first Smiles of Infant Innocence.

Sense as harmless as the first smiles of an infant is not likely to be loaded with significance. As the externalization of the innermost workings of personality, poetry is essentially immodest; the poetess, who must proceed tentatively, and cringe away from any hint of self-revelation, ends up writing this kind of thing.

> What's innocence? A brighter gem
> Than e'er enriched a diadem,
> A gem that bears a price so high
> As crowns and empires cannot buy.
> Yet by the poorest mortal's breast
> This matchless treasure is possessed,

> A treasure not like other wealth,
> That liable to fraud or stealth.
> No soul of this can be bereft
> By open force or secret theft.
> Safe in its cabinet 'twill stay,
> Till by the owner thrown away.

The appeal of this doggerel is guaranteed by the title as given by the editors of *Miscellanea Sacra* (1696): 'Innocence or the Inestimable Gem. Written by a Young Lady'. Youth was already an essential characteristic of the successful female poet; it is in the nature of the case that the indiscreet young did not pause to consider what would ensue when they were no longer young. They heard the vicious lampoons heaped on poets like Aphra Behn, who continued their gallantries into what was then thought to be middle age, and imagined that they would never suffer a like fate. The pattern, of the courtship of the young and beautiful poetess followed by persecution and vilification when she is no longer young, is repeated time and again in the annals of women's verse. In dozens of instances women published poetry when they were young enough to get away with it, only to turn to churning out novels and religious tracts or give up writing altogether in maturity. The poetess was genuinely incapable of development because she lacked the tools of self-criticism and prevented from developing by the sexism that did not allow her to grow up.

When her brother-in-law collected the miscellaneous works in prose and verse of Mrs Elizabeth Singer Rowe for publication in 1739, he included nothing from her first book, *Poems on Several Occasions written by Philomela*. He explained that she felt guilt and remorse for 'the harmless gaieties of a youthful muse':

Though many of these poems are of the religious kind and all of them consistent with the strictest regard to the rules of virtue, yet some things in them gave her no little uneasiness in advanced life. To a mind that had so entirely subdued its passions, or devoted them to the honour of its maker, and indued with the tenderest moral sense, what she could not absolutely approve appeared unpardonable, and, not satisfied to have done nothing that injured the sacred cause of virtue, she was displeased with herself for having writ anything that did not directly promote it.

Philomela's youthful effusions are in fact embarrassing, both in themselves and because they placed the poet in the hands of the bookseller John Dunton, who bandied her name around until long after she had married a clergyman and became known as a pious writer. When she was nineteen Dunton had sold her to the readers of *The Athenian Mercury* as 'beautiful', 'witty' and 'ingenious' and she had unwittingly added piquancy to the package by insisting on hers as an 'Infant-muse'. Curll, the Grub Street bookseller, republished Philomela in the year of her death, greatly enhancing the appeal of his volume by pharisaical defences of her virginal indiscretions in the 'heat of youth'. Mrs Rowe's insistence on the promotion of virtue as the only excusable aim is understandable because by the 1730s only the woman who wrote for God's glory rather than her own was safe from calumny and the kind of literary pimping that she had suffered all her life.

Religion remained the principal subject-matter of women's verse, the principal justification for women's writing and the best guarantee of a poetess's success for two hundred years. The works of Katherine Philips most admired by her contemporaries were not her occasional poems of female friendship, but her religious meditations. Many women versified as an aid to meditation on the scriptures, with no intention of publishing; often their husbands or fathers published their work after their deaths, as part of the testimony of an exemplary life. In 1689 Mary Astell, the champion of women's education, sent a collection of poems to Archbishop Sancroft that included one promisingly entitled 'Ambition', which concludes:

> Let me obscured be, and never known,
>   Or pointed at around the town.
>   Short-winded fame shall not transmit
> My name, that the next age may censure it.
> If I write sense, no matter what they say,
>   Whether they call it dull or pay
>   A reverence such as Virgil claims,
> Their breath's infectious. I have higher aims.
>
> Mean-spirited men! that bait at honour, praise,
>   A wreath of laurel or of bays.
>   How short's their immortality!

But Oh! a crown of glory ne'er will die!
This I'm ambitious of, no pains will spare
    To have a higher mansion there.
    There all are kings; here let me be
Great, O my God, great in humility.

This exact sentiment is to be found in Astell's *Serious Proposal to the Ladies* and in a dozen other defences of women's education. Such an argument contains its own refutation, for it is not information that guarantees salvation. The double standard demanded that a woman's poetry be pious, insipid and impersonal; she had virtually to repel her readers rather than turn them on. She might have a momentary vogue as improving reading for children and servants, and might even acquire a little prestige, but in doing so she had to sacrifice all passion, all imaginative daring.

The defences of women that appeared in English in the mid-seventeenth century, mostly translated from the French, compounded the problems of the woman poet by insisting that women were more sensitive and 'of purer plastical ingredients' than men, with such natural volatility and eloquence that they would only suffer by acquiring any kind of self-discipline. According to Poulain de la Barre, whose treatise was translated three times and was seldom out of print for a hundred years,

> Women ... express neatly and in order what they conceive. Their words cost them nothing; they begin and go on at their pleasure, and when they have their liberty, their fancy supplies them always with inexhaustible liberality.

The woman who confessed to working on her poetry would appear by this token to de-sex herself. If she wrote verse it could not be for ambition, or a desire to compete or to display her 'intellectuals', but because it came naturally, because she could not help it, in which case her male contemporaries would be perfectly justified in ignoring it. At first the argument from spontaneity was a fairly transparent fiction, but with the ballad revival and the unleashing of the romantic imagination, women came actually to believe that they sang as naturally as birds. In 1761, ten years after she had had an enviable success with her *Miscellanies* and been dubbed the best poet since

Katherine Philips, Mary Jones refused a commission with an apparently sincere disclaimer: 'All I ever did in the poetic field was spontaneous, or by mere accident – I sought not the numbers, but the birds sung and the numbers *came*.'

Even feminists have been seduced into taking Poulain de la Barre's arguments about female superiority as pro-feminist, when in fact they are not, because they insist upon sexual apartheid. If women have natural faculties superior to men's, goes the argument, any competition between men and women would be unequal and training women in the skills of men would be detrimental to their natural gifts of sensibility, modesty, tenderness, purity, etc. The unknown author of 'The Emulation' argues against the exclusion of women from serious intellectual pursuits, but justifies their acquisition of learning as the best way

> to enslave
> Those passions which we find
> Too potent for the mind.
> 'Tis o'er them only we desire to reign,
> And we no nobler, braver conquest wish to gain.
>
> We only so much will desire
> As may instruct us how to live above
> Those childish things which most admire
> And may instruct us what is fit to love.

Female learning, according to this argument, which seems to the present writer to be very unlikely to be by a woman, should be aimed at reinforcing good female behaviour. Women who had a little learning capitulated by demonstrating that it had not unfitted them for women's traditional roles. The more information they had acquired, the more necessary it was for them to display innocence. Mary Evelyn, wife of the diarist, summarized the situation, without rancour:

> Women were not born to read authors and censure the learned, to compare lives and judge of virtues, to give rules of morality and sacrifice to the Muses. We are willing to acknowledge all time borrowed from family duties is misspent . . . if sometimes

it happens by accident that one of a thousand aspires a little higher, her fate commonly exposes her to wonder, but adds little of esteem.

The only suggestion that Mrs Evelyn felt at all oppressed is the use of the word 'higher' to indicate the realm in which the ambitious woman chose to operate. The literary woman might meet with a certain success, but only as long as she was a novelty and excited wonder. Esteem was offered to the woman whose literary activity exhibited domestic virtues of humility, purity, piety and patience, and took second place to the demands of her station in life. A hundred years later, Annabella Blount wrote to Lady Pomfret explaining that she had burnt her youthful poetic efforts and had given up writing verse but, fully aware of the contradiction, she chose to do so in rhyme. Phoebus Apollo appears to her in the form of her brother to say:

> 'Why wilt thou, Nan, so ill employ thy wit
> In manly works, for ladies' hands unfit?
> Of all thy sex that sought the poet's fame
> Is there one character thou dost not blame?
> And wilt thou vainly misemploy thy days
> In what ne'er was the virtuous woman's praise?
> Turn thou thy sense to housewife's wiser cares,
> Mind well thy needlework, and say thy prayers:
> Secure in this advice that I have given
> Of peace on earth, and endless peace in heaven.'

When all the rewards were given for not trying, the woman who struggled towards literary excellence had to be some kind of an oddity, counter-suggestive to a fault, perhaps, 'a little distracted'. Most of the women whose work has survived capitulated to other people's expectations and only took up their work when there was absolutely no other claim on their attention and their time. Even then, they hastened to demonstrate their lack of seriousness. In presenting the world with her *Divine Songs and Meditations* in 1653, An Collins excused herself thus:

> Yet sith it was my morning exercise
> The fruit of intellectuals to vent

> In songs or counterfeits of poesies,
> And having therein found no small content,
> To keep that course my thoughts are therefore bent
> And rather former works to vindicate
> Than any new conception to relate.

She claims that it was her daily religious exercise to versify and to ditty, that is, to write new words for old songs and, because she enjoyed it, she continued to do it. She specifically excludes the possibility of originality, and goes on in zigzag phrases to deny ambition as well:

> Now touching that I hasten to express,
> Concerning these, the offspring of my mind,
> Who, though they here appear in homely dress,
> And, as they are my works, I do not find
> But, ranked with others, they may go behind,
> Yet for their matter, I suppose they be
> Not worthless quite while they with truth agree.

Aphra Behn competed with men less for empty praise than for solid pudding; when she inveighed against the shortcomings of her education it was because, once her novelty and notoriety had faded, she was ill-equipped to compete in the literary market-place. She was followed by a raffish group of professional women writers who never achieved even as much reputation or respectability as Behn could boast of. Delarivier Manley, who was ruined by a bigamous marriage when she was still a child and lived with her husband for three years after he had confessed his crime, so that she was never allowed into polite company, had little choice but to write for a living. While she was young and a novelty she got by with verse; she is probably the author of 'A Pindaric to Mrs Behn on her Poem on the Coronation. Written by a Lady', with its conventional disclaimer:

> Accept, thou much-loved Sappho of our isle,
> This hearty wish and grace it with a smile,
> When thou shalt know that thy harmonious lyre
> Did me, the meanest of thy sex, inspire,
> And that thy own inimitable lays

> Are cause alone that I attempt thy praise,
> Which in unequal measure I rehearse
> Because unskilled in numbers, grace or verse.
> Great Pindar's flights are fit alone for thee;
> The witty Horace's iambics be,
> Like Virgil's lofty strains, alas, too hard for me.
> And if enough this do not plead excuse,
> Pity the failings of a virgin muse,
> That never in this kind before assayed.
> Her muse till now was, like herself, a maid.

As Mrs Behn included this poem in an anthology she put together a year before her death, we must assume that she thought that it was not without merit, though to the modern taste its coyness and mock-modesty appear repulsive. A poet who presents herself as a curiosity and touts her own youth and virginity plays both pimp and whore. (If the poet is Delarivier Manley, within a few years she had given up peddling her youth and femaleness and taken to merchandising scandal in *romans-à-clef*.) Virgins are in great demand as prostitutes and virgin muses were no exception. There was always a market for works by gullible damsels whose very ineptitude was a selling-point, did they but know it. Elizabeth Teft, alias Orinthia, was in business at the same stand in 1747, when she pleaded for her *Miscellanies*.

> Every error generously excuse;
> Consider, Sir, a simple virgin's muse.

Laetitia Pilkington, separated from husband and children in conse-quence of her own indiscretion, 'once had the misfortune of writing for a Printer who never examined the Merit of the Work but used to measure it'. Though she wrote songs and three ballad operas for James Worsdale, who published them as his own work, and was personally acquainted with far more of the *habitués* of White's than any lady of reputation should have been able to name, she was imprisoned for debt in the Marshalsea in 1742. Every woman who sold her pen was also suspected of prostituting her person. As she did it for dire necessity, the imputation was often but by no means always justified. Nowadays the word 'professional' implies 'serious, committed'; in the eighteenth century it meant merely 'venal'.

'Shall I', wrote Mrs Mary Jones to her friend Lady Bowyer,

> Shall I go late to bed and early rise,
> To be the very creature I despise?
> With face unmov'd my poem in my hand,
> Cringe to the porter, with the footman stand?

When the great lord who might give her a couple of guineas for a dedication had the servants declare him not at home, she must wait in the servants' hall –

> Sick at the news, impatient for my Lord,
> I'm forc'd to hear, nay, smile at every word.

The professional poet of either sex had to 'smile, lie, eat toads and lick the dust'. And Mrs Jones needed the money, even while she sat 'in garret high',

> Out-soaring flatterers stinking breath
> And gently rhyming rats to death.

It must not be thought, however, that the women who were forced to write for a livelihood fared worse than the men. If they lost their respectability, they at least acquired notoriety, which was saleable. Curll's translators were paid so little that three of them worked side by side in the only bed in their squalid, unheated lodging. Charles Gildon was a gifted man whose talents were distorted by want; after a desperate career of misappropriation, servile flattery and outright forgery, he died in pathetic circumstances after years of being destitute and blind. Male poets acquired enduring reputations despite lives of the most crushing misery; some who ended in madness or suicide are still read. The factors that militated against female excellence in poetry led not to despair and death, but to mediocrity, often complacent mediocrity.

Women could find champions. Dr Johnson spent ten years arranging a subscription for the works of the blind poet Anna Williams, who lived in his house off and on for thirty years. Before her *Miscellanies in Prose and Verse* could finally emerge, he and his friends had to contribute their own work. Priscilla Pointon too was blind; a subscription was raised for her *Poems on Several Occasions* in 1770 and for another volume which was duly published in 1794, although there was no legible copy-text. Nothing can be further from the truth than the common notion that until our own day women had difficulty finding a publisher. The difficulty they had was of a different order, a difficulty in taking poetry seriously, in understanding what was involved in making a poem. Flattery, protectiveness and chivalry all added to that difficulty. When Dr Johnson learned several stanzas of Helen Maria Williams's 'Ode on the Peace' and repeated them to her at dinner, we must believe that he had been struck by sincere admiration, but what he admired in her work he would have despised in the work of a man. In his *Lives of the English Poets* he included not a single woman. A woman's work could charm him, but it was unlikely to impress him.

Pope's attitude to women poets illustrates the whole gamut of the reactions produced in the male literary establishment by the phenomenon of female talent. As well as his attempt to patronize Lady Winchilsea in an 'Impromptu' in answer to her remonstration with him for sneering lines in *The Rape of the Lock*, we have the sincerest compliment he ever paid any woman, namely his imitation of Elizabeth Rowe's elegy on her husband in 'Eloisa to Abelard'. Pope both acknowledged his indebtedness when the poem was published in 1719 and reprinted the text of Mrs Rowe's elegy, possibly because he was well aware that the comparison would prove that he made a better woman than she did. Eighteen-year-old Judith Cowper immediately responded with a poem of her own, 'Abelard to Eloisa'. Intrigued and flattered by her attention, Pope managed to meet her in 1722, in Charles Jervas's studio, where she was sitting for her portrait. He acquired her portrait for himself, corrected her verse, encouraged her writing and wrote a poem to her. We do not know what he hoped might develop from their relationship, but he was never considered as a suitor. The discovery in November 1723 that Judith was to marry Martin Madan brought the development of their friendship to a halt. Pope later reworked his verses to her in order to palm them off on Martha Blount and published his letters to Judith as *Letters to a Lady* in 1769. Lady Mary Wortley Montagu was a better poet than Rowe or Cowper and her relationship with Pope is correspondingly more difficult. Lady Mary collaborated with Pope and Gay on the town eclogues that were published by Curll as *Court Poems* in 1716, but by

1729 Pope was libelling her with a ferocity which implies pique beyond the usual in a man who was given to it. As an aristocrat Lady Mary could exhibit no interest in publication or in earning either fame or money from her literary activities, but she was intensely aware of being condemned to second-rateness by the deficiencies of her education. Pope, for his part, appears to have been convinced that excellence as a poet should cancel out all inequality of rank and lack of personal attraction. Never at any stage did he think of any of the women poets he befriended as a potential rival, though at least two appear to have appealed to him as potential sexual partners, poetesses to his poet.

The younger, lowlier and more ignorant the poet, the more easily she could be persuaded that she was a prodigy, the sole exception to the rule of female mediocrity. Teased by flattery, the poetess works her thin and narrow seam over and over, foundering into fearful postures of pertness and sprightliness. Mary Leapor, Mira to her readers, was never deceived, perhaps because she was without narcissism and the accompanying faculty for self-deception, being 'extremely swarthy and quite emaciated, with a long crane-neck, and a short body, much resembling, in shape a bass-viol'. Leapor wrote drolly of herself 'disrob'd with dirty shoes',

> And apron ragged as the Muse
> In night-cap tight and wrapping gown

biting her pen in chagrin at having refused a fee of ten pounds that day, for false modesty and vainglory because she was sporting a new top-knot. Pope might have sneered at her, but among the sixteen books she owned were most of his. She learned his style to mock herself. She wrote a fable on herself in the style of Gay, called 'The Sow and The Peacock', in which a swine exceeding witty

> And for the beauties of her Mind
> Excelling all her bristled kind

is rejected by a peacock who, fopling that he is, will not consent to roll in her sty. Vulgarity is no path to vigour for a woman, but Leapor's grotesque little poem can be guaranteed to make a reader laugh aloud. This insignificant piglet of poetry was a gardener's daughter who wrote to keep him alive, until the measles carried her off at the age of twenty-four. Her father was assisted in outliving her by the posthumous publication of her poems on subscription. Women poets being merchandised as freaks of nature, the greater the novelty the greater the acclaim. Mary Leapor is by no means the only servant-poetess of the eighteenth century. Mary Collier, whose *Poems on Several Occasions* were published in 1762, was a washerwoman. Ann Yearsley, who had considerable success in the 1780s, was a milk-seller. Elizabeth Hands, author of *The Death of Amnon* (1789), was a black-smith's wife. The most remarkable was Phillis Wheatley, 'brought from Africa to America in the year 1761, between seven and eight years of age'. In 1773 her poems were published, preceded by an attestation that she was genuinely 'under the disadvantage of serving as a slave in a family' in Boston. There is not much to choose between the effusions of the slave and the pastiche written by any other self-educated poet, male or female.

> 'Twas mercy brought me from my pagan land,
> Taught my benighted soul to understand
> That there's a God, that there's a saviour too.
> Once I redemption neither sought nor knew.
> Some view our sable race with scornful eye,
> 'Their colour is a diabolic dye.'
> Remember, Christians, Negroes, black as Cain,
> May be refined and join th'angelic train.

The degree of Wheatley's alienation from herself and her identification with an alien culture which sees her as inferior, so striking to a late twentieth-century mind, is hardly greater than the alienation of all the women who struggled to express themselves in a poetic language they had played no part in making. Wheatley is writing in a style already ossified, in a vocabulary that carries no hint of immediacy or individuality; hundreds of women poets did the same thing for the same basic reason, but we have still to understand the nature of their case.

By the second half of the eighteenth century women poets were so numerous that their writings had lost all novelty value. People began to imagine that the age of the female poet had finally dawned. Deserving oddities could still rely on compassionate support by way of subscriptions, but an important group of women poets set about striving for recognition from the literary establishment on something like equal terms. Curiously, the more successful they were, the less interesting we find them today. No one now reads Anne Laetitia Aikin, whose *Poems* (1773) were much admired and went through several editions. The reasons for her success and for her eventual failure are suggested in her short poem 'On a Lady's Writing':

> Her even lines her steady temper show,
> Neat as her dress, and polished as her brow,
> Stong as her judgment, easy as her air,
> Correct though free, and regular though fair,
> And the same graces o'er her pen preside
> That form her manners and her footsteps guide.

Miss Aikin also celebrated a female friend whose 'ready fingers plied with equal skill,/The pencil's task, the needle, or the quill'. Poetry in the young lady's scheme of things was on a par with needlework and the taking of views, a virtuous pastime and no more. Believing that a woman's highest calling was to be a companion to a man and mother to his children, Aikin showed her fitness for this great work by writing devotional literature for children. When in middle age she departed from the flowery purlieus of poetessery and, as Mrs Barbauld, attempted a long satiric poem entitled *Eighteen Hundred and Eleven*, the hostility of its reception shocked and shamed her into giving up poetry for ever.

Children's literature was invented in the late eighteenth century and poetesses were its most important and successful practitioners. Jane and Ann Taylor became famous as the authors of *Original Poems for Infant Minds* in 1805 and *Rhymes of the Nursery* in 1805. Ann Taylor used to say in old age that the feeling of being a grown woman let alone an old woman did not come naturally to her. Successful poetesses retain their affinity with childhood, and write nothing that a child could not safely read. Few people realize that these quatrains, described by E. V. Hale as the best-known verses in the English language,

> Mary had a little lamb,
> Its fleece was white as snow,

And everywhere that Mary went,
  The lamb was sure to go.

It followed her to school one day,
  Which was against the rule;
It made the children laugh and play,
  To see a lamb at school.

And so the teacher turned it out,
  And still it lingered near,
And waited patiently about
  Till Mary did appear.

Why does the lamb love Mary so?
  The eager children cry;
Why, Mary loves the lamb, you know,
  The teacher did reply.

constitute the masterpiece of the American poet Sara Josepha Hale, first published in the *Juvenile Miscellany* for September 1830, of which she was the editor, and then in her *Poems for our Children*. Mary Howitt (the female Wordsworth) scored a lesser hit with 'The Spider and the Fly'.

From one point of view writing and publishing for children simply take over from the ancient female pursuit of making up and singing poems to children, but there is an important difference. Children's literature was part of the construction of childhood as a period of innocence and powerlessness; toys are decoys from engagement with real life and the poetry of childhood was equally phoney. The literature of the nursery insisted on the nursery's separateness from the sphere of adults; no anxiety, no threat, no guilt was allowed to intrude. What survives of the ancient poetry of childhood in fossil form in traditional nursery rhymes shows that children shared in their parents' factionalism, their poverty, their anxiety, their persecution, their vengefulness, their morbid curiosity and their sexuality. The poetesses set to with a will, interposing a screen of monosyllabic verbiage between the children and understanding, manufacturing and preaching childish faith and simplicity. Nevertheless it is no small distinction to have penned a poem which has been known by heart by hundreds of millions of children. That we make nothing of it, and even apologize for it, indicates with blinding clarity just how little value we put on childish things. Sarah Catherine Martin, who penned *Old Mother Hubbard* in 1804, is not noticed by *The Dictionary of National Biography*.

The poetesses are even more conspicuous as writers of hymns, and especially hymns for children. Charlotte Elliott's *Hymns for a Week* sold 40,000 copies; her most famous hymn, 'Just as I am', is still sung in churches all over the world. Everybody knows 'All things bright and beautiful' and 'There is a green hill far away' and 'Once in royal David's city', but not everybody knows that they are part of the prolific output of Mrs C. F. Alexander or that 'We plough the fields and scatter' is by Jane M. Campbell. Sarah Flower Adams appears in *The Dictionary of National Biography* as 'poetess', and the genus is accurately delineated in an unusually rhapsodic entry by Richard Garnett: after enthusing about her verse play *Vivia Perpetua*, he continues:

> The authoress, however, was more happily inspired in her hymns, which, as simple expressions of devotional feeling, at once pure and passionate, can hardly be surpassed. 'Nearer to thee' – often erroneously attributed to Mrs Beecher Stowe – is known wherever the English language is spoken; and the lines beginning, 'He sendeth sun, He sendeth shower', are even more exquisite in their blended spirit of fervour and resignation. All who knew Mrs Adams personally speak of her with enthusiasm; she is described as a woman of singular beauty and attractiveness, delicate and truly feminine, high-minded, and in her days of health playful and high-spirited.

Mrs Adams went into a decline and died at the age of forty-three, before her playfulness, high-spiritedness, purity, passion, fervour, resignation and so forth should begin to pall, or her beauty, delicacy, femininity and attractiveness to give way to middle age.

Hymn-writing is a version of dittying in which new words are put to old tunes. It is closely related therefore to the Scottish ballad revival in which poetesses were instrumental and in which they had enormous success for very little effort. The ballad revival, like the discovery of nursery rhymes, was part collection and part invention. 'Hardyknute', one of the earliest ballads to be published, when it created a sensation, in 1719, was either written or rewritten by Elizabeth, Lady Wardlaw, who is possibly also responsible for the versions of 'Sir Patrick Spens' and 'Gilderoy' that later appeared in *Percy's Reliques of Ancient Poetry*. In 1753 Jane Elliot dittied on the old ballad 'The Flowers of the Field', turning it into a lament for Flodden which many believed to be traditional. The same ballad was dittied by Alicia Cockburn some years later and much admired by Robert Burns. Isobel Pagan, who is represented in anthologies by 'Ca' the Yowes to the Knowes', is not a typical poetess, because she was misanthropic, lame and lived alone on the proceeds of whisky-selling. Her 'uncouth lyrics', a by-product of evenings spent in bibulous company, were published in 1805. Burns's 'Hark! the Mavis' is dittied on Pagan's original. By contrast Lady Anne Lindsay's explanation of the composition of her famous ballad 'Auld Robin Gray' reveals the poetess *par excellence*.

> I was melancholy, and endeavoured to amuse myself by attempting a few poetical trifles. There was an English–Scotch melody of which I was passionately fond. Sophy Johnstone . . . used to sing it to us at Balcarres. She did not object to its having improper words, though I did. I longed to sing old Sophy's air to different words, and give its plaintive tones some little history of virtuous distress in humble life, such as might suit it.

When the ballad was published anonymously a number of people, including a clergyman, claimed it as their own, but Lady Anne kept her secret until two years before her death at the age of seventy-five.

Besides such enduring popular success, poetesses also met with acclaim from the more discerning which proved more fugitive. Dr Johnson declared that Hannah More was 'the most powerful versificatrix in the English language'. When she died aged eighty-eight in 1833 she left a huge fortune of £30,000 to be divided among seventy charities, all the proceeds of her literary activity. Charlotte Smith's *Elegiac Sonnets*, first published in 1784, went through six editions and won her golden opinions from the best poets of her generation. Hannah Cowley had enormous success as a playwright. Wordsworth addressed his first published poem to Helen Maria Williams. The most lionized of all was Joanna Baillie, whose *Series of Plays in which it is attempted to delineate the Stronger Passions of the Mind* was deemed the best dramatic writing since Shakespeare.

Anna Seward, the Swan of Lichfield, took her own poetic impulse so lightly that she yielded without a murmur to her parents' prohibition of versifying and swapped poetry for ornamental needlework, at which she worked just as hard. Her editor, Sir Walter Scott, betrays no twinge of disgust when he notes that, while she was distinguishing herself as a needlewoman, her time rolled on ten years. Scott finds a motive only for praise in her readiness to abandon her writing, and the way in which she sacrificed her own prospects of an independent life to care for her parents, who had been desolated by the death of her sister. But if you can be bothered to struggle through the great drift of indifferent verse she eventually wrote, you might find the odd couplet which gains a strange tension from its denial of Sir Walter's triumphant smugness:

> How many duteous Maids to filial cares,
> Yield unbecoming all their rosy years? . . .

> Through trials as hard as these, how oft are seen
> The tender Sex, in fortitude serene;
> Revenge unsought, and injuries unrevealed,
> Each wrong forgiven and each fault concealed . . .

Anna Seward's inverted egotism expressed itself as desperate shyness, but she was able to write as long as she was able to cloak her inward despair and frustration in a heavy wrap of piety – the substitute that female writers had to use for morality because they were prevented by the dictates of modesty from direct traffic with the truth and so with the naked flesh of ethics.

The women who threw off the wraps of decency and faced squarely on to the behaviour and the reality of their circumstances were brutalized by their struggle and fared no better ultimately. Most were content to illustrate their fealty to Anna Seward's recommendation:

> Designed for peace and soft delight,
> For tender love and pity mild,
> O seek thou not the craggy height
> The howling Main, the desert wild!

> Stay in the shelter'd valley low,
> Where calmly blows the fragrant air,
> But shun the Mountain's stormy brow,
> For darken'd winds are raging there . . .

Anna Seward knew the real courage and muscle that women have to wield in the exercise of this kinder love and pity mild, for she tended an apoplectic and paralysed father for ten years. By the time he died it was too late to seek a more demanding intellectual milieu. Seward seldom stirred from dreary Lichfield, although she knew that she needed some greater stimulus.

> Then should Fame or Pleasure to my ear
> Whisper that talent blooms neglected here,
> Lure to the circles where congenial fire
> Might emulation's generous warmth inspire,
> Yet here the spirit of departed joy
> Shall chain my step, shall fascinate my eye,
> Chase with his local spells awakening powers,
> Each languid consciousness of wasted hours.

The truth was that Anna Seward was afraid, deadly afraid of what she saw as the brutality and hardness of men, their cold exploitation of female susceptibility, the peremptoriness of their ambition and above all the different way they felt about all kinds of matters, especially love and loyalty. Even the great Dr Darwin, whom she utterly admired and who influenced her verse for the irretrievably worse, stole poems of hers and fixed them to his *Botanic Garden*. Somewhere in her ran a thin vein of iron, for she demanded that Scott put right the attribution and, as the poems had been published previously under Seward's name, he had no choice but to oblige her. She would not fight with Dr Darwin while she lived, but she made sure that the stain on his memory persists. Her discretion may after all have been the better part of valour; at least she lived and died her allotted span in honour.

Felicia Hemans was, like Anna Seward, too 'poetic' for the society of men, in all the mawkish Victorian meaning of that term.

> Her birth, her education, her genius . . . combined to inspire a
> passion for the etherial, the tender, the imaginative, the heroic,

in one word, the beautiful ... it was poetry she sought in history, scenery, character and religious belief ... She was a Muse, a Grace, the Italy of human beings.

Translated in terms of contemporary literary taste, we discover that this means that Hemans was sentimental, pious and prone to thread-bare exotic and romantic fantasy, a fantastic picturesque and all quaint bric-à-brac of the mind. The bitterest irony of all is that by his desertion Captain Hemans effectively blighted Mrs Hemans's gift, for she was so busy churning out popular poetry to pay for her sons' education that she could never take sufficient pains to bring her poetry up to her own standard. Not only was her secret heart unknown and undeveloped, her poetic gift died overworked and undeveloped too. Both Mrs Hemans's and Miss Seward's genius were strangled in the toils of rigid self-discipline. They forced themselves either to write as impersonal narrators or to convolute all their yearning into some inward spiral of aspiration for heaven and sanctity, achieved through wordless suffering and self-abnegation. They exalted a muteness which is the antithesis of poetry. They beat their language into quaintness and insipidity, strained off the black bile and the rage and prided themselves upon the pure mush that they were then able to offer the complacent public, whose certainties they were endorsing at such secret and unremitting cost to themselves. How could they resist this pressure, exerted from every contact they could expect to make in their poetic lives? They would be praised for nothing in their poetic achievement so much as they might have been in its renuncia-tion. Even an artist as discerning as Dickens could find no higher praise for Adelaide Procter than

> She never by any means held the opinion that she was among the greatest of human beings; she never suspected a conspiracy on the part of mankind against her; she never recognised in her best friends, her worst enemies; she never cultivated the luxury of being misunderstood and unappreciated. She would far rather have died without seeing a word of her composition in print than that I should have maundered about her as 'the poet' or 'the poetess'.

Those women who felt their poetic vocation as something peremp-tory, who whispered fiercely to themselves that they were *poets*, were obliged to consider the dread possibility that the normal gratifications of a woman's existence were lost to them, sacrificed to the higher destiny that had become the poet's. As Mrs Hemans wailed in the person of Properzia de'Rossi:

> Tell me no more, no more
> Of my soul's lofty gifts! Are they not rain
> To quench its haunting thirst for happiness?
> Have I not loved and striven and failed to bind
> One true heart unto me whereon my own
> Might find a resting place, a hope for all
> Its burden of affections? I depart,
> Unknown though Fame goes with me . . .

Paranoia had become the poet's birthright. No one now was content merely to rhyme, to write witty occasional verse, or to write poetry as a complete man's elegant recreation, or to speak in a public voice. The romantic poet was bard, seer, prophet, visionary, and could only become so by hallucinating himself with hunger and fatigue and self-denial, pushing himself to the outer extremities of experience. Insofar as the poetesses clung to the language of Thomas Gray and William Collins, they shunned this higher duty. Where poets sought glory amid glaciers in the cragged hills, poetesses enacted piety, humility, fairy fantasy and the domestic affections. Now that it seemed impossible that a woman would take on the mantle of poet, it had to be done.

At fourteen years old Elizabeth Barrett had no doubt that she was a poet. She chose no less than Homer for her model and, undaunted by her innocence of classical learning or warfare, wrote *The Battle of Marathon*. At twenty she wrote 'An Essay on Mind'. The ambition overbalanced the skill as obviously as the most uncharitable critic might expect, but Elizabeth's great ego struggled on, battling through avalanches of ideas she only half understood, turning inward upon her in its hunger for experience and shaking her small body with hysterics, paroxysms and convulsions. Baffled and deflected from any public arena, she took the egotist's classical refuge in outrageous shyness, pressed her whole family into service upon her palpitations and read, read, read, wilfully sacrificing her beauty and her chances of health to her hunger for the power of knowledge. She threw away ten years in the service of a blind pedant, chipped away with the poetesses at stagy pieces for Mary Russell Mitford's contemptible annuals, until she burst forth in her own image with another hubristic attempt, an account of the Redemption in verse. She won a considerable reputation, but she had not yet satisfied her own requirements of herself. She was desperately ill and dependent on opium but she felt that her poetry was a destiny to be worked out. We must be thankful that there was nobody in a white coat ready to destroy our poet's creative tension by shock treatment, for she went to the frontiers of death and madness and back again, with nothing but her opium to help her. Her brother Edward was drowned, and Elizabeth realized how parasitic she had been on his short and utterly unrealized existence. She struggled as she had never struggled before to turn to the best account a life that had already cost so much. In her sealed room in Wimpole Street she crossed the frontiers that virtuous women had always respected. She made poetry about illegitimate birth and infanticide.

Elizabeth Barrett knew better than to say that there is no sex in mind; she knew that the mind was conditioned, shaped by the destiny of the body, through which it learned all it knew just as she knew that the female sensibility of her time was as sharply differentiated from the male as might be. 'Poets needs must be/Or men or women, more's the pity' she was to write. Nevertheless, she was different from the poetesses of her time. She did not write to live, or as a diversion or elegant accomplishment, or to project herself as feminine, virtuous and desirable. She lived to write and she was rashly prepared to sacrifice all the traditional gratifications of women.

> Day and night
> I worked my rhythmic thought and furrowed up
> Both watch and slumber with long lines of life
> Which did not suit their season. The rose fell
> From either cheek, my eyes globed luminous
> Through orbits of blue shadow and my pulse
> Would shudder along the purple-veined wrist
> Like a shot bird.

The sacrifice of youth and health and beauty is part of her rejection of all more partial forms of knowledge, which she considered the

duty of a poet. She struggles to gaze impudently into the face of
eternity but too often falls back to banality and impotence.

> Such ups and downs
> Have poets.
> Am I such indeed? The name
> Is royal, and to sign it like a queen,
> Is what I dare not, –
> . . . 'tis too easy to go mad
> And ape a Bourbon in a crown of straws;
> The thing's too common.

For Elizabeth Barrett there was no art but the best, but she was
well aware of the role that poetry had played in women's past:

> Many fervent souls
> Strike rhyme on rhyme, who would strike steel on steel
> If steel had offered, in a restless heat
> Of doing something. Many tender souls
> Have strung their losses on a rhyming thread,
> As children, cowslips: — the more pains they take,
> The work more withers.

Browning's heroine, Aurora Leigh, is moved by a desire to utter
essential truth, not to depict the picturesque or the exotic, to tangle
fine tales for the readers of the illustrated poetry annuals, but to get
something so right that it would stay right for ever. For her image of
truth she uses Alexander's similitude of the colossal statue of a man,
which appears to the normal-sighted as just another mountain.
The peasants gathering brushwood in his ear have not discerned the
form or feature of humanity in the huge figure – it is the poet who
must describe it aright.

> . . . poets should
> Exert a double vision; should have eyes
> To see near things as comprehensively
> As if afar they took their point of sight,
> And distant things as intimately deep
> As if they touched them.

Surely things are different now! Surely woman poets will not have to wait for the chance of finding a poet as sensitive as a woman, like the one who took Elizabeth Barrett Browning out of her live interment and set her poetry free in this sudden mad spate of fine, muddled, headlong, sometimes grotesque but unmistakable poetry? Now that a woman may aspire with the best of men, may claim her cultural heritage with the same insolence as any poetaster of the age? We may speak now of wombs and blood and birth and bitterness, may we not, and be known for it? One look back at Elizabeth Barrett Browning's colossal statue should remind us where we have seen its unyielding masculine lineaments before. It is none other than Sylvia Plath's *Colossus*.

THE TRANSVESTITE POET

There is a version of the Judaeo-Christian creation myth which holds that Adam before the creation of Eve was both male and female, in other words, androgynous. Adam, out of whose body Eve was born, was and remains the one and only parturient man in our tradition. The male poet considers himself a creative androgyne, his female part being externalized as his muse while, like Eve, the woman poet remains female and female only. Male nature may comprehend female but female does not comprehend male. Consciousness of gender as limitation has prompted the development of an androgynous ideal, be it angelic or pagan or merely post-feminist. For those who believe the soul/mind to partake of angelic nature and to be neither male nor female, to overcome gender it is necessary merely to transcend the body. For women, but not for men, this usually meant sacrificing their reproductive opportunities. However, my concern is not here to follow the platonic or neoplatonic ideal of androgyny through its many historico-literary manifestations but to consider some aspects of the contradictions inherent in the idea of overcoming sexuality and/or gender as they presented themselves to the female poet. The very use of the term female poet rather than poetess suggests a willed androgyny.

It is a curious fact that there are many more men who claim the right to be female than there are women claiming the right to be male. Such men may shave their faces, legs and chests, dress as women, use women's cosmetics, take hormonal preparations and eventually have themselves castrated and surgically reconstructed in a fashion resembling female anatomy, giving birth to the female from their own bodies as it were by Caesarean section. Such men are apt to say that they had been women trapped inside a man's body until, by excision of male secondary sexual characteristics, they set themselves free. Women who are so biologically are very well aware that the constructed femaleness of men who have had what is erroneously called a sex-change operation is extremely artificial, that they are exaggeratedly feminine rather than actually female. What they are assuming is feminine gender, which is culturally constructed, rather than female sex, which is biological. One of the arguments of late twentieth-century feminism is that women too are being asked to impose feminine gender upon femaleness, to impersonate the feminine by belying the female. The feminine signifier is the virginal bosom; how far the contemporary female has capitulated to the gender ideal rather than the corporeal real can be gauged by the fact that mastectomy is associated with disfigurement and despair, while the psychological sequelae of hysterectomy are unexpected and often remain undiagnosed. Losing a breast involves a minor operation and little risk to life, but the sufferer considers herself and is considered a tragic heroine. Hysterectomy, on the other hand, though a major operation, is accepted as routine. Both men and women are tormented by the disjunction between their gender and their sex, but it is not women who have constructed the masculinity that so many men find a bad fit. Men have constructed both masculinity and femininity; in no field of human endeavour is this more apparent than it is in literature.

From the beginnings of poetry, male poets have assumed the right to write as women, laying bare – or, rather, inventing – the most intimate feelings of women. The consumers of poetry, who are in large measure, if not dominantly, female, have unconsciously absorbed what is in fact less a *description* of female nature than a *prescription*. The poet, whether he be Homer writing the speeches of Andromache or Virgil setting forth the passion of Dido or the prophet speaking as the beloved of Solomon, has presented a version of femininity that has been assumed to be not simply authentic but stereotypic. When literacy was the privilege of a small élite, these prescriptions had little in the way of damaging effect. The vast majority of working, childbearing women were quite unaware of the heroines whom they resembled not at all and could not be mocked by awareness of their shortcomings, their smelliness, their hairiness, their vigour and joviality. Men might dream of white-armed Venus but they realized that they were married to mere mortals who knew nothing of their dreams, especially as the literature that men were nourished on was written in languages that women never learned to read. Women began to capitulate to literary notions of womanhood only after the invention of printing and the rise of vernacular literatures, when the classic texts themselves were translated expressly so that ladies could read them, gentlemen being still expected to read them in the original. All the while male poets had been ventriloquizing as females but now women at the most susceptible stage in their personal development began to share the masculine fantasy of womanhood. No matter how mute and helpless the female, the male poet gives her artfully plangent voice to sing her victimhood.

> The maidens came
>
> When I was in my mother's bower;
> I had all that I would.
> > The bailey beareth the bell away,
> > The lily, the rose, the rose I lay.
>
> The silver is white, red is the gold,
> The robes they lay in fold.
> > The bailey beareth the lull away,
> > The lily, the rose, the rose I lay,
>
> And through the glass window shines the sun.
> How should I love, and I so young?
> > The bailey beareth the lull away,
> > The lily, the rose, the rose I lay.

Any poet is everywhere and always ventriloquizing: the male poet may know little more of the spiritual reality of a soldier on the battlefield or a king on the throne than he does of a woman, but he shares both the conditioning of males as males and their endocrine reality. He does not think of men as the object of his desires but as versions of himself. The male, conceiving himself as the norm from which the female is the departure, sees himself as containing all human life, and capable of all varieties of human experience; the female, as object of male desire, is defined not by her potentialities but by her limitations.

The level of contrast between masculine and feminine is, however, anything but constant. Though all cultures differentiate between male and female characteristics and fields of activity, sexual polarization, no matter how weightily institutionalized, cannot be fixed. Activities considered masculinizing or feminizing change from generation to generation, and the fragility of sexual identity can be greater or lesser from decade to decade. The area of overlap between masculine and feminine behaviours can be vast or virtually non-existent. What seems clear from a study of the evolution of late twentieth-century concepts of gender is that notions of masculine and feminine have become both more sharply contrasting and more intransigent.

According to the nursery rhyme, little boys are grubby and horrid and little girls are clean and sweet.

> What are little boys made of?
> Frogs and snails
> And puppy-dogs' tails,
> That's what little boys are made of.
>
> What are little girls made of?
> Sugar and spice
> And all that's nice,
> That's what little girls are made of.

Nursery rhymes are anything but timeless; this one was first published in the mid-nineteenth century as part of the invention of modern childhood. Though the construction of boyhood required a rigorous school system, a boys' literature and an intense culture of rough-and-tumble games, the result was thought by many to be as timeless as nursery rhymes. Sir Sidney Lee believed 'that the nature of boys is a pretty permanent factor in any society'. Issue was taken by W. Robertson Davies:

> It is true that many boys are characterised by an oafishness which their elders find agreeable because it makes the boys less troublesome than if they are acute. During the latter half of the nineteenth century, and even yet in many circles, the influence of public school education and the spirit of the age tended to make boys conventional and scornful of vigorous expressions of emotion, exalting intellectual stagnation and Red Indian stoicism above all other virtues.

Boys were not always so boyish. In Shakespeare's time both little boys and little girls wore skirts until the boys were old enough to be 'breeched'. Then their mothers wept, knowing that their little ones had begun the long, hard induction into masculinity. In many cultures boys live in the women's houses until they are old enough to be initiated into the men's activities. In Shakespeare's world a version of this still prevailed. It is often very difficult to decide in the iconography of sixteenth- and seventeenth-century child portraiture whether the subject is a girl or a boy. In the diaries of the time both mothers and fathers habitually refer to a son or daughter as 'the child'. Nowadays, though the word 'baby' is still ungendered, sexual differentiation is evident from a very early age. A parent will refer to a child as 'my little girl' or 'my little boy' rather than 'my child'. This is an important change, for it reflects the way in which we have come to think of gender as inherent in the same way that sex is. If a tiny baby is to be seen as a little man and fundamentally different from his sister, similar behaviours will be interpreted in contrasting ways. All our studies of mothers' behaviour shows rigid distinctions in responses to child signals; if a mother believes that a child is a boy she will respond more rapidly to its crying and she will feed it more readily than when she believes it is a girl. In Shakespearian times, when babies of both sexes were often sickly, a little girl was more likely to be praised and admired for the lustiness of her crying and her appetite than she is now. In popular thinking, it was mother's milk that feminized little boys, who would not begin to be male until it was out of them. An insufficiently masculinized man is still called a 'milksop'. In Shakespeare's time, boys greatly outnumbered adult men. As the 'hardening of youth' into manhood was a long, arduous process that in a significant number of cases was never completed, there was a clearer perception in Elizabethan times of the contrast between grown man and male child. Every stage in the process, from weaning to majority, when the boy was old enough to carry arms, involved a transformation.

> At first the infant,
> Mewling and puking in the nurse's arms.
> Then the whining schoolboy with his satchel
> And shining morning face, creeping like snail
> Unwillingly to school. And then the lover,
> Sighing like furnace, with a woful ballad
> Made to his mistress' eyebrow. Then, a soldier . . .

The sighing Elizabethan boy was by our lights an extremely effeminate creature who wore his hair hanging in soft curls and wept, blushed and laughed as easily as any girl. As a figure of Eros he was the proper object of the desire of both sexes and at the same time susceptible to the soft passion himself. Ben Jonson, impersonating his mistress, gives this account of the kind of man who would have better success with her than he:

> Young I'll have him too, and fair,
> Yet a man; with crisped hair
> Cast in thousand snares and rings
> For Love's fingers and his wings: . . .
> Chin, as woolly as the peach,
> And his lip would kissing teach . . .
> He would have a hand as soft
> As the down and show it oft,
> Skin as smooth as any rush,
> And so thin to see a blush
> Rising through it ere it came;
> All his blood should be a flame
> Quickly fired as in beginners.

The Elizabethan theatre unnerved its critics because it was essentially subversive; one of the institutions it destabilized was gender. It did this not only by having men play women and play them seductively, but by confounding male and female behaviours so that men were as labile and voluble as women. *A Midsummer Night's Dream*, for example, plays strange tricks with gender. It opens with the preparations for the wedding of Theseus with the Amazon queen. The iconography of Amazons in the masques of the period shows them dressed as warrior women. Theseus refers to an unconventional courtship, claiming to have wooed Hippolyta with his sword and won her love doing her injuries. The dimorphism that we are used to in bridal couples, the man in body-hugging black, the woman frothy and light in white, cannot be seen in this conjoining of two warriors or in the matching of the two speeches that open the play. Titania describes Hippolyta as 'the bouncing Amazon', a 'buskin'd mistress' and a 'warrior love', as if she were standing toe to toe with Theseus in wedding-as-combat.

Oberon is passing fell and wrath with Titania

> Because that she, as her attendant, hath
> A lovely boy, stol'n from an Indian king.
> She never had so sweet a changeling; . . .

The child is, as it were, the child of a same-sex marriage between Titania and his mother, the votaress of her order. Oberon and Titania cannot rear him together because marriage is out of their sphere. Such a pair as they might as well be same-sex lovers. As they can have no bodily connection, the only child they can have has to be born of an earthly man and woman. Oberon's plot to cause Titania to fall in love with something else so that, while she is otherwise obsessed, he can 'make her render up her page' to him makes clear that Titania is in love with her pretty child as if he were a catamite; she treats him, the fairy has told us, as she will be seen to treat Bottom, 'crowns him with flowers, makes him all her joy'. Relationships in fairyland have become so distorted partly because, as the fairies have no bodies, there is no kind of behaviour that is natural to them. Wayward love is tamed by its consequences and fairies cannot breed. True love is dependent upon death and fairies can never die. Both Titania and Oberon have had unconsummated adulterous affairs, Titania with Theseus, Oberon with Hippolyta. As there is nothing to hold them together, each is compelled to follow the endless ramifications of erotic fantasy for ever. Sex is one way to anchor fantasy in reality and marriage is the means by which both are civilized. Neither is available to the spirits who throng the wood outside Athens. The best that Titania can do for Bottom is to purge his 'mortal grossness' so that he can 'like an airy spirit go', condemning him to the restless covetousness of the fairies, who can only steal children not make them. Bottom treats the fairies that Titania sends to wait upon him, a gaggle of four little sexless pages, Peaseblossom, Cobweb, Moth and Mustardseed, as gentlemen, but he cannot prevent himself from speculating on what they have never had, a cut finger, a father and a mother, and a meal of roast beef.

The icon of same-sex union presented by Titania and her votaress is repeated in Helena's description of her relationship with Hermia:

> We, Hermia, like two artificial gods,
> Have with our needles created both one flower,
> Both on one sampler, sitting on one cushion,
> Both warbling of one song, both in one key,
> As if our hands, our sides, voices, and minds,
> Had been incorporate. So we grew together,
> Like to a double cherry: seeming parted,
> But yet an union in partition,
> Two lovely berries moulded on one stem.
> So, with two seeming bodies but one heart . . .

This is the language of spiritual union, of marriage. It belongs to the same frame of reference as Shakespeare's hymn of perfect love, 'The Phoenix and the Turtle', which floats on the surface of Shakespeare's deep understanding of the metaphysics of gender, apparently clear and transparent and actually totally mysterious.

> So they loved as love in twain
> Had the essence but in one,
> Two distincts, division none.
> Number there in love was slain.
>
> Hearts remote yet not asunder,
> Distance and no space was seen
> 'Twixt this Turtle and his Queen.
> But in them it were a wonder.
>
> So between them love did shine
> That the Turtle saw his right
> Flaming in the Phoenix' sight.
> Either was the other's mine.
>
> Property was thus appalled
> That the self was not the same.
> Single nature's double name
> Neither two nor one was called.

The Phoenix is here the Queen, the Turtle is her male mate; putting the Phoenix first is like referring to the Queen and King in that order. The turtledove, like a Rajput widow, has elected to be consumed by the phoenix's funeral pyre, and this time the phoenix will not rise. She too has accepted annihilation and sacrificed immortality to remain with her faithful dove. The poem recognizes otherness, for two creatures could hardly be more sharply contrasted than the one and only phoenix and the common turtledove, but the otherness cannot be understood as an encoded way of referring to gender difference. Nor is one bird beauty and another truth, for only both together can make truth-and-beauty.

The youth's propensity for love was seen by Elizabethans not as evidence of masculinity but as a function of his immaturity, when the high level of his gonadal activity dictated both susceptibility and incontinence. The process of maturing was the gradual achievement of the masculine virtue of continence, verbal, emotional and spermatic. Love is the special bane of 'breeching scholars in the schools'. Both Demetrius and Lysander in *A Midsummer Night's Dream* are referred to as youths; Lysander too claims that he changes his affections to Helena because he is young and not yet ripened to reason. In *The Merchant of Venice*, before Portia sets off for Belmont she brags to Nerissa:

> I'll prove the prettier fellow of the two,
> And wear my dagger with the braver grace,
> And speak between the change of man and boy . . .
> > and tell quaint lies
> How honourable ladies sought my love,
> Which I denying, they fell sick and died . . .
> And twenty of these puny lies I'll tell,
> That men shall swear I have discontinued school
> Above a twelvemonth . . .

Troilus too is 'a brave boy', the youngest son of Priam, 'not yet mature', who 'has not above three or four hairs on his chin' and is 'very young', 'an admirable youth who ne'er saw three-and-twenty'. The proper pastimes of this age are the games and arts of love. Troilus is nervous about the superior attractions of the Grecian youths, who

> are full of quality,
> Their loving well composed, with gifts of nature flowing,
> And swelling o'er with arts and exercise.

Troilus

> cannot sing,
> Nor heel the high lavolt, nor sweeten talk,
> Nor play at subtle games. –

These kinds of amorous display are all proper to the 'unhardened youth' described by Rosalind in *As You Like It*:

> I, being but a moonish youth [would] grieve, be effeminate, changeable, longing and liking, proud, fantastical, apish, shallow, inconstant, full of tears, full of smiles; for every passion something, and for no passion truly anything, as boys and women are for the most part cattle of this colour –

Celia reminds Rosalind that tears do not become a man, but Rosalind is never described as a man. She is Ganymede, cup-bearer to the gods, a celestial page. Other characters refer to her as a youth, a word that applied to both male and female in Shakespeare's time, a sweet youth, a peevish boy. 'The boy is fair'. Phoebe describes Ganymede as 'a pretty youth':

> He'll make a proper man. The best thing in him
> Is his complexion; and faster than his tongue
> Did make offence, his eye did heal it up.
> He is not very tall; yet for his years he's tall.
> His leg is but so-so; and yet 'tis well.
> There was a pretty redness in his lip,
> A little riper and more lusty-red
> Than that mixed in his cheek. 'Twas just the difference
> Betwixt the constant red and mingled damask.
> There be some women, Sylvius, had they marked him
> In parcels as I did, would have gone near
> To fall in love with him; . . .

Interestingly, Orlando, to whom Ganymede is actually married on stage, is described in very similar terms.

Shakespeare's was a time of flamboyant male display, not of oiled muscles and bulging G-strings, but of shape exaggerated by padding, embroidery, jewels and lace. A boy's beauty consisted of delicate skin, changeable colouring, lustrous eyes, glossy curls and a good leg. In *Hero and Leander*, Hero is described as a dressmaker's dummy loaded with elaborate costume, while Leander's beauty is the beauty of the naked boy:

> His dangling tresses that were never shorn
> Had they been cut, and unto Colchos borne,
> Would have allured the vent'rous youth of Greece
> To hazard more than for the Golden Fleece . . .
> His body was as straight as Circe's wand;
> Jove might have sipped out nectar from his hand.
> Even as delicious meat is to the taste,
> So was his neck in touching and surpass'd
> The white of Pelops' shoulder. I could tell ye
> How smooth his breast was, and how white his belly,
> And whose immortal fingers did imprint
> That heavenly path with many a curious dint
> That runs along his back . . .

Some might object that this evocation of the beauty of the boy is a pederast's self-indulgence. In fact, both men and women were supposed to be moved by lust for the beauty of the pubescent boy. Though the boy may be considered pre-masculine, in that he has not yet accumulated authority and seniority or muscle power, he is an erotic and erotically interesting figure, more so if he is beautiful. Oberon wanted to acquire Titania's page because of his beauty. A personable page made a good emissary; the best messenger of love is Eros himself. In Thomas Middleton's *A Mad World My Masters*, Harebrain announces that he has conveyed away his wife's 'wanton pamphlets, as *Hero and Leander, Venus and Adonis*; oh, two luscious marrow-bone pies for a young married wife'. It surprised no one in Shakespeare's audience that Phoebe should fall in love with Ganymede/Rosalind, or Olivia with Cesario/Viola. The male object of female desire is seen in, if anything, even more corporeal terms than the female object of male desire, whose legs are never referred to. In the housewife's second wanton pamphlet Venus loves 'rose-cheeked' Adonis because he is 'thrice fairer' than herself:

> Stain to all nymphs, more lovely than a man,
> More white and red than doves or roses are –

The tender boy responds to her bold wooing with blushes and pouting, burning with 'bashful shame'. When he smiles with disdain, the appearance of dimples in his 'hairless cheeks' makes Venus more desirous than ever. When Flute, playing Thisbe, sings the beauty of his/her lover, he/she might be parodying Venus's celebration of Adonis:

> Most radiant Pyramus, most lily-white of hue,
> Of colour like the red rose on triumphant brier . . .

Clearly Shakespeare's notion of sexual difference was not so polarized as to find the word 'beautiful' unsuitable for application to a man, who in today's English is usually called 'handsome', a word which refers rather to behaviour rather than appearance. Both Venus and the boar that sank his tusk into it marvelled at the lily-white softness of Adonis's flank. Nowadays the bodies of both men and boys are expected to be hard. Adonis's hairlessness makes him kissable; his lips are at least as soft, sweet and easily bruised as a woman's.

It has been argued that the sensuous portrayal of the male love object is simply a feminization of that object, but this is not in fact a fair or accurate description of what goes on either in *Venus and Adonis* or whenever Shakespeare's lovers celebrate each other's beauty. If both partners in heterosexual congress are feminized, then something important is being said about sexuality itself, or more properly perhaps about sensuality. Shakespeare's Venus is allowed sensuality; she is expected to desire to embrace male beauty in exactly the same way that men are attracted by female beauty. We learn more about this series of assumptions when Venus tells Adonis that she did not yield to Mars until he had abandoned his martial bearing for the arts of love:

> Over my altars hath he hung his lance,
> His battered shield, his uncontrollèd crest,
> And for my sake hath learned to sport and dance,
> To toy, to wanton, dally, smile and jest, . . .

Clearly such pastimes are not proper to the 'soldier':

> Full of strange oaths, and bearded like the pard,
> Jealous in honour, sudden and quick in quarrel,
> Seeking the bubble reputation
> Even in the cannon's mouth.

In this case it was clearly not Venus who was feminized, being female already, but the lover, who had to abandon his hyper-masculine postures for a new playful mode. We have only to try to imagine Clint Eastwood managing such a transition to realize how much has changed. For Elizabethans sexual activity itself was feminine; no one doubted the existence of female libido or that it was potentially insatiable, possibly because they assumed that it partook of the nature of the sensuality of the boy, which only became controllable when he passed out of his teens and became a man. It was the duty of a man to withstand the blandishments of both boys and women. The concern of the moralists of marriage was to avoid waking the sleeping giant of concupiscence by imposing chastity and delay upon both spouses. The incontinence of young men was a persuasion against rather than for allowing them to marry. Heroes, when they succumb to the sway of the goddess of love, shed their armour and become soft in body and in mind. It is as true to say that they regress to a childish condition as that they are feminized. In Book II of *The Faerie Queene* the noble knight Cymochles, in his flight from Acrasia's Bower of Bliss, where he

> has poured out his idle mind
> In dainty delices and lavish joys,
> Having his warlike weapons cast behind,
> And flows in pleasure, and vain pleasing toys,
> Mingled amongst loose ladies and lascivious boys.

Though to us the notion of flowing might indicate the triumph of masculinity, such incontinence was taken by Elizabethans to cause languor and loss of virility. When the soldier detumesced in the embrace of the enchantress, were 'All his force forlorn and all his glory done'. The young man sleeping beside Acrasia in the Bower of Bliss is called Verdant, a name which places him in the springtime of his life; he

> seemed to be
> Some goodly swain of honorable place,
> That certes it great pity was to see
> Him his nobility so foul deface;
> A sweet regard and amiable grace,
> Mixed with manly sternness did appear
> Yet sleeping, in his well-proportioned face,
> And on his tender lips the downy hair
> Did now but freshly spring, and silken blossoms bear.

Awareness of women's active libido lay behind the refusal to allow women to play themselves upon the stage; Elizabethans realized the importance of the clitoris in releasing the full fury of venery in women and they knew where to find it. They knew better than to decide that the clitorally responsive female was motivated by penis envy, infantile or fixated. Their idea of a generalized erotic sensibility is very different from the modern concept of butch and bitch; as their only forms of contraception involved coitus reservatus or coitus interruptus, they did not place the same importance on penetration that we do. For them penetration was only one form of intimacy and possibly not the most pleasant. All these considerations play some part in explaining the relatively large segment of Renaissance emotional experience that was open to both sexes, in an area that we might label androgynous.

By the time Shakespeare was writing *The Tempest*, the ground seems to have shifted. Once again Shakespeare juggles notions of gender. Prospero and Ariel's is a one-sided love story in which the consummation will be the letting go, the conferral of liberty upon the beloved and the acceptance of loneliness, abandonment and, eventually, death.

> Do you love me master, no?
>
> Dearly, my delicate Ariel.

In this love affair both sex and gender have been specifically ruled out. Prospero is an old man and Ariel is more angel than human. Even for the humans in *The Tempest*, though sex is imminent and immanent, gender has been obscured. Neither Miranda nor Caliban has learned a behaviour appropriate to the social perception of their sex. Caliban sees in Miranda not a love object but a way of passing on his genes and peopling the isle with Calibans. Miranda for her part has no notion that as a woman she ought to play the role of love object rather than lover. Prospero is concerned that she may act too spontaneously in her dealings with the young prince, who will expect from her the behaviour appropriate to modest women and may misinterpret her innocence as easiness of virtue. When Miranda beholds Ferdinand, she begins to speak to him and about him in the way that Lucentio speaks of his first sight of Bianca in *The Taming of the Shrew* or Antipholus of Syracuse to Luciana in *The Comedy of Errors*. She is protective of him too, defending him against her father's wrath, saying that he is gentle, not frightening. When she sees him carrying logs, she begs him to rest while she carries the logs for him.

> it would become me
> As well as it does you: and I should do it
> With much more ease

Miranda is a woman without gender. Her womanhood is unlimited either by conventional expectations or internalized self-image. When Alonso sees her playing chess with Ferdinand, itself a wonderful icon of equality and ungendered activity, he calls her 'goddess'. As a dramatist, Shakespeare spoke as both male and female, young and old, as well as the occasional ghost, fairy or androgyne. The same sort of imaginative freedom was displayed by Sir Philip Sidney, whose characters, apart from being in many instances transvestites themselves, are equally prone to express themselves in verse regardless of gender. What is even more remarkable is that Sidney's niece, Lady Mary Wroth, exercised the same freedom in *The Countess of Montgomery's Urania*. In one notable case she takes a poem she originally wrote about Penshurst and puts it into the mouth of Dolorindus, King of Negroponte.

It would be quite wrong to conclude from the freedom of Shakespeare, Jonson and Fletcher to set their imaginary actions in unmapped territories of gender ambiguity that their epoch was free from anxieties about questions of sexual identity. The Puritan attack on the stage was typified by intense anxiety about what it meant 'For a boy to put on the attire, the gesture, the passions of a woman'. Anglophile

Eutho, under which sobriquet lurked Anthony Munday, greatly deplored the corruption of 'young boys, inclining of themselves unto wickedness, trained up in filthy speeches, unnatural and unseemly gestures, to be brought up by these School-masters in bawdry and in idleness'. Stubbes was of the opinion that the boys were actually debauched:

> Then, these goodly pageants being done, every mate sorts to his mate, every one brings another homeward of their way very friendly, and in their secret conclaves (covertly) they play the Sodomites or worse.

Prynne too was concerned for the virtue of the young men in the theatre industry.

> Pity it is to consider, how many ingenuous, Witty, comely youths, devoted unto God in baptism, . . . are oftimes by their graceless Parents, even wholly consecrated to the Stage (the *Devil's Chapel*, as the fathers phrase it) where they are trained up in the *School of Vice* the playhouse . . . to the very excess of all effeminacy, to act these womanish, whorish parts, which Pagans would even blush to personate.

Prynne quotes the Epistles of Cyprian, pleading for the excommunication of one who

> did train up boys for the stage, for that he taught them against the express instruction of God himself, how a male might be effeminated into a female, how their sex might be changed by Art, so that the devil who defiles God's workmanship, might be pleased by the offices of a depraved and effeminated body . . . For since men are prohibited by law to put on a woman's garment, and such who do it are adjudged accursed. How much more greater a sin is it, not only to put on women's apparel, but likewise to express obscene, effeminate and womanish gestures, by the skill or tutorship of an unchaste art?

Puritans did not see the theatre presenting, as it should, the highly polarized world of Judaeo-Christian religion; they saw the stage and its purlieus as the haunt of smooth-bodied non-men whose histrionic skills rendered them highly seductive. Puritans, with their insistence upon cropped heads and severely cut clothing, were retreating from what Gordon Rattray Taylor once called the matrism of Elizabethan society towards something more authoritarian and patriarchal. They could not contemplate the theatre, where all distinctions were confounded and a mountebank could make a better king than the actual monarch, without acute anxiety.

> Yea, men are unmanned on the Stage: all the honour and vigour of their sex is effeminated with the shame, the dishonesty of an unsinewed body. He who is most womanish and best resembles the female sex, gives best content.

Prynne was the more anxious because he found the theatre spectacle acutely erotic:

> Lastly, this putting on of woman's array (especially to act a lascivious, amorous, whorish, Love-sick Play upon the Stage) must needs be sinful, yea abominable: because it not only excites many Adulterous filthy lusts, both in the Actors and the Spectators; and draws them on to contemplative and actual lewdness . . . but likewise instigates them to self-pollution (a sin for which Onan was destroyed): and to that unnatural Sodomitical sin of uncleanness . . .

Women too were aroused by the dressing of pretty boys as women. Ben Jonson's *Epicoene* opens with a scene between Clerimont and his page, whom Clerimont has been sending to the house of Lady Haughty, where much has been made of him.

> The gentlewomen play with me and throw me on the bed, and carry me in to my lady; and she kisses me with her oiléd face, and puts a peruke on my head: and asks me an I will wear her gown? and I say no: and then she hits me a blow o'the ear, and calls me Innocent!

Prynne did not see the theatre as a mirror of manners but as corrupter of manners.

For whence is it that many of our Gentry are lately degenerated into a more than Sardanapalian effeminacy; that they are now so fantastic in their Apparel, so womanish in their periwigs, love-locks and long effeminate powdered pounced hair; so mimical in their gestures; so effeminate in their lives; so player-like in their deportment, so amorous in their embracements; so un-manly, degenerous and un-English in their whole conversation?

To be player-like in deportment is to be exhibitionist and outgoing. Today, when women wish to pass as men, they discover that they have consciously to control their gestures because men make fewer and more deliberate movements than women; too much movement betrays the masquerade. The Elizabethans permitted men more variety of gesture than modern Englishmen do, but they were very clear that volubility and lability were unbecoming in a mature man. Prynne's anxiety was eventually to prevail. The attack on the theatre was part of the movement that culminated in the attack on the crown, which brought about the closing of the theatres in 1642. When they reopened in 1660, though women had made their first appearance on the stage, it was twenty-year-old Edward Kynaston who made the most endur-ing impression of glamour. When Pepys saw him at the Cockpit in 1660 he was ravished:

> to the Cockpit play, . . . *The Loyal Subject*, where one Kynaston, a boy, acted the Duke's sister but made the loveliest lady that ever I saw in my life – only her voice not very good.

Colley Cibber said Kynaston 'was so beautiful a youth that the ladies of Quality prided themselves on taking him with them in their Coaches to Hyde Park in the theatrical Habit after the Play'. John Downes said that he

> being then very Young made a Complete Female Stage Beauty, performing his parts so well, especially *Arthiope* and *Aglaura*, being parts moving Compassion and Pity; that it has since been Disputable among the Judicious, whether any Woman that succeeded him so Sensibly touched the Audience.

Kynaston was clearly an intersexual figure who was able to keep at bay the unmistakable attributes of adult masculinity until he was in his twenties. The young lover of the Restoration made even more flamboyant display of his attractions and was expected to be even more beautiful than the gallants of Elizabethan and Jacobean England. Pepys saw Kynaston play Epicoene in Jonson's play in 1661:

> Kynaston, the boy, had the good turn to appear in three shapes: first, as a poor woman in ordinary clothes, to please Morose; then in fine clothes as a gallant, and in them was clearly the prettiest woman in the whole house, and lastly as a man; and then likewise did appear the handsomest man in the house.

The masculine anxiety of Prynne and his intellectual heirs had by no means gone away. The introduction of women players was made by Sir William Davenant precisely in order to avoid the suspect eroticism of transvestite display. Unfortunately for the high-minded Davenant, whose actresses lived at his house under the chaperonage of his wife, his rival manager Thomas Killigrew, who began by employing Kynaston, was only too happy to run the Theatre Royal as a showcase for the most glamorous recruits to the oldest profession, so much so in fact that his lubricious comedy, *The Parson's Wedding*, was played by an all-female cast.

When Ben Jonson was writing his poetry in the first years of the seventeenth century, there was little in the way of a specifically feminine education. Women either acquired the same learning as men or none at all. As well as the women of his own family, Jonson knew a number of women who had a measure of authority over him and enough intelligence and education to demand the best of him, among them, his patron Lucy, Countess of Bedford, Elizabeth, Countess of Rutland, Susan Herbert, Countess of Montgomery, Katherine, Lady Aubigny, Lady Jane Paulett, Marchioness of Winchester, his muse, Lady Venetia Digby, and two poets, Lady Mary Wroth and Alice Sutcliffe. Jonson's poem of renunciation 'To the World', subtitled 'A Farewell for a Gentlewoman, Vertuous and Noble', is written in the persona of a young woman who is resolved to tread upon the throat of public life as the Blessed Virgin tramples the serpent:

> I know thou whole art but a shop
> Of toys and trifles, traps, and snares,

> To take the weak, or make them stop:
>   Yet thou art falser than thy wares.
> And, knowing this, should I yet stay,
>   Like such as blow away their lives,
> And never will redeem a day,
>   Enamoured of their golden gyves?

This voice would not be easy to distinguish from the voice of Fulke Greville or Sir John Davies. It is lineally descended from the sibylline utterance of the Virgin in one of the greatest poems ever written in English, the *Canticus Amoris*. In the same direct and downright way that the gentlewoman apostrophizes the world, the Virgin admonishes her doubting devotee:

> Mother of mercy I was for thee made,
> Who needeth it but thou alone?
> To get thee grace I am more glad
> Than thou to ask it. Why wilt thou none?
> When said I nay, tell me, to anyone?
> Forsooth never yet to friend nor foe.
> When thou askest nought, then make I moan,
> Quia amore langueo.

> I seek thee in weal and wretchedness,
> I seek thee in riches and poverty,
> Thou man, behold, where thy mother is,
> Why lovest thou me not since I love thee?
> Sinful or sorry now ever thou be,
> So welcome to me there are no mo.
> I am thy sister, right trust on me,
> Quia amore langueo.

These lines are not from the version of the *Canticus Amoris* that most people know. The fourteenth-century version collected by Sir Arthur Quiller-Couch for *The Oxford Book of English Verse* in 1900 is spoken in the person of the Saviour rejected by his beloved, the Soul. The Virgin speaks directly to the faithful; the Saviour complains to a bystander of his mistress's cruelty. A study of the relationship between the two canticles would illuminate, not only the shift away from what is known as Mariolatry, in this case the Catholic doctrine of Our Lady as mediatrix of all graces, to the rejection of the notion of intercession itself, but the intensification of patriarchalism in the emerging Protestant world. By the time Jonson is impersonating women in poems written in the last years of Elizabeth's reign, even the idea of the soul as the female beloved of a male Christ is fading from consciousness.

In an interesting group of three female-voiced poems, Jonson writes first as womankind sick of false praises and demanding the right to be heard:

> We have both wits, and fancies too,
> And if we must let's sing of you.

In the second, womankind defends her right to 'range', to acquire a variety of sexual experience so that she may find the right partner, and in the third, Jonson writes as a woman in love who dares not tell her lover's name. To write these poems Jonson had no more need to assume a mincing gait than Shakespeare had to write falsetto for his female characters. Jonson did not add to the mass of conventional poems rather unfortunately called 'female complaints', as Shakespeare, Spenser, Daniel and Drayton did, and Lovelace, Cartwright and Marvell after them. Jonson's female personae were of a tougher-minded breed altogether. His contemporary the Countess of Pembroke could write versions of the psalms in the same way as her brother, Sir Philip Sidney, without bothering to project herself as a female voice. Lady Mary Wroth, though intensely aware of herself as a cast-off mistress and mother of two children by her faithless lover, did not need to claim anything other or more intense than the helpless grief of the lamenting lover. The male as well as the female lover was to be known by his 'Sighing like furnace, with a woful ballad/Made to his mistress' eyebrow'. Poetry was the verbal incontinence that matched his physical susceptibility. To unpack one's heart with words is of a piece with other womanish qualities such as cowardice, as Hamlet observed. The wailing love poet then is a feminized figure and as such in a measure androgynous.

With Henrietta Maria came a different notion of female accomplishment; noblewomen were no longer expected to acquire classical learning but to sing, dance, read a vernacular language or two, write nothing beyond unpunctuated letters and books of household recipes, and do curious work with the needle. The subsumed area of overlap between male and female emotional and erotic experience was diminishing fast, as a new notion of female delicacy and fragility took hold. Yet even a poet of as staunch a Presbyterian background as Rochester had absorbed the old-fashioned idea that his soul was feminine.

Rochester, who was physically frail, emotionally volatile, blushed often and painfully and was extremely vulnerable in love, adopted female personae relatively often. Daphne in 'Strephon and Daphne' is probably the first of Rochester's female impersonations; she, in love with Strephon, who is tired of her, woos him in vain, for he has found that 'Change has greater charms than she'. Daphne learns from this that

> Womankind more Joy discovers,
> Making fools, than keeping Lovers

– a discovery not unrelated to the argument of Rochester's most popular poem, 'A letter from Artemiza in the Town to Chloe in the Country', published twice in broadside in 1679 and to be found in more than twenty manuscript anthologies. In this poem Rochester invented the female poet, a rebarbative virgin as witty, worldly wise and idealist as himself. Rochester also masquerades as a nymph in the Song addressed to the 'Injurious Charmer of [her] vanquished heart', asking him to 'invent some gentle way to let [her] go':

> For what with Joy thou didst obtain,
> And I with more did give;
> In time will make thee false and vain,
> And me unfit to live.

The inventiveness of Rochester's female impersonations is impressive, from the 'very young Lady' wooing 'her Ancient Lover' to 'the Platonick Lady' eschewing penetrative sex:

> I love a youth will give me leave
>   His body in my arms to wreathe,
> To press him gently and to kiss,
>   To sigh and look with eyes that wish,

> For what, if I could once obtain,
> I would neglect with flat disdain.

Rochester also assumed the identity of one of the Queen's Maids of Honour to write the 'Letter from Mistress Price to Lord Chesterfield', meant to upbraid him for boasting of favours he had never received. Lastly, there is the considerable fragment in Rochester's holograph beginning 'What vain unnecessary things are men . . .' To turn from Rochester's female personalities to Marvell's 'The Nymph complaining for the death of her Faun' is to be shocked by the contrast. Marvell's nymph is the utterer of simple prayers, who sets herself to play her solitary time away with the white faun her faithless lover gave her. The faun, whose love was 'far more better than/The love of false and cruel men', slept on beds of lilies and ate nothing but roses until passing soldiers shot it. The poem's short four-stressed lines use a deliberately restricted vocabulary of white on white to project an image of such plaintive inanity and helplessness that the reader suspects some satirical intent. The explanation seems to lie in Marvell's notion of himself; in the 'Dialogue between the Resolv'd Soul and Created Pleasure' his soul is not only masculine but a warrior, balancing its sword against the fight. Marvell's nymphs are all infantile, entirely undifferentiated as characters. He and his contemporaries, Waller, Cowley, Dryden, were all unable or unwilling to use a female as alter ego. The woman poet, for her part, had mostly to write as herself, whether under a sobriquet or not, if only because her publisher was using her sex as a selling-point. Even so, Aphra Behn was able to confound male and female to the point of virtual indistinguishability. Mostly she called attention to herself as a woman writing, claiming kinship with Rochester's Artemiza rather than Marvell's nymph, but when she writes in a male persona there is no obvious alteration of style or idiom, as may be seen in anyone of the eclogues to be spoken by nymph and shepherd in alternation. In the songs 'A Pox upon this needless scorn' and 'The Invitation', she persuades a young woman to waste no more time but consent to make love, much as a woman composer might compose an amorous serenade for the male voice. 'In Imitation of Horace' describes a love-worthy boy in three androgynous terms of an earlier era.

> What mean those amorous curls of jet?
>   For what heart-ravished maid
> Dost thou thy hair in order set,
>   Thy wanton tresses braid?
> And thy vast store of beauties open lay,
> That the deluded fancy leads astray?

(It is to be remembered that when a Walloon gentleman visited the young Duke of Gloucester at his lodgings in Brussels in 1659, he came upon him having curling papers removed from his hair.) When Behn gazed at 'Lysander at the Music-Meeting', she tells him:

> I saw the softness that composed your face,
> While your attention heightened every grace,
> Your mouth all full of sweetness and content,
> And your fine killing eyes of languishment.

'A Voyage to the Isle of Love' is the telling by Lisander to Lysidas, his friend, of the story of his heart – adapted from De Tallemant. 'Lycidus or the Lover in Fashion' purports to be his reply. *La Montre* consists of 'The Lover's Watch', written in the person of Iris, followed by 'The Case of the Watch' and 'The Lady's Looking-Glass', purporting to be by her lover, Damon, who makes as much use of exclamation points and breathless hyperbole as Iris. The explanation is partly to be found in the French original by De Bonnecorse; Dryden, for one, was to reject French heroes as finical and effeminate. The *ne plus ultra* of gender ambiguity comes in 'To the fair Clarinda, who made Love to me, imagin'd more than Woman'.

> Fair lovely maid, or if that title be
> Too weak, too feminine for nobler thee,
> Permit a name that more approaches truth,
> And let me call thee, lovely charming youth.
> This last will justify my soft complaint,
> While that may serve to lessen my constraint,
> And without blushes I the youth pursue,
> When so much beauteous woman is in view.
> Against thy charms we struggle but in vain
> With thy deluding form thou giv'st us pain,

While the bright nymph betrays us to the swain.
In pity to our sex sure thou wert sent,
That we might love, and yet be innocent,
For sure no crime with thee we can commit,
Or – if we should – thy form excuses it,
For who that gathers fairest flowers believes
A snake lies hid beneath the fragrant leaves?

Thou beauteous wonder of a different kind,
Soft Chloris with the dear Alexis joined,
Whene'er the manly part of thee would plead,
Thou tempts us with the image of the maid,
While we the noblest passions do extend,
The love to Hermes, Aphrodite the friend.

By the time Behn died such Frenchified manners were anathema; her female successors had little choice but to avoid writing of love altogether. The example of the women playwrights, who were a raffish bunch and severely treated by the change in social values that produced the Whig ascendancy, served rather to discourage than encourage the women poets of succeeding generations. Those who had little choice but to publish were exploited by booksellers who capitalized upon the fact of their sex. Elizabeth Singer Rowe lived to regret the way in which John Dunton introduced her to his public as 'the Pindaric Lady', Philomela; Elizabeth Thomas, who was exploited by Curll, was reviled as little better than a prostitute. Throughout the eighteenth century, with the growth of the middle class and the withering away of the woman's sphere of work, the feminine stereotype gained ground. There was no dearth of women poets, but the sphere of their operations was deliberately circumscribed; they wrote of family, the domestic affections, their social lives, and of piety. They gave up writing of love; they had never written of war. When they generalized in moral poetry, they referred to humanity in the same terms that men did. Mary Whately, after describing ignorance as the cloud that envelops 'the sapient sons of men' and asking pity for 'man's deserted cheerless breast' and disdaining 'fraud unmanly', continues:

But let me bless the providential hand
Which kindly formed me female and denied
Superior genius and superior pride.

From the mid-eighteenth century we may date the growing conviction that the poet is not merely an accomplished human being but a creature of another order, an *Übermensch*. Mary Whately accepts that, as a woman, she is born incapable of achievement of the highest rank. In the revolutionary era, a few women dared to assume the bardic voice of the poet as seer. Even so, Anna Seward and Anne Laetitia Barbauld wrote hymns and poems as portentous as anyone's. Hannah More's *Slavery, A Poem* is an impassioned exhortation in accents of the loftiest and most impersonal. Charlotte Smith and Helena Maria Williams wrote sonnets that inspired Wordsworth's emulation. Ann Yearsley, milkwoman turned poet, challenged men's belief in their own superiority.

> Why boast, O arrogant, imperious man,
> Perfection so exclusive? Are thy powers
> Nearer approaching Deity? canst thou solve
> Questions which high Infinity propounds,
> Soar nobler flights, or dare immortal deeds,
> Unknown to woman if she greatly dares
> To use the powers assigned to her?

For most of Yearsley's contemporaries, and their daughters and granddaughters, the notion of the poet was more like that of the American Mary E. Lee:

> The poets! The poets!
> Those giants of the earth;
> In mighty strength they tower above
> The men of common birth;
> A noble race – they mingle not
> Among the motley throng,
> But move with slow and measured step,
> To music-notes along!

When the first volume of Joanna Baillie's *Plays, in which it is Attempted to Delineate the stronger Passions of the Mind* appeared anonymously in 1798, it was assumed that the author was a man. Sir Walter Scott dubbed her the 'best dramatic writer since Shakespeare and Massinger'. Women had always had the choice of publishing anonymously and trying their luck in the literary market-place alongside men, but booksellers almost always gave clues of the age, rank or sex of the unnamed writer, as a way of encouraging interest. 'A Lady' could be relied upon to sell reasonably well, 'A Young Lady' even better. Both were prolific authors in the early eighteenth century. After Elizabeth Carter published her *Poems on Several Occasions* under her own name in 1762, it was easier for respectable women to follow her example, though Clara Reeve still judged it best to publish her *Original Poems on Several Occasions* as by 'C. R.' in 1769. Despite the horrors of publicity, and the factionalism of literary criticism in the period, no woman poet before the later nineteenth century assumed a masculine pseudonym. Even so, male impersonation by women writers was becoming increasingly common, in that more and more chose to venture beyond the female sphere and to address topics of the weightiest, undeterred by their ignorance of the world of men and of the classics. The most important of them was the best-selling poet of the Victorian era, Felicia Hemans.

Mrs Hemans was born Felicia Dorothea Browne in Liverpool in 1793. Like Elizabeth Barrett and Christina Rossetti, she began writing poetry almost as soon as she could write anything; like them she was encouraged by her family. It is sobering to reflect that we have no boy prodigy to equal them. Only females, it would seem, can write poetry without the benefit of any kind of training. Felicia was an accomplished poet by the time she was fourteen.

> New sources of inspiration were now opening to her view. Birthday addresses, songs by the seashore, and invocations to fairies, were henceforth to be diversified with warlike themes; and trumpets and banners now floated through the dreams in which birds and flowers had once reigned paramount. Her two elder brothers had entered the army at an early age, and were both serving in the 23rd Welsh Fusiliers. One of them was now engaged in the Spanish campaign under Sir John Moore; and a vivid imagination and enthusiastic affections being alike enlisted in the cause, her young mind was filled with glorious visions of British valour and Spanish patriotism.

The young poet chose to write 'England and Spain or Valour and Patriotism, a Poem' in heroic couplets with a vocabulary composed

almost entirely of magnificent abstractions propped up by an extraordinary number of exclamation points.

> O glorious isle! – O sovereign of the waves!
> Thine are the sons who 'never will be slaves!'

She was well aware that her assumption of the grand patriotic, also
known as the jingoistic, style was in itself a curiosity and inserted
herself in the poem as the bird-like treble behind the megaphone:

> Oh, could my muse on seraph pinion spring,
> And sweep with rapture's hand the trembling string!
> Could she the bosom energies control,
> And pour impassion'd fervour o'er the soul!
> Oh, could she strike the harp to Milton given,
> Brought by a cherub from the empyrean heaven!
> Ah, fruitless wish! ah, prayer preferr'd in vain,
> For her – the humblest of the woodland train;
> Yet shall her feeble voice essay to raise
> The hymn of liberty, the song of praise!

She was never to remind her readers of her age or sex again. It can
be no surprise that the teenage girl fell in love with a dashing Irish
captain who had served with the King's Own Regiment in Spain; in
1812 her parents, seeing no alternative, gave their consent for her to
marry him. Felicia bore Alfred Hemans five sons before the couple
separated in 1818. Mrs Hemans was never to see her husband again,
but all her life she remained under the spell of her own dream of
military life. She wrote elegies for dead soldiers, and choruses for
Highlanders and Crusaders. She even assumed the persona of an aged
Indian begging his enemies to kill him:

> These feet can no more chase the deer,
>   The glory of this arm is flown; –
> Why should the feeble linger here
>   When all the pride of life is gone?
> Warriors! why still the stroke deny?
> Think ye Ontara fears to die?

She described, or rather prescribed, the hero's death:

> His was a death whose rapture high
>   Transcended all that life could yield;
> His warmest prayer was but to die
>   On the red battlefield.

In 1819 a prize was offered for the best poem on the subject of Wallace inviting Bruce to assume the crown of Scotland. Mrs Hemans entered with a rollicking poem in hudibrastics and bore off the prize from the other fifty-seven competitors, most of whom were Scots. In the person of Wallace, Mrs Hemans exulted:

> The nurture of our bitter sky
> Calls forth resisting energy;
> And the wild fastnesses are ours,
> The rocks with their eternal towers.
> The soul to struggle and to dare
> Is mingled with our northern air,
> And dust beneath our soil is lying
> Of those who died for fame undying.

Mrs Hemans was now famous for the power of her pen. She capitulated by writing in the personae of Welsh, Irish and Scots, and Spartan and Austrian heroes, and throngs of dying (male) bards, travelling in imagination far beyond her own obscure circumstances, translating from Portuguese, Spanish, Italian and German, to produce a rarefied literature of heroism. In 'The Forest Sanctuary', her favourite of her own poems, she imagined herself a (male) Spaniard who has fled religious persecution to North America with his son. Nowadays, she is remembered, if at all, for 'Casabianca', which retells the story of the death of the Admiral of the Orient in the Battle of the Nile.

> The boy stood on the burning deck
>   Whence all but he had fled;
> The flames that lit the battle's wreck
>   Shone round him o'er the dead.

The boy will not leave his post until his father gives him word, but his father lies unconscious and the word does not come. Seven stanzas later –

> There came a burst of thunder-sound –
>   The boy – oh! where was he?
> Ask of the winds that far around
>   With fragments strewed the sea!
>
> With mast, and helm, and pennon fair,
>   That well had borne their part;
> But the noblest thing that perish'd there
>   Was that young faithful heart.

Mrs Hemans clearly played a part, though perhaps not a crucial one, in the invention of manliness. One of her most admired poems, 'The English Boy', developed a hint from Akenside: 'Go, call thy sons; instruct them what a debt/They owe their ancestors . . .' After thirteen stanzas of exhortation of the English boy to gaze upon the landscape, ancestral halls and hallowed fanes whose freedom was maintained by his forebears, the poem ends:

> Lift up thy heart, my English boy!
>   And pray like *them* to stand,
> Should God so summon *thee*, to guard
>   The altars of the land.

By the time she wrote these lines, Mrs Hemans was as famous in the United States, where Norton had published an edition of her work in 1825, as she was in England. Caroline Gilman responded with thirteen quatrains of her own entitled 'The American Boy':

> Look up, my young American!
>   Stand firmly on the earth,
> Where noble deeds and mental power
>   Give titles over birth.

The poet exhorted her young male compatriot to remember the battles of the War of Independence.

> And when thou'rt told of knighthood's shield,
>   And English battles won,
> Look up, my boy, and breathe one word –
>   The name of Washington.

No woman poet in either country thought to capitulate by addressing a similarly patriotic effusion to a girl, yet, clearly, women were as passionately involved in the propaganda of patriotic heroism as men. In penning 'The Battle Hymn of the Republic' Julia Ward Howe was following a path trodden by a succession of women poets.

In 1820, when she was fourteen, Elizabeth Barrett produced and dedicated to her father four books of Hemansesque heroic couplets, called *The Battle of Marathon*. In her preface, under two epigraphs, one from Akenside and one from Byron, she declares poetry the 'noblest of the productions of man', part of the culture of the soul in which 'man displays his superiority to brutes'.

> This humble attempt may by some be unfortunately attributed to vanity, to an affectation of talent, or to the still more absurd desire of being thought a *genius* . . . Now, even the female may drive her Pegasus through the realms of Parnassus, without being saluted with the most equivocal of all appellations, a learned lady, without being celebrated by her friends as a Sappho, or traduced by her enemies as a pedant; without being abused in the Review, or criticised in society; how justly then may a child hope to pass unheeded!

Rather than class herself as a female, Barrett insists on an androgynous identification as a child, to whom the masculine pronoun may refer.

> He who writes an epic poem must transport himself to the scene of action, he must imagine himself possessed of the same opinions, manners, prejudices, and beliefs; he must suppose himself to be the hero he delineates, or his picture can no longer be nature, and what is not natural cannot please.

So Childe Barrett imagines herself to be Aristides, Themistocles, Miltiades, Clombrotus and assembled gods and goddesses. Elizabeth Barrett claimed to have learned to translate Greek at sight, by sitting at the back of the children's schoolroom while her brothers were having their lessons. Though at the age of fourteen she must have been aware of herself as a woman and she says she had not meant to exhibit herself as a genius, she certainly laid claim to being a child prodigy.

> I confess I have chosen Homer as a model, and perhaps I have attempted to imitate his style too often and too closely . . .

Pope's translation of the *Iliad* is a much nearer source than anything in Greek and there may be at least that much dishonesty in Elizabeth Barrett's claim to have taken Homer as a direct model. Gina Lombroso seized upon the curious fact of Mrs Browning's classical education by default to make a curious point.

> Mrs Browning, who learned Greek by listening to lessons given to her brothers, confessed that she had no idea how it happened, but that she was able to translate Greek at sight. This way of learning things has many advantages. Above all, it entails no fatigue. However, science acquired in this way is not stable and never gives a woman the same assurance that a man gets from his slow and laborious methods of acquiring knowledge.

Women who have amassed the crumbs of an education offered to others have no confidence in the exercise of their knowledge, and so they are not assured. Extraordinarily gifted people can learn complicated subjects without apparent effort, as Mozart did, regardless of sex. The difference might be that the women never consider themselves prodigies, but mere amateurs and interlopers, and so are easily persuaded to submit their work to correction or even to suppress it. Not so Elizabeth Barrett: her frigid and dazzling literary exercise was destined from the first for print. The Battle of Marathon is presented in epic tradition as the continuation of the battle between Minerva and Venus; the poem is a succession of rumbustious speeches relieved by an occasional glance at the battlefield, which is usually described in grandiose extended similes. The child-bard does not shrink from violent depiction:

> But great Cynaegirus his danger spies
> And lashed his steeds – the ponderous chariot flies

> Then from its brazen bulk he leaps to ground,
> Beneath his clanging arms the plains resound,
> And on the Persian rushes fierce and raised
> The clattering axe on high, which threatening blazed,
> And lopped his head; out spouts the smoking gore,
> And the huge trunk rolled bleeding on the shore.

Despite the uncontrolled tone of this passage with its suggestion of burlesque and the zigzag alteration of tenses, the wonder of Elizabeth Barrett's *Battle of Marathon* is, not that it is a bad poem, but that it is not a worse one. It is utterly unrelieved by any touch of observation or any original reflection, yet within its chill decorum of apotheosis, epic sacrifice, the arming of the heroes and so forth, it moves with a sort of giddy alacrity. It is an extremely old-fashioned exercise, even for 1820, but Elizabeth Barrett's exaltation moves it out of the ruck of dreary epic verse in heroic couplets which so abounded in the second half of the eighteenth century and sheds upon it a new, if ghastly, radiance.

Miss Barrett had certainly never seen a battle; her description of the battle of Marathon is a purely literary exercise. Two hundred years earlier the Duchess of Newcastle must have seen a battleground as women see it, when they search among the dead and wounded for their fathers, sons and brothers. Her description is the polar opposite of Miss Barrett's rhetorical flourishes:

> Some, their legs hang dangling by the nervous strings,
> And shoulders cut, hang loose, like flying wings.
> Here heads are cleft in two parts, brains lie mashed,
> And all their faces into slices hashed,
> Brains only in the pia mater thin
> Which quivering lies within that little skin,
> Their skulls all broke and into pieces burst
> By horses' hoofs and chariot wheels to dust.
> Others, their own heads lies on their own laps,
> And some again, half cut, lies on their paps,
> Whose tongues out of their mouths are thrust at length,
> For why, the strings are cut that gave them strength.
> Their eyes do stare, the lids wide open set,
> The little nerves being shrunk, they cannot shut,

And some again, those glassy balls hang by
Small slender strings, as chains to tie the eye,
These strings when broke, eyes fall, which trundling round
Until the film is broke upon the ground.
In death their teeth strong set, their lips left bare
Which grinning seems as if they angry were.

The Duchess looks steadily on the horror that is war, just as she looks hard at the reality of that other male pursuit, hunting, in order to render it in all its brutality. The last thing Miss Barrett wanted to present would have been a woman's critique on the reality of war; she has accepted the rhetoric of military heroism and is concerned to show that she can function within the tradition. Of the two, the crazy Duchess has much the securer sense of self.

Having conquered the heroic poem, Miss Barrett addressed herself to the lofty preoccupations of ethical poetry, for which her qualifications were every bit as scant. Her subject was 'The Mind':

Thou thing of light! thou warm'st the breasts of men,
Breathes from the lips, and tremblest from the pen!

Though Childe Barrett has now accepted her fate and become Miss Barrett, she still inhabits a world without women. Her model is once more Pope, which augurs well for the soundness of her poetic taste but remains an extraordinarily conservative choice in 1826. 'The Mind' celebrates all the minds that have formed Miss Barrett's, all of them male. Over all towers Byron, 'the Mont Blanc of intellect'. In a short poem written at much the same time, the young poet speaks as an old Roumeliot soldier who, on hearing Byron's name, burst into tears.

Name me the host and battle-storm,
    Mine own good sword shall stem;
Name me the foeman and the block,
    I have a smile for them!

But name him not, nor cease to mark
    This brow where passions sweep –
Behold, a warrior is a man,
    And as a man may weep!

These lines reveal that the easy tears of the Elizabethan boy have long dried up, for in insisting that a man may weep for Byron without unmanning himself, Barrett reveals that otherwise he may not. In 'Riga's Last Song' she assumes the voice of a Greek patriot:

> And I bend my brows above the block,
> Silently waiting the swift death shock;
> For these lips shall speak what becomes the free –
> Or – Hellas, my country! farewell to thee!

Another poem, or fragment, called 'The Tempest' has as its speaker a Siegfried figure living in the forest who discovers the body of his mortal enemy and learns to cast away 'the low anxieties that wait upon the flesh – the reptile moods'. In the other poems of her first publication Barrett takes Byron as her model:

> There is a silence upon the Ocean.
> Albeit it swells with a fearful motion;
> Like to the battle-camp's fearful calm,
> While the banners are spread and the warriors arm.

In 'A Vison of Poets' Barrett sees Homer, Shakespeare, Aeschylus, Euripides, Sophocles, Hesiod, Pindar, Theocritus, Aristophanes, Virgil, Lucretius, Ossian, Spenser, Ariosto, Dante, Alfieri, Boiardo, Berni, Tasso, Racine, Corneille, Calderon, Lope de Vega, Goethe, Schiller, Chaucer, Milton, Cowley, Drayton, Browne, Marlowe, Webster, Fletcher, Jonson, Burns, Shelley, Keats, Byron, Coleridge

> And Sappho, with that gloriole
>
> Of ebon hair on calmèd brows.
> O poet-woman! none forgoes
> The leap, attaining the repose!

and another

> One set her eyes like Sappho's – or
> Any light woman's!

Miss Barrett the poet observes the male poet-pilgrim kissed by the muse, and overhears the poet's vow, and retails the poet's courtship of Lady Geraldine, but when she came to write 'The Runaway Slave at Pilgrim's Point' for the first time she represented herself as, like the black slave, female so that she could use a female authority in describing the slave's killing her white child. It was a bold step towards the recognition of a female reality that was as heroic as anything that could be imagined for men. At much the same time Elizabeth Barrett recognized the existence of her fellow poets Felicia Hemans and L. E. L. From then on she was content to be a woman-poet, and struggled no longer to present herself as a freak of nature. The change in her orientation is illustrated strikingly by the second of her two sonnets celebrating George Sand:

> True genius, but true woman! dost deny
> Thy woman's nature with a manly scorn,
> And break away the gauds and armlets worn
> By weaker women in captivity?
> Ah, vain denial! that revolted cry
> Is sobbed in by a woman's voice forlorn! –
> Thy woman's hair, my sister, all unshorn,
> Floats back dishevelled strength in agony,
> Disproving thy man's name! and while before
> The world thou burnest in a poet-fire,
> We see thy woman-heart beat evermore
> Through the large flame. Beat purer, heart, and higher,
> Till God unsex thee on the heavenly shore,
> Where unincarnate spirits purely aspire.

Aurore Dupin began to call herself George Sand in 1832 and to appear in public in a version of masculine attire. Her bold assertion of androgyny, which is specifically denied by Mrs Browning, inspired others. In 1846 the Brontë sisters published a small volume of verse as Acton, Currer and Ellis Bell, becoming the first English women poets to publish under male pseudonyms. Curiously the use of the male pseudonym allowed them to utter a woman's reality more freely. When the fact of their sex came out, after the publication of *Wuthering Heights* and *The Tenant of Wildfell Hall*, critics were bemused that they could write in so unfeminine a fashion. Transvestism appears to have permitted these women to escape from the imposed piety, modesty and insipidity of the stereotype. Where other women had had to ape the gait of male poets and make huge gestures towards subjects of which they knew nothing, the poets who took men's names could defy the double standard and write spontaneously. Still it is remarkable how few women took the option. Despite the enormous public veneration for George Eliot, the few women who took men's names after her also took on male clothing. Some, like Vernon Lee, were virginal; others, like Radclyffe Hall, considered themselves intersexual and took women as lovers; in the case of Michael Field, one male poet's name hid two women who were lovers.

The post-Romantic claim that the great artist does not write consciously as a member of either sex but as a representative of humanity is actually insidious and absurd. When Flaubert says, 'Madame Bovary, c'est moi', he should be understood as saying that his character is a male creation, not that he has pre-empted female nature. It cannot be true that the poet's sexuality does not become subject-matter for him until it becomes threatened, by mechanized civilization, by raucous women or by harrowing male competition; his sexuality colours everything he writes, even the very act of writing itself. To deny this is to deny to the sex that is acutely conscious of its otherness all right to artistic expression. A man does not write/sculpt/paint as a man, goes the lie, therefore a woman may not write/sculpt/paint as a woman. Women who fall for this line refuse to be included in anthologies of women's work. Elizabeth Bishop's executors consider themselves bound by the poet's will to refuse all permissions for her work to be discussed in the context of other work by women, because Bishop considered, like Miss Felicia Browne and Miss Elizabeth Barrett Barrett, that she had transcended her sex. Bishop would have been a better poet if she had lived to realize that to transcend one's sex is not only impossible but undesirable. Gender is another matter. Only by the full disclosure of sex potentiality can the miserable fraud that is gender be seen for what it is.

THE ENIGMA OF SAPPHO

Sappho is supposed to have flourished in the 42nd Olympiad (612/608 BC) or been born then – the Greek word in the source can be used either way. The source is the *Suda*, a lexicon written in the tenth century AD, a mere sixteen hundred years later. The *Suda* account fits with Eusebius, who says that Sappho and Alcaeus were both famous in the 45th Olympiad, in 600/599 BC. He was writing in about AD 300 – a mere nine hundred years after the event. The Parian marble stele mentions her in an entry following the entry on Alyattes, father of Croesus, and that was carved in 264/263 BC or so. On these grounds classical scholars accept Sappho to have been a real woman who lived round 600 BC in Lesbos. Her name and image featured at different times on the coinage of Mytilene, principal city of Lesbos.

We know nothing of the circumstances of poetic composition on the island of Lesbos in the seventh century before Christ. We do not know if there were public gatherings at which poets performed, whether they sang their songs accompanying themselves on their own instruments, whether they improvised or burned the midnight oil. We do know that they wrote on papyri but not a single Lesbian papyrus of the seventh century BC has survived. What has survived is the Florentine ostracon – a potsherd used to write on – of the third century BC which contains verses identified as Sappho's because Hermogenes quotes two of the lines on it in *Kinds of Style* as by Sappho, 'And round about cold water babbles through apple-branches.' Actually two of the eight words quoted by Hermogenes are different. In the same period Athenaios, the miscellany writer, quoted the same poem and his version is different again. If such changes occur in Sappho's text over 500 years, we must ask ourselves what has happened to it in 2,600 years. The chances that what we make of what we have bears any resemblance to the sounds once uttered by a woman poet of Lesbos are practically non-existent. The text we now associate with Sappho is derived from papyrus fragments of the second and third centuries AD, from a version of a poem quoted by Dionysius of Halicarnassus in about 20 BC and another by Longinus in the first century AD, together with isolated lines, phrases and single words quoted by metricians and grammarians.

It has been suggested that Homer is not a man but a group of men. The notion is not popular but it cannot be refuted. Sappho too could have been a group, the Lesbian Women's Poetry Co-operative perhaps. There is in this idea nothing intrinsically improbable, except to those people who believe that great artists are superhuman individuals. The idea of the *Übermensch* is dear to the heirs of nineteenth-century individualism but there is nothing classical about it, unless you consider intellectual fascism to be part of the classical heritage. Certainly none of the commentators on Sappho doubted her to be a single, actual, individual woman but it must be borne in mind that all of them were further away from her in time than we are from Shakespeare, and in the case of Shakespeare there is deep disagreement about the number of people actually involved in the generation of the Shakespearian text. Shakespeare is less than four hundred years dead. We have, if no birth certificate, a record of his baptism and, if no death certificate, his will. We also have tax records and court cases that mention a person called William Shakespeare. Yet Shakespeare is still a mystery. The autobiographical content of the sonnets, if indeed there is such a thing, is beyond us to determine, though, as in the case of Sappho, we greatly enjoy talking about it. More importantly, in Shakespeare's case we have a text, or rather we have a number of texts of varying degrees of authenticity. Scholars variously disintegrate the accretive texts and end up with what they consider to be lumps of authentic text connected by tracts of forgery or confer authenticity on parallel texts. Arguments about the precise meaning of thousands of passages have occupied millions of teaching hours. The problems would be exacerbated rather than solved if a substantial Shakespeare autograph were ever to be found.

Sappho is supposed to have called herself Psappha, a word meaning, if after a millennium or three we can be sure of anything so fugitive as a word meaning, lapis lazuli. Word meanings, even when they have been stabilized by print, mutate astonishingly fast. (Just think of the metamorphosis of the word 'gay' in our time.) What complicates the picture is that Psappha wote in the Aeolian dialect, which did not become, as Homer's Greek did, a literary language. Apuleius found Sappho's language rustic and quaint; Camille Paglia praises its melody.

To the the literary scholar only the connected texts can yield anything of interest; the most important of these for the history of Sapphistry are the 'Hymn to Aphrodite', which was quoted in full, we think, by Dionysius of Halicarnassus in about 20 BC, and φαίνεταί μοι, which was quoted in full or in part by Longinus a century later. However, as the great Lobel has said, 'The only correct procedure is to approach the quotations by way of the book texts,' i.e. the papyri. What Lobel is saying is that the papyrus texts, though dating from the second and third centuries AD, are more authentic than the earlier scholar's citations. Lobel gives as his reasons that the papyri

> are obviously written by scribes trained to their business, and, apart from slight surface corruptions such as inevitably attend this method of reproduction, are for the most part – at any rate prima facie – of a remarkable correctness. It is however unfortunately the case that the book texts, owing to the circumstances of their preservation, are often disfigured by the most serious lacunae or are difficult in various degrees to decipher.

How did Lobel arrive at an impression of the texts' correctness? He could hardly have derived it from comparison with known quotations, for he has already said that the papyri should be considered more authentic than the quotations, and in any event the degree of overlap is slight. If he means that the Greek is correct, it is a small enough claim in sooth. If the scribes were scrupulous in rendering an archaic provincial dialect, they were very unusual scribes indeed. A text surviving only by manuscript transcription could have been preserved from modernization over a thousand years, but only if the scribes themselves were illiterate and were not prompted to correct and systematize as they went along. This is not the case, for evidence from the papyri themselves shows that the texts attributed to Sappho were arranged by an Alexandrian scholar in nine books. The truth seems to be that Sappho was alternately lost and found over those thousand years; each rediscovery probably included its own element of re-invention. One of the elements in the reinvention was almost certainly the absorption of a number of Lesbian women poets into a single figure.

The *Suda* tell us that Sappho had pupils three, Anagora of Miletus, Gongyla of Colophon and Eunica of Salamis. The tone of this *Suda* entry and the names it adduces seem facetious. The second-century biographer, Philostratus, has Apollonius of Tyana name another pupil, Damophyla. The Gorgo and Andromeda mentioned in the orations of the second-century rhetorician Maximus of Tyre, are supposed to have been her rival craftswomen. Sappho's fame virtually guaranteed that any Sapphics written in Aeolian dialect and presenting a female speaker would be attributed to her. The tendency of great reputations is to amass works; the tendency of small reputations to lose them. Sappho is above all things a token woman; her function is to be always the single, the only one. Her existence is as the exception that proves the rule, therefore her freakishness will always be stressed, to the extent of turning her into an intellectual and emotional hermaphrodite.

Nearly all the Sappho papyri were found amongst a huge mass thrown away by the inhabitants of Oxyrhynchus, nowadays el-Behnesa, 200 kilometres south of Cairo, on the edge of the Western Desert. Why the inhabitants of Oxyrhynchus kept on throwing their papyri into the same dumps over centuries is a mystery. The dumps contain papyri of all kinds, legal documents, laundry lists, accounts, personal letters; as only a small proportion are literary in character, no thrilling hypothesis of an iconoclastic blitz can be entertained. Perhaps the papyri were meant to serve as cartonnage for mummies and were simply never used: 'Caprice governs the survival of papyri of any epoch.' Most of the pieces of the jigsaw are missing. Common sense should dictate to scholars that all we have are half-texts; if these are to serve as touchstones for assessing the authenticity of the texts that have survived in other ways, they must not be tampered with. However, Lobel's inference is quite different: 'The chief problem [the papyri] present is, therefore, the problem of filling up gaps.' In other words, what we do not have we will make up. This is an astonishing approach to a literary text. Reconstruction of any poet's work by anyone, whether poet or not, will give you a new poem, probably a bad one. (Ninety-nine per cent of all mutations are fatal.) If the substitutions are made according to likelihood or predictability, what you will get will be a series of clichés. The late great Professor Turner put it quite succinctly:

It will be thought a truism to point out that to restore words in a text — that is to say, to determine what were the words which have been torn away or perhaps eaten by worms — is only possible if you know what was there. And you can only know something formulaic.

The Sappho of Oxyrhynchus is in large degree formulaic.

Professor Turner has scant mercy for the restorers of Sappho, pointing out that Grenfell and Hunt had not only restored but read Oxyrhynchus 1,231, fragment 1, column 1, wrong. Their mistake came to light only because Lobel identified two tiny scraps belonging to this papyrus and fitted them into the lacunae. Their version read: 'Helen acclaimed outstanding among immortals for her beauty judged him best who destroyed the whole majesty of Troy.' The addition of the new bits provided: 'Helen who left behind the best of husbands and went off across the sea to Troy.'

Oxyrhynchus 7 is a comparatively big fragment measuring 20 centimetres more or less by 10. The text on it is described by Blass as

> Part of a poem in Sapphics written in the Aeolic dialect. Portions of twenty lines are preserved, *a foot and a half being lost at the beginning of each line* [my italics] besides occasional lacunae. In spite of its mutilated condition, however, enough remains of the poem to determine its subject and authorship with tolerable certainty . . . The reference to the poet's brother who is returning home across the sea (stanza 1) [a very rare circumstance for island dwellers to be sure], the tone of gentle reproach for some misdeed committed by that brother in the past which the poet now wishes to bury in oblivion [which is why she's mentioning them], the dialect and metre, the obvious antiquity of the poem as shown by the presence of the digamma in line 6, the resemblances in thought and phrase to the known fragments of Sappho — combine in favour of the hypothesis that we have here part of an ode addressed by Sappho to her brother Charaxus.

Lurking under this is an assumption that no modern literary scholar would ever make, namely, that poems are autobiographical documents. A singer of songs may sing as a girl bewailing her lost lover or as a lover bewailing his lost girl or as a pebble in the brook trodden by the cattle's feet. Ballad form, to take an ancient example based upon roughly the same elements as Homer's sung narrative, contains long stanzaic interpolations in the voices of a number of characters. There is no reason whatever to believe that Sappho is unique among the poets of all time in that she wrote poetry only as herself and about herself. Nowadays Blass's fillings in of the gaps, in which he mined most of his gentle reproach and therefore most of the grounds of his attribution, are left as lacunae.

The most important Sappho document is Oxyrhynchus 1,231. It appears to consist of fifty-six fragments from a single roll; the last fragment ends with the words $\mu\epsilon\lambda\hat{\omega}\nu$ a – 'songs 1' and the number 1,320, which is taken to refer to the number of lines transcribed. At first it was thought that the first fragment, made up of twenty small pieces, constituted a poem of some thirty-four lines, almost none complete; more recent scholarship disintegrated this into two poems by collation with another version to be found in Oxyrhynchus 2,166(a). The same papyrus provides the song beginning $\pi\lambda\acute{a}\sigma\iota o\nu$ $\delta\grave{\eta}$ and what appear to be fragments of ten more, too exiguous even for the restoratory talents of Lobel, Hunt, Blass, Wilamowitz and Co.

Surely this is hopeless. Though we may agree that there was a famous woman poet who flourished in Lesbos and perhaps too in Sicily round 600 BC, we have also to admit that we have lost her. What we have is more myth than literary history, but it is not in human nature to leave well alone. If Psappha is there buried beneath the sands of time – a.k.a. the Western Desert – submerged by the flood of 2,600 years, we believe that we can dive for her, that there is a trail to be followed and something genuine to be found, something true.

In the case of Psappha there is virtually no text and what is attributed to her could not by any stretch of the imagination be called authentic. The worst of the bad quartos of Shakespeare were based upon memorial reconstructions of the texts in performance; even when notes of speeches were made at the time, the degree of corruption is significant and intolerable. In the case of Psappha we are asked to accept memorial reconstructions and transcriptions made hundreds of years after the texts were originally spoken. Scholars occasionally refer to Psappha publishing; the only circumstance imaginable is that verses when composed were given to a scriptorium where copies were made for distribution to a clientele. In fact we have no evidence that Psappha had a clientele. Nobody has ever named a patron; nobody has left any record of being present when Psappha performed or of any public occasion upon which Psappha performed. Psappha may have lived and loved on Lesbos; what has been made of her in the 2,600 years or so since is legend. Nevertheless, classical scholars nonsensically debate the authenticity of one or other version of Sappho. The Sappho industry is enormous; a bibliography of Sapphistry would be massive.

From a dozen or so of the Oxyrhynchus papyri we have fragments of fifty or so poems. Remarkably, fragments of only seven or eight poems appear on more than one papyrus and there are few fragments that appear to relate to poems which are mentioned in the other great Sappho resource, the works of the grammarians, which should suggest some dubiety about the ascriptions. Inevitably the attribution of some of the papyrus fragments is disputed between Alcaeus and Sappho.

We have what we think is one complete poem out of nine books of Sapphics, one of which contained 330 stanzas, say, seven stanzas out of 3,000 or so, and that thanks to Dionysius of Halicarnassus's 'On Literary Composition'. Here for once the evidence of the papyri bears out the claim to authenticity of Dionysius's version, as far as it goes, which is not far.

> ποικιλόθρον' ἀθανάτ' Ἀφρόδιτα,
> παῖ Δίος δολόπλοκε, λίσσομαί σε,
> μή μ' ἄσαισι μηδ' ὀνίαισι δάμνα,
> πότνια, θῦμον,*

The first difficulty faced by translators into English is the Sapphic stanza: three lines, each composed of two sets of paired trochees separated by a dactyl, with the epic tag of a dactyl and a spondee. Worse, Greek is not supposed to be stressed – certain syllables can be uttered on rising or falling inflections which dictate meaning and grammatical relationship – though how this was supposed to work in sung Aeolian dialect is hard to tell. The rising and falling inflections do not always coincide with the metrical rhythm, which leads me for one to regard the current conventions of Greek pronunciation as arbitrary artefact. How we are meant to make any judgement whether

---

* elaborately seated deathless Aphrodite
child of Zeus wile-weaver, I implore you
do not me with distress or anguish subdue
lady, heart

any of this is good or not is unclear to me at least. Nevertheless, what we have is interesting. Aphrodite seems to be presented not as a seductress but as a tyrannical and resourceful entrapper, in terms that are more intellectually teasing than immediately appealing. This fits with Joan DeJean's reading of the poem as showing the eternal non-reciprocity of love. The original is uncclichéd but virtually all the versions made since 600 BC have been either formulaic or absurd. How anyone can make 'lower-apparelled' out of 'ποικιλόθρον', I cannot see. Barnstone goes for 'On your dazzling throne Aphrodite', Groden decides that 'ποικιλόθρον" means 'rainbow-throned'; while Mary Barnard plumps for 'Dapple-throned', Duban for 'apparelled in flowered allure'. Why, one might wonder, does Sappho refer to Aphrodite's chair at all? At least Davenport realizes that something more perplexing is going on and splurges on a conflation of ποικιλό θρον' with δολόπλοκε, to provide 'a whittled perplexity in your bright abstruse chair'.

> ἀλλὰ τυίδ' ἔλθ', αἴ ποτα κἀτέρωτα
> τὰς ἔμας αὔδας ἀίοισα πήλοι
> ἔκλυες, πάτρος δὲ δόμον λίποισα
> χρύσιον ἦλθες
>
> ἄρμ' ὐπασδεύζαισα· κάλοι δέ σ' ἄγον
> ὤκεες στροῦθοι περὶ γᾶς μελαίνας
> πύκνα δίννεντες πτέρ' ἀπ' ὠράνωἴθερος
> διὰ μέσσω,
>
> αἶψα δ' ἐξίκοντο· σὺ δ', ὦ μάκαιρα,
> μειδιαίσαισ' ἀθανάτῳ προσώπῳ
> ἤρε' ὄττι δηὖτε πέπονθα κὤττι
> δηὖτε κάλημμι,
>
> κὤττι μοι μάλιστα θέλω γένεσθαι
> μαινόλᾳ θύμῳ· τίνα δηὖτε πείθω
> ἄψ σ' ἄγην ἐς Fὰν φιλότατα; τίς σ', ὦ
> Ψάπφ', ἀδικήει;
>
> καί γὰρ αἰ φεύγει, ταχέως διώζει·
> αἰ δὲ δῶρα μὴ δέκετ', ἀλλὰ δώσει·
> αἰ δὲ μὴ φίλει, ταχέως φιλήσει
> κωὐκ ἐθέλοισα.

> ἔλθε μοι καί νῦν, χαλέπαν δὲ λῦσον
> ἐκ μερίμναν, ὄσσα δέ μοι τέλεσσαι
> θῦμος ἰμέρρει, τέλεσον· σὺ δ᾽ αὔτα-
> σύμμαχος ἔσσο.*

The second and much more influential poem in the Sappho canon has come down to us as remembered by Longinus in *De Sublimitate:*

> φαίνεταί μοι κῆνος ἴσος θέοισιν
> ἔμμεν᾽ ὤνηρ, ὄττις ἐνάντιός τοι
> ἰσδάνει καὶ πλάσιον ἆδυ φωνείσας
> ὐπακούει
>
> καὶ γελαίσας ἰμέροεν, τό μ᾽ ἦ μὰν
> καρδίαν ἐν στήθεσιν ἐπτόαισεν·
> ὡς γὰρ ἔς σ᾽ ἴδω βρόχε᾽, ὡς με φώναισ᾽
> οὐδ᾽ ἒν ἔτ᾽ εἴκει,

* but come to my side, if ever before
while listening alert from afar as I cried
you came from your father's house door
golden came

drawing lovely sparrows to the chariot's rein
who swiftly drew you down to darkened earth
whirling their wings through the air
of the middle

quickly they arrived and you O blessed one
a smile on your immortal face were asking
what I suffered this time, why this time
this time I summoned

and what it was did long for most
my maddened heart; who this time persuasion
shall bring as love captive, who O
Sapph' does you wrong?

and if she flees at first soon pursue will
she; the gifts she has spurned she will soon bestow
the love she flouts she will soon languish for
without willing

come to me even now, from crushing anxiety
me free that to me grant
heart should long for, yourself
fellow fighter be

ἀλλὰ κὰμ μὲν γλῶσσά ⟨μ᾽⟩ ἔαγε, λέπτον
δ᾽ αὔτικα χρῷ πῦρ ὑπαδεδρόμηκεν,
ὀππάτεσσι δ᾽ οὐδ᾽ ἓν ὄρημμ᾽, ἐπιρρόμβεισι δ᾽ ἄκουαι,

κὰδ δέ μ᾽ ἴδρως κακχέεται, τρόμος δὲ
παῖσαν ἄγρει, χλωροτέρα δὲ ποίας
ἔμμι, τεθνάκην δ᾽ ὀλίγω 'πιδεύης
φαίνομ᾽ ἔμ᾽ αὔτ[ᾳ.*

Edmonds and Tollius are responsible for this version of line 7, ὡς γάρ
ἔς σ᾽ ἴδω βρόχε᾽, Codex P rendering it ὡς γὰρ σἴδω βρόχεώς. Bergk
thinks that ἐπιρρόμβεισι should be ἐπιβρόμεισι. All hell breaks loose at
lines 9 and 10, where Longinus's Greek does not correspond to
Catullus's 'lingua sed torpet, tenuis sub artis flamma demanant'. Some
commentators emend it by restoring the digamma to ἔαγε,; followers
of Sitzler insert ⟨μ᾽⟩ apostrophe before ἔαγε,; the MSS of Plutarch's
'Progress in Virtue' which quote the lines ἀλλὰ κὰμ μὲν γλῶσσά ⟨μ᾽⟩ ἔαγε,
λέπτον δ᾽ αὔτικα χρῷ πῦρ ὑπαδεδρόμηκεν, either suppress the δ᾽ before
αὔτικα or render it in full before instead of after the word λέπτον. A
papyrus commentary of the early third century however presents
a variant that should make us question all the assumptions we
make about papyri, for the actual structure of the stanza is altered,
line endings appear at different points and one word is suppressed
entirely.

* seems to me that one equal to the gods
to-be, who face-to-face with-you
sits and your beautiful voice
listens to

and laughter charming. truly that my
heart in breast shakes
for when I look at you at-once my speech
quite fails me

but certainly my tongue unstrings, a subtle
under my skin fire slips
my eyes are darkened, hum
my ears

down from me water oozes, trembling
all over grips me, greener am I made
than grass. of death little short
seem I to myself

χλωροτ[έρα δὲ
π]οίας ἔμμι, τεθ[νάκην
δ᾽ ὀ]λίγω [[δ]] ἐπιδε[ύης
φα]ίνομ᾽ ἔμ᾽ αὔτ[αι

Apollonius Dyscolos in his *Pronouns* quotes by way of illustrating the Aeolian habit of prefixing οι (to himself) with a digamma,
φαίνεταί Ϝοι κῆνος. The evidence of corruption is undeniable, hence
the relegation of this, Sappho's best-known poem, to the second rank
of texts. A more disturbing thought, however, occurs when we realize
that the text being praised by Longinus must have been different.

> Are you not amazed how at one and the same moment she seeks
> out soul, body, hearing, tongue, sight and complexion, as though
> they had all left her and were external, and how in contradiction
> she both freezes and burns –

Well, in short she doesn't. There is no freezing in the text as quoted.
This has been taken to mean that Longinus misread the text he is
describing. It is much more likely that in the vicissitudes of copying,
the scribes misread Longinus, I am afraid. Some of the editors have
tried to get ψῦχρος back into the poem – simply by rewriting it, a
procedure which no literary historian of any other period would
countenance. What should also be taken into account is that a
semantic element of freezing could have disappeared from another
word in the sequence.

Any argument based upon a close reading of a text so corrupt
should be expressed throughout in conditional terms, but classical
scholars tire sooner than most of the particles 'may', 'might' and 'could'.
Joan DeJean, to quote a recent example, gives this account of what is
going on in Psappha's original poem:

> The poem recounts what appears at first to be a rather banal
> story: the narrator is a voyeur, observing from a distance the
> woman who is the object of desire while this woman is demon-
> strating her love for a man.

The poem is not a narrative, but a thoroughly dramatic lyric which
enacts a state of mind-body in immediate terms. DeJean also misinter-

prets the behaviour attributed to the beloved, who is simply talking and laughing. It is the observer who characterizes the words and the laughter, neither of which by implication she can hear, as tender and tempting. The observer is observing a love object who is giving her attention to anyone, even everyone, but the observer; the observer's distance contrasted with the nearness of others implies an inability to command the same kind of attention, perhaps because she is female, perhaps not. The fact that the observer is female is not given away until the feminine form χλωροτέρα is used, that is, in the fourteenth line. What DeJean says is that it is not 'immediately stressed'. I would have thought a more accurate account would point out that it is not stressed at all. The poem would have less power if it did not describe a familiar experience, familiar, not as DeJean would seem to have it, only to homosexual women, but to all those who have had an intense and painful crush on someone who was unaware or even repelled. Children in love with older children, or teachers, people too ugly or too poor or too old or crippled, clowns, waiters, all those people who are not to be taken seriously as potential lovers, have all experienced the psychosomatic uproar that Psappha enacts. The teacher who puts a question to a twelve-year-old pupil who blushes purple and cannot speak and begins to shake like a leaf knows what she is up against. She turns aside from the child, whose pitiful emotional state she cannot be seen to encourage, and asks someone else who gets her smile and her approval and appears to the trembling victim of the ignominious crush equal to the gods in her superiority and good fortune.

Sappho's poem presents pretty well the state of mind-body that causes twelve-year-old teenyboppers to liquefy all over the chairs at pop-concerts, to sob and scream and wet themselves: κὰδ δέ μ' ἴδρως κακχέεται. ἴδρως is normally taken to mean sweat, but, as the word is also used for the gum that oozes from trees, perhaps we ought to understand it, especially in close proximity to κακχέεται, as another kind of oozing. Though wholesale liquefaction by love-sick females is well known to pop-concert promoters, who have to undertake to re-cover the seats after rock concerts, it is not discussed in polite society. The parents of today's dripping maenads would not recognize them if they saw them in their frenzy. The spectacle of uninhibited female libido is terrifying. It is usually expressed to people who resemble Sappho's mythical beloved, Phaon, androgynous, erotic, but actually male figures. In the sixth century BC the Greeks had a word for it. Nowadays, though there is a widespread and uneasy suspicion that female libido is bottomless and deeply disorderly, the evidence is filed away unexamined. Sparagmos is enacted every time screaming teenage girls rip bits off a singer's clothes, or indeed body, but the phenomenon is marginalized and ignored. Ecstatic obsession with a stranger is clearly a sexual condition but genital contact will hardly gratify it, if indeed genital contact is sought. All those teachers – of either sex – who know that a schoolgirl is in love with them, know too that to exploit her susceptibility by seeking genital contact is destructive behaviour – and thoroughly unprofessional. Not that I meant by this that Sappho was a perpetual pre-teen; the condition of female libidinous frenzy was better known to the Greeks than it is to us. If it was accepted as part of female sexual identity, the capacity for incontinent emotional riot may well have endured into maturity. Meanwhile the object of these unbearably intense feelings is unaware.

Clearly, φαίνεταί μοι does not describe mass female libidinous frenzy but an isolated and repressed case of similar tumult. The real focus of the poem is not a relationship – no relationship is posited. The poem is about the self that has generated this heart-quake. DeJean's amazing reading continues:

> The appearance of the narrator's signature as a woman comes therefore as a shock, an invasion. The poem is meant to be initially mistaken for just what Catullus turns it into, the most common literary love triangle, in which a man desires a woman when he sees her in the arms of another man.

From being opposite the beloved and hearing her voice and laughter, the equal of the gods now has her in his arms. Which returns us to the voyeur, with whom DeJean's argument began, for she has assumed that the observed encounter is intimate when no evidence for such a supposition can be got from the poem. Such a reading vastly limits the poem's relevance even before DeJean announces that the poem's erotic geometry evokes 'the man in order to demonstrate his super-fluousness: the erotic experience concerns the two women alone, united by bonds that are purely personal'. This reading seems largely to have come about because DeJean appears less interested in poetry, which she dismisses as 'a subset of metrics', than in the novel. She must treat the poem as a novel in little, extrapolating all kinds of seminal novelistic strategies from it. A dramatic lyric often predicates an encounter in a series and simply illuminates its place in a sequence, but the best ones are incantations that illuminate a whole range of human emotional experience far beyond the confines of a particular narrative. In the rubble of this short lyric we can still discern Psappha's achievement in evoking by touches at once exact and inclusive an immediate emotional crisis and expressing it in terms of embarrassing concreteness, a concreteness very seldom achieved by translators who quail before the connotation of a word like κακχέεται. The paralysis and liquefaction are rendered by Sappho in terms so physical that translators are bound to euphemize, unwilling to confront female endocrine reality.

Camille Paglia's vivid and extremely perceptive insights into Sappho are unfortunately inconsistent and largely incompatible with each other.

> The great Sappho may have fallen in love with girls, but to all evidence she internalized rather than externalized her passions. Her most famous poem invents the hostile distance between sexual personae that will have so long a history in western love poetry. Gazing across a room at her beloved sitting with a man, she suffers a physical convulsion of jealousy, humiliation and helpless resignation. This separation is not the aesthetic distance of Apollonian Athens but a desert of emotional deprivation.

No poet can be said to internalize passion. Nor is the distance hostile. Nor is the poet deprived of emotion. She is literally awash with emotion which comes from looking at the beloved for even the shortest time. Her emotional potency is on display, and implicitly compared with the nullity of the man who sits opposite her idol and hears her voice and laughter. Mysteriously, Paglia also says:

> The silvery sweetness of Herbert's simple style is exactly like Sappho's. If you want to know how Sappho sounds in Greek, don't read her pedestrian translators: read Herbert. Herbert discourages anything abrupt or emphatic – that is masculine.

Elsewhere Paglia claims that Emily Dickinson is less melodious than Sappho. This is the more risky because commentators who were two thousand years and rather more miles closer remark that it is not for the melody that Sappho's songs were valued, but for the complexity of the thought, for what the seventeenth century would call wit. Nevertheless, both Paglia and DeJean make an important point – and it is the same point, though Paglia's misreading of the 'Hymn to Aphrodite' conceals it from her. Sappho understood that there is no reciprocity in love, that harmony is not the human condition and that the gods are not on our side. To love and to sing are the same; the thing sung will always be τὸ καλόν, the unenjoyed ideal.

While these texts are not so authentic as to assure us of the enduring greatness of Sappho's poetic talent, they are substantial enough to remove the possibility of regarding her simply as a chimaera. There is nothing for it but to admit that Psappha lived and Psappha wrote. Nowadays the most authoritative statement on when she lived and when she wrote is taken to be Oxyrhynchus papyrus 1,800 of the late second or early third century AD, most of which is missing.

> Sappho was a Lesbian by birth, of the city of Mytilene. Her father was Scamander or, according to some, Scamandronymus, and she had three brothers, Erygius, Larichus and Charaxus . . . She had a daughter Cleis, named after her own mother. She has been accused by some of being irregular in her ways and a woman lover (κ[α]τηγόρηται δ' ὑπ' ἐν[ί]ω[ν] ὡς ἄτακτος οὖ[σα] τὸν τρόπον καὶ γυναικε[ράσ]τρια). In appearance she seems to have been contemptible and quite ugly (τὴν δὲ μορφὴν [εὐ]καταφρόνητος δοκεῖ γε[γον]έναι κα]ὶ δυσειδεστάτη[[ν]]), being dark in complexion and of very small stature ([τ]ὴν μὲν γὰρ ὄψιν φαιώδης [ὑ]πῆρχεν, τὸ δὲ μέγεθος μικρὰ παντελῶς) she used the Aeolic dialect – wrote nine books of lyric poetry and one book of elegiacs.

The reference to her contemptible and swarthy appearance and low stature is one of the least mutilated parts of the papyrus.

Sappho's work was known to all literate Greeks and later to the Romans. All the commentators agree that her poetry is unsurpassed; where they disagree is in their assessment of her person and character. Whatever else she was, she was the 'the poetess' as Homer was 'the poet'. One, probably apocryphal, story has it that Solon of Athens, who was Sappho's contemporary, when he heard a song of Sappho's sung after dinner asked the boy who sang it to teach it to him so that he might 'learn it and die'. Her literary reputation was well established by the time Plato had Socrates speak of her in the *Phaedrus* as one of the wise ancients and called her beautiful because of the beauty of her lyrics. In the *Anthologia Palatina*, compiled at the end of the tenth century from earlier collections of epigrams, Plato is credited with a somewhat unlikely one: 'Some say the muses are nine – how careless – behold Sappho of Lesbos is the tenth!' The *Anthologia Palatina* contains a version of the same commonplace in a eulogy by Antipater of Sidon. In the same tenth-century collection a poem attributed to Dioscorides also salutes her as the Aeolian Muse from Eresus, ending 'greeting to you, lady, as to the gods; for we still have your immortal daughters, your songs'. In such praises there is nothing ironic, though the imputation of musehood rather than poethood contains certain inferences that bode ill for the female poet as conscientious and self-conscious artificer. The idealization of the Sappho portraits was unavoidable, for the beauty of the head was shorthand for the beauty of the poetry, but the tendency flowed backward into assumptions made about Psappha. Tenth Muses abound in the history of women's poetry in western Europe; the compliment was more often than not cynical, and in every case it was used to unseat former claimants to the title, for there can only be one tenth Muse, not only at a time but for all eternity.

When Aristotle quoted Sappho in the *Rhetoric* (1367a, 1398b) historic fact about Psappha had begun to decompose. If Athenaios is to be believed, Chamaeleon of Heraclea in Pontus wrote a treatise 'on Sappho' in the fourth century BC which mistakenly presented Sappho and Anacreon as contemporaries. By the time Sappho's reputation reached its zenith in the Hellenistic Age, all kinds of confused claims are being made for her. We know from Cicero's speech against Verres that Sappho's statue by Silanion, '*tam perfectum, tam elegans, tam elaboratum*', used to stand before the town hall of Syracuse until it was stolen. According to the *Anthologia Palatina*, another effigy of Sappho was to be seen in Constantinople. The last thing that any of these were likely to be images of a swarthy, dark, contemptible-looking female. Nowadays any graven image of a woman whose shoulders seem a mite broad, whose breasts seem less ebullient than usual and whose jaw is a little heavy is apt to be called 'a Sappho'.

Cicero's freedman Tullius Laurea wrote an epitaph for Sappho:

As you pass the Aeolian tomb, stranger, do not say that I, the Mytilenaean poetess, am dead: human hands built this, and such works of men disappear into swift oblivion; but if you judge me by the divine Muses, from each of whom I set a flower beside my nine, you will know that I escaped the gloom of Hades, and that no day will ever dawn that does not speak the name of Sappho, the lyric poetess.

So might he write in 60 BC or so. Relatively early in the development of Sappho's reputation, her lyric poetry seems to have taken precedence over other forms and her love lyrics over the other kinds. Her epigrams, elegiacs and iambics have fared less well, and her hexameters were considered inferior to those of Corinna. It is inevitable that an exclusively male literary establishment would cast its single female member as a capitulator to their own advances or as the object of their own sexual interest. Sappho had become the lyricist *par excellence* of love by the time Horace mentions her in *Carmina* 2,13:

> *Aeoliis fidibus querentem*
> *Sappho puellis de popularibus**

In *Carmina* 4, 9 Horace refers to her as the Aeolian girl, conferring on her the endless youth and beauty that may be granted to the Muses but is not the lot of any human being:

> *spirat adhuc amor*
> *Vivuntque commissi calores*
> *Aeoliae fidibus puellae†*

Sappho was now consigned by her admirers to endless girlhood. Even Petrarch would refer to her in the fourth *Trionfo d'Amore* as '*una giovane greca*'. It was left to the satirists to depict her as a mature

---

* to her Aeolian lyre complaining
  Sappho of the girls of her city

† breathes still the love
  and live entrusted the heats
  of the Aeolian to the lyre girl

woman, in other words, a grotesque. To her admirers, male and female, feminist and not, she would always be *Aeolia puella*. Her passion could be viewed positively or negatively. Horace's contemporary Plutarch seems not to have meant the epithet 'burning' Sappho as pejorative any more than Byron did when he wrote 'The Isles of Greece'. Plutarch found it appropriate to include Sappho as an exemplum in *Of the Virtues of Women*, not because he was unaware that she wrote of sexual passion, but because he accepted the Protean nature of human sexuality; the future fortunes of Sappho's reputation will have more to do with the ebb and flow of sexual permissiveness under various political and religious regimes than with any kind of political fact. The Australian classicist T. G. Tucker was of the opinion that

> the most genuine lyric poet of Rome, Catullus, and its most skilful artificer of odes, Horace, both freely copied her. They did more than imitate; they plagiarized, they translated sometimes almost word for word.

Certainly many motifs that can be found even in the little Sappho we have can be found also in the work of both poets, but this may as well indicate the prevalence of a convention as direct influence. The poet most obviously influenced by Sappho must be Anacreon, and some of the Sapphic elements in Catullus and Horace clearly derive from him. If Sappho is one of the founders of the convention that love poetry follows still to some extent, she is a figure of immense importance and the loss of virtually all of her work must be seen as a catastrophe. In *Epistles* 1, 19 Horace calls her '*mascula Sappho*' and gave rise to some silliness on the part of the scholiasts, who generally participated in the characterization that Seneca gives of 'Didymus the grammarian', who vexed his head about useless questions including 'whether Sappho was a prostitute, and other matters that you would forget if you ever knew them'. Seneca's sneer indicates that though they had the text he and his contemporaries were puzzled about the facts of Sappho's life. The conditions under which she composed were no longer understood. As far as Seneca was concerned, the biography seems to have been of little importance; the implication is that the poetry was the thing.

Sappho's influence on the development of love poetry has always been acknowledged, and may have been far greater even than is acknowledged. We know, for example, that Catullus imitated φαίνεταί μοι with, to my ear, truly wonderful results.

> Ille mi par esse deo videtur
> ille, si fas est, superare divos,
> qui sedens adversus identidem te
>   spectat et audit
> dulce ridentem, misero quod omnis
> eripit sensus mihi; nam simul te,
> Lesbia, aspexi. nihil est super mi
>   [vocis in ore]
> lingua sed torpet, tenuis sub artus
> flamma demanat, sonitu suopte
> tintinant aures, gemina teguntur
>   lumina nocte. (etc.)*

Catullus keeps the Sapphic stanza – there is only one other poem in the Catullus canon in this form – but the fourth stanza is gone, to be replaced by a moral exhortation against love-in-idleness addressed by Catullus to himself. The down-flowing liquid is gone and so is the pallor paler than grass. The beloved on the other hand has been reintroduced, by the simple device of using her name and the second person pronoun. The poem makes a grammatical claim on her attention, suddenly closing the distance between the male poet and the object of his love. After contracting and compressing Sappho's

---

* In translating Latin however literally it is impossible to duplicate word order or the concision of the original because of the multiplicity of syntactical functions compressed into single Latin words.

> To me he seems to be the equal of a god,
> if one may say, to outdo the gods,
> who sitting face to face with you again and again
>   beholds you and hears
> your sweet laughing. Alas, the thought of all my wits
> deprives me; for whenever you,
> Lesbia, I gaze upon, nothing remains
>   [of the voice in my mouth] (*actually lacking in text*)
> my tongue is paralysed, subtle along my limbs
> a flame steals, inward hummings
> ring in my ears; in double night
>   my eyes are cloaked

heart-quake, drying it out so to speak, Catullus still finds it necessary to append a stanza reproving himself for allowing himself to become so unmanned. The charge of plagiarism and of having taken over Sappho and made her his own creature has been laid against Catullus for this effort. In fact he is doing no more than generations of poets were to do for their classical models. The original was too well known for the compliment to Sappho not to have been perceived. It is in any event underlined by Catullus's retention of the unusual and difficult metre. A poem translated is a new poem. Catullus's translation of Sappho not only gives us a good Latin poem but has served as well to illuminate the battered original. If we knew our Sappho better we would know whether Lesbia is not in fact a literary creation, the woman of Lesbos, Catullus's master in the art of love, *Sapphica musa*. I can see no ground for discounting the possibility that all twelve of Catullus's Lesbia poems are imitations of Sappho, and no way of verifying it either, except to point out that in 43 he sneers at the mistress of the bankrupt of Formiae, saying:

> tecum Lesbia nostra comparatur?
> o saeclum insapiens et infacetum!*

Strabo's 'Sappho is a marvellous creature ($\theta\alpha\nu\mu\alpha\sigma\tau\acute{o}\nu$ $\tau\iota$ $\chi\rho\hat{\eta}\mu\alpha$), in all history you will find no woman who can challenge comparison with her even in the slightest degree' reveals how easily Sappho's excellence can be used as a justification for the silencing of the rest. The relative merits of male poets old and new could be discussed, but women had already done their dash.

When we consider more closely the grounds on which Sappho was cried up, another kind of uneasiness insinuates itself. Dionysius of Halicarnassus described her mastery of the elegant or spectacular style that 'tries to fit each word together, taking great pains to have everything planed and rubbed down smooth and all the joints neatly dovetailed'. One would have more faith in his judgement if he had not spoken of a poem as if it was a cupboard and had not quoted the 'Hymn to Aphrodite' as an example of high-class poetic joinery. Many of the commentaries praise Sappho's use of lovely words and

---

* With you are we to compare our Lesbia?
O age unknowing and untaught!

her descriptions of lovely things, in what appears to be a prescription for the very worst kind of namby-pamby poetic. The figure adumbrated by these commentaries is hardly the sweaty creature of φαίνεταί μοι. As the sound of Psappha's voice faded from the recollection of the Greek-speaking world, for reasons that have more to do with the usefulness of standardized Greek as the lingua franca of an increasingly bureaucratized state than sexual politics, Sappho's identification with female passion became all that all save the most diligent scholars knew about her. The notion of Sappho as a 'female Homer' gradually gave way to Horace's 'Aeolian girl' and eventually transmuted to Wordsworth's 'Lesbian maid'.

By the twelfth century the text that the Augustans had known so well, and that had continued to exert its sway over the literary establishment, at least until the end of the third century, had disappeared. John Tzetzes, writing on the metres of Pindar, was obliged to forbear using examples from Sappho; 'the passage of time has destroyed Sappho, her works, her lyre and her songs'. Tzetzes was writing in Byzantium, where knowledge of Sappho's text is believed to have endured longest; if it had disappeared there we may assume, I think, that it was long gone from everywhere else.

It is bitterly ironic that, after her text had disappeared, Sappho should have made her way back into the European literary tradition via the *Epistula Sapphus*, not as a poet but as a literary character. The *Epistula Sapphus*, nowadays better known as no. XV of the *Heroides* of Ovid, is a verse letter written in the persona of Sappho as if to Phaon on the eve of her suicidal leap from the Leucadian rock. The story of Sappho's suicide for love goes back to Anacreon, Euripides, and Ausonius. Strabo's *Geography* quotes Menander on Leucas, 'where they say that Sappho first, hunting the haughty Phaon, threw herself in her goading desire from the far-seen cliff'. Photius lists the known leapers at Leucas with never a mention of Sappho. The legend holds that Phaon was an old ferryman who

> accepted money only from the rich. The goddess Aphrodite . . . assumed the appearance of a mortal, and spoke with Phaon about a crossing. He quickly carried her over and asked for nothing. The goddess transformed the old man and gave him youth and beauty. This then is the Phaon about her love for whom Sappho often sang in her lyric poetry.

Phaon is clearly not a historic personage but a personification of absolute and irresistible beauty, in much the same way as Adonis. The inclusion of Sappho amongst the victims of his beauty would seem to indicate that the poet too had become to some extent mythologized. The poet of Aphrodite becomes the victim of Aphrodite; the tenth Muse, the mortal muse, destroys herself for love of an eternal non-reciprocating love object. The scholars who have sought evidence that Psappha herself was in love with a local lad of that name seem once more to have confused the figurative with the literal. In the *Epistula Sapphus*, Sappho's homosexuality is stressed, as is the extent of her homoerotic activity. Names that can be found in no other source are listed; as well as Anactoria, Cydro and Atthis, Sappho here claims to have had hundreds of female lovers:

> nec me Pyrrhiades Methymniadesve puellae
>   nec me Lesbiadum cetera turba iuvant.
> vilis Anactorie, vilis me candida Cydro,
>   non oculis grata est Atthis, ut ante, meis,
> atque alie centum, quas hic sine crimine amavi.
>   inprobe, multarum quod fuit, unus habes.*

There is as usual a crux – some versions read, maddeningly, '*quas non sine crimine amavi*'. In his gloss on this passage Politian quotes Lucian on the lubricity and homosexuality of the Lesbians, Horace on '*mascula Sappho*' and the girls of the people, and Martial on Philaenis the tribade. Porphyrio, commentator on Horace, explains Epistle I.19.28 *temperat Archilochi musam pede mascula Sappho* either because she is famous for her poetry, in which men more often excel, or because she is maligned as having been a tribade: *vel quia in poetico studo est [incluta], in quo saepius viri, vel quia tribus diffamatur fuisse*. So Sappho the diesel became an erudite joke, a gem of scholarly pornography, a mantra to still masculine anxiety by provoking disgust and laughter.

The best known of Latin lampoons on homosexual women is Martial's caricature of Philaenis, who is bigger, stronger, more

---

* Neither Pyrrhan nor Methymnan girls
   Nor of Lesbians the rest of the throng delight me.
  Nothing to me is Anactoria, nothing dazzling Cydro,
   nor to my eyes pleasing is Atthis, as before she was,
    or the other hundred whom not entirely without reproach I loved;
   unworthy you, what was enjoyed by many, have to yourself alone.

gluttonous and more preremptory than any man. The *Epistula Sapphus* exaggerates the sexual gluttony of Sappho, in order to gain the maximum frisson from the idea of her pursuit of Phaon. Many readers of the poem were convinced that Sappho's sexual demands drove Phaon to Sicily, though nothing in the poem actually suggests this. Just as the inveterate lesbian Pussy Galore was effortlessly laid low by James Bond, Sappho the insatiable tribade is reduced to blubbering impotence by Phaon. Until Oxyrhynchus 1,800 was deciphered, the *Epistula* was the only source for the notion that Sappho was ugly and squat:

> If nature malign to me has denied the charm of beauty weigh in the stead of beauty the genius that is mine. If I am slight of stature, yet I have a name fills every land; the measure of my name is my real height.

The verification of this detail has justified scholars in the use of the *Epistula* as a biographical source in itself.

In the *Epistula* Sappho argues wittily for Phaon's love, pointing out that if he waits for his equal in beauty he will wait for ever and that the white pigeon is often mated with a pigeon of duskier hue. She reminds him that when she sang to him he used to steal kisses from her, and that she pleased him as a lover because of her inventiveness and wit. Now that Phaon has left her and gone to Sicily, she prays to Aphrodite for protection, reminding her that she lost her father when she was six and that her brother has wasted his substance on a harlot, and that she has a little daughter to look after. The explanation of her infatuation with Phaon is as complex and sophisticated as we might expect from the genuine Ovid:

> molle meum levibusque cor est violabile telis,
> et semper causa est, cur ego semper amem –
> sive ita nascenti legem dixere Sorores
> nec data sunt vitae fila severa meae,
> sive abeunt studia in mores, artisque magistra
> ingeniuim nobis molle Thalia facit.
> quid mirum, si me primae lanuginis etas
> abstulit, atque anni quos vir amare potest?*

> * Soft is my heart and easily pierced by the subtle dart
> and ever cause is, that I should ever love –

Sappho has been seduced by the beauty of youth, as men are. She implies that she had written of love without feeling it, and has evidently seduced herself. It befits the servant of Aphrodite that she should be the active and aggressive lover of an avatar of Adonis. Sappho's description of the woodland where they made love makes the parallel more vivid and reminds us that Adonis rejected the goddess because of the call of the hunt, love being an inferior form of predation. Perhaps we can take it as Ovid's compliment to Sappho that she bemoans the loss of her poetic gift:

> non mihi respondent veteres in carmina vires;
> plectra dolore iacent muta, dolore lyra.*

The explanation of her planned leap is that a Naiad told her that Deucalion cast himself down from the Leucadian rock for love of Pyrrha 'et inlaeso corpore pressit aquas' ... not only did he survive unhurt, his passion fled from him and he was heart-whole again. The purpose of Sappho's letter is to plead for a word from Phaon that will be enough to deflect her from such a desperate act.

The manuscript history of the *Epistula Sapphus* is quite distinct from that of the *Heroides* proper. In the Ovid MSS descended from the eleventh-century Codex Parisinus it is not to be found. It first appears in the thirteenth-century Codex Francofortanus, which originated in the Loire valley. The *Epistula Sapphus* first appeared as *Heroides* XV in Heinsius' edition of 1661. Heinsius' justification for this is that he had found citations from it in that position in the *Florilegium Gallicum*, a highly eclectic compilation that also stemmed from the Loire valley. The *Epistula Sapphus* seems to have been discovered at the beginning of the fifteenth century; from about 1420 onwards more than two hundred copies were made and widely

---

whether at birth the Sisters this law decreed
  and spun not my thread of life with resistant strands,
or whether manners yield to study, and the mistress of our art,
  Thalia, makes our natures soft.
what wonder then, if unfledged youth
undoes me, those years that rouse men to love?

*not to me respond my erstwhile powers of song
  my plectra with grief lie dumb, with grief my lyre.

distributed. In *De Claris Mulieribus* Boccaccio draws heavily on the *Heroides*. Whether he was also able to draw upon the *Epistula Sapphus* for 'Cap. xlv, Sappho, Poetress of Lesbos', is not clear. Copies of the *Epistula* do not begin to proliferate until the fifteenth century, more than sixty years after *De Claris Mulieribus* was written. Boccaccio's account is not only highly allegorized but also intentionally misleading, principally about his ability to read Greek.

> The poetess Sappho was a girl from the city of Mytilene in the island of Lesbos. No other fact has reached us about her origins. But if we examine her work, we will see that she was born of honorable and noble parents, for no vile soul could have desired to write poetry, nor could a plebian one have written it as she did. Although it is not known when she flourished, she nevertheless had so fine a talent that in the flower of youth and beauty she was not satisfied with writing solely in prose, but, spurred by the great fervor of her soul and mind, with diligent study she ascended the steep slopes of Parnassus, and on that high summit with happy daring joined the Muses, who did not nod in disapproval. Wandering through the laurel grove, she arrived at the cave of Apollo, bathed in the waters of Castalia, and took up Phoebus's plectrum. As the sacred nymphs danced, this girl did not hesitate to strike the strings of the cithara and bring forth melody. All these things seem very difficult even for well-educated men. Why say more? Through her eagerness she reached such heights that her verses, which according to ancient testimony were very famous, are still brilliant in our own day. A bronze statue was erected and consecrated to her name, and she was included among the famous poets. Certainly neither the crown of kings, the papal tiara, nor the conqueror's laurel is more splendid than her glory.

Clearly Boccaccio knew little more of Sappho than her name, but he did know the story of Phaon. His reference to mournful verses that she wrote for him might be thought to be a reference to the beginning of the *Epistula Sapphus*, where she claims to have abandoned the lyric for the elegiac mode. Boccaccio's account continues in gallant strain:

Are the Muses to be blamed? They were able to move the stones of Ogygia when Amphion played, but they were unwilling to soften the young man's heart in spite of Sappho's songs.

The professional poet Christine de Pisan, daughter of a court astrologer, drew upon Boccaccio for her account of Sappho, 'that most subtle woman, poet and philosopher', in *La Cité des Dames*, written in 1404.

The wise Sappho, who was from the city of Mytilene, was no less learned than Proba. This Sappho had a beautiful body and face, and was agreeable and pleasant in appearance, conduct and speech. But the charm of her profound understanding surpassed all of the other charms with which she was endowed, for she was expert and learned in several arts and sciences, and she was not only well-educated in the works and writings composed by others but also discovered many new things herself and wrote many books and poems. Concerning her, Boccaccio has offered these fair words couched in the sweetness of poetic language: 'Sappho, possessed of sharp wit and burning desire for constant study in the midst of bestial and ignorant men, frequented the heights of Mount Parnassus, that is, of perfect study. Thanks to her fortunate boldness and daring, she kept company with the Muses, that is, the arts and sciences, without being turned away. She entered the forest of laurel trees filled with many boughs, greenery, and different coloured flowers, soft fragrances and various aromatic spices, where Grammar, Logic, noble Rhetoric, Geometry, and Arithmetic, all live and take their leisure. She went on her way till she came to the deep grotto of Apollo, god of learning, and found the brook and conduit of the fountain of Castalia, and took up the plectrum and quill of the harp and played sweet melodies, with the nymphs all the while leading the dance, that is, following the rules of harmony and musical accord. From what Boccaccio says about her, it should be inferred that the profundity of both her understanding and of her learned books can only be known and understood by men of great perception and learning, according to the testimony of the ancients. Her writings and poems have survived to this day, most remarkably constructed and composed, and they serve as illumination and models of consummate poetic craft and composition to those who have come afterward. She invented different kinds of lyric and poetry, short narratives, tearful laments and strange lamentations about love and other emotions, and these were so well made and so well ordered that they were named 'Sapphic' after her. Horace recounts, concerning her poems, that when Plato, the great philosopher who was Aristotle's teacher, died, a book of Sappho's poems was found under his pillow.

In 1521 Christine's work appeared in English as *The Boke of the Cyte of Ladyes*. Mount Parnassus is to Christine a version of the groves of academe; what she chooses to stress is that Sappho was not excluded from education, Apollo presides not as the god of poetry but as the god of learning. It is learning that enables Sappho to equal the achievements of men. Christine certainly had no Greek and probably very little Latin. Heaven knows how she came by her cute canard about Plato's pillow. Most importantly, Christine resolutely suppresses any mention of Phaon, treating Sappho's love poetry as genre rather than biography, a tendency that should be encouraged. Her falsification even of her source can be explained by her didactic intent; just as contemporary feminist politics dictate categoric statements about Sappho, Christine's feminism demands the suppression of any detail that might prejudice her case. In case ladies should think learning appropriate only to dowdy women, Sappho is declared beautiful. No suggestion can be tolerated, by ladies or gentlemen, that she was anything but chaste.

Even as Sappho's work was becoming better known in the vernacular the scholars were proceeding with their own investigations of Sappho, still based upon the *Epistula Sapphus*. Georgio Merula published *In Sapphus epistolam interpretatio* in Venice in 1471; another commentary, by Domizio Calderini, was published in Brescia in 1476. In the spring of 1481, Politian lectured on the *Epistula Sapphus* to his students in Florence. Politian's lecture notes, in Latin, preserved in the Munich Staatsbibliotek and published in Florence in 1971, make impressive reading. In introducing Sappho to his students he quotes Strabo and all Plato's mentions of Sappho. He provides a summary biography based on the known sources, listing her family, her pupils, and Atthis, Telesippa, Anactoria, Gyro or Gyrinna and Megara, quoting the *Suda*, 'And she got a bad name for her impure friendship with them' – in Greek – without further comment. In the course of his lectures he quotes from the known fragments sixteen times. Politian takes Sappho intensely seriously as a poet and is more interested in the *Epistula Sapphus* as evidence of her literary activity than as a cautionary tale or soft-core pornography.

Ovid's authorship of the *Epistula Sapphus* was questioned by virtually all the Italian humanists, though they disagreed about the grounds for denying the attribution. Politian suggests in fact that the *Epistula Sapphus* might be a free translation of a poem by Sappho herself, a hypothesis that has resurfaced at irregular intervals ever since. Like most of the hypotheses associated with Sappho, it can be neither proved nor disproved. Politian does not doubt that she nourished a criminal passion for women, or that she was reduced to utter humiliation by her infatuation for Phaon, but he does not doubt either that she was a great poet. His whole discussion is coloured by an unstated optimism that her nine books of poems would eventually be found.

When Sessa published a vernacular translation of *Epistole del famosissimo Ovidio vulgare in octava rima* in Venice in 1508 he did not include the *Epistula Sapphus*, which appeared in 1517, with no mention of Ovid, in the back of a volume entitled *Timone comedia del magnifico Conte Matheo Maria Boiardo, Conte de Scandiano, traducta de un dialogo de Luciano*. The text is immediately preceded by an 'Escusatione de Iacobo Philippo Pelle Negra de Troia in la sua epistola di Sappho', still without acknowledgement of Ovid, though Pelle Negra de Troia (surely an academy sobriquet) is described as '*interprete*'. Pelle Negra does not mince words when it comes to describing Sappho's homoerotic past:

> Piu il furor de le muse non mi honora
> Ne il piacer de le Druade mi tene
> ne de le mie Tespiade amiche ancora
> Cidno e Amithone che furo il mio bene
> Hor le desprezo: & de Atthi il dolce viso
> El mio occhio mirar non piu sostiene
> E da cento altre il mio core hai diuiso
> Sclerato Phaon che sol la cosa
> Che fu de molte & molte hor hai conquiso . . .*

* More the fury of the muse not me honours
  Nor the pleasure of the Druids me holds
  nor of my Thespian girlfriends even
  Cidno and Amithone who were my sweethearts

Scholarly contempt for Sappho was based on four judgements, that she was oversexed, that she was incontinent, verbally, emotionally and sexually, that she was a suicide and that she was a lover of her own sex, in more or less that order of importance.

At first even vernacular versions conveyed what scholars took to be the whole truth about the Sappho of the *Epistula*. George Turbervile, translating Ovid's 'Heroical Epistles' in 1567 for his patron, Thomas, Lord Howard, Viscount Byndon, appears utterly unembarrassed by Sappho's same-sex love affairs.

> Within a while this lad the lasses had allured,
> But wanton Sappho least of all his beauty's beams endured.
> She loved him passing well; he forced her not a rush:
> Her, silly nymph, enraged with love, a thousand cares did crush.
> 'Pyrino is forgot, nor dryads do delight
> My fancy: Lesbian lasses eke are now forgotten quite
> Not Amython I force, nor Cydno passing fine:
> Nor Atthis as she did of yore, allures these eyes of mine.
> Nor yet a hundred more, whom (shame ylaid aside)
> I fancied erst: thou all that love from them to thee has wried.'

Thirty years later, John Donne took the commentaries by the horns and wrote an imitation of the *Epistula Sapphus*, called breathtakingly 'Sappho to Philaenis'. It was never printed in his lifetime but, though some editors have suppressed the most suggestive passages and others have denied his authorship, it is true Donne. Sappho has recovered from her love for Phaon and now addresses a woman whose name means 'lover of girls'. The name Philaenis would have suggested Martial's tribade to all his colleagues, but Donne's entire argument is based upon her being an exact replica of Sappho herself. His fascination is with the notion of narcissism *à deux*, more comprehensible and more aesthetically satisfying than any engagement between beauty and a 'harsh rough man'.

---

now [I] despise them: and of Atthis the sweet face
My eye to behold no longer bears
And from a hundred others my heart [you] have divided
Rascal Phaon who alone the thing
That was for many and many now have overcome . . .

In 1509 Raffaelle Sanzio of Urbino joined the team of painters redecorating the apartments of the soldier pope Julius II. To Raphael were entrusted the frescos in the Stanza della Segnatura. The pope was no more a scholar than Raphael, but it was decided that the stanza should display Theology, Poetry, Philosophy and Jurisprudence as beautiful female personifications in the ceiling, with the themes worked out in emblematic scenes on the walls beneath the appropriate figures. When Marcantonio Raimondi copied the design for Parnassus, exemplifying poetry, the only female figures in it were the Muses. When Raphael came actually to paint it, he included the figure of Sappho in the foreground. By painting Sappho as if she is leaning into the room, he makes her the largest of the figures of the poets of love, one of the most dominating figures in the whole composition.

Whoever advised the inclusion of Sappho in 1509 or so was ahead of his time. While Sappho's personal reputation was both defined and degraded by the highly accessible *Epistula Sapphus*, her reputation as a poet was maintained at first by the scholarly commentaries and then by a series of publications in Greek, in Latin and in the vernacular, of the two texts as quoted by Dionysius of Halicarnassus and Longinus. The 'Hymn to Aphrodite' was published in Greek in France in 1546 by Robert Estienne; Estienne's son Henri reprinted it at the end of his Greek–Latin edition of Anacreon in 1554. In subsequent editions in 1556, 1560 and 1566 the 'Hymn' was translated into Latin. The Greek version as published by the Estiennes leaves the gender of the love object in the fifth and sixth stanzas indeterminate. It was in 1554 too that φαίνεταί μοι was published twice, once in Basel in Robertello's edition of Longinus's *De Sublimitate* and again in Venice in Muret's commentary on Catullus. A translation into Italian by Francesco Anguillac was published in 1572. Gabriel de Petra translated Longinus into Latin in about 1600; Gerard Langbaine published an edition at Oxford in 1636. The 'Hymn to Aphrodite' made little impression but φαίνεταί μοι took the literary world by storm. It was immediately translated into French by Remi Belleau, who for once follows the Greek rather than Catullus. De Baif and Ronsard wrote other versions of it.

> Je suis un demi-dieu quand, assis vis-à-vis
> De toi, mon cher souci, j'écoute des devis,
> Devis entre-rompus d'un gracieux sourire,

> Souris qui me retient le coeur emprisonné:
> Car, en voyant tes yeux, je me pâme étonné
> Et de mes pauvres flancs un seul vent je ne tire.
> Ma langue s'engourdit, un petit feu me court
> Frétillant sous la peau; je suis muet et sourd
> Et une obscure nuit dessus mes yeux demeure;
> Mon sang devient glace, l'ésprit fuit de mon corps,
> Je tremble tout de crainte, et peu s'en faut alors
> Qu'à tes pieds étendu sans âme je ne meure.

The erotic vision of the poets of the Pleiade is highly sophisticated, and in part constructed upon literary precedent; the sixteenth-century school of love taught a kind of behaviour and a language of feeling that were *précieux*. Much of the subsequent history of Sappho's reputation is in fact dictated by her identification with *préciosité*. *Préciosité* disfigures Belleau's reading of φαίνεταί μοι. The directness of Sappho's language of passion is simply unavailable to him. The love of a Petrarchist, who had inherited the erotic tradition founded by Sappho in a deeply mutated and conventionalized form, was always unrequited; it was inevitable that the rediscovery of Sappho's depiction of erotic self-torment should have been conceived as part of the same schema. Eternal non-reciprocity, which DeJean sees as Sappho's insight into the nature of love, is a fundamental tenet of the Petrarchist philosophy of love.

The mid-sixteenth-century Sappho craze in France probably inspired Lyly's curious court comedy of *Sapho and Phao*. Lyly's notion of the Sappho/Phaon story is probably derived from the same sources as Abraham Fleming's contemporary *Registre of Hystories*, namely Aelianus's *Varia Historia* crossed with the *Epistula Sapphus*, but essentially his play develops an idea from Churchyard's entertainment for the queen at Norwich, published in 1578, in which Dame Chastity subdued Cupid and gave his quiver into the keeping of the queen. In Lyly's play Cupid and Venus worst the princess Sapho, who is a personification of Chastity, by making her love Phao. Sapho defeats theirobject by refusing to give way to her passion, though it is so violent as to make her sick, and finally she too gains control over Cupid and supplants his mother. When the play ends Phao is in love with Sapho and indifferent to Venus, who is in love with him; Cupid too is in love with Sapho and obedient to her command. Sapho, having conquered her own obsession is absolute, and can afford to pity Phao, control Cupid and disdain Venus. For Lyly to be able to offer the queen such a compliment there can have been no common caricature of Sappho in circulation in England at the time.

A French prose translation of the *Heroides* published in 1621, made 'pour le contentement de deux princesses' ten years previously, included a version of the *Epistula Sapphus* at the end, which is doubly odd, because all things considered it might have been easier to have omitted it altogether. It is preceded by a curious synopsis of the myth, which can be traced through a number of translations in other vernaculars, including English. A similar account of the beautification of Phaon is given by Lyly for example.

> On fait un conte qui excuse un peu la folle passion que Saphon témoigne en cette lettre, & Pline même attribue cette faveur a la vertu d'une herbe que Phaon lui avait donnée ... dont cette déesse voulant se revancher, lui donna une boîte pleine d'une fard si excellent que dès qu'il s'en fut servi seulement une fois, il devint le plus beau de tous les hommes de son temps; pendant qu'il était en la fleur de cette parfaite beauté il fût aimé de Saphon, mais si éperdument qu'elle en était toute folle . . .*

As Saltonstall pointed out in 1636 in the dedication of his translation of the *Epistula Sapphus* to 'The vertuous ladies and gentlewomen of England', the poem 'which most Gentlemen could read before in Latin, is for your sakes come forth in English . . .' The ladies' Sappho was a far less disturbing creature than the one the gentlemen already knew in Latin; it was to protect the innocence of women that sexually explicit passages in all kinds of treatises continued to be expressed in Latin or Greek until the early twentieth century. The version boiled down for the French princesses renders Ovid's account of Sappho's homoerotic past in these terms:

---

* A story is told that excuses a little the mad passion that Sappho displays in this letter, and Pliny himself attributes this charm to the power of a herb that Phaon had given to him . . . the goddess wishing to do something in return gave him a box full of a cosmetic so excellent that after he had used it only once, he became the most beautiful of all the men of his time; while he was in the flower of this beauty he was beloved of Sappho, but so distractedly that she was quite mad with it . . .

[Je] suis si affligée, que je ne me saurais même plaire en la compagnie des Dames de Lesbos, qui m'était autrefois si agréable: je ne fais plus de cas d'Anactoire, ny de Cidnon dont j'étais presque amoureuse, autant en puisse - je dire de la belle Athis, et de beaucoup d'autres, avec qui je passais le temps avec tous les contentements du monde: maintenant je ne me plais avec les unes, ni avec les autres, et pour ne penser qu'en vous je les ai toutes effacées de mon âme pour vous mettre tout seul à la place qu'elles y avoient toutes ensemble.

Sappho's loves have here been transformed into *amitiés sentimentales*. Saltonstall, unlike his predecessor Turbervile, takes the same course. The argument of the *Epistula* which clearly relates to sexual intimacy is blurred to imply that the manageable sisterly affection that Sappho felt for many had been combined into a single overwhelming sexual obsession.

> A quiet mind doth verses best beget.
> The dryads do not helpe me at this time,
> Nor Lesbian nor Pierian Muses nine.
> I hate Amython, and Cydnus white,
> And Atthis is not pleasant in my sight.
> And many others that were lov'd of me,
> But now I have plac'd all my love on thee.

In 1652 John Hall, Cromwell's pamphleteer, published an English translation of Longinus with the first English translation of φαίνεταί μοι in the English version of the Sapphic stanza, namely, three lines of unrhymed iambic pentameter followed by a hemistich of trimeter. This extraordinary circumstance passed virtually unnoticed. When Katherine Philips's *Poems* were published posthumously in 1667 the unknown editor, who was probably the bookseller, opined:

We might well have call'd her the English Sappho, she of all Poets of former Ages, being for her Verses and her Vertues both, the most highly to be valued . . .

Cowley, a classicist of no mean order, in his elegy upon Katherine Philips, refused to draw any such comparison.

> Of female poets who had names of old,
> Nothing is known but only told,
> And all we hear of them perhaps may be
> Male-flattery only, and male-poetry.

Cowley was exceptionally unsympathetic to women, even for an Englishman, but his insight into the Sappho phenomenon was a true one. In four dyspeptic lines he dismissed all the Sapphistry of his day. This salutary example was not followed: in 1684 when Oldham praised Katherine Philips again, as

> soft Orinda, whose bright shining name
> Stands next great Sappho's in the ranks of fame

a minivogue for sanitized Sappho had begun, in response to the French precedent set by Boileau's translation of Longinus, *On the Sublime*, in 1674. Though he had Longinus before him, Boileau's version seems to me to owe more to Catullus than the Greek:

> Heureux qui, près de toi, pour toi seule soupire;
> Qui jouit du plaisir de t'entendre parler;
> Qui te voit quelquefois doucement lui sourire!
> Les dieux dans son bonheur peuvent-ils l'égaler?
>
> Je sens de veine en veine une subtile flamme
> Courir par tout mon corps sitôt que je te vois;
> Et dans les doux transports ou s'égare mon âme,
> Je ne saurais trouver ni langue ni voix.
>
> Un nuage confus se répand sur ma vue;
> Je n'entends plus; je tombe en douces langueurs,
> Et pâle, sans haleine, interdite, éperdue,
> Un frisson me saisit, je tremble, je me meurs.

After the word '*pâle*', Boileau has a note: '*Le grec ajoute "Comme l'herbe" mais cela ne dit point en français.*'* A note on the last line explains a second censorship: '*Il y a dans le grec une sueur froide; mais le mot sueur en français ne peut jamais être agréable, et laisse une vilaine idée a*

---

* The Greek adds 'like grass', but that says nothing in French.

*l'ésprit.'** Boileau's translation was translated into English by John Pulteney in 1680. Boileau's notions of decorum were to dictate English poetic taste and practice for more than fifty years. Sappho had proved once more too strong for gentlemanly stomachs. The ladies had no way of knowing how their heroine had been bowdlerized.

Madame Dacier and Madeleine de Scudéry had little choice in the circumstances. To have admitted Sappho's amorous complexion, not to mention her same-sex love affairs, would have blackened them by association and done their cause more harm than good. In the sex war, as in all other wars, the first casualty is truth. Male scholarship demonstrated its greater probity, seriousness and authority by insisting on Sappho's abnormality, and thus killed two birds with the same stone; the implication that the demonstration of great talent in poetry proved innate masculinity was immediately useful in repelling women who might seek to trespass on the male preserve. No seventeenth-century student of human nature would have supposed that women were not capable of behaving lasciviously together or that women who did so were unable or unwilling to couple with men. Lubricity implied promiscuity, which implied lecherous intention *vis-à-vis* men, boys, women, girls, infants and animals. What is defended by Dacier and de Scudéry is not Sappho's 'normality', which was not in question, but her 'virtue', without which she could not then be taken seriously. At the same time that they attempted to purge all taint of grossness from her character, they exalted her capacity for intense feeling within non-genital relationships. The *amitié sentimentale* included all the emotional manifestations that we nowadays associate exclusively with sex, including obsession, jealousy and fear of abandonment, as well as sighs, tears and rapture.

There is a less edifying aspect of the scholarly insistence on Sappho being amorously involved only with women which becomes comprehensible when we recall what an astonishingly high proportion of commercial heterosexual pornography features two women displaying erotic interaction for the titillation of men. If women did not experience homoerotic feelings, male fantasy would have invented them. The early scholars who teased out homoerotic implications in Sappho's work were indulging their own voyeurism, the same voyeurism that

---

* The Greek says 'a cold sweat', but the word 'sweat' in French can never be pleasant, and leaves an ugly idea in the mind.

amassed enormous collections of Fescennine literature and artefacts, scholars for the use of, not to be displayed before women, children or domestics. As it happens, women can be powerfully attracted to women and Psappha was, but to define her and to value her works exclusively as exhibiting homosexual priorities and values is once more to co-opt her and to isolate her from other women.

Though Madame Dacier's father, Tanneguy LeFevre, admitted Sappho's homosexual affairs and refused to credit tales of Kerkula or Phaon, Madame Dacier, in the biography that she prefixed to her translation of the *Poésies d'Anacréon et de Sapho*, published in 1681, presents her as a married woman who loses her husband while she is still young, has numerous suitors and finally kills herself for love of Phaon by leaping off the cliff. Madeleine de Scudéry, both through her 'harangue de Sapho' in *Les Femmes Illustres*, and the character of Sapho in *Artamène*, which was read by every lady of fashion for the next hundred years, brought the transformation of Psappha's physical love for whomever into *amitiés sentimentales* between women to a high polish. Sanitized Sappho survived alongside idolatry of her perversity well into the twentieth century. The American sculptress Vinnie Ream made her name with a demure life-size figure of Sappho in 1860. When she died in 1914 a bronze replica of this, her masterpiece, was set up over her grave.

Artamène, more commonly referred to as *Le Grand Cyrus*, was read almost as much in England as it was in France; at first the prestige of Sappho was hardly questioned. In 1675 Edward Phillips, in *Theatrum Poetarum*, gave an admirably fair and concise statement of the case:

Sappho, a Lesbian (the daughter of Scamandarus and wife of Cercilas, a rich man of Andros, by whom she had a daughter named Clio) not inferior in fame to the best of lyric poets and said to be the first composer of that sort of lyric verse, which for her is called Sapphic; in which some are extant under her name, besides which she is said to have written epigrams, elegies, iambics and monodies, and to have flourished in the 42nd Olympiad, and invented the plectrum. Moreover, being a poetess herself, she is likewise the subject of poetical tradition, if at least it were the same Sappho (for there have been imagined others of the same name) who falling in love with Phao the Ferry Man, and finding her self slighted, was possessed with a worse than poetic madness to throw herself headlong from the rock Leucus into the Sea. Ovid, Statius, and others of the Latin poets acknowledge but one Sappho.

In *The Illustrious History of Women*, published eleven years later, John Shirley confused everything but his eulogistic intention.

Sappho for her poetry was famous, and was as Elianus affirmeth, the daughter of Scamandronius, as Plato of Aristan, Suidas and other Greek writers say, there were two of that name, the one called Erixa, a much celebrated poetess, who flourished in the time of Tarqinius Priscus, and by many is imagined to be the inventress of lyrick verses. The other was Sappho Mitylaena, who published many poems among the Greeks, though some-what extravagant yet for her ingenuity had the honour to be styled the Tenth Muse and of her Antipater Sidonus thus writes 'When Sappho's verse he did admiring read,/ Demanded whence the Tenth Muse did proceed.'

Aphra Behn, who was herself called Sappho in a complimentary way by John Evelyn in *Numismata* in 1697, included in her *Miscellany* of 1685, 'Verses made by Sapho done from the Greek by Boileau. And from the French by a lady of quality'.

> Happy who hears you sigh, for you alone
> Who hears you speak, or whom you smile upon:
> You well for this might scorn a starry throne.

John Adams, in a prefatory poem to Behn's *Poems upon Several Occasions* of 1684, praised her above Sappho:

> 'Twas vain for man the laurels to pursue,
> (E'en from the god of wit bright *Daphne* flew)
> Man, whose coarse compound damps the Muses' fire,
> It does but touch our earth and soon expire;
> While in the softer kind th'ethereal flame,
> Spreads and rejoices as from heaven it came:
> This Greece in *Sappho*, in *Orinda* knew
> Our isle; though they were but low types to you . . .

Behn herself did not seek to supplant Sappho, but asked simply in her versification of the English translation of that part of Cowley's *De Plantarum* that dealt with the laurel tree:

> Let me with *Sappho* and *Orinda* Be
> Oh ever sacred nymph, adorn'd by thee:
> And give my verses immortality.

These lines were published in the year of her death. As one of the popularizers of French literary culture in Britain, Behn's reputation fell foul of the anti-French feeling that had developed as the Treaty of Dover became common knowledge and intensified after the flight of James II into exile at Saint-Germain. Though she mentioned Sappho with respect, most of her contemporaries, including her fellow poet Anne Wharton, used the name as a term of opprobrium.

When Jacob Tonson published *Ovid's Epistles Translated by Several Hands* in 1680, he did not place at the head of the volume, which was edited by Dryden, one of Dryden's elegant translations of the *Heroides* but a perfunctory version of the *Epistula Sapphus* by Sir Carr Scrope, who makes of the poem's 220 lines a mere 96, beginning with a version of lines 10–11, followed by lines 8–9.

> While Phaon to the flaming Etna flies,
> Consum'd with no less fires poor Sapho dies.
> I burn, I burn, like kindled fields of corn,
> When by the driving winds the flames are born.
> My muse and lute can now no longer please,
> They are th'employments of a mind at ease.
> Wandring from thought to thought I sit alone
> All day, and my once dear companions shun.
> In vain the Lesbian maids claim each a part,
> Where thou alone hast ta'en up all the heart . . .

As we have come to expect in vernacular compilations made up for ladies' perusal, the implications of '*quas hic sine crimine amavi*' are suppressed. But though the concern might be to protect the ladies from perversion, it is not to protect them from corruption, for Carr Scrope's intention is fundamentally pornographic. This is Scrope's version of lines 43–50, which is actually slightly longer than the original.

> Delighted with the music of my tongue,
> Upon my words with silent joy he hung,
> And, snatching kisses, stopped me as I sung,
> Kisses, whose melting touch, his soul did move,
> The earnest of the coming joys of love.
> Then tender words, short sighs, and thousand charms
> Of wanton arts endeared me to his arms;
> Till, both expiring with tumultuous joys,
> A gentle faintness did our limbs surprise.

Revulsion followed swiftly. A university poetaster called Matthew Stevenson – who had published a volume of poems in 1664 in which he had referred to a Sapho who 'summ'd up all her joy/In the embrace of a Sicilian boy' – rushed into verse with a burlesque of Dryden's anthology entitled *The Wits Paraphras'd*, which was published post-haste by William Cademan. The dedication, 'To Mr Julian Principal Secretary to the Muses', reveals it as emanating from the Whig satire factory, bankrolled by the Earl of Dorset. Stevenson's attack is levelled at the Tory poetasters led by Dryden, but it is Sappho who takes the brunt.

> While Phaon to the hot-house hies,
> With no less fire poor Sapho fries.
> 'I burn, I burn, with nodes and poxes,
> Like fields of corn with brand-tail'd foxes.
> My bag-pipes can no longer please,
> Nor can I get one minute's ease.
> Grunting all day I sit alone . . .'
>
> Naught behind was left by thee
> But shankers, shame and infamy.

To Tonson's horror the burlesque proved a faster seller than the original anthology, so he turned to a young Tory gentleman of Gray's Inn, Alexander Radcliffe, to reply to Stevenson with a burlesque on the burlesque, *Ovid Travestie*, printed the following year. After a withering preface in which he mocks Stevenson on the same grounds that Stevenson mocked Scrope, namely for his cavalier treatment of his Latin original, Radcliffe takes off in a burlesque that is not only a much closer parody of the Latin, but is also a satire on London lowlife. Once again, in a quarrel between Grub Street hacks, Sappho gets the worst of it. Radcliffe's synopsis goes like this:

Sapho was a lady very eminent for singing of ballads, and upon an extraordinary pinch, could make one well enough for her purpose. She held a league with one Phaon, who was her companion and partner in the chorus; but Phaon deserted his consort for the preferment of a rubber in the bagnio. Sapho took this so to heart, that she threatens to break her neck out of a garret window which, if effected, might prove her utter destruction. Authors have not agreed concerning the execution of her design but, however, she writes him this loving and terrifying epistle.

The first lines follow the *Epistula Sapphus* closely:

> When these my doggerel Rhimes you chance to see,
> You hardly will believe they came from me,
> Till you discover Sapho's name at bottom,
> You'll not imagine who it is that wrote 'em: . . .

For another essay of Radcliffe's Latin and his talent in burlesque, I offer his version of lines 41–50, in which Sappho struggles to remind Phaon how much pleasure they used to have together.

> I am not very beautiful – God knows;
> Yet you should value one that can compose;
> Despise me not, though I'm a little dowdy,
> I can do that – same – like a bigger body:
> Perhaps you'll say, I've but a tawny skin;
> What then? You know my metal's good within.
> What if my shoulder's higher than my head?
> I've heard you say, I'm shape enough a-bed.

Behn's preferred sobriquet was Astraea; when her enemies called her Sappho they reviled her as harlot and erotomane. The name was also applied to 'Ephelia' for the same reasons. Delarivier Manley availed herself of the same two-handed libel; by the time Sara Fyge

was called Sappho in 1700, the name had become a label too
dangerous to use. Meanwhile, Grub Street was touting the arous-
ing properties of Sappho's and Aphra Behn's verse: in 1691 in
The Athenian Mercury, a biweekly constructed out of answers to
phoney questions purporting to come from members of the public,
John Dunton replied to the question 'whether Sappho or Mrs Behn
were the better poetess':

> Sappho writ too little and Mrs Behn too much for us to give 'em
> any just or equal character . . . but yet one fragment consisting
> of but a few lines which we have of Sappho's carries something
> in it so soft, luscious and charming . . . that we wish Mrs Behn
> herself had translated 'em before she went to Elysium to meet
> her . . .

The force of this lies in the word 'luscious', which in context means
'gratifying to lascivious taste'. Though the upper servants to whom
Dunton was addressing himself might not have realized the fact, his
fellow Athenians would have relished the insinuation that both Sappho
and Aphra Behn were able pornographers. Dunton underlines it by
going on to say that Behn's 'soft strain' proved 'her a great proficient
both in the theory and practice of that passion' that passion being of
course love. To a lovesick correspondent in 1694 he replied:

> Thus Aphra, thus desparing Sappho mourned;
> Sure both their souls are to your breast returned.
> By the same tyrant-passion all enslaved,
> Like you they wrote, like you they loved and raved.
> But ah! the virtue vanished, what remained?
> Their verse as spotted as their glory stained.
> They lost that gem with which Orinda shined,
> And left a sullied name and works behind.

After her death Aphra Behn's literary property passed somehow or
other into the hands of Charles Gildon, who repaid her by exacerbat-
ing her notoriety to the best of his parasitic ability. In 1694 he
published an anthology called *Chorus Poetarum*, in which a version of
φαίνεταί μοι appeared with the title 'Sappho addrest to his Grace the
Duke of Buckingham'.

The Gods are not more blest than he,
Who fixing his glad eye on thee,
With thy bright Rays his senses chears,
And drinks with ever thirsty ears,
The charming musick of thy tongue
Does ever hear and ever long,
That sees with more than humane grace
Sweet smiles adorn thy angel face.

So when with kinder beams you shine,
And so appear much more divine,
My feebled sense and dazzled sight
No more support the glorious light,
And the fierce torrent of delight.
O then I feel my life decay,
My ravish'd Soul then flies away;
Then faintness does my limbs surprise,
And darkness swims before my eyes.

Then my tongue fails, and from my brow
The liquid drops in silence flow;
Then wandring fires run thro my blood,
Then cold binds up the languid flood;
All pale and breathless then I lie,
I sigh, I tremble, and I die.

This poem had already been published eleven years before, as the work of William Bowles, who almost certainly translated it from the Greek, but the piquancy of foisting it on to Behn was irresistible. Bowles stands at the head of a long tradition which required schoolboys to translate φαίνεταί μοι as part of their Greek exercises. It is interesting to reflect that Sappho's description of amorous susceptibility probably influenced the sexual development of generations of upper-class Englishmen – indeed, it might explain why they were so often convinced that women needed no wooing and were ever-ready to seduce themselves.

The end of the Whig versus Tory contest in which Sappho's name was the ball that they batted back and forth was Pope's translation of the *Epistula Sapphus*, first published in 1712. Pope followed the trend illustrated by Carr Scrope; his version of the *Epistula* is elegant titillation with a spice of perversity. Elsewhere Pope used the name Sappho as an insult, particularly but not solely for Lady Mary Wortley Montagu, who was herself a good poet and would have written more and more openly, if Pope's unremitting malice had not warned her that Grub Street is no place for a woman, let alone a lady.

Felicia Hemans, the best-selling poet of the nineteenth century, never mentioned Sappho, though she made a speciality of writing in the personae of learned and creative females of the past. Elizabeth Barrett Browning read Greek but she chose to imitate Homer rather than Sappho. In 1846, when she was sixteen, Christina Rossetti wrote a poem called 'Sappho' that proves that for all her religiosity she is a poet of the decadence. The revival of interest in the perverse Sappho is usually dated back to *Les Fleurs du Mal*, which was not published until 1857, but at sixteen Rossetti knew herself for an *âme damnée*, consumed by a passion that no earthly relationship could satisfy. In 1848 she wrote a poem called 'What Sappho would have said had her leap cured instead of killing her'. It ends in the algolagnia beloved of Swinburne:

> Oh come again, thou pain divine,
> Fill me and make me wholly thine.

Rossetti's first Sappho poem was printed in *Verses: dedicated to her Mother* on her grandfather's private press. The second was never printed in her lifetime.

The Sappho who became the heroine of the decadence is the poet as monster, born out of the invention of sexual psychopathy. Same-sex love between women was nothing new or alarming to the people who visited the Ladies of Llangollen. They lived an orderly, busy and intensely social life; their deep love for each other had in no way doomed or maddened them. No one blanched or fainted when they heard them call their little dog 'Sappho'. Where Byron could experiment with deviant sexuality without undue anxiety, some of his immediate successors presented it to themselves as an abyss into which they were obliged to leap and from which they could never return. The post-Romantic poet needed to accumulate memories of unbearable poignancy, and an addiction to pleasures of potentially fatal intensity whether of the genital or of the psychedelic variety. The search for the exotic dictated an intensification and proliferation of all kinds of fantasy.

Balzac's *Fille aux Yeux d'Or* and Gautier's *Mademoiselle du Maupin* fed the developing vogue of sexual deviance. The Sappho Baudelaire invented was descended from Byron's burning Sappho less directly than she was from Childe Harold himself. The myth of her self-destruction was absolutely essential to the cult. Strangely these elements are already present in Rossetti's poem; the love stronger than hate, the pleasure that is keenest pain, the suggestion of cherished but potentially fatal addiction are all there. The influence of Dante Gabriel Rossetti on Simeon Solomon produced the gouache called 'Sappho and Erinna at Mytilene' in 1864, in which Sappho bears an uncanny resemblance to Christina. When Solomon was arrested for homosexual offences in 1873, Rossetti, Swinburne and all the other aesthetes recoiled from him in horror. He gave way to drink and dissipation and ended his days as an alcoholic in the St Giles Workhouse. What the Fleshly School of Poetry taught was not acting out of deviant fantasy but the elaboration of deviant fantasy. Both Christina Rossetti and Algernon Swinburne recoiled from relationships. She retreated into reclusiveness and the self-torture of self-denial; Swinburne paid women to beat him. Beneath the imagery of the androgyne there was a retreat from physicality. The defining experience of the aesthetic movement was not with bodies but with drugs, as the poet of *Goblin Market* well knew. Unfortunately for Sappho her name took on the whole colouring of the movement towards androgyny, including the sterility, the mania and the morbidity. If she had been like Baudelaire, or either of the Rossettis, or Simeon Solomon, for that matter, Sappho would, like them, have borne no child. She was valued more for her perversity by the Symbolists, who took over her imagery from the Pre-Raphaelites, than she was for her poetry. The new papyrus fragments were scoured for every indication of same-sex love; poetry itself became a wasted, hollow-eyed *fricatrice*. The Greek satirists who wrote comedies about Sappho as a middle-aged, bibulous female wit with a healthy appetite for slim-flanked youths of either sex would never have recognized her.

After Swinburne's death, in 1914 *The Living Age* printed this statement by him:

Judging even from the mutilated fragments fallen within our reach from the broken altar of her sacrifice of song, I for one have always agreed with all Grecian tradition in thinking Sappho to be beyond all question and comparison the very greatest poet that ever lived. Aeschylus is the greatest poet who was also a prophet; Shakespeare is the best dramatist who was also a poet, but Sappho is simply nothing less — as she certainly is nothing more — than the greatest poet who ever was at all.

THE REWRITING
OF KATHERINE PHILIPS

Of all the women poets of the seventeenth century, Katherine Philips, the 'Matchless Orinda' would seem to present the fewest problems. Despite her protestations that she detested the very notion of publication, we know a good deal about her, much more than we know of Aphra Behn or 'Ephelia'. Autograph manuscripts of both poems and letters survive; her work was known and responsibly discussed not only by members of her coterie but in a wider literary milieu. As Peter Beal puts it in his *Index to English Literary Manuscripts*, 'hers is . . . one of the best documented centres of manuscript publication in the 17th century'. Beal finds her unusual among her contemporaries in that she left 'a substantial body of works in her own hand'.

Chief among these is what Beal calls the Tutin manuscript, an autograph collection of 'over fifty-five of her poems made in the late 1650s'. Before her death in 1664 Philips wrote more than 130 poems, seventy-four of them after she made this autograph collection of her own work. The question of the authenticity of texts of poems not to be found in the Tutin manuscripts presents one kind of problem, while the relationship of these early versions to later versions of the same poems must also be questioned. Though we have little evidence of Orinda herself correcting and refining her work, we do know that she solicited corrections and emendations from others. If the Tutin autograph is to be considered unassailable as a source, it is only because there is no later autograph which might be thought to represent the author's final intention. As no such autograph has been found, the Tutin manuscript must remain the copy-text for all the complete poems to be found in it. Two of the missing leaves from this little book have turned up at the University of Kentucky. Other poems in Philips's autograph are juvenilia found among the Orielton manuscript at the National Library of Wales, a copy in her own hand of 'Rosania to Lucasia on her Letters' in the British Library and an autograph copy of 'To the ... Countess of Carbery' among the Ellesmere papers in the Huntington.

The juvenilia consists of two poems, one on each side of a single sheet: one, beginning 'No blooming youth shall ever make me err', dedicated to Mrs Anne Barlow and signed with her maiden name, C. Fowler, may with reasonable certainty be attributed to Orinda; the other, which begins 'A married state affords but little ease', presents a problem. These sixteen lines appear as part of a longer poem beginning 'Madam, I cannot but congratulate' in four manuscript versions, all of which date from the 1680s; the extract, if such it is, in Philips's hand dates from 1646–7. We shall probably never know whether a later poem simply incorporated a pre-existing sixteen lines, as would not have been in the least unusual, or whether Philips copied out sixteen lines from a poem that had caught her eye of which we have not found a surviving copy of the earlier date.

The first poem by Philips to appear in print is 'To the Memory of the most Ingenious and Virtuous Gentleman Mr. William Cartwright, my much valued Friend', which appeared as the first of the commendatory poems in *Comedies, Tragicomedies, with other Poems by Mr. William Cartwright*, published by Humphrey Moseley in 1651. The political purpose of this royalist printing on the eve of Charles II's invasion is made obvious by the inclusion of fifty-four commendatory poems, with Philips's, signed K. P., chivalrously placed before those of the men, who are presented in descending order of rank, beginning with the Earl of Monmouth. The version published in 1651 differs in important respects from the version recorded by Philips in the Tutin autograph, most significantly in the line:

Rescue us from our dull imprisonment,

which as printed read:

Shall rescue us from this imprisonment.

The printed version is less flabby than the version in the autograph. It seems likely that it was tightened by the same hand that dubbed Cartwright Philips's friend, though she was little more than twelve years old and at school in London when he died of camp fever during the siege of Oxford. It is rather less likely that Philips later weakened her own original by including a bathetic word. In the copy made by Philips's friend Sir Edward Dering, variants to be found in none of the printed texts or the surviving autograph make their appearance, when he changes 'fancys' to 'fancy' and 'glorys' to 'glorie'. Patrick Thomas, who uses Dering's transcriptions as copy-texts for twenty-three of the poems in the Stump Cross Books edition, considers that Dering would have copied them when he and Katherine Philips were both in Dublin, between July 1662 and July 1663, and that Dering is a reliable copyist. In fact, the manuscript, which is at the Humanities Research Centre in Austin, Texas, appears to have been written at the same time, using sheets from the same batch of paper, as the Dering letter-book in the library of the University of Cincinnati, in which Dering, who died in 1684, twenty years after Orinda, is clearly ordering and transcribing scattered papers many years after they were originally written. Dering also has some tricks of substitution which alter Philips's style: for example, he habitually writes 'doth' for 'does' and 'hath' for 'has', fogging the characteristic directness of Orinda's tone. If Dering is to be considered the best source for twenty-three poems, it can only be because there is no better source.

In 1655, four years after the Cartwright poem, two more of Philips's poems appeared in Henry Lawes's *Second Book of Airs and Dialogues*. The first book had been dedicated to the Countess of Carbery and was commended in poems by Orinda's friend John Jeffreys, or 'Philaster', as well as Waller and others. Though others of the contributors to the second book appeared merely as initials, Katherine Philips's poem 'To the much honoured Mr Henry Lawes on his Excellent Compositions in Music' was signed with her full name, which also appeared on the setting of a poem of hers entitled 'Mutual Affection between *Orinda* and *Lucasia*', more usually known as 'Friendship's Mysteries'. The text of the former as printed departs from Orinda's autograph in nine instances, one of which ('Scarrs' for 'stars') is an obvious corruption, while five of the other variant readings can be found in no other source. The text of the second disagrees with the autograph in three cases, one of which, 'Graces' for 'Grows', is an obvious corruption. In this collection Orinda was surrounded by her coterie; not only did Philaster contribute to this volume as well as the first, three poems by 'Silvander', otherwise known as Sir Edward Dering, appeared in settings by his wife, Orinda's friend Mary

Harvey, together with a poem addressed by Cratander, Sir John Birkenhead, to Lucasia, Philips's closest friend, Anne Owen. In the case of Cartwright's *Comedies, Tragicomedies* and Lawes's *Airs and Dialogues* it would seem that in 1655 neither Orinda nor her circle had serious objections to appearing in print, even in rather garbled versions.

The next of Philips's works to appear in print was her translation of Corneille's *La Mort de Pompée*, printed in Dublin in 1663. Presumably Philips, who was in Dublin in connection with legal business regarding confiscated estates in Ireland, was herself involved in the preparation of this work for the press, which seems at some stage to have involved a good deal of rewriting, which, whether by Philips herself or not, must be assumed to have had her sanction. The text of the translation as it appears in the manuscript copy of Philips's *Pompey* held by the National Library of Wales is very different from what was eventually published. There can be no question of the copy representing work in progress or a first draft; it is written throughout in a neat, non-professional hand with few corrections or elisions, as if for presentation. The possibility exists that it is an early draft that was later rewritten by the author for it lacks the songs, which were written last, in order to provide an excuse for music and dancing between the acts. This possibility is rendered less likely because the songs are added at the end of the manuscript in another hand. At the end of the song that closes Act III, Katherine Philips herself has added the stage direction:

> Then follows a military dance, as part of Cornelia's dream, after which she starts up in amazement and says
>> What have I seen and whither is it gone?
>> How great the vision and how quickly done!
>> Yet if in dreams we future things can see,
>> There's still some joy laid up in fate for me.

The only conclusion from this evidence is that Katherine Philips had this copy in her hands after the details of the staging had been settled, which cannot have been much before the first performance. We must ask ourselves, then, whether the text as printed was actually the text that was played and, if so, who did the rewrite. The collation of the manuscript with the printed versions shows more than 120 lines substantially altered; what is more, the manuscript version is based on an early edition of Corneille; the printed version takes account of Corneille's revisions for the collected edition of 1660. If Philips herself is responsible, we must ask why the revisions were not incorporated in the surviving manuscript. Perhaps the editors of Philips's plays for the Stump Cross Books edition should have used the manuscript rather than the Dublin printing as their copy-text. However, they proceeded upon the assumption, which is usually justifiable, that Philips personally sanctioned the changes that appear in the printed text.

There is little likelihood that Philips herself is responsible for the revisions. Act IV, scene iv, ll. 21–2 originally read:

> No Pompeys blood forever must deny
> All Correspondence between thee and I.

In print, in order to avoid the blunder of using the incorrect nominative pronoun in place of the dative, this was changed to:

> No, *Pompey's* blood must all commerce deny
> Betwixt his Widow and his Enemy.

Unfortunately for Orinda's peace of mind, other grammatical errors survived the revision and appeared in print. In June, 1663, she wrote to Poliarchus:

> Sir Edward Dering has desired me to ask your opinion concerning these two lines in the last scene of the Play
>> I know I gain another diadem
>> For which none can be blamed but heav'n and him
> His objection is, that *him* is scarce grammar; he says it should be *he*: I am not critic enough to resolve this doubt, and therefore leave it wholly to your determination.

These words would appear to show that whoever did correct ungrammatical usages in Philips's original, it cannot have been Philips herself. Another class of problem was presented by pronunciation. Several times in the manuscript the copyist elides the 'e' in power to make a monosyllable, with the result that the line does not scan. Twice the 'e' is restored in a fashion that resembles the interpolations recognizable as Philips's autograph. After he saw the translation in December 1663, Sir Charles Cottrell, whom she dubbed Poliarchus, appears to have written to Orinda regarding the use of certain words as bisyllables, for she replied on 10 January 1663:

> As for the words 'heaven' and 'power', I am of your opinion too, especially as to the latter; for the other may, I think be sometimes so placed, as not to offend the ear, when it is used in two syllables.

However, by April 1663, Orinda was embarrassed about her occasional bisyllabic pronunciation of both words; she wrote to Poliarchus:

> By my Lady Tyrrell, who took shipping last Friday for Chester, I have sent you a packet of printed Pompey's to dispose of as you think fit. Be pleased to get one bound and present it to the Duchess; and if you think the King would allow such a trifle a place in his closet, let him have another; but before you part with any, pray mend these two Lines, Act 5. Scene 2.
> > If Heaven, which does persecute me still,
> > Had made my Power equal to my Will.
> My objection to them is, that the words 'heaven' and 'power' are used as two syllables each; but to find fault with them is much easier to me, than to correct them.

As the copies were already printed Sir Charles would have had to have made his correction by hand, if at all. No surviving copy of the Irish or the English printing of *Pompey* has been so emended. As Orinda points out, correcting such faults is no easy matter, for it involves the rewriting of the whole couplet, as was done in many instances before the play was printed.

Where the manuscript has:

> And he who then would equity obey
> Must not his reason but his power weigh.

in which 'power' is pronounced as two syllables, the printed version has:

> And he who then affairs would rightly weigh
> Must not his reasons, but his power obey.

In the original version of Act II, scene i, one line reads:

> Sure love in you does little power show

In the printed version the unfortunate bisyllable was simply changed to 'empire'. Another line,

> Since too much power will their strength o'erwhelm

was altered to:

> Those too much power would quickly overwhelm.

The person who prepared *Pompey* for the press also corrected examples of 'heaven' scanned as a bisyllable:

> When she her Pompey's murder did perceive,
> Her woeful hands to heaven she did heave.

became:

> By dreadful shrieks, she tried his life to shield,
> Then hopeless up to heav'n her hands she held.

If we assume that Philips saw and authorized the changes made in the text of *Pompey* between the making of the fair copy and the printing, editors could feel quite safe in accepting the printed text as authentic. However, the survival of the unamended text in a fair copy together with its completion with the matter prepared for the actual performance suggest that perhaps Philips paid little attention to the text as it was altered for its appearance in print. As we have seen, she did not insist on the right to authorize the final version of the text if it were to be amended by Cottrell. Philips's contemporary the Duchess of Newcastle was offended when her printers did *not* reorganize her work. In soliciting corrections from better-educated gentlemen, Philips was both exercising common sense and following the custom.

It would have been a rasher gentlewoman than she who would expose herself in print without taking such a precaution. As we have seen, both Cottrell and Dering offered emendations, but when Lord Orrery deigned to utter an opinion, it had power to override them both. After begging Cottrell in December for a correction to an unfortunate couplet in the first scene of *Pompey* and evidently getting an altered version from him in January, Orinda wrote in April:

> I would fain have made use of your Correction, and thrown away the word 'effort', but my Lord Orrery would absolutely have it continued, and so it is, to please his humour, though against my will, and judgment too . . .

only to write again within days, begging him once again to alter the couplet before *Pompey* went to press. The couplet remained unaltered.

The belief that Katherine Philips was concerned about the authenticity of her published work is founded upon what is usually taken to be her extreme reaction to the projected publication of *Poems by the Incomparable Mrs K. P.* in 1664. A close reading of the documentary evidence suggests that the initiative to suppress the book may not have come originally or spontaneously from the poet. She did not shrink from appearing a few months before as the star of *Poems by Several Persons*, which was printed by the same printer for the same bookseller as the Dublin edition of *Pompey*.

She wrote to Poliarchus on 15 May 1663:

> I intend to send you by the first opportunity a miscellaneous collection of poems, printed here, among which, to fill up the number of his sheets, and as a foil to the others, the printer has thought fit, though without my consent or privity, to publish two or three poems of mine, that had been stolen from me, but the others are worth your reading.

Though Philips is careful to dissociate herself from the appearance of her work in print, there is no hint here of outrage. We may suspect that, despite her disclaimers, she should have been delighted to find her work not only included in a volume with Orrery's and Cowley's but celebrated by both of them. Orrery's complimentary poem to Philips, bearing the title 'To *Orinda*', is the second item in the miscellany which also contains Cowley's ode 'On *Orinda's* Poems'.

The poems by Philips are 'Ode, On Retirement', 'To the Right Honourable, the Lady Mary Butler, at her Marriage to the Lord Cavendish' and 'The Irish Greyhound', all described in the list of contents as 'By a Lady'. For the Stump Cross Books edition Patrick Thomas used the version of the text to be found in the collection made by Sir Edward Dering, which Thomas takes to be the earliest and best source. Thomas did not know of the survival of a single exemplum of *Poems by Several Persons* but, even if he had, it is no easy matter to decide whether he should have used it. In the retirement ode, the third line, in Dering's version:

And me too long thy football made

has become:

And me too long thy restless ball hast made.

This version appears in no other source, and must be considered the Dublin editor's emendation, as must other substitutions, 'wilt' for 'dost', 'mortals' for 'worldlings', 'And where bright angels gladly would resort' for 'Where angels would officiously resort' and 'subjects' for 'subdues'. The wedding poem for the Lady Mary Butler exhibits one variant to be found in no other version, 'always' for 'still do' (a change prompted by political tact). The text of 'The Irish Greyhound' has also been tinkered with. 'By which' becomes 'From whence', 'And', 'But', 'does make', 'hath made' and 'Man's Guard would now be, not his sport' becomes 'He would Man's Guard be, not his sport'. Katherine Philips appears neither to have complained about these substitutions nor to have incorporated them in her own copies of her poems. Cowley was either less easily pleased or more outspoken. When Herringman published Cowley's *Verses written upon Several Occasions* later, in 1663, a note signed by him was included on the second leaf:

Most of the verses, which the author had no intention to publish, having been lately printed at Dublin without his consent or knowledge, and with many, and some gross mistakes in the impression, he hath thought fit for his justification in some part to allow me to reprint them here.

Cowley forms the link between this apparently unproblematic episode in Philips's publishing history and the next. His ode, with the elaborated title, 'To the most excellently accomplished Mrs. K. P. upon her Poems', appears at the head of the compilation of seventy-four of her poems that Marriott published in 1664. This text exhibits corruptions that Cowley could not have countenanced, many of which it shares with the Dublin printing, which is the most probable source. If we ask who provided the Dublin printer with his copies, we are obliged to conclude that it was the same source that provided Marriott with the text he printed in 1664.

Marriott's proposed publication was entered in the Stationers' Register on 5 November 1663. The volume was advertised for sale in *The News* of Thursday, 14 January 1664, but an apologetic note by Marriott in *The Intelligencer* of 18 January announced that it had been withdrawn. Two weeks later, on 29 January, Orinda wrote to Poliarchus:

> I am so obliged to you for the generous and friendly concern you take in the unfortunate accident of the unworthy publishing of my foolish rhymes, that I know not which way to express, much less to deserve, the least part of so noble an obligation. Philaster gave me a hint of this misfortune last post, and I immediately took an opportunity of expressing to him the great but just affliction it was to me, and begged him to join with you in doing what I see your friendship had urged you both to do without that request, for which I now thank you, it being all that could be done to give me ease, but the smart of that wound still remains, and hurts my mind. You may be assured I had obeyed you by writing after my old ill rate on the occasion you mention, had you not in your next letter seemed to have changed your opinion, advising me rather to hasten to London and vindicate my self by publishing a true copy. Besides, I considered it would have been too airy a way of resenting such an injury, and I could not be so soon reconciled to verse, which has been so instrumental to afflict me, as to fall to it again already. However, if you still think it proper, I will resign my judgment and humour to yours, and try what I can do that way. Meanwhile I have sent you inclos'd my true thoughts on that occasion in prose, and have mixed nothing else with it, to

the end that you may, if you please, show it to anybody that suspects my ignorance and innocence of that false edition of my verses, and I believe it will make a greater Impression on them, than if it were written in rhyme. Besides, I am in too great a passion to solicit the Muses, and think I have at this time more reason to rail at them than court them, only that they are very innocent of all I write, and I can blame nothing but my own folly and idleness for having exposed me to this unhappiness.

This letter is a *reply* to one from Sir Charles telling Philips that he has taken action to stop Marriott publishing; Philips tells him that John Jeffreys had let her know of the 'unfortunate accident' by the last post, i.e. only days before – and she had begged him in a letter by return of post to join Sir Charles in intervening to stop the appearance of the book, only to find that they had already done so *without instructions from her*. This is the true sequence of events behind the general perception that the 1664 edition of her poems was withdrawn in answer to Philips's earnest entreaties. Philips now had to dissociate herself from the whole ill-advised enterprise, which she did at length in the enclosure sent with the same letter on 29 January.

Your last generous concern for me, in vindicating me from the unworthy usage I have received at London from the press, doth as much transcend all your former favours, as the injury done me by that publisher and printer exceeds all the troubles that I remember I ever had. All I can say to you for it, is, that though you assert an unhappy, it is yet a very innocent person, and that it is impossible for malice itself to have printed those rhymes (you tell me are gotten abroad so impudently) with so much abuse to the things, as the very publication of them at all, though they had been never so correct, had been to me, to me (Sir) who never writ any line in my life with an intention to have it printed, and who am of Lord Falkland's mind, that said,

> He danger feared than censure less,
> Nor could he dread a breach like to a Press.

And who (I think you know) am sufficiently distrustful of all, that my own want of company and better employment, or others' commands have seduced me to write, to endeavor rather that they should never be seen at all, than that they should be exposed to the world with such effrontery as now they most unhappily are. But is there no retreat from the malice of this world? I thought a rock and a mountain might have hidden me, and that it had been free for all to spend their solitude in what reveries they please, and that our rivers (though they are babbling) would not have betrayed the follies of impertinent thoughts upon their banks; but 'tis only I who am that unfortunate person that cannot so much as think in private, that must have my imaginations rifled and exposed to play the mountebanks, and dance upon the ropes to entertain all the rabble, to undergo all the raillery of the wits, and all the severity of the wise, and to be the sport of some that can, and some that cannot read a verse. This is a most cruel accident, and hath made so proportionate an impression upon me, that really it hath cost me a sharp fit of sickness since I heard it, and I believe would be more fatal but that I know what a champion I have in you, and that I am sure your credit in the world will gain me a belief from all that are knowing and civil, that I am so innocent of that wretched artifice of a secret consent (of which I am, I fear, suspected) that whoever would have brought me those copies corrected and amended, and a thousand pounds to have bought my permission for their being printed, should not have obtained it. But though there are many things, I believe in this wicked impression of those fancies, which the ignorance of what occasion'd them, and the falseness of the copies may represent very ridiculous and extravagant, yet I could give some account of them to the severest Cato, and I am sure they must be more abused than I think is possible (for I have not seen the book, nor can imagine what's in't) before they can be rendered otherwise than Sir Edward Dering says in his Epilogue to Pompey.

> ——No bolder thought can tax
> Those rhymes of blemish to the blushing sex,
> As chaste the lines, as harmless is the sense,
> As the first smiles of infant innocence.

So that I hope there will be no need of justifying them to virtue and honour; and I am so little concerned for the reputation of writing sense, that provided the world would believe me innocent of any manner of knowledge, much less connivance at this publication, I shall willingly compound never to trouble them with the true copies, as you advise me to do: which if you still should Judge absolutely necessary to the reparation of this misfortune, and to general satisfaction; and that, as you tell me, all the rest of my friends will press me to it, I should yield to it with the same reluctancy as I would cut off a limb to save my Life. However I hope you will satisfy all our acquaintance of my aversion to it, and did they know me as well as you do, that apology were very needless, for I am so far from expecting applause for any thing I scribble, that I can hardly expect pardon; and sometimes I think that employment so far above my reach, and unfit for my sex, that I am going to resolve against it for ever; and could I have recovered those fugitive papers that have escaped my hands, I had long since made a sacrifice of them. The truth is, I have an incorrigible inclination to that folly of rhyming, and intending the effects of that humour, only for my own amusement in a retir'd life; I did not so much resist it as a wiser woman would have done; but some of my dearest friends having found my ballads, (for they deserve no better name) they made me so much believe they did not dislike them, that I was betray'd to permit some copies for their divertisement; but this, with so little concern for them, that I have lost most of the originals, and that I suppose to be the cause of my present misfortune; for some infernal spirits or other have catch'd those rags of paper, and what the careless blotted writing kept them from understanding, they have supplied by conjecture, till they put them into the shape wherein you saw them, or else I know not which way it is possible for them to be collected, or so abominably transcribed as I hear they are. I believe also there are some among them that are not mine, but every way I have so much injury, and the worthy persons that had the ill luck of my converse, and so their names exposed in this impression without their leave, that few things in the power of fortune could have given me so great a torment as this most afflictive accident. I know you, Sir, so much my friend, that I need not ask your pardon for making this tedious complaint; but methinks it is a great injustice to revenge myself upon you by this harangue for the wrongs I have received from others . . .

Strangely, every one of the poems in Marriott's edition is an authentic work by Orinda. This is not what one expects from a seventeenth-century edition, in which poems associated with the author and circulated in manuscript with the author's work are usually transcribed pell-mell. Though Orinda may have been told that the poems were abominably transcribed, and may have believed it, in fact they were not. As seventeenth-century editions go, *Poems* 1664 is unusually reliable. The proportion of corruptions and emendations is actually smaller than we have seen Philips tolerate in other printings. Obvious corruptions include lines dropped in three poems, 'his' for 'her', 'Bellows' for 'billows', 'Prodigy' for 'Progeny' and 'Oracle' for 'O race', 'watch' for 'reach' and 'Beauty' for 'bounty', 'count' for 'court', 'generally' for 'generously' and 'Leons hill' for 'Zion-hill' 'Light' for 'Right', 'his' for 'my', 'his' for 'thy' and 'Virge' for 'Verse', 'made' for 'read', 'it' for 'in', 'change' for 'chain', 'change' for 'chance', 'Truth' for 'trash', 'poore and just' for 'poor unjust'. Some of these corruptions, most notably 'Leons hill' for 'Zion-hill', are shared with all the printed texts and with some manuscripts, most notably the Worcester College manuscript, which follows dozens of 1664 readings, though the order in which the poems are copied is completely different. If we compare *Poems* 1664 with the Tutin autograph we will find that 1664 often agrees with the autograph against the 1667 edition, most notably in the cases where lines have been suppressed by the 1667 editor.

It is the more curious, then, that Cottrell should have advised Orinda to hasten to London in order to arrange for a more correct edition. In her protestation Philips says that she has not seen the edition; if she was convinced that the texts were corrupt, it must have been Jeffreys and Cottrell who convinced her. Correctness, as we have seen, was not an area in which Orinda felt herself secure. The last thing she would have felt able to do is to oversee the publication of a correct text. The truth is that once it had been made clear to her that her mentors considered publication an injury to herself and her reputation, Philips had no option but to clamour for the book's withdrawal.

In a letter to Dorothy Temple dated 22 January, a week before the two letters were sent to Poliarchus, Philips referred to her instructions to Philaster:

some most dishonest person hath got some collection of my rhymes as I hear, and hath delivered them to a printer who, I understand, is just upon putting them out, and this hath so extremely disturbed me, both to have my private follies so unhandsomely exposed, and the belief that I believe the most part of the world are apt enough to have, that I connived at this ugly accident, that I have been on a rack ever since I heard it and though I have written to Colonel Jefferies, (who first sent me word of it) to get the printer punished, the book called in, and me some way publicly vindicated, yet I shall need all my friends to be my champions to the critical and malicious, that I am so innocent of this pitiful design of a knave to get a groat, that I was never more vexed at anything, and that I utterly disclaim whatever he hath so unhandsomely exposed. I know you have goodness and generosity enough to do me this right in your company, and to give me your opinion too, how I may best get this impression suppressed and myself vindicated, and therefore I will not beg your pardon for troubling you with this impertinent story, nor for so long a harangue as this . . .

By the 'knave' so anxious 'to get a groat' Orinda might be thought to be referring to the publisher, Richard Marriott. As the son of the distinguished literary publisher, John Marriott, Marriott had inherited an impressive list of literary copyrights to which, since the beginning of the 1640s, he had added more of his own, including works by Donne, Quarles, Wotton and Richard Brome. He published the first and twelve of the succeeding editions of Izaak Walton and the first authorized edition of *Hudibras*. Some of his activities in the 1660s, by which time he was one of the distinguished senior members of his profession, suggest a direct link with Orinda: in 1660 and 1661 he published editions of compilations by John Ogilby, who directed the production of Philips's *Pompey* in Dublin; at the beginning of 1663 he published *The Assembly-Man* by Sir John Birkenhead, Orinda's Cratander. If his edition of Orinda's *Poems* was in fact unauthorized, it is the only instance of Marriott's being connected with a pirated work. Only days before the Orinda débâcle, he had taken space in *Mercurius Publicus* to warn the public against 'a most false imperfect copy' of *Hudibras* to which he had exclusive copyright. The withdrawal of the whole printing of Orinda's poems must have cost him much more than a groat, and much more than mere money. The exact wording of the withdrawal notice is worth attention:

> Publication being made upon last Thursday of the Poems of Madam Catherine Philips newly printed for Richard Marriott, it is now the wish and desire of the said Richard Marriott to notify that whereas he was fully persuaded both of the correctness of the copy, and of that ingenious lady's allowance to have them printed, that now he finds neither the one nor the other, according to his expectation: which is a double injury, and that he intends to forbear the sale of them, being not without hope, that this false copy may produce the true one.

All Marriott offers to do here is to delay the sale of his books. His hope that the true copy might appear could be taken as a challenge, for no truer copy was likely to be forthcoming even from the author herself as Marriott probably knew. The printer was never punished and history records no attempt to punish him; neither was an order given for the copies to be destroyed.

If the edition was not corrupt and all the works were by the reputed author, there must have been another reason behind the prompt and decisive intervention of Cottrell and Jeffreys. Orinda's is mostly occasional verse; occasional verse is written to each other by members of cultivated society for their private amusement. The more celebrated examples of versified table-talk might have been copied and circulated extensively in manuscript, and a venal copyist might eventually have made a copy of such poems for sale to a publisher but, though Philips says that fugitive copies had been distributed randomly, the extent of Philips's manuscript publication was not great. Besides, Marriott's compilation is not based upon rags of paper but on a careful transcription from a collection of seventy-four poems, all of them probably in the same hand, given the uniformity of orthography and elisions. Despite the difference in the ordering of the poems, the Worcester College manuscript seems very close to *Poems 1664*; it lacks the same two poems, while containing all but the last two of the rest; like *Poems 1664* it reads 'bounty' as 'Beauty' in one poem, and accidentally drops the same line in two others.

No individual with pretensions to gentility, let alone a female, could be seen to tolerate her verse letters being exposed to the vulgar gaze, but in 1664 the Philipses were in severe financial difficulty, occasioned by James Philips's investments in sequestered property and crown lands which were forfeit at the Restoration. Aubrey records that years later Katherine Philips's uncle Oxenbridge was imprisoned for a debt incurred on behalf of his niece and her husband. Katherine Philips had tried to gain royal favour and the odd royal guinea by writing celebratory verses; the money to be made from the clandestine sale of her verse to a publisher might well have seemed irresistible, if not to her then to her husband or someone near to him who was aware of the intense distress caused him by the collapse of his fortunes both fiscal and political.

There were examples of successful publication of occasional verse fairly close to home, notably James Howells's *Poems on several choice and varied Subjects*, first published in 1663, with another edition in 1664, Cowley's *Verses lately Written on Several Occasions*, twice published in 1663, and Herringman's 1664 edition of Waller's *Poems*, first published in 1645. Richard Marriott had published the first edition of Henry King's *Poems, Elegies, Paradoxes and Sonnets* in 1657. Martin Llewellyn, one of the contributors of commendatory verses for the 1651 Cartwright, published a collection called *The Marrow of the Muses* in 1661. When such publication is contemplated, however, it is important to protect the privacy of the individuals whom the poet addresses. One of the functions of the coterie name, after all, is that it identifies the individual only to members of the coterie and not to outsiders. The only outlandish aspect of *Poems* 1664 is its indiscretion in fully identifying the private individuals to whom Orinda's poetic attentions were addressed, 'the worthy persons that had the ill luck' of knowing Orinda, 'and so their names exposed in this impression without their leave'.

In *Poems* 1664, Anne Owen is named in full and identified as Lucasia; Rosania is identified as 'Mrs M. Aubrey', her 'private marriage' is referred to and she is identified in the title of another poem as 'now Mrs Montagu'; Regina and John Collier, Mary Carne and John Jeffreys are named in full; Malet Stedman is named as Mrs M. Stedman; Palaemon is identified as Francis Finch; Silvander as Sir Edward Dering. That these identifications are accurate is itself cause for astonishment; if we begin to ask how the unauthorized editors could have come by them, we are faced with a very limited number of possibilities. Presumably, Orinda herself can hardly have needed to remind herself who Lucasia and Rosania were; if she made these identifications in her own papers, it must have been because she expected outsiders to see them, whether in print or in manuscript. Any one of the individuals whose privacy was breached by the publication of these poems, whether John Jeffreys, then married to another woman, here revealed as the disappointed suitor of Mary Carne, or Mary Montagu, revealed as a disloyal friend and an unacknowledged wife, or Anne Owen, now Viscountess Dungannon and far removed from Orinda's coterie, could have objected in forceful terms. Sir Charles Cottrell, himself a disappointed suitor for Anne Owen's hand, is unlikely to have waited until this indiscretion came to her attention before taking action to protect her.

Within weeks of the withdrawal of the book, Orinda was in London, where in June she died of smallpox. The next important Philips source must be what Beal calls the Rosania manuscript, which contains ninety-six poems and all Philips's translations, namely *Pompey* and 'Horace', two madrigals, Saint-Amant's *La Solitude*, the eclogue from *Almahide*, and a fragment of Corneille's versification of *L'Imitation de Jésus-Christ*. This collection, copied in 'a single, neat, but somewhat varying, non-professional hand throughout', was made for presentation to Philips's friend, Mary Aubrey, shortly after the poet's death. A dedicatory letter, 'To the Excellent Rosania', signed 'Polex'', explains to some extent the circumstances of its compilation:

Madame
Orinda, though withdrawn, is not from you. In lines so full of spirit sure she lives, and to be with you, is that only spell can share her with the bright abodes, your eyes, her heaven on earth, your noble heart her centre. Admit that Lethe washes cares away, yet there's no passage to Elisium debarred her joys, and the sweet intercourse your souls maintained was of a nature so refined, of the fruits of Paradise, a taste of those above! And so entirely seized of Orinda's soul, no more to be devested with mortality. Cease then, adorable Rosania, to afflict your beauteous mind for that privation which being hers is your advantage, and freely sympathise in her beatitude. So her enlarged knowledge views your graces and, with undazzled optics, in you behold that fullness, whose but imperfect discovery was so much her wonder; and now displayed, both justifies and enter-

tains her admiration. Nor can she feel your absence, whose pure thoughts she sees already, so familiar in those glorious mansions, and your candid breast, so fit and loved, a receptacle for her own. Here is a beatific converse! Angels, thus, are still ascending and descending. It was this Orinda's matchless pen aspired and, having bequeathed you these clear streams, you see how soon she thither took her flight, whence the rich vein derived. To appear in print, how un-inclined she was! (I confess an edition, now, would gratify her admirers, and 'twere but a just remeriting that value which (in hers, and in their own right) was the universal consent.) You, whose passionate concern so frankly exposed your admirable beauty to that spiteful disease (whence all our grief) led by the generous dictates of as inimitable friendship, you, whose solicitous devoirs, whose bleeding anguish, showed how readily you would have been her Ransom! You, in whose pious memory she shines, next to her lustre amongst the stars! You alone were her ambition, as her love. Enjoy these dear remains, no more as a sad monument nor to remind her past but present state. Thus, will her raptures be to your harmonious soul a Jacob's staff, to level at her glories. Nor can these charming poems, so absolute over our affections, be themselves utterly insensible, how sovereign a bliss it is to be yours, . . .

There is no reference in any of Orinda's poems or letters to a 'Polexander'; the pseudonym is derived from the hero of a romance by Gomberville, translated as *The History of Polexander* and published in 1647 with another edition in the following year. 'Polexander' cannot be identified as the editor of the 1667 edition of *Poems by the most deservedly Admired M^{rs}. Katherine Philips, The matchless Orinda*, because the manuscript includes a poem which does not appear in that edition, as well as exhibiting significant variants in the versions of the poems that do appear. Both Sir William Temple and Sir Charles Cottrell have been suggested as candidates for Polexander, but the breathy incoherence of the letter and the fulsomeness of its flattery are not characteristics to be found in any of the writing of either.

As the letter makes clear, 'Rosania', Philips's old schoolfriend Mary Aubrey, now the wife of William Montagu, had nursed Philips in her last illness. It seems likely, therefore, that the presentation copy was made fairly soon after the event. Thomas is loath to use it as a copy-text for the poems because a significant number of lines have been dropped but, as the lines dropped usually comprise a self-contained syntactic unit, they must be supposed to have been deliberately excised. The first excision occurs in the second poem in the collection, 'A sea voyage from Tenby to Bristol', in the following passage:

> One of the rest, pretending to more wit,
> Some small Italian spoke, but murdered it,
> For I (thanks to Saburra's letters) knew
> How to distinguish 'twixt the false and true,
> But to oppose them there as mad would be
> As contradicting a presbytery.
> 'Let it be Dutch', quoth I, 'e'en what you please'.
> For him that spoke it might be bread and cheese.
> So softly moves our bark which none controls,
> As are the meetings of agreeing souls . . .

In the Rosania manuscript the two couplets beginning 'But to oppose them . . .' have been suppressed. In such a case there is no question of four lines being accidentally dropped; we must suppose that someone decided that the four lines did not fit and constituted a blemish on the body of the poem. Similarly two couplets are deleted from the third poem in the manuscript, a quatrain from the fourth, from the sixth eleven couplets, two couplets from the eighth and from the eleventh, from the twelfth seven quatrains, three couplets from the fourteenth, one couplet from the fifteenth, five couplets from the sixteenth reducing it by a third, four quatrains from the eighteenth, four couplets from the nineteenth and so on. Of a total of ninety-one poems, twenty appear to have been pruned in this fashion. The question is, by whom? By the copyist, by the poet or by someone who was asked by the poet to edit her work?

One of the more curious aspects of this collection is that it contains all but two of the poems originally addressed to Rosania. As 'Lucasia, Rosania & Orinda, parting at a Fountain. July 1663' and 'A Farewell to Rosania' appear in no other manuscript sources and were not printed in *Poems* 1664, two possibilities suggest themselves: that the source is either Orinda herself, or Rosania, who at one stage must have had copies of all the poems addressed to her. Thomas assumes that one of the Rosania poems, 'On Rosania's Apostacy and Lucasia's Friendship', was omitted from the collection made for Rosania on grounds of tact, but the omission of another, 'To Mrs M. A, upon Absence. 12 Decemb. 1650', which was printed, as were all but the two mentioned, in 1664, cannot be explained upon the same grounds. As Thomas notes, 'Rosania's private Marriage' is copied into the manuscript in a different hand, and appears to be a transcription from a printed source. The pruning of the other Rosania poems seems to stem from tact of another kind, for it is clearly intended to abate the exaggeration of Orinda's flattery for the sake of decorum and taste.

The Rosania manuscript is the most comprehensive collection of Philips's work to appear before the 1667 edition, for it contains, besides a transcription of *Pompey* as printed in 1663, the exactness of which is further evidence that the excisions from the twenty poems represent deliberate editing by someone other than the copyist, Philips's translations of shorter poems and extracts, and of Corneille's *Horace*. The fact that no attempt has been made to smooth the roughness of the 'Horace', which is unfinished and a first draft, strengthens the case for the copyist's having made an exact transcription of texts of the poems as he or she found them. There may be little or nothing to choose between Dering's transcriptions and Polexander's after all. If it could be proved that the editing of the poems was done by Orinda or with her consent Polexander's would have to be accepted as definitive.

Polexander's letter makes clear that an edition of Philips's work was not yet in preparation. At the beginning of 1667 Marriott turned all rights to Orinda's poems over to his friend and colleague Henry Herringman. In mid-1664 Marriott and Herringman had collaborated on the second edition of Henry King's *Poems, Elegies, Paradoxes and Sonnets*, Marriott having published the first in 1657. Though only Herringman's name appeared on the title-page, he and Marriott both signed the letter from 'The Publisher to the Author', in which they begged pardon for publishing without his permission.

The best we can say for ourselves is, that if we have injured you it is merely in your own defence, preventing the present attempts of others, who by their theft would (by their false copies of these poems) have added violence, and some way have wounded your reputation.

Because the collection contained one poem, 'The Pink', that was not by Henry King, an erratum notice was printed on the verso of the last page of text before the Elegies, which were bound in separately. In this Marriott and Herringman display a far higher level of editorial scruple than was usual with their contemporaries.

In view of this collaboration between the two leading publishers of the decade, it is not surprising that the 1667 edition of Orinda's poems is based upon the edition of 1664. Like 1664, 1667 begins with the poems addressed to the king and members of the royal family, and follow the same order until poem 24, when it skips two poems, which it reincorporates in a slightly different order, so that the same order is resumed ten poems later and maintained until after poem 67, at which point 1667 includes two poems not before printed, before resuming the same sequence as 1664 until poem 77, which was the last to be printed in 1664, after which forty-one additional poems are printed in no obvious sequence. Not only do the 1667 texts of the seventy-five poems agree with 1664 against the manuscripts in far more instances than they diverge, some of the corrections of obvious corruptions in the 1664 version indicate that the 1667 had no more authoritative version to hand. For example, in 1664 the line

> The intermitted storms returned as fast

was dropped from 'On the fair weather at the Coronation'. It was substituted in 1667 by:

> The storm returned with an impetuous haste.

In 'La Grandeur d'Esprit', where the 1664 compositor had read 'company' for 'constancy', the word was corrected to 'honesty'. The new editor did not limit himself to correction of faults that had escaped in the printing of 1664; whole couplets accurately transcribed from the original in 1664 are excised or rewritten. In 'On the numerous access of the English to waite upon the King in Holland' (poem 2), line 4,

> As Pompey's residence made Afrique Rome.

was rewritten as:

> As Pompey's camp, where'er it moved, was Rome.

It is of course possible that both Dering and Polexander, whose versions agree with 1664 against 1667, were copying from that edition, but on balance it seems more likely that the 1667 editor is supplying his own improvements. An awkward couplet in 'To the Queen on her Arrival at Portsmouth':

> We did enjoy but half our King before;
> You us our prince, and him his peace restore.

was dropped, while another,

> (For Fortune would her wrongs to him repair,
> By courtships greater than her mischiefs were:

was rewritten as:

> (For Fortune in amends now courts him more
> Than ever she affronted him before:

From 'In Memory of . . . Mrs Mary Lloyd of Bodidrist' one couplet (lines 41–2) was dropped and another,

> She lost all sense of wrong, glad to believe
> That it was in her power to forgive.

appears as:

> She grew to love those wrongs she did receive
> For giving her the power to forgive.

Five couplets were dropped from 'Rosania shadowed' and another,

> She scorns the sullen trifles of the time
> But things transcendent do her thoughts sublime;

appears as:

> Transcendent things her noble thoughts sublime
> Above the faults and trifles of the time.

As the autograph, Polexander and Dering agree with 1664, it is all but certain that what we have here is another of the 1667 editor's smoothings out of Philips's choppier and more interesting sense and sound. In 'A Friend' the difficult parenthesis:

> (As liquors, which asunder are the same)

becomes:

> (As a far stretched out River's still the same)

The most astonishing of these revisions, to be found in no pre-1667 version of the poem, occurs at the end of 'Friendship', when the concluding couplet:

> Free as first agents are true friends, and kind,
> As but themselves I can no likeness find.

becomes:

> What shall I say? when we true friends are grown,
> W'are like – Alas, w'are like ourselves alone.

Such cases as these increase the probability that the problem with 1664 was not that it was an incorrect transcription but that it was a transcription from an unvetted original. By contrast, the text of *Pompey*, which had been corrected before its original publication, is allowed by the 1667 editors to stand, whereas 'Horace' is extensively rewritten. As transcribed for the Rosania manuscript 'Horace' is stylistically very close to the manuscript of *Pompey*. Though pieces have been chopped out of the poems, all but a couplet or two of the French has its equivalent in the Rosania manuscript transcription of 'Horace'. As printed in 1667, however, Act III, scene vi was completely recast, more than 150 lines of the rest were rewritten and a character's name was changed from Curiace to Curtius throughout. The recasting of Act III, scene vi is so far completely inexplicable.

inexplicable. The recast version bears little resemblance to Corneille, but the reordering of lines and exchanges does not suggest censorship of the original. The rewriting might have been required as a condition for the performance of the play at court. If so, the grounds of the stipulation remain mysterious. When Tonson decided to publish Philips's text in parallel with the French original in his 1710 edition of Orinda's works, he realized that the text of this scene did not run parallel to the French. As Sir John Denham's completion of the translation renders 346 lines for 458 in the original, Tonson had to resort to Charles Cotton's translation of 1665 for both Act III, scene vi and the continuation from where Orinda left off. Denham may have been required to produce a shorter play-text in order not to overtax the memories of the noble amateurs who were to play the completed translation at court, but even this consideration goes no way to explaining the reshuffling of the elements of Act III, scene vi.

In this case, the decision of editors of the Stump Cross Books edition was relatively easy; they decided to use the Rosania manuscript as their copy-text both for 'Horace' and the translated poems, which in the 1667 edition had been tidied up by the same smoothing hand. At least one of them must confess to an animosity against the editor who could change the lovely line in the elegy on the death of Orinda's infant son:

I did but touch the rosebud and it fell

to

I did but pluck the rosebud and it fell.

The case of Katherine Philips's letters is even more opaque; four letters appeared in a collection of *Familiar Letters* in 1697. The collection is sometimes called 'Rochester's letters' because twelve hitherto unpublished letters by Rochester are included in it. It also contains the first printing of the spurious letter 'Against Bribery and Arbitrary Government' attributed to Algernon Sidney. The publisher was Samuel Briscoe, the editor, Tom Brown, a celebrated composer of letters in the style, the idiom and the personae of his betters. The four letters from Orinda to Berenice, who was probably Elizabeth Ker, daughter of the Earl of Ancram, were almost certainly spruced up and modernized by Brown. When forty-eight letters from *Orinda to Poliarchus* were published in 1705, they too had been modernized, as can be seen by a comparison of the 1667 text of letter 45, which appeared in the bookseller's preface to *Poems* 1667 and the version published in 1705. A conflation of the two versions showing how thorough and skilful is the revision can be seen in Vol. 2 of the Stump Cross edition.

What has passed down to us as the authentic work of Katherine Philips adds up to a heavily revised publication of *Pompey* with revisions she may not have authorized, an autograph manuscript which is probably less authoritative than supposed, as well as a transcription of unknown date by a friend with a trick of substitution and another of 1664–5 which is remarkably faithful to the printed *Pompey*, and just as faithful to the first draft of 'Horace', but takes what seem to be extraordinary liberties with the poems, an unrevised but good edition which has always been known as a bad edition (*Poems* 1664), and a supposedly good but heavily revised edition which is less authoritative than the bad one (1667), and two post-humously printed collections of letters that have been so heavily revised as to be virtually rewritten.

Katherine Philips is a major poet of the Restoration period, yet only now are academics beginning to invest energy and resources in establishing her text. The problems that continue to present themselves at every turn are by no means unusual; when it comes to Aphra Behn we have even less reason to suppose that the versions we have before us now are in any sense authentic. Feminist scholars who clamour for women's work to be included in the canon assume that there are texts attributed to women that actually represent what women wrote and the way they wrote it. The further back we go from our own time, the more unlikely that is. A single new discovery could discredit a great deal of the close textual criticism upon which feminist academics have staked their reputations and their careers.

DID APHRA BEHN EARN
A LIVING BY HER PEN?

Aphra Behn is rightly considered to be a heroine of women's liberation. Journalist and author Yvonne Roberts described her in these
terms:

> Seventeenth-century adventurer, all-round bad girl, poet, satirist,
> a spy for Charles II, a debtor, the author of 17 plays and 13
> novels, Aphra Behn was an abolitionist, a believer in free love
> 'between equals', an enthusiast for the education of women.
> Lowly born, she valued herself highly, did as she pleased, upheld
> her own principles, stirred up trouble, altered (some) male
> perceptions and had a bloody good time in the process.

Ever since Virginia Woolf dubbed Behn the first Englishwoman to
make a living by her pen, though she had no evidence that Behn was
born in England or that her writing actually earned her a living, the
struggle to unravel the facts about Aphra Behn's life and literary
career has been complicated by the necessity of respecting a role
model. Biographers of Aphra Behn tend to project her as a kindred
spirit. Seduced by her occasional representation of herself as a free and
self-regulating character, they fail to test the enforced insouciance of a
professional wit against the real grimness of the situation of an
unattached woman in Restoration society. Restoration actresses did
not embark upon a theatrical career to avoid prostitution, but to
attract a better class of protector. On stage, even in a minor role, a
woman could most easily project her attractions of body, face, voice
and style before an audience that included gentlemen of all ranks,
often even the king himself. In order to 'be fine', that is to be
sumptuously dressed in the latest fashions, actresses had to make a
considerable investment in clothes which cost as much comparatively

as a car might do today. As they were paid no more than 20 to 30 shillings a week, plus the proceeds of an annual benefit, there was no chance that they could go gay on their earnings when a pair of gloves could cost as much as fifteen shillings. Indeed, one of the most frequent offences with which actresses were charged was borrowing fine clothes from the wardrobe for their own use. Angeline Goreau quotes as an example of actresses' insecurity the case of Elizabeth Farley, pretty and 'fine' enough to catch the eye of the king, then kept by a Gray's Inn man who deserted her, whereupon her creditors descended. Pregnant, she continued on stage with the King's Company as long as she could, because to leave would have removed the protection of the king, which was all that stood between her and debtors' prison. Though Aphra Behn moved in theatrical circles, she apparently never took any kind of role herself, though other women playwrights did. This circumstance seems odder if one considers that, according to her contemporary, the actor Bowman, Behn was beautiful and spirited and coached Elizabeth Barry, who became the greatest tragic actress of her time, in her part for *The Rover*. Though the apparent contradictions could all be explained if we knew more, they complicate the indistinctness of Aphra Behn's identity.

The suffragettes needed to produce a role model for the female writer that would not immediately alienate the opponents of women's education. Though women striving for the right to become independent career women needed a considerable figure who avoided dishonour by making a living by her own efforts, at the end of the twentieth century it should be unnecessary to refute or deny the imputation of loose living to Aphra Behn in order to esteem her as a literary figure. She will be no less important for today's women when we have understood the grim reality of her struggle against destitution, even if we must come to the conclusion that she turned to writing as a way of making a living when she could no longer rely upon the generosity of a protector. In a poem published in broadside twice in 1679 Rochester has given a chilling yet oddly sympathetic insight into the life career of the unattached witty beauty:

> That wretched thing Corinna, who had run
> Through all the several ways of being undone,
> Cozened at first by love, and living then
> By turning the too-dear-bought trick on men:

Gay were the hours, and winged with joys they flew,
When first the town her early beauties knew,
Courted, admired, and loved, with presents fed,
Youth in her looks, and pleasure in her bed,
Till Fate, or her ill angel thought it fit,
To make her dote upon a man of Wit,
Who found, 'twas dull, to love above a day,
Made his ill-natured jest, and went away.
Now scorned by all, forsaken, and oppressed,
She's a Memento Mori to the rest.
Diseased, decayed, to take up half-a-crown
Must mortgage her long scarf, and Mantua gown.
Poor creature! Who unheard of, as a fly,
In some dark hole must all the winter lie,
And want and dirt endure a whole half year,
That for one month she tawdry may appear.

Aphra Behn doted on the Gray's Inn lawyer John Hoyle, called by her 'a wit uncommon and facetious,/A great admirer of Lucretius'. According to gossip of 1687, it was 'publickly knowne that Mr Hoyle 10. or 12. yeares since kept Mrs Beane' – that is to say, from about 1675 to 1677, when she was already writing plays. According to Alexander Radcliffe, it was known that

> The plays she vends she never made.
> But that a Grey's Inn lawyer does 'em,
> Who unto her was friend in bosom.

Radcliffe's poem was published in 1682; in a poem of January 1684 Aphra Behn regretted missing an assignation with Thomas Creech, because she wished to introduce him to Hoyle:

> To honest H[oy]le I should have shown ye,
> A wit that would be proud t'have known ye.

This evidence would seem to indicate that Behn's association with Hoyle continued for many years after she was known as his mistress. In *Humours and Conversations of the Town* (1693) James Wright described the fate of women left destitute by men of wit 'at best in an old tattered manto, carrying news about, from one acquaintance to another, for a meals-meat and a glass of wine'. Later commentators have assumed that, because Mrs Behn was having plays performed and published, she would neither have needed nor enjoyed the protection of a gentleman. In fact, income from the playhouse was both irregular and uncertain and not all gentlemen wished or could afford to be generous to the women under their protection. Delarivier Manley is known to have lived with Alderman Barber at the same time that she was penning sensational exposés of her betters. It is always assumed that such a relationship is sexual, though it is by no means unimaginable that a needy woman would have been happy to be housed as an upper servant at the same time that she sought a little fame and an independent fortune by the exercise of her pen. At this stage we do not know whether Aphra Behn was ever concubine or housekeeper to John Hoyle.

Some might find in the fact that Hoyle was arraigned before a Grand Jury on a charge of sodomy in 1687 evidence that his relationship with Aphra Behn was platonic. The verdict in the case was one of Ignoramus, which means that the act was never proved to have taken place, but even if it had been, the fact would in no way disqualify Hoyle as the lover and protector of Aphra Behn. It was a lucky woman who kept the same protector all her life; to be kept by one man involved being kept by others afterwards usually, but not always, in descending order of rank and social status. What every 'miss' dreaded was the downward slide that ended in the miserable existence of a common prostitute. Aphra Behn may have turned to writing as a way of avoiding a career that was certain to lead to brutalization, disease, destitution and early death. How successful she was is further matter for concern. There is no need to assume that Rochester's Corinna is actually Aphra Behn – the sad spectacle presented by the toast of the town once she had begun to show signs of wear and tear was common enough – but the vividness of his evocation of what poverty meant adds a new dimension to Aphra Behn's complaints. Behn too may have had to mortgage her fine clothes to eat and have been unable to redeem them until she had got an advance from a playhouse or a publisher. In the Prologue to *The Feign'd Curtezans*, performed in the same year that Rochester's broadside was published, an actress in ragged finery complains:

Yet I am handsome still, still young and mad,
Can wheedle, lie, dissemble, jilt – egad,
As well and artfully as e'er I did;
Yet not one conquest can I gain or hope,
No prentice, nor the foreman of a shop,
So that I want extremely new supplies;
Of my last coxcomb, faith these were the prize;
And by the tattered ensigns you may know,
These spoils were of a victory long ago:
Who would have thought such hellish times to have seen,
When I should be neglected at eighteen?

The Feign'd Curtezans is dedicated to Nell Gwyn, the comedienne who had risen from obscurity to become the mistress of a king by the power of her wit and her beauty, according to Mrs Behn, a woman so charming that it seemed that she had been 'made on purpose to put the whole world into good humour'. Seen from this viewpoint courtesanship is the pinnacle of virtuoso female performance. As Killigrew observed in 'Thomaso', a successful courtesan has to be 'an humour, a dancer, a wit, a shape, a voice . . . so that it is comedy to see or hear her'.

Like Rochester's Corinna and Nell Gwyn, Behn seems to have been a woman totally without connections; scholars have found no property owned by her, no taxes paid by her, no will. A woman of no substance could only inhabit the fashionable world if she found someone to pay her day-to-day expenses for food, clothes and lodging, in which case she would leave no trace in the records. A woman who succeeded in supporting herself would appear somewhere in the record, as a tenant, a tax-payer, a debtor or a creditor. If we look for evidence that the younger Behn had the kind of income that would have obviated the necessity to find a protector, we can find nothing, unless it be the reference to the Widow Behn as one of the parties involved in case of the ship *Abraham's Sacrifice*, seized during the second Dutch War. The Widow Behn is understood to be an agent for the insurers of the cargo; whether she was Aphra Behn cannot be ascertained from the scanty fragments of the documentation of the case that have survived.

Rochester may actually have known Mrs Behn. In a poem written after his death in 1680 in answer to one from the poet's half-niece,

Anne Wharton, congratulating her on the elegy she wrote on the occasion, Behn describes her vision of Anne Wharton as the reincarnation of Rochester:

> It did advance, and with a Generous Look,
> To me Addrest, to worthless me it spoke:
> With the same wonted Grace my Muse it Praised,
> With the same Goodness did my Faults Correct;
> And careful of the Fame himself first raised,
> Obligingly it Schooled my loose Neglect.

In these lines Behn claims to have enjoyed Rochester's praise, to have been schooled as a poet, promoted and encouraged by him as well. These are large claims and possibly no more than self-serving, but there is some evidence to support them. Mrs Wharton, who did not tolerate presumption, did not appear to doubt them, for she remained proud of the poetic correspondence with Mrs Behn despite the disapproval expressed by her mentors.

If we look for hard evidence that Behn and Rochester were confederates there is none, unless we count the fact that, when Rochester impersonated a quacksalver in order to write a description of the diseased state of the body politic, he took the name, 'Alexander Bendo'. At the time the initials 'A. B.' were often assumed to indicate a person or persons unknown, as in 'Any Body', but Rochester may have been gesturing towards a companion mountebank. Otherwise, the only contemporary to couple Behn with Bendo was Behn herself. Later, in her commendatory poem for Thomas Creech's *Lucretius*, she praises Rochester, Creech's predecessor at Wadham, in purely generalized terms as '*Strephon*, the Soft, the Lovely and the Great'. Her attempt to claim an association at the time of his death may simply have been a desperate attempt to climb on to a very successful publishing bandwagon, but an association persists between three of Behn's best poems, 'On a Giniper Tree cut down to make Busks', 'The Disappointment' and 'On the death of Mr Grinhil, the Famous Painter', and poems by Rochester. The MS miscellany entitled 'Songs & Verses Upon severall occasions', which was used as the copy-text for the first edition of *Poems on Several Occasions, By the Right Honourable the E of R.* in 1680 contains all three poems, which she did not publish as her own work until 1684, long after they had appeared in print as the work of Rochester. By including these well-known poems in her own *Poems on Several Occasions*, Behn was laying claim to an association with the most admired wit of her generation. In the miscellany she collected in 1685 she included a hitherto unpublished poem as by Rochester. On such evidence Rochester's editor, Keith Walker, dubs her Rochester's friend. Another piece of evidence is that Mrs Behn was invited to write the Prologue for the first day's performance of the revival of *Valentinian* in 1685. As the other people associated with that project, Elizabeth Barry, John Grubham Howe and Robert Wolseley, were known associates of Rochester, we may assume that Mrs Behn was too.

Daniel Defoe, writing in 1706, thought Mrs Behn had been Rochester's mistress. By that time, partly because of the activities of her posthumous editors and publishers and partly because of the successes of the Whig propaganda machine, Aphra Behn's name had become synonymous with immorality. Rochester's mistress in the 1670s was the actress Elizabeth Barry. Behn certainly knew Barry, who became identified with key roles in Behn's plays. She was first cast disastrously in Otway's *Alcibiades*, but in 1676 she was successful in playing Leonora in Behn's play *Abdelazer* and Hellena in *The Rover*. She outgrew *ingénue* roles like Hellena and began to specialize in heavy roles. She became Angelica Bianca, whom she played in the frequent revivals of *The Rover* for more than twenty-five years, Cornelia in *The Feign'd Curtezans* (1679), La Nuche in *Rover* II (1681), Lady Galliard in *The City Heiress* (1682) and Lady Fulman in *The Lucky Chance* (1687). Both women exploited the connection between them in the struggle for self-promotion, and both encouraged the confusion between the stage roles and their real-life careers. But there is an important difference: in December 1677, Barry bore Rochester a child and called her Hester. Rochester's estate was encumbered with debt; his marriage to an heiress, though it provided for his children, did not result in sufficient personal income to cover his liabilities. For years after his death his executor stayed away from London in order to avoid the importunities of his creditors. This being the case, Rochester was unable to provide handsomely for his paramours. When Elizabeth Barry was brought to bed Henry Savile wrote to congratulate Rochester and to utter a reproach: 'I doubt she does not lie in much state.' If Behn was ever Rochester's mistress, she would still have had to turn the association to her advantage in the market-place; certainly she was happy to be part of the circle that included gentlemen with their mistresses rather than their wives. If she herself did not scruple to be numbered with women of ill-repute, modern scholars have no right to distinguish and separate her from them. The belief that Behn was the sole virginal *habituée* of the un-chaste world of the theatre has no basis in the facts as we know them.

The poet was called variously A. Behn, Mrs Behn, Mrs A. Behn, Mrs Ann Behn, Astraea, Sappho and only very rarely Aphra. The first mention of her, if it is a mention of her, is as Astraea, in a letter of 14 March 1664 from Willam Byam, lieutenant governor of Surinam, to Sir Robert Harley. Astraea is a name with very specific connota-tions, either by way of classic mythology or by way of Honoré D'Urfé. It ought never to be applied to an ever-married woman. Throughout her spying career Mrs Behn was called Astraea, signed herself Astraea in her letter to Arlington (22? September 1666) and the last documentation of her life, the record of her burial in the cloister of Westminster Abbey, calls her 'Astrea Behn'. She generally signed herself Mrs Behn, or Mrs A. Behn. Both Edward Verney, who began compiling the huge collection of broadsheets and pamphlets known as the Verney Papers, and his brother John, who took over, thought the A. Behn who wrote the Pindarics on the death of Charles II, and the mourning of his wife and the coronation of his brother in 1685, was called 'Anne' and filled in the initial 'A' four times in this fashion and repeated it four times in full in the handwritten list of items on the fly-leaf of the collection. Yet the Verneys haunted Covent Garden; if Mrs Behn's given name was 'Aphra' they must surely have known. One possibility that has never been examined is that there was more than one Mrs Behn. As both married and unmarried women were called Mistress, abbreviated to Mrs, the name Mrs Behn could be applied to both a mother and a daughter, or two sisters, or all three. Conversely, Astraea, Aphra and Anne may all be names for the same person. It must not be thought that if Aphra Behn lived with her mother she would have been chaperoned by her; on the Continent courtesans were typically inducted into their profession by their mothers, who acted as their managers and agents.

What kind of a name is 'Aphra' after all? It is known from the epigrams of Martial; more people would have known the name from the *Golden Legend*, where Afra is the umpteenth example of prostitute-turned-saint, with the difference that she was not a beautiful courtesan but a common prostitute of the lowest rank who achieved sanctity without leaving the brothel. Aphra may have been a common name in Kent in the 1640s; it was not so common by the 1660s that anyone could make sense of it. In the state papers it is rendered in various ways, the most peculiar being 'ffyhare'.

The letter that first mentions Astraea is couched in terms that would hardly be appropriate to a respectable unmarried girl or young widow:

> I need not enlarge but to advise you of the sympathetical passion of the Grand Shepherd Celadon who is fled after Astrea, being resolved to espouse all distress or felicities of fortune with her. But the more certain cause of his flight (waving the arrow and the services he had for the lodger) was a regiment of protests to the number 1000 of pounds sterling drawn up against him.

Another undated letter from Byam tells us that he found

> a ship full freighted bound for London, on whom I sent off the fair shepherdess and Devouring Gorge but with what reluctancy and regret you may well conjecture.

We must, I suppose, translate 'Devouring Gorge' as Duffy does, to mean the fair shepherdess's mother, but rather than take 'Gorge' as a version of the family name Gorges, I would suggest that she was either a glutton or a gorgon or both. No one has conjectured about Byam's reluctancy to see the last of the 'fair shepherdess' — is the reference ironic or is it not? The implication of both letters is surely that 'Astraea' had been a well-known personage in the buccaneering off-shore cavalier society of Surinam. William Byam was one of the first post-colonial despots, who began in classic fashion as the elected lieutenant-governor and quickly transformed himself into a gangster who both patronized and pillaged the resident Sephardic community. Two things are clear: Mrs Behn hated Byam — see *Oroonoko passim* — but she loved his boon companion, George Marten. In *Oroonoko* she describes Marten as:

> a man of great gallantry, wit and goodness, and whom I have celebrated in a character of my new comedy by his own name

in memory of so brave a man. He was wise and eloquent, and, from the fineness of his part, bore a great sway over the hearts of the whole colony.

George Marten was the brother of Sir Harry Marten, called by Behn 'the great Oliverian'. Behn's precise memory of the location of his plantation is one of the grounds for believing that she really knew her Surinam. The play Behn wrote about him, *The Younger Brother*, probably had some relationship, however coded and tangential, with her life but, as it was not acted until 1696 in a *rifacimento* by Charles Gildon, who not only removed all Behn's Tory propaganda but also removed all specificity from the characters and all suggestion of a real context, it is useless as a biographical source. Who can the Astraea have been whose departure was of such concern to Byam? In *Oronooko* Behn herself says that she, her sister, her brother and her mother had gone to Surinam with her father, who was to be governor but died on the voyage. As no such individual can now be identified, it seems this claim is fiction – unless it relates to someone coming not from England but elsewhere and not to Surinam originally but to somewhere else in Central America or the Caribbean.

Information concerning Surinam in the 1660s is sparse and contradictory. The Puritan settlers who were desperately petitioning the parliaments at home for some protection from Byam's illegal rule did not share the poet's esteem for Marten, but denounced him as an atheist in league with the Jews. A pamphlet published in 1662 described 'Byam and Marten [as] being wrought on by the tears of a Jew, who had great prevalencies with them . . .' According to this account, Marten 'offered himself the hangman of any at the Governours single command'. The author was scandalized by Marten's 'Witty prophanations of . . . religion, atheistically with scoffs, seldom sparing his God in jest'. This is not the only instance of Mrs Behn's displaying sympathy with a confessed atheist. The commendatory poem that she wrote in 1683 for Thomas Creech's translation of Lucretius was so outspoken in its mockery of 'dull Religion' and 'Faith, the last Shift of routed Argument' that it was understandably bowdlerized when Creech's book was published. Unabashed, and frankly annoyed by this presumption, Mrs Behn printed the authentic text in her *Poems on Several Occasions* (1684). Though there has been a good deal of discussion of Mrs Behn's possible Catholicism, there has been very little discussion of her manifest scepticism. The truth seems to be that she was a convinced sceptic with a background of entrenched Catholic enculturation. Any examination of the imagery of her celebrations of the divine right of kings in the Pindarics reveals a trick of exaggeration that approaches blasphemous hyperbole, almost as if she were using the imagery of Mariolatry and the Passion and Crucifixion against itself. The atheist/papist/Jew was not only a chimaera of the Puritan imagination. Mozart's librettist Lorenzo da Ponte and his great rival the Abbate Casti are both historical examples of the same cultural hybrid. That Behn was an atheist/papist/Jew is no more unlikely a hypothesis than that she was an innocent Protestant lass from Kent who went off like Puss-in-Boots to make her fortune in London by the sole exercise of her enchanted pen.

Behn's biographer, Maureen Duffy, not only invents a flight from Kent to London but interprets it:

> For a woman of fairly obscure birth who wished to make some impression on the world Kent was an impossible place to stay. The dominance of the local gentry, while it gave a patriarchal sense of security, would have made no accommodation for the phenomenon of a dowerless poet who in any case had little inclination to support herself by what she regarded as the legalized prostitution of arranged marriage.

The greatest mystery clouding our image of Mrs Behn will always be how, when and where she turned into 'a dowerless poet', acquiring a level of literary culture more polished and various than any of her contemporaries, even the most gifted. Nobody understood French salon culture better than she; nobody could write in so many forms with the same lightness and elegance. This proficiency was not acquired at a dame school in Kent, or in any of the girls' boarding schools in suburban London, or sitting on the knee of some Huguenot émigré in Canterbury. In *Oroonoko* the poet asks us to believe that she went to Surinam with her father, her mother, her sister, her brother and her maid; more reliable documentary evidence shows that both her brother and her mother were with her in London in 1666. The notion of Aphra Whittington becomes more difficult to swallow, if we imagine her trudging along the roads of Kent with her whole family trailing behind her, not to mention the maid. The likelihood that Aphra Behn came to England from somewhere else via Surinam should at least be considered before we can conclude that she was an Englishwoman.

The next documented episode in Mrs Behn's life is her spying mission to Antwerp, which, according to Duffy, she undertook to prove that she could survive without becoming a 'miss', being by that time a widow – or so it is assumed. Her mission was to lure William Scot, the 'Celadon' she had known in Surinam, to Antwerp and milk him for information about the English republicans and the degree of their Dutch support, promising him both a pardon and a reward. She arrived in Antwerp with her brother at the beginning of August 1666 with a bill of exchange for a mere £50, which was changed at four-fifths of the rate she expected. She met with Scot on 15 August, finding him so uneasy that she was obliged to hire a coach and take him on a day-trip into the country and then to give him money to pay for his trip back to Holland. After their second meeting she was obliged to pawn a ring. Within weeks she was a hundred pounds in debt; before Christmas Scot was imprisoned for debt and Mrs Behn likely to be so. When she was ordered to return to England, she had to borrow £150, to pay her debts and finance her passage from Colonel Edward Butler, the Duke of Ormonde's Latin secretary. For a year she waited for money from the crown to repay Butler, who eventually gave her a week to pay or go to prison. In her third petition she revealed that the order for her arrest had been made. Maureen Duffy assumes that Behn was in fact imprisoned, though no record of an imprisonment has been found.

In December 1670 Behn's first performed play, *The Forc'd Marriage*, had a six-day run at the Duke's Theatre in Lincoln's Inn Fields. The takings for each third day were the playwright's due; Mrs Behn would have made more money when the text was sold to the publisher, James Magnus, who brought it out in quarto the next year as by 'A. Behn'. According to Downes, the prompter, Mrs Behn gave the part of the old king to Thomas Otway.

> He not being used to the stage, the full house put him to such a sweat and tremendous agony, being dashed, spoilt him for an actor.

The Prologue of *The Forc'd Marriage* argues that it is the product of

a woman who has turned her wit to advantage because her beauty has
faded:

> this art
> Retrieves (when beauty fades) the wandering heart;
> And though the airy spirits move no more,
> Wit still invites, as beauty did before . . .
> The poetess too, they say, has spies abroad,
> Which have dispersed themselves in every road,
> I'th' upper box, pit, galleries, every face
> You find disguised in a black velvet case.

If Behn could choose her cast, we may assume that she could also
choose her prologue. If she did not wish to be known as an ageing lady
of pleasure, she certainly capitulates to such a notion in this prologue,
in which an actress enters to claim solidarity with and superiority
to the vizards. Women in Restoration England aged early.

> At twenty five in women's eyes
> Beauty doth fade, at thirty dies.

The Forc'd Marriage may not have been the first play Behn wrote.
The dedicatory epistle of *The Young King*, published in 1683, describes
it as the work of a virgin, i.e. unpublished, muse:

'Tis the glory of the great and good to be the refuge of the
distressed; their virtues create 'em troubles; and he that has the
god-like talent to oblige is never free from impunity. You,
Philaster, have a thousand ways merited my esteem and veneration, and I beg you would now permit the effects of it, which
could not forbear, though unpermitted, to dedicate this youthful
sally of my pen, this first essay of my infant-poetry to your self.
'Tis a virgin-muse, harmless and unadorned, unpractised in the
arts to please . . . Three thousand leagues of spacious ocean she
has measured, visited many and distant shores, and found a
welcome every where . . . A thousand charms of wit, good
nature, and beauty at first approach she found in *Philaster* and,
since she knew she could not appear upon the too-critical
English stage without taking choice of some noble patronage,
she waited long, looked around the judging world, and fixed on

you. She feared the reproach of being an American, whose country rarely produces beauties of this kind. The muses seldom inhabit there or, if they do, they visit and away, but for a variety a dowdy lass may please. Her youth too should atone for all her faults besides, and her being a stranger will beget civility . . .

The epistle is addressed to 'Philaster', a name meaning 'lover of Astraea'. Dedications earned money from the dedicatees, who both accepted the honour and paid a couple of guineas for it. The use of a sobriquet here implies that the circumstances are unusual, but whether it was the dedicatee who demanded anonymity or the author who conferred it cannot now be known. The name 'Philaster' can be associated with George Villiers, second Duke of Buckingham, who made a version of Fletcher's play *Philaster*. The epistle – and the play – clearly date from a much earlier period when Behn could describe herself not only as young and, unpublished author, but also as a stranger, a newcomer, even an American . . . In *The London Stage* a hint from the last page – 'After a dance of Shepherds and Shepherd-esses, the Epilogue is spoken by Mrs Barry as a nymph; at his R. H. second exile into Flanders'– is taken to indicate that performance dated from 1679, when the Duke of York was sent to Flanders. The description of herself that the author gives in the dedicatory epistle could not have applied to her in 1679 either. The composition of the play and its presentation to 'Philaster' must be dated very much earlier. Among Behn's published *Poems upon Several Occasions* she included one 'On a Copy of Verses made in a Dream, and sent to me in a Morning before I was Awake'. Though the lover who sent the verses is here called Amyntas, the boy who brought them is called Bellario, which is the name of Philaster's page in the play.

In 'On Desire' printed a few years later, the speaker apostrophizes Desire in terms that suggest that she had once had admirers of princely status:

> Where wert thou, oh, malicious sprite,
> When shining honour did invite?
> When interest called, then thou went shy . . .
> When princes at my feet did lie . . .
> When thou couldst mix ambition with thy joy . . .

The suggestion that Buckingham may have acted as Behn's protector and patron is offered with diffidence; their names were
never linked in contemporary gossip. When Charles Gildon edited
Chorus Poetarum for publication in 1694, he printed William Bowles's
paraphrase of Sappho as 'By Madam Behn'; in *State Poems* 1703 the
same poem appeared as 'On Madam Behn'; when the poem appeared
in *The Dramatick Works of his Grace George Villiers, late Duke of
Buckingham* in 1715, it bore the title 'Sappho addressed to his Grace
the Duke of Buckingham, in the Year 1681 Translated by Mrs Behn'
and was followed by 'To the Memory of the most Illustrious Prince,
George, Duke of Buckingham. By Mrs. Behn, in the Year 1687'.
Gildon had included the elegy, first printed in 1687 by the Whig
publisher Richard Baldwin as an unattributed broadside, in *Chorus
Poetarum* without attribution. What the later printings represent is a
concerted attempt by the miscellany writers of Grub Street to build a
connection between two notorious figures of the bad old days of
Charles II. Modern scholars should probably avoid the temptation,
especially as Behn aligned herself with Buckingham's enemies in the
years before his death. For his part, Buckingham satirized Behn's play
The Amorous Prince in *The Rehearsal*.

A careful reading of Wycherley's 'To the Sappho of the Age,
Supposed to Lie in of a Love-Distemper, or a Play' suggests some
other possibilities.

> Once, to your shame, your parts to all were shown,
> But now (though a more public woman grown,)
> You gain more reputation in the town;
> Grow public, to your honour, not your shame,
> As more men now you please, gain much more fame
> ... Barren wits envy your head's offsprings more,
> Than barren women, did your tail's before.
> Thus, as your beauty did, your wit does now
> The women's envy, men's diversion grow;
> Who to be clapped, or clap you, round you sit,
> And tho' they sweat for it, will crowd your pit;
> Since lately you lay in, (but as they say)
> Because you had been clapped another way;
> But, if 'tis true, that you had need to sweat,
> Get, (if you can) at your new play, a seat.

This is usually taken to be straight invective; actually the tone is more complex and subtle. Wycherley claims that the playwright has been a woman of pleasure, and implies that though her 'parts to all were shown' she lived relatively privately, in comparison to the notoriety that she enjoys as a woman of the theatre. He credits her with success in living by her beauty, but even greater success in living by her wits. Where once her clients might sweat as part of taking a cure, now they have to sweat to get a seat at one of her plays. Moreover, he implies that Behn produces plays the way that women of pleasure produce children – there is no hint here of Radcliffe's greater libel that 'the play she vends she never made'. The tone, though ironic and scurrilous, is actually one of congratulation, one mountebank saluting another. It is not after all as if Mrs Behn sought to conceal her career of dalliance under a veneer of respectability; she claims a variety of lovers and demonstrates solidarity with a brother of the pen being treated for venereal infection.

The one possibility that has never been discussed is that Aphra Behn began her career in the Americas or in mainland Europe as a courtesan. Courtesans were trained in a demanding profession by their mothers who, when their daughters were entertaining their clients, held the door and ran the household. In societies where women of rank and breeding could not mix with the male friends of their husbands or sons, all the entertaining for foreign dignitaries had to be done in the houses of courtesans, and both secular and religious authorities both subsidized the ladies of pleasure and made use of their services. The courtesans of Venice, who were universally acknowledged the most opulent and accomplished of all, enjoyed the patronage and the protection of some of the most powerful men in Europe. The heroine of *The Rover* is a courtesan with the same initials as Mrs Behn, who ruins herself for her profession by falling in love, just as the heroine of Rochester's poem does, just as the persona of 'On Desire' does.

In 'A Session of the Poets', thought to be by Elkanah Settle, or by Rochester and/or Buckingham and convincingly dated by Veith November 1676, Behn is paid a curious back-handed compliment.

> The Poetesse Afra, next showed her sweet face,
> And swore, by her poetry and her black ace,
> The laurel by a double right was her own,
> For the plays she had writ, and the conquests she had won.

Apollo acknowledged, 'twas hard to deny her,
But, to deal frankly and ingeniously by her,
He told her, were conquests and charms her pretence,
She ought to have pleaded a dozen years since.

It is a curious fact that Behn echoes these exact words in the
interpolation she makes in her versification of the English translation
of the sixth book of Cowley's *De Plantarum*:

Among that number, do not me disdain,
Me, the most humble of that glorious Train.
I by a double right thy bounties claim,
Both from my sex, and in Apollo's name:

'A Session of the Poets' was very well known in its time; in listing
her among the most respected poets of her generation, Settle paid Mrs
Behn a considerable compliment, especially as she had by then written
only three plays and edited one miscellany. If the dating is right, Behn
reigned as a beauty in 1664 or so, ten years before she is supposed to
have been kept by Hoyle. Behn seems not to have resented being
referred to in such terms. Nowhere does she register a protest about
such characterization of herself, though she does object to condemna-
tion of her work as obscene. Rather she invites her audiences and her
readers to see her as a member of the raffish milieu of beaux and
gallants and their lady-friends. In the Epilogue to *The City Heiress* she
asks:

What is't you see in quality we want?
What can they give you which we cannot grant?
We have their pride, their frolics, and their paint.
We feel the same youth dancing in our blood;
Our dress as gay – all underneath as good.
Most men have found us hitherto more true,
And, if we're not abused by some of you,
We're full as fair – perhaps as wholesome too.

To publish one's own occasional verse was to invite the world to
share in one's friendships and intimacies: Aphra Behn identifies her
faithless lover as Mr J. H. but places him in a context of coterie

names, Amyntas, Lysander, Lycidus, Damon, Alexis, names which may or may not be interchangeable but suggest no regard for either chastity or monogamy. The commendatory poems by Charles Cotton, Nahum Tate, George Jenkins, Richard Ferrer or Farrer, John Cooper of Buckden, J. Adams, Thomas Creech, 'J. W.', 'F. N. W.' and 'H. Watson' all refer to her skills in the art of love, her 'Pen sheds flames as dangerous as her Eyes'. She is 'Love's great Sultana'. Jacob Tonson allowed himself to ask,

> Whoe'er beheld you with a heart unmoved,
> That sent not sighs and said within he loved?
> I gazed and found, a then unknown delight,
> Life in your looks, and death to leave the sight.
> What joys, new worlds of joys has he possessed,
> That gained the sought-for welcome of your breast?

A woman who did not wish herself to be thought of as an adept in love would hardly have welcomed such commendatory poems as these.

Behn herself, then, would have no objection to being known as having had more than one and perhaps more than a few lovers; she might, on the other hand, have been bemused to learn that she was considered to have earned sufficient to live on. After her first appearance as a playwright with *The Forc'd Marriage*, Behn tried her hand again with *The Amorous Prince*, 'a damned intrigue of an unpractised muse', adapted from *The City Night-Cap* of Robert Davenport; this too was relatively successful. Wycherley's suggestion that Mrs Behn was being treated for venereal disease is borne out by a note to himself in the diary of her friend Jeffrey Boys of Gray's Inn for 29 May 1671: 'g. Astrea 5s for a guinea if she live half a year'. Astraea, who is identified as Behn because she later sent Boys a copy of her play, has borrowed five shillings against twenty-one shillings if she should be alive to pay it in six months. If Behn was raising money by this means, she must herself have had little hope. If this is the case we must ask ourselves what had become of the earnings from the two plays she had had performed. After the union of the companies she explained to Tonson that she was desperately short of money because 'a body has no credit at the play-houses for money as we used to have, fifty or 60 deep or more'. If Behn borrowed at such a rate, it would be unsurprising if she was left with very little to live on even after a well-attended third day.

Boys's note indicates that Aphra Behn was so ill in 1671 that her recovery was not certain. This is evidence of a different kind from allegations in satires and lampoons that Behn was infected with pox. Behn seems to have had as little squeamishness in referring to love-distempers as Wycherley. Her joking poem to 'Damon', thought to be the playwright Ravenscroft, about his treatment for syphilis, supplies details of his treatment ('coddling in a cask'), and diet that argue a certain familiarity with the occupational disease of gallants male and female. Behn's biographers assume that all descriptions of her illness are merely libellous, but the assumption is hardly a safe one. An epistle of 1686–7 to 'Julian', chief distributor of libellous lampoons, asks:

> Doth that lewd harlot, that poetic quean,
> Famed through Whitefriars, you know who I mean,
> Mend for reproof, others set up in spite
> To flux, take clysters, vomits, purge and write?
> Long with a sciatica, she's besides lame,
> Her limbs distortured, nerves shrunk up with pain,
> And therefore I'll all sharp reflections shun,
> Poetry, poverty, pox are plagues enough for one.

Robert Gould refers to Behn as 'Sappho, famous for her gout and guilt'.

In 1672 we find Behn taking on the compilation of the anthology *Covent Garden Drollery*. The very rare first issue carries on the title-page the wrong initials, R. B., and also the designation 'Servant to his Majesty'; the second issue not only corrects 'R. B.' to 'A. B.' but removes the designation as well. Why was Aphra Behn in 1672 forced to take on a piece of anonymous literary hackwork? She was known as a playwright for the Duke's Theatre; both her plays had been published as by A. Behn, then Mrs A. Behn; why should the bookseller James Magnus, who published the plays and the anthology, not have capitalized on the fact? *Covent Garden Drollery* contains songs of Behn's that were not used in plays until after the volume was published. It seems obvious, therefore, that Behn wrote playful songs and *vers de société* before she was obliged to make a living by her pen; did she use her plays as showpieces for the peotic effusions of an earlier time? The shortcoming of all the biographies of Aphra Behn is that they do not begin to address such problems.

In the next year, 1673, only Behn's play *The Dutch Lover*, badly cast and acted, failed outright. If Mrs Behn earned a living by her pen that year, or the next or the next, she must have done so anonymously, for nothing was played or published as by her. Nevertheless, in 1675 Behn is called 'poetess' in Edward Phillips's *Theatrum Poetarum*. In July 1676 her *rifacimento* of *Lust's Dominion, Abdelazer or the Moor's Revenge* was successfully staged at the Duke's Theatre, partly because Nell Gwyn brought a party to see it. Angeline Goreau assumes, on no evidence that she cites, that at this time Mrs Behn

> kept company with court wits like Buckhurst . . . Sedley and most particularly Buckingham. She pleased Charles II and gained the patronage of his brother, James Duke of York, as well as the friendship of his mistress, Nell Gwyn. The patron and friend she seems to have valued most, though, was the Earl of Rochester . . .

If Behn was keeping this kind of company, we may be sure that it must have cost her way above her earnings as an occasional dramatist and literary jobber to keep up with the pace and style they set. If she was actually acquainted with such people, she can hardly have spent much time with them. She was acutely conscious of the gulf in rank even between her and low-born Nell Gwyn; in 1679, in the dedication of *The Feign'd Curtezans* to Gwyn, she writes with the excessive obsequiousness that earned her Johnson's contempt:

> I make this sacrifice with infinite fear and trembling, well knowing that so excellent and perfect a creature as yourself differs only from the Divine powers in this, the offerings made to you ought to be worthy of you . . .

Though panegyric is the medium of these dedications, Behn's effusiveness here must be taken as evidence of insecurity and desperate need. Thomas Otway, Behn's friend, became tutor to Gwyn's sons in 1680 and she too may have hoped for some sinecure in Gwyn's household. The king knew how precarious was the position of a woman of pleasure once she had lost her protector. He had Lucy Barlow,

Monmouth's mother, on his conscience already; no wonder that on his deathbed he asked his brother to 'let not poor Nelly starve'.

In 1676, with *Abdelazer* playing in July and in September *The Town Fopp*, which was a success, Behn was dominating at the Duke's Theatre, yet a year later, when *The Rover*, her reduction of Thomas Killigrew's semi-autobiographical play 'Thomaso, or, The Wanderer' took the stage at the Duke's Theatre, her authorship was not acknowledged. The Prologue, 'by a Person of Quality', referred to the author as 'he'; when the play was published it sported neither dedication nor attribution. Only when *The Rover* had been hailed as a runaway success did Mrs Behn own herself the author. Six months later, in the address to the reader printed with *Sir Patient Fancy*, successfully produced at the Duke's Theatre in January 1678, Behn found it necessary to defend herself from the charge of bawdiness, stating roundly that it was her unhappiness that she was

> forced to write for bread and not ashamed to own it, and con-
> sequently ought to write to please (if she can) an age which has
> given several proofs it was by this way of writing to be obliged,
> though it is a way too cheap to be pursued by men who write for
> glory and a way *even* I despise as much below me [my italics].

Behn herself was aware that she was prostituting her pen, writing bawdy because nothing else would sell. No other play followed until *The Feign'd Curtezans* in 1679. No performance of a Behn play is recorded before Part II of *The Rover* was staged in 1681. However, 1682 saw the production of three plays by her, *The Roundheads*, *The False Count* and *The City Heiress*.

In the winter of 1683–4 Mrs Behn wrote a hudibrastic epistle to Thomas Creech, the translator of Lucretius, explaining why she had missed an appointment with him:

> From Whitehall, Sir, as I was coming,
> His Sacred Majesty from dunning;
> Who oft in debt is, truth to tell,
> For Tory farce, or doggerel . . .
> Near to that place of fame call'd Temple, . . .
> Against that sign of whore call'd scarlet,
> My coachman fairly laid pilgarlic.

Having sold her pen to the court party, Behn was having difficulty in getting paid for it. A lady of fashion would have sent a servant on such an errand, especially during the great frost of the winter of 1683–4, but Behn was obliged to go herself. The coach that overturned in the ice was certainly a hackney.

By this time Rochester was dead and Buckingham had withdrawn to the country to die of dissipation and disappointment. The people Behn had then to woo were not the great court wits but the likes of Thomas Creech, a jobbing translator like herself, and the vegetarian proselytizer Thomas Tryon. At the same time as Mrs Behn was writing anti-Whig satires, with reflections upon the Duke of Monmouth so unmistakable that she was actually arrested, she was also writing for the trimmers. There can be little doubt that she took the Earl of Mulgrave's shilling for writing 'Ovid to Julia', ironically celebrating his successful wooing of the Princess Anne in 1682. We may assume that Mulgrave was an irresistible patron because he actually coughed up; he also 'gave her guineas' for her translation of De Bonnecorse's *Journey to the Isle of Love*, which contained a flattering account of him as one of the suitors to the Princess of Hope. Yet in 1684 we find Mrs Behn pleading with Jacob Tonson for an extra five pounds for her *Poems on Several Occasions*. The letter repeats itself almost hysterically:

> As for the verses of mine, I should really have thought 'em worth thirty pound; and I hope you will find it worth twenty-five; not that I should dispute at any other time for 5 pound where I am so obliged . . . I vow I would not lose my time in such low gettings, but only since I am about it I am resolved to go through with it though I should give it . . . good dear Mr Tonson, let it be 5 pounds more, for I may safely swear I have lost the getting of 50 pounds by it, though that's nothing to you or to my satisfaction and humour, but I have been without getting so long that I am just on the point of breaking . . .

The letter makes sad reading; Tonson is offering £20; the compiler thinks the book worth £30, but will settle for £25. On the one hand she tries for a little hauteur, the sum she is pleading for is after all a mere bagatelle; but on the other hand she has 'been without getting' for so long, she is on the point of 'breaking', having to declare herself unable to pay her debts. The desperateness of such a struggle could hardly be exaggerated. Failure to pay her debts would mean summary arrest. Wycherley had languished in debtors' prison for years. Behn struggled on: she completed her collection of poems, contributed her prologue for the revival of *Valentinian* and wrote the first part of *Loveletters between a Nobleman and his Sister*, but by August 1685 she was in financial trouble again and had to pledge her future earnings.

> Whereas I am indebted to Mr Bags the sum of six pound for the payment of which Mr Tonson has obliged him self ... if the said debt is not fully discharged before Michaelmas next, to stop what money he shall hereafter have in his hands of mine, upon the playing my first play till this aforesaid debt of six pounds be discharged ...

There was no shortage of work for Aphra Behn, but it seems as if the rates paid by the booksellers were much lower than the successful playwright might expect from a good third day. Two years were to pass before *The Emperor of the Moon* and *The Lucky Chance* were successfully staged. In the meantime, in a desperate attempt to gain royal patronage and perhaps a pension, she had turned her hand to writing Pindarics on the death of Charles II and the coronation of James II. In October 1687, Behn wrote to the daughter-in-law of the poet Edmund Waller: 'I am very ill, and have been dying this twelve month ... I write this with a lame hand scarce able to hold a pen ...' In her elegy for Waller she described herself:

> I, who by toils of sickness am become
> Almost as near as thou art to a tomb,
> While every soft and every tender strain
> Is ruffled and ill-natured grown with pain.

Yet despite her infirmity she had been working ceaselessly over that year, producing, as well as two plays and more Pindarics, a third and last part of *Loveletters between a Nobleman and his Sister*. Before she was released by death in April 1689, she was to go on to produce *Lycidus, Oroonoko, The Fair Jilt, The Lucky Mistake, The History of the Nun*, translations of *La Montre, Agnes de Castro*, Fontenelle's *Histoire des Oracles* and *Entretiens de la Pluralité des Mondes*, and the *Maximes* of de la Rochefoucauld. How a sick woman can have produced so much for the booksellers and under what duress is unimaginable.

What the hard facts add up to is not an account of 'a bloody good time'. Aphra Behn kept smiling, for light-heartedness was her stock in trade, but we owe it to her to look deeper and to confront her reality squarely. In 1699 Dryden wrote to Elizabeth Thomas, whom he dubbed Corinna, warning her against 'licences Mrs Behn allowed herself of writing too loosely', telling her that she was 'too well-born to fall into that mire'. Elizabeth Thomas was the daughter of a lawyer, who died when she was two, leaving her to be brought up in lodgings by her mother and grandmother, no higher in the social scale in fact than Elizabeth Barry. After a hand-to-mouth existence nursing a sick mother and waiting to marry a sick fiancé for seventeen years, Thomas languished three years in the Fleet for debt, and died destitute and alone two years later. Dryden knew Behn, and if Thomas's connections such as they were struck him as so very superior, Behn's connections with the Kent gentry must have been invisible, at least to him. It is more likely that Mrs Behn's was a milieu without social status, possibly an *émigré* community, perhaps Jewish or even Creole. Certainly she had an internationalist culture which was quite un-English.

After her death, Behn's papers came into the hands of Charles Gildon, who at twenty-five, having run through his inheritance and contracted a rash marriage, was embarking on an undistinguished career as a literary jobber. Gildon was unencumbered by scruples about the use he might make of Behn's literary estate; he had no hesitation in publishing as hers work he must have known was not by her or in permitting himself to fictionalize and sensationalize the facts of her life. It is impossible that the works that Gildon and his confederate Samuel Briscoe published after Behn's death were lying by unpublished during the months of frantic activity that preceded Behn's death which, according to Gildon, came about because of want of care in her physician. Gildon was a follower of Charles Blount, who preached the moral acceptability of suicide. There is a distinct possibility that, exhausted, destitute and racked with terrible pain, Aphra Behn herself put an end to her 'bloody good time'.

APHRA BEHN AS GHOSTWRITER

Aphra Behn's masterpiece is agreed to be the *The Rover*, which opened to rapturous applause at the Duke's Theatre in Dorset Gardens on 24 March 1677. When the play appeared in print in August it carried a Post-script:

This Play had been sooner in print, but for a report about the town (made by some either very malicious or very ignorant) that 'twas 'Thomaso' altered, which made the booksellers fear some trouble from the proprietor of that admirable play, which indeed has wit enough to stock a poet and is not to be pieced or mended by any but the excellent author himself. That I have stolen some hints from it may be a proof that I valued it more than to pretend to alter it. Had I had the dexterity of some poets, who are not more expert in stealing than in the art of concealing, and who even that way outdo the Spartan boys, I might have appropriated it all to myself, but I, vainly proud of my judgment, hang out the sign of Angelica (the only stolen object) to give notice where a great part of the wit dwelt, though, if the play of 'The Novella' were as well worth remembering as 'Thomaso', they might (bating the name) have as well said, I took it from thence. I will only say the plot and business (not to boast on't) is my own. As for the words and characters, I leave the reader to judge and compare 'em with 'Thomaso', to whom I recommend the great entertainment of reading it, though had this succeeded ill, I should have had no need of imploring that justice from the critics, who are naturally so kind to any that pretend to usurp their dominion, they would doubt-less have given me the whole honour on't. Therefore I will only say in English what the famous Virgil does in Latin: I make verses and others have the fame.

'Thomaso, or The Wanderer' is an enormously long play that had been published by Henry Herringman in a complete edition of *Comedies and Tragedies written by T. Killigrew, Gent.* in 1664. In Restoration times copyright rested with the publisher, which meant that Herringman was the proprietor referred to in Behn's Post-script. The author, Thomas Killigrew, was not only a Gentleman of the King's Bedchamber and manager of the King's Theatre, where he might have been expected to produce his own play, but Master of the Revels. Even if he had not been known to be a vengeful man, booksellers had every reason to fear getting on the wrong side of him. As it happened, Killigrew did not intervene to prevent the performance and Herringman made no attempt to protect his copyright. Behn's play was duly licensed for printing on 2 July. Though both the Term Catalogue entry and the Stationer's Register list Behn as the author, *The Rover* was published anonymously. No name appeared on the title-page, there was no dedicatory epistle and the Post-script was unsigned. Behn's name was not added for the second issue but some copies show an interesting variant in that the words 'especially of our Sex' are added into the Post-script, revealing for the first time that the author of the play was a woman. The third issue carries Behn's name on a cancellans title-page. As the title-page of *Sir Patient Fancy*, licensed 28 January 1678, announces that the play is 'Written by Mrs A. Behn, the Author of the *Rover*', we may conclude that she had waited for the success of the play to be confirmed before claiming it.

The Prologue to Behn's play, which purports to have been written by 'a Person of Quality', describes *The Rover* as 'a new play, whose author is unknown' and implies that 'he' is 'a young Poet' and male:

> As for the Author of this coming play,
> I asked him what he thought fit I should say . . .
> He called me fool . . .

Aphra Behn was neither unknown, young nor male. Her play, *The Forc'd Marriage*, had been a success for the Duke's Company in December 1670 and a year later she had another success with *The Amorous Prince*, followed in 1673 by *The Dutch Lover*. No new play by Behn appeared before the summer of 1676, when the Duke's Company played *Abdelazar, or the Moor's Revenge*, which was followed in the autumn by *The Town Fop*, if Summers and Duffy are right, and *The Debauchee* and *The Counterfeit Bridegroom* are Behn's as well, she produced four playscripts within a year, and must have been working under pressure. *The Debauchee*, a *rifacimento* of Brome's *Mad Couple Well Match'd*, and *The Counterfeit Bridegroom*, another of Middleton's *No Wit, No Help Like a Woman's*, were played and published anonymously. If one or other or both are by Behn we must assume that her name had ceased to be bankable. The fact that 'Astrea Behn' was one of only four women writers mentioned by Edward Phillips in *Theatrum Poetarum* in 1675 proves that she had a reputation; her anonymity in 1676 implies that for some reason neither she nor her paymasters wished to exploit it.

The Post-script to the original anonymous publication is anything but straightforward, but it clearly dares the reader to examine 'Thomaso' in order to ascertain what of *The Rover* can be found in it. *Comedies and Tragedies* was a handsome folio volume of which many copies have survived. Behn's contemporaries would have had no difficulty whatsoever in finding a copy, even though it was published thirteen years earlier. The library of the University of Columbia holds what appears to be Behn's own copy, with the name A. Behn entered on the separate title-pages of all the plays. What is obvious from even the most cursory examination of 'Thomaso' is not only that Behn has taken many elements from Killigrew but that she has not troubled to conceal her borrowing. This she was well able to do. Revivals, which cost half as much to license as new plays, were the staple of the Restoration theatre. Behn adapted the anonymous *Lust's Dominion*, itself a version of *The Spanish Moor's Play* by Dekker, as *Abdelazar*, modernizing her original line by line, suppressing four supernumerary characters, and adding a virtually mute female character 'Elvira, Woman to the Queen', probably in response to stipulations by the company. *The Town Fop* was a much more radical *rifacimento* of *The Miseries of Enforced Marriage* by George Wilkins. Behn introduces a major new character, Sir Timothy Tawdrey's kept woman or 'miss', Betty Flauntit, and changes the names of all the other characters. Though her Celinda is based upon Clare in the original, she is not allowed to die of a broken heart. Sir Timothy resembles his antecedent, Sir Francis Ilford, so little that he may fairly be called a new character. Behn also recasts the tavern scenes of Act IV in a *bagnio*.

Strangely, Behn took little or no pains to conceal her borrowings from 'Thomaso'. Of the dramatis personae she chose to change only the names of the cavaliers. The name Lucetta 'a famous Curtezan' is given to 'a jilting Wench'; Philippo, her 'Paramour' according to Killigrew, is her 'Gallant' according to Behn; and Sancho, her 'Bravo' according to Killigrew, her 'Pimp' according to Behn. Callis is now a governess rather than a servant, Diego page to Don Antonio rather than servant to Don Pedro, Stephano servant to Don Pedro rather than friend to Don Mathias. Though the scene of the play is now Naples rather than Madrid, the rivals of the English cavaliers are Spaniards, and one of them carries the same name as Killigrew's original. Their Spanishness is explained by the fact that the other, Don Antonio, is the son of the Spanish Viceroy. Instead of having one sister, Serulina, Don Pedro now has two, Florinda and Hellena (whose name was borne by 'an old decayed Curtezan' in 'Thomaso').

So many details that could as well or even more easily have been altered stand like signposts in the text that we must conclude that Behn was not afraid of her work's being associated with Killigrew's. It is almost as if she was taking up a challenge of some kind, deliberately demonstrating how much of the unplayable original she could leave in. Even more striking than the details of the casting taken over unchanged from *Thomaso* are the verbal parallels; no fewer than 500 lines of Behn's short play are quotations from 'Thomaso', most paraphrased, many verbatim in whole or in part.

The play opens with a scene between Hellena and Florinda, two virtuous women in place of Killigrew's one; Florinda is in love with Belvile, who performed for her the same service that Thomaso did for Serulina in 'Thomaso'. Speech after speech is replicated in the new context with only minor changes:

> *Serul.* I know not Sir. Calis, when was he here? I considered it so little myself, I have forgot when 'twas.

becomes:

> *Flor.* I know not, Sir – Callis, when was he here? For I consider it so little, I know not when it was.

Serulina's suitor too had 'a Passion for' her, and Serulina's prays to her brother not to presume upon 'the ill customs of our Countrey so far as to make a slave of [his] Sister'. Behn also uses Pedro's speech from 'Thomaso':

> I only beg to be ranked in your esteem with Don Thomaso; why do you frown and blush? Is there any guilt belongs to the name of that Wanderer?

And Florinda answers with some of the exact words of Serulina's answer. Behn's method is not to follow the structure of any scene of 'Thomaso' for after quoting and paraphrasing parts of Act III, scene iv she then puts into Pedro's mouth part of a speech of Serulina's from 'Thomaso' Part II, Act II, scene i:

> What Jewels will Don *Thomaso* present his wife with? Those of his eyes and heart.

The scene proceeds with more scraps from the same scene between Harrigo and Serulina, but this time Harrigo's cynicism is being displayed by the minx Hellena, who has hardly lived long enough to accumulate it. This is Harrigo's version:

> *Harr.* When? by Moonshine? I'm sure you dare not meet Signor *Sol* abroad . . . 'Tis enough for your *Alphonso* and his Indian breeding to endure such stabs as the sun strikes in the dog-days . . . signs of favour I can assure you; and such as you must not hope, unless your woman be out of the way; and that honour being past, the giant stretches himself, yawns and sighs a belch or two, stales in your pot, farts as loud as a musket for a jest; and then throws himself under the rug, and expects you in his foul sheets . . . and ere you can get into the bed he calls you with a snore or two; and are not these fine things in a ladies' bed . . . yet this man you must kiss; nay, you must none but this, and muzzle through his beard to find his lips; and this you can submit to for threescore year for a jointure . . .

This Hellena's:

> When? By moonlight? For I'm sure she dares not encounter

with the heat of the sun; that were a task only for Don *Vincentio* and his *Indian* breeding, who loves it in the dog-days . . . Signs of favour, I'll assure you, and such as you must not hope for, unless your woman be out of the way . . . That honour being past, the giant stretches it self, yawns and sighs a belch or two as loud as a musket, throws himself into bed, and expects you in his foul sheets, and e'er you can get your self undrest, calls you with a snore or two – Are not these fine blessings to a young lady? . . . And this man you must kiss, nay, you must kiss none but him too, and nuzle thro his beard to find his lips – and this you must submit to for threescore years, and all for a jointure.

Act I, scene ii of *The Rover* contains scraps of Act I, scenes i and v of Part I of 'Thomaso'; Act II, scene i is a patchwork of elements from Act II, scene ii and of Act I, scene iii of 'Thomaso' e.g.

Edwardo. Prithee, where do these lady whores live?
Thomaso. Where no constable, lousy watch-man, beadle, or saucy bell-man dares to break into their chambers. These will not be kicked neither, nor suffer your blades, inspired with sack, to break their windows . . . yet they are doxies . . .

becomes:

Will. Pox on't, where do these fine whores live?
Belv. Where no rogue in office yclept constables dare give 'em laws, nor the wine-inspired bullies of the town break their windows; yet they are whores . . .

Quotations from 'Thomaso' are so frequent in *The Rover* that the recollections seem almost unconscious; there is no obvious reason Frederick should echo the statement of one of the three 'Monsieurs without cloaks' that Angelica's fee is 'a portion for the Infanta' or the Bravo's statement that Angelica's is 'a trade . . . that cannot live by credit'. Angelica's first appearance in *The Rover* uses material from three scenes of 'Thomaso', namely Thomaso's speech from Act II, scene iii, Angelica's description of Don Pedro in Act II, scene i, and the dialogue about her immunity to love from Act II, scene iii:

Anna. I was thinking what sullen star reigned at your birth, that has preserved your youth from being in love, that green-sickness of the heart that vexeth all our sex, early or late.

Angelica. A kind and thrifty star, to which I owe my chief happiness ... How should I become a lover, that have not so much leisure as to wish or long for any man? ...

The scene continues along the lines of the original, with Angelica singing to the theorbo, with the important difference that in this case Angelica's song is an original composition. The encounter between Willmore and Angelica is likewise a selection of paraphrases from Act II, scene iv of 'Thomaso'; with some extracted chunks of prose crudely transmogrified as verse. 'Thomaso' says:

Not that I despise you, but to secure myself. All those flames I feel now are but so many lusts. I know them by their sudden bold intrusion. The impatiency and sauciness of the flame betrays it, still devouring till it be devoured. Had it been love's pure dart, I should have pined at your feet in silence, ere found a daring to tell you so ...

Willmore has somehow to recite:

> But that secures my heart and all the flames it feels
> Are but so many lusts,
> I know it by their sudden bold intrusion.
> The fire's impatient and betrays; 'tis false –
> For had it been the purer flame of love,
> I should have pined and languished at your feet,
> Ere found the impudence to have discovered it

In 'Thomaso' the scene ends with the bitter animadversions of the courtesan's maid:

Love was always fatal to our trade ... to dote upon a beggar, a soldier-beggar, a trade as ill as our own, as poor too, and as impossible to be made rich; one that thinks it a dishonour to get or save; we shall never eat again neither, for he'll have all in drink; nay, 'tis an English soldier too, and one of the King's party, three titles to perpetual poverty, a race of men who have left praying, or hoping for daily bread, and only rely upon nightly drink.

Behn's paraphrase, which buries Killigrew's closing quip, is notably weaker than the saturnine original.

> Now my curse go with you – Is all our project fallen to this? To love the only enemy to our trade? Nay, to love such a shameroon, a very beggar; nay, a pirate-beggar, whose business is to rifle and be gone, a no-purchase, no-pay tatterdemalion, an English picaroon; a rogue that fights for daily drink, and takes a pride in being loyally lousy – O, I could curse now if I durst – This is the fate of most whores.
>> Trophies, which from believing fops we win,
>> Are spoils to those who cozen us again.

Behn's Act III continues with a highly condensed version of Killigrew's Act III, scene ii in which virtually all of Willmore's observations have close parallels in the original; Behn's Act III, scene ii uses material from Act V, scenes v, vi, vii and xi of 'Thomaso'. For scene iii of Act III, Behn returns to Act IV, scene ii, from which she puts the dialogue between Edwardo and Serulina in the mouths of Willmore and Florinda, with interesting results for the characterization of her hero, who takes on the added dimension of a drunken rapist. In 'Thomaso' Edwardo is the one Englishman who is not a supporter of the exiled king, having compounded for his estates; his sexual boorishness is meant to be contrasted with the streetwise rakishness of the cavaliers. By giving Willmore so many of his lines, Aphra Behn seriously confuses the issue. If her intention was, as Jones De Ritter argues, to expose rakishness as a social evil, she signally failed, for Willmore was universally agreed to be a devilish attractive figure. The rest of Act III is all original material concerning the assault by Willmore on Antonio and the arrest of Belvile, and the arrangement with Antonio for Belvile to fight in his stead; the subsequent business takes up the first and second scenes of Act IV until the entry of Angelica, whereupon Thomaso's speeches from Act IV, scene i, reappear. Angelica's verse lament for her lost reputation which ends this scene has no parallel in 'Thomaso'. Act IV, scene iii is based largely upon 'Thomaso', Part II, Act II, scene iv, with the added unpleasant complication that where Serulina was threatened with a single rape, Florinda is menaced by two men.

It is odd that modern Behn scholarship makes no account of the Killigrew material transported holus-bolus into *The Rover*, ignoring Langbaine's stringent judgement:

> These are the only comedies, for the theft of which I condemn this ingenious authoress; they being so excellent in their original, that 'tis pity they should have been altered: and notwithstanding her apology in the Postscript to the first part, I cannot acquit her of prevarication, since *Angelica* is not *the only stolen Object*, as she calls it, she having borrowed largely throughout.

So much is incontrovertible. What follows is more puzzling.

> The truth is, the better to disguise her theft, she has (as the ingenious *Scarron* observes . . .) *Flayed the eel by beginning at the tail* . . . and therefore could not justly call these plays her own.

If Aphra Behn had been anxious to conceal her borrowings, only Langbaine would have found them, but in her Post-script to the published version of *The Rover* Behn actually tells her readers where to look. When it is realized that the text of her play is studded with unmissable quotations, misquotations and paraphrases of 'Thomaso', what emerges in the Post-script is a fascinating game of double-bluff. Nowhere does she refer to the author of 'Thomaso' but only 'the proprietor'. 'Wit enough to stock a poet' is a strange phrase, which could be taken to imply that a poet had helped herself to the wit of a non-poet. Behn goes on to identify 'the play of "The Novella"' as the ultimate source for the device of the sign of Angelica, although both might have been said to have drawn upon historical events and situations, for the advertising of a courtesan's charms was actual practice. 'The plot and business is my own' could be taken to imply that Behn was not concerned to lay claim to the dialogue, which is a patchwork of adapted borrowings, but to the structure of the intrigue. If her challenge to the reader to make the comparison with Killigrew's work is not a breathtakingly impudent piece of double-bluff, it must be an indirect boast of her own ingenuity. She concludes by remarking that if her play had failed it would have been attributed to her.

Killigrew was not only an important courtier, he was also a well-known raconteur. Reading the comic speeches in 'Thomaso' is like reading the transcript of a stand-up comedian. Here is his 'What we did in the Interregnum' routine:

> *Johan.* ... the Louvre and the Pale-Royal have been sad enchanted castles to [the exiled cavaliers]. They have kept a Lazarillo's court there; darkness, loneness, and the nest of poverty, but two loaves a day, and without fish, to work the miracle. Yet the gallery was a Christian coney-warren, filled with cavaliers of all trades, and, unless they fed upon their children, 'tis not visible what they ate.
>
> *Carlo.* They are now removed to the Palais-Royal, where they eat so seldom and dung so small, you may as soon step in a custard as a turd in the court. They that do shit save it for their own pig. There is not a blade of grass left in the garden, nor a drop of oil in the Madonna's lamp. Sacrilege and their salads make it burn dim. They are happy that swim, they dive in the pond and steal the fish. The younger stomachs browse upon the copse as high as they can reach ... the grasshoppers are grown pismires now, and are abroad as early as the day, and industrious as the ant for food. Brown-bread and old Adam's ale is current now; yet if little Eve walk in the garden, the lean starved rogues neigh after her as if they were in Paradise. There's their resident too; his arms are up still, but 'tis long since he had the supporters. 'Tis thought he ate the unicorn last Passover ...

Though 'Thomaso' is written in dialogue it is a series of comic routines of this kind. Both Killigrew's real-life antagonist Richard Flecknoe and Harbage, Killigrew's biographer, assume that 'Thomaso' is autobiographical and that Thomaso is Killigrew himself. Yet, though an autobiographical element is present in 'Thomaso', it is as risky to treat it as straightforward autobiography as it would be to take a stand-up comedian literally. The immediate historic context of the action of 'Thomaso' shifts confusingly, probably deliberately, for the covert activities of the royalists in the 1650s had consequences that were still politically sensitive in the 1660s. The entirely unnecessary statement on the title-page that 'Thomaso' was 'written in Madrid' is almost certainly false. Though Thomaso refers to 'seven years' misery' that have altered him chiefly by the addition of a periwig and Paulina too says that Englishmen have 'an ill name in the world this last seven years', which would appear to place the action in 1650, Act V, scene vii of Part II of 'Thomaso' refers to an historic meal of sucking pig that could not have taken place before July 1652:

> *Edw.* I remember 'twas at the Saint John's Head, and it proved the purest babe of grace. It would have tempted a Jew as it lay in the dish. Old Satan of the *Disser*, and a Scot his Host, in spite of *Moses* fell to the roast.

Satan was the nickname of William Murray, created Earl of Dysart in 1651, identified as '*L.* Disser' in the margin. Ferdinando adds more details:

> *Ferd.* 'Twas where we met Ambassador Will, and Resident Tom, with M. Sheriff's secretary, John the Poet with the Nose; all Gondibert's dire foes; from Poland laden with the spoils of what do you lack, sir, and all the Scotch pedlars' packs on their backs, sir.

These three are identified in the margin as 'Will Crofts, T. Killig. Jack Denham'. Clearly this meeting took place after Sir John Denham and William Crofts returned from their successful fund-raising expedition to Poland and after Killigrew's return from his disastrous career as Charles II's resident in Venice. By grouping them as 'all Gondibert's dire foes', Killigrew claims on their behalf the authorship of *Certain Verses written by severall of the Author's Friends; to be reprinted with the second Edition of Gondibert* published in 1653.

Harbage interprets a reference to the Dutch peace with Cromwell and another to Prince Rupert's brief stint as Master of the Horse as *termini ad quem*, placing the composition of 'Thomaso' firmly in the April and May of 1654, when Killigrew is thought to have been with the king in Paris, though he had time enough in The Hague to court the heiress Charlotte van Hesse, whom he married on 28 January 1655. The likelihood is that 'Thomaso' is composed of reminiscences drawn from different circumstances over four or five years, eventually grouped together rather unhappily under the overarching plots of Serulina and the Mexican monsters, which have the same relevance to its real concerns as the love story in *Horsefeathers*. The Angelica Bianca plot, by contrast, is intrinsic to the depiction of the peculiar milieu of the exiled English agents and mercenaries in Catholic Europe. De Ritter, who shares neither Killigrew's saturnine view of male sexuality nor his social anthropological interest in prostitution as a social system, finds the accounts of the life career of *le cortigiane oneste* in 'Thomaso' completely unconvincing, when in fact they are borne out to the letter by abundant historical documentation.

Killigrew himself tried to shape 'Thomaso' for performance for the stage without success. His marked-up copy of *Comedies and Tragedies* can be seen in the library of Worcester College, Oxford. Pencil lines in the margin show that he would have ended Act I at the beginning of Act I, scene iv, ended new Act II at the beginning of old Act II, scene iv, slightly cut the next scene and ended new Act III at the end of old Act III, scene ii, noting, 'The 3. Acte ends here ad the 3 ackts ar 34 sides 4 Acte begins here', ending it at the end of old Act IV, scene i, a total of forty-six pages or 'sides'. Act IV, scene ii, which introduces Lopus the Mountebank, Celia, Scarramucha and Hellena, was to have been cut altogether, as well as Act IV, scene iv and half of Act V, scene i, the remainder making up a new Act V. In Part II the cuts become confused and a scribal hand appears, possibly that of the intriguing 'Miss Hancocke', whose task it was to write out the parts for the actors. In the margin of page 399 the new editor remarks 'First Act ought to end here'; three whole pages are then cut and material from page 403 is marked to be moved to replace the beginning of Act II, scene iii two pages further on. There follow some short tussles between Killigrew and the scribe, who is obliged to restore speeches without which the plot would be imcomprehensible. Act III, scenes viii, ix, xi, and Act IV, scene i, are eliminated. The scribal hand begins to indicate entrances and exits, cuts are more frequently debated, with Killigrew writing his own instructions in the margin in 'red lead', using the same monogram, like a long-stemmed trefoil, that he used to authenticate his secret correspondence. The result of both Killigrew's repeated exertions, in pencil, ink and 'red led', and the scribe's neat interpolations is still unactable. Though like Killigrew Behn chose to eliminate the Lopus scenes and the intrigue of the Mexican monsters, *The Rover* paraphrases material which Killigrew had selected to be cut and appears to bear no relation to Killigrew's attempted reduction.

The marginalia in the Worcester College copy of *Comedies and Tragedies* reveal something more surprising. Killigrew appears to have been afflicted with a degree of illiteracy more commonly associated with gentlewomen than gentlemen. His writing is extraordinarily clumsy, with missing upstrokes and downstrokes and many unrecognizable characters, while his spelling is wildly inconsistent. At the end of *Claricilla*, for which he has indicated – mostly impenetrably illegibly – the altered staging necessary for the Drury Lane Theatre, he writes:

Here must be a shorte songe of ioey 4 liens is a nuffe

A substitution in 'The Parson's Wedding' ('The Parssens Vedding' according to Killigrew) reads:

Yet a mite hafe over cum my a verssion

The word 'bawd', though it is printed 'Baud' in the text, appears as 'baed' and 'bude'. Odder still is the fudging of the writing of his own name, which is made less legible by his habit of writing 'e' as 'ω'. Harbage noticed from the transcriptions by R. N. Worth from Killigrew's entries in the family Bible that he did not spell the word 'son' the same way twice, in one instance arriving at an extraordinary version 'suenne'. He also notes Henry Bennett's commendatory poem in *The Prisoners and Claracilla*, published in 1641, which praises 'his most honoured uncle' for making plays that are not

> . . . enriched by others' cost or pain,
> But like *Minerva*, raised from your own brain.
> I cannot choose but wonder how your parts
> Gained this perfection without books or arts;
> . . . your thoughts have read
> Men that are living rules, whilst books are dead . . .

Harbage does not dwell on the implications of this odd praise, or those of Robert Waring's compliment to the '*Auctoris ab ipso cultu*' or Cartwright's to 'the ingenious fountain [that] clearer flows/And yet no food besides its own spring knows'. References to 'The Parson's Wedding' in the epilogue as a play made by an 'illiterate Courtier'

... 'one that can scarce read, nay, not his own hand' are likewise dismissed, though this play too has an autobiographical element, indulging as it does Killigrew's hostility towards his learned brother, Henry Killigrew, D.D. Oxon. The Parson sneers at the Captain, Killigrew's avatar:

> ... rail, do rail, my illiterate Captain, that can only abuse by memory; and should I live [till] thou couldst read my sentence, I should never die.

Two more of Killigrew's brothers, Robert and William, went to Oxford, but Killigrew was left to run wild in the streets of Lothbury.

Perhaps Killigrew remained illiterate all his life because attempts to teach him his letters had failed. Though dyslexia has only recently been recognized as a congenital learning disability, it is by no means a new phenomenon. Killigrew's inability to copy words he had before him on the same page suggests that he suffered from a significant degree of word-blindness. Dyslexia has a genetic element, being often found in boys together with left-handedness. Another of Killigrew's brothers, Charles, also received no education and, like Killigrew, preferred to spend his time with players and lackeys. He wandered around Europe, living as well as he could by his wits, and died young in Rotterdam in 1629. 'Thomaso' describes himself as 'thrown from his cradle into other men's grounds, naked and unthought of by his parents and friends'. Killigrew's father, a man of high culture and a close friend of Constantijn Huygens, probably saw in his sons' inability to get their letters only simple delinquency and just as probably had them soundly thrashed for it before giving up on them and turning them loose to roam the world. Killigrew's literary ambitions fit nicely into the picture of a rejected son revenging himself on his bookish brothers by proving that he was their intellectual equal, even their superior. As most literate gentlemen availed themselves of the services of a secretary, there would have been little in Killigrew's doing so to excite remark, as long as the extent of his reliance upon his amanuensis was not known. The pattern of producing literary works by dictation was probably set when Killigrew recounted his experiences with the possessed nuns of Loudun in December 1635 for a letter to Lord Goring of which no copy in his own hand has been found; the version of events that is familiar from numerous MS copies has been virtually 'novelized' by a professional.

The fact that Killigrew was illiterate had come to the knowledge of his enemies. In *The Life of Tomaso the Wanderer* (1667) Richard Flecknoe sneers:

> 'Tis a great commendation for a man to be tam marte quam mercurio . . . and so was he, for he was good at neither, yet he would be writing though he could not spell, and be an author without rhyme or reason, and without any other learning, than only that of vice and debauchery.

In *Athenae Oxonienses*, Anthony à Wood quotes Sir John Denham:

> Had Cowley ne'er spoke, Killigrew ne'er writ,
> Between the two, they'd made a matchless wit.

Faithorne's engraved frontispiece to *Comedies and Tragedies*, which has been described as a portrait of 'the dramatist at work on his plays', shows Killigrew seated at a table upon which are stacked seven closed volumes with the names of his plays lettered on the sides. On a lectern close by stands another book, closed by bands tied in a bow. Killigrew holds in his right hand a blank page of a blank book, and rests his head upon his left, as he looks rather wistfully out of the picture. There is no pen to be seen. The picture seems indeed to be telling us that Thomas Killigrew did not 'write' his seven plays at all.

Illiteracy would go a long way to explaining Killigrew's failure as resident in Venice and as manager of the King's Theatre where he could not exercise authority over his actors or keep track of finances. According to Hotson, from 1663 he was forced to delegate direction of his plays. He managed to avoid sharing the Mastership of the Revels with Davenant, who would soon have exposed him, by doing a deal by which Sir Henry Herbert effectively retained the office until his death in 1673. Killigrew had the reversion and announced that he would exercise it, but he is not known to have censored a single play. On 24 February 1667, he was forced to hand over the managership of his theatre and the Mastership of the Revels to his sons, who were both literate.

What must now be considered is the possibility that the amanuensis who helped Thomas Killigrew put together 'Thomaso' for publication in 1664 was Aphra Behn. In August 1666 Behn knew Killigrew well enough to write to him familarly from Antwerp:

> I presume to take a freedom with you more than any, and the sooner because 'twas from you as well as any I received my business and from you I shall expect a favour.

When in 1668 she was in great difficulty as a result of the failure of the king's secret service to meet the expenses of her mission to Antwerp, she wrote once more to Killigrew at his lodgings in Whitehall, ending her letter in terms that suggest that she still had some claim upon him:

> Sir, if I have not the money tonight, you must send me something to keep me in prison, for I will not starve.

Killigrew seems to have come to the rescue and satisfied her creditors, for there is no record of Aphra Behn serving any time in prison. In 1672, if modern scholarship is correct, Behn edited the anthology *Covent Garden Drollery*. As a playwright she was exclusively associated with the Duke's Theatre, but this anthology features verse associated with Killigrew's Theatre Royal, including the Prologue and Epilogue for the revival of Killigrew's play 'The Parson's Wedding'. Behn could have secured this material by taking it down in shorthand during performances, but the bookseller would have been taking a risk if she had not acquired the material legitimately. Was it Killigrew who made it available to her? Was he once more coming to her rescue? Though Behn is commonly thought to have earned a living by her pen, she had produced no work since February 1671. In May of that year Jeffrey Boys had lent Behn five shillings to be repaid at 320% interest if she lived to repay it at all. It is possible, even probable, that Killigrew, who knew what it was to live perpetually on the edge of ruin, came to Behn's aid again before her six months were up, providing her with material towards a collection that she could sell to a bookseller. The title-page of the first issue of the first edition of *Covent Garden Drollery* claims that the 'Choice Songs, Poems, Prologues, and Epilogues, (Sung and Spoken at Courts and Theatres)' were 'Collected by R. B. Servant to His Majesty'; the 'R. B.' was smartly corrected to 'A. B.' and the title 'Servant to His

Majesty' as smartly dropped. Killigrew, as a Gentleman of the Bed-chamber, was of course a servant to His Majesty.

If Aphra Behn was ever Killigrew's mistress, she was not so for long, for Killigrew adhered to the captain's and Thomaso's creed, that variety provided the interest in sex. His promiscuity was legendary and he is not known to have paid for the support of any woman, except the wench he hired to serve 'eight or ten' of his actors at 20 shillings a week. What seems more likely is that Aphra Behn, like Miss Hancocke in real life and Secret in 'The Parson's Wedding', had worked for Killigrew as his amanuensis. In the Prologue to *The Rover* the unknown Person of Quality, whose style bears a marked similarity to Behn's own, tells us:

> Some write correct indeed, but then the whole
> (Bating their own dull stuff i'th' play) is stole: . . .
> Some write their characters genteel and fine,
> But then they do so toil for every line,
> That what to you does easy seem, and plain,
> Is the hard issue of their labouring brain.
> And some th'effects of all their pains we see,
> Is but to mimic good extempore . . .
> In short the only wit that's now in fashion
> Is but the gleanings of good conversation.

Killigrew was the acknowledged master of 'good extempore' and 'Thomaso' a compilation of his extemporizings; when Killigrew's spoken gems turned literary gems were gleaned and adroitly reset in a romantic comedy format, the result was *The Rover*. The last line of the Post-script could be taken to mean that the original translation of Killigrew's spoken word into the text of 'Thomaso' was the work of Aphra Behn. Two things are certain: Killigrew made no public claim to his intellectual property, though he was himself in financial diffi-culty at the time, and when Aphra Behn wanted to capitalize upon the success of *The Rover* four years later, she returned to 'Thomaso' for her material, safe in the knowledge that her claim to it would not be challenged.

ROCHESTER'S NIECE

The important poets of the Restoration period used to be three: Cowley, Waller and Dryden. Beyond and, some think, far above them, set in a firmament of petty lights, glittered another trio, the Duke of Buckingham, the Earl of Dorset and the wicked Earl of Rochester. Though Waller was a gentleman, he was also a professional poet who personally supervised the publication of his work. Cowley was the son of a stationer, dependent all his life upon patronage, and he too saw his work through the press. Gifted with an unusual combination of business acumen, taste, authority and poetic talent, Dryden gradually, and with many reverses, raised the profession of versifier to respectability, opening the way for the public poets of the Augustan age. Contrariwise, the noblemen were obliged to eschew the market-place; their poetry-making was supposed to be a diversion, undertaken to while away an idle hour. To sell their work would have been to make of their minds 'a common shore', that is, a sewer, used by all and sundry; noblemen wrote for the amusement and appreciation of their peers. Often they improvised together, leaving an insoluble riddle for the scholars of the twentieth century, who like their poetry to come in 'author-shaped parcels'. The most notorious and most brilliant nobleman-poet was John Wilmot, second Earl of Rochester. His poems began to circulate in manuscript before he had finished working on them. Booksellers were desperate to get their hands on Rochester's copies to publish them as broadsides. When he died in 1680, worn out by his own frenetic dissipation, collections of poems purporting to be his sold out as fast as the printers could put them together. In the judgement of the late twentieth century, it is Rochester who emerges as the most significant literary talent at the court of Charles II, despite the scrappiness of his oeuvre.

There is no good biography of Rochester. Few scholars are aware that Rochester had a niece who wrote poetry, much of it showing the effect of her charismatic uncle's closeness. He was twelve years old when she was born in the same house as he was, Sir Henry Lee's house at Ditchley, where the Countess of Rochester was obliged to live, the Wilmot house at Adderbury being uninhabitable. The Countess was in mourning for the death of the master of the house, her first son by her first marriage to an elder Sir Henry Lee. His young widow was also grievously ill; when she went into labour no one expected her or the baby to survive. They christened the little girl with her mother's name, which was also her grandmother's name, Anne. With her dying breath Lady Anne Lee placed her two little girls in the care of her mother-in-law, Rochester's mother. Unlike the young Earl, new-born Anne and her eighteen-month-old sister were rich, partly because their father had charged the estate he passed on to his brother with large dowries for them, mostly because their mother was heir-at-law to the vast estates of the great Earl of Danby.

Lady Rochester was rich in her own right, for she had inherited estates in Wiltshire from her father, Sir John St John of Lydiard Tregoze, as well as a handsome jointure settlement from her first husband, but her income was not equal to her ambition to live 'as the top of all'. Though her second husband's house at Adderbury was only leased from the Bishop of Winchester, she spent vast amounts rebuilding and refurbishing it. In 1664 she was appointed Groom of the Stole to the Duchess of York. The Groom of the Stole (pronounced 'stool') was responsible for Anne Hyde's chamberpot and, as the most intimate of the great lady's body servants, took precedence over all the other ladies-in-waiting. Lady Rochester was a natural choice for the position, for she had had close connections with the Hyde family all her life; the Duchess's father, Edward Hyde, the new Earl of Clarendon, had been her principal trustee after her father's death. Moreover, in the carve-up of the Danby and related estates at the Restoration, Hyde had been allowed to take possession of Danby's most extensive and valuable property, Cornbury Park, and his son to assume the grace title of Viscount Cornbury. In return, some estates of the regicide Sir John Danvers, Danby's brother, had been settled on the Lee girls. As Groom of the Stole, Lady Rochester was granted an apartment in Whitehall, where her little granddaughters stayed with her when she was in attendance on the Duchess. Otherwise she and they and Rochester lived at Adderbury.

Lady Rochester has both been called a puritan and accused of adultery with her cousin Sir Allen Apsley, who held, besides other lucrative offices, that of Master of the Duchess's Horse and was thought by Aubrey to be Rochester's actual father. The Countess was a Presbyterian, as were many courtiers in the court of Charles II. Her religion was genuine, but her lust for magnificence and her passionate nature were at least as genuine. Though her son's escapades must have grieved her, she never remonstrated with him; though he was floundering in a morass of debt, she made no attempt to curb his extravagance or her own. Masses of letters in a very distinctive hand with characteristically emphatic expression show that Lady Rochester possessed literary skill though she did not care to exercise it. We do not know what tutors were provided for her granddaughters at Whitehall, but it is likely that they were taught by the Countess's chaplain or perhaps one or other of the many dissenting clergymen who enjoyed her protection. By the time Eleanor Lee was six she wrote a very fine hand; though her little sister always wrote in a jagged fashion with often bizarrely idiosyncratic spelling, she prided herself as much as her uncle might on never penning a dull or predictable line. From the time she was very small Anne was determined to be a woman of wit and fashion.

Rochester never mentions his step-niece; she was to write about him at length in an elegy on his death in July 1680. In it she claimed that Rochester was her pride, the 'cause' of all her 'hopes and fears', and her guide. Speaking of herself she said:

> He led thee up the steep and high ascent
> To Poetry. The sacred way he went
> He taught thy Infant Muse . . .

It is not easy to think of Rochester instructing a girl poet until we remember that on the relatively rare occasions when Rochester was obliged to spend time at Adderbury, he and his young wife, Elizabeth Malet, diverted themselves by exchanging verses and working on compositions together. Among the Portland manuscripts at the University of Nottingham are drafts of poems in Rochester's hand and in his wife's; copies of the same poems kept at Longleat have written among the names in the margin 'Mrs Whorton', the married name of Anne Lee, which seems to indicate that she was sometimes a member of the versifying crew at Adderbury.

It would be strange if little Anne Lee had not been more than a little in love with her glamorous uncle, whom she saw mostly in his element at court, where no one was wilder, no one more amorous and no one funnier. She knew of his bravery at sea against the Dutch, and of his courtship of Elizabeth Malet, his attempt to kidnap her, and his spell in the Tower as a consequence, and exactly when his reluctant bride succumbed. She must have been there when the king and queen saw Rochester and his bride abed at Whitehall.

Apart from his close friends, few men liked Rochester, but women adored him, partly because he was fascinated by them. When he was in love, he was irresistible, but he seldom remained in love for long. If little Anne Lee was in love with her uncle, she almost certainly decided to emulate him, if only to be a little closer to him. The most ambitious way of doing that was to write poetry. We do not know how old Anne Lee was when she wrote this elegant pastoral song:

> How hardly I concealed my tears,
>   How oft did I complain,
> When many tedious days my fears
>   Told me I loved in vain.
>
> But now my joys as wild are grown,
>   And hard to be concealed:
> Sorrow may make a silent moan,
>   But joy will be revealed.
>
> I tell it to the bleating flocks,
>   To every stream and tree,
> And bless the hollow murmuring rocks,
>   For echoing back to me.
>
> Thus you may see with how much joy
>   We want, we wish, believe;
> 'Tis hard such passion to destroy,
>   But easy to deceive.

Rochester used this metre many times, both in such amorous songs as 'An age in her embraces past' and 'Phyllis be gentler I advise' and in parodies of the convention, such as 'By all love's soft yet mighty powers'. More revealing of her uncle's influence, however, is the sharp modulation of the exultant tone of the song in the very last line. The poem is suddenly flipped over by the terse suggestion that the happiness in the poem is, in Rochester's phrase, 'The perfect joy of being well-deceived'.

By the time she wrote this song Anne Lee was almost certainly married, for she was matched in haste in September 1673, when she was fourteen, to Thomas Wharton, the son and heir of a Presbyterian nobleman and exactly the same age as her uncle. Thomas was no courtier but a sportsman who was heavily involved in breeding and training horses at his stables at Winchendon and in racing them against all comers but principally against his political opponents, the court party. According to his eccentric brother, Goodwin Wharton, Anne Lee was already sexually experienced when she was married to Thomas Wharton. In his unpublished autobiography, Goodwin claimed that she was debauched 'for money when mighty young by Lord Peterborough'. The Lord Peterborough in question is Henry Mordaunt, second Earl of Peterborough, Groom of the Stole to the Duke of York. Goodwin was often deranged and always gullible, but he was also utterly sincere. If he believed that Anne had been deflowered by a courtier thirty-five years older than she, modern scholars have no information to refute it. His informant must have been his brother, unless it was Anne herself. The oddness of the circumstance that she was debauched for money adds to the plausibility of the allegation; Anne Hyde's court was more elegant than that of the king. Though Anne's half of the Danby estate was worth more than £50,000, she may well have had very little cash to spend on the fine clothing necessary to cut a decent figure among the best-dressed women in the kingdom. Perhaps Goodwin actually means that Peterborough paid a servant to give him access to the child and simply raped her.

There is no indication in the surviving documentation of the family that anyone else so much as suspected such a horrible possibility. The memoirs of the Comte de Grammont tell of a child called Sarah Cooke who was debauched at Whitehall by one of the Duchess of York's Maids of Honour. She was rescued from corruption by none other than Lord Rochester and according to Grammont, though still a child, became his mistress. Perhaps Rochester's poem 'A Song of a young Lady' is a document in this episode of Anne's life:

Ancient Person, for whom I
All the flattering youth defy,
Long be it ere thou grow old,
Aching, shaking, crazy, cold,
But still continue as thou art,
Ancient person of my heart.

On thy withered lips and dry,
Which like barren furrows lie,
Brooding kisses I will pour,
Shall thy youthful heat restore,
Such kind show'rs in autumn fall,
And a second spring recall,
Nor from thee will ever part,
Ancient person of my heart.

Thy nobler part, which but to name
In our sex would be counted shame,
By age's frozen grasp possessed
From his ice shall be released
And, soothed by my reviving hand,
In former warmth and vigour stand.
All a lover's wish can reach
For thy joy my love shall teach
And for thy pleasure shall improve
All that art can add to love.
Yet still I love thee without art,
Ancient person of my heart.

The odd combination of innocence and corruption in this poem is exactly what one would expect of a child who seduced and was seduced by an old gentleman. Rochester had imagination enough to have invented it, but it may be that he actually witnessed something like it. As for the possibility that Rochester took his niece away from her seducer and made her his mistress, Goodwin's character of Anne goes on to say that she had an affair of long duration with her uncle Rochester. Grammont is a falsifier, if only because the law of libel required him to conceal the actual identity of some of the characters in his memoirs. Lord Peterborough was alive and holding important office at court when Grammont was writing; Anne and her uncle

Rochester were both dead. The child in Grammont's story is supposed to be the niece of the Mother of the Maids; the story he tells might have been as true of the granddaughter of the Groom of the Stole. The possibility that Anne Lee was abused at Whitehall is distressing to contemplate; it becomes tragic when we realize that Lord Peterborough, who had served in the navy and as Governor of Tangier, died an old man, but riddled with venereal infection. A satirist of 1690 or so saw him in these terms:

> A walking mummy in a word;
> Moves clothed in plasters aromatic,
> And flannel, by the help of stick,
> And like a grave and noble peer
> Outlives his sense by sixty year; . . .
> By pox and whores long since undone,
> Yet love it still and fumbles on.

Anne Wharton had her first recorded serious illness in March 1670, when she was almost eleven. Her sister had had smallpox in November; the letters of the Countess and the trustees refer to the girls' having survived 'smallpox and measles', so we may be sure that Anne's affliction involved skin lesions, though it seems odd that she was ill so long after her sister if she was suffering from the same diseases. What was wrong with her may have been primary syphilis. She was never to bear a child that we know of; by the time she was twenty she had begun to be troubled by 'convulsion fitts', attacks of severe and very painful cramping in her muscles, and then by 'imposthumes' or swellings in her throat that threatened to suffocate her, intense headaches and inflammations of her eyes. She died in dreadful agony after months of suffering on 29 October 1685. She was twenty-six. Six months before she died she made over her whole estate to her husband, to the intense chagrin of her family and friends, who considered that Wharton had neglected her and knew that he had been unfaithful to her. If Anne had been syphilitic at the time of her marriage or had contracted the disease outside marriage, her husband would have had the right to put her away and to take her settlement lands for his sole use. Perhaps Anne gave her estate away to avoid the scandal that revelation of the truth would have given, as well as to make up to her husband for the wrong done to him. And perhaps all this speculation is unwarranted.

Though we have only Goodwin Wharton's allegation to prove that Anne Wharton had a sexual relationship with her uncle Rochester, her poetry is proof that she felt a deep intellectual and spiritual affinity with him. She began her poetic career as a libertine in her uncle's mould. She believed as he did that 'The poet's talent is to love and rail', and love and rail she did. Like her uncle she was deeply sceptical. When she was brought to her conjugal dwelling at Winchendon, the court came into the country, and religion went out the door. Anne may have expected to live much as she had done at Whitehall and at Adderbury, but if so she reckoned without her husband's power to keep her rusticated for months at a time. The £600 a year that she was to have for her personal maintenance was not paid for years on end. It was not long before her poetry took on the cynical, almost despairing tone of Rochester in his blackest mood.

> Raising my drooping head, o'er charged with thought,
> Having each scene of life before me brought;
> I chid myself because I durst repine
> At nature's Laws, or those that were divine.
> Throughout the whole creation 'tis the same,
> The fuel is devoured by the flame;
> Each peaceful, harmless, unoffending thing
> Is to the offender made an offering . . .

The grief and anger of this poem, called 'My Fate', are nothing as simple as self-pity, for the poet specifically rules out the suggestion that she has been unusually unlucky. The thread of her argument is interrupted by an admonition to herself to presume not the ways of God to scan, in which the reflection that the innocent son of God was made a 'victim to the vilest' simply reinforces her main point. She continues:

> The harmless dove the falcon doth betray;
> The lamb is to the wolf become a prey;
> And man whom free will Heaven doth impart,
> To follow still the counsels of his heart,
> Is wracked with doubt; if harmless, he designs
> Peace to his heart, and still his wish confines,
> Justice to peace, and love to quiet joins.

> Why then, the dove-like fate will sure be his;
> Short is his life, unsettled is his bliss.
> Hard fate! that choice we eagerly pursue
> Is or to be undone or to undo.

We may wonder at the precise cause of so much bitterness in a woman so rich and so young. Women of Anne's class did not expect to marry for love or that their husbands should be faithful, but they did expect to bear their husbands' children. Their dignity too was to be upheld; they were not to be humiliated by obvious neglect. One recurring theme in Anne Wharton's work that is not to be found in her uncle's is that of intense loneliness. Though she was surrounded by servants, some of whom, her waiting gentlewomen for example, may have expected to be her friends, she felt herself to be living in complete isolation. In a poem addressed to her friend Lady Anne Coke, she talked of 'Treading the maze of doubtful fate alone' for nine years until she had the good fortune to meet with her friend again:

> Why did we meet so soon again to part?
> Though patient as a god, 'twould break my heart.
> With greater ease the body might resign
> Her wedded soul and grow to earth again.
> 'Tis natural to love as well as live;
> Nature joins them. Love does our union give;
> And much I fear the knot so firm was tied,
> The fatal Sisters do the thread divide.
> Why say I fear? Joy with my life I'll twine
> And, if one breaks, the other I'll resign.

Lady Anne was something of a libertine herself. Within a year of her marriage to the 'great Coke of Norfolk' she is supposed to have been found in bed with the Duke of Monmouth. Subsequently she was rusticated like Anne, and compelled to live on her husband's estate in Norfolk and bear his children, until he died of smallpox in 1679.

As Mrs Wharton fretted and pined in the country, she wrote an odd autobiographical poem about the twisted thread of her life:

> Ah for what crimes am I condemned to live?
> Else I might wander through unbounded air
> And learn to comprehend the secrets there,
> What rules are kept by every spark of light,
> Which forces day instead of shady night,
> What makes each day revive and still seem new
> And makes the working Sun one track pursue,
> What makes a gay variety appear
> Through all the seasons of the fertile year.

Anne's notion that she would have enjoyed life more as a disembodied spirit exploring the universe and investigating the principles of its organization is hardly a Christian one. In Rochester's satire 'Of Mankind' there are two distinct voices. One argues a case rather like Anne's view of spiritual inquiry:

> Reason, by whose aspiring influence,
> We take a flight beyond material sense,
> Dive into mysteries, then soaring pierce
> The flaming limits of the universe,
> Search heaven and hell, find out what's acted there,
> And give the world true grounds of hope and fear.

The other, principal voice in the poem rejects this view for a distrust of human intellectual activity as intrinsically self-deluding. According to Gilbert Burnet, Rochester and his closest friends occasionally attended an atheist conventicle in a nobleman's house; there is no obvious reason Anne Wharton could not have taken part in their discussions. Perhaps Rochester was the only person who cared sufficiently to encourage her to express her doubt and despair or to argue with her about the relative merits of faith and reason. If this was in fact the case, Anne's celebration in her elegy of her uncle as her moral preceptor can be seen to be no more than the truth.

> Weep drops of blood, my heart, thou'st lost thy pride
> The cause of all thy hopes and fears, thy guide.
> He would have led thee right in wisdom's way,
> And 'twas thy fault whene'er thou went'st astray.
> And since thou strayed'st when guided and led on,

> Thou surely wilt be lost when left alone . . .
> He civilised the rude and taught the young,
> Made fools grow wise, such artful magic hung
> Upon his useful, kind, instructing tongue.

The idea of 'unbounded air' as her element preoccupied Anne's imagination; she was to return to it again and again, sometimes longing to fly on the viewless winds and sometimes dreading it. She could not comprehend God and she knew it was not her fault that she could not.

> How should a finite creature know the store
> Of infinite, who is himself so poor?

She would do the will of God, if only she could understand what that will might be:

> That will so darkned o'er with mystery.
> We know not what his will exacteth here,
> Less can we know what 'twill command us there.
> Here I'm lost again. Never the dead
> Return'd to tell what was a soul when fled.
> Of what we there may do we here may boast,
> But there for ought we know all thought is lost.

When she came to show this poem to Burnet he told her he was sorry to find her quarrelling with her maker. Instead of taking issue with her and taking care to refute her argument, he scolded her. He showed the poem to the Whig *salonnière* Lady Ranelagh, and she was equally put out. They all knew her uncle's great sceptical poems, especially 'Of Mankind' and 'Upon nothing' and so did Anne, but there was an important difference between her and her uncle in this regard. He knew the world of men; she knew only her own blighted, limited, sequestered life.

Like her uncle Rochester, Anne Wharton was intensely interested in the theatre. Rochester adapted Beaumont and Fletcher's *Valentinian* for the stage and wrote a completely original play called 'Sodom'. Anne wrote an equally original play called 'Love's Martyr'. She took for her plot the entirely fictitious love affair between the great poet

Ovid and Julia, supposed to be the daughter of Augustus Caesar. Out of it she made a verse tragedy of more than 3,000 lines, about a quarter of them rhyming couplets. In the play all beholders believe that Julia is the most beautiful creature ever to exist on earth; she is destined to be the chaste spouse of her father's elected heir, Marcellus, but, though her father thinks she 'has not learnt to love', she has given her heart to Ovid.

> Doubt not my Ovid, but I'll still be true;
> No monarch e'er possess'd such charms as you.
> Let meaner souls the diadem admire,
> 'Tis wit not crowns can set my heart on fire.

Among the notions that Anne and her uncle held in common was the idea of the man – or woman – of wit. In the seventeenth century 'wit' was the name given to the faculty of active discrimination; it dictated both taste and morality. To be dull was to be gross, heavy, bestial; to be witty was to be light, graceful, puzzling and exciting. The man of wit would risk all for a wicked observation; if his desire to coruscate on thin ice led him so far that his *jeux d'esprit* became public, he risked utter disgrace. In the poem that was best known to his contemporaries Rochester has a female poet, called Artemiza, animadvert on the perils that lay in the path of the man of wit:

> How many bold Advent'rers for the bays
> Proudly designing large returns of praise,
> Who durst that stormy pathless world explore,
> Were soon dashed back and wrecked on the dull shore,
> Broke of that little stock they had before?

Love and wit went together; the man of wit was always in love but only for as long as he was not bored. Anne's understanding of the distinction between the amorous wit and the unfeeling fool could have been learned at her uncle's knee.

> There is an art in loving fools ne'er know;
> A fool can neither be discreet nor true.
> Love all his charms to witty men reveals
> But from the dull his smallest arts conceals.

The same could be argued for the woman of wit. Julia is in love with Ovid because he is the wittiest man in Caesar's court, and therefore can appreciate not only her beauty but her sparkling intelligence. The dog-like devotion of her betrothed, Marcellus, does not move her; rather than become Marcellus's wife, she has chosen to become Ovid's mistress. Ovid is duly sensible of the honour done him:

> I nothing can return but constancy
> For all those blessings which you daily give,
> For all those ecstasies which I receive,
> And when I fail in that, to every slave
> May I become a scorn, may I be prized
> By fools, and by all witty men despised.

Anne Wharton's love idealism owes more to French novels like *Artamène: Le Grand Cyrus* than it does to Rochester, but her insistence upon the importance of 'kindness', that is, sexual generosity, does not derive from French notions of gallantry. Not only does she suggest that sexual enjoyment is an end worth pursuing in itself, she implies that only the witty can master the 'arts of pleasure'. Ovid exults over the natural lover Tibullus:

> Sure you are not a poet. Them we call
> Love's priests, but you (I'm sure) ne'er understood
> The mysteries of that delightful god.
> 'Tis love alone exalts. Were she I love
> The meanest thing on earth, when loved by me
> She then becomes (to me) not only princess
> But goddess, such is love's exalted power.

Any reader of 'Love's Martyr' is sorely tempted to discern contemporary references in it. The Ovid–Julia motif was adopted by Aphra Behn in order to write about the courtship of the Princess Anne by John Sheffield, Earl of Mulgrave, in 1682. Mulgrave was a poet of sorts, especially when he availed himself of the collaboration of Dryden, but he was also the implacable and bitter enemy of Rochester. Anne Wharton may have heard of Mulgrave's challenge to Rochester in November 1669, and must have encountered Mulgrave's endless elaboration of the unsubtantiated story of Rochester's cowardice on that occasion; she probably knew of Rochester's caricatures of Mulgrave in 'A Very Heroical Epistle in Answer to Ephelia' and 'My Lord All-Pride'. Anne Wharton's editors date 'Love's Martyr' to 1679, which is too early for any reference to Mulgrave's ambition to marry a member of the royal family. What is more, the representation of a princess of the blood as a poet's complaisant mistress would have been a clear-cut case of *scandalum magnatum*.

A better candidate for Ovid might be Rochester's young protégé John Grubham Howe, who was disgraced and banished from the court in 1679 for claiming to have enjoyed the favours of the Duchess of Richmond.

> Jack How, Sir Jervois How's brother, a young amorous spark of the Court, has for some months declared a very great veneration for the Duchess of Richmond; but her Grace, neither regarding Will of the Wisp nor his feigned fires, has at length converted the Squires soft passion into revenge. Whereupon he has of late reported that he has had testimonies of her kindness, as well by letters as otherwise. As soon as the Duchess understood this malicious report she forthwith made her application to the King, who was pleased to refer the matter to the Duke of Monmouth, the Earl of Essex, my Lord Sunderland and the Earl of Halifax. Upon inquiry, their lordships found that, amongst the many evidences of her Grace's favour that Mr. How had boasted of, he could only produce one letter, which the King, as soon as he saw, said was neither her hand nor style; whereupon his majesty was pleased to give order that he forthwith refrain from coming to Court.

Not everybody was convinced by the king's defence of the reputation of *la belle* Stuart, whom he had courted unsuccessfully for himself. The satirists continued to include Jack Howe among the recipients of the duchess's favours for years afterwards. Howe and Anne Wharton shared an aunt, but more important than this connection must be Howe's friendship with Anne's uncle Rochester. According to the satirists, it was Rochester 'who soothed him first into opinion of being a wit'. Howe was coupled with Rochester by Dryden and Mulgrave in *The Essay on Satire* as well. An anonymous satire of 1680 says of him:

> His whole design is to be thought a wit,
> Therefore this freedom takes to farther it . . .
> His person he too much admires and strove
> Once to be thought renowned for feats of love.
> But to his constancy and trust in those,
> Churchill reports and Richmond too well knows.

Jack Howe's poetry has never been collected but, as well as satires, it includes a couple of cavalier songs in the same mode as Anne Wharton's, and a dialogue in a similar spirit, beginning 'You say 'tis love creates the pain'. The Mary Howe to whom 'Love's Martyr' is dedicated may have been Jack Howe's sister. The dedication claims, in what one hopes is an exaggerated compliment, that she alone made the happiness of Anne's life.

The possibility that Ovid contains elements of Rochester should not be automatically discounted. Rochester's translation of *Amores* 2.9 circulated extensively in manuscript; even better known was 'The Imperfect Enjoyment', an exercise in the vein of *Amores* 3.7. Rochester was several times banished from the court. He was sent to France in 1669 for boxing Tom Killigrew's ears in the royal presence. In 1674 he inadvertently showed the king a libel upon himself and was obliged to withdraw; in 1675 he smashed the king's sundial and was probably rusticated again. In the late summer of 1675 he was banished from court for a prolonged period as a result of offending the Duchess of Portsmouth, in what way we do not know. It was probably during these suspensions of his duties as courtier that Anne Wharton saw the most of him in the years after her marriage. After his appointment as Keeper of Woodstock Park in 1674, Rochester lived at High Lodge when he was in the country, rather than with his mother, his wife and his four children at Adderbury. Echoes of Rochester abound in 'Love's Martyr', which is more fulsome and less ironic than anything Rochester permitted himself to pen on the subject of sexual relations. However, the germ may be in one of Rochester's most imitated passages, the praise of love in *A Letter from Artemiza in the Town to Chloe in the Country*.

> Love, the most generous passion of the mind,
> The softest refuge innocence can find,
> The safe director of unguided youth,

Fraught with kind wishes and secured by truth;
That cordial drop heaven in our cup has thrown
To make the nauseous draught of life go down;
In which one only blessing, God might raise
In lands of atheists, subsidies of praise,
For none did e'er so dull and stupid prove
But felt a god and blest his power in love.

Artemiza, the young and witty woman poet, could be thought to bear some resemblance to Anne Wharton, though 'Love's Martyr' demonstrates the opposite of Artemiza's conviction that women prefer fools as lovers. In 'Love's Martyr' there are many versions of Artemiza's praise of love; the most obviously related to Rochester's is spoken by Tibullus in Act IV:

Almighty love, how powerful is thy sway.
The wisest souls thy gentle snares betray.
Unpolished statesmen mild and gentle grow,
When once they to thy mighty sceptre bow,
And the rough warrior, when to thee he yields,
Quits all the fierceness he hath learnt in fields,
Changing his warlike frowns for sighs and tears.
Nay, the fair sex quit all their wonted fears,
And grow as bold as men, when once their breast
By that all conquering victor is possessed.

Ovid is probably also Ovid, but Mrs Wharton's notion of the court of Augustus is anything but historical. The poets Tibullus and Cornelius Gallus are contemporaries of Ovid only in Jonson's play *Poetaster*, which may have been one of Mrs Wharton's sources. She may also have been influenced by Nat Lee's play *Gloriana*, but her Julia is not the virtuous heroine of *Gloriana* but reviled in the play as 'queen of prostitutes'. Throughout the play Julia and Ovid talk of dying for love, of love and during love, in an extraordinary confusion of the semantics of orgasm and death, but it is Julia who, when she hears that Ovid is banished, fatally stabs herself in the last scene. The court of Rome is an idealized version of Whitehall, which Anne Wharton remembered as the realm of love and wit; of Charles II she was to write in a poem advising Burnet to cast himself upon the king's mercy:

> His anger like the wrath of heav'n is slow
> And all his actions his compassion show.
> Injustice never can his temper suit;
> Love, gentle Love, is his blessed attribute.
> A soul inclined to such a peaceful charm,
> No fear of danger could his soul alarm;
> Plot upon Plot, intended or devised,
> He smiled to see, looked over and despised.
> When every subject at his danger shook,
> His thoughts flowed easily as a summer's brook.
> He pardoned still and when, unruly, they
> Forced him the Sword of Justice to display,
> Unwillingly he punished to obey.
> I say to obey for, might he still command,
> Garlands of peace would grow within his hand.
> Then love and wit, in which he does excel,
> With peace and plenty here would ever dwell.

This is an uncritical view of Rochester's 'easiest king and best-bred man alive', who 'never said a foolish thing' if he never did a wise one. Charles II probably was the nearest thing to a father Anne Wharton ever had. She grew up with his many bastard children; her grandmother was the Duchess of Cleveland's friend; when she was to be married the king wrote urging that she be married to the son and heir of his loyal servant Sir Richard Arundel of Trerice. If Caesar is a figure of Anne's father surrogate, perhaps Julia is an account of Anne herself. If so, Ovid could well be a figure of Rochester, though it must be pointed out that in the third and last part of his character of his sister-in-law, Goodwin Wharton alleges that she had a brief affair with Jack Howe as well. None of these parallels should be over-strained; their relevance could only emerge if we learned more about both Anne and Rochester, and probably not even then.

Mrs Wharton's first attacks of serious illness probably came upon her while she was working on her play. In 1680 a long episode of repeated seizures from April to May left her too weak to leave London. At Woodstock, Rochester lay dying, while his mother battled for his soul, assisted by her chaplain, Robert Parsons. In June Anne was well enough to be brought to Winchendon, but so weakened by the long bout of illness that she could do no more than send a servant the twenty miles or so to inquire after her uncle. When he died on 26 July, she penned his elegy.

> He was – but I want words and ne'er can tell,
> But this I know he did mankind excel.
> He was what no man ever was before
> Nor can indulgent nature give us more
> For to make him, she exhausted all her store . . .

Of all the people affected by the news of Rochester's deathbed conversion, none took it more to heart than Anne Wharton.

> God saw and loved him, saw this chiefest part
> Of his creation from his precepts start,
> Blessed him with dying pains and gave him more
> In that last mournful gift than all before,
> Gave him a penitence, so fixed, so true,
> A greater penitence, no saint e'er knew
> Which done, the merciful Creator said
> 'This creature of my own is perfect made,
> No longer fit to dwell with men below,
> He'll be a wonder amongst angels now.'

The image of union in death that was the staple of 'Love's Martyr' she now adapted for her love for her uncle.

> With ecstasy these thoughts inflame my mind.
> Methinks I leave this case of flesh behind
> And to him, winged with joy, out-fly the wind.

Jack Howe and Aphra Behn too wrote elegies on Rochester, and Mrs Wharton's brief literary career began with poetic exchanges with both of them. She was so involved in following her uncle's spiritual journey that she wrote a paraphrase of Isaiah:53, the chapter of the Old Testament that had so vividly affected her dying uncle 'that he did ever after as firmly believe in his Saviour as if he had seen him in the clouds'. The syntax of her imitation reveals that faith came less easily to her.

> Who hath believed on earth what we report?
> Our breath to flying wind's become a sport.
> Thy wonders Lord can never be concealed
> And yet, alas, to whom was this revealed?

Within weeks she was desperately ill with her seizures again, this time with the complication of an abscess in her throat which her attendants thought would kill her, but Anne was strong. It was decided that her husband should take her to Paris for specialist treatment. By the time she left, in late February 1681, she had begun to look forward to death as a release; the storminess of the crossing brought peace instead of terror to her heart. Once she was settled in Paris, Thomas returned to London for the sitting of Parliament. Though she was struggling with a paraphrase of Jeremiah and still pursuing the elusive consolations of faith, as well as enduring the appalling tortures of the treatment, Anne wrote to her husband the light, polite letters of a woman of wit and fashion, mocking herself in Rochester's vein.

The first surviving letter is dated 22 March.

Forgive me for giving you the trouble of a letter every post, but I am indeed grown so fond a fool that I can't help it; the other day, in a fit, I almost beat my brains out against the pavement and found the want of boards. For a little more and it had eased you of the inconvenience of a wife. But, *à propos de bottes*, that day your brother Hampden met Mr Savile in my lodging and, not knowing him, began extremely to complain of the King's ambassador for not giving an information which he thought necessary. The fat person, wanting temper, began too quick to clear himself and so discovered himself to the lean person, and spoiled a hopeful adventure. And then laid the fault upon innocent I who sat harmlessly meditating a quarrel between famine and plenty. As it happened there was no more but an excuse made by your friend, which was odd enough, but yet not worth giving you the trouble of relating. He seemed troubled for not seeing you before you left Paris, but I told him you did not know where to find him or had certainly seen him. He is much recovered, which signifies no more than the rest. You see how loth I am to leave off. These are fine things to

I. Sappho, the oldest known image, from a sixth-century BC Greek vase

2. Sappho, a fin-de-siècle version by Félicien Rops;
the frontispiece to Mallarmé's *Les Poesies*

3. 'The Nine Living Muses of Great Britain', by Richard Samuel, 1779.
The sitters are (standing, left to right): Elizabeth Carter, Anna Laetitia
Barbauld, Elizabeth Anne Sheridan, Hannah More, Charlotte Lennox;
(seated, left to right): Angelica Kauffmann, Catharine Macaulay,
Elizabeth Montagu, Elizabeth Griffith
(*By courtesy of the National Portrait Gallery, London*)

4. (*Left*) Veronica Franco
(1546–91)
5. (*Below*) Gaspara Stampa
(*c.*1523–54)

6. Katherine Phillips, 'the matchless Orinda' (1632–64)
(*By courtesy of the National Portrait Gallery, London*)

7. Lady Mary Wroth (1587–1653)
(Reproduced by permission of Viscount De L'Isle, from his private collection)

8. (*Right*) Anne Wharton (?1632–85)
9. (*Below*) Anne Killigrew (1660–85),
   a self-portrait (*By courtesy of the
   National Portrait Gallery, London*)

10. Aphra Behn (1639–89). It was not uncommon for engravings to lose or change their identifications. These two engravings are clearly of different women: (*left*) an engraving by R. White after Riley; (*below*) an engraving by Fittler (*By courtesy of the National Portrait Gallery, London*)

11. Margaret Cavendish, Duchess of Newcastle (*c.*1624–74)
(*By courtesy of the National Portrait Gallery, London*)

12. Anne Finch, Countess of Winchilsea (1661–1720)
(*By courtesy of the National Portrait Gallery, London*)

13. Laetitia Landon (L. E. L.) (1802–38),
engraving after Daniel Maclise, from 'Maclise's Portrait Gallery'

14. 'Regina's Maids of Honour', engraving after Daniel Maclise. The sitters are (anti-clockwise, from right): Lady Blessington, Caroline Norton, Jane Porter, Harriet Martineau, Mary Russell Mitford, Anna Marie Fielding, Letitia Landon, Lady Morgan (*By courtesy of the British Library*)

15. Felicia Hemans (1793–1835) (*By courtesy of the National Portrait Gallery*)

16. (*Above*) Elizabeth Barrett Browning with Pen, Rome, 1860
(*The Master and Fellows of Balliol College, Oxford; photo: Thomas Photos*)

17. Christina Rossetti (1830–94). (*Facing page, above*) At seventeen, a
Pre-Raphaelite beauty, painted by her brother Dante Gabriel Rossetti (*private
collection*); (*facing page, below*) a year later, a portrait by James Collison, the
suitor who was soon to be rejected on religious grounds

18. Amy Levy (1861–89)

entertain you with, but rather than say nothing, I could talk all
day idly to you, as if you had no more business or sense than

Your obedient humble servant

Thin John Hampden was Thomas Wharton's political colleague;
fat Henry Savile, Rochester's good friend and correspondent, was the
ambassador. Thomas did not trouble himself to reply. Anne wrote as
often as she could.

Though I never hear from you, I cannot give over the custom
of writing to you every post, but I think I may complain a little
of you for it. I was at Charenton on Easter day and was here
shrewdly censured to be a Presbyterian for forsaking Mr Savile's
congregation. But the true reason was I went not to Church for
company, and therefore thought myself better amongst forty
thousand strangers, that it was probable would take little notice
of me, than five hundred that I knew ... I am threatened
mightily I shall be visited. I give it out 'They do me a great deal
of honour but I shall return none, not being able', and can
hardly keep myself from being rude, which for your sake I
would avoid, it not becoming one who hath the honour of
being your obedient wife & humble servant.

Like her uncle, Anne made a point of bearing herself like a person
of quality. The more upset she was, the more coolly she wrote.
Though Thomas ignored her letters, she continued to write, apologizing only for not following the protocol that required her to wait for a
reply before writing again. Her next surviving letter, dated 4 April,
was endorsed: 'These For the Honourable my Spouse if he pleaseth'.
In that letter she told Thomas that 'Mrs Loftus goeth to Bourbon on
Friday and into her lodgings (the same day) go I.' Her next letter
contained the macabre news that Mrs Loftus had succumbed to the
disease and/or the treatment and she had taken over the same bed:

I have been yesterday, tonight, and all this morning, so ill that I
was very likely, from Mrs Loftus's bed, to have taken the long
journey which she took out of it. And I therefore resolved as
soon as I was a little better to write to you, (lest I should never

do it more) . . . I hear the poor House of Commons were very
roughly dealt with. They have no virtue left (that I know of)
but patience, to make use of, and they say that is the coward's
virtue but yet I hope they will practise it in their affliction,
which I cannot be very sorry for, because I am the more likely
to see you here. You see how public misfortunes bring private
satisfactions. Goodbye my dear best dear. Pardon me that I say
no more for I am so very ill I can hardly hold the pen, or know
what I write . . .

Despite Thomas's silence, Anne persevered.

To begin a letter orderly and discreetly, I must first beg your
pardon for writing so often and then make an excuse for saying
so little as I shall be now forced to do, being just let blood and
not well able to stir my arm. This is orderly, but I think 'tis
enough of both. I will then go on to tell you that I was
yesterday at St Germain's which is not worth seeing, and fell
down on the top of the house and strained my leg . . . pray send me
some news. I know nought but that Mrs H's nose is red & her
husband's blue. My Doctor forbade me wine and let me drink
nothing but barley water and liquorice and improve daily in
patience. If I writ not this you'd think me drunk for the rest.

In the next surviving letter, dated 14 May, Anne gave a wry
account of the Countess of Rochester:

My grandmother writes me very many kind letters and, I find,
is very impatient to have me home again, telling me that I have
an odd fate upon me to fly my friends, neglect my health, and
not care to live, for if that were my design I should not have left
England, that I get no health, and upon all other accounts, if I
thought so, she thinks I were better there.

Though Anne wanted to stay in France, and to travel south to
Montpellier, being sure she would die if forced to return to England,
her husband required her at home. Days after her return Rochester's
widow died suddenly 'of an apoplexy'; in November, when the
young Earl of Rochester died, three months before his eleventh

birthday, Anne wrote another elegy and once more celebrated her uncle:

> That wondrous wit which graced his father's breath
> He did to him by legacy bequeath,
> And, though ten winters he had never told,
> He seemed in wit and sacred learning old.

By the summer of 1682, Anne's health had seriously deteriorated again and it was becoming clear that her illness was terminal. Still under the spell of Rochester's conversion, she sought the acquaintance of Gilbert Burnet, who had rushed into print with an account of Rochester's deathbed and was by now famous as the mediator of his conversion. Anne immediately invited him to do the same for her, for despite her pious exercises her faith was as unsteady as ever. Burnet evidently did not understand that her interest in him was primarily dictated by her obsession with everything that concerned her uncle. For her part Anne did not even pretend to be convinced by his arguments for natural religion; she was much more preoccupied with her own inability to perceive the workings of an active providence. In vain Burnet remonstrated with her, and advised her to strike out the offending passages in the poems she sent him:

> The use of knowledge is to find it poor;
> We know 'tis less by seeking to know more.
> We seek and wish, but all we can obtain
> Is to be sure we've sought and wished in vain.
> The life of man on time's swift wings does fly;
> We snatch at all in haste but, ere we die,
> Can only reach at dark uncertainty.
> In ignorance the busy world rolls on;
> The spark of life so soon away is blown.
> We live to doubt and, ere that doubt's resolved,
> In death's dark mists the working soul's dissolved.
> He's happiest who ne'er has reach'd so far,
> Who, blind with ignorance, ne'er feared despair,
> Submits to guides and thinks their way is clear,
> For, if he aims to see, it is to find
> Not only he but all his guides are blind.

> Unhappy then, benighted and undone,
> He wildly wanders and himself would shun,
> Courts Death like me, and thinks there may be light,
> Would venture gladly for it through the night,
> But when 'tis near he starts and fain would know,
> Before he ventures, whether he's to go,
> And what it is he to death's altar brings,
> Asks why Heaven makes these weak, imperfect things,
> And, till he knows, would pinion time's swift wings.
> All's one, murm'ring or pleased he still obeys,
> Death claims his right, and weary life decays.

If Burnet recognized this as an imitation of Rochester's satire 'Of Reason and Mankind', he did not say so. Anne Wharton's rejection of human knowledge is a slip from the stock of Rochester's attack on reason, the will-o'-the-wisp,

> Which leaving light of nature, sense behind,
> Pathless and dang'rous wand'ring ways it takes
> Through error's fenny bogs and thorny brakes,
> Whilst the misguided follower climbs with pain
> Mountains of whimsies, heaped in his own brain,
> Stumbling from thought to thought falls headlong down
> Into doubt's boundless sea . . .

The dissolution of the soul in death's dark mists is Anne's version of Rochester's soul drowning in doubt's boundless sea, but unlike her uncle she does not see doubt as the result of a misguided use of intelligence. Rochester's rejection of reason was a continuation of the old Christian homiletic theme 'de contemptu mundi'. Anne Wharton's mental anguish was caused by ineradicable doubt of the goodness of God. If God created man to know, love and serve him, why has he at the same time made man incapable of knowing him at all, truly loving him or faithfully serving him? Her conclusion, that the unquestioning soul is the happy soul, is the same as Rochester's but her meaning is blacker and more hopeless than anything Rochester permitted himself. Rochester too envisions a soul that has groped towards the wrong conclusion:

> Then old age and experience, hand in hand,
> Lead him to death, and make him understand
> After a search so painful and so long
> That all his life he has been in the wrong . . .

Anne was such a soul, but she was never to accumulate the old age or the experience.

Burnet may seriously have meant to help Anne Wharton confront her grim destiny of intense suffering and early death by imbuing her with Christian faith, but he went quite the wrong way about it. Instead of crediting her genuine struggle to make sense of her life, he reprimanded her for entertaining ungodly thoughts, in brusque authoritarian words that he would not have permitted himself to use with Rochester. Unable to choose between a manner sickeningly obsequious, grotesquely gallant or simply bumptious, he alternately grovelled, simpered and nagged. His worst mistake was to insist not only that Anne read 'An Essay upon Poetry', in which Rochester was belittled and derided, but that she agree with him and the entire anti-Rochester cabal that it was 'one of the perfectest pieces of poetry . . . ever writ'. Burnet confessed to disagreeing with a couple of lines that related to her uncle. Those lines were more than a couple:

> Such nauseous songs as the late convert made,
> Which justly call this censure on his shade;
> Not that warm thoughts of the transporting joy.
> Can shock the chastest, or the nicest cloy;
> But obscene words, too gross to move desire,
> Like heaps of fuel do but choke the fire.
> That author's name has undeserved praise,
> Who palled the appetite he meant to raise.

Anne seldom answered Burnet's screeds and the answers, when they came, were short and sometimes disobliging. Her excuse was that she was once more very ill, but Burnet noticed that she could write at length when the subject was poetry. She complained of headaches, told him she felt that death was near. Her throat abscess flared up again, but she still found energy to write sharp criticisms of *An Essay upon Poetry*. Burnet responded unabashed:

> I do not submit to your censure of the *Essay of Poetry*; and to let
> you see that it is probable I am in the right, I know all the wits
> in the town, not excepting *Dryden* for all his being ill used, are
> of my mind, that it is incomparable.

Not only Dryden but, according to Burnet, Waller 'commended
the Essay of Poetry as the most extraordinary thing that ever was
writ' and the Marquis of Halifax too, 'thought it the greatest poem,
that ever was writ'. Burnet's labouring of the point by such name-
dropping can only have infuriated Anne, even before he imparted
information that can have done him no good whatever:

> I shall next tell you, what I knew long ago, but as a secret, that
> the Earl of Mulgrave is the author of the *Essay on Poetry*.

Anne must have known that Rochester hated Mulgrave; she had
probably heard the libellous allegations of cowardice on Rochester's
part that Mulgrave continued to elaborate and repeat until his dying
day. It was because Mulgrave could not stomach the fact that Rochester, with so little apparent effort, was so much better a poet than he
that he found it necessary to revile him on every conceivable pretext.
Apart from the hiccup of his courtship of Princess Anne, which was
of a piece with his manipulation of the other court ladies who could
advance his career, Mulgrave was steadily accumulating wealth and
power, yet he still found it necessary to revenge himself upon a dead
man.

Rochester's friends could not let Mulgrave blacken Rochester's
reputation with impunity. The counter-attack involved the revival of
Rochester's *rifacimento* of Fletcher's *Valentinian* for a sumptuous per-
formance by the United Company at the Theatre Royal on 11
February 1684 with three prologues, the 'Prologue spoken by Mrs
Cook the First Day' by Aphra Behn, and the 'Prologue . . . spoken by
Mrs Cook the Second Day' by John Grubham Howe and a third
anonymous 'to be spoken by Mrs Barry', together with an Epilogue
'Written by a person of quality'. Both Howe and Behn had been
associated with Mrs Wharton in the writing of elegies on Rochester.
Jack Howe had also written a poem in praise of Mrs Wharton's
elegy.

Thus, of his dear Euridice deprived,
In numbers soft the faithful Orpheus grieved,
Thus charm'd the world, while he his pains relieved.

To hear his lyre the beasts and forests strove,
But yours alone can men and angels move,
Can teach those how to write, these how to love.

You only could deserve so good a friend,
And to be thus lamented by your pen,
Was only due to the wittiest, best of men.

His soul to heav'n he willingly resigned,
But kindly left within your matchless mind
A double portion of his wit behind.

Equal to this is the return you give,
Lofty as clouds, which did his soul receive;
His well-sung name does in your poem live.

The part of Lucina was taken by Rochester's mistress, Elizabeth Barry. The person of quality who wrote the Epilogue was probably William Fanshawe. According to Fanshawe, Rochester was demented when he visited him at Woodstock and the conversion story was hogwash. Her own experience of Burnet had probably brought Mrs Wharton to much the same conclusion.

Soon after its successful revival the play was published by Timothy Goodwin as *Valentinian. A Tragedy. As 'tis Alter'd by the late Earl of Rochester, And Acted at the Theatre-Royal with a Preface concerning the Author and his Writings. By one of his Friends*, with a date of 1685, although the book may have been printed in 1684. The friend who supplied the Preface is usually taken to be Robert Wolseley, whose slender poetic talent was fostered by Rochester, if we may take William Wharton's word.

Remember the great Rochester is dead.
Thy wit was but repeating what he said.
Of thee a necessary tool he found,
Still proud to father all that he disowned,
For which he let thee of his jests dispose
As servants flutter in their lords' old clothes . . .

He taught thee not the art to think but rhyme
Though like a clock he sometimes made thee chime
Now he can't wind thee up, thou still strik'st out of time . . .

Anne had probably known Wolseley, the eldest of the seventeen children of Lord Wharton's old friend and colleague Sir Charles Wolseley, for many years, for he had acted as tutor to William Wharton, Philip Lord Wharton's only child by his third wife, born in 1662:

Will, a pert youth, a scandal-scribbling elf
Whom Bob had bred up dully like himself.
He taught his feeble hand to trail a quill,
And nicely did direct him to write ill . . .

Wolseley's 'Preface' is less a defence of Rochester's writings than a concerted attack on *An Essay upon Poetry*. Mrs Wharton wrote a poem congratulating Wolseley 'On his Preface to Valentinian':

To you, this generous task belongs alone,
To clear the injured and instruct the town;
Where but in you is found a mind so brave
To stretch the bounds of love beyond the grave?
Anger may last, but friendships quickly die,
For anxious thoughts are longer lived than joy.
Yet those whom active fancy has misled
So far as to assault the mighty dead,
Now taught, by your reproof, a noble shame,
Will strive by surer ways to raise their fame . . .
Such are the paths to fame in which you tread,
You baffle envy, while you nobly aid
The helpless living, and more helpless dead.

The beginning of the poem has the grammar of the conferring of a commission and a persuasion to accept it. Mrs Wharton may be merely responding to the appearance of Wolseley's Preface, but the manner in which she does it suggests a more active complicity. Who could the 'helpless living' be if not she herself? Wolseley replied with ninety-nine grateful lines 'To Mrs Wharton: On a paper of Verses she did me the honour to write, in praise of the Preface to Valentinian'.

While soaring high, above Orinda's flights,
Equal to Sappho, famed Urania writes,
And, fearless of an host of biass'd men,
In my defence draws her all-conquering pen.
While forcing every caviller to submit,
Her approbation stamps my questioned wit,
And, a new way, by all the nine inspired,
Commending mine, she makes her own admired.
While that kind balm's restoring virtue cures
The critics' bite and lasting life assures,
Delight extreme, rewarding all my pain,
Spirits my genius, and improves my vein.
A useful pride the unhoped honour brings,
Like that which from a sense of virtue Springs.

In his rapture at Mrs Wharton's condescension, Wolseley was thought by some to have overdone the flattery.

Oft when, perplexed wth timorous doubt's unrest,
I read her praise in which my Muse is dress'd,
With all the grace and all the power of poetry express'd,
Raptures so strong my happier thoughts employ
As pain perception and oppress with joy.
The rich ragoût, wits's too profuse expense,
A flavour gives that conquers human sense,
A taste too high for weak man to digest . . .

The concluding passage of the poem could be thought to point to Mrs Wharton as Rochester's literary executor as well as the inheritrix of his wit.

His perishing goods to others let him leave;
To her his deathless pen he did bequeath:
And if my humble Muse, whose luckless strain
Was us'd alone of beauty to complain
And sing, in melancholy notes, love's unregarded pain,
Rais'd by that theme above her usual height,
Could clear his fame, or do his virtue right;
How well does she the trifling debt acquit,

> She whose resembling genius shows her fit
> To be his sole executrix in wit.

The satirists well knew who was involved in the mounting of the defence of Rochester against Mulgrave and there was a good deal of sympathy mixed in with the usual libels. One of the many 'Letters to Julian', a hawker of copies of anonymous satires, who was called the 'Secretary of the Muses', describes the whole undertaking, adding further names:

> Jack Howe, thy patron's left the town,
> But first writ something he dare own,
> A prologue lawfully begotten
> And full nine months maturely thought on,
> Born with hard labour and much pain;
> Wolseley was Dr Chamberlain;
> At last from stuff and rubbish picked,
> As bear cubs into shape are licked.
> When Wharton, Etherege and Soame,
> To give it the last strokes were come,
> Those critics differed in their doom.
> Some were for embers *quenched with pages*,
> And some for *mending servants' wages*.
> Both ways were tried, but neither took,
> And the fault's laid on Mrs Cook;
> Yet Swan says he admired it 'scaped,
> Since 'twas Jack Howe's, without being clapped

If the satirist is right, the revival of *Valentinian* was first mooted in June 1683, four or five months after the last surviving letter from Burnet to Mrs Wharton. The Wharton who helped to edit the Prologue is probably William. The satirist well understood that the point of the *Valentinian* project was to defend Rochester's reputation against Mulgrave's cowardly attack:

> Some say his lordship had done better
> To answer Roger Martin's letter,
> Or give Jack Howe his bellyful,

> Who justly calls him a dull owl
> For quoting books he never read,
> And basely railing at the dead.

Wolseley is now mostly known for his literary squabble with his erstwhile pupil, which ended tragically in a duel on 9 December 1687, when Wolseley dealt Wharton a wound in the buttock of which after four days he died. There is some slight evidence that this furious animosity had its genesis during the months of Anne Wharton's decline and derived some of its intensity from Wolseley's resentment of the Whartons' treatment of her. In the second poem of the sequence that led up to Dorset's poem 'The Duel', Wharton ironically congratulates Wolseley's 'costive Muse' for having at last laid down 'her painfull burden'.

> 'Tis not yet full two years since 'twas begun.

Wharton tells Wolseley to desist from certain activities, not to

> . . . heal departed souls with wit's ragoûts,
> Write verses to fair ladies when they're dead
> And prefaces which tire men to read.

Anne's life was rapidly drawing to its close but in her case we hear nothing of deathbed conversions. She may have reopened Rochester's dialogue with the deist Charles Blount, which would explain the posthumous appearance of some of her work in an anthology published by Blount's friend and protégé Charles Gildon. In May 1685, she signed the deed that gave her estate to her husband. The only personal legacy she made was to Hester Barry, Rochester's illegitimate daughter by the actress Elizabeth Barry, to whom she left the staggering sum of £3,000, presumably as a dowry, so that she could make the kind of match that befitted Rochester's daughter. The little girl, whom Anne may have met when her mother was rehearsing for the revival of *Valentinian*, did not live to enjoy her windfall.

Like her uncle, Anne was buried under a plain stone without a marker. The widower, who made no pretence of grief, afterwards, in Steele's authorized biography, *Memoirs of the life of the Most Noble Thomas late Marquess of Wharton*, gave the world to understand that his first wife's person and temper were unattractive. The world assumed therefore that she must have been an older woman of repellent piety. *The Dictionary of National Biography* adduced a birth-date for her that made her older than either of her parents, decided that her grandmother was her mother's aunt and Rochester a distant relation. Anne Wharton may or may not have been the lover of her half-uncle Rochester, but she was undeniably his most earnest admirer and disciple.

WORDSWORTH AND WINCHILSEA:
THE PROGRESS OF AN ERROR

Now that metaphysical poetry is a part of the well-trodden way of literary studies and the poetry of wit no more a curious side-track, it is no longer fashionable to treat Anne Finch, Countess of Winchilsea, as a precursor of Wordsworth. As long ago as 1945, Reuben A. Brower remarked rather crossly that,

> If Lady Winchilsea is 'prophetic' in poems such as 'Fanscombe Barn', 'The Petition for an Absolute Retreat', and 'A Nocturnal Reverie', she is prophetic of Thomson, Young, Gray and Akenside, rather than of Wordsworth.

He went on to show convincingly that her work shows clear lines of descent, finding echoes of Marvell's 'The Garden' in both 'A Nocturnal Reverie' and 'The Petition for an Absolute Retreat'. In fact 'The Petition' is written in full consciousness of Marvell's poem, and might profitably be considered an Augustan rejoinder to it. Brower correctly sees that Winchilsea is writing her own version of Marvell's extravagant description of co-operant nature in lines like

> Cherries, with the downy peach,
> All within my easy reach;
> Whilst creeping near the humble ground,
> Should the strawberry be found
> Springing whereso'er I strayed,
> Through those windings and that shade.

Brower might have taken his argument a good deal further, for Winchilsea is not here attempting what Marvell had already achieved. Rather she is civilizing him by eschewing his deliberate oddities and subjecting her own treatment of the retirement theme to the laws of taste and common sense. Not for her a garden where one is nudged by queer peaches and brought to earth by aggressive melons, or for that matter a garden which is the projection of human fantasy, replete with sexual imagery as well as platonic conundra. Her imagination dwells not on paradisaical emblems and their possible correlates in life and art, but on the actuality of country life. She writes with full awareness of her own matter-of-factness, taking as much pleasure in it as many an earlier poet might have taken in his own astonishing ingenuity. Where Marvell's intention was to show something of the mystery of the spiritual world, Winchilsea's is at least partly to characterize the world that is to be rejected, for she is quite incapable of Marvell's blithe disregard of the social dimension. So she enumerates and encapsulates the inconveniences that she trusts to be spared,

> No intruders thither come!
> Who visit, but to be from home . . .
>
> News, that charm to list'ning ears;
> That false alarm to hopes and fears;
> That common theme for every fop,
> From the statesman to the shop,
> In those coverts ne'er be spread,
> Of who's deceased, or who's to wed.
> Be no tidings thither brought,
> But silent, as midnight thought,
> Where the world may ne'er invade,
> Be those windings, and that shade.

Winchilsea's poem is inscribed to 'Arminda', the Countess of Thanet, and is far more in the nature of a communication than a meditation. The distinction is deliberately observed, for the theme of the poem is not simply retirement but retirement as an aid to communion between free and equal souls. Winchilsea's way of enunciating it sounds like a challenge and perhaps an imputation of ungodliness to Marvell.

> Give me there (since Heaven has shown
> It was not good to be alone)

A partner suited to my mind,
Solitary, pleased and kind;
Who, partially, may something see
Preferred to all the world in me;
Slighting by my humble side,
Fame and splendor, wealth and pride.
When but two the earth possessed,
'Twas their happiest days, and best; . . .

Lady Winchilsea's method of dealing with the poetical tradition which she inherited, if only in a woman's portion, is typical of her time. She does not shrink from mitigating the brilliance of its barbaric effects by imposing upon it the social creed of the post-Lockean era. Her writing is often looser and blunter, and almost always weaker, than Dryden, but their sensibility is the same. Indeed, Dryden might himself have envied the austerity, firmness and elegance of her expression in occasional successes like the short poem 'On Myself'.

Good Heav'n, I thank thee, since it was designed
I should be framed, but of the weaker kind,
That yet, my soul, is rescued from the love
Of all those trifles, which their passions move.
Pleasures, and praise, and plenty have with me
But their just value. If allow'd they be,
Freely and thankfully as much I taste,
As will not reason, or religion waste.
If they're denied, I on myself can live,
And slight those aids, unequal chance does give.
When in the sun, my wings can be displayed,
And in retirement, I can bless the shade.

The praise of equanimity as a way of transcending fortune is a theme as old as English vernacular poetry: in forging this poem of statement, Winchilsea has skilfully adumbrated the vast and multifarious region of unreason which presses upon her and threatens her poise, the more tellingly because she is female and sagacity is not to be expected in her. There is no hint of stridency or protest, nor of rhetorical attitudinizing. The couplets clutch the dense syntax, so that the spare, unpatterned phrases must push steadily against the returning chime, subtly building up the tone of quiet determination and ultimate confidence, ending in the ghost of an old conceit, as Winchilsea's soul like Marvell's spreads, or folds, her wings.

It cannot be said, then, that Lady Winchilsea in any sense passed herself off as a precursor of Romanticism. The faint undertone of irritation with which scholars consign her to the companionship of Prior, Gay, Pomfret, Thomson, Young, Akenside, Phillips, Parnell, Ramsay, Flatman, Ayres, Dyer or Tickell, with none of whom she herself would have objected to being numbered, is not actually of her deserving, for she did not claim to be of the tribe of Wordsworth. It was rather Wordsworth who was anxious to claim her, even at the cost of misrepresenting her. It was in his 'Essay, Supplementary to the Preface' in 1815 that Wordsworth first named Lady Winchilsea, saying that her 'Nocturnal Reverie' and Pope's *Windsor Forest* alone of all the poetry written between *Paradise Lost* and *The Seasons* contained new images of external nature or represented 'a familiar one from which it can be inferred that the eye of the Poet had been steadily fixed upon his object'. Evidently Wordsworth had already acquired his copy of the *Miscellany Poems* of 1713. In 1819, he had certain poems copied by his sister-in-law, Miss Hutchinson, for an album which he presented to Lady Lowther. In his introduction to the edition of the album published in 1905, Harold Littledale claims that the album, which contains gobbets of twenty-two other poets, including William Julius Mickle and John Langhorn, Philip Doddridge and Thomas James, 'is one more refutation of the stupid remark that Wordsworth cared for no one's poetry but his own'. Lady Winchilsea's work amounts to one-third of the total volume, which includes poems by Laetitia Pilkington, Jane Warton and Anne Killigrew as well. The selections are not made simply with an eye to excellence, for most are more estimable for the sentiments which they seek to impart than for any beauty of expression. Lady Lowther's album is the scion of the long tradition of bowdlerized anthologies considered suitable for the perusal of ladies by those concerned for their moral improvement. It cannot therefore be taken as a book of poetic touchstones; nevertheless, in Wordsworth's treatment of Winchilsea's work, we may see what it was that he prized in it, and how much of it was beyond his power to appreciate, as was all of Dryden, whose language, he said, 'cannot be the language of the imagination'. In his editing of Winchilsea, we may see how partial a view he had of her imagination and how cavalierly he dealt with those parts which he did not understand.

The first poem represented is Winchilsea's Pindaric ode 'The Spleen', if a poem of 150 lines can be said to be represented by eight lines which do not even make up a full sentence in the original. Wordsworth's version goes thus:

> In the Muses' paths I stray;
> Among their groves and by their sacred springs
> My hand delights to trace unusual things,
> And deviates from the known and common way;
> Now will in fading silks compose,
> Faintly the inimitable rose,
> Fill up an ill-drawn bird, or paint on glass
> The threat'ning angel, and the speaking ass.

'The Spleen' is a difficult poem, crabbed and jerky, as disordered in its progress as the disease which it mimics, but it is not, as Seccombe has called it, 'unbearable'. The images used to characterize the disease are extravagant and charged with a kind of hysterical disgust for their own extremeness:

> Now a Dead Sea thou'lt represent,
> A calm of stupid discontent . . .
> Trembling sometimes thou dost appear,
> Dissolved into a panick fear . . .

The unreasonable disjunction between mind and matter leads to brusque paradoxes:

> Now the jonquil o'ercomes the feeble brain;
> We faint beneath the aromatic pain,
> Till some offensive scent thy pow'rs appease,
> And pleasure we resign for short, and nauseous ease.

For Anne Finch, the spleen was not an affectation. She was not writing, as Elizabeth Carter was to do sixty years later, of the pleasures of melancholy. She would not have understood how Keats could court melancholy and associate it with the special pleasure we derive from evanescent things. For her it was mental disease, more like acute clinical depression, with all its miseries of deathly lassitude, physical disgust, sleeplessness, hallucinations and anxiety. Then as now, women were its commonest victims. She saw it as a consequence and a resource of women's servile station:

> In the imperious wife thou vapours art,
>   Which from o'erheated passions rise
> In clouds to the attractive brain . . .

> Till lordly man, born to imperial sway,
> Compounds for peace, to made that right away,
> And woman, armed with spleen, does servilely obey.

In the next section of the ode, she deals with the real and pretended melancholy of artistic people and their imitators, returning to the *punto dolente* of women's spleen.

> O'er me alas! thou dost too much prevail:
>   I feel thy force, whilst I against thee rail;
> I feel my verse decay, and my cramped numbers fail.
> Thro' thy black jaundice I all objects see,
>   As dark and terrible as thee,
> My lines decried, and my employment thought
> An useless folly, or presumptuous fault:
>   Whilst in the Muses' paths I stray,
> Whilst in their groves, and by their secret springs
> My hand delights to trace unusual things,
> And deviates from the known and common way,
>   Nor will in fading silks compose
>   Faintly th'inimitable rose,
> Fill up an ill-drawn bird, or paint on glass
> The sovereign's blurred and undistinguished face,
> The threat'ning angel, and the speaking ass.

Wordsworth's rewritten version takes on a completely different character once its missing parts and the context are restored; it becomes part of a protest against contempt and ridicule of her preference for writing poetry to the usual feminine pursuits. Her susceptibility to the spleen is seen to be at least partly caused by the conflict and the ensuing crisis in her self-confidence.

The poem continues with a description of the drunkenness and promiscuity caused by the disease, and then with an account of religious doubts and scruples, and the inefficacy of all proposed remedies, tea or coffee, music or physic. Wordsworth's selection, if it can even be called a selection, from this gallery of horrors described in the true horrid vein, is no more representative than the flower in a gangster's buttonhole is representative of him. As it stands, however, the stanza is one which Wordsworth might have wished that he had written, especially if the frigid glitter of his dedicatory sonnet to Lady Lowther was the best that he could manage at the time.

The next poem that Wordsworth chooses is 'The Petition for an Absolute Retreat', or rather sixty-three lines of it. The inscription and all mention of Lady Thanet are suppressed, along with 230 lines of the original, which is rather a moralized landscape, interpreted as an emblem of human life rather than the hymn of breathy longing for rural seclusion which Wordsworth makes of it. Every aspect of the society of two set up by these ladies (and not the primal couple as implied in Wordsworth's version) is described in detail, right down to the preferred mode of dress and the eschewal of all chemical scents; but the climax of the poem, missing altogether from the version given to Lady Lowther, is the emblematic description of the forest with Ardelia herself a withered vine until Arminda revives her, which then moves into a coda dealing with historical figures who came to grief because they abandoned their seclusion. The poem moves slyly from literal to figurative sense, from prosopopoeia to direct address, constantly changing perspective in a way that has much more to do with the wit of Cowley and Marvell than it has with the lyrical expression of piety which Wordsworth extracts from it.

It would matter little if this misleading image of Lady Winchilsea had been communicated to no one but Lady Lowther. Unfortunately, Wordsworth's remarks in the Preface of 1815 had been widely read; the Reverend Alexander Dyce had quoted them in his *Specimens of British Poetesses* in 1825, and his selection goes to show that he was allowing Wordsworth's taste to guide him, for he chose, as well as 'The Spleen' and 'The Atheist and the Acorn', 'Life's Progress' and 'A Nocturnal Reverie'. Wordsworth no sooner heard that such a book existed than, without bothering to examine it, he wrote to the editor, offering to select the Countess of Winchilsea's work for him, in a manner which seems to indicate a certain amount of proprietary feeling. Dyce sent him a copy and was favoured in return with a list of the 'best passages' in her work, which bears a strong resemblance to the content of Lady Lowther's album.

> The most celebrated of these poems, but far from the best, is 'The Spleen'. 'The Petition for an Absolute Retreat', and the 'Nocturnal Reverie', are of much superior merit. See also for favourable specimens . . . 'on the Death of Mr. Thynne' . . . ('Moral Song') and 'Fragment' . . .

he wrote, giving the page numbers of the 1713 edition.

Wordsworth advises the same elisions from 'The Petition' as he had already stipulated for the album, and even 'A Nocturnal Reverie' was not to escape unscathed, for the moralizing reference to the glow-worms and the compliment to Anne Tufton, the Countess of Salisbury, were to be cut out. In another letter to Dyce he wrote:

> her style in rhyme is often admirable, chaste, tender and vigorous, and entirely free from sparkle, antithesis, and that over-culture, which reminds one by its broad glare, its stiffness and heaviness, of the double daisies of the garden, compared with their modest and sensitive kindred of the fields.

Lady Winchilsea might well have understood what Wordsworth meant, for her own attacks upon artificiality and glare, especially as they were personified in the fashionable life of the town, are made with conviction, but she would not have understood the notions of simple piety and the solemnity of nature which had stifled the comic spirit in verse. Her poems were mostly conversational, mostly written in the middle style, easy, familiar, elegant and witty, proud to call themselves occasional and to dignify themselves by association with the names of the Countess's aristocratic and cultivated friends. The adoption of a different posture instead of bardic superiority did not mean that the poet was any less meticulous in working up her poems, but rather that the poems had an added function, as another of the delicate sinews which bound the fragile society of the coterie together. While she wrote her fair share of hymns, prayers and versified psalms, Winchilsea had the highest opinion of the didactic function of comic poetry, and gave much time and effort to it. In selecting from her work for their *Poems by Eminent Ladies* (1755), George Colman the Elder and Bonnell Thornton chose no fewer than nine of her Fables, as well as 'The Spleen', a charming poem 'To Mr. Finch now Earl of Winchilsea, Who, going abroad, had desired Ardelia to write some Verses upon whatever subject she thought fit, against his return in the evening', in which she describes the consternation caused on Parnassus by the news that she intends to write about a husband, and Pope's fulsome 'Impromptu' with her reply. Like Wordsworth's, their selection was made from the *Miscellany Poems* of 1713, and the transcription is remarkably accurate. None of the poems is shortened by so much as a word; compared to Miss Hutchinson's rather slipshod efforts, the punctuation is impeccable. Nevertheless, Wordsworth's judgement is severe:

> British poetesses make but a poor figure in the 'Poems by Eminent Ladies.' But observing how injudicious that selection is in the case of Lady Winchilsea, and of Mrs. Aphra Behn (from whose attempts they are miserably copious) I have thought something better might have been chosen by more competent persons who had access to the volumes of the several writers . . .

Because the principles which guided Colman and Thornton in their selection were nothing akin to his own, Wordsworth does not scruple to label them incompetent, if only relatively, yet it must be said that they have assembled remarkably pure texts and made few errors in the slender biographical details which they supply. Their aim was, presumably, to produce a light and amusing book, which might expect a popular sale. Their selections function as a sort of appetizer by way of slightly offhand introduction of eighteen literary freaks. Colman was a playwright, and he leans naturally to the most entertaining of his ladies, Aphra Behn, while the epigraph from Cowley would give the game away even if the editors were not quick to warn us whenever the ladies' work is 'of a serious cast, and less adapted to the generality of readers'. However, even in rushing to defend Colman and Thornton against any suggestion that they had rudely transmogrified the work of the women whom they had chosen to promote, it must be admitted that their selections do not at all represent what was most characteristic or most successful in the women's work. Their predilection for lightness and easiness easily leads them into preferring girlishness and insipidity over difficulty or intensity, but even so, it does not occur to them to tailor any poem to fit in with their notions of acceptability. While Lady Winchilsea might well have wished that they had chosen to include more ambitious work, she would not have had the indignity of seeing her work curtailed or rewritten – except for her answer to Pope's 'Impromptu'. Pope had used the sheets on which she had written to transcribe part of his translation of the *Iliad* and had published Lady Winchilsea's poem as corrected by him in his *Miscellanies* of 1717. It was not uncommon for ladies to send their work to eminent gentlemen poets for correction, and a lady who had her work corrected by the most distinguished poet of her time was unlikely to be ungrateful. Lady Winchilsea might have recorded her objections and published her own authentic version, but she never did.

Such correction was made in the spirit and taste of the time; it was assumed that all persons of discrimination would agree that the corrections were improvements. Dean Swift, Dr Delany, the Pilking-tons and Constantia Grierson corrected the poems of Mary Barber for publication by subscription, and she had every reason to be grateful to them. The cosmetic surgery to which Wordsworth subjected Winchil-sea's work and which he would have had duplicated by Dyce is quite a different matter, for Wordsworth's corrections were not made in the taste or the spirit of the time. He tailored Lady Winchilsea in his own likeness, so that for 100 years she was regarded as an impostor. The publication of all her work, except for the poems in the Dowden, now the Wellesley Manuscript, was deemed to be a disaster because it refuted her claim to historic importance, when she herself had never made any such claim.

There can be little doubt that 'A Nocturnal Reverie' is Winchilsea's most significant achievement. In seeing this, Wordsworth was simply proving the soundness of his own judgement; nevertheless, his way of regarding the poem as if it had been written by himself, has led to a persistent habit of misreading it. For Lady Lowther, Wordsworth had excised four offending lines, and he gave Dyce the same advice: '. . . omit "When scattered glow-worms", and the next couplet.'

As in 'The Petition for an Absolute Retreat', Winchilsea does not allow herself or the reader to forget the social world from which this twilight ramble is an escape. The poem begins in a classical manner, despite the echoes of *The Merchant of Venice*, with the conceit of the

more boisterous winds confined in their caves, and confuses personified Zephyr with the anthropomorphized nightingale and owl, confounding any expectation of vivid perception of nature in the creation
of a fusion and continuity between disparate images. The shock of
recognition which greets the waving moon and trampled grass straight-
ening as the humid evening air restores its turgidity does indeed enact
a particular experience rather than convey the generality which
characterizes most eighteenth-century nature poetry, and Winchilsea's
remarking the changing colour values of twilight further fines down
the experience to a single moment. But the experience is shared. The
four lines which Wordsworth would have suppressed suddenly remind
us that at least two pairs of eyes are perceiving all this minutiae.

> When scattered glow-worms, but in twilight fine,
> Show trivial beauties watch their hour to shine;
> Whilst Sal'sbury stands the test of every light,
> In perfect charms and perfect virtue bright . . .

After establishing the still harmony of the evening by means which
even Wordsworth had never been quite able to eschew, and moving
through the classical abstraction to the immediate life of the scene,
Winchilsea suddenly twitches us back to the fashionable world and
what the evening hours generally mean in town, evoking and rejecting the context of high society all at once. She recognizes her fellow
fugitive from town life, the Countess of Salisbury, and drops a quick
curtsy enlivened with a spark of malice against the painted beauties of
the *haut ton*, thus preparing the way for her introduction of the
participants in this experience, the *we* of the poem. The ladies are not
customs officials on a weekend ramble, but the denizens of the great
house, which is no further away than it ever is in Gainsborough's
portraits of the rural gentry. The ladies join in the carnival of the
other domestic animals, if rather timorously; in the gloom which has
deepened wonderfully since the beginning of the poem they are
aware that the horse is 'loos'd', the sheep 'at large', the cattle 'unmolested', although a moment's reflection makes it clear that their
freedom consists solely in the fact that no *men* are by. It would be
contrary to the spirit of the poem to overemphasize this tinge of
rebellious feeling, but it reinforces the oddity of finding these high-
born ladies rambling amongst the animals in the fields at night. That

impression is as much a part of the poem's achievement as the
recognition of grass and foxgloves.

> Their short-lived jubilee the creatures keep
> Which but endures whilst Tyrant-Man does sleep;
> When a sedate content the spirit feels,
> And no fierce light disturbs whilst it reveals;
> But silent musings urge the mind to seek
> Something too high for syllables to speak;
> Till the free soul to a compos'dness charmed,
> Finding the elements of rage disarmed,
> O'er all a solemn quiet grown,
> Joys in th'inferior world, and thinks it like her own: . . .

It is true that Man is a generic term, and that the use of the
feminine pronoun for the soul is as normal for Marvell as it is for
Winchilsea; nevertheless the Countess of Salisbury's fleeting presence
in the poem gives an extra colour to the notion of female creatures
being unmolested only when man sleeps. At all events the *we* of the
poem sees sleeping man as alien to itself and curiously associates the
carnival of the animals with the freedom of the soul, an irony which
might easily be missed.

While the poem has something in common with Wordsworth's
sonnet 'The World is too much with Us', its message is after all not
the same message, and the *we* of Winchilsea's poem is not the same
as the *we* of Wordsworth's poem. The hint of defiance is magnified
slightly in the suggestion that the poet stay out all night; on one level,
'Let me abroad remain' is simply a conventional suggestion, but on
another, not too deeply hidden, it is also a demand. 'A Nocturnal
Reverie' is a much more subtle and various poem than Wordsworth
was willing to recognize. He responded to the element of natural
piety in it, but was repelled by the suggestions of the coterie of learned
aristocratic ladies and their slightly delinquent attitude to their social
duties. The counterpoint of ironic suggestion which troubles its
surface harmonies could be ignored, especially if the four lines
about the Countess of Salisbury were simply regarded as a lapse.
Even when they are suppressed, however, the contemplative mood
cannot be sustained without impoverishing the effect of certain
ironic juxtapositions within the poem. To Wordsworth's mature

taste, such impoverishment may have been indistinguishable from simplicity, but simplicity is not a characteristic which may be imposed upon a work.

Lady Lowther's album is a curious volume: its purpose seems not so much to whet her appetite for the poetry of Wordsworth's predecessors as to present a reductive view of all that is worthwhile in it. No one with even the haziest notion of the real personality of Laetitia Pilkington, for example, could fail to be aware that the turgid lines on sorrow which represent her in the album are utterly untypical of the impudence and wit that endeared her to Swift. The strangely lugubrious and pious cast of the album is derived from Wordsworth's unconscious assumption of the posture of preceptor of women, a posture which he assumes even when dealing with Lady Winchilsea. It may be stupid to say that Wordsworth liked no poetry but his own, but it is by no means obviously stupid to say that he only liked the poetry of others when they wrote, or when he fancied that they wrote, like he did. His readiness to alter Winchilsea's work, which extended beyond the album to his advice to Dyce, and even to a projected edition of her work which fortunately never materialized, argues a considerable degree of arrogance, together with the unshakeable conviction that his own way was the true way of poetry. In Wordsworth's view, in Winchilsea's

> style and versification there is a good deal of resemblance to that of Tickell, to whom Dr Johnson justly assigns a high place among the minor poets, and of whom Goldsmith rightly observes, that there is a strain of ballad-thinking through all his poetry, and it is very attractive.

There is no strain of ballad-thinking, attractive or not, in Lady Winchilsea's make-up. Her poems are never impersonal, vatic utterances projected into history, but the expression of a finely tuned social intelligence, content to live and die with the community of sympathy which was their chief inspiration. That they survive and have survived their brief period of transvesture is indicative of the degree to which Winchilsea succeeds in giving life to her ideal society in her poetry. There is little point in striving to find evidence of her influence upon later generations of poets, unless it be in the work of Wordsworth himself, and even less in lamenting the non-Romantic character of her work. It can be no praise to say that she wrote lines that might have been written by Thomson or Tickell, for she wrote them in contexts that could have been invented by neither. On the other hand, Wordsworth often wrote no better than Thomson or Tickell and might well have wanted Lady Winchilsea's light touch for his own.

SUCCESS AND THE SINGLE POET:
THE SAD TALE OF L. E. L.

The story of Letitia Landon is the story of the exploitation and destruction of an extremely talented but uneducated young middle-class woman at the hands of the London literary establishment of the 1820s and 1830s. As long as she was a young poetic female she was a marketable commodity; because she was marketed she became conspicuous; because she believed in the freedom and spontaneity of the artist she behaved indiscreetly; because taste changed and she aged and the men who manipulated her had enemies, she became the target of vicious gossip and enduring contempt. The reality of her life was daily work, endless deadlines, poor pay and no power whatsoever, even to express what she really believed. Grub Street destroyed her personal integrity, worked her to exhaustion and then turned on her. The poetry so cynically puffed is nowadays unread. Her story illustrates in a concise and appalling way the complex of causes that have excluded women from a full participation in literary culture. If the truth were that women were simply denied access to print and the literary establishment, there would be no problem to solve; the problem that confronts the student of women's creativity is not that there is no poetry by women, but that there is so much bad poetry by women. The factors that worked first to create and then to destroy the 'poetess' were never deployed in more spectacular fashion than in the story of L. E. L.

Letitia Landon was born when the Romantic movement which Wordsworth and Coleridge had initiated had weathered and become the official mode. Its most celebrated representatives were not Shelley and Keats but Southey, Scott and the Byron of *Childe Harold*. A taste for the exotic and the thrilling had displaced the love of simple, noble verse. Wordsworth's concept of poetic language as the ordinary language of men had been vulgarized. Fairy poems, love lyrics and picturesque landscape pieces proliferated. The hunt was up for young, spontaneous, untutored genius. The literary reviews were only too happy to print the first poetic lispings of infant poets. Popular taste was, as always, undiscriminating and even Wordsworth found that the currency of his own verse had been devalued by the extension of his own argument. The clarity and directness that he laboured for were assumed to exist in insipidity; critics nurtured in his own poetical system praised extravagantly the untutored responses of ignorant and incompetent poets, who glittered as luminaries of a season and fell from sight as suddenly as they came. 'We wish very much to hear more of the Girl whose verses you have sent us,' wrote Dorothy Wordsworth to her benefactress Lady Beaumont in May 1805, 'for they have interested us exceedingly.'

> The command of language and versification is really surprising, and there is, I think, a great deal of fancy, and of the eye of a feeling being in the Fairy Pastoral ... She could not have thought of stealing the golden rings from the tail of a wasp without a rare fancy, and a mind delighting in looking at and seeking after beautiful objects. There is a childishness about the poem, the conception, the manner of it, the little fairy green, etc., that makes one love the girl and her verses. I could have kissed her for giving the fairies a cake. I hope you have some influence over her parents; if so you will use it I am sure, in endeavouring to keep her out of the way of being spoiled; and above all take care that her productions are not printed and published as wonders. Should this be done, farewell all purity of heart, all solitary communion with her own thoughts for her own independent delight! She will never do good more.

History shows numerous examples of girl poets who, at first overpraised and sought after as curiosities, were then exploited by those who had anything to gain and denied opportunities for full development. The alternative, for this little poet, at any rate, was to remain mute and inglorious. She is lost to the most painstaking researches of the Wordsworth Society, who must note sadly in the editions of the Wordsworth correspondence that they cannot find out who she is. Miss Wordsworth may have been right; the little poet may have lived and died happier for the reticence of her parents. Then again ...

Letitia Landon composed poems from a very early age, but neither she nor her parents had the option of letting her genius develop in quiet communion with herself. The collapse of her father's business meant that she had to find some way of earning money. She began to seek publicity and to drudge towards it when she was fifteen. Nowadays L. E. L. is all but forgotten; the few authorities who make mention of her speak of her as a woman ruined by recognition, a vain, credulous, silly being whose head was so thoroughly turned by adulation that she behaved injudiciously, lost her virtue, sought refuge in an unsuitable marriage and died. The vague detraction that blighted her life persists after her death. In a footnote to the life of one of her friends, we can read that he may have had an affair with her, although there is no proof one way or the other. Someone else's biographer may permit himself to sneer at her in passing, as a 'luckless, and transient Sappho'. For anyone who cares to know what becomes of a little girl who bargains with her baby brother to get him to listen to her verses, who is transported with delight when her parents agree to listen to her recital of one of her poetic narratives in the drawing-room after dinner, it is important to see through the fog of gossip the real face of a woman whose documentation is a curious compilation of breathy eulogy and coarse innuendo.

The 'snub-nosed Brompton Sappho' was not beautiful; neither could she claim the blessed immunities of ugliness. She was, unfortunately for her, attractive to a degree, and she tried hard to increase that degree. She laughed, showing her small, even, very white teeth, a little too readily. She tried to offset the effect of her short neck by exposing the fair expanse of her plump bosom. She looked too meltingly with her fine, dark-lashed, deep grey eyes. Those who liked her, responded gallantly to the kittenish charm that she lavished upon them; those who did not, found it servile and vulgar, forced and irritating. When the damped muslin gowns of the Regency Incroyables had given way to the stiff rustlings of approaching Victorianism, L. E. L.'s too-evident desire to love and be loved became a cause of embarrassment. The soft approachability of Miss Landon was the more inappropriate because she was a bluestocking, albeit a bluestocking with a difference. The other ladies of her generation who indulged in the dubious pastime of versifying were careful to preserve themselves from all taint of Byronism by rampant prudery, and of Shelleyism by unbending piety. Miss Landon was from the first associated with the most conservative political elements in her society, but they, alas, were not at all proper in their manners, being given to facetiousness, gallantry and drink.

Lady poets were not at all a rare phenomenon in L. E. L.'s. day. From 1762, when she was seventeen, until her death in 1833, Hannah More wrote sensible moralizing poems and hymns and verse tragedies on historical and sacred themes. Helen Maria Williams, the sonneteer beloved of Wordsworth, died when L. E. L. was twenty-one. Eleanor Anne Franklin thrilled the world with historical narratives, rather in the mixed style of L. E. L.'s own. Anna Laetitia Barbauld, the unimpeachable widow of a dissenting minister, retired from the literary world as a result of some unjust and unkind criticisms of her work which appeared in 1812, when she was already sixty-nine. Hester Piozzi, Anne Hunter and Ann Radcliffe all wrote poetry. In 1802, the year of Letitia Landon's birth, Amelia Opie published her *Poems*. Joanna Baillie first published verse in 1790; when Letitia Landon was growing up, Baillie's verse *Plays on the Passions* were earning her the reputation of a 'female Shakespeare'. Margaret Holford and Mary Russell Mitford emulated her success with historical dramas in blank verse. Mary Howitt on the other hand chose a simpler more Wordsworthy strain, as the poet of the young, the humble and the poor, the fireplace and the field. Caroline Anne Bowles published her first metrical tale in 1820. In 1829 fourteen-year-old Elizabeth Barrett wrote *The Battle of Marathon*; Felicia Hemans published her first volume of poems in 1809 and in 1820 a collection of dim and graceful poems *On the Domestic Affections*, before financial hardship forced her to step up the pace of her productions, mostly on moral and religious subjects. Maria Abdy became a well-known name in the annuals and magazines; as befitted a clergyman's wife she consecrated her poetic gift to the service of religion. To L. E. L. she gave advice which was neither solicited nor heeded. When L. E. L. gnashed her teeth and complained:

How often have I exclaimed, – I am not beloved as I love!

Mrs Abdy sympathized:

> Daughter of song! how truly hast thou spoken!
>   Yet deem not that to thee alone belong
> Sad memories of Idols crushed and broken,

Of wounding falsehood, and of bitter wrong:
Oh, in thy cares, thy trials, I can trace
The lot appointed for thy gifted race . . .

For Mrs Abdy and for nearly all of L. E. L.'s female contemporaries
there was only one way beyond the delusiveness of human love:

. . . there is One, on whom its (Genius's) deep affection,
In fearless trusting ardour may repose;
Exhausting all the riches of its store,
Yet ever in return receiving more.

Yes: let it safely guard its true devotion
From the low commerce of the worthless sod
Laying each fond and rapturous emotion
A tribute at the holy shrine of God:
Oh! where can gifted spirits wisely love,
Save when they fix their hopes on One above?

However bossily Mrs Abdy might instruct L. E. L. to stop deeming
that she was the only gifted female in the world and adopt the
common colouring of piety, L. E. L. could not. She had put herself
on the record as wanting to love wisely but greatly, to experience all
the rapture and all the pain that is possible on earth. Her yearning for
incandescent passion was so strong that it terrified at least one man,
who suspected that she was mad. She did not seek the domestic
affections or the pale sweets of devotion. Love was the only adventure
open to her and she meant it to dazzle and appal. As she passed the
first flush of youth L. E. L. tried to wean herself from her erotic
subjects and write pious poetry, but conviction was utterly wanting.
She tried to be refined and dull, but she failed. Her idea of passion,
which was her one living and breathing idea, was truly Byronic, and
she would not relinquish it. She detested, as he did, pettiness and
cowardice and hypocrisy, but she had not his weapons with which to
fight them. Her token revolts, usually expressed in trivial improprie-
ties, brought her under heavy fire, with no defence but the plea of her
own innocence, a true but pusillanimous resource.

L. E. L. was not like the other poetesses. She could not blunt the
edge of passion and turn it into bland affection and self-denial. She

could not write smooth and even harmonious, elegant verse. Her mind was too choked with images, mostly images of herself and the man she loved, moving through fantastical, luxury landscapes like those of Angria, the hothouse world created by the adolescent Brontës. Once her surrogates had found their form in her dense, choppy verse, she was powerless to refine it. The impetus was spent, and she was hurrying on to the next permutation of a pattern that remained essentially unaltered. She was obsessed, like all those of the generation which clutched at the Byronic hero. She took the psychic process begun by the general love affair with *Childe Harold* and took it one palpitating step further. The speaker was now not the Childe himself, but the woman he was making love to, a being every bit as combustible as himself, although obliged by circumstances to wait and sigh and repine in a white heat of devotion. The world that lost its head for Childe Harold lost it again for the Improvisatrice, but shame was quick to follow. Lord Byron had soured the public appetite by turning upon his readers and sneering at their prurient predictability. He made his name and fortune by exploiting sex in the head; the same people who thrilled at the shadow of dissipation cast upon the Childe's cheek, turned upon his creator savagely when they had anything like evidence of actual dissipation. When the old mad king died and the Regency was at an end, prurience became a rule, and L. E. L. fell foul of it. She herself angrily repudiated the suggestion that her poems were improper. Lost in her painfully vivid narcissistic fantasies, she knew only that she had never yielded to another's passion for she had never encountered any feeling as sublime as her own. Most of her heroines died virgins, as it is very probable their creator did.

If L. E. L. had been noble like Mrs Norton and Lady Caroline Lamb, she might have damned them all and forged ahead. If she had had £500 a year, if she had not been estranged from her mother, if one man had loved her well enough to protect her, she would probably have been no less forgotten but she would certainly have lived a less miserable life. L. E. L.'s poetry forms a curious nexus between the work of Coleridge and Keats and Tennyson. Her model was Scott, although her inspiration was Byron, but the something direct and pictorial in her imagination brings us pell-mell into the Victorian era. Her imaginary tableaux are dense and dramatic, all the space crowded like a Pre-Raphaelite painting with flowers and luxury effects. Her visual imagination forms a continuum with that of the painters who are only now coming to be appreciated, Henry Fuseli, Daniel Maclise and his devout imitator and spiritual heir Richard Dadd. No other woman of her time had anything like her vigour in imaginings, and few men could equal her headlong kaleidoscopic rush through scene after scene to her almost unfailingly tragic conclusion. The verse may have been garbled, the rhythms approximate, the texture of the whole blurred and uneven, but there is still a glimmer of something more than prolixity and conventionality, the track of an intense, unhealthy inner life, the spurious mysticism of love. L. E. L. served its false creed faithfully all her life long, and was in the end sacrificed to it.

Mary Wollstonecraft's *A Vindication of the Rights of Woman* appeared ten years before Letitia Landon was born; five years later its authoress was dead, and public reaction to the publication of her husband Godwin's *Memoirs* made it clear that she had lived long before her time. The detractions which were then uttered represent the prevailing attitude towards her up until the time of L. E. L.'s death; L. E. L. herself was too insecure to make her own acquaintance with the philosophy of that great woman. The view that her book would 'be read with disgust by any female who has pretentions to decency' would have sufficed to convince poor L. E. L., one of the most disappointed and oppressed of women, that she had better not read the book at all. The suicide of Mary Wollstonecraft's illegitimate daughter, Fanny Imlay, the elopement of Mary Godwin with Shelley, the suicide of Shelley's first wife, Harriet Westbrook, the scandals attaching to the ménage of Shelley and Byron in Switzerland with Godwin's other daughter, Claire Clairmont, all kept alive in the public mind both the notion that Mary's race was degenerate and the fear of their Jacobinical associations. Even the elopement of Mary's ex-pupil Mary King with her cousin, who was shot by Lord Kingsborough, was also put down to the baneful influence of her teacher. In the years that followed the fall of the Bastille, feminists made a considerable contribution to the revolutionary movement in France, until the Convention closed the women's clubs in 1793, but the notoriety of women like Olympe de Gouges, Etta Palme von Aedelers, Théroigne de Méricourt and Claire Lacombe did nothing to allay the fears of the appalled English, who had bitter cause to repent their own short-lived revolutionary fervour of the 1790s. Massive recantations of the simplest liberal principles inspired the repressive politics of the beginning of the nineteenth century, and as feminism was allied with easing of marriage laws and irreligion it languished under the darkest cloud of all. Saint-Simonian notions of free love were anathema.

Anna Doyle Wheeler, the mother of L. E. L.'s friend Rosina Lytton, described by Disraeli as 'something between Jeremy Bentham and Meg Merrilies', 'very clever but awfully revolutionary', had the extraordinary courage to join a band of English expatriates in Caen, where she reigned as the Goddess of Reason, but her example only deterred the next generation from interesting itself in the problems of women in any measure at all. The eminence of Mrs Hannah More supplied the necessary corrective to Mary Wollstonecraft's impiety. The bluestockings were content to live and move within a self-imposed pale of propriety. Much later Mary Shelley was to be criticized for failing to espouse the cause that her mother had so eloquently pleaded, but in L. E. L.'s lifetime it existed only as a butt for calumny and ridicule. After the passing of the Reform Bill in 1832, the question of women's rights was revived and from 1833–40 three new editions of *A Vindication of the Rights of Woman* appeared, too late to have been of help to baffled, penurious, exhausted L. E. L.

The happiest year of L. E. L.'s life was the year of Byron's death. In 1824 she was paid £300 by Messrs Hurst and Robinson for a volume of verses entitled *The Improvisatrice*, of which within the year no fewer than six editions were published. No poet had had such a smash hit since Lord Byron 'awoke one morning' in 1812 and found that *Childe Harold* had made him famous. The young author basked in her celebrity. Her literary career had begun only four years earlier, when three poems, 'Rome', 'The Michaelmas Daisy' and 'Vaucluse', were published anonymously in *The Literary Gazette*. Soon after she sent off to a Mr Warren of Bond Street a whole book of poetry entitled 'The Fate of Adelaide, a Swiss Romance', for which she would have been paid fifty pounds if the publisher had not gone bankrupt. The book was noticed by *The Edinburgh Magazine*, *The Lady's Magazine*, *The New Monthly Magazine* and *The Literary Gazette*, but, though the new poet was launched, nothing more appeared from her pen that year except the unsigned piece 'Air-Fire-Water-Shame' and the poem 'Bells', the first to be signed with the initials 'L. E. L.', followed in November by six rather unmaidenly songs of love, and three further poems. In 1822 *The Literary Gazette* printed forty-seven poems by L. E. L., in 1823 no fewer than ninety. Even before the publication of *The Improvisatrice*, L. E. L. was a cult heroine, if we may believe Bulwer Lytton:

> We were at that time, more capable than we are now of poetic enthusiasm; and certainly that enthusiasm we not only felt ourselves, but we shared with every second person we met. We were young, and at college, lavishing our golden years, not so much on the Greek verse and mystic character to which we ought, perhaps, to have been rigidly devoted, as
>   'Our heart in passion, and our head in rhyme'.
> At that time poetry was not yet out of fashion, at least with us of the cloister; and there was always in the reading-room of the Union a rush every Saturday afternoon for the 'Literary Gazette;' and an impatient anxiety to hasten at once to that corner of the sheet which contained the three magical letters 'L. E. L.' And all of us praised the verse, and all of us guessed at the author. We soon learned it was a female, and our admiration was doubled, and our conjectures tripled. She was young? She was pretty? . . . But the other day, looking over some of our boyish effusions, we found a paper superscribed to L. E. L., and beginning with 'Fair Spirit!'

In February 1822, when a poetic encomium upon L. E. L.'s poetry had been sent to *The Literary Gazette*, the editor seized the occasion of the author's dithering over whether to say 'his' or 'her' to point out that 'the sweet poems under this signature are by a young lady yet in her teens', thus setting off the legend of the 'Child of Song'. He went on to claim the role of guide and mentor:

> the admiration with which [her verses] have been so generally read could not delight their fair author more than those who on the Literary Gazette cherished her infant genius.

The 'Child of Song' was to pay dearly for having been identified from the outset as the creature of *The Literary Gazette*. The owner-editor of *The Literary Gazette* was the Landons' neighbour William Jerdan:

My cottage overlooked the mansion and ground of Mr Landon
... at Old Brompton, a narrow lane only dividing our resi-
dences. My first recollection of the future poetess is that of a
plump girl, grown enough to be almost mistaken for a woman,
bowling a hoop around the walks with a hoop-stick in one
hand, and a book in the other, reading as she ran, and as well as
she could manage, taking both exercise and instruction at the
same time.

When Jerdan was first shown the girl's poems by her mother he
had difficulty reconciling the poet's persona with the child who
played with his own daughters. *The Literary Gazette* seems to have
existed principally to notice or snub new works, to puff some authors
and execrate others. Most literary periodicals in London at the time
applied criteria which were far from literary or disinterested. Jerdan
moved in elevated literary circles – in fact he was something of a
doyen, for Bates, Maginn and Maclise agreed to put him at the head
of their portrait gallery of literary notables. He knew and worked
with 'Crabbe, Barry Cornwall, Miss Mitford, Alaric Watts, Dr.
Maginn, Mrs. Hemans and Thomas Campbell', all shining lights of
the resident London literary establishment. On the face of it Jerdan
was L. E. L.'s protector and patron, a friend who 'put much reviewing
in her way' so that she could earn a living and support her family.
Henry Chorley was to take a different view:

At the time when I joined the *Athenaeum*, its vigour and value
to the world of letters were not acknowledged as they have
since been. The *Literary Gazette*, conducted by Mr Jerdan, who
was the puppet of certain booksellers, and dispensed praise or
blame at their bidding, and it may be feared 'for a consideration',
was in the ascendancy; and its conductors and writers spared no
pains to attack, to vilipend, and to injure, so far as they could,
any one who had to do with a rising journal so merciless in its
exposure of a false and demoralising system.
    It would not be easy to sum up the iniquities of criticism (the
word is not too strong), perpetrated at the instance of publishers,
by a young writer and a woman, who was in the grasp of Mr
Jerdan, and who gilt or blackened all writers of the time, as he
ordained. When I came to London to join the *Athenaeum*, she 'was

flinging about fire' as a journalist in sport, according to the approved fashion of her school, and not a small quantity of the fire fell on the head of one who belonged to 'the opposition' camp, like myself. It is hard to conceive any one, by flimsiness and by flippancy, made more distasteful to those who did not know her, than was Miss Landon. For years, the amount of gibing sarcasm and imputation to which I was exposed, was largely swelled by this poor woman's commanded spite. That it did not make me seriously unhappy was probably an affair of temperament; those who would have been pained by it were, happily, beyond reach of hearing. But that these things most assuredly had a bad influence on my power as a worker, I do not entertain the slightest doubt.

It is to be hoped that matters were not quite as squalid as Chorley suggests. At first L. E. L. was probably too flattered by the invitation to judge the works of others to notice that she was embarking on a career which would cost her much in reputation and tranquillity. When she was older and wiser she gave a harrowing account of how a poet can be forced into venal journalism, in the subplot of her novel *Ethel Churchill* (1836). To friend and foe alike L. E. L. soon became known for her disregard of literal truth. S. C. Hall, whose loyalty to her is beyond question, in a memoir which virtually gags itself in its determination to say nothing which could harm her memory, was obliged to deplore her practice of 'saying things for "effect" – things in which she did not believe'.

> Certainly no advocate of Miss Landon can affirm that the 'bright ornament of truth' was hers. It was no use telling her this; she would argue that a conversation of facts would be as dull as a work on algebra, and that all she did was to put her poetry into practice.

The Literary Gazette made L. E. L. a famous name, and she capitulated, naturally, by doing her best to fit in, to be charming and entertaining, even though her store of experience was tiny and she was naturally shy and terrified of rejection. Never at any time in her career did she find the security to defy her public or even to appear sullen and recalcitrant before it. She always took refuge, if refuge was possible, in a lie. Although she was overworked from the outset she frequented the parties of the literary set and wore herself out being their life and soul. When she was alone, she either worked or dashed off letters to all and sundry, until one wonders how such feverish activity could have been kept up. Spiritually, she was exhausted, for she had never been fed or replenished with genuine intimacy, either to give or to receive. The outraged organism began to revenge itself. Her hidden neurasthenia burst out in strange diseases, epileptoid fainting fits, asthmatic seizures, 'spasms'.

Jerdan can hardly have blamed himself for his exploitation of this girl of slender means. Her own willingness to please clamoured for more and more work. Not only did Jerdan 'make' her, he also helped her to manage her finances, and if she was always poor, he claimed that it was not because he had neglected to see that she was properly rewarded for her work but because her relatives had prior claims. Much is made by her biographers of the help she gave her mother which apparently only began after her sister's death and amounted to £50 a year, and of the fact that she put her brother through Oxford. Jerdan summed up her earnings after her death at around £250 a year, saying that for magazine contributions over ten years she had earned £200. As magazine contributions were largely anonymous, so that L. E. L. could not exploit her name, she might have been advised to have left off such journalism, and have worked much harder on her poetry, but as a magazine owner-editor Jerdan was hardly likely to suggest such a course of action.

L. E. L. was very conscious that, if she had not become a famous name through the columns of *The Literary Gazette*, *The Improvisatrice* might never have been published. As she explained herself:

> The *Improvisatrice* met with the usual difficulties attendant on a first attempt. It was refused by every publisher in London. Mr Murray said peers only should write poetry; Longmans would not hear of it; Colburn declared poetry was quite out of his way; and for months it remained unpublished. In the meantime the fugitive poems with my signature, L. E. L., had attracted much attention in the *Literary Gazette* and Messrs. Hurst and Robinson agreed to publish it. I may say without vanity that its success was complete, and I have never since found any publishing obstacles.

L. E. L.'s Improvisatrice lives in a palace in Florence, a palace moreover with the kinds of appointments we would expect to find in some Oriental nabob's dwelling:

> Amid my palace halls was one,
> The most peculiarly my own;
> The roof was blue and fretted gold,
> The floor was of the Parian stone,
> Shining as snow as only meet
> For the light tread of fairy feet;
> And in the midst, beneath a shade
> Of clustered rose, a fountain played,
> Sprinkling its scented waters round,
> With a sweet and lulling sound, –
> O'er oranges, like Eastern gold . . .
> . . . And ever as the curtains made
> A varying light, a changeful shade,
> As the breeze waved them to and fro,
> Came on the eye the glorious show
> Of pictured walls where landscapes wild
> Of wood and stream, or mountain piled,
> Or sunny vale, or twilight grove,
> Or shapes whose every look was love . . .

How the oranges and roses grow under the fretted roof and through the marble floor, and what the running rose-water did to the frescos and the curtains is not of course to be considered in the faery world of poesy. Florence is not Seville, and even if it were, it is unlikely that an extempore poet would be given apartments in the Alhambra. L. E. L.'s Improvisatrice is not simply a millionairess and a poet, but also a painter whose canvases have been hung in a public gallery. One depicts Petrarch gazing upon Laura, another Sappho and another, painted in the course of the heroine's unhappy love affair, the abandoned Ariadne. Each subject, like the poem itself, deals with doomed love and occasions an ancillary treatment of the main theme.

In developing the idea of the professional female composer-reciter of extemporaneous verses, L. E. L. was on the one hand indulging her own fantasy and on the other capitulating to the marketing of herself by *The Literary Gazette* as the 'Child of Song'. Her own verse was virtually improvised:

> I like to show how much I can do in little time. I wrote the *Improvisatrice* in less than five weeks and during that time I often was two or three days without touching it. I never saw the MS till in proof sheets a year afterwards, and I made no additions, only verbal alterations.

When the Improvisatrice strikes her lute and holds her listeners spellbound, the words she sings are L. E. L.'s own. She is free of family ties, for no other inhabitant of her palace is mentioned, not even a duenna or a servant. The totally imaginary freedom of manners which allows this young and beautiful woman to roam Florence as she pleases never characterized Florentine society at any time, even in the heyday of the Renaissance. The spontaneity and opulence of the Improvisatrice's existence were just what L. E. L. would have wished for herself. The most striking element in the wish-fulfilment fantasy is the way in which the Improvisatrice conquers the affections of the man of her dreams. And what a man!

> 'Twas a dark and flashing eye,
> Shadows too that tenderly,
> With almost female softness, came
> O'er its mingled gloom and flame.
> His cheek was pale; or toil or care,
> Or midnight study had been there,
> Making its young colours dull,
> Yet leaving it most beautiful.
> Raven curls their shadow threw,
> Like the twilight's darkening hue,
> O'er the pure and mountain snow
> Of his high and haughty brow.

Neither Byron nor Childe Harold himself could have exercised more dubious fascination than this figure, the equivalent in verse of a Regency pin-up. L. E. L. likens him to Apollo in her first description and then to the statue of Antinous:

> He leant beside a pedestal.
> The glorious brow, of Parian stone,
> Of the Antinous by his side,
> Was not more noble than his own!
> They were alike: he had the same
> Thick-clustered curls the Roman wore –
> The fix'd and melancholy eye –
> The smile that passed like lightning o'er
> The curved lip.

One evening, as the Improvisatrice glides over the waters of the Arno (presumably in a boat, although no means of locomotion is actually mentioned), the public, designated only as 'they', interrupts her reverie to demand a song. Unlike most *improvvisatrici*, this one accompanies herself on the lute, to which she sings a long narrative poem in iambic tetrameter subtitled 'A Moorish Romance', which calls forth the breathless adulation of the assembled company, among whom is the fatal youth, Lorenzo, who is soul-struck by her harrowing tale of the doomed love of Leila and Abdalla. Leila, daughter of a Christian mother and a Moorish father, awaits the lover whom she rescued from slavery in her father's house. He, the Christian Abdalla, is to arrive and take her with him to Italy. He arrives and takes her on board his ship. A brief idyll follows, but the ship is wrecked by a storm and they are found drowned in each other's arms on an Italian beach. Lorenzo's reaction to all this passion and pathos is exactly as the poet would wish:

> He spoke not when the others spoke,
> His heart was all too full for praise;
> But his dark eyes kept fixed on mine,
> Which sank beneath their burning gaze.
> Mine sank – but yet I felt the thrill
> Of that look burning on me still.
> I heard no word that others said,
> Heard nothing but one low-breathed sigh.

In the dream-world of Florence, women artists may, like male artists, be loved and courted for their achievements, rather than despite them. Lorenzo is first and foremost a fan, but not simply a fan – he is the most appreciative of the Improvisatrice's talent, and the most responsive to the feelings that she strives to evoke. His burning glance incinerates her maidenly calm.

> As yet I loved not; – but each wild,
> High thought I nourished raised a pyre
> For love to light and lighted once
> By love, it would be like the fire
> The burning lava floods that dwell
> In Etna's cave unquenchable.

The minstrel's poetic preoccupations were rendering her more and more susceptible to the grand passion, which when it came would be in the nature of a cataclysm. This notion connects with L. E. L.'s highly romantic notion of genius as a capacity to feel more strongly than other folk and hence to figure forth emotions and emotional states in an especially moving way. L. E. L. had been writing self-indulgent love poetry since she was fifteen; her head, like the Improvisatrice's, was full of it. Her self-induced susceptibility must have been obvious to most men; her youth and eminence must have made her interesting to many. Her great forte was writing of the mental torture of women who had been rejected. Like the other Romantics, she believed that the 'sweetest songs are those that tell of saddest thought', but she took the notion so literally that she made herself incapable of happiness.

At first all seems to go well for the Improvisatrice. The day after she sees Lorenzo on the Arno, she goes to the picture gallery to sketch and lo! he is there. They pass the morning in animated converse about Art and are transported with rapture in each other's company although no word is breathed of love. That night there is a fancy-dress ball at Count Leon's, and the Improvisatrice goes as a Hindoo girl and blights the festivities with an appalling tale of suttee, magnifying the shock-effect by pretending that the lovers have met again alive, before revealing that Azim is dead. Suttee is depicted as marriage with a corpse, and the funeral as a wedding bed; just as the consummation of Leila's union was drowning in Abdalla's arms, Zaide is joined to her lover on the pyre. This done, she leaves the company and happens upon Lorenzo, who plants a burning kiss – upon her hand. As soon the hand is flung away, and Lorenzo rushes off.

> We did not meet again – he seemed
> To shun each spot where I might be:
> And it was said, another claimed
> The heart – more than the world to me!

Once the artist has admitted to herself that she loves the die is cast. The interpolated tales all illustrate either that love is a disaster by natural law or that the only love worth discussing ends in utter tragedy. No female poet before L. E. L. had ever written of women's passion as she did. It was not like the love plaints of men, but the fierce, impotent, inward-turning tumult of a woman's heart, the agony of a creature unable to speak or act, forced to wreak her vengeance upon herself, to refuse to live.

> No! I did not speak:
> My heart beat high, but could not break.
> I shrieked not, wept not; but stood there
> Motionless in my still despair;
> As if I were forced by some strange thrall,
> To bear with and to look on all, – . . .

Her description of the Improvisatrice's love for Lorenzo was shocking; not until the unmentionable Brontës would the world read anything quite like it:

> I loved him, too, as woman loves,
>   Reckless of sorrow, sin, or scorn:
> Life had no evil destiny
>   That, with him, I could not have borne! . . .
> I loved, my love had been the same
>   In hushed despair, in open shame.
> I would rather have been a slave,
>   In tears, in bondage, by his side,
> Than shared in all, if wanting him,
>   This world had power to give beside!
> My heart was wither'd, – and my heart
>   Had ever been the world to me:
> And love had been the first fond dream,
>   Whose life was in reality.

> I had sprung from my solitude
>> Like a young bird upon the wing
> To meet the arrow; so I met
>> My poisoned shaft of suffering.

This is the real leitmotif of *The Improvisatrice*; all the scene changes merely allow for another outburst in a similar strain. Her animadversion upon love apropos of Petrarch is the first emergence of the theme, which is developed in the portrait of Sappho driven to suicide by Love's despair, and in Sappho's song. Ida, abandoned by Julian,

> A cold white statue; as the blood stood
> Had, when in vain her last wild prayer,
> Flown to her heart, and frozen there.
> Upon her temple, each dark vein
> Swelled in its agony of pain.
> Chill, heavy damps were on her brow;
> Her arms were stretched at length, though now
> Their clasp was on the empty air:
> A funeral pall – her long black hair
> Fell over her; herself the tomb
> Of her own youth, and breath, and bloom.

The more powerful, gifted or passionate the woman, the more inevitable the agony. Nearly all of L. E. L.'s heroines are, like herself, dark and intense. They are often supplanted by insipid blondes, like the woman Julian married for money, and the girl that Lorenzo married out of duty. The blind and reckless passion of the dark females was not a part of the accepted stereotype in Letitia Landon's day; woman's love was seldom if ever expressed before the proprieties had been satisfied, and then it was modest and tremulous. These wilful creatures were a new species, and their creation was to cost Letitia Landon dear. Their immediate popularity was little more than a thoughtless response to novelty; it is very doubtful if anyone, not excepting L. E. L. herself, had any clear idea of the nature of the protest that was being made through their impassioned outpourings.

> I must my beating heart restrain –
> Must veil my burning brow!

> O, I must coldly learn to hide
>   One thought, all else above –
> Must call upon my woman's pride
>   To hide my woman's love!
> Check dreams I never may avow;
> Be free, be careless, cold as thou!

Woman's fate, at least as L. E. L. saw it, was to live through her emotions, to mate with a stranger and to be eventually spurned, whether within or beyond the conventions. Her readers responded to L. E. L.'s crazy vision of the world in a snobbish and sentimental fashion. They were moved to copious tears by the plaints of Ida and Sappho and Cydippe, but they did not see any cause for concern in L. E. L.'s inability to imagine any other kind of sexual communion but that of corpses lying side by side. Such writing was evidence of a powerful imagination, as far as they were aware, and not of obsession. They were enchanted to find that the virgin prodigy was not as heavy-going socially as her published verse might have indicated; beyond that they did not care to look. Miss Landon's spasms, which seem to have been quite severe attacks resembling epilepsy, and her frequent nervous illnesses were not much discussed.

The Improvisatrice had painted Petrarch, not because he was one of the greatest poets who ever lived, but because he was a great lover.

> I ever thought that poet's fate
> Utterly lone and desolate.
> It is the spirit's bitterest pain
> To love, to be beloved again;
> And yet between a gulf which ever
> The hearts which burn to meet must sever.
> And he was vow'd to one sweet star,
> Bright yet to him, but bright afar.

But if Petrarch is a great lover, it is also because he is an artist.

> O'er some, Love's shadow may but pass
> As passes the breath stain o'er glass; . . .
> But there are some whose love is high,
> Entire, and sole Idolatry:

Who turning from a heartless world,
Ask some dear thing which may renew
Affection's several links and be
As true as they themselves are true.
I loved him as young genius loves.

The Improvisatrice's next painting was of another poet, Sappho, whom she also celebrates rather as a great unhappy lover than as a poet, painting her on the brink of the cliff she is supposed to have jumped off for love of Phaon. Sappho's song from *The Improvisatrice* has often been put into the mouth of L. E. L.:

Farewell, my lute! – and would that I
  Had never waked thy burning chords!
Poison has been upon thy sigh,
  And fever has breathed in thy words.

Yet wherefore, wherefore should I blame
  Thy power, thy spell, my gentlest lute?
I should have been the wretch I am,
  Had every chord of thine been mute.

It was my evil star above,
  Not my sweet lute that wrought me wrong;
It was not song that taught me love,
  But it was love that taught me song . . .

There is some truth in L. E. L.'s account of the poet's motivation. Considered at its basest level, artistic aspiration and hence artistic activity do seem to be functions of the libido. The artist, especially the romantic artist, does exhibit himself with a view to obtaining fame and honour and love, but he is not often satisfied either with his achievement or with his reward. He has two love affairs going on at once, one with his medium and the other with his public, and neither results in a stable or contented relationship. In this sense every artist is thwarted in love and L. E. L. can be interpreted as speaking of this general struggle of artists with the unsynthesized manifold, but she is also speaking of the fate of the artist in a philistine, commercial community, and in particular of the special suffering reserved for the female artist. The theme of the suffering of

the gifted female is one that was frequent enough in the poems of
L. E. L.'s contemporaries. Mrs Hemans saw in the story of Properzia
De'Rossi, the incarnation of the problem, as did Ouida after her.
Elizabeth Barrett gave the matter thought and so did equable, practical
Miss Mitford. Letitia Landon was so convinced that the spirit of the
female poet was too sensitive and fastidious for this nether world that
she hardly ever omitted a mention of her sufferings in any poem that
she wrote. Wishing and believing eventually made it so, but both
were helped along by the real circumstances in which the poet found
herself.

Events as tragic as those narrated in the words the Improvisatrice
sang when heart-whole can hardly become more dire when she
discovers that she is suffering the wasting disease of love. The last
song that the Improvisatrice sings tells of Cydippe pining for Leades,
who is over the sea taking a last leave of his native land, until she
eventually dies of waiting for him to return. She is no sooner buried
than he arrives, and then he in his turn pines away and dies upon her
tomb. This is the last song the Improvisatrice ever sings; one evening
she wanders into the 'Cathedral of San Marco' and accidentally
witnesses Lorenzo's wedding to a 'pale and lovely girl'. Thereafter she
plays and paints no more, but goes into a full-time decline. One
evening Lorenzo is suddenly at her side as she sits by the window,
holding her hand and explaining everything. He had been betrothed
since his childhood to an orphan girl brought up in his own household.
He did fall in love with the Improvisatrice but could not disappoint
his betrothed. She, once duly wed, obligingly faded away. Having
buried her, Lorenzo comes to claim his love. All seems set for a happy
ending, but alas! the canker of love unrequited has eaten away the
Improvisatrice's heart and Lorenzo is too late to do aught but watch
her die.

Though *The Improvisatrice* may seem little more than a phantasma-
goria of sentimental sillinesses, the poem is more than the story. It is
not without energy, even a certain gnashing dramatic power. The
simplicity of L. E. L.'s basic patterns occasionally becomes a sort of
crazy stylization which allows her genuine intensity and oddness to
emerge. Her habit of dividing her poem into scenes divided by bands
of decorative description and an occasional impassioned apostrophe is
not altogether unsuccessful. The poem was reviewed no fewer than
sixteen times, usually in the most favourable terms.

And I was happy; hope and fame
Together on my visions came,
For memory had just dipp'd her wings
In honey dews, and sunlit springs –
My brow burnt with its early wreath,
My soul had drunk its first sweet breath
Of praise, and yet my cheek was flushing,
My heart with the full torrent gushing
Of feelings whose delighted mood
Was mingling joy and gratitude.
Scarce possible it seemed to be
That such praise could be meant for me –
Enured to coldness and neglect,
My spirit chilled, by breathing checked,
All that can crowd and crush the mind,
Friends, even more than fate unkind,
And fortunes stamped with the pale sign
That marks and makes autumn's decline.
How could I stand in the sunshine,
And marvel not that it was mine?
One word, if ever happiness
In its most passionate excess
Offers its wine to human lip,
It has been mine that cup to sip.
I may not say with what deep dread
The words of my first song were said,
I may not say how much delight
Has been upon my minstrel flight.

What L. E. L. construes as discouragement and neglect of her poetic gift was in fact the patchy education offered young middle-class women, which taught young ladies to write copperplate not couplets. As the first child of John Landon, partner in the army agency of Adair in Pall Mall, and his wife, Catherine Jane Bishop, Letitia was unlikely to have been given any systematic education. Little Letitia was taught to read by an invalid neighbour by the strangely advanced method of scattering letters on the carpet, having the little girl pick them up as she named them and giving her a reward for getting the right combinations. Her younger brother, Whittingdon, was later to write:

If she came home without a reward, she went upstairs with her nurse, of whom she was particularly fond, to be comforted; but when she brought her reward with her, she never failed to display it in the drawing-room and then share it with me . . . she seldom came empty-handed, and I soon began to look for the hour of her return, for which I had such very good reasons.

When she was five she was sent to Miss Rowden's famous school at Hans Place, where Lady Caroline Lamb and Mary Russell Mitford had studied before her, but within months she was spirited away to live at East Barnet on a farm into which John Landon had poured far too much money. There Letitia was given her lessons by her cousin Miss Elizabeth Landon, who freely admits in her letter to L. E. L.'s biographer Laman Blanchard that often her little pupil grasped and retained more of the matter that they were studying than her teacher. Apart from the essential grammars and catechisms and Gradgrind geographies that children's brains were racked with, little Letitia read

Rollins Ancient History, Hume and Smollett, Plutarch's Lives, the Fables of Gay and Aesop, the Life of Josephus, Montesquieu's Spirit of the Laws, Dobson's Life of Petrarch

and so forth. Her retentive and greedy brain gorged itself on this heavy diet and then dreamed in fantastical visions.

We are indebted to shadowy Cousin Landon for the only mention of Letitia in the company of her mother.

At so early an age as this, she would occupy an hour or two in the evening amusing her father and mother with accounts of the wonderful castles she had built in her imagination . . .

Letitia Landon herself addressed a single unprinted sonnet to her mother and never wrote a line of poetry ostensibly about her or about the sickly sister who was born in 1814. Perhaps she was simply jealous of the new baby in a way that she had not been about Whittingdon, but slowly the conviction grew in her that her mother did not love her, that she was treated cruelly. Perhaps a conflict arose between her parents as a result of John Landon's mismanagement of

his affairs in which Letitia's passionate love of her father blinded her
to the difficulties of her mother's position. Certainly the new baby,
who was very sickly, did absorb much of Mrs Landon's time and
energy and Letitia, who was ravenous for love from the outset, did
not forgive it. She remembered Whittingdon and herself as neglected
children shut up in the big house, sniffing Sunday dinners being
brought from the cookhouse and knowing there was none for them,
running wild through the rooms playing games of extravagant make-
believe. In the story of Frances Beaumont in *Traits and Trials of Early
Life*, L. E. L. tells of a girl who must support her helpless mother and
deaf-mute sister, while her mother does nothing but sit and complain
about the treatment she has received.

> I have known little else than privation, disappointment, unkind-
> ness, and harassment. From the time I was fifteen, my life has
> been one continual struggle in some shape or another against
> absolute poverty, and I must say not a tithe of my profits have I
> ever expended on myself . . . No one knows but myself what I
> have had to contend with.

Letitia and Whittingdon must have had much time on their hands,
for despite Cousin Landon's embargo on poetry and novel reading,
the children managed to read somewhere between 100 and 150
volumes of Cooke's *Poets and Novelists*. Despite the strongest indica-
tions that little Letitia was lacking in manual dexterity, it was
considered essential that she learn penmanship and music. When she
failed to make any progress in either and revolted against useless
perseverance, her little brother was locked in a dark closet, Letitia's
father having early discovered that she would endure anything herself,
but could not bear to see him suffer. So Letitia went back to her
straggling pot-hooks and her five-finger exercises, accepting torture
and humiliation so that her innocent brother might be freed. The
pattern of oscillation between utter determination and self-abnegation
which was to characterize her behaviour all her life was very early set.
Whittingdon Landon has given us an early example:

> I petitioned my father for three shillings, when he offered me,
> by way of compromise, a new eighteenpenny-piece if I would
> learn and repeat to him the ballad –

> Gentle river, gentle river
> Lo! thy streams are stained with gore,' &c.

But as this ballad was some thirty verses long, and the payment inadequate, I struck for the three shillings, and would learn no ballad for less. I was in disgrace accordingly. Without saying a word my sister went out, came back in a very short time, and repeated the ballad for me – asked for the three shillings – got them, and a kiss or two besides. She then persuaded me to learn it, teaching it me verse by verse. I forget whether I ever said it; but I do not forget that she gave me the three shillings.

When she was only seven, Letitia would ramble through the unkempt garden with a long stick which she called her measuring stick, replying to playful demands with, 'Oh, don't speak to me, I have such a delightful thought in my head.' She would pace up and down the lime-tree walk, musing or repeating her verses aloud, plotting long stories of adventure and probably even then of love, to which Whittingdon would be compelled to give ear that night. Eventually they had to strike a bargain; one day he was to listen while she talked and another day she was to play at Spartans, bows and arrows, trap-ball and hoops.

> On her days, I had to undergo either the account of 'the island', that is, of what she would do as another Robinson Crusoe, or some fairy tale or verses of her own composition; or perhaps the battle scene from the 'Lady of the Lake' for the whole of that poem I think she knew by heart.

As soon as she could write at all, Letitia carried everywhere her little slate. It went to bed with her instead of a teddy bear. It seems that she would write down her thoughts in the dark. She would sit quietly for hours if anyone played or sang, writing busily away upon her slate. She was fascinated by words, and set herself to help the gardener, Mr Chambers, plumb the mysteries of the dictionary that he carried in his hat. When her cousin Captain Landon came back from America, she narrated his adventures on her slate and regaled the family with them piece by piece for months. She was fascinated by heroism and travels to remote, wild lands. Her father's glamour was increased by the wonderful associations of the adventure story 'Sylvester Tramper' which he put into her hands. For a while it eclipsed even Robinson Crusoe, until it too was overshadowed by *The Arabian Nights*, as she narrates herself in 'The History of a Child'.

Whether the pathetic anecdotes in 'The History of a Child' represent objective fact, they certainly represent subjective fact, namely the image of herself as a child that Letitia Landon entertained as an adult. The sentimental education of L. E. L. presented itself to her adult imagination as the slow realization that she was unlovable. Those who should have loved her according to the rights and duties of nature were negligent; the servants who supplied their places were promiscuously tender and basically indifferent. The affection that was manifested to her could be neutralized by a single instance of brusqueness. In childhood as in later life Letitia Landon would entertain an impossible idealism of love which would effectively prevent her from finding any satisfactory intimacy of any duration with any living soul. This morbidity she was to construe as genius.

When she was thirteen the family left the farm and returned to Fulham, and then to Old Brompton. Her father was ruinously embroiled financially and it seems that Letitia's lessons had long since been given up.

The embarrassed state of my father's circumstances made us live in great seclusion at Old Brompton, and also led to a thousand projects for their amelioration – among others, literature seemed the resource, which it only seems to youth and inexperience. With what wonder in after years we look back on how we used to believe and expect! My course of reading had been very desultory – principally history and travels, and I especially remember a life of Petrarch which perhaps first threw round Italy that ideal charm it has always retained in my eyes. The scene of his being crowned at the Capitol was always present to my mind and gave me the most picturesque notion of the glory of poetry. *The Odyssey* was another work that I never tired of reading. It was the same sort of pleasure that I derived from reading Scott – an excitement, a keener sense of existence, and a passionate desire of action. Were I to be asked the writer who has exercised the greatest influence in forming style, I should say – Walter Scott.

The Improvisatrice was still selling like hot cakes when L. E. L. presented Messrs Hurst and Robinson with *The Troubadour*, for which she received the princely sum of £600, the most she was ever to earn for a single work. During its composition, John Landon died, leaving his family in severe financial straits. His wife and her consumptive youngest child retired to the country, where they seem to have lived in great misery. Letitia Landon decided to stay in London. She had stayed with her grandmother in Sloane Street 'for a year or two' before her father's death, but she did not return to her mother and sick sister ever afterwards. That matters had come to a painful pass in the Landon family before her father's death might be gathered from the passionate dedication which concludes *The Troubadour*:

> My page is wet with bitter tears –
> I cannot but think of those years
> When happiness and I would wait
> On summer evenings by the gate,
> And keep o'er the green fields our watch
> The first sound of thy step to catch,
> Then run for the first kiss and word –
> An unkind one I never heard.
> But these are pleasant memories,
> And later years have none like these:
> They came with griefs, and pains, and cares,
> All that the heart breaks while it bears;
> Desolate as I feel alone,
> I should not weep that thou art gone.

Even so soon after her debut, delight in her literary success was not unalloyed, if we may take these lines to be inspired by her own experience. She here speaks of poetry as a taskmaster:

> Yet ah! the wreath that binds thy shrine,
> Though seemingly all bloom and light,
> Hides thorn and canker, worm and blight.
> Planet of wayward destinies,
> Thy victims are thy votaries!
> Alas! for him whose youthful fire
> Is vow'd and wasted on the lyre –

> Alas! for him who shall assay,
> The laurel's long and weary way!
> Mocking will greet, neglect will chill
> His spirit's gush, his bosom's thrill;
> And worst of all, that heartless praise
> Echo'd from what another says.

When these lines were reworked from a fragment published earlier in *The Literary Gazette* L. E. L. had not yet suffered any public obloquy, though she had certainly run the gamut of the reviewers and of those people who gush at authors without ever having read a word they have written. She may even have had an inkling of what was not perfect in her poem, seeing as she was so ready with criticism of the poetry of others. She had probably too had ample opportunity to reflect that fame does not necessarily add anything to a woman's power to charm, especially to charm men.

> . . . it was properly disseminated that I was 'the London Author-ess'. The consequence was that, seated by the only young man I had beheld, I acted upon him like an air-pump, suspending his very breath and motion; and my asking him for a mince-pie, a dish of which I had been for some time surveying with longing eyes, acted like an electric shock – and his start not a little discomposed a no-age-at-all, silk-vested spinster whose plate was thereby deposited in her lap – and last not least, in the hurry, he forgot to help me!

The Troubadour emerged, and the money was paid, and the public settled down to luxuriate in another far-fetched tale in verse, this time the story of the soldier-poet Raymond. The simple plot of *The Improvisatrice* is here abandoned for something much more Gothic. Raymond is still the fatal man, a sort of Byron transposed to fourteenth-century Toulouse, but he has dealings with a cluster of contrasted female characters. The opening of the poem is quite impressive, for L. E. L. draws an extraordinary Caspar David Friedrich landscape, of a tower black against the red sky at the last phase of twilight, while the river runs past reflecting the vivid light of the sky through the 'death-black ocean' of the pine forest. Only after her poetic eye zooms in on one of the lighted windows to give a résumé of the landscape as seen from the castle do we enter the great hall to meet our hero, upon whose pale cheek we discern something of 'pride and gloom' ill-sorting with his youth. The companion of his reveries is Eva, one of L. E. L.'s pallid blondes, daughter of a faery lover, taken to wife by Sir Amirald in a manner clearly indebted to Scott's *Bride of Lammermoor*. Eva's skin is very rarely reddened by the heart's blood because of her daemon heritage, but exactly what is meant by this is never explained. Raymond has barely sung Eva a tragic ballad when a summons comes from the Lady Clotilde to lead men into battle for her right. Raymond hesitates not, for this will be his entry upon knighthood. Eva is hurt by his willingness to abandon her:

> O, she had yet the task to learn
> How often woman's heart must turn
> To feed upon it's own excess
> Of deep yet passionate tenderness!

Raymond spends the night before his ordeal straying about his favourite haunts with Eva, who seems to have no thought of compromising herself. She gives him an 'amber scented chain' with a cross on it as a parting gift and watches him ride off. Canto II begins with six lines of Byronic pastiche:

> The first, the very first; O! none
> Can feel again as they have done;
> In love, in war, in pride, in all
> The planets of life's coronal,
> However beautiful or bright –
> What can be like their first sweet light?

Then Raymond hurls himself into the fray, in which he wins glory and a seat beside the raven-haired Lady Adeline, who kindles his very soul within him. He sings her the fatuous tale of Lady Elenore fled to the forest with Eginhard the minstrel, and discovered there by her grieving father after the passage of years. Adeline is merely trifling with Raymond's feelings, so he flees away as fast as his horse can carry him, until it drops,

> And deep shame mingled with remorse
> As he brought the stream to his fallen horse.

As he raves, recites and maddens about, he encounters his erstwhile commander, De Valence, *en route* for Marseilles to ship for the Crusades. Before joining them, he bethinks him of Eva and gallops off to the castle, takes his leave and dashes off to the Crusades, singing a final song for Canto II as he goes.

In Spain Raymond saves the life of Eva's father, who tells how Eva's mother died and he was driven mad, apparently as a punishment for trying unsuccessfully to burn his wife's body so that the worms should not be intimate with it. Raymond is called to battle and falls and Amirald returns to Toulouse to bring the sad news to Eva. Raymond is flung into a Moorish dungeon in Granada, from which he is rescued by one of L. E. L.'s Christian Moors, Leila, who takes him to the house of her Christian aunt Elvira, miraculously saved from death after leaping off a cliff to avoid the Moor who would marry her by force. Raymond collapses with brain fever and Leila nurses him to health, whereupon he departs to claim Eva as his bride, while Leila goes to her favourite bower and dies by the fountain.

Raymond speeds homeward, passing Lady Adeline's castle, which has been laid waste, and learning by the by that the Lady had fallen in love with Raymond's brother, who trifled with her and eventually spurned her as she had done Raymond. Now she has returned to a convent, to expiate her sins of vanity. Raymond finds that Eva is to judge the contest of the Golden Violet. She is pining for him, but Raymond remains incognito, not knowing if she remembers him. He sings a song of the 'Chagrin d'amour', Eva rises to give him the Golden Violet and faints upon his neck. And thus abruptly ends the tale.

> But what has minstrel left to tell
> When love has not an obstacle?

With 'The Troubadour' were bound sheets containing some of the 'Poetical Sketches of Modern Pictures' which had appeared in *The Literary Gazette*, and four 'Sketches from History'.

The Troubadour went through three editions and was almost as extensively reviewed as *The Improvisatrice*, but already the fact that

L. E. L. had been identified as Jerdan's creature was exposing her to the grossest of calumnies. In an attack on Jerdan as one of the 'Quacks of the Day' a fly-by-night satirical magazine called *The Wasp* included the following gross libel on L. E. L.

> Jerdan has been mainly assisted in his poetical efforts by his *literary* and *personal* friend, Miss LETITIA ELIZABETH LANDON, whose contributions have been productive of as much comfort to the *Literary Gazette* as her society has been to its editor. This young lady is a most useful and indefatigable contributor, and the salubrious air of Sloane Street and Brompton Row (between which places she passes her time) has been of peculiar advantage both to her *mental* and *bodily* health. With respect to the latter, it is a singular circumstance, that although she was a short time since as thin and aereal as one of her own sylphs, she in the course of a few months acquired so perceptible a degree of *embonpoint* as to induce her kind friend Jerdan to recommend a change of air, lest her health and strength should be affected. She followed his advice, and strange to say, such was the effect of even two months' absence from Brompton, that she returned as *thin* and poetical as ever!

The truth seems to be that L. E. L. spent the weeks leading up to and after Christmas, as she had the preceding year, with her uncle, the Reverend James Landon, at the rectory of Aberford, near Wetherby, in Yorkshire. From there she wrote to her friend Katherine Thomson, a novelist and the wife of her medical attendant, Dr Anthony Todd Thomson, and to Rosina Wheeler. While she was in the north she visited her mother, whom she was shocked to find reduced to skin and bone by poverty and the fatigue of nursing her consumptive daughter in her last illness. From that time onwards she supported her mother as well as her brother by her work.

The editors of *The Wasp* were never taken to task for their gross imputation. Indeed Jerdan may even have enjoyed the laddishness of the situation; in 1852, he attempted to mend his failing fortunes by publishing an *Autobiography* in which he went so far as to claim that the chief well-spring of L. E. L.'s creativity was her passion for him.

Thus it befell with my tuition of L. E. L. Her poetic emotions and aspirations were intense, usurping in fact almost every other function of the brain; and the assistance I could give her in the ardent pursuit produced an influence not readily to be conceived . . . The result was a grateful and devoted attachment; all phases of which demonstrate and illumine the origin of her productions. Critics and biographers may guess, and speculate, and expatiate for ever; but without this master-key they will make nothing of their reveries.

Jerdan's recollections continue in this repellent vein for several pages. He does not shrink from assuming the entire responsibility for the development of L. E. L.'s literary talent and the direction of her career, and even boasts that for him 'the return of services was great' and that she was soon doing little less for his magazine than he did himself, apparently more for love than money. He gives no sign that he was aware that her close association with him had exposed a vulnerable young woman to the slander of his enemies, let alone that he might regret the fact. A later number of *The Wasp* repeated the charge; L. E. L.

(alias Letitia Languish) was next called up, charged with having written a sentimental elegy on the Swellings of Jordan. She pleaded that the flood had gone off; but the plea was overruled and she was ordered into the country to gather fruit, and to deliver an account thereof on her return.

The *Sun* newspaper too attacked her savagely with ridicule and calumnious insinuation, touching what so far no reviewer had mentioned, the 'immoral tendency' of L. E. L.'s poetry.

Consultations were held by her friends as to the steps to be pursued. Mr Jerdan advised an action being threatened if an instant contradiction did not appear.

No retraction appeared, and no one was ever sued. In June 1826, L. E. L. wrote to Katherine Thomson:

I think of the treatment I have received until my soul writhes

under the powerlessness of its anger. It is only because I am
poor, unprotected and dependent upon popularity, that I am a
mark for all the gratuitous insolence and malice of idleness and
ill-nature. And I cannot but feel deeply that had I been possessed
of rank and opulence, either these remarks had not been made,
or if they had, how trivial would their consequence have been
to me.

What the fashionable demi-mondaine could do with impunity, the
bankrupt army agent's daughter could not. As for her suggested
relationship with Jerdan, which has been described by modern biographers as an absurdity and an impossibility which, prejudices about
age and youth aside, it certainly was not, Letitia Landon had this to
say:

As to the *report* you named, I know not which is greatest – the
absurdity or the malice. Circumstances have made me very
much indebted to the gentleman for much of kindness. I have
not a friend in the world but himself, to manage anything of
business, whether literary or pecuniary. Your own literary pursuits must have taught you how little, in them, a young woman
can do without assistance. Place yourself in my situation. Could
you have hunted London for a publisher, endured all the alter-
nate hot and cold water thrown on all your exertions; bargained
for what sum they might be pleased to give; and, after all,
canvassed, examined, nay quarrelled over accounts the most
intricate in the world? And again, after success had procured
money, what was I to do with it? Though ignorant of business, I
must know I could not lock it up in a box. Then, for literary
assistance, my proof sheets could not go through the press
without revision. Who was to undertake this I can only call it
drudgery – but someone to whom my literary exertions could
be in return as valuable as theirs to me? But it is not on this
ground that I express my surprise at so cruel a calumny, but
actually on that of our slight intercourse. He is in the habit of
frequently calling on his way to town, and unless it is Sunday
afternoon, which is almost his only leisure time for looking over
letters, manuscripts, &c., five or ten minutes is the usual time of
his visit . . .

At the time when this was written, William Jerdan had known and collaborated with L. E. L. for eight or nine years. It would not be so remarkable if, at the beginning, the teenage girl who so loved her father, had been love-struck by the famous man who was so kind to her. Jerdan may well have treated her as if she was younger than she actually was, and unwittingly encouraged her in some sort of infantile, self-abnegating obsession, but no tensions ever developed in the intimacy between L. E. L. and the whole family, and it would seem on those grounds wiser to reject the likelihood of any physical intimacy having taken place between William Jerdan and his protégée. This does not however exclude many other kinds of intimacy; callow as she was L. E. L. may have seen herself as a Laura to Jerdan's Petrarch, with very little encouragement.

Even impartial observers were bemused by the manner in which L. E. L. capitulated to the fiction of the 'Child of Song'. Jerdan had begun it by his insistence that she was still in her teens, when she was in fact just out of them. Mrs S. C. Hall, better known as the novelist Anna Marie Fielding, supplies an unintentionally grotesque account of the demeanour of the poet of female passion, who must at the time have been twenty-three years old.

> I first saw Letitia Landon – in her grandmother's modest lodging in Sloane Street – a bright-eyed, sparkling, restless little girl, in a pink gingham frock, grafting clever things on commonplace nothings, frolicking from subject to subject with the playfulness of a spoiled child, her dark hair put back from her low, yet broad forehead, only a little above the most beautiful eyebrows a painter could picture, and falling in curls about her slender throat. We were nearly the same age, but I had been a year married, and if I had not supported myself on my dignity as a matron, should have been more nervous on my first introduction to a 'living poet', though the poet was so different from what I imagined. Her movements were as rapid as those of a squirrel. I wondered how one so quick could be so graceful. She had been making a cap for her grandmother and would insist upon the old lady's putting it on, that I might see 'how pretty she was'. To this grandmamma (Mrs Bishop) objected. She 'couldn't', and she 'wouldn't' try it on; 'how could Letitia be so silly?' Then the author of the *Golden Violet* put the great be-flowered,

be-ribboned thing on her own dainty head with a grave look –
like a cloud on a rose – and folding her pretty little hands over
her pink frock, made what she called a 'Sir Roger de Coverley'
curtsy, skipping backwards into the bedroom; and rushing in
again, having deposited out of sight the cap she was so proud
of constructing, she took my hands in hers and asked me 'if
we should be friends.' 'Friends!' I do not think that during
the long intimacy that followed the childlike meeting, extending
from the year 1825 to her leaving England in 1838, during which
time I saw her nearly every day, and certainly every week –
I do not think she ever loved me as I loved her – how could
she?

Katherine Thomson believed that L. E. L. was only fifteen when
The Fate of Adelaide was published in 1821, when in fact she was
nineteen. In 1836 Thomas Hood described Bettina von Arnim in a
letter to Dilke as quite notorious in Berlin.

> After the manner of L. E. L. she affects to be the girl – so young
> and innocent that she lays her head on gentlemen's bosoms or
> sits on their laps . . .

All her life, friends were to insist on L. E. L.'s kittenish charm.
Rosina Wheeler found it jarring and artificial and her playful style of
dressing absurd. Chorley thought that her adoring public would
instantly see through the tirades of blighted love and super-sentiment
once they actually saw the giggling miss who produced them by the
yard. The Quaker Mary Howitt had heard that she was

> a most thoughtless girl in company, doing strangely extravagant
> things; for instance, making a wreath of flowers, then rushing
> with it into a grave and numerous company, & placing it on
> [Jerdan's] head

but went on to say that such behaviour must be excused in 'a girl
of twenty' and 'a genius'. In fact when these words were written
L. E. L. was twenty-three. Bulwer Lytton who saw her often at
Miss Spence's and Miss Benger's soirées in 1826 judged her to be
eighteen.

One remark in Mrs Hall's description of her relationship with
L. E. L. could be a clue to much about the poet that has never been
intelligibly discussed. L. E. L. was convinced that she was unloved
partly because she did not notice the strong and durable affection of
loyal friends like Mrs Hall. L. E. L. was also convinced that she was a
woman of strong passions but she was never tempted to return the
love of those who loved her. The paradox of emotional impotence
masquerading as emotional superiority is a common female syndrome,
originating probably in the defect in narcissism which characterizes a
sex conditioned to think of itself as inferior.

Ever since the success of *The Improvisatrice* L. E. L. had been much
in demand at the social gatherings of literary London, where young
women were at a premium. She was, of course, an oddity, being
totally without family or connections as far as most people could
judge. Her grandmother was all her life a dear friend of Mrs Siddons
and had kept a circle of select acquaintance, so that Letitia's manners
were not without polish, although we are given to believe that at first
she dressed very oddly.

> When I first knew her, and for some time after, she was
> childishly untidy and negligent in her dress. Her 'frocks' were
> tossed on, as if buttons and strings were encumbrances; one
> sleeve off the shoulder, the other on, and her soft, silky hair
> brushed 'anyhow'.

When Rosina Wheeler came to call upon L. E. L. at her grandmother's house in Sloane Street, she took exception to her dress on
somewhat different grounds:

> I was surprised, and somewhat scandalised when I first saw her;
> for, though only 2 p. m. she had her neck and arms bare, a very
> short, but elaborately flounced white muslin dress, and a flower
> in her hair – but I thought, of course, that authoresses, like
> 'charming women', might dress themselves just as they pleased.
> In later years her dress was tamed to the conventional standard,
> but her manners were never entirely broken in.

Rosina Wheeler had come to call on L. E. L. to thank her for the
stanzas relating to an exploit of her great-uncle, Sir John Doyle, with

whom she was living in Somerset Street, Portman Square. She was one of many people who sought the poet out at her grandmother's house.

> The drawing-room of these lodgings was sometimes filled with gay ladies of rank in the morning, and with men of letters and literary ladies in the evening. L. E. L. was a social being; and young as she then was little more than twenty-three had the gift, so perfect in France, so rare in England, of receiving well. Nothing could be more lively than these little social meetings and nothing more unexceptionable . . . It was at this period that she was seized with her first attack of serious illness, inflammation of the lungs. She suffered much, and her constitution never perfectly rallied afterwards. It was about this time, also, that the first attempt to injure her character was made in the *Sun* newspaper.

However diverse the characters of literary gentlemen, it would seem that they behaved themselves in Mrs Bishop's house. It was at this house that Rosina Wheeler 'first beheld all the curious specimens of the literary menagerie'. Apparently the only colour of respectability was supplied to these gatherings by the presence of one Mrs Roberts, widow of the headmaster of St Paul's school. Rosina Wheeler may have had ample reason to inveigh against the slough of literary society and to sneer at the 'strange and questionable people' one met at L. E. L.'s perhaps, but her own antecedents and conduct were not such as to place her beyond inclusion in any list of strange and questionable people. Together the poet and the beauty went the rounds of the literary soirées, or 'menageries' as they called them. One of the most indefatigable hostesses was Miss Spence,

> who on the strength of having written something about the Highlands, was decidedly '*blue*' . . . She had a lodging of two rooms in Great Quebec Street, and 'patronised' young *littérateurs*, inviting them to her 'humble abode', where tea was made in the bedroom, and where it was whispered that the butter was kept cool in the wash-hand basin!

The chief attraction at Miss Spence's gatherings was the frequent presence in her 'humble abode' of Lady Caroline Lamb, who was still invested with the glamour of her association with Byron.

The other literary salon where L. E. L. and Rosina Wheeler might be found was that of Miss Benger, another of the 'turban'd Turks', authoress at the age of thirteen of *The Female Geniad* (1791). Rosina Wheeler describes in her ill-natured way the figure cut by L. E. L. in this assembly.

> Fortunately, 'L. E. L.' arrived; but was some time before she made her way over to me, for she had to shake every one by both hands *chemin faisant*; for never was there any one, even among the *literati*, who had such an exaggerated and enthusiastic way of expressing what she did not feel . . .

L. E. L. was deeply impressed by Rosina Wheeler, who seemed to be all that she herself was not. Statuesque and comely, haughty to the point of insolence, with a literary gift she hardly cared to use, Rosina fascinated the plainer girl. For a while they were bosom friends, until Rosina began to court Lady Caroline Lamb, to whom L. E. L. could not afford to come too close.

Although L. E. L.'s reputation was severely damaged by gossip, there was no thought in her mind of retirement from public life. However much she might complain of the miseries of fame, she had, in the interests of her career and her dependants, to put a brave face on things and struggle on. The parties were as necessary an adjunct to the publishing industry then as they are now. Besides, L. E. L. had never been able to come out in society in the usual way. Literary society was all she knew and all she was eligible for. If she hoped to find friends and a husband, those awful parties of Miss Benger's and Miss Spence's were her only chance.

L. E. L. gave expression to her sincere admiration for Rosina Wheeler in *The Golden Violet*. Rosina wrote to her friend Mary Greene, who had expressed fears about L. E. L.'s being a fit companion for her:

> I do not feel justified in sending you L. E. L.'s lines on me as they form part of the new poem which is coming out in May when you will have the gratification of seeing my portrait in full length, and so beautifully unlike as not to be able to

recognise anything but the name. She gets £1000 for this her third volume. And now on the score of her being too impassioned for my friend (N.B. she never was in love in her life) I would give you one little piece of advice, which is never to decide that because in writing poetry a person summons 'thoughts that breathe and words that burn' that they are as a matter of course practically to illustrate what they describe . . . To set your mind at rest and prove to you that she is almost as prudent as yourself, I enclose you a lecture I got from her a week ago about poor dear Lady Caroline Lamb who is the most fascinating, bewildering attractive creature I ever knew – one whom the more I know of her the more convinced I am has been 'more sinned against than sinning'.

And now to show you what *prudent* people are . . . Three days after I was out of bed, and one day after she was out of hers, she insisted on my going to a ball with her . . .

L. E. L. had been seriously ill with what Dr Thomson diagnosed as 'inflammation of the lungs', aggravated in this case by her distress at the evil reports that were circulating about her. Rosina was wrong about the price that L. E. L. was paid for *The Golden Violet*, which according to Jerdan's figures earned a mere £200. The book did not come out in May, but in December 1826. Even her grandmother had not understood that it was necessary to leave L. E. L. locked up in her bedroom, where she wrote on a small table at the foot of her narrow white bed, surrounded by books and papers on the floor, because her writing case left no room on the table for them. She thought that so much sitting and poring over papers was bad for Letty's health and she was right. L. E. L. decided that she could function better as a boarder than she could as a grandchild and left her grandmother's house:

Perhaps in not returning to her mother, L. E. L., as an authoress, was right; as a member of society she was wrong. As an authoress she required quiet; entire freedom from irritation; absence from small worries incidental to a home of privation. Advice that she could not always follow, yet dared not, lest altercation should arise, dispute. After a lapse of years these considerations seem valid, and constitute a plea for that which was constantly urged against her – her absence from her mother's protection. It was, in point of fact, all that could be urged to her detriment.

It would have been the correct and most convenient arrangement for L. E. L. when she left her grandmother's house to bring her mother to live with her, but this was not done. Mrs Hall comments in a maddenly cryptic way which suggests that it was Mrs Landon who refused to live with her daughter:

Her mother I never saw. Morally right in all her arrangements, she was mentally wrong, and the darling poet of the public had no loving sympathy, no tender care from the author of her being. She had endured the wrongs of a neglected child-hood, and but for the attachment of her grandmother she would have known 'next to nothing' of the love of mother-hood. Thus she was left alone with her genius; for admiration, however grateful to a woman's senses, never yet filled a woman's heart.

L. E. L. returned to the house in Hans Place where she had been a scholar for such a brief time as a child. It was now run by the three Misses Lance and their father, people of the utmost respectability.

L. E. L. established herself in a small attic looking out into the square, with its small, well-guarded circles of shrubs and turf, and there slept and wrote, often till the depth of winter, without a fire. She dined with the school, drank tea in the parlour with old Mr Lance and his daughters, and received her visitors in the long, low room in which in her careless infancy she had seen Lady Caroline Lamb deliver the prizes. The chief trouble she gave was in the continual opening of the door to coroneted carriages, or loungers from the clubs, or those killers of one's morning, intimate friends, who think they are privileged to look in early, and ruin their hosts with the interruption. Then, at night, some lady would often call and take the poetess to some gay fete.

They were staid and serious, and felt deeply the responsibility of their calling, and had received Miss Landon on the terms and in the character of a parlour-boarder, as much from affection for her, as from interest; and, indeed, I think the incessant callers, notes, and messages which ensued must have put these excellent ladies out of their way. But they all loved her; and she, in return, was the most considerate of human beings, and respected their wishes and their convenience as much as if they had been duchesses. The aged gentleman too was cheered by that flow of good-humour, which whether in the hilarity of a prosperous and flattering career, or in the gloom of secret anxiety, was exhaustless to him, and to all who, like that individual, were dependent upon the solace of kindness for cheerfulness and comfort. How well do I remember the drawing-room fire-place, beneath what had been a window, but which was con-verted into a recess, lined with shelves, and paved with shells, and teacups and saucers of delicate china, and teapots, and small vases! How we used to sit there, over an expiring fire, she unwilling to have it replenished, because the day's seance was nearly over: − the little square was in gloom, the afternoon London mist had overspread it: 'There will be no more callers to-day,' was her usual speech; and, when not engaged, L. E. L. always, in the winter at least, sat with the family in a small square parlour, lined with good book-shelves, and furnished with less precision than the guest-chamber. She composed and wrote, she told me, in a small attic at the very top of the house, looking upon the octagon garden of Hans Place, dotted by the handful of children who play therein; upon the turning, too down from Hans Street . . . And numerous were the visitors; ladies of quality, who had read the sonnets of the poetess on 'terraces by moon light'; critics, and their victims; grave travel-lers, who had issued their quartos; young prodigies, old cox-combs, American tourists, briefless barristers, and profitless cu-rates, all found an entrance into that long parlour, opening behind into a drear enclosure of a garden. How often have I found my friend, taking breath in that dingy garden, from the hot presence of a reviewer, or the chilling address of a disap-pointed author!

It might be supposed that living in such circumstances, with no more privacy than a boarder in school, L. E. L. would have been beyond the reach of scandal, especially as she was working harder than she ever had before.

Although Rosina might have abandoned her for the more apparent charms of Lady Caroline Lamb, L. E. L.'s attachment seems not to have waned. In April 1826 at a party of Miss Benger's, Rosina Wheeler met Edward Bulwer Lytton and next year, quite against old Mrs Bulwer's wishes, she married him. In 1828 Jerdan was the unconscious cause of further traduction of L. E. L.'s character, for he took her with him to visit the Bulwers at Woodcot. Mary Greene wrote in her diary of how she was shocked by the apparent philandering between Letitia Landon and Edward Bulwer. We may assume that Mary's Kilsallaghan upbringing had ill prepared her for the freedom of London manners and she misunderstood the meaning of L. E. L.'s behaviour. However, Rosina Lytton was to terminate her friendship with L. E. L. on account of her closeness with her husband and to write very scurrilously of her more than twenty years after the event. L. E. L. was honoured to visit the Lyttons at 36 Hertford Street, the most glittering salon in London, where she might meet Augusta Leigh, Lord Normanby (then Lord Mulgrave), William Godwin and Benjamin Disraeli. Bulwer Lytton was becoming associated with the reform party and the Benthamites, and so was being brought into conflict with L. E. L.'s old colleagues, the Tories, and in particular her evil genius, William Maginn.

Undoubtedly the worst turn that William Jerdan did for L. E. L. was to bring her into close and prolonged contact with William Maginn. Maginn's extraordinary career had begun in Cork, when he took over his father's school upon his sudden death and ran it so effectively that at the age of twenty-three he was given a Doctorate of Laws from Trinity College, Dublin. After sending occasional contributions to *Blackwood's Magazine* in Edinburgh, he became a virtual fixture with *Noctes Ambrosianae*, which ran from 1822 to 1835, most of which he wrote himself. By 1823 he was so much in demand as a journalist that he left Ireland for London, where his first mailing address was care of William Jerdan, and worked regularly for *The Literary Gazette*. There can be little doubt that young Miss Landon was dazzled by this extraordinary figure. His wildness and irresponsibility only enhanced his brilliance and at thirty his careless good looks had not yet degenerated into squalor. He was a fine prose writer, perhaps the best of his generation, but he turned his pen to virtually anything, including the worst campaigns of the Tory cabal. If L. E. L. had needed a model for her own brand of literary immorality, Maginn was just the man.

Even though Maginn had what L. E. L. had not, a refined and disciplined intelligence, his intellectual arrogance and reckless improvidence led to mismanagement of all his affairs, bringing him to the same end, oblivion and premature death. His epitaph was effectively penned by his old ally and boon companion Lockhart in 1842.

> Here, early to bed, lies kind William Maginn,
> Who, with genius, wit, learning, Life's trophies to win,
> Had neither great Lord nor rich cit of his kin,
> Nor discretion to set himself up as to tin;
> So his portion soon spent, (like the poor heir of Lynn),
> He turned author, ere yet there was beard on his chin –
> And whoever was out, or whoever was in,
> For your Tories his fine Irish brain would he spin,
> Who received prose and rhyme with a promising grin –
> 'Go ahead, you queer fish, and more power to your fin!'
> But to save from starvation turned never a pin.
> Light for long was his heart, though his breeches were thin,
> Else his acting, for certain, was equal to Quinn;
> But at last he was beat, and sought help of the bin
> (All the same for the Doctor, from claret to gin),
> Which led swiftly to jail, with consumption therein.
> It was much, when the bones rattled loose in his skin,
> He got leave to die there, out of Babylon's din.
> Barring drink and the girls, I ne'er heard of a sin,
> Many worse, better few, than bright, broken Maginn.

Chorley, who blamed these early associations for L. E. L.'s subsequent misfortunes, may not have been far out in his estimate of the harm that was done her.

If she was unrefined, it was because she had fallen into the hands of a coarse set of men – the Tories of a provincial capital – such as then made a noise and a flare in the 'Noctes Ambrosianae' of

Blackwood's magazine, second-hand followers of Lockhart and Professor Wilson, and Theodore Hook; the most noisy and the most reprehensible of whom – and yet one of the cleverest – was Dr Maginn. Not merely did they, at a very early period of the girl's career, succeed in bringing her name into a coarse repute, from which it never wholly extricated itself, but, by the ridiculous exaggeration of such natural gifts as she possessed, (no doubt accompanied by immediate gain), flattered her into the idea that small further cultivation was required by one who could rank with a Baillie, a Tighe, a Hemans – if not their superior, at least their equal.

It seems likely that, if Maginn made overtures to Letitia Landon, he would have done it when she was fresh to fame and most impressionable, but gossip does not link his name with hers until after Jerdan. Maginn was known as a womanizer; perhaps he did try to include his colleague in his list of conquests. Perhaps he was not entirely unsuccessful; she may have encouraged him unwittingly. Somehow she seems to have placed herself in his power, for even the loyal Halls admit that there was something between them:

> Undoubtedly the wicked slander that associated the name of Maginn with that of L. E. L. had some foundation. She had written to that very worthless person a letter, or letters, containing expressions which she ought not to have penned. They aroused the ire of a jealous woman and led to much misery.

A persistent tradition among Maginn's biographers holds that he was in love with her and remained so all his life.

> Certain it is that Maginn was deeply attached to Miss Landon; his feeling for the fair poetess constituting, according to his biographer, Kenealy, 'one of the most remarkable features of his life'. He is said to have contributed at least a fourth of the poetry in the *Drawing-Room Scrap-Book*, when it was under her guidance; he was disconsolate at her death, and almost lost his senses for two days; and he fancied that he saw, and conversed with, her attendant spirit, in the last hours of his life.

L. E. L.'s good friend Katherine Thomson begins her recollections of literary characters with a ruefully admiring portrait of Maginn in which she mentions L. E. L. in passing, in a fashion which implies less than if she had omitted to mention her at all. Maginn contributed material to *Fisher's Drawing-Room Scrap Book*, which was being edited by L. E. L., as late as 1836 and 1837. If there was some sort of amorous relationship between L. E. L. and Maginn, it seems very odd that it should have continued in such an amicable fashion for more than ten years, at least until L. E. L. gave up the editorship of the *Drawing-Room Scrap Book* in 1837. Bulwer Lytton's biographer, Michael Sadleir, erects a fascinating but fairly ill-founded structure of conjecture upon the few facts that are known. The new scandal arose, he says, out of anonymous letters which appeared in 1830, saying that the 'Child of Song' was actually the mistress of a married man. Sadleir reconstructs the following sequence of events:

> In the middle twenties the Doctor made overtures – maybe applied direct pressure – to Miss Landon, and had been repulsed. A definite part in his discomfiture had been played, not only by Bulwer, but by Rosina also . . . The Bulwers were told by their friend of the persecution to which she was being subjected, and deliberately took a hand in thwarting the unwelcome lover. Maginn relinquished an intrigue which threatened to cause more trouble than it was worth, but did not forget Bulwer's interference or the lady's evasion of capture. He determined on a double revenge – a public one on Bulwer, a private one on L. E. L. The very purposeful belabouring of Bulwer at the hands of *Fraser's* was the former; the anonymous letters were the latter. These letters were written by Maginn (even more probably at Maginn's instigation by Westmacott, who was an adept at this sort of meanness . . .) and the identity of the married man was left purposely and conveniently vague.

Unfortunately for Sadleir's hypothesis no such letters have ever been found, nor are they mentioned in any other source. Reckless and improvident Maginn may have been, and unscrupulous to a degree, but hardly so small-minded and vindictive. The worst crime that can with certainty be charged against him is that of having written twice in one day on the Norton–Melbourne scandal, once from one side, with all due righteousness, and once from the other. That he should cold-bloodedly have arranged the ruination of L. E. L., knowing that she was his sister in adversity, at the same time as he was helping her with her chores for the annuals, simply does not add up.

Nevertheless there was a connection between L. E. L. and William Maginn, although it may not have been overtly sexual. Perhaps they imagined that they were in love with each other; perhaps he was in love with her. Perhaps there was some idealistic relationship which Letitia Landon betrayed when she announced her engagement. Somehow she could not disentangle herself from the wretched man and his jealous wife, but she had no idea of the extent of her vulnerability until she had the foolhardiness to become engaged to an eminently respectable, highly promising younger man. Then all hell broke loose.

The catalogue of Daniel Maclise's retrospective exhibition at the National Gallery in London in 1872 says that 'his relationship with Letitia Landon might have been disinterested'. L. E. L.'s biographers can only throw up their hands in despair at yet another innuendo which by its very nature cannot even be investigated let alone proved or disproved. Maclise arrived in London in 1827. Like all the other children of his shoe-tanning ex-soldier father, he was exceptionally good-looking. Moreover, he was very young and already acknowledged as a brilliant painter, Guido come to life. L. E. L.'s friend Samuel Carter Hall had come across him in Cork and, impressed by his work, had suggested that he study in the newly opened Cork Academy. Then Maclise came to London, and was enrolled at the Royal Academy School where he carried off all the prizes. He was soon taken up by the other members of the Halls' circle and became one of the most picturesque Byronic attendants at their gatherings. He was also moody, hypochondriacal and an incorrigible flirt. Women adored him, and it seems that Maclise adored being adored.

Maclise certainly knew L. E. L. They frequented the same houses, were intimate with the same people, but oddly enough, none of their mutual acquaintance thought it worthwhile even to deny that L. E. L. had behaved disreputably with Maclise. The matter never really arose, until it was suggested in 1834 that she had written four-and-twenty love letters to Maclise, who had offered one of them to her arch-enemy, Mrs Maginn. Mrs Hall wrote to L. E. L. begging her to comment upon the slanders that were circulating. L. E. L. was a good enough writer to know how to make something seem incredible without actually denying it. She pretends that the later scandal involving her with Maginn is merely a different version of the first preposterous suggestion, flung off by the whirling brain of Mrs Maginn. She mentions the precise figure of twenty-four letters, as if the very notion of a series contains its own refutation.

Maclise painted L. E. L. 'three or four' times. One portrait hangs in the National Portrait Gallery, another was engraved by Thomson and published by Fisher, and another engraved by Finden, published by Saunders and Otley in 1835. A caricature (by the same hand) appeared in *Fraser's*. Maclise certainly drew L. E. L. better than Pickersgill did in 1822, but he probably had a more interesting subject. What Rossetti called his 'funnily-drawn' portrait in *Fraser's*, the water-colour study for which is preserved in the British Museum, emphasizes the tininess of L. E. L. The fragility of the small hand extended towards the viewer and the delicacy of the small, elegant head with its strange top-knot are cleverly conveyed by a strange play of proportions within the whole drawing. All of the series called 'Maclise's Portrait Gallery', bar two or three, are excellent likenesses, with just the right touch of caricature. Most of them have become standard images of their subjects for use in encyclopedias and such. Everyone knows for example the exquisite drawing of Disraeli, leaning against a mantelpiece, gazing though his curls with an air of disdain and one tiny foot propped on the taper tip of his pump. Maclise's brilliance as a draughtsman would be amply attested by these drawings, most of which seem to have been executed in oddly candid situations – Miss Porter pours tea, Mr Rogers is asleep in his chair, Bulwer Lytton is shaving before a pier glass. Where and when and if L. E. L. was alone with Maclise for the various studies that he did of her, we do not now know, but the works themselves throw some light on the subject. Maclise did paint L. E. L. with a certain ironic tenderness, and she seems to have posed for him in a strangely forthcoming way. Very few of the faces in the 'Portrait Gallery' are actually looking straight out of the picture, but L. E. L.'s eyes are bent directly upon her beholder. Her expression contains all the lightness and good humour and easiness of manner which her friends enjoyed and her enemies called by other names like 'unrefined gaiety'. Her features good and bad are all recognizable, her high shoulders, low brow, retroussé nose ('one of the most homoeopathic, ignoble little snubs that ever attempted to do duty for that juste milieu of facial population'), her well-set, brilliant grey eyes and 'perfect' eyebrows, even her slightly prognathous jaw. The effect is of a very 'bonny' little woman, as Hogg pronounced her, with more than a common share of grace and charm.

If L. E. L. had been unimpressed by Maclise she would have been unique among his female acquaintance. For her, in any case, the artist was a superman, and this one even looked like a superman, with his noble broad brow under its Corinthian curls, his wide-set compelling eyes and powerful but elegant figure. His physical appeal was to ensnare many a woman with much more to lose and much more experience than Letitia Landon, although he was never to establish a relationship of any depth with any woman. Like L. E. L. he was an emotional incompetent. If any man of her acquaintance was to play Lorenzo to her Improvisatrice, Maclise was typecast. Handsome, passionate, arrogant and young, he was her Antinous to the life. *The Painter's Love* deals with the sad fate of an Italian peasant girl who elopes with a painter who betrays her. In one of the 'Miscellaneous Poems' appended to *The Venetian Bracelet*, L. E. L. tells the romantic story of Canova's love for the model of his Ariadne, who died. In 1835, when the engraved portrait of L. E. L. by Maclise was published and drew a delighted response from her fans, L. E. L. responded by writing a long poem on the subject of Maclise's painting *The Vow of the Peacock*, exhibited at Somerset House in 1835.

It seems likely that L. E. L. developed a crush on Maclise, and he would have at first responded and then, tiring of the emotionalism and the histrionics, simply let her slide out of his life. There probably were letters, pathetic, compromising, desperate letters, like the ones that Mary Wollstonecraft sent to Fuseli. Possibly the seduction of L. E. L. was the kind of affair which Maclise knew he could take up or leave off at any time, for the obsessiveness of his lover's nature was pretty evident. It would have been an easy matter to keep such an affair clandestine; L. E. L. was used to wearing a mask in public. Few circumstances are more degrading than to love fervently a perfectly nice man who simply does not care, especially when that man occasionally gratifies his ego by offering some easy encouragement, and when everybody else is in love with him too. In the year that Letitia Landon died, Maclise was discovered *in flagrante delicto* by the husband of Lady Harriet Sykes. L. E. L. would have liked the irony of that situation, but she would have liked better the fact that Maclise kept one of his portraits of her, which was not sold until the artist's sale in 1868.

In 1829 L. E. L. brought out a new book of poetry, *The Venetian Bracelet*. The title-poem is a melodrama, of black-haired Amenaide, a peasant beloved of Leoni, elevated to high rank and riches during his absence. Comes the glad day of his return and she is aghast to discover that he brings with him his blonde English bride, Edith. After a night of severe mental anguish she buys a trick bracelet from a pedlar, and at the first opportunity she slips the poison from it to Edith, who dies forthwith. Leoni is suspected and then judged guilty. Amenaide goes to him in the dungeons, her cheek already livid from the poison's action, and tells him that all has been set right. In the introduction L. E. L. takes on her traducers:

> I allude to the blame and eulogy which have been equally bestowed on my frequent choice of love as my source of song. I can only say, that for a woman whose influence and whose sphere must be in the affections, what subject can be more fitting than one which it is her peculiar province to refine, spiritualise and exalt? I have always sought to paint it self-denying, devoted, and making almost a religion of its truth; and I must add, that such as I would wish to draw her, woman actuated by an attachment as intense as it is true, as pure as it is deep, is not only more admirable as a heroine, love is that of light amusement, or at worst of vain mortification. With regard to the frequent application of my works to myself, considering that I sometimes portrayed love unrequited, then betrayed, and again destroyed by death – may I hint the conclusions are not quite logically drawn as assuredly the same mind cannot have suffered such varied modes of misery. However, if I must have an unhappy passion, I can only console myself with my own perfect unconsciousness of so great a misfortune.

Such pleading is clearly disingenuous, especially in view of the fact that the poem it seeks to preface deals with an attachment so pure and deep and spiritual that it ends in murder and suicide. L. E. L. is arguing that obsession is more ennobling than affection guided by common sense. Purity means for her not freedom from any taint of carnality but from any sordid considerations of convenience or social utility. The sensuous trappings of her settings, the numerous perfumed couches whereupon her lovers fling themselves when their strength fails, insist upon sensuality as an ultimate value. What is truly perverse about L. E. L.'s avowed position is that, while she insists that her poetry does not relate in any way to her own experience, she insists on dragging herself into the poems in such a way that she invites discussion of her own emotional experience. She begins *The Venetian Bracelet* by discussing her own non-existent acquaintance with Italy, then congratulates herself for never having been there and for being totally ignorant of the language:

> Thou (Italy) art not stamped with that reality
> Which makes our being's sadness and its thrall!
> But now, whenever I am mix'd too much
> With worldly natures till I feel as such –
> (For these are as the waves that turn to stone,
> Till feelings keep their outward show alone) –
> When wearied by the vain, chill'd by the cold,
> Impatient of society's set mould –
> The many meannesses, the petty cares,
> The long avoidance of a thousand snares,
> The lip that must be chain'd, the eye so taught
> To image all but its own actual thought –
> Deceit is the world's passport: who would dare
> When work, my nature struggling with my fate,
> Checking my love, but, O, still more my hate –
> Why should I love? flinging down pearl and gem
> To those that scorn, at least care not for them:
> Why should I hate? as blades in scabbards melt,
> I have no power to make my hatred felt;
> Or, should I say, my sorrow: I have borne,
> So much unkindness, felt so lone, so lorn,
> I could but weep, and tears may not redress,
> They only fill the cup of bitterness –
> My spirit turns to thee (Italy) . . .

For one who insists that her personal experiences are utterly irrelevant to her poetry, this gargantuan adverbial clause, with its flying buttresses of parentheses ought to find no place at all in the poem. The morose and crabbed style is not in itself attractive and the most scrupulous critic must be pardoned for harbouring a suspicion that the 'Child of Song' is getting something off her chest. The headlong tumbling of the syntax gives an ineradicable impression of spontaneity and the hit-and-miss versification verifies it. L. E. L. did put herself into her poetry – she had nothing else to put in it. What she was quite right in objecting to was the crassness of the public attempts to interpret her reflections as confessions of some peccadillo or another. She was not talking about a month in the country, but about her image of her whole life and all her circumstances, her 'nature' struggling with her 'fate'. The other two long poems published in *The Venetian Bracelet* are much more concerned with L. E. L.'s own dilemmas, in particular, the fate of the genius which cannot disentangle itself from popularity. 'The Lost Pleiad' uses a strange allegory of the youngest of the Pleiades, who falls in love with a promiscuous earthling, and is henceforth unable to play her lyre. 'The History of the Lyre' tells the story of the poetess Eulalie, exhausted by acclaim and public life, whose spirit withers from frigidity and impotence. Both provide L. E. L.'s partial diagnosis of her spiritual disease, and both bear the unmistakable stylistic signs of arrested development and artistic frustration. That the poems are not better is the proof of their argument. That they are not worse is a painful indication of what might have been.

The political ferment of 1829–32 must have reached even L. E. L., buried as she was in her own imaginative and emotional experience and snug behind the school doors in Hans Place. The hotting up of the campaign for and against the Reform Bill induced Maginn to add to activities for *Blackwood's* and *The Literary Gazette*, and his editorship of the scurrilous gossip sheet *The Age*, a new venture of the bluest Toryism, *Fraser's Magazine*, in which he baited all the eminent reformists of his day. L. E. L. on the other hand was slowly being taken over by the opposition. She clung to her 'Tory principles', although the idea of a Tory principle was by that time in a fair way to becoming a contradiction in terms, but she continued to frequent the company of the literary avant-garde, who were for the most part liberal and reformist in their ideas. The Halls, the Thomsons, the Lyttons all supported the Bill. The assemblies at Hertford Street were frequently ridiculed, much gossiped about by those excluded from them and sometimes by those who attended. L. E. L. was unfortunately utterly dazzled and quite uncritical, whether of the insolence of Rosina Lytton, which amounted to downright rudeness, or the foppish radicalism of her host.

Taste was changing; L. E. L.'s stock in trade was no longer as palatable as it had been. The dubiousness of her sense of moral discrimination was becoming more apparent as the age of decency loomed nearer.

> Was she to go on writing Troubadours and Golden Violets all her days – apostrophizing loves, memories, hopes and fears, for ever, in scattered songs and uncompleted stanzas, and running the chance of weakening the effect of her past music by monotony of note? That she was in danger of doing this was indicated by the tide of criticism that set in against her. It stimulated her to a gradual change of poetic note that had acquired for her more popularity than she could permanently retain. Her thoughts found a deeper channel and flowed still more freely; her observation took a wider range, and scanned the features of life as they presented themselves to her earnest gaze . . .

Unfortunately perhaps L. E. L. did not in her novels scan the features of the life she knew. She was no Austen, although in the pertness of her reported conversation she may have had something of Fanny Burney's sprightliness. She did not write, as Charlotte Brontë would have done, of the Misses Lance and their father, or of her fellow parlour-boarder, Miss Emma Roberts, who took the trouble to help Miss Landon to dress herself in less fanciful ways and in fact succeeded in rendering her at last well coifed and even elegant. L. E. L.'s novels were nearly as far-fetched as her poems; after her first attempt she gave up all idea of portraying her own generation and the life that other people knew so much better than she did, and built up painful mosaics of a bygone age, introducing all the most glamorous characters she had met in books.

If she had sought to evade ridicule and parody by writing in prose, she utterly failed of her object. Perhaps she misjudged the political situation, perhaps she wished to treat it with open contempt but, in directly portraying the Lyttons as twin deities in her novel *Romance and Reality*, she blundered straight into the hands of the Tory lampoon-ers. Bulwer Lytton's biographer is scathing:

> The syntax is a little indeterminate; the compliments are ludi-crously over-pitched, as were all the ingratiations of this luckless and transient Sappho; but with due allowance for their author's saccharine servility and remembering that Bulwer had been one of the several daylight lovers she had incautiously allowed herself, we may take the description of 'Emily Arundel's' sight of them as fairly representative of the opinion held of Edward and Rosina among sympathetic blues.

So is history made. There is no proof that L. E. L. ever had a lover by day or night, let alone several. One would like her rather better if she had, but she seems, however reckless in her superficial manner, to have been deeply reserved about any act of physical committal. What Rosina Lytton said twenty years after the event, and Mary Greene wrote at the time, does not add up to evidence of any significant involvement of L. E. L. with Bulwer Lytton. She may, of course, have been being manipulated by him because of some effect he wished to produce in his wife, with whom he was at the time (1828) still infatuated. The chief witness to L. E. L.'s servility is in fact Rosina Lytton, who knew that she could rely upon her beauty and sexual power to achieve effect and admiration – until her husband cast her off and had her committed to an insane asylum, that is. L. E. L. knew that she could not afford to offend, and literally had to please to live. By 1830, when she was seriously harassed and unwell, her un-steady demeanour with her patrons is too easily explicable. To make matters worse, Bulwer Lytton, possibly unaware that the world would recognize in L. E. L.'s panegyric his wife and himself, gave the novel an extremely favourable review in the *New Monthly Magazine*. The absurd incestuousness of the situation gave abundant justification to enemies of the clique; L. E. L. and Bulwer Lytton found themselves pilloried together in *The Age* for mutual backscratching, and anything else that prurience would assume to be thereby entailed.

As the editor of *The Age*, Maginn must have had a hand in the abuse of Lytton and L. E. L.; he may even have written the squib in question. Perhaps Sadleir is right to assume jealousy in an attack of so personal a nature. It is obvious that L. E. L.'s hero-worship rankled

with Maginn, for he brought it quite unnecessarily into the portrait of
Bulwer Lytton that he prepared for Maclise's 'Portrait Gallery':

> L. E. L. in her *Romance and Reality* has so completely depictured
> Bulwer (we shall not say '*con amore*' lest that purely technical
> phrase should be construed literally) that it would be useless.

Romance and Reality ought to have proved at once that L. E. L. had
very little idea of rhythm or pace in prose writing. The opening is
quite witty in a Dickensian and image-laden way, but it flags and
loses focus continually. The effort to write in a clear, connected and
intelligible fashion was taxing her.

> I can only say that writing poetry is like writing one's native
> language and prose, writing in a strange tongue.

It was all too clear that the novel had had absolutely no guidance
through the press. L. E. L. had to prefix it with an embarrassing
apology for muddling the name of one of her characters, an inauspi-
cious beginning to a new career as a novelist.

In the same year that saw the emergence of L. E. L. into the field of
novel writing, she also began her acquaintance with the annuals,
described by Thackeray as 'a little sham sentiment with a little sham
art'. *Fisher's Drawing-Room Scrap Book* was a handsome quarto, containing upwards of thirty poems, illustrative of an equal number
of engravings. The exigencies of her situation now demanded that
L. E. L. write about subjects dictated by others. The poetic gift that
she had exercised as naturally as she breathed when a little girl had
now become her slavery. She was not insensible of the degradation:
each one of her set poems cost her more labour than the ones that
had made her famous, and gave her none of the pleasure that self-
expression had been. Her unsteady health began to deteriorate and her
public appearances took a heavier toll of her reduced store of vitality.
Paradoxically, she seems to have become more handsome; she lost
weight and became positively delicate-looking, something she had
never been before. Her complexion, always transparent, became more
ethereal. By dint of hard labour and constant suffering she was
turning into one of her old heroines.

I confess the changing spirits of L. E. L. did not surprise me. Her health was broken, and she rested solely on her own efforts. Her immediate relations also depended upon her exertions; and, believe me, the daily task-work, the beautiful lines for the 'Easter Offering', the 'Drawing-room Scrap Book', and other undertakings, were often penned when the throbbing head would gladly have reposed upon her pillow, and the over-excited and restless mind would scarcely fix itself on its appointed theme; and that with the loathing of a slave – a literary slave – to the enforced subject. Heavens! What a profanation to bow down that sweet Muse to such subjects as the tastes of the day suggested! Sometimes flesh and blood rebelled against it – she had promised, on one occasion, a sonnet to some periodical; worn out, the night before, by previous exertion, she had retired to rest without writing it. She slept long, as one exhausted sleeps – perhaps her dreams were of some happier days, for she awoke refreshed. It was late; the emissary of the journal had arrived – the poem was to go to press that morning. The poetess sprang up – knelt down to her little writing-table, and, whilst the boy waited below, in a quarter of an hour's space, wrote some exquisite stanzas, and sent them off to the printer.

But, in spite of great and constant success, she was always poor.

Other eyes saw clearly what was happening to Letitia Landon; the absence of gushing in Chorley's bitter observations gives a much more vivid sense of what was happening to her as the flimsy ground of her reputation slid away from under her.

As years went on, the ephemeral success of Miss Landon's verses subsided: and, indeed, she had rendered herself next to incapable of anything like a sustained effort, though some of her smaller lyrics were more earnest and more real in their sentiment and sweetness than her earlier love-tales and ditties had been. There was amendment, too, in her versification. She attempted drama, in the tragedy, I think, of 'Castruccio Castrucani', but without the smallest success. She wrote a volume of sacred verse, which was sentimental rather than serious. She took Annuals in hand, but the result was the same, and it must have been felt so by herself. At last she began to write imaginative prose; and the coterie who supported her blew the trumpet before her first novel, *Romance and Reality*, as no one would do nowadays were a new Dickens, or a new Bulwer, on the threshold. But she held out bravely; wearing out life, and health, and hope, as all who work on ground which is not solid must do; bravely holding up those who looked to her for position and subsistence in life, and keeping up before such of the friends she retained, and such of the society as she mixed in sparingly, those hectic, hysterical high-spirits, which are even more depressing to meet than any melancholy. There was a certain audacious brightness in her talk; but it was only false glitter, not real brilliancy, it was smart, not sound.

The truth of Miss Landon's story and her situation had for some time oozed out; it was felt that her literary reputation had been exaggerated; that her social position was, so to say, not the pleasantest in the world. Those who had, in some measure, compromised her, were in no case to assist her; those who had stood aside, had become aware of the deep and real struggle and sorrow which had darkened her whole life, from its youth upwards, and the many, many pleas for forbearance implied in such knowledge.

L. E. L. was aware of the crippling of her mind and the disappearance of any possibility she may have had of developing to a real poet long before anyone else. Her despair found utterance in the poems printed with *The Venetian Bracelet* but she did not spell out unambiguously the story of her own disfigurement until she came to write the only novel that has any touch of greatness, *Ethel Churchill*, which follows almost ruthlessly the gradual stages of the destruction of Walter Maynard. Maynard, like L. E. L., was forced to earn a living in Grub Street.

'I cannot help,' said Walter Maynard, as he gazed, listlessly, from one of the upper windows, 'reading my fate in one of those little boats now rocking on the tide, only fastened by a rope, scarcely visible to the passer by. So am I tossed on the ebbing tide of life – now in sunshine, now in shade – seemingly free, yet, in reality, fettered by the strong, though slight chain of circumstance. For a small sum, any passenger may enter that boat and direct its course; and here again is similitude. I am at the beck of others. I may scarcely think my own thoughts, they must run in whatever channel public taste may choose; and that puts me in mind how I promised Curl his pamphlet this very night. How weary I am of exhausting the resources of language in dressing up the vague commonplaces of party, or giving plausibility to sophisms I feel to be untrue! but it must be done:' and, muttering to himself,

> 'For inspiration round his head,
> The goddess Want her pinions spread',

he drew his table towards him, and began to write.

The scene of his labours, and his own appearance, were much changed since his first lodging in London. Still, there was an air of careless discomfort in his room; nothing was in its place; books, foils, papers, and clothes, were scattered together, and a female mask lay beside his inkstand. He was fashionably dressed; but looked, as was really the case, as if he had not been in bed the previous night. His face was worn, and one red flush burnt on each cheek; though even that could scarcely animate the sunk and heavy eye. After a few minutes passed, first in writing, then in erasing what he had written, 'It is of no use,' said he, flinging down the pen, 'I am not worth a single phrase; alas! I want motive – the mere necessity of exertion is not enough. Would that I could dream as I once dreamed! that I could still think fame the glorious reality I once held a whole life's labour would cheaply purchase! But what does it matter, whether there be a name or no on the tombstone that weighs down our cold ashes? Ah! I promised Marston his verses to-morrow: I sell my opinions, I may as well do the same with my sentiments;' and again he drew the paper towards him.

At first, he wrote mechanically, and flung aside one sheet of paper, and then another; it was no longer the eager and impassioned writer, who, in his early composition, forgot want, cold, and misery: no, the real had eaten, like rust, into his soul. Last night's excess had left him weary and feverish; yet of all shapes that temptation can assume, surely that of social success is the most fascinating.

L. E. L.'s social life was still proceeding at its old pace. In between toiling away for *The Literary Gazette* and the annuals and her novels, and occasionally penning the spontaneous poems which only S. C. Hall would publish for her in *The New Monthly*, she kept up her attendance upon the Lyttons and upon their standard-bearers, the Halls, in whose house she met more and more literary lions, including even the Wordsworths and Mrs Edgeworth, for whom her preference had once led her into the suspicion of immorality. She met the vivid and enigmatic Mrs Jameson and Barry Cornwall and Allan Cunningham and Michael Thomas Sadler and Hogg, the Ettrick Shepherd, but none of these acquaintances became genuine friendships. None of these authors, perhaps because L. E. L. was already famous and seemed so little to need guidance and constructive criticism, or perhaps because she had not the courage to seek them out or perhaps because she really was a repellent phenomenon, was interested in offering her support or friendship. She returned the hospitality of others; her social life, despite the rather forbidding surroundings of Hans Place, seems to have been a success. On one occasion she managed to give a fancy-dress ball, to which even the Lyttons were happy to come.

In her own little home, however, she had her votaries and her throne. It is now long since forgotten, how in the long, low room, papered as it was with one of those dim papers of the last forty years, which make 'darkness visible', L. E. L. gave a fancy ball, which was attended in fancy dresses by Sir E. and Lady Bulwer, and other friends – some proportion of whom were editors and publishers, for L. E. L. never forgot that she had to depend on the press for support. Sometimes she received a small reunion of all her regiment of authors and journalists, the Misses Lance her chaperons, or some lady of consequence and often rank. Lady Stepney was one of her most indulgent friends; Mr and Mrs Hall also gave her their support. Not even Hannah More brought to life could have found anything to challenge censure in these agreeable and irreproachable evenings; but whilst this may be called the sunshiny day of her brief and unquiet maturity, she was often sad at heart.

In 1835 L. E. L.'s friends were delighted to learn that she was engaged to be married. She would no longer be the ageing boarder at Hans Place, which establishment anyway was about to break up or had broken up. She was, at the ripe old age of thirty-three, to be married. According to her publicity, she had had above two hundred offers by 1825 but, as she said herself, they were offers like the North Passage or Wordsworth's cuckoo, 'much talked of but never seen'. The prospective bridegroom was a distinguished and eminently suitable young man, perhaps a little too young, for he was eleven years younger than L. E. L., but none of her friends thought that detail worth commenting on. His name was John Forster. He had been trained to the law, but had chosen a literary way of life, and, despite his youth, had been appointed editor of *The Examiner*.

The news of the engagement had hardly begun to circulate when the cloud of gossip and slander about L. E. L. gathered and burst. Well-wishers felt it incumbent upon them to warn the young gentleman that his promised wife had rather an unenviable reputation. At first he was shocked and tried to track the evil reports back to their source, but the whispering was indomitable. Nobody who spoke to him believed what was being said, of course, but they had heard that L. E. L. had for a long time been the mistress of a married man. Rosina Lytton wrote in 1855:

It appears that that loathsome satyr, old Jerdan, in one of his drunken fits at some dinner let out all his liaison with Miss Landon and gave her name coupled with some disgusting toast: this Sir Liar told me. Whereupon I was so indignant, and still so staunch to Miss Landon that I went to her and said, 'Your only way to clear yourself in the eyes of the world is forever to shut your doors against this infamous man and on no pretext literary or *other business* ever admit him'. She affected to be furious, made a real scene and swore . . . that Jerdan would never again darken her doors. I said she could do no less; therefore imagine my consternation and disgust when a fortnight after, going to call on her in Hans Place, the servant threw open the door suddenly to announce me – and what did I see but Miss Landon seated on old Jerdan's knee with her arm around his neck!

When these words were written Rosina Lytton was a very angry woman; because in the same letter she accused L. E. L. of affairs with

Maginn and with her own husband, her testimony is usually discounted.

Forster, after an embarrassing confrontation with Alaric A. Watts, who seemed to be one of the fountain-heads of this gossip, finally gave up trying to deal with it himself and confronted L. E. L. There was no defence against what was being suggested, except to beg her husband-to-be to investigate further and to satisfy himself of the truth or falsehood of the charges. L. E. L. would not stoop to plead or explain, but released him from any obligation until he should be satisfied about the honour of the woman he (presumably) loved. He made his inquiries.

It had been a hard year for L. E. L. Besides writing *The Vow of the Peacock*, which was published in the autumn, she had been contributing reviews to the *Court Journal*. She had contributed to Mr Ackermann's illustrated volume *Flowers of Loveliness* and to *Heath's Book of Beauty* (both edited by the Countess of Blessington), as well as fulfilling her duty of versifying the accompaniments to the engravings in *Fisher's Drawing-Room Scrap-Book*. Harsh reality had driven her dear world of pure affections and devastating heroes beyond the horizon. Mr Forster's offer was at least

> a prospect of being domesticated with a man whose abilities she almost reverenced, and of living on that scene and that society which she had always preferred to any other – the literary society of London.

We know nothing of the courtship, or even of how John Forster and Letitia Landon met. Mrs Thomson tells us only that Forster's

> personal character was unexceptionable – an honourable, warm-hearted and highly-talented man. He was sincerely attached to L. E. L.; but no sooner was he accepted than *Friends* stepped forward to tell him a thousand tales of her supposed imprudences and even criminalities.

Blanchard, Hall, Wharton and Thomson all affirm stoutly that John Forster was satisfied after his inquiries that L. E. L. was not guilty as charged, and was perfectly happy to go ahead with the proposed marriage. Miss Landon however withdrew her consent, because she felt it unfair for so young a man to be shackled to a wife who could attract such calumny and because, said Mrs Thomson, Forster had been so uncertain of his choice as to distrust her. The broken engagement is never omitted from L. E. L.'s biography. John Forster's biographers, on the other hand, tend to deny in the teeth of unmistakable evidence to the contrary that John Forster was ever connected with her. All L. E. L.'s biographers insist that he behaved handsomely, that he never wavered in his readiness to honour his undertaking to take her under his protection and to give her his name, which is uncommonly good of them, because it seems, very definitely, not to have been the case.

I have already written to you two notes which I fear you could scarcely read or understand. I am today sitting up for an hour, and though strictly forbidden to write, it will be the least evil. I wish I could send you my inmost soul to read, for I feel at this moment the utter powerlessness of words. I have suffered for the last three days a degree of torture that made Dr Thomson say 'You have an idea of what the rack is now.' It was nothing to what I suffered from my own feelings.

I look back on my whole life – I can find nothing to justify my being the object of such pain – but this is not what I meant to say. Again I repeat that I will not allow you to consider yourself bound to me by any possible tie. To any friend to whom you may have stated our engagement, I cannot object to your stating the truth. Do every justice to your own kind and generous conduct. I am placed in a most cruel and difficult position. Give me the satisfaction of, as far as rests with myself, having nothing to reproach myself with. The more I think the more I feel I ought not – I cannot – allow you to unite yourself with one accused of – I cannot write it. The mere suspicion is dreadful as death. Were it stated as a fact, that might be disproved. Were it a difficulty of any other kind, I might say, Look back at every action of my life, ask every friend I have. But what answer can I give, or what security have I against the assertion of a man's vanity, or the slander of a vulgar woman's tongue? I feel that to give up all idea of a near and dear connection is as much my duty to myself as to you. Why should you be exposed to the annoyance, the mortification of having the name of the woman you honour with your regard coupled with insolent insinuations? You never would bear it.

I have just received your notes. God bless you! – but – After Monday I shall, I hope, be visible; at present it is impossible. My complaint is inflammation of the liver, and I am ordered complete repose – as if it were possible! Can you read this? Under any circumstances, the

Most grateful and affectionate of your friends,

'L. E. LANDON.'

We do not know the date of this letter, or at what stage in the affair it was written, but we do know that John Forster accepted its terms and went out of L. E. L.'s life for ever. If he had been convinced that she had not done what the gossips said, he would surely have waited. His behaviour, however correct, was more that of a man relieved to escape from an uncomfortable situation than of a man outraged by the traduction of his beloved fiancée's character. The public was not deceived.

Bulwer Lytton wrote begging L. E. L. to reconsider her decision; she replied:

I prefer writing to speaking. When I speak I become ashamed and confused and never say precisely what I mean. Misunderstanding there certainly is, if you suppose that I wish all connection between Mr Forster and myself at an end on account merely of the steps he has taken in the last most miserable business . . .

From all I can learn, the cruel slander is old; was well known to have originated in the very lowest portion of the Press; was put down by the kindly countenance of friends – and I may add by the whole tenor of my life. It was forgotten by most and scorned by all. I will not admit that Mr Forster *vindicated* my conduct inasmuch as there was nothing to vindicate. Still, holding as I do this opinion, I should not consider it a sufficient justification of my resolve that the gentleman can never be to me more than a friend. Mr Forster states that he will not consider me as bound to him if I can prove that he mentioned the report to any to whom it was previously unknown! Yet there was one person it was utterly unknown to – one person to whom if he had common feeling or delicacy he would not have named it – and that is myself. If his future protection is to harass

and humiliate me as much as his present – God keep me from it
. . . The whole of his late conduct to me personally has left
behind almost dislike – certainly fear of his imperious and
overbearing temper. I am sure we never could be happy together. He is clever, honourable, kind; but he is quite deficient
in the sensitiveness to the feelings of another, which is to me an
indispensable requisite. I bitterly regret what has passed and any
pain my determination may inflict on him, but we are quite
unsuited to each other and the proof is the very first question of
opinion – feeling – that arises between us. How differently do
we view it!

William Macready was another person who had not heard the
slander before John Forster repeated it to him.

Called on Forster, and stayed some time listening to a tale of
wretched abandonment to passion that surprised and depressed
me. That rumours and stories pressed in such number and
frightful quality upon him that he was forced to demand explanation from one of the reported narrators or circulators, Mr A. A.
Watts – that his denial was positive and circumstantial, but that
it was arranged between themselves and their mutual friends
that the marriage should be broken off. A short time after
Forster discovered that Miss L— made an abrupt and passionate
declaration of love to Maclise, and on a subsequent occasion
repeated it! It has lately come to light that she has been carrying
on an intrigue with Dr Maginn, a person whom I never saw,
but whom all accounts unite in describing as beastly biped; he is
married and has four children. Two letters of hers and one of his
were found by Mrs Maginn in his portrait, filled with the most
puerile and nauseating terms of endearment and declarations of
attachment! I felt quite concerned that a woman of such splendid
genius and such agreeable manners should be so depraved in
taste and so lost to a sense of what was due to her high
reputation. She is fallen!

As a barrister, Forster must have had some understanding of the
rules of evidence; we must assume then that when he told Macready
of the declarations of love to Maclise and of the notes to Maginn, he

was convinced that he was speaking of facts. Neither circumstance offers any evidence of 'criminal behaviour', that is, of sexual inter-course between Letitia Landon and either Maclise or Maginn, but for Macready what he had heard necessarily implied 'wretched abandon-ment to passion'. Macready and Forster were both Victorians, al-though the great queen herself was as yet uncrowned. The permissive and free-thinking aristocratic mileu of the romantic Regency was for them a period against which to react, the bad old days. The solid, cautious, hypocritical bourgeoisie was in the ascendant and, although some would hanker after the Byronic era, most would condemn and ridicule it. In fear of the consequences, Thomas Moore burnt Byron's autobiographical novel. Lady Blessington might have been entertain-ing brilliantly in the elegant surroundings of Gore House, but only men attended, and the storm that was eventually to exile her to France was gathering. For Forster and Macready it was enough to know that Letitia Landon had so far fallen in love as to forget her dignity and maidenly modesty and declare the fact, to know also that she was a depraved woman. Her descriptions of the feelings of passionate women were, if not ridiculous, improper, her ideas of the sovereignty of deep feeling old-fashioned and wrong. In the future as represented by Forster and Macready there was no place for L. E. L. She knew it, but exhausted by overwork, and emotional tension, she somehow could not care. She made no bid to ingratiate herself with the new men, but shrank back into the care of Mrs Sheldon, who had taken her in when the school at Hans Place had been broken up. Her illness dragged on, but as soon as she could she drove herself back to work.

The breaking off of her engagement gave the gossips new heart. The whispers that had come to John Forster's ears became a roar. L. E. L.'s friends were aghast; so emphatic and detailed were the accounts from one source, namely Mrs Maginn, that some of her friends felt obliged to ask L. E. L. to explain them. In June 1836, L. E. L. wrote in answer to Mrs Hall:

> You are quite right in saying that you owe me no apology for your letter, though I own I am surprised at its contents; for, from all that has been said to me, I had no idea that the least importance was attached to the slanders of a violent and malevo-lent woman. Mrs Maginn is too well-known in her own circle;

she speaks but of me as she speaks of everyone else. She has for some time past taken a great dislike to me, and first one spiteful invention and then another was its consequence – always however, fawning and flattering to my face. She seems to have quite a mania about my letter-writing; for the first shape in which it reached me was, that I had written four-and-twenty love-letters to Mr Maclise, and that he had offered her one of them. As to the new fancy about her husband, I cannot even call it jealousy – for jealousy implies some degree of feeling; it is sheer envy, operating upon a weak, vulgar, but cunning nature. As to the idea of an attachment between me and Dr Maginn, it seems to be too absurd even for denial. The letters, however, I utterly deny. I have often written notes, as pretty and as flattering as I could make them, to Dr Maginn, upon different literary matters, and one or two on business. But how any construction but their own could be put upon them I do not understand. A note of mine that would pass for a love-letter must either have been strangely misrepresented, or more strangely altered. Dr Maginn and his wife have my full permission to publish every note I ever wrote – in *The Age* if they like. I regret I ever allowed an acquaintance to be forced upon me of which I was always ashamed. The fact was I was far too much afraid of Dr Maginn not to conciliate him if possible; and if civility or flattering would have done it, I should have been glad so to do. As it has turned out, I have, I fear, only made myself a powerful enemy; for of course, on the first rumour that reached me, I felt it incumbent on me to forbid his visits, few and infrequent as they were. I have met both since, and the only notice I took was to cut Mrs Maginn decidedly . . .

What is my life? One day of drudgery after another; difficulties incurred for others, which have ever pressed upon me beyond health, which every year, by one severe illness after another, shows is taxed beyond its strength; envy, malice, and all uncharitableness – these are the fruits of a successful literary career for a woman.

In this letter L. E. L. allows herself to say just a little too much. Her certainty that Mrs Maginn cared nothing at all for her husband – apart from being most probably quite wrong for it is difficult not to have any feeling about a man with whom one has four children – can only have come from Maginn himself, and is not at all the kind of thing that she ought to have allowed him to discuss with her. The acquaintance with Maginn had been 'forced upon' her by Jerdan, who was still her dear friend, and it had not always been so embarrassing an intimacy. When Letitia Landon first met him Maginn was young, brilliant, successful and debonair. As his improvidence and arrogance began slowly to undo him, he became more reckless and certainly more often drunk. He resorted to less and less savoury shifts to keep the wolf from the family door and it seems possible at least blackmailing L. E. L. was one expedient that occurred to him and that he practised with success. Certainly he had power over her, and he used it. I doubt that he persecuted Bulwer Lytton for her sake, but it seems certain that he manipulated her in various kinds of ways, at the same time, I suspect, as he nurtured some kind of feeling for her.

> She then informed me that a certain person, known to me only by report, had made use of his influence in the literary world to obtain power over her for her personal seduction. He was the editor of a newspaper and a magazine, and, as a leading critic, she was to listen to the inducements he had held out to her, and thus has become completely compromised and at his mercy. In short, the young and clever debutante in the literary world had this terrible choice set before her, writing as she was to maintain her mother. Her personal and secret acquiescence in the vile proposition was to be the price of her public praise, and her refusal the cause of overwhelming blame, and this at the hands of a reviewer self-elected and set up to guide the opinions of the world. He was an Irishman of considerable talent, but, like many of his countrymen, possessed an extraordinarily plausible, and, if vulgar, still to some a persuasive tongue. She, an inexperienced girl, had believed his professions – indeed, had placed implicit reliance on his honour – till she had made the astounding discovery that he was a married man, and that he was by nature as false as he was unprincipled.
>
> As soon as she became aware of her fatal position, she declared to me that she endeavoured to break off all intimacy with this man, but that hitherto his proceedings had made such a course impossible. He persecuted her perseveringly, threatened to

expose her, forced from her the greater portion of the proceeds of her pen, and, in short, so compromised her, that her life had become a burthen.

The writer is an uproarious sporting character calling himself the Honourable Grantley Berkeley, whose account of his dealings with Letitia Landon has always been most energetically pooh-poohed by all who have chosen to write on the subject. No critic, they argue, could have made or marred L. E. L.'s prospects in 1835, but they do not notice that Berkeley does not say when the pressure was applied; L. E. L. first met Maginn when she was unable to find a publisher for *The Improvisatrice*; she might well then have been susceptible to some such threat. Berkeley says not that she gave in to the attempted seduction but that she listened to it, which I understand as meaning that she entered into some sort of amorous interchange which then gave Maginn all he needed in order to extort money and anything else that he required. He could certainly have ruined her prospects at any time, not by damning her writing, but by revealing that she was immoral. As the editor of *The Age* he had the organ of her destruction at his command.

What Berkeley has to say about Maginn's charm lends itself more to the supposition that L. E. L. did entertain Maginn's advances at first for their own sake, and then recoiled when she discovered that he was married, but by that time having given Maginn ample material with which to compromise her. As she was attempting to persuade Berkeley to challenge Maginn on her account, she was hardly likely to have minimized his blackguardism, and she was certainly not going to lay herself open to a rebuff which she might have got if Berkeley had got the idea that her present dilemma was simply her own fault.

All I was enabled then to establish was that the person I had undertaken to oppose, and thwart, and punish should it be necessary, was a literary adventurer who lived a hand-to-mouth existence on what he gained by writing for newspapers and magazines, was as often in prison as out, and much more frequently drunk than sober, and that latterly the chief object of his persecution really was to force Miss — to pay his debts, and afford him the means of carrying on his habits of dissipation without the daily labour he every day found more and more irksome, and for which his brain was beginning to fail.

Berkeley also says quite clearly that Maginn had 'forced from her the greater proportion of the proceeds of her pen'. Certainly L. E. L. was always poor although she worked like a dozen beavers. Her contributions to her mother's upkeep were not enormous and did not start until 1825, and her brother's education must have finished at some time. The money must have gone somewhere.

L. E. L.'s favourite way of dispelling doubts as to her purity was to point out that she had always been chaperoned, and had always lived with the same people, who would vouch for her blamelessness in this respect. If one considers that fact from another angle, it might well seem extraordinary that L. E. L. was always so closely chaperoned; if she was being pursued and pressurized by Dr Maginn, her best defence lay in interposing company between herself and him. He could continue to threaten her with exposure and even to extort money from her, but he could hardly force his physical attentions upon her in the drawing-room of the Misses Lance. From there she went to the protection of Mrs Sheldon's household and from hers to Mrs General Fagan. Other lady writers, Mrs Jameson, Mrs Inchbald, Miss Spence and Miss Benger, might live alone, but not L. E. L. Perhaps it seems absurd, to suggest that a woman lived for more than ten years in fear of a man like Maginn, in fear of both his love and his hate, but Maginn was no ordinary man. If he did love and terrorize L. E. L. (and the two are far from incompatible) it would more than explain Mrs Maginn's campaign against her.

L. E. L.'s biographers indignantly reject the idea of her having called upon a known swaggerer and bully like Berkeley to act as her strong-arm man and drive Maginn out of her life. Many a woman has smarted under the knowledge that a good thrashing would disencumber her of a nuisance like Maginn, and that all she lacks is strength of arm. Lady Caroline Lamb after all had tried to persuade Grattan to challenge Byron; according to Captain Medwin, Byron wrote in a blank leaf of *Vathek*: 'She offered young Grattan her favours if he would call me out.'

If she chose, L. E. L. chose more wisely than Lady Caroline. Her champion was courageous and stupid and vainglorious to a degree. He did not pause to verify her story, but he did not act upon it at once either. The immediate cause of Berkeley's duel with Maginn was the libellous review that Maginn wrote of his novel *Berkeley Castle* in *Fraser's Magazine* in August 1836. After flogging Fraser on the footpath outside his shop with a racing whip and appearing before the magistrate, Berkeley was gratified to receive Maginn's card. The connection with L. E. L. was presumably that upon his instructions L. E. L. had refused to receive Maginn's visits, whereas Berkeley's chestnut mare was often to be seen at the door; therefore, Maginn attacked *Berkeley Castle*. So far it seems as if Maginn ran about madly tilting at all who might have been more favoured by L. E. L. than he was, which may have been something of the case. It was doubtless very improper of the Honourable Grantley Berkeley to have told the story of his duel with Maginn in his *Memoirs*, although he is careful not to mention Miss Landon by name, but simply as 'Miss —'. Her friends, while they do not dispute the identity of 'Miss —' angrily reject the story; in the *Art-Journal*, Laman Blanchard called it an 'invention', whereupon Berkeley threatened him and then attacked him in a second edition of the *Memoirs*. The Reverend J. B. Landon wrote to the *Pall Mall Gazette*:

Mr Grantley Berkeley's statements would long since have been met with an indignant denial on the part of the relations of L. E. L., had they not felt that the amount of credit likely to be attached to any statement that gentleman might make was hardly such as would justify them in giving currency to the slander by taking the trouble to deny it. They would have been satisfied to leave him to the profound contempt of all right-thinking persons which he has already incurred, and the reproaches of an accusing conscience which may yet await him. As, however, others have generously stepped forward in L. E. L.'s defence, they feel that silence on their part might be misconstrued; and I therefore lose no time in declaring their conviction that there is not the slightest foundation for the story which Mr Grantley Berkeley's morbid vanity has led him to concoct.

Other correspondents to the *Gazette* accused Berkeley of using L. E. L. in his campaign against Maginn, on the grounds that, if what he had written was true, as a *chevalier sans peur et sans reproche* he should have kept silent about it until death. Posterity would have less to complain of, if only the Victorians were less prone to suppress all that might reflect badly upon L. E. L. whether they are for her or against her. It is certainly inconceivable to all of them that another age with different mores might feel more indignant at her victimization by Maginn than shocked or disgusted by the way it came about. I doubt that Berkeley's story is pure invention, because I cannot see that he would have involved himself in so much contumely just for a peg to hang a story on. His morality is that of a harum-scarum aristocrat, much less concerned for the conventions than L. E. L. could afford to be. He was an *habitué* of Gore House, and the Countess of Blessington first put him on the track of Maginn. Besides, he includes in his book the text of a couple of notes from L. E. L.

All these consequences followed much later. For L. E. L., after the battle to recover her health, there was nothing for it but to go on working, oblivious of the triumph of the gossips who considered that her ruptured engagement was their vindication. She had not been in love with Forster; the fact seems plain enough. Soon she had put him, at least, if not the rest of the awful business, quite out of her mind.

> After the deed was done, as is almost always the case, her sentiments somewhat changed – a state of exasperation came on. Alas! Was it not augmented by the wanton hints of the careless or the mischievous? She became irritated against him who, of all that ever paid her the attentions of a lover, perhaps most truly loved her. Upon being told that the late Allan Cunningham, whom she appreciated, as all who knew him must have done, as a noble specimen of mankind, stated to a friend of hers the circumstances here related, adding that the engagement was likely to be renewed, she repelled the idea with great vehemence, and, in a tone and manner very unusual to one of so gentle a nature, begged that the subject might never be mentioned to her again.

She was not short of things to do. In 1836 Colburn published her *Traits and Trials of Early Life*, containing a selection of gloomy tales for children, interspersed with poems. The last tale, *The History of a Child*, was claimed by her to be autobiographical. She began a series of essays on Scott's female characters which were to be issued over two years in *The New Monthly Magazine*. She contributed, free of charge, to Mr Schloss's *Fairy Almanack* and, most important, she finished her novel *Ethel Churchill*. The novel has two interconnected plots: one deals with the struggle, defeat and death of the poor poet, Maynard, and the other with the fate of Henrietta Marchmont, married to a cold, punctilious, ambitious man and seduced by another whose letters were written by Walter Maynard. When she discovers that she has been duped, for Maynard brings her back her own letters, which her seducer has given to his actress mistress, she concocts prussic acid and poisons both husband and lover.

The iron was entering Letitia Landon's soul. She was beginning to register the real nature of her suffering and to glimpse its ultimate cause. She was no longer internalizing all her griefs and disappointments; somewhere in her private world was obtruding the possibility of punishment and revenge. The description of the death of Henrietta's lover is luxuriously ghastly; there is no hint of dismay or pity as she makes him grovel on the grass of St James's Park, dying alone like a dog that has been given a bait. Her heroine moves with utter premeditation and assurance to bring vengeance on the men who have degraded her in their very different ways. Only at the last, and unconvincingly, is she white-haired and mad. It seems somehow a small price to pay. We cannot suppose that L. E. L. was about to defy the schizophrenic society that had so tormented her. As usual her fantasy life impinged very little on her actual behaviour. She still exhibited her 'warmth of heart, her exuberance of gratitude, . . . her buoyant spirits', but some found them hectic and strained more than usual. Chorley went to see her to discuss an appointment for her brother Whittingdon:

He had rested on her support. It was right that her devotion to her own family should not be allowed to drag her down; that her literary industry should be recognised – especially now, when it was failing of its reward. It was felt among some of us, that, in this matter, there was a claim to be upheld. I had to see her on the subject. It was, for both of us, an awkward visit. She received me with an air of astonishment and bravado, talking with a rapid and unrefined frivolity, the tone and taste of which were most distasteful, and the flow difficult to interrupt. When at last, I was allowed to explain my errand, the change was instant and painful. She burst into a flood of hysterical tears. 'Oh!' she cried, 'you don't know the ill-natured things I have written about you!' From that time I saw her occasionally, and am satisfied of the sincerity of her feelings. Then, I came to perceive how much of what was good and real in her nature had been strangled and poisoned by the self-interested thoughtlessness of those who should have shielded her. Some growing conviction of this it was, I have always thought, which drove her into a desire for escape.

She did not think to stand and fight. She was already beaten. She had tried to escape into marriage and had been driven back. Next time she must run further.

In October 1836 she met George Maclean. After an undistinguished military career, in 1826 Maclean purchased an unattached lieutenancy in the Royal African Colonial Corps,

> one of the so-called 'condemned corps' into which defaulters from other regiments were drafted and the War Office was in fact at its wits' end to know how to recruit officers for it.

The chief problem seems to have been the mortality rate; all that was required for promotion was the ability to survive the climate and the teeming diseases of the African Coast.

> The Commander-in-Chief himself had declared that 'no individual can with propriety to serve on the coast of Africa and to forfeit his half-pay, if he should decline that which is viewed as little better than condemnation to death, as indeed it has proved in one half of the cases.'

Maclean arrived in Freetown, Sierra Leone in December 1826. More than half the soldiers brought out in 1823 had died by the end of the next year, and 'only forty-two of them had been killed in action. Even for a Penal Corps, this was too much . . .' Accommodation for the troops was ramshackle, uncompleted and utterly inadequate. As might be expected, the soldiers turned to liquor as a protection against fear, depression and disease. Discipline had collapsed. Maclean acquitted himself with credit in Sierra Leone, although the value of his contribution was hardly recognized by the Colonial Office, where there was little grasp of the intricacies of balancing the local tribal antagonisms in order to achieve some security for the beleaguered white settlements. The spread of English influence had as its ostensible object the prosecution of the slave traffic. The exigencies of army life were such that many a slave liberated from a slave-ship by the British found himself made a soldier with no very clear notion of how it came about. Distinctions which seemed fundamental in England were almost imperceptible in Africa, and from the outset Maclean discreetly strove for some balance between ideal and reality. When the Governor of Sierra Leone died, Maclean was made private secretary to the new acting Governor, Lumley. He was then twenty-six. Unfortunately Lumley was refused the governorship, which went to his junior, Denham, who died a month after taking up his appointment. Lumley and Maclean both became seriously ill that summer, and in September 1828 Maclean had to return to England for a year's leave of absence.

In October 1829, the Council of Merchants of Cape Coast Castle told the committee of London merchants that monitored its affairs that it desired Mr Maclean to succeed the retiring President of the Council, John Jackson. The suggestion was accepted by the Colonial Office and Maclean arrived at Cape Coast in February 1830. His position was as ambiguous as the role played by the British force on the African coast. He was not a governor, although he could make treaties; he was not a member of the civil service either, although his activities had to meet with the approval of the Colonial Office. His military position was unclear, especially as he had neglected to inform his commanding officer of his acceptance of the post. However deficient the bureaucrats in London found him he seems to have been an able and resourceful governor of his scattered domains. His duty was to see that trade was not jeopardized by tribal ways and local misrule. He had no brief to colonize the interior, and he made no attempt to, his only expedition being dictated by the absolute necessity of making a show of strength. He was successful because he survived, and because he never used two words where one would do. Much of his activity, too much of it for the convenience of the Colonial Office, was quite unrecorded. He acted upon expedient and his own understanding of the situation, neither of which were respected by the bureaucrats at home. There is no doubt that he was ignorant of many things which he ought by rights to have known, but there was no blueprint for the contradictory situation in which he found himself. He had little choice but to act in a manner which might seem both oracular and dictatorial.

> George Maclean was almost a legend on the Gold Coast in his own lifetime. In Ashanti a contemporary wrote, 'so necessary did the King consider him for the peace of the country, that he was in the habit of making prayers and sacrifices to his fetish, for a continuance of his health and friendship.' In October 1856, the Rev. Daniel West recorded a conversation with an African at Anomabu ... he noted that the African's 'admiration of Governor M'Lean was boundless: "He was worth more than one hundred governors and four times as many soldiers."' One of the governors thus summarily assessed was ready enough to admit the inferiority of Maclean successors and to affirm that there was general agreement on the coast in 1857 that conditions had deteriorated sadly since that time ... Maclean passed into the vernacular: as *Badayi*, which might be freely rendered as 'the Peacemaker'; in Ashanti *Obrodie Badaie*, 'the White Man in whose time all men slept sound'; or as *Apamfy Bronyi*, 'the White Man with a Council', or perhaps 'of Wise Counsel'.

When Maclean went to the Gold Coast, the British government had practically abandoned the settlements to their fate. His daily work was complicated by the necessity of making long and detailed explanations of his policy and practice to those who were only interested in finding faults. He was constantly hampered by the lack of money, and by the refusals to ratify the treaties that only he, by deft manipulation of circumstances, was ever able to make. Bulwer Lytton remembered him as a 'dry, reserved, hard-headed Scotchman, of indefatigable activity – not of much perceptible talent'. His talent was not for dazzling the drawing rooms of London, nor for explaining himself to the Colonial Office. He was at home as the Laird of Cape Coast Castle, daily using his ingenuity to enact his own notion of justice. He must have known that he was writing on water; a political decision in England, another illness, foreign manipulation of the tribal situation, any of these would suffice to wipe him out and before long

Africa would claim her own. Nevertheless he delighted in his work and, it seems, in very little else.

Maclean came to England on leave of absence in the autumn of 1836, and found that, in some circles at least, he was received as a hero. The Colonial Office was bristling with unanswerable questions and malicious reports, but London society knew nothing of these. He was generally called Governor Maclean, as he wished to be, although he had no claim to the title. Generally his fans had only the dimmest notion of his actual claims to admiration. Mrs Thomson was firmly convinced that 'Mr Maclean had just then distinguished himself by great judgement, and some considerable amount of personal valour, in quelling an insurrection of Ashantees'. One writer in a public journal, who claimed to have known Maclean since boyhood, was happy to mislead his readers with this report:

> When very young, we do not think he was eighteen years of age, he was appointed secretary to the governor of Sierra Leone, and had not been long there when he was made governor himself . . . His elevation to governor, when, from his personal appearance, he could not be looked upon in any other view than as a boy approaching manhood, did not in the least alter his disposition . . .

Clever London society was unaware that Cape Coast Castle and Sierra Leone were different places, and that only the latter deserved the title of the White Man's Grave. Ironically enough, Maclean applied for the post of Lieutenant-Governor of Sierra Leone, aware as he was after a year as private secretary to the acting Governor of its horrors, and was refused.

In October 1836, the Matthew Forsters gave a party for the conquering hero, and they invited Miss Landon.

> In her enthusiasm she wore a Scotch tartan scarf over her shoulders. She had a ribbon in her hair, and a sash also, of the Maclean tartan; and she set out for the soirée in great spirits, resolved on thus complimenting the hero.
>
> Mr Maclean was much struck by her appearance. In looks L. E. L. was improved by being more delicate than ever in form

and complexion. The rich hues of the tartan over her white muslin dress became her neck.

Maclean seems to have been pleased and flattered by the compliment and not to have found her dress 'fanciful'. L. E. L., who had dreamed of Africa ever since her father had related his adventures as a runaway midshipman, was ready, willing and able to draw Maclean out. He had certainly never read anything of L. E. L.'s; he reacted to her as he would have done to any charming little woman, and she for the time was just as happy that it should be so. It was not long before he had proposed to her, and she accepted.

To some commentators, it appeared as if L. E. L. accepted Maclean simply to escape from her invidious situation. She had been very ill and depressed before she met him, and had struggled in vain to silence the whispers that now followed her wherever she went. Only a few months before she met Maclean she felt obliged to write to Mrs Thomson:

> To those who indulge in a small envy, or a miserable love of gossip, talk away my life and happiness, I can only say, if you think my conduct worth attacking, it is also worth examining ... I have no answer beyond contemptuous silence, an appeal to all who know my past life, and a very bitter sense of innocence and of injury ...
>
> God knows my path has been a very hard one! What constant labour, what unceasing anxiety! yet I never felt dejected until lately. But now I feel every day my mind and my spirits giving way; a deeper shade of despondency gathers upon me. I enter upon my usual employments with such disrelish; I feel so weary – so depressed; half my time so incapable of composition; my imagination is filled with painful and present images ...

From the time of L. E. L.'s eulogy of Sir John Doyle she had rarely missed an opportunity to flatter military exploit. Maclean might not have been the flamboyant, passionate type to whom her heroines had always made love, but perhaps L. E. L. was ready to realize that beauty and arrogance do not necessarily qualify a man for the role of a husband.

Maclean has been described as verily repulsive, mostly well and truly after the event. L. E. L.'s biographer Mrs Enfield describes him as a 'short, pale, heavily built man, with black hair brushed across a low forehead'. This description she must have extrapolated from Mrs Thomson's:

> He was a grave, spare man, between thirty and forty when he became engaged to L. E. L., but he looked very much older. His face, without being very plain, was not agreeable. It was pallid: and his dark hair fell upon a brow by no means of an elevated or intellectual cast. His dark-gray eyes were seldom raised to meet those of another. He was very taciturn, and still spoke his native Scotch, when he did speak, which was seldom: never, if he could help it.

He seemed to Grace Wharton like 'one who had buried all joy in Africa . . .' The portrait of him which is preserved at Elgin would be considered as that of 'a very fine and fashionable man in the prime of life', which is how L. E. L. herself had described him. The portrait must have been painted at the time of his return to Urquhart in 1837, and possibly it was more or less trumped up, but in 1834 Alexander had described him in terms more consonant with the portrait at Elgin that Mrs Thomson's as a 'tall, sparely-made gentleman' with 'regular features and fair hair . . . apparently in the prime of life'.

Maclean's offer of marriage seems to have been fairly hasty; we know certainly that it was made between the first meeting in October and the end of the same year. Then Maclean went to Urquhart. His letters ceased. He did not return. L. E. L. found herself in the same class as Cydippe, pining for the return of her betrothed from a visit to his family.

> There is a grief that wastes the heart
>   Like mildew on a tulip's dyes –
> When hope, deferred but to depart,
>   Loses its smiles, but keeps its sighs;
> When love's bark, with its anchor gone,
>   Clings to a straw, and still trusts on . . .
>
> O, absence is the night of love!
>   Lovers are very children then!

Fancying ten thousand feverish shapes,
 Until their light returns again.
A look, a word, is then recalled
 And thought upon until it wears,
What is perhaps, a very shade,
 The tone and aspect of our fears.
And this is what was withering now
 The radiance of Cydippe's brow . . .

She thought on the spring days, when she had been,
Lonely and lovely, a maiden queen:
When passion to her was a storm at sea,
Heard 'mid the green land's tranquillity.
But a stately warrior came from afar;
He bore on his bosom the glorious scar
So worshipped by woman the death-seal of war.
And the maiden's heart was an easy prize,
When valour and faith were her sacrifice . . .

He came not! Then the heart's decay
Wasted her silently away –

L. E. L.'s friends watched her sinking into deep depression. Ever
since the Forster affair her health had been shaky. At one point her
hair was cut off. By January 1837, she was mending but Dr Thomson
was still a regular caller at Hyde Park Street. As Maclean stayed in
Scotland she began to sink again. By the summer she was seriously ill.

Weeks passed away – weeks of that time when everyone is away
from London, and the few humanised creatures in it draw closer
together. I called every day to inquire in Berkeley Street – 'a
little better – not so well – at last downstairs.' I saw her. No
news from Scotland? No: but a thousand surmises, a thousand
hopes and conjectures, a certainty of anything but that he meant
to withdraw, were hurriedly expressed; her cheek flushed as she
spoke; I dropped the subject. A few weeks elapsed: I was a
privileged person, and called to take L. E. L. a drive in my cab.
She came gaily out, but looked shattered, thin, and was careless
in her attire. We drove round the inner circle of Regent's Park;
it was a soft and bright morning, and the air blew freshly on the

delicate cheek beside me. There was upon her face, nevertheless, that peculiar look of suffering which I never saw on any other countenance; as if every nerve had the *tic douloureux* – as if every moment were torture. She abandoned herself to dejection, and spoke not. At last I took the privilege of a friend, and gently remonstrated with her. I pointed out to her that she was unreasonable to indulge in sorrow for a man who had evidently given up all thoughts of her; that it was inconsistent with the dignity due to herself – it was unworthy – unwise – distressing to her friends. She answered me – I did not dare to look at her face as she spoke – (we drove round and round); but I hear her voice now; it was very low, and inexpressibly plaintive, as she said, 'But I have never loved anyone else.' This was her reasoning, poor child of song! and she proffered no other. I answered not – she sank into silence. We drove on – the air seemed to soothe her – when suddenly she declared that she was tired and faint, and begged me, somewhat hastily, to take her home.

Mrs Sheldon wrote to Maclean that she was afraid his behaviour might result in the poet making an attempt on her own life, interpreted by Maclean's biographer as a 'suicide threat' from the person he insists on calling 'Letty Landon'. Maclean, it seems, was employing the kind of tactics that succeeded brilliantly in dealing with tribal politics in Africa. By ignoring L. E. L. he was hoping that she would eventually tire and go away. Once the first flush of gratified vanity and sexual excitement had worn off, he had realized that he was in no financial condition to undertake to keep a wife. His family would not have been slow to point out the unwisdom of taking a wife in his circumstances, for his life in Africa had been conducted on the principle of maximum frugality. His reconsiderations were so alarming that he could or would not communicate them even to L. E. L. Her hysterical reactions to his letters on much less touchy subjects had repelled him. He took refuge in his old habit of silence, until a 'hard letter' from Matthew Forster, in whose house had had first met Miss Landon, brought forth some sort of an explanation. He replied:

Everybody makes a fool of himself once in his life, and I candidly admit that I have done so to perfection. *A priori* I should have said that there did not exist a man in the world less likely to 'fall in love' (as it is called) than myself. Nothing could be more 'out of my way' and nothing, I am free to acknowledge, could be more foolish or ill-judged – situated as I am. But what will you have? I was destined, I suppose, to make a fool of myself, and have done so effectually. I feel the truth of every word you say; no person could be less fitted for a poor man's wife than Miss L—, and looking at the matter as I now do, in a common sense point of view, I am only surprised at my own folly in having ever dreamed of such a plan. Nevertheless, it is equally true, that both verbally and in writing, I am pledged to the lady; that is, I left her with the understanding that I was to marry her on my return to London, unless my love should be cooled by the cold winds of the north. I must confess also, that I would have married her when in London – at least I think I would – and I must do the lady the justice to say that she refused to allow me to enter into any engagement until I should have had an opportunity of knowing my own mind. I must further confess that I have since then become acquainted with various matters which have somewhat altered my opinion of Miss L—; or rather, I should say, I have had an opportunity of reflecting more seriously upon various matters to which I before paid perhaps but too little attention. What the devil I am now to do is another matter. I suppose, as you say, that I must pay the penalty of my own folly and precipitation, and marry the girl. I find waiting me here a letter from Mrs Sheldon, telling me that if I do not write Miss L— will kill herself. What on earth under such circumstances can a man do but say something very sooth-ing and tender? But her applying to you most certainly has both surprised and disappointed me exceedingly. It shows a want of delicacy which I could not have conceived possible, and corrobo-rates strongly the impression made upon my mind by some circumstances which came to my knowledge when in Edin-burgh. I feel that I am in a scrape. I cannot, I suspect, retire honourably, and cannot go forward with safety. However, I must make up my mind in some way or other. But I am anxious to know, in the first place, whether Miss L—'s happiness would really be affected seriously and permanently were I never to see her again. Literally speaking, I am not bound by any express engagement – for she refused, in fact, to give or receive any pledges on the subject until I should have visited Scotland – but morally speaking I do conceive myself bound to marry her or to give some good reason why.

Maclean may not have heard the rumours about L. E. L. in London, but he had certainly heard something to her discredit in Edinburgh, which, notwithstanding all the statements made by L. E. L.'s biographers, he was disposed to believe, especially after she had had the indelicacy to beg their mutual friend to intervene in order to determine Maclean's intentions. However, more out of his respect for his own honour than his regard for the 'girl', he did write to her in June 1837. Foolishly, perhaps, she made some pathetic attempt to stand on her dignity, hopelessly compromised by the rashness of sending Forster out to hunt him up. She also apparently countered any misgivings Maclean might have been having about her reputation, with a few suspicions of her own.

Since I last wrote to you I have had a letter from Miss L— wherein she wonders at my impudence in having written to her so kindly, and intimates her intention of closing the correspond-ence. She alludes to various reports which, she says, have reached her, respecting me, and which have led to, or at least confirmed her present resolution.

Obviously, such a response to kindness from a man who had asked her to marry him and then disappeared is very unreasonable. Mr Maclean's biographer is probably quite right to sneer at it, but one is somewhat baffled to understand why he is not more concerned to consider the behaviour of his principal subject, who seems to have been something currish for his own part, however upset and irrational his victim's behaviour. Maclean ought to have sympathized with L. E. L. as the victim of destructive gossip, for he himself was having a great deal of trouble refuting the shocking allegations made by one Captain Burgoyne, and part at least of his difficulty stemmed from the fact that Burgoyne's accusations, while substantially false, were not entirely unrelated to the truth. Now, besides the awkward questions being asked in the Colonial Office, came a series of further queries to which Maclean never supplied any public answer. One rumour was that

McLean had been engaged to a lady in Scotland, which engagement he had withdrawn; and that she was in the act of sealing a
farewell letter to him, when her dress caught fire, and she was
burnt to death.

More material was the suspicion that Maclean had a native wife at
Cape Coast Castle and was not free to marry anyone, for British law
states that marriage contracted in any British colony by the law of the
place is binding in British law also. There was no concern at the time
to establish whether Maclean was pure or not, but simply whether he
was eligible. A better illustration of the grossness of the difference
between the standard morality of man and of woman can hardly be
imagined. L. E. L. was rendered ineligible by the merest suspicion of
an indiscretion; Maclean could have had fifty whores and as many
diseases; as long as he was not legally entangled he was a desirable
match. Metcalfe avers staunchly that Maclean was not 'grossly given
up to all the vices of the coast' but he adds:

> At a time when 'country marriages' were almost universal
> among European residents on the coast, it would be surprising
> rather than otherwise if Maclean had not contracted such an
> alliance . . .

Blanchard states quite firmly that some liaison had existed: when
faced by L. E. L. with the 'confident assertion' that he had 'a native
wife living at Cape Coast, who was then or at least had been the
occupant of the Castle', Maclean immediately and voluntarily
explained

> that no such matrimonial connection had ever existed; and no
> connection at all, that had not been terminated some considerable
> time before in a manner the most unequivocal and final.

Metcalfe can find no historical evidence that any woman acted in the
capacity of wife to George Maclean, which simply leaves the matter
open, for discretion was very much a part of Maclean's valour and he
would hardly have mentioned his concubine in dispatches.

Now after all – stating the case as strongly as it can be stated –

wherein have I acted so blamably? I have never for a moment denied her claims – nor to herself have I ever said an unkind word. I have never even pleaded, which I might have done fairly and without challenge – that I left her avowedly and by her own express desire (as Mrs Forster can testify) free and unengaged; in short, she would have nothing to say to me until I had paid my visit to Scotland – where, she always predicted, I would change my mind. When in Edinburgh, I certainly had time to look at matters in a more common sense way than I had before done – and the more I reflected on the subject, the less could I bear the idea of subjecting a girl, accustomed to all the elegancies and refinements of London society, to the villainous realities of a passage to and residence at C. C. Castle. Besides, the late accounts of the mortality there made the thoughts of such a plan more and more revolting. I ought perhaps to have told her all this, but I well knew she would instantly ascribe it to a very different motive from the real one; particularly as she had only a short time before, in a fit of jealousy at something I had said in one of my letters, accused me of some such scheme. Under the influence of these feelings, I became uneasy and half distracted as to what I should do – for there is not a greater ignoramus in the world on all that relates to womankind than myself. The natural result was that the correspondence on my side slackened, et hinc illae lachrymae. Neither will I deny that perhaps absence did in some degree – assisted by the cold air of the north – cool the ardour of my 'early love'. But she never saw or was made aware of this; and as I have already said, I really do not see that she was justified in kicking up any dust about the matter. It would be sheer madness, after what we have lately heard, in her to even wish to go to Cape Coast Castle, and it would be worse than madness in me to allow her. But no one shall be able to say that I acted unfairly by her, or any one, nor will I insist upon my admitted right to draw back, if I choose. I have therefore written to her to say that I will do anything she wishes, and if I marry her, she may depend upon being made as comfortable as is in my power. But I really wish you would explain to her the impossibility (as I may say) of her going to the coast. Were I to do so, she would at once say that I merely wanted an excuse for my fickleness. One reason – which I am very unwilling to mention, even to you – has held great weight with me in the matter; do you know that I cannot help suspecting that the lady has a 'bee in her bonnet' – as we say here. She possesses wit, talents, and powers of literary composition in no ordinary degree – but you have no conception of the violence of her temperament when excited. In mere fun, I happened to mention that a lady in Edinburgh had won my heart by her exquisite singing; and in her reply she was, as she herself said, quite frantic, and declared that it was the last letter I should ever receive from her. In her very last letter she tells me that she fainted I know not how often on my previous letter having been brought in to her. Now 'unaccustomed as I am to ladies in general' I do not know but all this may be usual and proper; but to me it does not appear consistent with common sense. However, as you say, 'I am in the stocks' and am ready to do all that is right and proper with a good grace. But you would really oblige me by explaining to her the state of matters at C. C. C. As to my own feelings, respecting which you appear to be in doubt – I scarcely know myself what they are. Were I differently situated I think I am sufficiently in love to marry the lady, with much compunction; but the extreme imprudence of my marrying her as matters stand, has had the effect of materially cooling my passion.

In August, 'Governor' Maclean was at last back in London. In the months that followed, when he had to delay his return to the Gold Coast while he wrangled with the Colonial Office about the manifold ambiguities and suspicions attaching to his actions as President of the Council, his courtship was renewed. The marriage was on again.

The engagement was stormy, but the wavering in intention seems mostly to have been expressed by the lady. Maclean stood firm by his promise that he would not abandon her, which she held him to, even though she had declared herself that he was not bound by any obligation. In his first letter to Matthew Forster, there is one sentence which from a proud and reserved man like Maclean indicates a depth of feeling for L. E. L. which was consistently belied by his conduct. His anxiety to know whether Miss Landon would be affected seriously and permanently if he broke the engagement is also a desire to know if she really loved him. Much of Letitia Landon's emotional skirmishing with him was probably an attempt to find out much the same thing, but her fainting fits and outbursts of frantic jealousy simply annoyed and bewildered him. As the wedding drew nearer she seems to have sunk into a mood of joyless resignation. Where her friends thrilled and despaired at the thought of Cape Coast Castle, she barely expressed any concern. Just before her wedding L. E. L. had called upon Harriet Martineau, who had a cousin in Sierra Leone, to ask advice about dressing for the tropics:

> . . . it was all so sad that my mother and I communicated our sense of dismay as soon as the ladies were gone. Miss Landon was listless, absent, melancholy to a striking degree. She found she was all wrong in her provision of clothes and comforts – was going to take out all muslins and no flannels, and divers pet presents which would go to ruin at once in the climate of Cape Coast. We promised that day to go to Dr Thomson's and hear her new play before she went; and I could not but observe the countenance of listless gloom with which she heard the arrangement made. Before the day of the visit came round it was discovered that she had been secretly married and we saw her no more.

The 'new play', L. E. L.'s blank verse tragedy *Castrucio Castrucani*, was not printed in her lifetime. It represented a determined effort to break away from the stereotypes of her own imagination and of the commercial versifications that she had for so long been toiling over – although she also had her eye on Macready and a sumptuous production. It is written in a style which is unusually chaste, and her care for the blank-verse cadence occasionally results in real elegance. Her hero, Castrucani, is the ruler by popular consent of Lucca, besieged by Florentines without, and by faction within. The Lucchese nobles, led by Count Arrezi, are plotting with the Florentines against him, because he has destroyed too many of their ancient privileges and enfranchised the common people. The plot bears some vague relation to the political struggles of the early sixteenth century when the communes of Tuscany fought against Florentine empire-building and papal interference. The plot is too intricate and predictable to be related in detail, but the tragedy concerns not Castrucio but Claricha, his long-lost love who is also the daughter of his arch-enemy, Arrezi.

The great prestige of the blank-verse tragedy as a genre is doubtless what drew L. E. L. to it. The model is clearly Shakespeare, although in the clarity, regularity and abstraction of her style L. E. L. reminds one more, if only very faintly, of Jonson. These five acts make more of a neo-classical Roman drama than a poetic drama in the Shakespearian style. In attempting verse drama, L. E. L. was pulling herself up by her bootstraps to the level of Hannah More, who impressed her contemporaries, if not posterity, with tragedies like *The Inflexible Captive*, *Percy* and *The Fatal Falsehood*. The mantle of Miss More fell upon Joanna Baillie, who was lionized until her death in 1851.

L. E. L.'s bid for poetic weight and respectability was made too late. The excellent Miss Mitford had a resounding public success in the 1820s and early 1830s with *Julian*, *Rienzi*, *Charles the First* and *The Vespers of Palermo*, but L. E. L.'s effort was 'without the slightest success'.

Despite all the emotional strain of her on-again-off-again courtship and the fluctuations of her health, L. E. L. worked steadily away at her series of portraits of Scott's female characters and fulfilled her usual chores for the annuals, while she struggled with her tragedy, which was recast several times. Maclean tried to dissuade her from the idea of coming with him to Cape Coast Castle, as well as begging others to do so for him, but L. E. L. was not to be shaken off so easily. She probably realized that she was exploiting Maclean's sense of honour by holding him to their engagement, but there was nothing else for it. She could not face another disgrace and more calumny. She struggled to prove to herself and to her fiancé that she did love him, luxuriated in the idea of braving exile, peril and hardship for his sake, all the time trembling at the least sign of flagging interest or contempt. Maclean for his part probably loved her, without liking or understanding her, and the growing hostility shown him by her friends did nothing to help. He had his own problems, which probably appeared to him, as they did to his biographer, much more important than Letitia Landon's vapours. He went to The Hague on a diplomatic mission connected with the African colonies as part of the long and delicate process by which he won some confidence from the Colonial Office. The time of his return to Cape Coast Castle was eventually fixed for 5 July.

On 7 June 1838, Letitia Landon was married by her brother, Whittingdon, to George Maclean at St Mary's, Bryanston Square. The bride was given away by Bulwer Lytton, and the couple spent the night at the Sackville Street Hotel. Then Miss Landon returned to her lodging with Mrs Fagan. The marriage had been delayed, because George Maclean, understandably, did not want the expense of setting up house in London when he had a perfectly good habitation awaiting him at Cape Coast Castle. He would have delayed until the very eve of his departure, had not Miss Landon's relatives protested that they wished to be present and to fête the bride. The wedding

> was by Mr Maclean's wish, so strictly private that even the family with whom L. E. L. resided did not know that it had taken place until a fortnight afterwards. Mr Landon, the bride's brother, performed the ceremony: Sir Edward Bulwer Lytton gave the bride away. After the service, all who were present at the church, except the bride and bridegroom, made their congratulations and went away. Mr and Mrs Maclean went to the Sackville Street Hotel; but on the following day L. E. L. returned to her friend's house, and entered into society, as usual, under her maiden name. It is impossible to avoid suspecting that this arrangement was the result of some fear in Mr Maclean's mind lest the event should be known too soon at Cape Coast; but the reason he alleged was his dislike of congratulations and festivities, and the great amount of business which he still had to transact at the Colonial office before his return.

Maclean gave a different account of his reasons to his uncle, Sir John Maclean, an account which does not do any great credit to him, for it seems to indicate a degree of furtiveness and indecison and even weakness which is hardly what one expects from the Solon of the Gold Coast.

> In fact my marriage . . . was so often likely and then unlikely, that I did not like to admit anything about it until it was finally resolved upon. I was intimate with her before I went to Scotland, but when there the matter was entirely broken off and was not resumed till long after my return. Again, when it was finally resolved on and I wrote to you about it, I took it into my head — in fact I was told — that you did not approve of it at all — which made me act very foolishly. Equally foolish were the

circumstances of the marriage itself. We had always determined not to be married till I was on the point of leaving town, in order to save the expense of taking up house. But then came the two nearest relatives who begged that the ceremony might take place privately at least – without the marriage being announced – in order to enable them to be present; which they could not be if it was postponed till the time of my departure. In this way it was that Miss Landon continued Miss Landon after the marriage had actually taken place. But it came out prematurely, and in such a way that no person could understand the meaning of the whole affair.

Whether indignation and interference caused the announcement of L. E. L.'s marriage to appear in the newspapers against Maclean's wish, we cannot now know. None of her husband's family was at the wedding, there were no festivities, and the honeymoon in the Sackville Street Hotel was no more than a one-night stand before a return to single life for both of them until they should meet again on the *Maclean*.

L. E. L.'s last public appearance was made in a white muslin dress and a white bridal bonnet, as if she wished despite everything to make one showing as a bride. The occasion was the coronation of Queen Victoria; L. E. L. had a seat at Crockford's to watch the procession, and apparently some of the processors watched her as she waved her handkerchief to the Lancers. That evening there was a farewell party for her at Hyde Park Street.

The gay, the literary friends, the lovely daughters of the house – now, alas! gone save two – the early friend of her girlhood, Sir Edward Lytton Bulwer, Mr Disraeli, and many others, lingered long to wish her happiness and a safe return. It was understood that she was only to remain three years at Cape Coast, and the delicacy of her lungs rendered it, on that account, even desirable for her to go to a warm climate, as she had been threatened with asthma. At supper, Sir E. L. Bulwer, in a graceful speech, proposed the health of 'his daughter', alluding to his having acted as a father at her marriage.

Samuel Carter Hall remembers a different farewell party.

The last time I saw L. E. L. was in Upper Berkeley Street, Connaught Square, on the 27th June, 1838, soon after her marriage, when she was on the eve of her fatal voyage. A farewell party was given to some of her friends by Mrs Sheddon, with whom she then boarded, Misses Lance having resigned their school. When the proper time arrived, there was a whisper round the table, and as I was the oldest of her friends present, it fell to my lot to propose her health. I did so with the warmth I felt. The 'chances' were that we should never meet again; and I considered myself free to speak of her in terms such as could not but have gratified any husband, except the husband she had chosen. I referred to her as one of my wife's most valued friends during many years of closest personal intimacy, and sought to convey to McLean's mind, and to the minds of her other friends, the high respect as well as affection with which we regarded her. There were many at the table who shed tears while I spoke. The reader may imagine the chill which came over that party when McLean had risen to 'return thanks'. He merely said, 'If Mrs McLean has as many friends as Mr Hall says she has, I only wonder they allow her to leave them.' That was all: it was more than a chill – it was a blight. A gloomy foreboding as to the future of that doomed woman came to all the guests, as, one by one, they rose and departed, with a brief mournful farewell. Probably no one of them ever saw her again.

If Mr Hall's recollection has not played the fool with him and if he is not simply being wise after the event, it still seems possible that Maclean's response was the response of a shy man to what he might justifiably have seen as emotionalism and self-indulgent eloquence. He was too well aware that Cape Coast Castle required a good housekeeper of frugal habits and equable temperament to feel any great glow of pride in L. E. L.'s literary achievements. Her charm and popularity were certainly not enough to keep her from trailing out to Cape Coast Castle with him. Having her head turned and perhaps her heart too turned against him on the eve of their departure was hardly the most auspicious beginning. Forster joked that Letitia Maclean would be on the first boat back to England, but he did not reckon on the woman's determination to win Maclean's love and admiration, and to redeem a life which she had begun to fear had been entirely wasted. But the masochistic, self-dramatizing part of her was still blocking her way to a clear view of what was really due to herself and to others. The ill-informed who saw her dragged off by a dour tyrant to sweeten raffish seclusion in the White Man's Grave were probably gratified by expressions of exquisite melancholy and the sparkling of unshed tears.

In one of her essays on the female characters of Scott, L. E. L. does show that she understood Maclean's character better than her friends did:

> the habits of a man accustomed to command – especially on a foreign station, would necessarily be reserved and secluded. Not only accustomed to implicit obedience, but aware of its imperative necessity under the circumstances in which they had been placed, such are apt to expect it from all. How, what is but the necessary authority in official life, and with man over man, seems harshness when extended to woman. How often, perhaps, must Colonel Mannering's decision have seemed sternness, his reserve coldness, his abstraction indifference, and his authority tyranny, to a young, spoilt and pretty woman. Her attachment would not be diminished, for his high qualities ensured that respect needful for the duration of affection; but he had also those which keep the imagination alive, and of that, feminine love is 'all compact'. We can also believe that Colonel Mannering was very fond of his wife, though shy of showing it, even to herself; above all his pride would revolt from any of that display before others in which she would take an excusable vanity. Pride on the one hand – petulance on the other, would soon lead to a misunderstanding.

This essay was written during her short married life and in common with its fellows it shows a further stage in the Victorianization of Letitia Landon. She expresses pious, unexceptionable sentiments; nowhere does she permit herself those sudden outbursts of theatrical cynicism which had disfigured her novels. Her style is pared down, striving more for authority and justness than for effect. I think we may fairly assume that Mrs Maclean was determined not to fall into petulancy, but to become a fitting wife for George Maclean of the Gold Coast. This was to prove more difficult and less gratifying than she would ever have foreseen.

L. E. L. spent the three weeks between her wedding and the departure arranging her affairs. She arranged to produce another novel for Mr Colburn, and to continue the series of Scott's female characters for the *New Monthly Magazine*, later to be published as a book by Heath. She was anxious to retain the editorship of *Fisher's Drawing-Room Scrap-Book*. Maclean left all her literary affairs to her and all the income therefrom was likewise hers to dispose of. She still had the responsibility of her mother, which Maclean might have found very difficult to discharge, and it seems as if L. E. L.'s relations with her mother improved as a result of her marriage.

On 4 July she set off for Portsmouth, her husband apparently having boarded their ship in London. She was accompanied on the journey by her brother and Mr Hugh Maclean and they slept that night in Portsmouth. George Maclean, as was usual with him apparently, slept very late. The morning passed rapidly for L. E. L. for she spent it scribbling notes and compiling lists of presents for Whittingdon to deliver, lists that were never completed, to his embarrassment. In the afternoon a cutter took them out to the *Maclean*, and Letitia gave her brother her purse to keep, asking him to take as good care of it as ever she had.

Once she had recovered from the shock of the salute which the crew of the brig fired for Maclean and his lady, she found that the *Maclean* had been made much more comfortable than it had been when she visited the ship in London, for which she undoubtedly had Maclean to thank. There was moreover female company in the shape of Mrs Bailey, the steward's wife, whose presence mitigated the unpleasant effect of Maclean's refusal to allow his wife to bring a maid with her to Africa. L. E. L. kept her spirits up and gave no expression to any of the fear and desolation she must have felt. Apart from her months with her uncle at Aberford and other visits to friends, and her visit to Paris in 1834, she had never travelled. The prospect of a long voyage in a small vessel must have daunted her. Even on board the brig, Maclean and his wife were separated at night and during the day can have had little or no privacy. Seasickness does not make for good company, and Mrs Maclean seems to have had her fair share. Nevertheless, her journal of the voyage is as brave and hearty as anyone could wish.

Friday, 10 August brought them in sight of Cape Coast Castle. During the night the brig fired guns and impromptu fireworks to attract attention until a fishing boat put off from the shore to fetch the 'Gubbernor', who surprised everyone by going ashore in the surf at two in the morning. This was later considered to have been a very sinister act. The President's secretary had just died, and Maclean might well have wished to bring a little order to the ensuing chaos and to see if it was quite safe to bring his lady ashore. He might also have wished to see that the fort was in some sort of a fit condition to receive a European lady, something which had rarely been seen there.

Already L. E. L. was suffering from loneliness. She who had always been surrounded by people was suddenly without anyone to talk to. Her image of Maclean strolling the decks with her like Abdalla with Leila was far from reality. She was the only person with time for strolling and entertaining melancholy thoughts about the disappearing Polar Star. Her husband seems to have been utterly absorbed by the intricacies of navigation, although it can hardly have been his responsibility. Possibly he found her more than ever embarrassing, this fervent woman with her exaggerated responses to everything, including him. He did what he always did, withdrew, held his peace and waited, for the conquering of his own shyness and the calming of her ridiculous susceptibilities, and she bore it, with just the faintest trace of annoyance.

L. E. L. was agreeably surprised by the Fort:

The Castle is a very noble building, and all the rooms large and cool, while some would be pretty even in England. That where I am writing is painted a deep blue, with some splendid engravings – indeed, fine prints seem quite a passion with the gentlemen here. Mr McLean's library is fitted up with bookcases of African mahogany, and portraits of distinguished authors. I, however, never approach it without due preparation and humility, so crowded is it with scientific instruments, telescopes, chronometers, barometers, gasometers, &c., none of which may be touched by hands profane. On three sides, the batteries are dashed against by the waves; on the fourth is a splendid land view. The hills are covered to the top with what we should call wood, but is here called bush. This dense mass of green is varied by some large, handsome, white houses, belonging to different gentlemen, and on two of the heights are small forts built by Mr McLean . . . All my troubles have been of a housekeeping kind, and no one could begin on a more plentiful stock of ignorance than myself. However, like Sinbad the Sailor in the cavern, I begin to see daylight. I have numbered and labelled my keys – their name is legion – and every morning I take my way to the store, give out flour, sugar, butter, &c., and am learning to scold if I see any dust, or miss the customary polish on the tables. I am actually getting the steward of the shop, who is my right hand, to teach me how to make pastry. I will report progress in the next. We live almost entirely on ducks and chickens; if a sheep be killed, it must be eaten the same day. The bread is very good, palm wine being used for yeast; and yams are an excellent substitute for potatoes. The fruit generally is too sweet for my liking, but the oranges and pineapples are delicious. You cannot think the complete seclusion in which I live, but I have a great resource in writing, and I am very well and very happy.

It is not easy to understand why the duties of victualler and housekeeper should have devolved upon L. E. L. Presumably someone had done the giving out of provisions for the day's meals before her arrival but she willingly assumed the unfamiliar responsibility and spent a good deal of energy in trying to bring the bachelor establishment to order. Moreover, Maclean was ill after his ill-advised landing in the night. His wife did as Victorian wives must and sat up with her husband for several nights, until his sufferings abated. It was also her job to supervise the housekeeping. The cleaning was carried out by the prisoners – most of them debtors confined for unspecified terms in the fort prison – under the supervision of a soldier with drawn bayonet. Like most slaves, they worked badly.

However willingly L. E. L. undertook her work, her inexperience must have made it more exhausting and worrying than it ought to have been. Apparently Maclean was better able to see the deficiencies in her performance than he was to discern the efforts and the progress she was making. She became disheartened, and even slightly rebellious, but there was no dispute between the spouses, not ever, on any subject, and that mere fact might give some idea of the strangeness of their situation. Mrs Maclean, like a junior officer, had no option but to beg pardon and struggle on. As before, they did not sleep in the same room, nor did they keep the same hours. L. E. L.'s day began at seven while her husband slept late: even if there were departing guests the next morning he would not put in an appearance. At seven in the evening they met for dinner.

For some reason, Maclean would not allow his wife the use of one of the empty rooms in the fort as a study. She had brought with her a desk which was quite inappropriate for a sitting room and was obliged to write to her brother asking for a little 'show-desk' where she might keep her papers. Another letter to Whittingdon dated 27 September does show her in slightly rebellious mood. She mentions the anxiety about her husband's having an affair with a native woman:

> I can scarcely make even you understand how perfectly ludicrous the idea of jealousy of a native woman really is. Sentiment, affection, are never thought of – it is a temporary bargain – I must add that it seems to be quite monstrous.
>
> Now he gave me not one real idea of what I was coming to – half the time bestowed in fancying unreal horrors, would have made me mistress of all I needed to know. I do not know what Scotch girls may do, but I am quite sure any English girl would be puzzled ... You would be surprised at the pains I have taken ...

The *African* brought a letter for L. E. L.'s mother, in which she describes Maclean's second illness. Her husband had never been quite well since his wetting, although L. E. L. declared herself perfectly healthy, except for deafness in one ear and abscesses which kept forming in it and bursting. All her letters tell the same story of loneliness and drudgery, however stoutly she asserts that she is happy and in good health. That she was disheartened can well be assumed, and Maclean seems to have done little to warm her heart. When they met in the evenings, they dined, then she read or worked while he played his fiddle. 'At ten we go to bed. I suspect I sleep for both, for he reads or writes half the night.'

Of what she wrote, her 'nonsense' verses, Maclean seems to have asked not a word, although L. E. L. drank in the praise of her husband that she heard when other colonial functionaries and passing sea captains dined at the fort. If she was pleased to play the role of first lady at those social gatherings, she did not find it so pleasant when she was faced with Maclean's criticism.

He expects me to cook, wash and iron; in short, to do the work of a servant. He says he will never cease correcting me until he has broken my spirit, and complains of my temper, which you know, was never, even under heavy trials bad.

In late September Maclean was ill again, though not seriously, and suffered much pain. L. E. L. slept on the floor of his apartment wrapped in a shawl. On 14 October she entertained some of her husband's fellow officers. She seemed, as she took care always to seem, happy and well.

The next morning she rose at six, took tea and arrowroot to her husband, and, saying she was tired, went back to bed for an hour and a half. Then Emily Bailey went to her to collect a present, for she was leaving for England on the return voyage of the *Maclean*. Mrs Maclean asked her to return to help her dress when she called. Some time between eight and nine Mrs Bailey went to her room with a note from Maclean and found her on the floor by the door unconscious. She called Maclean and, by his order, the surgeon, who tried to revive her with ammonia, but L. E. L. was dying. Within a few minutes she was dead.

No one will ever know how or why L. E. L. died. She was thirty-six years old, and a bride of little more than four months, in better health than she had been for years. The news came to London with the *Maclean* and was published on New Year's Day, 1839: 'Died ... suddenly ...' and that was all. Apparently no attempt had been made by Maclean to send any more personal and explanatory communications to any of his wife's family, nor had it occurred to him that his wife was sufficiently well known in London to necessitate some kind of explanation. The Reverend Whittingdon Landon obtained the inquest papers from the secretary to the Western African Company, but what they had to tell was hardly reassuring. The body was not opened, nor was anything approaching an autopsy performed. Emily Bailey, whose testimony was to alter so much over the next year as to be virtually useless, said that she found Mrs Maclean lying on the floor with an empty bottle in her hand labelled 'Acid Hydrocyanicum Delatum, Pharm. Lond. 1836. Medium Dose Five Minims, being about one-third the strength of that in former use, prepared by Scheele's Proof'. Obviously Mrs Bailey cannot have remembered all this; the bottle was actually produced in evidence. Mrs Maclean, it seems, was subject to spasms, and used to take a drop or two of prussic acid in water. She had had the spasms the night before, but had not complained that morning. One of her letters to Mrs Hall was produced in corroboration of Maclean's testimony. Mr Cobbold, the surgeon, was so convinced that the contents of the bottle in Mrs Maclean's hand had been the cause of her death that he convinced also James Swanzey, acting as coroner, and the thirteen other gentlemen on oath, who found that L. E. L. died of an overdose of prussic acid, incautiously administered by her own hand.

L. E. L. was very interested in poison. In many of her poems an unfaithful lover or his new wife is poisoned, and sometimes her protagonist poisons herself. In *Ethel Churchill* Henrietta Marchmont actually brews prussic acid from a tincture of bitter almonds, all the time holding before her face a glass mask, for even L. E. L. knew that prussic acid fumes are dangerous to inhale. If she had administered the fatal dose in water, the mistake might have been feasible, but if she had brought the phial of acid to her mouth, she must have done so either in a state of considerable confusion or deliberately. Interestingly enough, although Maclean says that he was against her use of the medicine, he also said that he did not know that it was prussic acid. To add to the confusion, Dr Thomson wrote to the papers, denying that in all his long dealings with L. E. L. he had ever given her delated hydrocyanic acid and that in the medicine chest made up for her by Mr Square there was no such thing. There was, however, henbane, *Hyoscyamus niger*, an effective but dangerous anti-spasmodic, which according to one source is what was originally thought to be in L. E. L.'s mysterious bottle. There was no smell of bitter almonds, and death seems to have been too gradual to have been occasioned by a massive overdose of prussic acid. Perhaps L. E. L. fell, as she sometimes did in one of her fits, spilt the bottle and actually died of inhaling it, but even then the odour would have been present. There had been no vomiting or convulsions.

A distinguished physician asked to comment upon the inquest spoke very harshly about Cobbold's manifest incompetence:

> We dare not trust ourselves to comment upon this extraordinary inquest ... We should also animadvert of the jury, in finding the verdict on the evidence before them. In England, could such

an inquest have been tolerated, the verdict would have been simply 'found dying'.

Any suspicion that later arose, that Maclean had suborned the jury and managed the inquest, is belied by the obvious fact that the incompetence of the proceedings damaged him more than a more thorough examination of the circumstances would have done. Any 'Governor' with a moderate amount of guile would see that in such a case justice must be seen to be done, and Maclean was, in all that did not relate to Letitia Landon at least, a far-sighted and astute man. Moreover, most of his daily business involved courts, the rules of evidence and the law. He must have seen that the inquest was a shambles and that the examination of witnesses had been conducted very sloppily. For these reasons there exists still the possibility that L. E. L. did die of natural causes, which the coroner simply did not take into account.

The only explanation of the muddle which fits in with the character of Maclean as a wily manipulator, which in his dealings with both traders and natives he most certainly was, is that muddle was the only alternative to an unpalatable certainty. Maclean must have known that eventually the jungle claims its own. In a transient community like Cape Coast Castle, bodies are unlikely to be exhumed and inquests reconvened because they have been conducted incompetently. He may have reckoned without the inadvertent launching of a full-scale scandal in London by a bemused Methodist missionary, but the gamble was a reasonable one and eventually, when both Lord Russell and Lord Normanby had had to cry off because of the impossibility of gathering reliable evidence, he won. The only circumstance which makes sense of the evident blundering of all involved is their certainty, well founded or otherwise, that Letitia Maclean had committed suicide. Only by not raising the question of death by natural causes at the inquest would death by natural causes remain a possibility. Brodie Cruikshank decided long after the event that L. E. L. died of a heart attack, which he was hardly entitled to do seeing that he was one of the jury who accepted the original verdict. Maclean at the time rejected the charge that the jury was not conscientious as disgraceful. Maclean's biographer tends to the same conclusion for no good reason. In the very long term, Maclean's techniques seem to have been justified. If George Maclean did wish to conceal the motive and manner of his wife's death, his motives need not have been entirely selfish. Suicide was an appalling crime in the Victorian canon, the final act of atheistical despair. The cheerfulness of L. E. L.'s letters is adduced by all her friends as evidence that she was too courageous and level-headed to do anything so godless and violent, but they do not notice that all the letters paraphrase the same story of her rising at seven, giving out the provisions, lunching on yam, writing in the afternoon, meeting her husband back from court in the evening.

L. E. L. had learned the hard way to quell her own discontents and disappointments, because there was no one attached to her for any other reason than his own entertainment. She had gracefully flattered, acquiesced, adulated and courted everyone she ever knew. She was proud and secretive, but her pride and secretiveness expressed themselves as false light-heartedness. No one was to feel sorry for L. E. L. She might well have been desperately miserable, but she certainly would not have written about it in her letters home, for she felt no nearer to her friends than to anyone else. She had suffered far too much at the hands of friends, of even the most generous and affectionate friends, to make them privy to her last defeat. She would not have told Maclean either, for it was only too obvious that he was dismayed and repelled by the violence of her emotions. After years of schooling herself, we can well imagine her laughter as Maclean referred to her nonsense verses and twitted her about her furniture polishing or pastry making. Sir Edward Bulwer Lytton told the Colonial Office that L. E. L. had once before attempted suicide, but it was more typical of her nature perhaps to have avoided the showiness of attempts and to have quietly done it one morning when everything seemed quite normal. Henrietta Marchmont poisoned her husband with prussic acid in *Ethel Churchill* because he was a cold, punctilious, ambitious, heartless man.

> Lord Marchmont's coldness oftentimes comes over me with the effect of suddenly rounding a headland in one of our valleys, and finding the north wind full in my face. He takes not the slightest interest in aught I say, and I have continually thoughts and feelings which I am restless to communicate.

The day after the announcement of Letitia Maclean's death in the

London papers a curious letter appeared in *The Watchman*, announcing that missionaries ought not to be deterred from going to Cape Coast because of Mrs Maclean's death, which was not due to the climate or to fever. If Maclean had hoped that there would be no sensation about the poet's untimely demise, this letter set matters in a roar. When the finding of the inquest was known, the inference was too obvious to be missed.

Oddly enough, on 2 January Matthew Forster and Dr Quin came to visit Macready,

> afterwards poor Blanchard, in dreadfully low spirits; it now appears that L. E. L. the gifted creature, perished by her own hand! What is genius?

Their certainty about the manner of L. E. L.'s death must derive from some private source, for the public only knew that she had died suddenly of neither climate nor fever. Much of the mad speculation that was now unleashed was no more than an attempt to cloud the issue, just as had happened at the inquest. The morass of prudery and dissimulation in which Letitia Landon had floundered engulfed her even in death. Her friends seized upon a story of a cup of coffee brought to her by a native boy, after she had delivered her husband's tea and arrowroot, which cup was standing empty in her room when she was found. The only person in the colony who would have liked to murder her, it was assumed, would have been the native wife of George Maclean, but she was never traced by anyone more reliable than Dr Madden, who said he met her in Accra in 1841.

As early as February 1839 (five months after L. E. L.'s death), Maclean had written a long letter to her brother, which never reached him because of a 'mistake'. In August 1839, thirty-one folio pages did arrive, but Maclean desired their contents to remain private. Reverend Landon was particularly anxious to remove the stigma of suicide but he was informed by the Colonial Office in December 1839 that there would never be an answer to his questions. He had asked for the official papers and was told:

> The papers to which you allude, having, from their confidential nature, been diverted from passing through the ordinary official

channels, are at present mislaid, but will be returned to you as soon as they may be found.

Mrs Thomson was sure that the strange inability of the Colonial Office to order any investigation (not to mention the loss of all the documentation) was a result of the intervention of an MP on behalf of George Maclean.

The Secretary of State, now the Marquis of Normanby, saw fit to conduct the correspondence with Landon privately, and the papers subsequently disappeared.

Six hours after her death, L. E. L. was buried under the parade ground of the fort. Only one man, not her husband, stood by to see her interred. The Countess of Blessington offered a memorial tablet, but Maclean somewhat tardily announced that he would take care of it. He wrote to her mother, offering to double her allowance, and was stung by her reply that as long as she feared that her daughter was unhappy in her marriage, she could not accept his generosity. Maclean did not write again. Soon, Mrs Landon's circumstances were found to be so desperate that a public subscription was taken up for her by old friends of L. E. L. led by Bulwer Lytton.

L. E. L. has left us her own epitaph.

> The future never renders to the past
>   The young beliefs entrusted to its keeping;
> Inscribe one sentence – life's first truth and last –
>   On the pale marble where our dust is sleeping –
>   We might have been.

THE PERVERSITY OF
CHRISTINA ROSSETTI

It is ironic that it was not Dante Gabriel Rossetti but his retiring sister
Christina who in 1862 won recognition for the Pre-Raphaelite school
of poetry with *Goblin Market*. According to Swinburne (over whose
irreligious passages Christina Rossetti used to paste white paper), she
was the Jael who led their hosts to victory. Where once it was the
critical fashion to include Christina Rossetti in the larger tradition of
English religious poetry, recently she has emerged as, if not a feminist
poet, a poet important for feminists. Feminist readers tend to
concentrate on *Goblin Market* and the poems leading up to it, the
poems of Rossetti's rebellion and self-assertion seeming far more
interesting than those of her resignation and self-denial. An examination of her whole life's output reveals that Rossetti certainly considered herself a religious poet, but her religion is a matter of devout
sentiment, rather than an intellectual apprehension of the nature of
God or any mystical intimation of communion with him. As a
religious poet she must be listed among incorrigibly minor figures, a
bare cut above the horde of pious ladies who penned hymns in the
nineteenth century. The small devout poems that are to be encountered
in all kinds of anthologies may have won golden opinions from her
contemporaries and family, but the verdict of history is rather less
enthusiastic. By contrast modern readers are fascinated by *Goblin
Market*, even more so perhaps than its original readers. If *Goblin
Market* is a religious poem, it is a very strange one. No presiding deity
is ever invoked; pleasure and denial of pleasure appear to constitute
the only values.

Christina, who with her sister was educated at home by her
mother, began writing poetry when she was twelve:

On the flyleaf of the first of the seventeen black notebooks in which until 1866 she kept her poetry, her mother wrote, 'these verses are truly and literally by my little daughter, who scrupulously rejected all assistance in her rhyming efforts, under the impression that in that case they would not be her own'.

The first notebook, which like the others has thirty-two leaves, began with a poem to her mother 'on her Birth-day' dated 27 April 1842 and ended with 'Hope in Grief', dated 3 December 1845. Though Christina was not to be told how to write her poetry by her mother, she quite sensibily took literary models from the work of Herbert, Crabbe, Blake and Tennyson. At this stage she was serving a literary apprenticeship rather than a lay novitiate. There is every reason to believe that she worked at these early poems, making a conscious attempt to understand the dynamics of form, trying her hand at ballads and sonnets. She used a volume of religious poetry called *The Sacred Harp* as a poetic sampler. Not until she was satisfied with her poem would she copy it into the black notebook and date it. Sadly for those of us who would like to study her methods of composition, her foul papers were invariably destroyed. Her brother William Michael Rossetti describes her as writing 'rapidly as if from dictation'; if the poet of *Goblin Market* wrote so effortlessly, it must have been after the poem had been worked into its finished state in her mind. What seems more likely is that Rossetti's facility grew as she grew older, and as the poems became less literary and more religious.

Rossetti is not, as her male models were, a religious poet who used carnal experience as a metaphor for the soul's apprehension of God. Consciously or unconsciously she used the aspirations of piety as a metaphor for her own frustrated sexuality. As a Victorian woman poet she is simply typical in this respect. For dozens of literary women the passions of the heart, for which there was no acceptable expression, were diverted and subdued into piety with results as curious and sad as the garbled flutterings of Mrs Oliphant, Rossetti's fellow parishioner at Christ Church, Albany Street:

> On the edge of the world, I lie, I lie,
> Happy and dying and dazed and poor,
> Looking up from the vast great floor
> To the infinite world that lies above
> To God and Faith and Love, Love, Love!

Not that the real world does not supply the religious poet with all his materials, for the language that the poet disposes is itself a phenomenon of the real world and a metaphor of that world. Even when a poet writes directly of supernatural matters he must apply the grammar of mundane perceptions. Dante, the great bugbear of the baby Rossettis, explained this fourth and highest function of the poet, of presenting the unknowable in comprehensible terms, as the anagogic level of allegory. The anagogic use of language is what characterizes the mystic poet. For him the flesh is the unreal, the evanescent metaphor that clothes the immutable realities of eternity, obscuring them even while it makes them perceptible to mortal eyes: this paradox is the poet's glory and his grief. In true mystic poetry, the images of sexual intimacy serve as familiar, almost domestic analogues of the nearness and pervasiveness of God, and of the intense joy to be found in communion with him.

> Yet dearly I love you, and would be loved fain,
> But am betrothed unto your enemy:
> Divorce me, untie, or break that knot again,
> Take me to you, imprison me, for I,
> Except you enthral me, never shall be free,
> Nor ever chaste, except you ravish me.

This is the female soul of John Donne begging her male God to possess her, without any hint of coyness. There was no impropriety for Donne in the adoption of a feminine persona who wants to be redeemed from the toils of sin by the God whose name is Love. Francis Quarles celebrated his spiritual closeness to God in the euphoric terms much more typical of religious poetry than Rossetti's despairing and almost inarticulate longing for release from earth.

> E'en so we met; and after long pursuit,
> E'en so we joined, we both became entire;
> No need for either to renew a suit,
> For I was flax, and He was flames of fire:
> Our firm-united souls did more than twine;
> So I my Best-beloved's am; so He is mine.

George Herbert uses the image that we find turned topsy-turvy in *Goblin Market*: his loving God is beckoning him to a feast.

Love bade me welcome; yet my soul drew back,
    Guilty of dust and sin.
But quick-eyed Love, observing me grow slack
    From my first entrance in,
Drew nearer to me, sweetly questioning,
    If I lacked anything.

A guest, I answered, worthy to be here:
    Love said, 'You shall be he.'
I the unkind, ungrateful? 'Ah my dear,
    I cannot look on thee.'
Love took my hand, and smiling did reply,
    'Who made the eyes but I?'

'Truth Lord, but I have marred them: let my shame
    Go where it doth deserve.'
'And know you not,' says Love, 'who bore the blame?'
    'My dear, then I will serve.'
'You must sit down,' says Love, 'and taste my meat':
    So I did sit and eat.

The poets who write in this way about God are people for whom sexual pleasure is demystified, at ease in describing states of mind and heart which to Rossetti were entirely unknown. The relationship which they parallel to that of the Christian soul to God is the relationship of the spouses in marriage, elevated by the Protestant theologians to a position of high honour rather than the mere legalized concubinage that it seemed to the pre-Reformation Catholic Church. St Teresa of Avila used the image of marriage to describe the relationship between her reformed order of Carmelites and their divine Spouse, even to the extent of writing epithalamia based on folk forms for the profession of her nuns. The joyous note she sounded has nothing in common with the melancholy of Rossetti; even her famous lament 'I die because I do not die' has a double meaning, for St Teresa often died for hours at a time as Christ entered her and she floated in rapture, which was, if the term may be applied, the orgasm of her union with Christ.

Richard Crashaw could write in envy, probably after reading *The Flaming Heart*, a current English version of St Teresa's life:

O thou undaunted daughter of desires!
By all thy dower of lights and fires;
By all the eagle in thee, all the dove;
By all thy lives and deaths of love;
By thy large draughts of intellectual day,
And by thy thirsts of love more large than they;
By all thy brim-filled bowls of fierce desire;
By thy last morning's draught of liquid fire;
By the full kingdom of that final kiss
That seized thy parting soul and sealed thee His:
By all the heavens thou hast in Him
(Fair sister of the Seraphim!),
By all of Him we have in thee;
Leave nothing of my self in me.
Let me so read my life, that I
Unto all life of mine may die!

Rossetti was more successful than Mrs Oliphant in giving form to her emotional experience, but she suffers the same fundamental disability. Mrs Oliphant may have known how she felt, although she expressed it lamentably, but she certainly did not know what her feeling was. Rossetti's poetry is the direct colloquial expression of distinct emotional states, but the God who is the apparent object of all this carefully delineated feeling is not present in the poetry. Indeed, Rossetti can so far slide into Victorian muddle about God that she can call him 'the Eternal Smile'.

Though God is a phenomenon of human fabrication he is not simply an emotional whipping boy. The concept of the deity built up over two thousand years of Christianity and nourished by Platonic philosophy is an awe-inspiring construct comprehending many of the most sublime notions generated by human yearning for perfection, but Rossetti knew almost nothing of this complexity. Like a seventeenth-century ranter, she produced a God from her own psyche and worshipped him. The greater beauty and grandeur of the Mystical Body she perforce ignored. Christina Rossetti was not, as St Teresa of Avila was, a member of a venerable religious order, taking part in the great upheaval which galvanized the Catholic Church in the sixteenth century. She was separated from the intellectual traditions of Catholic mysticism by her own sectarianism, which was every bit as blind and terror-driven as her prudery. She laid her soul upon a bed, like the heroine of *The Eve of St. Agnes*, and waited for the divine lover who would lift the latch of her chamber door and carry her to heaven.

> They told her how, upon St. Agnes' Eve,
> Young virgins might have visions of delight,
> And soft adorings from their loves receive
> Upon the honeyed middle of the night,
> If ceremonies due they did aright;
> As, supperless to bed they must retire,
> And couch supine their beauties, lily white;
> Nor look behind, nor sideways, but require
> Of Heaven with upward eyes for all that they desire.

The poem appealed strongly to Rossetti and left its mark upon her work, especially her poetry of waiting, passive, dumb but unresigned, for the God who is love.

Rossetti was a Victorian, who had sucked guilt with her mother's milk and could not refer to her own body without embarrassment. Her sexuality was unknown to her: the more it loomed vast and polymorphous in her dreams, the less able she was to confront it in any recognizable form. What was called innocence in women like Christina Rossetti was in fact agonized self-consciousness. Later in her life she was to tell a much younger niece that when she was her age she was once so enraged at being prevented from having her way that, in her own words, she 'ripped up her arm with the scissors'. It is perhaps typical of her womanhood that she took out her anger upon her own body: Rossetti crushed herself more efficiently than anyone else could have. Appalled by the uncontrollable violence of her own nature, she resolved to stifle herself, no matter what the cost. At the age of fifteen, after enjoying perfect health all her life, she became an invalid. Her disease was diagnosed as angina pectoris, although nothing in her adult medical history would bear out such a hypothesis. Mackenzie Bell wrote in a copy of his biography of Rossetti that he had given to a friend that he debated with himself whether to include a note by the doctor in attendance when Rossetti was sixteen to eighteen years old declaring her to be insane, possibly suffering a 'religious mania'. The pains in her chest subsided to be replaced by a cough 'with symptoms which were counted ominous of decline or consumption, lasting towards 1867'. In 1871 she fell a victim to Graves's disease, exopthalmic bronchocele, which had permanent consequences for her health. However, she outlived all her family except William and his children, and died at sixty-four, after an operation for breast cancer. Constitutionally she seems to have been very tough, her lifelong poor health solely the result of the action of her own will.

Some of the symptoms of Rossetti's disorder seem to be hysterical. William Rossetti was not willing to expatiate but he does mention 'a sense of suffocation' which was characteristic of hysteria. William's veneration for Christina's patience under her afflictions, and her keen appreciation of the special privileges to which her invalid state entitled her, argues some gullibility on his part. Her illness allowed her to remain at home instead of teaching school or governessing, occasionally turning her hand to a little literary work that earned her no more than £10 a year until *Goblin Market* appeared, when her fortunes slightly changed. She was content to live at her family's expense, as her mother's companion and nurse for fifty-six years. Rossetti's invalidism was her idiosyncratic version of the enclosed life of a nun. Her sister undertook the discipline of an Anglican sisterhood but Christina preferred her life as an anchoress, perhaps because she was not prompted to bring herself under the intellectual and spiritual discipline of life in a convent, where her indulgence of personal fantasy would have been curbed. The life she chose was after all not greatly different from that of her mother, who existed solely within the walls of her own home and to go to church. It is at least possible that the female children of Gabriele Rossetti were expected to live as narrow and confined an existence as any middle-class Abruzzese women of the same period, regardless of the stirrings of new freedom in the country of their adoption.

The lonely self-torture of Christina Rossetti might be contrasted with the life of the sister to whom *Goblin Market* is dedicated. Maria Francesca was the elder, a practical, thorough sort of person, who distinguished herself by publishing a reputable study of Dante. While Christina's faith caused her great suffering, Maria Francesca's seems to have verily uplifted her and brought her the spiritual confidence and joy which is typical of a genuine mystic. As a member of a religious order, she would of course have been counselled and protected from the spiritual disease of scruples that so tormented her sister. It was pride that directed Rossetti's religious career, and tortured her with undying fears of unworthiness. Although she appeared to all the world self-forgetful to a marked degree, she was after all the daughter of mad Gabriele Rossetti, who said of himself in later life, 'I have become like one of those people of exaggerated piety who think that in their most insignificant action they have committed a mortal sin', and the sister of Dante Gabriel, whose declining years were tortured with guilt and terror. She had the Rossetti artistic ego, although she scorned to devote the extended effort that might have made her a great poet. In her very carelessness in composition, we may read not only her otherworldly indifference to excellence, but her own profound and perverse self-absorption. Wilfully, she set out to waste her life, ostensibly in order to enjoy eternal life, but eternal life appeared to her only fitfully in visions that increased her torment. Her assiduity in frittering her time away was unrelenting.

> One thing which occupied C. to an extent one would hardly credit was the making up of scrapbooks for Hospital patients or children this may possibly have begun before she moved to Torrington Sq. was certainly in very active exercise for several years ensuing – say up to 1885. When I called to see her and my mother it was 9 chances out of 10 that I found her thus occupied – I daresay she may have made up at least 50 biggish scrapbooks of this kind – taking some pains in adapting borderings to the pages etc etc.

Christina Rossetti first began to display signs of melancholy and contempt for the world at puberty, when she also produced in herself the symptoms of angina. 'Hope in Grief' was written on 3 December 1845, two days before Rossetti's fifteenth birthday:

> Tell me not that death of grief
> Is the only sure relief.
> Tell me not that hope when dead
> Leaves a void that nought can fill,
> Gnawings that may not be fed.
> Tell me not there is no skill
> That can bind the breaking heart,
> That can soothe the bitter smart,

> When we find ourselves betrayed,
> When we find ourselves forsaken,
> By those for whom we would have laid
> Our young lives down . . .

Rossetti's poetry is probably no more autobiographical than anyone else's. Nevertheless the reiteration in so many of the poems of the theme of bitter disappointment in love has led most students of Rossetti to posit a betrayal, but few have imagined it occurring before she was fifteen. Who was the person for whom Christina would have laid her young life down? Who could have forsaken her so long before that she was aware of 'Long, unmitigated pain'?

> Say not, vain this world's turmoil,
> Vain its trouble and its toil,
> All its hopes and fears are vain,
> Long, unmitigated pain.
> What though we should be deceived
> By the friend that we love best?
> All in this world have been grieved
> Yet many have found rest.
> Our present life is as the night,
> Our future as the morning light:
> Surely the night will pass away,
> And surely will uprise the day.

Rossetti may have been indulging in the fashionable morbidity of poets like the ill-fated L. E. L., but her death wish seems to have been genuine. She became so ill that her family believed that she was close to death.

Mrs Rossetti was clearly not moved to treat her daughter's poetry as autobiographical, or she would have been deeply perturbed by some of the poems presented to her in 1847. The teeth-grinding of 'Eva' could be thought to be explained by the reference to Maturin, if only one were not moved to wonder what the attraction of Maturin to a sixteen-year-old might have been:

> Yes, I loved him all too well,
> And my punishment is just . . .

Haughty in its humbleness;
  Proud in its idolatry:
Let the loved heel gall and press
  On my neck: so it should be.
'Twas in madness that I spake it:
Let him leave my heart or take it,
Let him heal my heart or break it;

But it still shall be for him,
  It shall love him only still.—
Nay it was no passing whim,
  But a woman's steadfast will.
And this word is aye returning:
And I cannot quell the yearning
That in breast and brain is burning.

Tears of mine may quench it never,
  Bitter tears shed all alone;
Dropping, dropping, dropping ever
  For the thought of him that's gone:
Dropping when none see or know.
Woe is me! they only flow
For the joys of long ago.

The themes of tainted joys long ago and 'love slighted not requited',
secret pining and penance and eventual reunion in heaven were
reworked many times throughout Rossetti's poetic career. 'Fair Margaret' develops another familiar motif, this time of the triangle, in
which the poet's persona is the true enduring love rejected for
another who is incapable of her passion:

For though I may not love thee,
Though calm as heaven above me,
  My thoughts of thee must be,
I cannot break so lightly
The chain that bound me tightly,
  Once bound my soul to thee.

In 'Divine and Human Pleading' a contrite man is comforted by a
female apparition who tells him that God forgave her:

> My youth and my beauty
> Were budding in their prime;
> But I wept for the great transgression,
> The sin of other time.

'Will these hands ne'er be clean?' deals with guilt; even 'The Dead Bride' is presented as one whose heart was won and held by 'tainted pleasure'. 'Zara', another poem relating to a reading in Maturin, deals with a love that was once noble and is now a crime; Zara warns the lover's new beloved that as she has sucked the honey of his love, she too will feel the sting of his rejection. What Zara cannot do is turn her wrath against her faithless lover. 'The Dream' is a recollection that recurs in poem after poem, of sitting beside a stream with a lover who has proved indifferent and gone away.

> I say: 'it is a joy-dream; I will take it;
> He is not gone; he will return to me.'

It is risky to attempt to identify the subject of a pubescent girl's fixation, but by the same token it is difficult to imagine who can have played such a role in the poet's early emotional life if not her brother. Gabriel, as Gabriel Charles Dante Rossetti was called by the family, was two years older than Christina. As the first-born son of an Abruzzese, he was certain to have been lionized and overindulged by his family; certainly he wielded immense influence over Rossetti as if by right. The experiences of childhood are always crucial for any artist, but for Rossetti, who renounced all adult adventures, they must have been even more important. Ellen Moers finds that the genre of female Gothic derives directly from the lawless society of the nursery and the sexual tension that builds up between pubescent children. In the Rossetti household the children were not segregated in a nursery where they could torment each other with impunity but, given Gabriel Senior's mad preoccupations and Mrs Rossetti's diligent churchgoing, much must have happened between Rossetti and her brother of which her parents were unaware.

Rossetti and Gabriel were alike in looks and temperament. Both passionate and wilful, they quarrelled violently and were as violently reconciled. All their lives Gabriel and Rossetti used a special style of language in speaking to each other that they did not use with anyone else. This is not to say that Rossetti was guilty of an incestuous passion, but simply that no other man ever came close to replacing her adored brother in her imagination. She followed his lawless life with grief, both sympathizing deeply with the other people who were despoiled by his egotism and instability, as the little sister herself had been, and tormented by jealousy that other, lesser women should have been so much closer to him and meant so much more to him than she did. It would be strange if adolescent sexuality had not been kindled within the relationship, perhaps before Rossetti had been aware. There may have been a pact between the children never to let any other relationship take precedence over their commitment to each other which the brother did not take as seriously as the sister. Rossetti may have only recognized the physicality of her longing for closeness with her brother when she encountered the physical pain of jealousy. The 'old familiar love' that so many of her poems present as being reborn in heaven could be the pre-adolescent love of brother and sister later corrupted by their nascent sexuality and abandoned by the brother for slightly more acceptable sexual liaisons, or some such. As an adult Gabriel was never without a lover; Rossetti was shown a series of potential spouses, none of whom exhibited any of Gabriel's angelic or demonic qualities, and rejected them all. There is less need to dwell on the abnormality of this kind of relationship than to realize its inevitability in a personality as narcissistic and obsessive as Rossetti's.

One of the recurrent aspects of the love that racks so many of Rossetti's personae is that it dare not speak its name. Some have taken this to mean that Rossetti was attracted to her own sex; though the number of Rossetti's love poems that feature a female beloved would give countenance to such an idea, it seems to me rather that she chose a male persona in order to utter the truth about her own complex feelings about sexual passion and about her brother. In 'The Dying Man to his Betrothed', written when she was fifteen, the speaker begs for his faithless lover's attention with a helplessness in the face of taciturnity that is more feminine than otherwise. Mrs Rossetti must have taken such monologues to be pure fictions; she was not to know that Rossetti would rework these themes all her life.

In the months following the printing of *Verses: Dedicated to Her Mother* Rossetti wrote three poems purporting to be uttered by an abandoned lover who awaits the step on the stair and a hand on the latch, knowing they will never come: 'Death's Chill Between', 'Heart's Chill Between' and 'Repining'. Many attempts have been made to discover the man (or woman) who was responsible for Rossetti's rejection of worldly love. William Rossetti claimed that Rossetti had rejected two suitors, James Collinson in 1849 and Charles Bagot Cayley in 1867, both on religious grounds. Lona Mosk Packer in her biography of the poet has gone most of the way to discrediting either as a feasible object of the poet's passions, at least partly so that she could erect another man in their stead, the poetaster William Bell Scott. A woman living in Rossetti's circumstances could be expected to have suffered violent infatuations fairly regularly and for various people, not necessarily male, not necessarily members of her circle of acquaintance. A bigot with her sense of guilt and terror of physical experience is likely to have magnified such feelings and given them a perverse sort of indulgence by fighting to suppress them. One thing is certain: Rossetti was passionately proud of her capacity for intense feeling. Behind the locked door of her chamber she cherished her passion, nourished it and gave it regular, encoded expression. The struggle to replace her idolatrous human love with a genuine love of God was long and exhausting. Isidora's guilty question, 'Paradise, will he be there?' was answered when Gabriel died in 1882. In 'Advent Sunday', first published in 1885, after Gabriel's death, consummation of joy in heaven is presented in new terms:

> His eyes are as a Dove's and she's Dove-eyed:
> He knows His lovely mirror, sister, Bride.

In 'Whitsun Tuesday' and 'Feast of the Annunciation', published in the same volume, the motif is repeated. If Gabriel and Christina are able to love with the 'old familiar love' in heaven, it will be because all taint of carnality is purged and they can love as innocently and as passionately as children.

Gabriel used Christina as the model for *The Childhood of the Virgin*, and William tells us that the likeness is good despite the changed hair colour. The Virgin sits listlessly pushing a needle through a tapestry, while the large form of her mother crowds close to her, cutting her off from the open window which gives on to a sunny landscape. The mother's hands are idle, her large eyes cast down, but the Virgin sits rigid, staring dully into space, her cheek hardly a foot from her mother's. William Rossetti tells us that Rossetti was one of the models for *Ecce Ancilla Domini* and that the Virgin's expression is typical of her. Again the look is shrinking and abstracted, the posture of the body crushed and helpless. Gabriel may have imagined that he was depicting sanctity, just as Rossetti imagined that she was attaining it, but he seems to have felt strongly that meek and self-effacing manners were the only ones that became women. That he had any real understanding of how Rossetti had imprisoned herself inside an iron maiden of her own devising is extremely unlikely. Once she allowed herself to cry out, in tones reminiscent of Elizabeth Barrett, in rage against the pettiness of her cramped existence. In 'The Lowest Room' two sisters offer contrasting images of acceptance and rebellion. The tale is told by the rebellious sister, who yearns for a more heroic age:

> 'Oh better then be slave or wife
>   Than fritter now blank life away:
> Then night had holiness of night,
>   And day was sacred day . . .
>
> 'A shame it is, our aimless life:
>   I rather from my heart would feed
> From silver dish in gilded stall
>   With wheat and wine the steed –
>
> The faithful steed that bore my lord . . .'

She is soundly defeated by her sister's arguments for calm domestic virtue, but Gabriel was disgusted that his sister should have written in such a way at all. He decried the 'modern vicious style' and 'falsetto muscularity' of the writing.

> Everything in which this tone appears is utterly foreign to your primary impulses . . . If I were you I should rigidly keep guard on this matter if you write in the future: and ultimately exclude from your writings everything (or almost everything) so tainted.

In the original notebook 'The Lowest Room' is called 'A Fight over the Body of Homer' and dated 30 September 1856; it was first published in *Macmillan's Magazine* for March 1864 without these opening stanzas:

> Amen: the sting of fear is past,
>   Cast out and no more burdensome;
> There can be no such pang as this
>   In all the years to come.
> No more such wrestlings in my soul,
>   No more such heart-break out of sight,
> From dawning of my longdrawn day
>   Until it draw to night.

A pencil stroke has struck these stanzas out. Of all the Rossetti texts this is one of the most heavily revised. The seventh (now fifth) stanza read originally:

> I may be second, but not first;
>   All cannot be the first of all:
> This weighs on me, this wearies me,
>   I stumble like to fall.

Now the stanza as printed reads:

> Some must be second and not first;
>   All cannot be the first of all:
> Is not this too but vanity?
>   I stumble like to fall.

In all fourteen stanzas were suppressed and another half-dozen radically altered, in an attempt to civilize the poet's rage at being prevented from writing epic poetry, not only for the stated reason that she was born in 'days of dross' to 'fritter now blank life away' but for the unstated reason that she is a woman. The theme of the contrasting fates of two sisters, one a wife and mother, the other not, one self-effacing and fulfilled, the other self-abasing but unresigned, points in a mysterious way towards *Goblin Market*, where the theme of women's fulfilment is developed in a manner far more disturbing but also much more efficiently veiled.

Much of Rossetti's poetry is a sort of mental tranquillizer, composed without heat in much the same way as she might have put together her therapeutic scrapbooks; at her best her poetry can be stirring and terrible, the cry of a woman of great talent, great passion and stronger will, who destroyed her life rather than live within the narrow bounds of what was possible. Again and again, Rossetti gives a heroic account of her own emotional capacity only to compare it with the pettifogging demands actually made upon it.

> How can we say 'enough' on earth –
>   'Enough' with such a craving heart?
> I have not found it since my birth,
>   But still have bartered part for part.
> I have not held and hugged the whole,
>   But paid the old to gain the new:
>   Much have I paid, yet much is due,
> Till I am beggared sense and soul.

Rejection of the love of mere mortals is expressed with bitter trenchancy:

> Of all my past this is the sum
> – I will not lean on child of man.
>
> To give, to give, not to receive!
>   I long to pour myself, my soul,
> Not to keep back or count or leave,
>   But king with king to give the whole.
> I long for one to stir my deep –
>   I have had enough of help and gift –
>   I long for one to search and sift
> Myself, to take myself and keep.

In Christina's notebook this poem, one of two with the title 'The Heart Knoweth its own Bitterness', is dated 27 August 1857. Despite its manifest quality, the poem was passed over for inclusion in any of the collections of Rossetti's verse published during her lifetime. A bowdlerized version of the first and last stanzas, together with a title 'Whatever is right, that shall ye receive', was published in 1885 by the Society for the Promotion of Christian Knowledge in *Time Flies: A Reading Diary*. William Michael, who wrote, 'few things written by Christina contain more of her innermost self than this', included the whole text in *New Poems Hitherto Unpublished or Uncollected* in 1896. Within the poem we hear the voice of Christina Rossetti's pride repelled by the mediocrity of human love. It is the cry of any woman revolted not only by the foolish games of courtship and servile domesticity but by her brother's fickle sensuality, yearning for a love that will sound the depths of her potency.

> You scratch my surface with your pin,
>   You stroke me smooth with hushing breath –
> Nay pierce, nay probe, nay dig within,
>   Probe my quick core and sound my depth.
> You call me with a puny call,
>   You talk, you smile, you nothing do:
>   How should I spend my heart on you,
>   My heart that so outweighs you all?
>
> Your vessels are by much too strait:
>   Were I to pour, you could not hold.
> Bear with me: I must bear to wait,
>   A fountain sealed through heat and cold.
> Bear with me days or months or years:
>   Deep must call deep until the end
>   When friend shall no more envy friend
> Nor vex his friend at unawares.
>
> Not in this world of hope deferred,
>   This world of perishable stuff:
> Eye hath not seen nor hear hath heard 'enough':
>   Here moans the separating sea,
>   Here harvests fail, here breaks the heart:
>   There God shall join and no man part,
> I full of Christ and Christ of me.

Aware that she was too much to handle, Rossetti tamed herself and drew herself into the most confined compass, to show that she could do anything, even the impossible. For her reward she took a divine lover, but her dread secret was that she loved him for self-love.

In 1858 she wrote another extraordinary poem, 'The Convent Threshold', which deals with one of her favourite themes, a young woman's rejection of the world and worldly love for the promise of joy in heaven, but this time the process of rejection itself is dramatized in a suggestive and compelling way. The poem is in the form of a dramatic monologue, spoken at the foot of a stair of gold, mounting 'to city and to sea of glass', apparently a metaphor for the conventual life which leads to heaven. The earthly love, who is addressed in the poem, has been abjured because there is blood between the lovers, father's love and brother's blood, an ambiguity which William Rossetti explains as a family feud, but which might also mean some taint in the love itself: 'Blood's a bar I cannot pass.' The novice's eyes are turned to the city of heaven, but it pales into remoteness next to the earthly beauties which attract her lover's eyes, beauties like those of the goblin fruits:

> You looking earthward, what see you?
> Milk-white, wine-flushed among the vines,
> Up and down leaping, to and fro,
> Most glad, most full, made strong with wines,
> Blooming as peaches pearled with dew,
> Their golden windy hair afloat,
> Love-music warbling in their throat.
> Young men and women come and go.

She pleads with him to renounce the world, repent and accept her cheerless life of expiation. The words used to describe her dreary days of unremitting self-denial are the words that Rossetti uses elsewhere to describe her physical desolation.

> How long until my sleep begin,
> How long shall stretch these nights and days?

As part of her plea for her lover's soul, in case she should feel a pang finding herself in heaven without him (a heretical notion, if she only knew), she recounts to him two dreams. The first is of a spirit 'with transfigured face' who mounted upwards through the heavens in a quest for more light, outstripping angels and archangels, until, once arrived at the summit of knowledge, he dashes his crown down and abandons his throne, because he has discovered that

Knowledge is strong, but love is sweet.

The second dream is quite different. It is Christina Rossetti's recurrent dream of being dead and buried, but this time the lover comes to her heroine, as so often she prayed that her divine lover would come to her, and speaks to her through the clay.

> I tell you what I dreamed last night.
> It was not dark, it was not light,
> Cold dews had drenched my plenteous hair
> Through clay; you came to seek me there,
> And 'Do you dream of me?' you said.
> My heart was dust that used to leap
> To you; I answered half asleep:
> 'My pillow is damp, my sheets are red,
> There's a leaden tester to my bed:
> Find you a warmer playfellow
> A warmer pillow for your head,
> A kinder love to love than mine.'
> You wrung your hands: while I, like lead,
> Crushed downwards through the sodden earth:
> You smote your hands but not in mirth,
> And reeled but were not drunk with wine.
>
> For all night long I dreamed of you:
> I woke and prayed against my will,
> Then slept to dream of you again.
> At length I rose and knelt and prayed.
> I cannot write the words I said,
> My words were slow, my tears were few;
> But through the dark my silence spoke
> Like thunder.

The motifs of this dreaming are so familiar from Rossetti's writing that we are even more shocked at the macabreness of this manifestation. The zone which is neither light nor dark is the genuine land of dreams, and the curious frustration of her being half-asleep and answering drowsily to her lover's egotistical question is most true to dream experience. She makes one last plea to him to join her in heaven, where she shall meet as once they met,

> And love with old familiar love.

And the poem ends. The situation is banal enough, but Rossetti's treatment of it is compressed and strident; the poem moves towards its climax with a deliberateness that is quite unusual in the work of a poet whose favourite form was the short lyric. William Rossetti had surprisingly little to say about this poem, but he did speculate upon the relevance of the vision of the spirit in quest of pure intelligence, saying that it would befit the circumstances of an Heloise and Abelard theme, but the poet makes no specific reference.

Goblin Market is not often examined in the context of Rossetti's other work. It was first published accompanied by sixty poems selected from the poetry Rossetti had been writing over the preceding twenty years, of which the earliest are four from 1848 and ten, the largest number from any single year, from 1849. One of the earliest is 'A Pause of Thought' written originally 'In memory of Schiller's *Der Pilgrim*', which begins:

> I looked for that which is not, nor can be
>   And hope deferred made my heart sick in truth:
>   But years must pass before a hope of youth
>   Is resigned utterly.

The despairing mood of this kind of writing can be considered a mere literary convention, by Byron out of L. E. L., but in the whole of the output for 1848 there are stranger, more despairing works. The next stanza develops a dimension of feeling which is fundamental in Rossetti's work:

> I watched and waited with a steadfast will
>   And though the object seemed to flee away

That I so longed for, ever day by day
I watched and waited still.

The last stanza admonishes the poet's persona:

Ah thou foolish one! alike unfit
For healthy joy and salutary pain . . .

Commentators have been puzzled by Rossetti's references to guilt
and guilty pleasures in her early poems; the cause of the failure of her
engagement in 1849 has remained and should remain a mystery, but
the possibility that Rossetti was incapable of 'healthy joy' should be
borne in mind. She was a child of tempestuous feelings; the most
tempestuous pleasure she ever felt may very well have been unhealthy
because it was connected with her equally stormy brother. This is not
to say that she had an affair with her brother, but simply that she
knew that she wanted to be the most important person in his life, that
she chafed that she could not share more of his life, that she longed
for his approval more than anything, that she was jealous of all his
other affections and intimacies, that every time he left the house she
watched the street for his return. To him she was only the little sister;
he may well have found her poetry the most interesting thing about
her, and she may have wooed him unconsciously in that poetry.

Lizzie Siddal came into Gabriel's life in 1850. Christina observed the
love affair, and how after four years of infatuation Gabriel's affection
began to wane. Ford Madox Brown, who was aware that Christina's
reactions were of importance, observed her: 'She works at worsted
ever, and talks sparingly'. Christina was not insensible to Lizzie's
beauty, which was to become the *beau idéal* of the Pre-Raphaelites,
nor to Lizzie's suffering as she gradually realized that her love for
Gabriel could not survive his fickleness and indifference. Christina's
reluctance to trust herself to the derisory love of humans may have
been reinforced by Lizzie's ruin. Lizzie died of an overdose of
laudanum in the same year that saw the publication of *Goblin Market*.

Rossetti wrote in a presentation copy of a later edition of *Goblin
Market*:

'Goblin Market' first published in 1862 was written (subject of
course to subsequent revision) as long ago as April 27, 1859, and

in MS was inscribed to my dear only sister Maria Francesca
Rossetti ... In the first instance I named it 'A Peep at the
Goblins' in imitation of my cousin Mrs Bray's 'A Peep at the
Pixies', but my brother Dante Gabriel Rossetti substituted
the greatly improved title as it now stands. And here I like to
acknowledge the general indebtedness of my first and second
volumes to his suggestive wit and revising hand.

Perhaps Mrs Rossetti was quite wrong about Christina's rejection
of 'all assistance'; it may have been only her mother's interference that
the poet sought to discourage. Perhaps the thought of her work being
exposed in public, unlike *Verses: Dedicated to Her Mother*, which was
privately printed by her grandfather in 1847, brought about a change
in Rossetti's attitude to editorial intervention. The heart of a seeker
after woman-as-text sinks at the implications of the words 'general
indebtedness' because for the most part we do not have markedly
different versions of the poems published in 1862 and 1866 and must
assume that once Rossetti had accepted Gabriel's emendations she
incorporated them in fair copies and threw her originals away. The
1859 holograph of 'A Peep at the Goblins' shows remarkably few
substantive departures from the text printed as *Goblin Market* in 1862.
The regularizing of punctuation accounts for most of the changes.
The repetition of 'Morning and evening' at line 32 is altered; 'cry' at
line 46 becomes 'call'. Four lines:

> Lizzie hid her eyes with hands
> That showed like curds or cream;
> Laura raised her golden head
> And spoke like music of the stream:

are improved to read:

> Lizzie covered up her eyes,
> Covered close lest they should look;
> Laura reared her glossy head,
> And whispered like the restless brook:

The mildly unfortunate second line here:

> How fair the vine must grow
> That swung those grapes luscious;

becomes:

> Whose grapes are so luscious;

In line 70, 'goblin' becomes 'merchant' in keeping with the altered emphasis of the new title. In line 82 the coinage 'innested', with its irrelevant horticultural connotation, becomes 'imbedded'.

> Like a silver poplar branch
> Which the moonshine dwells upon

is altered to

> Like a moonlit poplar branch,

'Quaint' becomes 'queer' in line 94 and 'brisk' at line 241, 'anguish' 'aguish' in line 491, 'he' 'she' in line 503; these four revisions are entered in the holograph in Christina's hand. An awkward passage at lines 180–81:

> Odorous indeed must be that mead
> Whereon they grow, and whose waters clear they drink

in the text as printed is smoothed to:

> Odorous indeed must be the mead
> Whereon they grow, and pure the wave they drink.

A barbarism at line 187, 'They laid down in their curtained bed' is corrected. 'Peered' in line 192 becomes 'gazed', 'songful' in line 213, 'warbling', 'farthest' in line 222 'furthest', 'darkness' in line 262 'dimness', 'hope deferred' in line 267 'baulked desire', 'heard' in line 272 'caught', 'glad' in line 316 'gay', 'queer' in line 337 'wry', 'flame' in line 414 'fire', 'Pulled' in line 427 'Kicked' and 'Kicked' in line 428 'Mauled'. Some of these changes reinforce alliterations and assonance; others avoid repetitions; others intensify the physicality of the imagery.

All must be assumed to have been made with Rossetti's consent, which is not to say that she made them or could have made them without prompting. In the last 140 lines of the poem there are only eleven such changes; if we disregard punctuation changes, only thirty-nine lines out of a total of 567 show any change at all between composition on 27 April 1859 and publication in 1862. If Gabriel's 'suggestive wit and revising hand' played as significant a part as Rossetti suggests, it must have been before the fair copy of 'A Peep at the Goblins' was made. Even so, the departures in the printed text are not mere corrections but genuine revisions of an authorial kind. If they are Gabriel's they argue an unusually masterful attitude to the work of another, even if the other was his little sister.

Goblin Market is often compared to *The Ancient Mariner*; certainly it displays a similar directness of speech and concreteness of imagery, but the manipulation of certain archetypes of repressed or infantile eroticism is completely original. The pretence that *Goblin Market* is a children's poem enables Rossetti to deal directly with complex notions springing fully armed from the dream-world of childhood, without the necessity of disguising them as more acceptable narrative preoccupations. Blake and Coleridge, both poets whom Rossetti knew well, used similar mythic and visionary structures to embody their version of the numinous world of pre-Augustan imagination. We have only to think of the compelling mystery of Blake's rose —

O Rose, thou art sick!
The invisible worm
That flies in the night,
In the howling storm,
Has found out thy bed
Of crimson joy,
And his dark secret love
Does thy life destroy.

— to recognize the world inhabited by Laura and Lizzie, where all is familiar and nothing explicable. Rossetti knew Blake; two of the poems in her first publication were imitations of Blake.

To this day ballads are considered fit for children's reading regardless of their subject-matter, possibly because ballads tell stories and are not susceptible to pompous exegesis. Most good teachers realize, as they take children step by step through the ambiguities of Lord Randall or Barbara Allen, that they are dancing on a tightrope. The depths they might fall to, if the rope should break, are unfathomable. *Goblin Market* is such a poem. Its story is a simple one, simply told, yet even the most unashamed of post-Freudian readers looks up from it in wonder and hesitates to offer any translation of its odd events. Now and then critics hint at what might be the poem's theme, but more often they are content to let it lie enveloped in its mystery, for fear that to unravel it would be to reveal more of the psychology of the unraveller than it would of the meaning of the poem itself.

It would be fatuous to attempt to prove that *Goblin Market* is simply a commentary upon Lizzie's destructive relationship with Gabriel; rather the poem embodies in a still undigested and unrationalized form all that Christina had learned about pleasure and pain and love. The poem is compelling because troubling ideas exist within it quite unanalysed, as they do in dreams. It is driven by the paradoxical motivations of Christina's yearning for ecstasy, her fear of male insensibility and rapacity and her repugnance for carnal intercourse. The work of art generated by these powerful and inexpressible forces succeeds in awakening in all of its readers a voluptuous guilt such as they would never feel if confronted by the most vivid and captivating erotic art. Ellen Moers is right: the poem does belong to the nursery; its preoccupations are all infantile and all thoroughly corrupt. It reminds us once for all that there is nothing innocent about childhood and so strikes at the root of a cherished adult fantasy. Part of the poem's eroticism derives from the presence of the poet-voyeur, who watches Lizzie and Laura:

> Crouching close together
> In the cooling weather,
> With clasping arms and cautioning lips,
> With tingling cheeks and finger tips.

Christina's point of view is the same as Gabriel's will be when he comes to illustrate the poem; we might wonder whether she is not wooing Gabriel in presenting him this fantasy:

> Laura stretched her gleaming neck
> Like a rush-imbedded swan,
> Like a lily from the beck,

> Like a moonlit poplar branch
> Like a vessel at the launch
> When its last restraint is gone.

As we know this is one of the passages altered by Gabriel's suggestive wit. Gabriel chose to illustrate the extended passage that depicts the two girls asleep in one bed:

> Cheek to cheek and breast to breast
> Locked together in one nest.

Lizzie and Laura are like most heroines beloved of children (if not of their parents) in that they have no families and live an entirely self-regulating existence. We know that they are maids, that is virgins, which implies puberty, and that they are beautiful. Laura has glossy golden hair, a gleaming swan-like neck and a body as white as snow. Laura is energy, whether she is braving the encounter with the goblin men or greedily sucking their fruit, or writhing in medicinal torment. Lizzie is hardly ever physically described, although she is included in the description of them both as equally white and equally golden-haired. Lizzie's strength is the strength of inertia and renunciation: she acts slowly but she does not swerve and carries her intention to its completion. She can wear out the goblins simply by relentless passivity. Both characters seem to have existed in Christina side by side – the child who ripped up her arm with the scissors and the woman who knitted her eternal worsted and spoke sparingly.

The goblins are like Christina's favourite animals, the small grotesque wronged beasts that she loved to play with. At first there is nothing sinister about them. Their cries have been identified partly with the street vendors' cries that the children would have heard in Charlotte Street, and it is only too easy to imagine how excited and envious they felt about the goodies that their struggling father could not hope to buy for them. Charlotte Street was then a seedy area, growing seedier, and we can also imagine how the parents badgered the children not to speak to strange men, especially the itinerant vendors. Rossetti builds up her picture of oral luxuries with very simple means but the result is literally mouthwatering. To identify the fruits at this stage with sexual pleasure is to reduce their effectiveness as an image. They are all that infantile libido yearns for, pleasure unlimited, eternal dessert. One might as profitably compare them to breasts or the fruit of the tree of knowledge, or foreplay, as when Porphyro visits the sleeping Madeline in Rossetti's beloved *Eve of St. Agnes*.

> . . . he from forth the closet brought a heap
> Of candied apple, quince, and plum, and gourd;
> With jellies smoother than the creamy curd,
> And lucent syrops, tinct with cinnamon;
> Manna and dates, in argosy transferred
> From Fez; and spiced dainties, every one,
> From silken Samarcand to cedar'd Lebanon.

Porphyro's candied apples are never eaten, but Laura does eat gluttonously the fruits of the goblins, which require no biting. Their skins may be simply sucked empty. The fruits are all globes filled with liquid, which is not like honey, but sweeter, nor like wine, but stronger, nor like water, but clearer. The magic fluid has properties more like those of a drug than nourishment. The Rossettis knew drugs pretty well, for many of the psychosomatic ailments of the nineteenth century were treated as a matter of course with habit-forming drugs. Christina must have known the warming effects of opium in some form or another, for drugs were one of the rewards of her kind of invalidism. Lizzie believes that she could eat the fruit for ever and never be sick of it, for it has the addictive characteristic that each use prompts further use.

Human beings are not organized for pleasure, although they are for dependence. Laura reels home, not knowing whether it is night or day, only to meet the homily of Lizzie, who brings the figure of Jeanie into the story. Jeanie died at the first snowfall after eating the goblin fruit: the suggestion that the pleasure of the goblin fruits is sexual is first made here, and then strengthened by the later reference to 'joys brides hope to have'. Rossetti claimed that the poem is not a systematic allegory, and we must agree with her; all kinds of premature and intense pleasure now seem included in the meaning of the juicy globes. Infantile sexuality is very little understood, especially the genital sexuality of infants. Suffice it to say that if there was no sex play among the Rossetti children they must have been unique in the annals of childhood. One has only to think of the inadvertent ecstasies of the nursery in contrast to the lethargic courtship of James Collinson to see that Christina Rossetti might have retained a half-verbalized memory which destroyed any appeal that conventional titillation might have had for her. The fact that her demeanour discouraged any liberties is no guarantee that she had not enjoyed them before her skirts were let down. Laura tastes intense pleasure once and ever after pines for it; we know that Rossetti pined ever after, but we shall never know whether she tasted intense pleasure once. Laura 'sat down listless' and 'would not eat'. The model for *The Childhood of the Virgin* seems anorexic.

The other perplexing thing about *Goblin Market* is the relationship between the two sisters, who sleep entwined in each other's arms like lovers. When the world loses all savour for Laura, who can only yearn for the fruits which she may not have again, Lizzie is slow to react. The fading of Laura resembles the fading of Lizzie Siddal, who was destroyed by her yearning for the guilty pleasures she had once had with Gabriel: as human beings are not designed for pleasure, it follows that if they experience great pleasure, they find everything that is not that pleasure unexciting by contrast. Then when they do attempt to repeat the experience, they find that it is not as gratifying as it was before. Rossetti's objection to worldly pleasure is that the unregenerate soul is incapable of prolonged ecstasy. Renunciation of the curtailed pleasures of earth for the eternal pleasures of heaven is a bargain, but as yet she was not resigned to it. Those who deny themselves pleasure can still hear its siren call; *only* they are still tempted. Those who indulge themselves in pleasure lose their sensitivity to it. The solution that Rossetti devises for this dilemma in the poem is simply fantastical. It is both a kind of redemption and a source of the perverse pleasure of resistance. Lizzie must follow the temptation to eat right to the utterance and still resist. She must, like Rossetti herself, force her soul through an extremely dangerous exploit. There is no moral to be drawn from it, even if the deliberate entertainment of temptation were not itself a sin. Rossetti simply indulges her own erotic version of resistance as Lizzie performs the obverse of Laura's sin: where Laura sucks in the juices, Lizzie stands within them, like a rock in a stream. It would not be illuminating to remark that Lizzie performs a male role where Laura has performed a female one, for that is both obvious and insignificant. More pertinent perhaps is that Laura's aggressiveness turns out to be weakness and Lizzie's passivity to be strength. So might Rossetti have contrasted her own life with Gabriel's. Nevertheless the vividness of the poem is still with Laura, who treats Lizzie like the goblin fruit. Her salvation is literally that she makes love to her sister. In that her first motive is terror that her sister may have destroyed herself as she has, we might argue that once the addict's self-centredness is broken into, cure is possible, but the stress is much more upon the ritual eating of Lizzie. The effect of this new oral experience is electric. The language of Laura's purging is the purgatorial language of Rossetti's own spiritual suffering, just as the fantasies of guilty pleasure and virtuous resistance are the twin fantasies of Rossetti's emotional life.

Goblin Market is a deeply perverse poem, which will, like Rossetti herself keep its secret for ever. It stirs in each reader the depths of half-remembered infantile experience, only to baffle her by withholding the means of verbalizing and externalizing the memories that are printed on her flesh. It inverts the Christian notion of salvation through the Eucharist, or eating the body and blood of Christ, and then rights it again in the image of Lizzie offering her pure body for consumption, but in such a way that we are still uncomfortable. Homosexuals may make superficially convincing cases that the poem is about the greater virtue of physical love between sisters, and those who believe that heterosex is fundamentally distorted and sadistic will want to agree with them. All of us, however, have grown up with the unexpressed incest taboo which regulated the degree of physical contact we think appropriate between brothers and sisters, and all of us have somehow violated it. The poem it seems is about guilt, and the pleasure of guilt. However we reduce the poem to expound our own philosophies, we are left with the overriding fact of its subtle perversity and our own complicity.

In 1896, when Christina's brother William published a collection called *New Poems by Christina Rossetti hitherto unpublished or uncollected*, he dedicated it:

To Algernon Charles Swinburne, a generous eulogist of Christina Rossetti, who hailed his genius and prized himself the greatest of living British poets, my old and constant friend . . .

Although some modern commentators have liked to think of William Rossetti as a patriarchal, censoring figure, the truth seems to be that he was well aware of his sister's deep and complex perversity, and respected her the more for it. In any case there was no hiding it, for in all her poetry that is not ritualized or perfunctory, it is to be found, even in this apparently harmless sonnet:

> O Earth, lie heavily upon her eyes;
>   Seal her sweet eyes weary of watching, Earth;
>   Lie close around her; leave no room for mirth
> With its harsh laughter, nor for sound of sighs.
> She hath no questions, she hath no replies,
>   Hushed in and curtained with a blessèd dearth
>   Of all that irked her from the hour of birth;
> With stillness that is almost Paradise.
> Darkness more clear than noonday holdeth her,
>   Silence more musical than any song;
> Even her very heart has ceased to stir:
> Until the morning of Eternity
> Her rest shall not begin nor end, but be;
>   And when she wakes she will not think it long.

This is Rossetti's most anthologized poem; she was not yet twenty when she wrote it and no actual bereavement has ever been suggested as an occasion for it. The 'she' of the poem might as well be 'I' for all the distance that is invoked between live poet and dead subject. The controlling thought is closely related to that of the equally well-known poem, 'When I am, dead my dearest', written six months before. There is more than elegiac convention in the exhortation to the earth to weigh and seal her eyes shut, and lie suffocatingly close, pressing upon and obliterating the woman who will neither speak nor answer. The massiveness of the lover-like figure pressing upon the woman has suggested to some readers an encoded reference to sexual abuse by her father; there is no need to posit an actual point of reference. The fantasy will suffice. Crushed under this enveloping presence the woman experiences a stillness that is almost Paradise, a notion that reduces Paradise to a figure of annihilation. The sestet of the sonnet inverts what is usually believed about life after death: the darkness of the buried self awaiting resurrection is more dazzling than the sun at the zenith; its silence is more musical than *any* song, which must include the diapason of the blest. Rossetti then inverts the concept of Eternity, describing the duration of the world until the resurrection of the body as a continuing 'now' and eternity as a return to duration. In this dim and suggestive sonnet Christina Rossetti's credo is recited backwards, like the Paternoster in a Satanic mass. The sonnet was printed many times in England and America; yet no one, least of all Rossetti herself, noticed its strangeness or objected that the rhetoric of belief had been inverted to signify the opposite.

EPILOGUE

It is tempting to end a rather jaundiced account of the careers of some of the most successful women poets with a rousing statement that, with improvements in the status of women, the female poet is better prepared for her social and cultural role and far more likely than her predecessors to write good and durable poetry. If this is the case, it has not long been so. Too many of the most conspicuous figures in women's poetry of the twentieth century not only destroyed themselves in a variety of ways but are valued for poetry that documents that process. No woman now embarking on a career in poetry can be unaware of these terrible precedents. Many must feel as Jeni Couzyn did in the 1960s:

> As I lurched through my twenties, conscious of the many women poets I admired who had taken their own lives – Sylvia Plath, Anne Sexton, Ingrid Jonker, Eva Royston, Marina Tsvetaeva – I deeply believed that the choice for me was between 'happiness' (i.e. home, husband and children) or poetry. The consequence of choosing 'happiness' would be losing the ability to write, and of choosing poetry would be an early suicide. This was not so much an idea as a tangible feeling within my life of the tug of opposing energies.

It is odd that the opposition presented itself to Jeni Couzyn in these terms, when Plath, Sexton, Jonker and Tsvetaeva were all married and had children. The female poet is not presented with the women's magazine standby of a choice between marriage and a career, but with the choice to be happy and mute or unhappy and articulate. Happy marriage and motherhood are not the raw material of poetry, let alone poetry of high seriousness. The consequences of this emphasis on suffering as the raw material of poetry are serious; the more literary a young woman's bent, the more insidiously she is inducted into failure and frustration. She will be pressured to cannibalize herself and to regard herself as utterly alone, an outcast on the earth, though she is in fact surrounded by spouse, family, friends and therapists, all of whom must be shown to be inadequate. Couzyn states as clearly as may be that she grew up believing that the happy woman had nothing to say. That situation seems now, but only now, to be changing. As Stevie Smith wrote wryly:

> Why does my Muse only speak when she is unhappy?
> She does not. I only listen when I am unhappy
> When I am happy I live and despise writing
> For my Muse this cannot but be dispiriting.

This is not to say that the woman poet must manufacture unhappiness, but rather that unhappy women will be attracted to poetry and that poetry will give their unhappiness permanent form in intransigent text.

The life of the Afrikaner poet Ingrid Jonker, whose poetry has been described as 'poetry of pure loneliness, perpetual longing', was difficult. Her parents separated before she was born, her father going on to become a leading nationalist politician, while Ingrid, her mother and sister struggled. Ingrid began writing poetry when she was six. When she was ten her mother died and Jonker and her elder sister, Anna, had to live with her father and his family by his third wife, who treated her as an outsider. (History does not relate how she treated them.) When she was sixteen she sent her first collection off to publishers, who rejected it. From the outset she was intensely ambitious, translating many of her poems into English so that they would reach a wider public. In 1956 a collection entitled *Ontvlugting* or 'Escape' was published. A year later she married the poet Pieter Venter and bore a daughter, Simone, before the couple split up and she moved back to the Cape. In 1963 she published *Rook en Oker* ('Smoke and Ochre') which had an international success and brought her a prize that enabled her to travel in Europe. She was preparing a third volume of poems when on the winter's night of 19 July 1965 she drowned herself in Three Anchor Bay. Her work has been compared to Sylvia Plath's, perhaps because she writes of the emotional ambivalence of being pregnant.

but sewer O sewer,
my bloodchild lies in the water.

I play that I'm happy:
look where the firefly sparkles!
the moon-disc, a wet snout that quivers –
but with the morning, the limping midwife,
grey and shivering on the sliding hills,
I push you out through the crust into daylight,
O sorrowing owl, great owl of the daylight
free from my womb, but besmeared,
with my tears all smeared
and tainted with grief.

Sewer O sewer,
I lie trembling, singing,
how else but trembling
with my bloodchild under your water . . .?

Another of Jonker's poems, 'From the wound in my side', written
in the person of the crucified Christ, begins 'I looked down from the
mountains and saw I was dead'. Jonker is unlike Plath in that her
poetry identifies with outcasts and underdogs, even with animals; part
of her gloom is politically engendered, but the poetry of the collection
published posthumously with the name *Kantelson* ('Setting Sun') is
the poetry of one who believes herself abandoned by the world and is
actually preparing to abandon it.

My black Africa
follow my lonely fingers
follow my absent image
lonely as an owl
and the forsaken fingers of the world
alone like my sister
My people have rotted away from me
what will become of the rotten nation
a hand cannot pray alone

The question is not whether Jonker had good reasons for feeling
miserable, for she certainly did, but what role poetry played in

intensifying her dissatisfaction, giving her as it were licence to torment herself rather than take part in any of the movements to free her country from a rotten political system. The misery of the poet *qua* poet is meant to be intractable; the poet is a misfit in this workaday world, too sensitive to take any action more physical than putting pen to paper. To be cured of the misery is to be cured of the poetry.

Poets have not always thought this way about themselves and what they were doing; poets were not recruited exclusively from the ranks of doomed youth until the nineteenth century. When the poet Cowper tried repeatedly to kill himself in 1763, the matter was concealed from his friends as squalid and shameful. The agony of the would-be suicide was intensified by his conviction that to succumb to the temptation would be to lose all hope of eternal life. By 1820, when Shelley wrote confidently that 'Our sweetest songs are those that tell of saddest thought', sadness, even to the pitch of madness, was not simply acceptable, but taken to be evidence of a higher sensibility. Among the manuscripts left by Keats, when he died in 1821 at the age of twenty-five, is a lugubrious sonnet that ends:

> Verse, Fame, and Beauty are intense indeed,
> But Death intenser — Death is Life's high meed.

By the time this sonnet and Keats's sonnet to Chatterton were published in 1848, anguish of all kinds had become the poet's stock in trade. Though Chatterton's contemporaries would have taken a different view of his suicide in 1770, Keats places the 'Dear child of sorrow – son of misery!' 'among the stars of highest heaven'. Coleridge and Shelley both celebrated Chatterton. Dante Gabriel Rossetti esteemed him, 'as great as any English poet whatever'. Chatterton's case presents significant parallels with the predicament of the woman poet. Like many a woman poet Chatterton, who had only a charity school education, began writing poetry when he hardly knew what it was. He 'never touched meat, drank only water and seemed to live on air'. He was still a child when he began producing texts in his own version of olde-worlde antique diction and invented an author for them, the fifteenth-century 'prieste of St. Johans, Bristowe', Thomas Rowley. These poems he tried to pass off on Horace Walpole, who refused to take up the young man's cause when he became aware of his humble origins. At the time Chatterton was apprenticed to a scrivener, whom he forced to release him from his indentures by threatening suicide, so that he could go up to London and be a writer; there a few weeks later he took arsenic. What Chatterton has in common with the woman poet, beside an inadequate education, poverty and isolation, is the necessity to invent himself as poet. A female contemporary could have written as he did:

> I must either live a slave, a servant to have no will of my own, no sentiments of my own which I may freely declare as such – or die, perplexing alternative.

It is not poetry that absorbs him, but the construction of the poetic self. To poison himself was as essential as putting an end to a poem. Seen from such an unflattering angle the young genius who could only write poetry *as someone else* is a kind of *idiot savant*, with an astonishing but ultimately disabling gift.

The effects of the poetic vogue for self-destruction can be seen even in the apparently triumphant career of Elizabeth Barrett Browning, who is thought to have made good poetry out of emotional fulfilment. She stands as the great exception to the rule that women will be loved in spite of their achievements rather than for them. Did Robert Browning not write to her after reading her *Poems*, published in 1844, 'I love your verses with all my heart, dear Miss Barrett, . . . and I love you too', four months before he clapped eyes on her? The story of the courtship of a well-known woman poet by a younger, little-known man poet has been told time and again. Theirs is assumed to have been a marriage of two great minds and hearts in perfect unanimity. A dispassionate reading of the evidence suggests something altogether less idyllic. In the weeks leading up to her elopement with Browning, Elizabeth Barrett poured out all her love in a series of sonnets, the last dated two days before their wedding. She did not show the sonnets to her husband until three years later. Browning was to tell his friend Isa Blagden: 'That was a strange, heavy crown, that wreath of Sonnets, put on me one morning unawares, three years after it had been twined . . .' It was Browning's idea that the sonnets should be published under the guise of translations from the Portuguese.

The poet Browning had fallen in love with was seriously ill, but not, as he supposed, with some disease of the spine. By dint of self-starvation and opiate abuse Elizabeth was so weak and thin that when they were eloping Browning had to lift and carry her from one conveyance to another; the jolting of the carriages bruised her so badly she was obliged to increase her usual dose of morphine. Within months she was transformed, walking, riding, eating and drinking 'like a young and healthy woman'. The explanation of the transformation is supposed to be that she wintered in Pisa rather than Wimpole Street, but winters in Pisa are hardly less severe than they are in London. Rather, with Robert by her side responding to her every need before she had time to articulate it, and with the beginning of sexual activity, Elizabeth abandoned her invalidism and decided to be well. In March 1847 she suffered a miscarriage and a year later another, but neither seems to have affected her health or spirits; within months she was pregnant again, carried the baby to term and gave birth after twenty-one hours of labour, during which she 'never cried out once nor shed a tear', although she was forty-three years old. By nature Elizabeth Barrett Browning was both unusually fertile and physically strong. A month before her son was born, she had kicked her morphine and ether habit. She wrote to her sister: 'Ours is a true marriage, and not a conventional match. We live heart to heart all day long and every day the same.' After Penini's birth her letters gradually filled up with his infantile exploits and tiresome transliterations of his baby talk; she mentioned her husband less and less.

In the early years of his married life Robert Browning found composition extremely slow and difficult; Elizabeth's obsessive personality had shouldered his concerns aside and he, believing her the better, as she was very much the better-known, poet, had abetted the process. Their sexual involvement with each other at this time was intense. Elizabeth conceived again and miscarried. She appeared to recover full health, but during her convalescence she returned to her old morphine and ether habit. For fear of future pregnancies sexual relations between the spouses eventually ceased. After their visit to England in 1851 Browning and Elizabeth began to discover that there was less harmony between their minds than they had believed. Browning was unnerved by his wife's increasing drug dependency; he realized that she ate even less than he thought, giving her food away under the table to her spaniel. They began to disagree and disagree passionately, about George Sand and then about Louis Napoléon, whom Elizabeth admired and Robert despised. Browning never shared his wife's intensely partisan feeling for Italy, nor did he approve of the way she was rearing their son. When they visited England for the second time Elizabeth was her old infirm, anorexic, drug-dependent self; her health obliged them to return to Florence, which Browning found increasingly dull. In the summer of 1853 Elizabeth became involved in spiritualism, of which her husband heartily disapproved; as the distance between them grew he recovered the will to write and began working on *Men and Women*, with its haunting studies of the progress of estrangement.

Elizabeth now allowed herself to become spectacularly frail. All comments mentioned her smudged eyes and the extreme slightness of her figure. Henriette Corkran wrote of her meeting with her in the summer of 1855:

> She panted a great deal and was very pale . . . How thin and small she looked lying back! I stared at her, overpowered by a kind of awe, wondering where the poetry was; and then I felt sure it was in her large dark eyes, like seas of light, and full of soul . . .

As she presented herself as a frail and delicate shadow wreathed in improbably black curls, Elizabeth displayed her son as a kind of ephebous pageboy:

> Penini, I remember, had long, golden ringlets; he wore white drawers edged with embroidery; these peculiarities impressed me, for I thought he looked like a girl . . . During most of her visit Mrs Barrett Browning kept her right arm round her little son's neck, running her long, thin fingers through his golden curls.

In photographs taken only a few months before his mother's death, when he was twelve, Penini's hair still hung down in long corkscrew curls and the embroidered drawers were still in evidence. He slept in his mother's room from his birth until her death.

Men and Women was badly received; Browning turned to helping Elizabeth prepare *Aurora Leigh* for the printers. It was to be as big a success as *Men and Women* was a failure. Elizabeth dedicated it not to her husband but to her cousin and patron, John Kenyon, who died shortly after it appeared, leaving her £11,000. In April 1857

Elizabeth's father died, without having reconciled himself to her marriage or recognized his grandson. In May Elizabeth wrote to her sister Henrietta: '. . . my heart goes walking up and down constantly through that house of Wimpole Street, till it is tired, tired'. Her emotional exhaustion is usually presumed to have a been a response to her father's death, but it is evident that Elizabeth's love for her husband was not sufficient to protect her from slipping into a depression that reduced her to 'a rag of a woman', 'brooding, brooding, brooding'. When Nathaniel Hawthorne met her in the summer of 1858, he found her

> a pale, small person, scarcely embodied at all . . . It is wonderful to see how small she is, how pale her cheek, how bright and dark her eyes. There is not such a figure in the world; and her back ringlets cluster down into her neck, and make her face look the whiter by their sable profusion. I could not form any judgment about her age; it may range anywhere within the limits of human life or elfin life.

Elizabeth was, in fact, fifty-two. After her sister's death in November 1860, she succumbed entirely to depression: 'I have sat here through two heavy months in the silence which was best for me . . .'

While Elizabeth retreated further into catatonic silence, Browning was the noisy life and soul of expatriate parties, spending as many as four evenings a week at Isa Blagden's villa at Bellosguardo when they were in Florence. Elizabeth grew weaker and weaker until she died of a combination of infections, after very little pain and a great deal of morphine, 'always smiling, happily, and with a face like a girl's', on 29 June 1861. Within weeks Casa Guidi had been abandoned and Pen's curls shorn and Browning was working on his poetry as he had not worked for years. Four years on his fame had eclipsed his wife's. Though he had many intimate friendships with women, some of whom may have expected to marry him, Browning was never to marry again. His excuse was his fidelity to the memory of Elizabeth; the explanation of his reluctance to enter into intimate commitment was certainly the memory of Elizabeth.

Among the poems of the bleak closing period in Elizabeth's life is 'My Heart and I'.

Enough! We're tired, my heart and I.
　　We sit beside the headstone thus,
　　And wish that name were carved for us.
The moss reprints more tenderly
　　The hard types of the mason's knife,
As heaven's sweet life renews earth's life
With which we're tired, my heart and I.

You see we're tired, my heart and I!
　　We dealt with books, we trusted men,
　　And in our own blood drenched the pen,
As if such colours could not fly.
　　We walked too straight for fortune's end,
　　We loved too true to keep a friend;
At last we're tired, my heart and I.

How tired we feel, my heart and I!
　　We seem of no use in the world;
　　Our fancies hang grey and uncurled
About men's eyes indifferently;
　　Our voice which thrill'd you so, will let
　　You sleep; our tears are only wet:
What do we here, my heart and I?

So tired, so tired, my heart and I!
　　It was not thus in that old time
　　When Ralph sate with me 'neath the lime
To watch the sunset from the sky.
　　'Dear Love, you're looking tired,' he said;
　　I, smiling at him, shook my head:
'Tis now we're tired, my heart and I.

So tired, so tired, my heart and I!
　　Though now none takes me on his arm
　　To fold me close and kiss me warm
Till each quick breath end in a sigh
　　Of happy languor. Now, alone,
　　We lean upon this graveyard stone,
Uncheered, unkissed, my heart and I.

Tired out, we are, my heart and I.
  Suppose the world brought diadems
  To tempt us, crusted with loose gems
Of powers and pleasures? Let it try.
  We scarcely dare to look at even
  A pretty child, or God's blue heaven,
We feel so tired, my heart and I.

Yet who complains? My heart and I?
  In this abundant earth no doubt
  Is little room for things worn out:
Disdain them, break them, throw them by.
  And if before the days grew rough
  We once were loved, used – well enough,
I think, we've fared, my heart and I.

To interpret such a poem as a personal statement is usually a solecism, but Elizabeth Barrett Browning's art was more of a piece with her life than usual. The autobiographical elements in *Aurora Leigh* have long been recognized. Like many other female poets, Elizabeth Barrett Browning is her own subject matter; first she constructs a self and then she writes about it. Later women poets, Natalia Ginzburg for example, have been aware of the process and have consciously reacted against it, refusing to write autobiographical or, as they put it, women's poetry, but reticent poets like Ginzburg, or Marianne Moore or Elizabeth Bishop are not the women poets who dominate the popular imagination.

It is usually thought that Browning must have been delighted with *Sonnets from the Portuguese*, but the decay in his relationship with his wife dates from the period of their publication. Feminist scholars have argued that critical esteem for *Sonnets from the Portuguese* derives from their celebration of sanctioned heterosexual union and have preferred to study, and to edit and republish, *Aurora Leigh* instead. In fact the *Sonnets'* emotional hyperbole exemplifies the 'lack of control' that contemporaries found embarrassing in Mrs Browning's poetry. There is no distance, not a hair's breadth, between the poet and the voice of the sonnets. They are personal documents of a kind that neither Browning nor any of his male contemporaries could have or would have wanted to have written. Life as text produces text as life; the existence of the literary version distorts the real intimacy in which it operates. In print sincerity becomes exhibitionism. Amongst Browning's last poems is one which we can only be glad that Elizabeth never saw:

> Shall I sonnet-sing you about myself?
>   Do I live in a house you would like to see?
> Is it scant of gear, has it store of pelf?
>   'Unlock my heart with a sonnet-key?'
>
> Invite the world, as my betters have done?
>   'Take notice: this building remains on view,
> Its suites of reception every one,
>   Its private apartment and bedroom too;
>
> 'For a ticket, apply to the Publisher.'
>   No: thanking the public, I must decline.
> A peep through my window, if folk prefer;
>   But, please you, no foot over threshold of mine!
>
> I have mixed with a crowd, and heard free talk
>   In a foreign land where an earthquake chanced:
> And a house stood gaping, nought to baulk
>   Man's eye, wherever he gazed or glanced.
>
> The whole of the frontage shaven sheer,
>   The inside gaped: exposed to day,
> Right and wrong and common and queer,
>   Bare, as the palm of your hand, it lay.
>
> The owner? Oh, he had been rushed, no doubt!
>   'Odd tables and chairs for a man of wealth!
> What a parcel of musty old books about!
>   He smoked – no wonder he lost his health!
>
> 'I doubt if he bathed before he dressed.
>   A brasier? – the pagan, he burned perfumes!
> You see it is proved, what the neighbours guessed:
>   His wife and himself had separate rooms.'
>
> Friends, the goodman of the house at least
>   Kept house to himself till an earthquake came:

'Tis the fall of its frontage permits you feast
   On the inside arrangement you praise or blame.

Outside should suffice for evidence:
   And whoso desires to penetrate
Deeper, must dive by the spirit-sense –
   No optics like yours, at any rate!

'Hoity toity! A street to explore,
   Your house the exception! "*With this same key*
Shakespeare unlocked his heart," once more!'
   Did Shakespeare? If so, the less Shakespeare he!

Browning uses the words of Wordsworth to sneer at the sonnet form, implying that his argument is with the other romantic sonneteers, but the revulsion he expresses must have assailed him when Elizabeth first placed her small book in his hand. The spurious attribution to a Portuguese original fooled nobody; those poems dogged Browning, whose interest in women was naturally of an unsentimental and specific kind. Elizabeth's emotional egotism, her neuroses and her self-destructiveness defeated him in death as they had in life. Elizabeth may have died thinking that she was the one who 'loved too straight to keep a friend', but her love was not enough to wean her off opium or her fixation on her father, cure her anorexia, dry her tears, allow her baby to turn into a boy or her hair to 'hang grey and uncurled'. As Elizabeth Barrett fashioned herself, she had also the option of annihilating herself. When the construct became impossible to maintain, she took the annihilation option, but in a form in which it did not have to be recognized. She simply allowed her established self-destructive habits to kill her in the guise of illness. Later poets would document their slow suicides in verse and would be praised for outspokenness and honesty, though they inculpated all the lesser mortals who had dealings with them.

Among male poets suicides are not only relatively few, but also peripheral. In the small throng of women poets the suicides represent a significantly higher proportion of the total number and are much closer to the mainstream. Sometimes, as in the case of Charlotte Perkins Gilman, who chose to end her life rather than live out the progress of her cancer, suicide is completely rational. When young, healthy people deliberately end apparently tolerable lives, the act cannot be seen as a rational response. Suicide notes are public statements that explain nothing; some of the best-known modern women's poetry consists of elaborated suicide notes. In such cases the interaction of personality and poetry must be seen to be pathological. The superstitious awe we now feel for suicide and our reverence for poetry combine to outlaw any suggestion that poetry is part of a pernicious process. To state baldly that the writing of poetry is intensely attractive to self-destructive women is to reveal oneself as an insensitive philistine. To insist that the evidence is overwhelming is to compound the offence. Most discussions of the careers of our poet-suicides see their fate as tragic evidence of the oppression of women and, even when the suicides are the subject-matter of the poetry, refuse to countenance the possibility of a suicide culture attracting the wrong women to the writing of verse. Our versifying suicides did not always write good poetry and, when they did, the subject was too often suicide. Without suicide, we might ask, what would their subject-matter have been?

The construction of the female poet who carves her verses on her wrists is mapped by the gradual dissemination of the myth of Sappho's suicide. The parts of the myth are three: the first is that Sappho is the greatest woman poet who ever lived; the second that she was sexually deviant in a nineteenth-century sense; the third that she committed suicide for unrequited love of a man. (It is of no consequence that parts two and three of the myth cannot both be true.) Originally the myth functioned to warn women off poetry and in particular the poetry of sexual passion. After Swinburne, it worked to dare the woman poet to expose or invent her innermost desires and to drive herself to the brink of madness and self-immolation. Who dared do less had no hope of entering the list of true poets. Few women poets had enough classical learning to disentangle history from fiction and ideology. Once the myth of Sappho's leap was popularized, the number of female poet suicides increased exponentially, not because of direct emulation but because the suicidal Sappho and the suicidal woman poet were both produced by the same complex of cultural factors. Before 1900 the phenomenon was rare. The German poet Karoline von Günderrode stabbed herself with a dagger in 1806. L. E. L. was found dying in 1838. In 1889 Amy Levy gassed herself in her parents' house.

Amy Levy was in many ways a remarkably fortunate young

woman. In 1881, while she was a student at Newnham College, Cambridge, she published a volume of verse, called *Xantippe* after the principal poem in it, in which Socrates' unhappy wife expresses her grief and rage at her exclusion from the circle of philosophers. Levy's picture of the beautiful Alcibiades being lionized by the elder philosophers is a vivid insight into traditional Cambridge that could apply to certain circles today. As a Jew and a woman in the Cambridge of the late 1870s Levy must have been snubbed and excluded from many but by no means all groups; she seems to have yearned most passionately for acceptance by the groups who were least likely to accept her. *Xantippe* contains as well an imitation of Swinburne called 'Felo de [*sic*] Se', which ends:

I am I – just a Pulse of Pain – I am I, that is all I know.
For life, and the sickness of life, and Death and desire to die –
They have passed away like the smoke, here is nothing but Pain and I.

In 1884 Levy published another small volume, *A Minor Poet*. The title poem is a dramatic monologue in the person of a suicidal poet whose first attempt was thwarted by his friend Tom Leigh, and his second by his own intoxication. He describes himself as

> A creature maimed and marred
> From very birth. A blot, a blur, a note
> All out of tune with the world's instrument.
> A base thing, yet not knowing to fulfil
> Base functions. A high thing, yet all unmeet
> For work that's high.

It is by no means easy to make this kind of utterance make sense; most people have no awareness of being either 'base' or 'high', let alone both at once. Delusions of grandeur can only coexist with delusions of abasement in seriously disordered personalities. An epilogue written in the person of Tom Leigh reveals that his friend's third attempt has succeeded.

> There was no written word to say farewell,
> Or make more clear the deed . . .

Leigh says that he did value 'the poet in him'.

> Nay, I sometimes doubt
> If they have not, indeed, the better part —
> These poets who get drunk with sun, and weep
> Because the night or a woman's face is fair.
> Meanwhile there is much talk about my friend.
> The women say, of course, he died for love;
> The men, for lack of gold, or cavilling
> Of carping critics.

Levy allows the suspicion to nag that her poet died because he was a poet. The theme of lost happiness replaced by bottomless misery is reiterated so often in Levy's tiny canon that the best-intentioned reader begins to feel that the misery stream was constant; unwitting love objects seem to have strayed into it and promptly out again as it flowed on unchecked. The suicide note is sounded even in short, unassuming lyrics like this one, which is to be found in several anthologies of the period:

> Deep in the grass outstretched I lie,
>   Motionless on the hill;
> Above me is a cloudless sky,
>   Around me all is still.
>
> There is no breath, no sound, no stir,
>   The drowsy peace to break;
> I close my tired eyes – it were
>   So simple not to wake.

A poet who announces firmly that she 'shall be glad no more' is determined to make her life as short as her lyrics. In 1889 Levy read the proofs of her new book of poems, *A London Plane-Tree*, but did not wait to see the book in print. When she killed herself a week later she was twenty-eight, the same age as the Russian poet Elisaveta Aleksandrovna Diakonova when she killed herself in the Swiss Alps in 1902. Renée Vivien (born an Englishwoman, Pauline Tarn) died of drink and starvation in 1909 aged thirty-two. In 1928 Charlotte Mew, 'the greatest living poetess' according to Virginia Woolf, drank Lysol.

In 1915 Mew, till then known as a writer of stories for *Temple Bar* and *The Yellow Book*, had a poem printed in *The Nation*. The poem, 'The Farmer's Bride', was a dramatic monologue in the person of the farmer who married a girl too young for him who 'turned afraid' of love and her husband and all things human and 'runned away'. Harold Monro of the Poetry Bookshop asked Mew to come and see him.

> When she came into the shop she was asked, 'Are you Charlotte Mew?' and her reply, delivered characteristically with a slight smile of amusement, was, 'I am sorry to say I am.'

Mew's younger brother and sister were both confined in mental hospitals; she and her sister Anne were convinced that they should never marry for fear of passing on a hereditary taint. It is easy to understand Virginia Woolf's high estimation of Mew's ability faced with writing like this:

> Red is the strangest pain to bear;
> In Spring the leaves on the budding trees;
> In Summer the roses are worse than these,
>   More terrible than they are sweet:
>   A rose can stab you across the street
>   Deeper than any knife:
>   And the crimson haunts you everywhere –
> Thin shafts of sunlight, like the ghosts of reddened swords have
>   struck our stair
> As if, coming down, you had spilt your life.

Mew's poetic output, virtually complete by the time Monro printed her first collection, was small; only sixty poems survive. 'The Farmer's Bride' met with distinct critical success; at the end of 1923 Mew was awarded a Civil List pension on the recommendation of John Mase-field, Walter de la Mare and Thomas Hardy. More often than is usual with even the most adventurous women poets, she assumed a mascu-line persona to express physical longing for a reluctant, even repelled, subject. Though Mew impressed most people as a light-hearted and witty individual, her poetry dwells on yearning, loss and death. The image of the Crucifixion is invoked again and again to signify human suffering as spectacle; any hope of redemption remains rhetorical. Behind the most seeming-innocent rural subjects stalks the spectre of the Great War. The felling of the great plane trees at the end of her street provides Mew with an objective correlative for all kinds of irreparable loss but her grief is not luscious mawkishness but the authentic death of the heart:

> Up here, with June, the sycamore throws
>   Across the window a whispering screen;
> I shall miss the sycamore more, I suppose,
> Than anything else on this earth that is out in green,
>   But I mean to go through the door without fear,
>   Not caring much what happens here
>   When I'm away –
> How green the screen is across the panes
>   Or who goes laughing along the lanes
> With my old lover all the summer day.

The everyday motif of the descent into the street from a tall London house here stands for leaving the world itself. After her mother's death, Mew went to live in the studio of her sister Anne, who slaved for a living painting furniture. After Anne's painful death from cancer Mew refused the hospitality of friends and took a dreary room with no view, already determined, one suspects, to end her life. From her childhood she had been a self-punisher; she never admitted her deviant sexuality and judged the sexual irregularities of others with great harshness. She was certainly in love with May Sinclair, who made a salacious anecdote out of her one attempt to achieve some kind of physical closeness. She may well have felt as alien to the emotional life around her as 'The Changeling':

> Why did They bring me here to make me
>   Not quite bad and not quite good . . .
> I shall grow up, but never grow old,
> I shall always, always be very cold,
>   I shall never come back again!

Alida Monro was out of her depth in dealing with a personality as complex as Mew's. One of the elements she left out of her account of Mew was guilt, which had tormented her ever since she was a child.

She always spoke of stacks of MSS. salted away in trunks, but after her death very little was found. Perhaps there was some truth in the remark she once made casually to me one afternoon at tea in Gordon Street. She was sitting making spills, which she used to light her endless cigarettes, and which were also made for the parrot to chew and amuse himself with. Seeing some writing on some of these, I asked if she used up old letters that way, and she replied – 'I'm burning up my work. I don't know what else to do with it.' Anne and I often wondered together whether she might be really destroying some original work, or whether it was just intended to whip us up. Who knows?

Alida Monro would have been justified in feeling very hurt by the consideration that Mew was destroying work she had never let her see. I think it unlikely that there were ever trunks full of unpublished work, or that Mew ever worked very hard, or that her failure to produce more was due to domestic cares. She was guilty that she had come by her reputation with so little effort, and became unbearably so when her sister's hard life ended in an even harder struggle. Most of Mew's poetry projects a special mood of bleak desolation which, we know from descriptions of her as a social being, visited her fairly infrequently. After years of writing nothing, she proved by drinking the lysol that she had been a poet all along.

Mew's death marks the beginning of an international vogue for poet suicide. The Portuguese poet Florbela Espanca seems to have killed herself with a drug overdose at the age of thirty-six in 1930. The American poet Sara Teasdale took an overdose of barbiturates in 1933. The Milanese poet Antonia Pozzi killed herself in 1938; in the same year the Argentine poet Alfonsina Storni walked into the sea after sending her suicide note in the form of a poem called 'Quiero Dormir' to a newspaper. The New Zealander Robin Hyde gassed herself in 1939.

Robin Hyde was born Iris Guiver Wilkinson in 1906 and educated at Wellington Girls' College. As is usual with female poets, she began versifying to great acclaim when very young. She also became lame in consequence of an undiagnosed disease and was obliged to use morphine for extended periods, suffered episodes of severe depression and attempted suicide several times. In 1926 she bore a child that died soon after birth and in 1930 a son who survived. After a breakdown

in 1933, she lived in a mental hospital for several years. In 1937 she
wrote an autobiographical novel called *The Godwits Fly*. In 1938 she
sailed for England but changed her mind in Hong Kong and went to
China instead. There, in an attempt to report the Sino-Japanese war,
she took extraordinary risks and was missing behind the lines for two
months. When she escaped, she was ill with psilosis and obliged to
leave China and travel on to England. In England she stayed with her
fellow New Zealander Charles Brasch, to whom 'she turned . . . for
reassurance'.

> But physically she repelled me; I could not respond more than
> in friendship. Feeling slighted and rejected, she went upstairs,
> lay down and swallowed half a bottle of her sleeping draught –
> all that was left of it.

The next day she was sick from the effects of the overdose and spent a
good deal of time in the bathroom.

> Suddenly she said to me, 'Shall I shock you?' I shrugged. She
> pulled up the sleeve of her dressing-gown and showed a huge
> open gash in her left arm, one of several gashes made with a
> razor-blade of mine in the bath . . . she had often mentioned
> cutting herself like this when miserable.

(Christina Rossetti too cut open her arm.) Hyde described herself as
'writing poems with the regularity of a model Orpington mother
laying eggs', implying that, like many other women poets, she was
temperamentally incapable of working up her poems. When she can
focus her mind on externals she is a remarkable poet of the New
Zealand land- and seascape. Among her poetry can be found the
occasional suicide note.

> Yet I think, having used my words as the kings used gold,
> Ere we came by the rustling jest of the paper kings,
> I who am overbold will be steadily bold,
> In the counted tale of things.
> I tell you this, I,
> The false magician who flourished Pharaoh's snake –
> Long the word may curl in the tamer's hand,

For the true tale's sake.
I who hastened for Pharaoh the beaten king,
(Call me bought or fool!)
Fighter with words, must clasp the prick of words,
Fawned on with words, sick at the heart with words
I shall look to drink and the well be foul with words;
(And these the words of the mouths that cannot sing,
Of the minds cold, not cool.)
I shall be struck on a futile mouth with words,
Capped with a word, in that hour I die.

The bumper year for poet deaths was 1941; both Virginia Woolf and the Swedish lyric poet Karin Boye committed suicide that year. On 31 August 1941 Marina Tsvetaeva hanged herself.

Tsvetaeva was then forty-nine; she had been evacuated to Elabuga in the Tartar Republic. She applied to be relocated at Chistopol and was humiliatingly interrogated before being granted permission. Though there were friends at Chistopol anxious to help her, she inexplicably returned to Elabuga. While her son and neighbour were absent on a day of forced labour, she hanged herself from a hook on the wall of her hut. However depressing her immediate circumstances, their relevance is somewhat weakened by an entry in her diary for 5 September the previous year:

> No one can see, no one knows that for a year (approximately) my eyes have been searching for a hook, but there aren't any, because they have electricity everywhere. No chandeliers. For a year I have been trying death on for size. Everything is ugly and terrifying. To swallow is disgusting, to jump is inimical, my inborn revulsion to water.

She had told a friend that she had understood that 'everything was over' when she set her foot on the gangplank of the ship that brought her from exile in Paris on the first stage of her return to Moscow in June 1939. Pasternak was to say that she sacrificed herself and her poetry for her sixteen-year-old son, for whose sake she had return-ed to Russia. The boy made no pretence of anything but disgust at the discovery of her suicide and did not attend her funeral. It seems equally likely that Tsvetaeva abandoned the émigré Russian community because it had abandoned her. Ever since her arrival in Berlin in 1922 she had been treated as a star; in 1938, from being the biggest name in Paris, she found herself ostracized as the wife of a Soviet agent. Though she later claimed to have been in despair, Tsvetaeva returned to Moscow expecting unrealistically to take up her old position at centre stage.

Tsvetaeva was her own heroine; much of her output was autobiographical or semi-autobiographical – or rather, purported to be so. Her attitude to fact was cavalier:

> She was a difficult person because she was, clinically speaking, certainly a mythomaniac. This helped her literature. But in her life, this was a catastrophe.

In the poems of *Mileposts I*, which purports to be a poetic record of the year 1916, she presented herself as a Pole and a noblewoman, when she was neither. When living in poverty in Czechoslovakia and Paris, she portrayed herself as a martyr to housework, when her apartment was so filthy that it stank. In the course of inventing herself as a heroine Tsvetaeva convinced herself that she was an unwanted child; the assertion that she was an outcast is made time and again throughout her life: 'In every group I am an alien, and have been all my life.'

No matter how generous her family and friends were, they were never generous enough. At some point all withdrew, unable to cope with the demands she made upon them. It was not society that refused to admit Tsvetaeva, but Tsvetaeva who could not see herself as a person like any other. In a poem she asked an ex-lover,

> How do you live with one of a
> thousand women   after Lilith?

Tsvetaeva began writing poetry when she was six and published her first book of poems, *The Evening Album*, herself. She dedicated it 'to the radiant memory of Maria Bashkirtseva', whose diary was dubbed by Simone de Beauvoir a 'case book study of female narcissim'. Elaine Feinstein, who is largely responsible for the recognition of Tsvetaeva in the west, wrote of her at fourteen:

Her huge green eyes were seriously myopic, though she seldom wore glasses. To remove the offensive signs of health from her cheeks, she cut down on food and drank vinegar.

Feinstein's passionate love of her subject is only too apparent in that misplaced 'though'. Rather than *see* the world through glasses, Tsvetaeva chose to *be seen* without them. A poem she wrote on her seventeenth birthday begs 'Christ and God' to let her die, ending

> Thou gavest me a childhood better than a fairy tale
> So give me a death at seventeen!

In 1913, at the age of twenty-one, she penned a series of poems on her own death. Published in the same collection with a cycle entitled 'Woman-Friend', which traced the poet's affair with Sophie Parnok; Tsvetaeva was to record all of her fierce emotional attachments in verse.

> Non-existent qualities were ascribed to a person of her choice, the person was saddled with desires or expectations he or she never had, hopes were vested in the incipient relationship that could not possibly come true. Tsvetaeva knew what was involved, but she could not stop because these emotional defeats were the raw material of her poetry.

The result may have been 'splendid poetry', but was the poetry worth the distortion not only of Tsvetaeva's own life but of the lives she touched? Tsvetaeva appears to have been in a sense autistic, unaware of the otherness of other people. She lived solipsistically, as befits a high myopic who refuses to correct her vision. Mandelstam, who fell under her spell in 1916, realized that to stay with her would have destroyed him. Her children too were to be constructed by her, first Ariadna, then Georgy was conceived as unique and wonderful, and prepared for an extraordinary destiny. (The middle child, Irina, died in the Russian famine.)

> Alya (Ariadna) is at a difficult stage. She is very talented, very intelligent. But completely different from me. Moor – he is *really* my son! He's wonderful!

Among the throng who were aware of her brilliance, there were those who were wary of her strangeness. One of her contemporaries in Paris wrote in his diary: 'I strongly dislike Tsvetaeva for her posturings, her ignoble character and her female irresponsibility. And for her extraordinary vanity.' Another wrote in a letter, 'I can't stand that psychopath, with her leaden eyes, gifted but lacking in shame, taste, etc.' (The intolerance of these observers might have been less if Tsvetaeva had been younger.) The poet's long-suffering husband was only prevented from seeking a separation by the conviction that Tsvetaeva could not survive without him; she thought that he could not survive without her. Tsvetaeva wrote of her death in an incredibily insensitive letter to Pasternak:

> Among your superhumans I was *merely* a human . . . Rilke died without summoning his wife, his daughter or his mother. Yet they all loved him. He was concerned for his *own* soul. When my time comes to die, I shall have no time to think of my soul (of myself). I shall be fully occupied: have my future pall-bearers been fed? Have not my relatives ruined themselves arranging it all? . . . I have only ever been myself (my soul) in my notebooks and on solitary roads (which have been rare), for all my life I have been leading a child by the hand . . . I myself chose the world of superhumans. Why should I grumble?

In hanging herself, in supreme disregard of what would become of her family (who were to suffer appallingly in the years that followed) Tsvetaeva proved herself a superhuman. In the third of a group of poems under the heading 'The Poet', Tsvetaeva asks herself a question:

> Now what shall I do here, blind and fatherless?
> Everyone else can see and has a father.
> Passion in this world has to leap anathema
> as it might be over the walls of a trench
> and weeping   is called a cold in the head.
>
> What shall I do, by nature and trade
> a singing creature (like a wire – sunburn! Siberia!)
> as I go over the bridge of my enchanted

visions, that cannot be weighed, in a
world that deals only in weights and measures?

What shall I do, singer and first-born, in a
world where the deepest black is grey,
and inspiration is kept in   a thermos?
with all this immensity
in a measured world?

When she strung herself up Tsvetaeva answered her own question. Elizabeth Barrett Browning too expressed resentment that her 'tears were only wet'. A personality driven back time and again on narcissism and egotism must eventually succumb to the law of diminishing returns. We must ask why we demand of poets that they be virtuoso sufferers, why we value only the documentation of misery. A 1916 poem of Sara Teasdale states the commonplace with a combination of tear-jerking hyperbole and near-comic baldness:

> My heart cries like a beaten child,
>   Ceaselessly, all night long;
> And I must take my own heart cries
>   And thread them neatly into a song.
>
> My heart cries like a beaten child,
>   And I must listen, stark and terse,
> Dry-eyed and critical, to see
>   What I can turn into a verse.
>
> This was a sob at the hour of three,
>   And this when the first cock crew —
> I wove them into a dainty song,
>   But no one thought it true!

Wordsworth constructed poetry out of 'emotion recollected in tranquillity' and was believed sincere and honest; Sara Teasdale's version presents her self observing her heart and taking verse notes on it only to be rejected as a poseuse. Though she is well aware of the self-defeating nature of the process and describes it at a third remove, Teasdale did in the end have no other subject matter than her own longings and disappointments. She too sees herself as a misunderstood freak, an outcast, though she knows full well that poems exist to be read and readers are as essential to poetry as egos are to poets.

In 1947 Anna Wickham hanged herself. Twelve years before she began an autobiography which was actually a suicide note.

> It is the fourth of March, 1935, and a fine early Spring morning. I begin my great house-clean ... For twenty-nine years I have been attempting to order the house; because of the pathological weakness of a betraying untidyness, I have not succeeded. For twenty-nine years I have been putting things away in loathsome sets of drawers: my self-discipline is complete enough. I shall have very pin, rag, tot and tittle in the villa in its place, and everything will be splendidly clean. But I am finished: I am utterly defeated: there is nothing before me but suicide. I order the villa for my death. When the stove is clean enough I shall turn on the gas.

Nowadays few people remember the name of Anna Wickham. In 1935, as she pointed out herself, she had 'a European reputation'; her 'poetry was mentioned with honour in the *Encyclopaedia Britannica*'. She writes of herself in terms that could have been used by Amy Levy:

> I feel that I am myself a profound mistake and that I was doomed from my conception by being myself: I feel that women of my kind are a profound mistake. There have been few women poets of distinction, and, if we count the suicides of Sappho, Lawrence Hope and Charlotte Mew, their despair rate has been very high.

The linking of the name 'Lawrence Hope' with Sappho and Mew implies a certain critical astigmatism. The name is one of the sobriquets adopted by Ada Florence 'Violet' Nicolson, wife of an Indian Army officer stationed in Madras. She was famous for her Indian love lyrics, which include 'Pale hands I loved beside the Shalimar' and are less indebted to Hindu sources than to Swinburne; because of the intensity of their expression of female desire these were sometimes described as 'Sapphic'. Hope killed herself when she was thirty-nine by swallowing perchloride of mercury, two months after the death of her husband in 1904.

Wickham is typical of the sterotypical poetess in that she began writing verses at the age of four for her father, who took her to see a then well-known poet to ask if she had what it took to be a poet like him. In answer, according to Wickham, he was told, 'She will be a poet if she has pain enough.' She was haphazardly educated at country schools in Queensland, at a Brisbane convent and a high school, and left off all systematic schooling at sixteen. She trained for a time as a singer, but in 1906, when she was twenty-two, became the wife of Patrick Hepburn instead. She had her first poems printed for her father as *Songs of John Oland* in 1911. In 1914 Harold Monro printed nine of her poems in *Poetry and Drama*. In 1915 *The Contemplative Quarry* and in 1916 *A Man with a Hammer* were published in London. In 1921 both were published in the United States and a new collection, *The Little Old House*, came out in London. Wickham was received into the confraternity of artists and hobnobbed with Ezra Pound, Augustus John, Nina Hamnett, the Lawrences, Jacob Epstein, Dylan Thomas, Malcolm Lowry and Natalie Barney. An important element in her success was Wickham's feminism; she declared that at the head of each of her books should stand this epigraph:

> Here is no sacrificial I,
> Here are more I's than yet were in one human,
> Here I reveal our common mystery:
> I give you *woman*.

Her publishers, thank goodness, decided otherwise. All the things that would later be said of Plath and Sexton were said about Anna Wickham. She was considered to have laid bare heterosexual womanhood and exposed the violence of women's subversive grief and rage. Her poems were inscribed on feminist banners. Much of her impassioned utterance described the dark side of her marriage with 'Croydon man', who could not give expression to his feelings, if indeed he had any. The perceived political importance of what she was doing greatly distorted contemporary assessment of her achievement. Where poetesses of old had been overpraised for insipidity and piety, Wickham was glorified as bold, outspoken, dauntless 'Woman'. Nowadays her free rhythms seem no rhythms at all; the clumsy rhymes seem to lead her thought by the nose; much of her writing is not shocking, but embarrassing.

It's so, good Sirs, a Woman-poet sings
Sick self and not exterior things,
She'd joy enough in flowers, and lakes and light,
Before she won soul's freedom in a fight.
Thus half creation is but half expressed,
And the unspoken half is best.
Note:
It will be seen this fact is stated,
Of such intrepid artists as are mated;
A maid, good Sirs, in many senses human,
As artist is a negligible woman.

Wickham wrote more than a thousand gusty versicles like these. She was both temperamentally and intellectually incapable of tightening them up or pointing them or working them into a scheme.

Let us consider the Superman,
Him who is to be more than human.
He must lie nine months alone
Hid in the dark with a woman.
Is she to be a thing of scorn
Before the prodigy is born?

Poor man who in the end ran mad
And died so less than human,
Saw you not the brain-wrecking absurdity
Of preaching superman and scorning women?

With Wickham poetry had 'to come spontaneously or not at all'. Most of the immediate feeling that fuelled her daily versifying was negative feeling; far from liberating her, the apparently accidental death of her much deplored husband in 1929 seems to have virtually silenced her. Wickham knew that she was cultivating and propagating pain, and ended her suicidal autobiography, which unaccountably stopped after the birth of her first son, with this paragraph.

As I look back over this long and melancholy road, I am ashamed. I try to think why I endured so much futile pain, and the truth is that I believed in pain. I believed that by suffering and endurance I was working out some salvation. Nearly all the relationships of my life have been tawdry, insincere and unsatisfactory. Many people were attracted to me, but I was intimate with nobody. I was not sufficiently like anyone to invite that self-identification which is the essence of true friendship and love.

The cynical reader might think that the underlying problem was that Wickham was not as different as she thought and that her demand for total identification with a lover was infantile. Anne Sexton's therapist might have understood what was going on rather better if he had had the chance to read Anna Wickham's 'Fragment of Autobiography'. For twelve more years Wickham was to be suicidal before, at the age of sixty-three, she completed the process. During that time, though she was known and celebrated as a poet, she seems to have written little poetry and published none.

In 1959 Sylvia Plath, whose suicide has been far too often discussed to need elaboration here, began to attend Robert Lowell's Boston University poetry workshop. She was attracted to Lowell because like her he had frequent breakdowns; she was to find herself drawn to another member of the group, Anne Sexton. Both women had attempted suicide, both more than once. The two women began going out for drinks after class, and trying death on for size, in Tsvetaeva's phrase.

Often, very often, Sylvia and I would talk about our first suicides; at length, in detail, and in depth between the free potato chips. Suicide is, after all, the opposite of the poem. Sylvia and I often talked opposites. We talked death with burned-up intensity, both of us drawn to it like moths to an electric light bulb. Sucking on it!

As 'the opposite of the poem', suicide is conceptually related to it. To succeed the poem must render its end inevitable much as the suicide plots her end. As Sylvia Plath said, 'Dying is an art.' We know from the epidemiology of suicide that the pattern includes a pronounced cultural element. Suicide confers order on a chaotic career, makes clear that the jugglers of truth and identity really meant what they said and did. Lowell and his contemporaries deliberately diced with death and madness, imagining that what they wrote on the verge of either was rawer or more alive than what occurred to them in their right minds. Lowell wrote to Roethke:

> There's a strange fact about poets roughly of our age, and one that doesn't exactly seem to have always been true. It's this, that to write we seem to have to go at it with such single-minded intensity that we are always on the point of drowning . . .

John Berryman alone of the group of male 'confessional' poets is known to have definitely ended his own life by jumping off a bridge. Manic depressive as he was, Lowell died in a taxi cab of heart failure; equally manic depressive Randall Jarrell was hit by a car and Theodore Roethke had a heart attack in a swimming pool. Delmore Schwarz was found dead of a heart attack in a seedy hotel room. Elizabeth Hardwick, who was then married to Lowell, said of Sylvia Plath that at the end of her life she was both the dramatist and the dramatic heroine of her 'murderous art',

> frighteningly there all the time. Orestes rages, but Aeschylus lives to be almost seventy. Sylvia Plath, however, is both heroine and author: when the curtain goes down, it is her own dead body there on the stage, sacrificed to her own plot.

A week before she ended her life on 11 February 1963, Sylvia Plath wrote 'Edge'. The poet presents herself to herself as a decorative colophon at the end of the book of her life, reducing herself to a motionless icon. She had verbalized herself so often that the kernel of truth was worn away; the only way to get it back was to make it come true. Her mother wrote bitterly:

> She has posthumous fame – at what price to her children, to those of us who loved her so dearly and whom she has trapped into her past. The love remains – and the hurt. There is no escape for us.

If the muse is also to be the poet, the result will be life-into-art, which is a net loss, for the poet should have both life and art. I could not agree less with Joyce Carol Oates, who wrote:

It is proper to say that Sylvia Plath represents for us a tragic figure involved in a tragic action, and that her tragedy is offered to us as a near-perfect work of art, in her books.

Even when the poetry is good, perhaps especially when the poetry of self-annihilation is good, the destruction of the woman is too high a price to pay. Sylvia Plath and Elizabeth Barrett Browning were both poets married to poets. Both women placed a high value on fecundity, but thought of their children as perpetual babies, like queen bees immobilizing them in imaginary cells. Both women expected devotion and disabled themselves in order to claim a greater share of the husband poet's attention – and both women exhausted their spouses' capacity for togetherness. Both were utterly monogamous and unsparingly self-righteous. Sylvia Plath wrote in her journal for 11 May 1958: 'Oh, only left to myself, what a poet I will flay myself into.' In 1982 the skinless woman poet was awarded a posthumous Pulitzer Prize. Since that time her fame has continued to grow; American college students and British undergraduates alike are fascinated as much by her suicide as by her poetry.

Anne Sexton was not married to a poet but, like Tsvetaeva, to a long-suffering cuckold. She liked to present herself as a housewife superstar, tall, broad-shouldered and sexy, given to stagy and exhibitionistic gestures.

Anne Sexton liked to arrive about ten minutes late for her own performances: let the crowd work up a little anticipation. She would saunter to the podium, light a cigarette, kick off her shoes, and in a throaty voice say, 'I'm going to read a poem that tells you what kind of poet I am, what kind of a woman I am, so if you don't like it you can leave.' Then she would launch into her signature poem.

Her signature poem, 'Her Kind', thrums with suicide threat.

> I have gone out, a possessed witch,
> haunting the black air, braver at night;
> dreaming evil, I have done my hitch
> over the plain houses, light by light:
> lonely thing, twelve-fingered, out of mind.

A woman like that is not a woman, quite.
I have been her kind.

I have found the warm caves in the woods,
filled them with skillets, carvings, shelves,
closets, silks, innumerable goods;
fixed the suppers for the worms and the elves:
whining, rearranging the disaligned.
A woman like that is misunderstood.
I have been her kind.

I have ridden in your cart, driver,
waved my nude arms at villagers going by,
learning the last bright routes, survivor
where your flames still bite my thigh
and my ribs crack where your wheels wind.
A woman like that is not ashamed to die.
I have been her kind.

Sexton's subject in this poem, as Teasdale's in hers, is herself *qua* poet; it is impossible to imagine a male poet presenting himself in such a guise or being concerned to project himself so immediately. Moreover, Sexton is constructing femininity as much as poet-ness; she is writing as 'other', treating her body programmatically. Her death is presented as a sensational public spectacle, the burning of a witch.

After writing poetry as a teenager Sexton gave it up until after she had a mental breakdown in 1956, when she produced more than sixty poems for her psychotherapist. When she could not remember her self-relevations from one session to another her psychotherapist taped them and gave them to her to study; when Diane Middlebrook used them in her biography of Sexton there was a great fuss but, in fact, what Sexton said in therapy was no more revealing or honest and hardly less artful than what she said in poetry. From the first she gave herself the special licence of a mad person. Like others of the Lowell generation she fell for the outrageous lie that drugs and alcohol free the creative imagination. In the words of Louise Bogan, another friend of Lowell:

Come drunks and drug-takers; come, perverts, unnerved!
Receive the laurel, given, though late, on merit; to whom
    and wherever deserved.

Parochial punks, trimmers, nice people, joiners true-blue,
Get the hell out of the way of the laurel. It is deathless
        And it isn't for you.

The fashion was self-exposure; if it had not been, Sexton would probably not have been drawn to it; she 'wrote openly about menstruation, abortion, masturbation, incest, adultery and drug addiction' and claimed to be the only confessional poet. The public could not get enough of it. When Plath killed herself, Sexton, already addicted to pills and alcohol, was envious and celebrated her envy in a poem, 'Sylvia's Death'. In the months that followed she thought about dying more and more; in 'Wanting to Die', she wrote unforgettably:

> But suicides have a special language.
> Like carpenters they want to know *which tools*.
> They never ask *why build*.

The collection published in 1966 that contains both poems was called *Live or Die*. A tetchy reviewer dismissed it: 'mere self-dramatization has grown a habit'. Sexton's needs were gargantuan and her needs were paramount; her family suffered as did the successions of therapists, advisers and soulmates she assumed and abandoned. George MacBeth judged her as one who 'was always anxious to be seen as striking'. Such a one was not likely to approach menopause and middle age with any degree of equanimity, regardless of the success and security she had achieved. Sexton killed herself on 4 October 1974; after more than forty years inventing herself she had run out of things to say. Adrienne Rich said at her memorial:

We have had enough suicidal women poets, enough suicidal women, enough self-destructiveness as the sole form of violence permitted to women.

Such a statement implies that a woman poet's suicide is merely a part of the misery of women and that, in a world that was less unjust to women, our poets would be less likely to destroy themselves. I would argue that poetry as presented by the male literary establishment, which Tsvetaeva, Plath and Sexton wooed all their lives, enticed the woman poet to dance upon a wire, to make an exhibition of herself and ultimately to come to grief. In the lethal potion that their souls imbibed, poetry was at least as important an ingredient as womanhood.

The effect of awareness of Sara Teasdale and Virginia Woolf on Plath and Sexton has never been traced, but it is palpable. Given the contagiousness of suicide, the poet Anne Stevenson took a great risk in putting together a full-length study of Sylvia Plath; and afterwards she wrote, in 'Making Poetry':

> And what's 'to make'?
>
> To be and to become words' passing
> weather; to serve a girl on terrible
> terms, embark on voyages over voices,
> evade the ego-hill, the misery-well,
> the siren hiss of *publish, success, publish,*
> *success, success, success.*

'To make' is the literal translation of the Greek root for the word poet, *'poein'*. In her definition of the term Stevenson acknowledges the poet's obligation to verbalize all experience, the maleficent influence of the muse (the girl). She insists on a trip away from self-consciousness, in terms that Mr Browning would have understood and Mrs Browning not. The way that the woman poet avoids the ego-hill and the misery-well is by developing what male poets always instinctively gravitated towards, a community of poets, a school, so that the isolated poet does not disappear into solipsism and cannibalize herself. Stevenson also encapsulates here the distorting pressure of celebrity, the siren hiss that draws the poet away from her work and at the same time undermines her capacity for self-criticism. Stevenson is conscious of herself as *a* woman poet rather than as *the* woman poet. She sees herself in a female tradition rather than as a female prodigy, but she is well aware of the appallingness locked in women's literary history. She looks to the forging of a new language in which women would not have to impersonate themselves:

> A long litany of astonishment
> would be, in this language,

a hymn of thanksgiving: 'Even as it died,
the sea made power out of its own pulse,
pounding to salt the poisoned cities
of the suicides.'

The new language has yet to be born, and its birth may well coincide with the death of print and dismantling of the literary establishment. Some feminist critics have seen the writing as women and the bringing of the immediate self into poetry as a necessary strategy of liberation; others have argued that such 'intimismo' and confessionalism are limitations that prevent the female poet from achieving power. The rhetoric of petulance locks women into their victim status and the personae of daughters, lovers, mothers, virgins, mothers and wives. The versifying of agony and rage was probably necessary until Marcuse's femalization should be accomplished and a female audience, in the midst of which men feel themselves as other as women had done in the literary world of yore, should emerge. Female collectivity makes possible a more poised and understated writing, a subtler and more complex manipulation of tone, the raising of the voice of female sanity. It is sobering to reflect, however, that even this has been seen before. In 1921, J. C. Squire wrote in the preface to *A Book of Women's Verse*:

To-day we scarcely bother about the distinction between men and women writers. With thousands of women writing, with women's verses in every magazine and women reporters in every newspaper office, *when literary women congregate in clubs* [my italics], and robust women novelists haggle with editors and discuss royalties with their male rivals, we take composition for granted as a feminine occupation.

In his anthology Squire included one poem each by Jean Ingelow, 'Violet Fane', Emily Lawless, Fanny Parnell, Rose Terry Cooke, Violet Jacob, Anna Bunston de Bary, Eva Gore-Booth, Katharine Tynan Hinkson, Rose Macaulay and Sylvia Lynd, two by Dora Sigerson Shorter and Moira O'Neill, three by Mary Elizabeth Coleridge, Margaret L. Woods and Frances Cornford, five by Alice Meynell – and *six* by Amy Levy. There can be no doubt in such a case that Levy's suicide at twenty-eight added glamour and gravitas to her reputation, for hers is not by any criterion the most impressive verse written by this group of women. Hundreds of good women poets now travel the length and breadth of our world, performing their work with wit and style. Their verse does not incessantly vibrate at the highest frequency; they have other subjects besides themselves; they do not see themselves as outcast and solitary or unique in their capacity to be miserable. Because they fail to flay themselves alive, they will be called minor, and forgotten as all but two or three of Squire's contemporary poets have been forgotten, until such time as we come to prefer our poets of all sexes with the skin on.

NOTES

PROLOGUE

p. xii Emily Dickinson (1830–86): *The Letters of Emily Dickinson*, ed. T. H. Johnson (Cambridge MA, 1958), 260–61.

Shulamith Firestone: *The Dialectic of Sex: the Case for a Feminist Revolution* (London, 1979), 157: 'The animation of women and homosexuals in the arts today may signify the scurrying of rats near a dying body.'

p. xiii Eata Extra Egga Day: this rune is attributed to distinguished novelist Fay Weldon.

lullabies: belated studies of lullabies include I. Tahir-Ul-Taq, *Das Lied der Juden in Osteuropäischen Raum* (Frankfurt-am-Main, 1978), L. Lambert, *Chants et Chansons populaires de Languedoc* (Marseille, 1983) and E. Gerstner-Hirzel, *Das Volkstümliche Deutsche Wiegenlied* (Basel, 1984).

p. xiv Dorothy Wordsworth: there are many current studies of Dorothy Wordsworth, *Dorothy Wordsworth* by R. Gittings and J. Manton (Oxford, 1988), *Dorothy Wordsworth, Writer* by P. Woof (Grasmere, 1988) and *A Passion for the Particular: Dorothy Wordsworth* by E. Gunn (London, 1981), as well as S. M. Levin, *Dorothy Wordsworth and Romanticism* (New Brunswick and London, 1987), and Margaret Homans, *Women Writers and Poetic Identity* (Princeton, 1980). Virginia Woolf on 'Dorothy Wordsworth', *Collected Essays* 3, 199–206, is as usual perceptive.

Marie de France: Very little is known about Marie de France who wrote in the last thirty years or so of the twelfth century and seems to have been living in England. Her *Lais* edited by A. Ewert were published in 1969. Translators include J. L. Weston (1900) and E. Rickert (1901). Scholars should consult G. S. Burgess, *Marie de France: An Analytical Bibliography* (London, 1977).

Mary Herbert, Countess of Pembroke (1561–1621) sister of Sir Philip Sidney was educated at the Sidney homes, Ludlow Castle and Penshurst.

She became the third wife of Henry Herbert, second earl of Pembroke, when she was fifteen and thereafter lived at Wilton, which she made the centre of a literary circle. J. C. A. Rathmell edited the *Sidney Psalms*, versions of the psalms that she worked on with her brother, in 1963; in 1977 G. F. Waller edited *The Triumph of Death and other unpublished and uncollected poems*. See also E. V. Beilin, *Redeeming Eve: Women Writers of the English Renaissance* (Princeton, 1987), R. Zim, *English Metrical Psalms: Poetry as Praise and Prayer 1535–1601* (Cambridge, 1987) and M. G. Brennan, *Literary Patronage in the Renaissance: The Pembroke Family* (London, 1988).

p. xv   Mehetabel Wright (1687–1750) was the daughter of Samuel Wesley and his wife Susanna, and sister of John and Charles Wesley, the founders of Methodism. Her poems were first printed in the *Gentleman's Magazine* in March and December 1836. Her most ambitious work, *Eupolis, a Hymn to the Creator*, was said by her brother to have been written by her father, who married her to a plumber after she had made an unsuccessful attempt to elope with a lawyer. See Roger Lonsdale, ed., *Eighteenth-Century Women Poets: An Oxford Anthology* (Oxford, 1989), 110, 115.

p. xvi   Sappho: see Chapter 4, *passim*.

Katherine Philips, the matchless Orinda (1632–64), wrote mostly occasional verse addressed to the members of her Royalist coterie. After the restoration she was persuaded to translate Corneille's *La Mort de Pompée* and *Horace* and addressed a number of celebratory poems to members of the royal family. Long after her death she became famous as the author of a series of 'Letters from Orinda to Poliarchus'. Her *Collected Works* have recently been published in three volumes by Stump Cross Books. See Chapter 5, *passim*.

Aphra Behn (1639–89): Maureen Duffy's biography of Behn, *The Passionate Shepherdess*, is still in print. Angeline Goreau's *Reconstructing Aphra* (New York, 1980) takes a different line. Both should be treated with caution. Janet Todd is at present working on the first comprehensive edition of all *The Works of Aphra Behn* (London, 1993–); an incomplete edition by Montague Summers (Oxford, 1915) was issued in facsimile in 1967. Separate editions of *Loveletters between a Nobleman and his Sister*, *The Rover* and *Oronooko and other Stories* are at present in print. *The Uncollected Verse of Aphra Behn* was published by Stump Cross Books in 1989. See also Chapters 6 and 7, *passim*.

p. xix   Lady Grisell Baillie (1665–1746): see p. xx.

Jane Elliot (1727–1805) is principally known for a ditty to the tune of 'The Flowers of the Forest' celebrating the fallen at the battle of Flodden (Lonsdale, 264). See p. 57.

Isobel Pagan (1740–1821): see p. 57.

Anna Laetitia Barbauld (1743–1825) won a high reputation with her *Poems* published in 1773 (*DNB*); see pp. 29, 54, 90 and 262 and Lonsdale, 299–300. See also Barbauld's *Works*, with a memoir by Lucy Aikin (London, 1825).

Fanny Greville (*c.*1724–89) born Macartney is the author of 'the most celebrated poem by a woman' of the time, the much anthologized 'Prayer for Indifference' (Lonsdale, 190–91).

Lady Anne Lindsay (1750–1825), eldest child of the fifth earl of Balcarres, wrote new words for an old Scottish ballad. As 'Auld Robin Gray' it was a universal hit, but Lady Anne did not reveal her authorship until 1821 (*DNB*). Lonsdale, 276–7.

Joanna Baillie (1762–1851), Scott's 'immortal Joanna', was educated at a boarding-school in Glasgow and published her first volume of verse anonymously in 1790. When the first volume of her *Series of Plays, in which it is attempted to Delineate the Stronger Passions of the Mind* was published in 1798 it too was anonymous and reviewed as the work of a man, who was by some suspected to be Sir Walter Scott. Her authorship became known in 1800 after one play had been successfully staged (*DNB*). *A Series of Plays* has been reissued in facsimile (Oxford, 1990). Walter Whyte, in a memoir for *Poets of the Century*, ed. A. H. Miles (London, 1898), vii, 4, states his opinion that her lyrics will continue to be read as her plays will not because they display the essential virtue of 'heartiness'. 'Of all English women-poets she speaks in accents least easily distinguishable from a man's'. See p. 29.

p. xx   Mary Lamb (1765–1847) fatally stabbed the mother of a servant when the balance of her mind was disturbed, and was placed in the custody of her brother, the essayist Charles Lamb, until his death in 1834. She collaborated with her brother on *Poetry for Children* (1810) (*DNB*).

The reputation of Carolina, Lady Nairne (1766–1845) is based on Jacobite songs such as 'Wha'll be King but Charlie' and 'Charlie is my Darling', 'The Land o' the Leal' and 'The Laird o' Cockpen'. Her work is almost all dittying, fitting new words to old airs, under the name of 'Mrs Bogan of Bogan'. Her poems were not published under her own name until after her death (*DNB*).

Felicia Hemans (1793–1835): see pp. 59–61, 91–4.

The Hon. Mrs Caroline Norton (1808–77), recognized by Richard Garnett (*DNB*) as 'poetess', was one of the three beautiful granddaughters of the playwright Sheridan. She began writing poetry when still a child and when she was twenty-one had a critical success with her Byronic tale,

The Sorrows of Rosalie. She had then been married to the Hon. George Norton for two years; she went on to earn as much as £1,400 a year by her poetry which was featured in the annuals. In 1836 her husband brought a clamorous case against her, alleging criminal conversation with Lord Melbourne. Though the case failed, Norton continued to persecute his wife and even to claim her income. She published *The Undying One* in 1830, *The Dream and other Poems* in 1840, *The Child of the Islands* in 1845, and her masterpiece *The Lady of la Garaye* in 1862, as well as several novels.

Jean Ingelow (1820–97) was educated 'at home'; she published her first volume of verse in 1850; the second, which contained her best-known poem, 'High Tide on the Coast of Lincolnshire 1571', went through four editions in 1863 and continued to be reprinted over many years. Her British success was replicated in America, where she sold 200,000 copies (*DNB*). Virginia Woolf points out in her essay 'I am Christina Rossetti' that while Ingelow's work went through eight editions, Rossetti earned £10 a year.

Alice Meynell (1847–1922), born Thompson, published her first volume of poems in 1875. Two years later she married Wilfrid Meynell and between 1879 and 1891 bore him eight children. In 1893 she published *Poems*, in 1896 *Other Poems*, in 1902 *Later Poems*, in 1917 *A Father of Women and other Poems*, in 1923 *Last Poems*. F. Page believed that she 'would rank among women poets with Emily Brontë, Elizabeth Barrett Browning and Christina Rossetti' (*DNB*).

The Hon. Emily Lawless (1845–1913) is not noticed by *DNB* though she was a well-known novelist and poet of the turn of the century. She was the daughter of Lord Cloncurry, and educated at home. Her first publications were anonymous; in 1886 she successfully published a novel under her own name. Stopford Brooke encouraged her to publish her poems, *With the Wild Geese*, in 1902. Her second volume of verse, *The Point of View*, was privately printed for the benefit of Galway fishermen in 1909. Her collected poems were published in 1965 (*The Feminist Companion to Literature in English*, ed. V. Blain, P. Clements and I. Grundy, London, 1990).

Dora Sigerson (1866–1918) was born in Ireland; though she married the London literary journalist Clement King Shorter in 1896, she remained true to the Irish Republican cause and the Celtic movement. She published more than twenty volumes of verse (*Feminist Companion*).

Margaret L. Woods (1856–1945) was born Margaret Bradley, daughter of the Master of Rugby school. She was educated at home and at Miss Gawthorp's school in Leamington. She married the Master of Trinity

College, Oxford and wrote novels as well as five volumes of verse (*Feminist Companion*).

Agnes Mary Frances Duclaux (1857–1944), who began her poetic career as A. Mary F. Robinson, is described by Arthur Symons in a memoir for *Poets of the Century*, ed. A. H. Miles (London, 1898), as 'the spoilt child of two literatures' whose Paris salon 'was one of the centres of Parisian letters and learning' (viii, 521). From 1875–80 she attended University College, London. A beautiful woman, she struck up a literary friendship with Julian Symonds and became a member of the circle of Vernon Lee. *A Handful of Honeysuckle* appeared in 1878, in 1881 *The Crowned Hippolytus and other Poems*, in 1884 *The New Arcadia and other Poems*, in 1886 *An Italian Garden* which was also successfully published in the United States. In 1888 she married James Darmesteter, Professor of Persian at the Ecole des Hautes Etudes, and published *Songs, Ballads and a Garden Play*. Symons' enthusiasm may be tinged with sarcasm: 'If she has attained or preserved any originality it is in spite of the kindness of Fate and her friends. Her surroundings have always been too perfect. She and her books have always been very fortunate. Her triste muse has had the task of inventing a delicate misery which (happily!) has never existed.' Darmesteter died in 1894; in 1901 the poet married sixty-one-year-old Emile Duclaux who died three years later. The only modern study of this poet is Sylvaine Marandon, *L'Oeuvre Poetique de Mary Robinson 1857–1944* (Bordeaux, 1967).

Mary Elizabeth Coleridge (1861–1907), great-niece of the poet, was educated 'at home' and began to write poetry and romances as a child; the poet Robert Bridges persuaded Oxford University Press to publish her first volume of poems, *Fancy's Following*, in 1896. After her sudden death, Henry Newbolt collected her *Poems New and Old* for publication the same year (*DNB*).

May Probyn is not mentioned in biographical dictionaries or companions to literature. She is responsible for three volumes of verse, *Poems* (London, 1881), *A Ballad of the Road, and other Poems* (London, 1883) and *Pansies: A Book of Poems* (1895).

Katherine Tynan Hinkson (1861–1931) had very little schooling because measles had affected her eyes; her father paid for the publication of her first novel, *Louise de la Vallière*, in 1885, and she went on to publish more than a hundred novels, as well as occasional collections of poems which were collected for an edition in 1930. She grew up in Ireland, moved to England in 1883 when she married Henry Albert Hinkson, and divided her later years between Ireland, England and the continent. The best source of information about her life is her five-volume autobiography (*DNB*).

Frances Bannerman is not mentioned in biographical dictionaries or companions to literature; Grant Richards, who also published Katherine Tynan Hinkson, Louise Imogen Guiney and Alice Meynell, published her *Milestones: A Collection of Verses* in 1899.

Emily Brontë (1818–48), best known for her great novel, *Wuthering Heights*, began to write poetry in early childhood; when a selection of her and her sisters' poems was privately printed in 1846 as *Poems by Currer, Ellis, and Acton Bell*, it was the first time that Englishwomen had published under male pseudonyms.

Elizabeth Barrett Browning (1806–61): see below, pp. 61–4, 95–100 and 394–401.

Christina Rossetti (1830–94): see Chapter 11, *passim*.

Edith Sitwell (1887–1964) is described by Fleur Adcock in *The Faber Book of Twentieth-Century Women's Verse* (1987) in these terms:

> Then there are the borderline cases, those whose originality went little deeper than surface tricks. Edith Sitwell was convinced, and convinced others (Yeats among them) that she had introduced a new note into English literature. Her games with sound, her dance-tune rhythms, her use of nonsense rhymes and synaesthesia, and her whole clutter of historical/mythological/folkloric paraphernalia enhanced the entertainment value of the Sitwell circus, but it is as entertainment that they should now be chiefly viewed.

Despite the sternness of these strictures Adcock included a single Sitwell poem in her anthology. Adcock might have preferred to include an example of the work of Laura Riding whom she recognized as a genuine innovator, if Riding had not specifically prohibited the printing of her verse in any anthology of women's work. Adcock does not so much as mention Anne Ridler or Kathleen Raine.

Though Anne Ridler (1912–) is still alive, her poetic reputation appears to have collapsed. Examples of her work were included in Ann Stanford's overview of *The Women Poets in English* in 1972, the same year that Professor Gardner included her in *The New Oxford Book of English Verse*, but little has been reprinted since then. She was born in Rugby, educated at King's College, London, took a diploma in journalism and married Vivian Ridler, printer to Oxford University. From 1935 to 1940 she worked as an editor for Faber & Faber; in 1951 she edited *The Faber Book of Modern Verse* (revised 1960). She began publishing her own poetry with *Poems* (1939), followed by *A Dream Observed* (1941), *The Nine Bright Shiners* (1943), *The Golden Bird* (1951), *A Matter of Life and Death* (1959) and *Selected Poems* (1961).

More than twenty years after the death of Stevie Smith (1902–71) examples of her work continue to be included in even the most progressive anthologies. She was born in Hull, moved to London, and attended North London Collegiate School. Until 1953 she worked for a publisher; her first book of poems, *A Good Time Was Had By All*, illustrated as were all her books by herself, was published in 1937, followed by *Tender Only to One* (1938), *Mother What Is That Man?* (1942) and *Harold's Leap* (1950). In the fifties she performed musical versions of her poems at literary festivals. In 1957 her best known volume, *Not Waving But Drowning*, appeared, to be followed by *Selected Poems* (1962), *The Frog Prince and Other Poems* (1966) and *The Best Beast* (1969).

Kathleen Raine (1908–), who studied Natural Sciences at Cambridge University, was one of a group of Cambridge poets that included William Empson, Ronald Bottrall, John Cornford, Julian Bell and Charles Madge. From 1955–61 she was a research fellow of Girton College. She edited the writings of the Platonist Thomas Taylor and Coleridge's letters, but is best known for her studies of Blake. *The Collected Poems of Kathleen Raine* were published in 1956, followed by *The Hollow Hill and Other Poems, 1960–1964* (1964), *Six Dreams and Other Poems* (1968) and *Ninfa Revisited* (1968).

p. xxi   Dr Johnson: *Boswell's Life of Johnson*, ed. G. Birkbeck Hill (Oxford, 1887), i, 463: 'Sir, a woman's preaching is like a dog's walking on his hinder legs. It is not done well; but you are surprised to find it done at all.'

Sir Walter Scott: Introduction to the third canto of *Marmion*.

p. xxii   Frederick Rowton: ed., *The Female Poets of Great Britain chronologically arranged: with copious selections and critical remarks* (London, 1848), xx–xxi.

'Miss Landon': see Chapter 10 *passim*.

Anne Finch, Countess of Winchilsea (1661–1720), born Anne Kingsmill, Maid of Honour to Mary of Modena until her marriage to Heneage Finch in May 1684, began writing poetry in 1685. Her poem 'The Spleen' preceded by an 'Epistle to Flavia' by Nicholas Rowe was published in Gildon's *Miscellany* in 1701, almost certainly without her permission. The publication of other verses by Delarivier Manley in *The New Atlantis* (1709) probably prompted the publication of a selection of her work in 1713 as *Miscellaneous Poems on Several Occasions*, at first anonymously, though her name appears on the numerous reissues. Myra Reynolds who edited her *Poems* in 1903 did not know of the existence at Wellesley College MA of an important MS which has since been edited by J. M. Ellis D'Alessandro (Florence, 1988). See Chapter 9 *passim*.

Mary Tighe (1772–1810), born Blachford, was apparently a very beautiful woman (*DNB*). The last three cantos of *Psyche, or the Legend of Love* were nonsensically claimed by Mackintosh to be 'without doubt the most faultless series of verses ever produced by a woman'. Other women's verse was 'less faultless' presumably. Tighe's poem is written in Spenserian stanzas, hence Rowton's claim.

'Mrs Grant' is Anne Grant of Laggan (1765–1838). She was born in America but returned with her family to Scotland in 1773 and married a Scots clergyman six years later. After her husband died in 1801 her poems were successfully published by subscription. She went on to publish letters and memoirs and further poems and to play a significant role in the literary life of Edinburgh (*DNB*).

Hannah More (1745–1833) enjoyed a degree of success seldom achieved by male poets. One of the three daughters of a Bristol schoolmaster who opened a boarding-school together in 1758, she was by her own account eighteen when she wrote *The Search after Happiness: A Pastoral Drama*, which was well-received when published in 1773. The next year she had a tragedy, *The Inflexible Captive*, successfully performed and published. In 1776 her 'legendary tales', *Sir Eldred of the Bower and the Bleeding Rock*, were published, and revised by Dr Johnson for republication in 1778. With the death of Garrick, who revised her enormously successful tragedy *Percy* and advised her on *The Fatal Falsehood*, her career as a dramatist came to an end and she turned her hand to *Essays on Various Subjects. Principally Designed for Young Ladies* (1777). *Sacred Dramas. Chiefly Intended for Young Persons, to which is added, Sensibility, A Poem* (1782) went into nineteen editions, followed by *Florio: A Tale for Fine Gentlemen and Fine Ladies* and *The Bas Bleu, Or Conversation: Two Poems* (1786); Johnson said of the poem *Bas Bleu* 'there was no name in poetry that would not be glad to own it'. *Slavery, A Poem* (1788) was followed by *Thoughts on the Importance of the Manners of the Great to General Society* (1791) which went through eight editions in four years. *An Estimate of the Religion of the fashionable World* (1791) went through five editions in two years. *Village Politics by Will Chip* (1792) was followed by *Strictures on the Modern System of Female Education* (1799) which went through thirteen editions and *Coelebs in Search of a Wife* (1809). See W. Roberts, *Memoirs of the Life and Correspondence of Mrs Hannah More* (London, 1834), M. A. Hopkins, *Hannah More and her Circle* (New York, 1947), S. Harstack Meyers, *The Bluestocking Circle: Women, Friendship, and the Life of the Mind in Eighteenth-Century England* (Oxford, 1990) and M. G. Jones, *Hannah More* (Cambridge, 1952).

Susanna Centlivre (?–1723) is a shadowy figure; little is known of her early life. Her first work was published under the name of Susannah Carroll. By 1707 when she married Joseph Centlivre, a cook in Queen

Anne's household, she was a successful playwright, with eight plays to her credit (*DNB*, Lonsdale, 74–8).

Ann Radcliffe (1764–1823) is principally known as a 'Gothic' novelist; she included verses in her novels, but poetry only became a preoccupation in later life when she wrote *St Alban's Abbey: A Metrical Tale*, published with one of her novels in 1826. Her collected *Poetical Works* were not published until 1834 (Lonsdale, 448–51).

'Mrs Browning': there has been no new edition of the complete works of Elizabeth Barrett Browning since the nineteenth century, though *Aurora Leigh* has been published several times as a feminist classic, in editions by C. Kaplan (London, 1978), M. Reynolds (Athens OH, 1992) and K. McSweeney (Oxford, 1993). See pp. 61–4, 95–101, 394–401.

Mary Howitt (1799–1888), born Botham, began writing verses at an early age; her works were first published with those of her husband William Howitt in 1827 in *The Desolation of Eyam and other Poems*. She is best known for her tales for children, but her name appears on more than 110 publications of all kinds. See *My own Story* (1845), *Mary Howitt: An Autobiography* (1889) and S. J. Kunitz and H. Haycraft, *British Authors of the Nineteenth Century* (New York, 1936). Howitt imitates *Lyrical Ballads* (1789) rather than Wordsworth.

'Mrs' Baillie was never married.

CHAPTER I: THE MUSE

p. 1   Robert Graves: *The White Goddess: A Historical Grammar of Poetic Myth* (revised ed. London, 1959), 14 cf. 5.

p. 2   Sigmund Freud: *A General Introduction to Psychoanalysis*, twenty-third lecture.

p. 4   Elizabeth Sacks: *Shakespeare's Images of Pregnancy* (London, 1980).

Robert Graves: *The Greek Myths*. See also *The White Goddess*, Chapter 22, *passim*.

p. 5   the pregnant poet: Terry Castle, 'Labring Bards: Birth Topoi and English Poetics 1660–1820', *Journal of English and Germanic Philology*, 78 (1979), 193–208; Susan Stanford Friedman, 'Creativity and the Childbirth Metaphor: Gender Difference in Literary Discourse' in *Speaking of Gender*, ed. Elaine Showalter (New York, 1989), 73–100, and Gershon Legman, 'Male Motherhood of Authorship', *The Rationale of the Dirty Joke: An Analysis of Sexual Humor*, i, 592–605.

'what is called': *The White Goddess*, 11–12.

p. 6   Cf. Petrarch, *Canzoniere*, cxc, 'una candida cerva . . .'

Christine de Pisan (1363– after 1429): C. C. Willard, *Christine de Pizan: Her Life and Works* (New York, 1984). *The Book of the City of Ladies* has been translated by Earl Richards. Scholars should consult Angus J. Kennedy, *Christine de Pizan: A Bibliographical Guide* (London, 1967).

p. 7   'Spenta è d'Amor . . .': the single surviving sonnet of Barbara Torelli (1475–*c*.1533) was published in Ferrara in 1713 among *Rime scelte de' poeti ferraresi antichi e moderni*.

p. 8   J. Burckhardt: *Civilization in the Renaissance* (London, 1944), 241. See also Margaret W. Ferguson, Maureen Quilligan and Nancy J. Vickers, eds., *Rewriting the Renaissance: The Discourses of Sexual Difference in Early Modern Europe*.

p. 9   the sex of mind: Londa Schiebinger, *The Mind has No Sex? Women in the Origins of Modern Science* (Cambridge MA and London, 1989).

Ludovico Ariosto, *Orlando Furioso*, canto xlvi, stanzas 3–10.

Vittoria Colonna (1490–1547) married Ferrante de Avalos, Marquis of Pescara in 1509. After his death in 1525 she dedicated her widowhood to celebrating his memory. Her *Rime* edited by Alan Bullock were published in 1982. See also Maud Jerrold, *Vittoria Colonna* (New York, 1969).

commendatory poems addressed to Orinda: *The Collected Works of Katherine Philips, the Matchless Orinda* (Stump Cross, 1990–93), iii, 182–222.

Margaret Cavendish, Duchess of Newcastle (*c*.1624–74) published her *Poems and Fancies* in 1653 with a revised version in 1664. 'They say it is ten times more extravagant than her dress' wrote Dorothy Osborne to William Temple on 29 March 1653, and decided after she had read it that 'there are many soberer people in Bedlam' (*Letters of Dorothy Osborne to William Temple*, ed. G. C. Moore Smith, Oxford, 1928, 37, 41). For more information about Cavendish see Virginia Woolf, 'The Duchess of Newcastle', *Collected Essays* 3, 51–8, K. Jones, *A Glorious Fame* (London, 1988), S. H. Mendelson, *The Mental World of Stuart Women* (Brighton, 1987) and pp. 39–41 and 97–8.

p. 10   The poetry of Veronica Gambara (1485–1550) was first published in Brescia in 1759; a more complete edition of her *Rime e Lettere* appeared in Florence in 1879, edited by P. M. Chiappetti.

p. 11   A very readable account of Elizabeth I in her own words can be found in M. Perry, *The Word of a Prince: A Life of Elizabeth I from Contemporary Documents* (Woodbridge, 1990). Most people know the famous utterance from her speech to the navy about to engage with the Armada, delivered in armour and on horseback at Tilbury, with the lines, 'I know I have the body of a weak and feeble woman, but I have the heart and stomach of a King, and a King of England'.

The *Rime* of Gaspara Stampa (*c.*1523–54) are kept in print by Rizzoli as Nos 687–8 of the Biblioteca Universale Rizzoli (first ed. Milan, 1954). See also Justin Vitiello, 'Gaspara Stampa: The Ambiguities of Martyrdom', *Modern Language Notes* 90 (January 1975), 58–71.

p. 12   'It was the woman': Fiora A. Bassanese, *Gaspara Stampa* (Boston, 1982), 31.

'This tale of love': Bassanese, 123.

p. 14   courtesans: Georgina Masson, *Courtesans of the Italian Renaissance* (London, 1975). See also Antonio Barzagli, *Donne o Cortigiane: la Prostituzione a Venezia* (Verona, 1980).

Veronica Franco (1546–91): Giuseppe Tassini, *Veronica Franco Celebre Poetessa e Cortigiana del Secolo XVI* (Venice, 1969) and Marcella Diberti Leigh, *Veronica Franco: Donna Poetessa e Cortigiana del Rinascimento* (Ivrea, 1988).

Laura Terracina published *Rime* in 1548, *Rime Seconde* in 1549, *Quarte Rime* in 1550, *Quinte Rime* in 1552 and *Seste Rime* in 1558. See A. Borzelli, *Laura Terracina: Poetessa Napoletana del Cinquecento* (Naples, 1924).

p. 15   Lady Mary Wroth (1587–1653): *The Poems of Lady Mary Wroth*, ed. with introduction and notes by Josephine Roberts (Baton Rouge and London, 1983), 33.

Margaret Cavendish, Duchess of Newcastle: *Sociable Letters* (1664; Scolar Press facsimile, 1969), Sig. b; see p. 9 and n.

Ben Jonson: *Underwood*, xxviii.

p. 16   Comtesse de Dia: Meg Bogin, *The Women Troubadours* (London, 1976), 84–6. See also Oscar Schultz-Gora, *Die Provenzalischen Dichterinnen* (Leipzig, 1888), J. Boutiere and A. Schultz, *Biographies des Troubadours* (Paris, 1964); G. Kussler-Ratyé, 'Les Chansons de la Comtesse de Die', *Archiv Roman*, i, 174; Biblioteca Estense, Modena, MS a R 4 4.

p. 17   Henriette de Coligny, Comtesse de la Suze (1618–73): *Les Poesies de Madame la Comtesse de la Suze* were published in Paris in 1666 and again in 1725 in *Recueil de Pièces galantes, en prose et en vers, de Madame la Comtesse De La Suze, et de Monsieur Pelisson*.

love poems by Aphra Behn addressed to men: see 'The Return', 'On a

Copy of Verses made in a Dream and sent to me in a Morning before I was Awake', Song, 'Ah what can mean that eager joy?', 'In Imitation of Horace', 'To Lysander, who made some Verses on a Discourse of Love's Fire', 'To Lysander at the Music Meeting', and 'On Mr J. H, in a Fit of Sickness', *The Works of Aphra Behn*, ed. M. Summers (Oxford, 1915), vi, 173, 174, 192, 195–6, 200–202.

John Wilmot, second Earl of Rochester (1647–80): *A Letter from Artemiza in the Town to Chloe in the Country*, published in broadside twice in 1679.

p. 18 Anne Bradstreet (1612–72): *The Works of Anne Bradstreet*, ed. Jeannine Helmsley (Cambridge MA, 1967), 5, 7. See also E. Wade White, *Anne Bradstreet: The Tenth Muse* (New York, 1971).

p. 19 Thomas Creech: 'To the Author on her Voyage to the Isle of Love', Summers, vi, 121ff. ll. 1–4.

'But now into such lab'rinths': Hensley.

p. 20 'My muse': Hensley, 192.

'If for thy father': Hensley.

p. 21 Robert Boyle, Earl of Orrery, 'To Orinda': *Philips*, iii, 186–8.

p. 22 Abraham Cowley, 'On Orinda's Poems': *ibid.*, 191–5.

p. 23 'Philo-Philippa', 'To the Excellent Orinda': *ibid.*, 197–204.

Sara Fyge (1670–1723): 'The Emulation', *Poems on Several Occasions* [1703], 35–6.

'a satiric poem': 'A Session of Poets', Bodleian Library, MS Don. b. 8; see also D. M. Vieth, *Attribution in Restoration Poetry: A Study of Rochester's Poems of 1680* (New Haven and London, 1963), 309.

'To Damon': Summers, vi, 347.

p. 24 *Poems by Mrs. Anne Killigrew* was published posthumously in 1686; a facsimile has been issued by Scholars' Facsimiles and Reprints (Gainesville, 1967). 'Upon the Saying that my Verses were made by Another' and 'To My Lord Colrane' can be found in *Kissing the Rod: An Anthology of Seventeenth-Century Women's Verse*, ed. G. Greer, S. Hastings, J. Medoff and M. Sansone (London, 1988), 305–8.

p. 25 John Dryden, 'To the Pious Memory of the Accomplished Young Lady Mrs. Anne Killigrew, Excellent in the two Sister-Arts of Poetry and Painting'.

p. 26 *The Nine Muses, or, Poems on the Death of the Late Famous John Dryden, Esq.* (London, 1700).

For concise biographies of Delarivier Manley (1663–1724), Catherine Trotter (1679–1749), Mary Pix (1666–1709), Sarah Fyge (1669–1722), Susannah Carroll (Mrs Centlivre, ?–1723), and Lady Sarah Piers (?–1720) see *A Dictionary of British and American Women Writers 1660–1800*, ed. Janet Todd (London, 1984). Examples of the verse of all six can be found in *Kissing the Rod*.

Elizabeth Thomas (1675–1731): 'The True Effigies of a Certain Squire: Inscribed to Clemena', from *Miscellany Poems on Several Subjects* (1722), R. Lonsdale ed., *Eighteenth-Century Women Poets: An Oxford Anthology* (Oxford, 1989), 37–9.

p. 27   Jean Adams (1710–65): 'To the Muse', *Miscellany Poems* (Glasgow, 1734), Lonsdale, 145.

Martha Sansom (1690–1736): Lonsdale, 84–91. See also *Epistles of Clio and Strephon* (1720).

Mary Leapor (1722–46): 'The Headache. To Aurelia', Lonsdale, 196–7.

p. 28   Henrietta, Lady Luxborough (1699–1756): 'Written to a near Neighbour in a Tempestuous Night. 1748', printed in Dodsley's *Collection of Poems* (1755), Lonsdale, 224–5.

Clara Reeve (1729–1807): 'To my Friend, Mrs. ——. On her holding an Argument in Favour of the Natural Equality of both the Sexes. Written in the year MDCCLVI', Lonsdale, 249.

p. 29   Mary Darwall née Whateley (1738–1825): 'On the Author's Husband Desiring her to write some Verses', Lonsdale, 261–2.

Anna Laetitia Barbauld (1743–1825): 'Washing-Day', Lonsdale, 308–10, see p. xix and n.

Joanna Baillie (1762–1851): 'An Address to the Muses', Lonsdale, 440–41. See p. xxi and n.

p. 30   Lydia Jane Pierson: 'My Muse', *The Female Poets of America*, ed. T. B. Read (Philadelphia, 1852), 63–4, 67. Mrs Pierson is known only for *The Forest Minstrel*, published in 1846.

p. 31   *The Poems of Laura Riding* (1901–) were republished in her own edition in 1980. It is worth noting in the context that 'Riding' claimed that all the ideas in *The White Goddess* were hers including presumably 'Woman is not a poet. She is either a muse or she is nothing' (444).

Raine, 'Invocation': *The Collected Poems of Kathleen Raine* (London, 1956), 5. In *The Collected Poems of Kathleen Raine, 1935–1980*, edited by the poet with the assistance of her daughter, this poem, the most anthologized of Raine's poems, does not appear. See p. xix and n.

p. 32   Mary Webb (1881–1927) is best known as the author of *Precious Bane*, now in print as a Virago Modern Classic. Few of her poems were published in her lifetime; a hasty selection, *Poems and the Spring of Joy*, appeared in 1928. See G. M. Coles, *The Flower of Light: a Biography of Mary Webb* (London, 1978).

Mary K. DeShazer: *Inspiring Women: Reimagining the Muse* (New York, 1986).

p. 33   'When, Lo!': D. Hopkins and T. Mason, *The Story of Poetry* (Bristol, 1992), 42.

'even while': Hopkins and Mason, 53.

'You, my Poet': Hopkins and Mason, 175.

p. 34   Carolyn Kizer, 'A Muse of Water': *The Ungrateful Garden* (Bloomington, 1961), 61–3. Kizer, born in Spokane, Washington, U.S.A. in 1925, founded *Poetry-Northwest*. Later books of poems include *Knock upon Silence* (1965), and *Midnight Was My Cry: New and Selected Poems* (1971).

Sylvia Plath, 'The Disquieting Muses', *The Colossus* (London, 1972), 58. For another discussion on this theme see Henry Nelson Coleridge, *Quarterly Review* (1836), 'The Modern Nine'.

CHAPTER 2: POET, POETASTER, POETESS

p. 36   A. Alvarez: review of *The Colossus* quoted on early Faber editions of Plath.

'The only truth-tellers': Elizabeth Barrett Browning, *Aurora Leigh*, i, 859–62, 86–7, 901–7.

p. 37   Mary, Lady Chudleigh (1656–1710): 'Of Knowledge', from *Essays on Several Subjects in Verse and Prose* (1710); *The Poems and Prose of Mary, Lady Chudleigh*, ed. M. Ezell (New York and Oxford, 1993), 251.

p. 38   Lady Chudleigh, 'To the Reader': Ezell, 247.

See *Poems of Queen Elizabeth I*, ed. L. Bradner (Providence RI, 1964).

Elizabeth, Queen of Bohemia (1595–1660): *Kissing the Rod: An Anthology of Seventeenth-Century Women's Verse*, ed. G. Greer, S. Hastings, J. Medoff and M. Sansone (London, 1988), 40–43.

Elizabeth, Viscountess Falkland wrote *The Tragedie of Mariam* in blank verse, published in 1613, and perhaps a verse *History of the Life, Reign and Death of Edward II*, published in 1680; *Kissing the Rod*, 54–60.

Lady Mary Wroth: see p. 15 and n.

p. 39   Rachel Speght (1597–?): *A Muzzle for Melastomus, the Cynical Baiter of and foul-mouthed Barker against Evah's Sex* (1617), *Kissing the Rod*, 68–78.

Mary Oxlie of Morpeth is known only by a dedicatory poem prefixed to the posthumous edition of *Poems* by William Drummond of Hawthornden (1656), *Kissing the Rod*, 79–82.

Lady Jane Cavendish (1621–69), 'Envoi', Bodleian Library MS Rawl. poet. 16, 84, *Kissing the Rod*, 106–18.

p. 40   'If my writing': Margaret Cavendish, Duchess of Newcastle, *Poems and Fancies* (1653) Sig. [A8]; see p. 9 and n.

Virginia Woolf, 'The Duchess of Newcastle', *Collected Essays* 3, 518.

Pepys, *Diary*, 26 April 1667: *The Diary of Samuel Pepys*, ed. R. Latham and W. Matthews (London, 1970–83), viii, 209 cf. 186–7.

Dorothy Temple: *The Letters of Dorothy Osborne to William Temple*, ed. G. C. Moore Smith (rept. Oxford, 1968), 41.

'I writ so fast': Newcastle, *Poems and Fancies* (1653), Sig. [A8].

p. 41   'Madam, I dedicate': Lady Alice Egerton, Huntington Library MS EL 8367.

Hester Wyat: 'A Poem made . . . in answer to one who asked why she wrote', Bodleian Library MS Rawl. d. 360, f. 53, *Kissing the Rod*, 5–6.

p. 42   Katherine Philips, letter of 29 January 1664: *The Collected Works of Katherine Philips*, ii, *The Letters*, ed. P. Thomas, 129; cf. the actual epilogue, iii, *The Translations*, ed. G. Greer and R. Little, 90.

'Innocence or, the Inestimable Gem. Written by a Young Lady': *Miscellanea Sacra* (1696), i, 4, *Kissing the Rod*, 279.

p. 43   Elizabeth Singer Rowe (1674–1737): *The Miscellaneous Works in Prose and Verse*, ed. T. Rowe (1739), xvi–xvii; cf. *Poems on Several Occasions written by Philomela* (1696) and *Philomela: or, Poems By Mrs. Elizabeth Singer* [*Now Rowe*] (1737). See also Henry F. Stecher, *Elizabeth Singer Rowe, the Poetess of Frome: A Study in Eighteenth-Century English Pietism* (Frankfurt, 1973).

p. 44   Mary Astell (1668–1731): Ruth Perry, *The Celebrated Mary Astell: An Early English Feminist* (Chicago and London, 1986), 405.

p. 45   François Poulain de la Barre: *The Woman as Good as the Man: Or, the Equality of Both Sexes. Written Originally in French, And Translated into English by A. L.* (1677), 31.

p. 46   Mary Jones (?–1778): letter of 16 March 1761 to Ralph Griffiths, Lonsdale, 156.

'The Emulation': *Triumphs of Female Wit* (1683), *Kissing the Rod*, 311.

Mary Evelyn: *The Diary and Correspondence of John Evelyn*, ed. W. Bray (London, 1818), ix, 31.

p. 47   Annabella Blount (fl. 1700–41): Lonsdale, 186–7.

An Collins: 'The Preface', *Divine Songs and Meditations* (1653), *Kissing the Rod*, 148–9.

p. 48   'A Pindaric to Mrs Behn on her Poem on the Coronation. Written by a Lady': *Lycidus: or the Lover in Fashion* [by Aphra Behn] *Together with a Miscellany of New Poems, By several hands* (1688), *Kissing the Rod*, 262–3.

p. 49   Elizabeth Teft (fl. 1741–47): 'On Learning. Desired by a Gentleman', *Miscellanies* (1747), Lonsdale, 218.

Laetitia Pilkington (1708?–50): *Memoirs* (1748), Lonsdale, 136–41.

p. 50   Mary Jones: see above, p. 46 and n., 'An Epistle to Lady Bowyer', Lonsdale, 158.

Mary Jones: 'Soliloquy on an Empty Purse', Lonsdale, 163.

The career of Charles Gildon (1663–1724) is noticed in *DNB*; the account of his activities by Paul Dottin in his edition of Gildon's pamphlet *Robinson Crusoe Examin'd and Criticis'd* (London, 1923) should be treated with caution.

Anna Maria Williams, (1706–83): Lonsdale, 240–44.

Priscilla Pointon (1740–1801): Lonsdale, 272–5.

p. 51   Dr Johnson and Helen Maria Williams: *Boswell's Life of Johnson*, ed. G. Birkbeck Hill (Oxford, 1887), iv, 282.

Pope and the Countess of Winchilsea: Anne Finch, Countess of Winchilsea (1661–1720) took issue with the younger poet about four lines about the spleen, subject of her best-known poem, in *The Rape of the Lock*:

> Parent of vapours and of female wit,
> Who give the hysteric or the poetic fit,
> On various tempers, act by various ways,
> Make some take physic, others scribble plays.

Pope replied to her defence of women poets with an Impromptu:

> In vain you boast poetic names of yore,
> And cite those Sapphos we admire no more:
> Fate doomed the fall of every female wit,
> But doomed it then when first Ardelia writ etc.

The Countess, rather too graciously, accepted the compliment.

> Disarmed, with so genteel an air,
>   The contest I give o'er,
> Yet Alexander have a care,
>   And shock the sex no more.
>
> We rule the world, our lives' whole race,
>   Men but assume that right,
> First slaves to every tempting face,
>   Then Martyrs to our spite.

The original copy of this poem in the Countess's autograph, with Pope's corrections for publication, can be seen in the British Library (MS Add. 4807, ff. 209, 210), because Pope later used the paper (an expensive commodity in those days) to write out part of his translation of Homer.

Judith Cowper (1702–81): Lonsdale, 93–95. Pope's poem to Judith Cowper was sent in his second letter to her, dated 18 October 1722, and published in *Letters to a Lady* (1769). The Sappho/sun referred to here is Lady Mary Wortley Montagu, then on good terms with Pope who had not yet expressed sympathy with those 'Poxed by her love or libelled by her hate' but, even so, Pope must make of the existence of another female poet a competition for his admiration.

> Though sprightly Sappho force our love and praise
> A softer wonder my pleased soul surveys,
> The mild Erinna, blushing in her bays.
> So while the sun's broad beam yet strikes the sight,
> All mild appears the moon's more sober light,
> Secure, in virgin majesty, she shines,
> And, unobserved, the glaring sun declines.
>   (*Minor Poems*, N. Ault ed., 306)

See Robert Halsband, *The Life of Lady Mary Wortley Montagu* (Oxford, 1956), 130ff, 140–42, 147–8, 149–52 and *passim*.

p. 52   Mary Leapor: see p. 27 and n. and biographical notice, Lonsdale, 194–5. A larger selection of her work appears in *Poems by Eminent Ladies*, ed. G. Colman and B. Thornton (1755), ii, 17–134.

Leapor, 'The Penitent. Occasion'd by the Author's being asked if she would take Ten Pounds for her Poems': *Poems upon Several Occasions* (London, 1748), 119.

Leapor, 'The Sow and the Peacock': *Poems upon Several Occasions*, 179.

p. 53   Mary Collier (1690?–1762): Lonsdale, 171–4.

Ann Yearsley (1752–1806): Lonsdale, 392–401; see also Moira Ferguson ed., 'The Unpublished Poems of Ann Yearsley', *Tulsa Studies in Women's Literature* 12, No. 1 (1993), 13–46.

Elizabeth Hands (fl. 1789): Lonsdale, 422–29.

Phyllis Wheatley (1753?–84): *The Collected Works of Phyllis Wheatley*, ed. John Shields (New York and Oxford, 1988).

p. 54   Anna Laetitia Aikin, later Mrs Barbauld (1743–1825): Lonsdale, 299–311. See also pp. 29, 90 and 262; and B. Rodgers, *Georgian Chronicle: Mrs. Barbauld and her family* (London, 1968).

Aikin: 'On a Lady's Writing', *Poems*, The Fourth Edition (London, 1774), 52.

Ann (1782–1866) and Jane Taylor (1783–1824): *DNB* and *The Oxford Dictionary of Nursery Rhymes*, ed. Iona and Peter Opie (Oxford, 1969), 60, 356, 398. Their best-known work is 'Twinkle, twinkle, little star'. See also Ann Taylor, *Autobiography*, I. Taylor, *Memoirs and Poetical Remains of Jane Taylor*, L. B. Walford, *Twelve English Authoresses*, Mrs H. C. Knight, *The Life and Letters of Jane Taylor* and Virginia Woolf, *The Common Reader, First series*.

p. 55   Sara Josepha Hale (1788–1889), née Buell, editor of *The Ladies American Magazine* from 1828 to 1837 when it merged with *Godey's Lady's Book* of which she continued as editor, also published a volume of verse, *Three Hours; or, the Vigil of Love* in 1847. *The Oxford Dictionary of Nursery Rhymes*, 42, 300.

Mary Howitt: see p. xxii and n. *The Oxford Dictionary of Nursery Rhymes*, 5.

p. 56   Sarah Catherine Martin: *The Oxford Dictionary of Nursery Rhymes*, 320–22. See Z. Moon, *Old Mother Hubbard. The Authoress buried at Longerton* (London, 1917).

Charlotte Elliott (1789–1871): *DNB*.

Cecil Frances Alexander (1818–95): *DNB*.

Jane M. Campbell (1817–78) is one of an interesting group of women who translated hymns from the German of whom Catherine Winkworth (1827–78, *DNB*) is the best known; Campbell's *The Garland of Song* (1862) was followed by *The Children's Choral Book* in 1869.

Sarah Flower Adams (1805–48): *DNB*.

Hymn-writing: Other successful lady hymn-writers include Harriet Auber (1773–1862), Charlotte E. Tonna (1790–1849), Jane Borthwick (fl. 1813), Mrs J. C. Simpson (1811–86, *DNB*), Jemima Luke (1813–1906, *DNB*), Mary L. Duncan (1814–40), Caroline M. Noel (1817–77), Mrs E. S. Alderson (1818–88), Mrs M. F. Maude (1820–1913), Elizabeth Charles

(1827–1906), Elizabeth Clephane (1830–69), Emily Miller (1833–1913), Emily E. S. Elliott (1835–97), Frances R. Havergal (1836–79, *DNB*), Mary Dunlop (1837–66), Mrs Frances M. Owen (1842–83), Mrs Dorothy Frances Gurney (1858–1932), Frances F. Fuller Maitland (fl. 1827), Mrs L. M. Willis (fl. 1864), Mrs A. J. Carney, Jane E. Leeson, Mrs A. Richter, Isabel S. Stevenson, Mrs E. Toke and Mrs D. Coote. See H. Martin, *They Wrote Our Hymns*, 126–39.

Elizabeth, Lady Wardlaw (1677–1727): *DNB*.

p. 57   Jane Elliot: see p. xix and n.

Alicia Cockburn (1713–94): Lonsdale, 262.

Isobel Pagan: *DNB*.

Lady Anne Lindsay: see p. xix and n.

Dr Johnson on Hannah More: Lonsdale, 323. For Hannah More see p. xxii and n.

Charlotte Smith (1749–1806): *DNB*, Lonsdale 365–72. See *The Poems of Charlotte Smith*, ed. Stuart Curran (New York and Oxford, 1993), F. M. Hilbish, *Charlotte Smith, Poet and Novelist* (Hughesville PA, 1941), K. M. Rogers, *Feminism in Eighteenth-Century England* (Brighton, 1982).

Hannah Cowley (1743–1809): Lonsdale, 385–8, *DNB*.

Helen Maria Williams (1761?–1827): entry by Janet Todd in *A Dictionary of British and American Women Writers, 1660–1800* and Lonsdale, 413–19.

Joanna Baillie: see p. xix and n., also Lonsdale, 429–4.

p. 58   Anna Seward (1742–1809): entry by B. Brandon Schnorrenberg in *A Dictionary of British and American Women Writers, 1660–1800*, ed. J. Todd, and Lonsdale, 311–19; H. Pearson, *The Swan of Lichfield* (London, 1936), R. A. Hesselgrave, *Lady Miller and the Batheaston Literary Circle* (New Haven, 1927).

Sir Walter Scott: 'Biographical Preface', *The Poetical Works of Anna Seward, with Extracts from her Literary Correspondence* (London, 1810), i, vii–viii.

'How many duteous': Seward, 'Epistle to Cornelia', *Poetical Works*, ii, 116.

p. 59   'Designed for peace': Seward, 'Address to Woman. From the Italian', *Poetical Works*, ii, 176.

'Then should Fame': Seward, 'Lichfield, an Elegy. Written May 1781', *Poetical Works*, i, 99.

The Darwin business: according to Scott, in her *Life of Darwin*, Seward 'laid her claim to the last fifty verses in The Botanic Garden, which she had written in compliment to Dr Darwin and which he had inserted in his poem without any acknowledgment. The correctness of Miss Seward's statement is proved by the publication of the verses with her name, in some periodical publications, previous to the appearance of Dr Darwin's poem; and the disingenuous suppression of the aid of which he availed himself must remain a considerable stain upon the poet of Flora' (*Poetical Works*, i, xx–xxi).

Felicia Hemans (1793–1835): *The Poems of Felicia Hemans* (Edinburgh, 1875), 694.

p. 60   Adelaide Procter (1824–64): Charles Dickens: preface to *Lyrics and Legends*. Dickens published the first work of Adelaide Procter in *Household Words* to which she sent them under the name 'Miss Mary Berwick' in 1853. She is best known today for the lyric of 'The Lost Chord', a staple of Victoriana concert performances (*DNB*).

p. 61   Hemans: 'Properzia Rossi', *Records of Women, Poems*, 393. Cf. L. E. L. in *The New Monthly Review*, August, 1835: 'Genius places a woman in an unnatural position; notoriety frightens away affection; and superiority has for its attendant, fear, not love'.

Recent studies of Browning include M. Forster, *Elizabeth Barrett Browning: A Biography* (London, 1988), R. Mander, *Mrs Browning: the Story of Elizabeth Barrett* (London, 1980), H. Cooper, *Elizabeth Barrett Browning: Woman and Artist* (Chapel Hill NC, 1988) and A. Leighton, *Elizabeth Barrett Browning* (Bloomington, 1986).

p. 62   'Day and night': Browning, *Aurora Leigh*, iii, 271–8.

p. 63   'Such ups and downs': Browning, *Aurora Leigh*, i, 933–6; i, 940–42.

'Many fervent souls': Browning, *Aurora Leigh*, i, 942–8.

'poets should': Browning, *Aurora Leigh*, v, 183–8.

Sylvia Plath, 'The Colossus', *The Colossus* (London, 1960), 20–21.

CHAPTER 3: THE TRANSVESTITE POET

p. 65   androgyny: A. Aurnhammer, *Androgynie: Studien zur einem Motiv der europäischen Literatur* (Köln, 1986), W. Doniger, *Women, Androgynes and Other Mythical Beasts* (Chicago, 1990), K. Weil, *Androgyny and the Denial of Difference* (Charlottesville VA, 1992).

p. 67   'The maidens came': *The Oxford Book of English Verse* (1939), 42, No. 30, 15–16th century.

p. 68   'What are little boys made of?': *The Oxford Book of Nursery Rhymes*, 100–101.

Sir Sidney Lee: *Shakespeare and the Modern Stage* (London, 1906), 19.

W. Robertson Davies, *Shakespeare's Boy Actors* (London, 1939), 24–5.

p. 69   'At first the infant': *As You Like It*, II. vii. 143–9. All Shakespeare quotations are taken from *The Complete Works*, ed. S. Wells and G. Taylor (Oxford, 1988).

p. 70   Ben Jonson: 'Her Man Described by her Own Dictamen', *The Underwood* (1640).

iconography of Amazons: P. DuBois, *Centaurs and Amazons: Women and the Pre-History of the Great Chain of Being* (Ann Arbor, 1991), M. Hammer, *Die Amazonen: vom Mutterrecht und der Erfindung des gebärenden Mannes* (Frankfurt-am-Main, 1981), S. W. Tiffany and K. Adams, *The Wild Women: An Enquiry into the Anthropology of an Idea* (Rochester VT, 1985), C. Berkson, *The Amazon and the Goddess: Cognates of artistic Form* (Bombay, 1987).

p. 71   'Because that she': *A Midsummer Night's Dream*, I. ii. 20–23.

Titania's affair with Theseus: *A Midsummer Night's Dream*, I. ii. 74–80.

Oberon's affair with Hippolyta: *A Midsummer Night's Dream*, I. ii. 68–73.

'purge his mortal grossness': *A Midsummer Night's Dream*, II. iii. 152.

p. 72   'We, Hermia. . .': *A Midsummer Night's Dream*, III. ii. 204–13.

'The Phoenix and the Turtle': ll. 25–40.

p. 73   'I'll prove. . .': *The Merchant of Venice*, III. iv. 64–76.

Grecian youths. . . : *Troilus and Cressida*, IV. v. 76–8, 86–8.

p. 74   'I, being but. . .': *As You Like It*, III. ii. 394–9; 'He'll make. . .': III. v. 116–27.

p. 75   'His dangling tresses. . .': Christopher Marlowe, *Hero and Leander*, First Sestiad, 55–69.

'wanton pamphlets. . .': Thomas Middleton, *A Mad World My Masters* (1608), I. ii. 43–5.

p. 76   'Stain to all nymphs. . .': *Venus and Adonis*, ll. 9–10.

'Most radiant Pyramus. . .': *A Midsummer Night's Dream*, III. i. 87–9.

'Over my altars. . .': *Venus and Adonis*, ll. 103–6.

p. 77   'soldier': *As You Like It*, II. vii. 150–52.

Cymochles: Edmund Spenser, *The Faerie Queene*, II, canto v, stanza 28.

p. 78   'Do you love me?': *The Tempest*, IV. i. 48–9.

p. 79   'it would become me. . .': *The Tempest*, III. i. 28–30.

'Sweet solitariness . . .': Lady Mary Wroth, *The Countess of Montgomery's Urania*, i, 109 cf. BL MS Add. 23229 ff. 91–2, 'Penshurst Mount'.

'for a boy . . .': Stephen Gosson, *The Ephemerides of Phialo . . . and a Shorte Apologie for the Schoole of Abuse* (London, 1579), 197.

p. 80   'young boys . . .': Anthony Munday, *A Second and Third Blast of retrait from Plaies and Theaters* (London, 1580), 110.

'Then, these goodly . . .': Philip Stubbes, *The Anatomie of Abuses* (London, 1583), Sig. [Lviiiᵛ].

'Pity it is . . .': William Prynne, *Histriomastix: the Players Scourge or Actors Tragedie* (London, 1633), 171–2, cf. 178–276, 584, 850, 859–89.

'did train up . . .': Prynne, *Histriomastix*, 168–9.

p. 81   G. Rattray Taylor, *Sex in History* (London, 1966), *passim*.

'Yea, men are . . .': Prynne, *Histriomastix*, 168.

'Lastly, this . . .': Prynne, *Histriomastix*, 208.

Ben Jonson: *Epicoene*, I. i. 11–15.

p. 82   'for whence . . .': Prynne, *Histriomastix*, 171.

Pepys: *Diary*, 18 August 1660, *The Diary of Samuel Pepys*, ed. R. Latham and W. Matthews (London, 1973–88), i, 224 and n.

Colley Cibber: *An Apology for the Life of Colley Cibber*, ed. B. R. S. Fone (Ann Arbor, 1968), 71

John Downes: *Roscius Anglicanus* (London, 1708), 19.

p. 83   Pepys: *Diary*, 7 January 1661, Latham and Matthews, ii, 7 and n.

Davenant: A. H. Nethercot, *Sir William D'Avenant, Poet Laureate and Playwright-Manager* (Chicago, 1938), 276–7.

Lucy Russell, Countess of Bedford (1581–1627), daughter of Sir John Harington, acted as patron not only to Jonson, but also to Donne, Chapman, Drayton and John Davies of Hereford (*DNB*); Elizabeth Manners, Countess of Rutland (1581–1615), daughter of Sir Philip Sidney; Susan Herbert, Countess of Montgomery (1587–1629), daughter of Edward de Vere, Earl of Oxford; Katherine, wife of Esmé Stuart, Seigneur d'Aubigné (d. 1627); Lady Jane Paulett, Marchioness of Winchester (1607–31); Venetia (1600–33), wife of Sir Kenelm Digby; Lady Mary Wroth: see p. 15 and n.

Alice Sutcliffe, author of *Meditations of Mans Mortalitie. Or, a Way to True Blessednesse* (London, 1633), *Kissing the Rod: An Anthology of Seventeenth-Century Women's Verse*, ed. G. Greer, S. Hastings, J. Medoff and M. Sansone (London, 1989), 90–93.

Ben Jonson: 'To the World', ll. 17–24, *The Forrest* (London, 1616).

'Canticus Amoris': for the original spelling version see in John Kerrigan, *Motives of Woe: Shakespeare and 'Female Complaint'* (Oxford, 1991), 90–91.

p. 85 Ben Jonson: 'In the person of Womankind. A Song Apologetique', ll. 5–6; 'Another. In defence of their Inconstancy' and 'A Nymph's Passion', *The Underwood* (1640).

Mary Herbert, Countess of Pembroke: see p. xiv and n.

Lady Mary Wroth: see p. 15 and n.

John Wilmot, second Earl of Rochester (1647–80): Rochester's poems are available in two good editions, one by D. M. Vieth (New Haven and London, 1967) and another by Keith Walker (Oxford, 1984). All quotations from Rochester are based on Walker, but have been modernized by the present author. 'A Dialogue between Strephon and Daphne', ll. 62, 71–2.

Rochester: 'A Letter from Artemiza in the Town to Chloe in the Country', Walker, 83–90.

Rochester: 'Injurious charmer of my vanquished heart', Walker, 28.

Rochester: 'Song of a Young Lady. To Her Ancient Lover', Walker, 32–3.

Rochester: 'The Platonick Lady', ll. 12–17, Walker, 24.

p. 87 Rochester: '[Letter from Mistress Price to Lord Chesterfield]', Walker, 61–2.

Rochester: 'What vain unnecessary things are men', Walker, 90–91.

Andrew Marvell: 'The Nymph complaining for the death of her Faun', *The Poems and Letters of Andrew Marvell*, ed. H. H. Margouliath (Oxford, 1927), 22–4.

Marvell: 'Dialogue between the Resolved Soul and Created Pleasure', Margouliath, 9–12. The contrast between Rochester's acceptance of his own feminine characteristics and blurring of gender distinction and Marvell's masculine anxiety corresponds to a contrast between royalist and republican culture that could be traced from the beginning of the century to the triumph of masculinism in the Whig supremacy. I would argue that the pendulum has not yet swung all the way back.

Aphra Behn: 'A Pox upon this needless scorn', sung by the page, Abevile, in IV. i of *The Rover*, Part II. Behn published it again in her *Poems on Several Occasions* (1684) as 'The Counsel. A Song. Set by Captain Pack', *The Works of Aphra Behn*, ed. M. Summers (Oxford, 1915), vi, 190.

Behn: 'The Invitation: A Song. To a New Scotch Tune', *Poems on Several Occasions* (1684), Summers, vi, 192–3.

Behn: 'In Imitation of Horace', *Poems on Several Occasions* (1684), Summers, vi, 195.

p. 88   Walloon gentleman: Konincklijke Bibliothek, The Hague, MS 75.J.51, F. 3ᵛ

Behn: 'Lysander at the Music-Meeting', *Poems on Several Occasions* (1684), Summers, vi, 207–8.

Behn: 'A Voyage to the Isle of Love', *Poems on Several Occasions* (1684), Summers, vi, 224–90.

Behn: *Lycidus or the Lover in Fashion &c* (1688), Summers, vi, 299–342.

Behn: 'La Montre', Summers, vi, 12–79; 'The Case for the Watch', 80–94, 'The Lady's Looking-Glass', 94–111.

Behn: 'To the fair Clarinda, who made Love to me, imagin'd more than woman', 'Poems appended to Lycidus', Summers, vi, 363.

p. 89   Elizabeth Singer Rowe and John Dunton: *Kissing the Rod*, 383–6. See p. 43 and n.

Elizabeth Thomas (1675–1731): *Kissing the Rod*, 429–31; see also *Eighteenth-Century Women Poets: An Oxford Anthology*, ed. R. Lonsdale (Oxford, 1989) 32–4, and p. 26 and n.

Mary Whately (1738–1825): 'Ode to Truth', Lonsdale, 166.

p. 90   Anna Seward (1742–1809): see p. 58 and n.

Anna Laetitia Barbauld (1743–1825): see p. xix and n.

Hannah More (1745–1833): *Slavery, A Poem* (London, 1788). See also p. xxii and n.

Charlotte Smith (1749–1806): see p. 57 and n.

Helen Maria Williams (1761?–1827): see p. 57 and n.

Ann Yearsley (1752–1806): 'On Mrs Montagu', Lonsdale, 395. See p. 53 and n.

Mary E. Lee (d. 1849): 'The Poets', *The American Female Poets of America*, ed. C. May (Philadelphia, 1853), 466.

Joanna Baillie: see above, p. xix and n. Samuel Rogers was only one of the people who reviewed *Plays of the Passions* as the work of a man.

p. 91   Elizabeth Carter (1717–1806): Lonsdale, 165–70.

Clara Reeve (1729–1807): Lonsdale, 247–50.

Hemans: *Memoir of Mrs. Hemans by her Sister Mrs. Hughes* (London, 1839), 10.

'England and Spain; or, Valour and Patriotism': *The Poems of Felicia Hemans*, The Complete Copyright Edition (Edinburgh, 1875), 5, 6.

p. 92   Hemans: 'The Aged Indian', *Poems*, 57.

p. 93   Hemans: 'The Hero's Death', *Poems*, 59.

Hemans: 'Wallace's Invocation to Bruce', *Poems*, 65.

Hemans: 'The Forest Sanctuary', *Poems*, 316–37.

Hemans: 'Casabianca', *Poems*, 369.

p. 94   Caroline Gilman (1794–?): 'The American Boy', *The Female Poets of America*, ed. T. B. Read (fifth edition, Philadelphia, 1852), 106–8.

p. 95   Julia Ward Howe (1819–1910): 'The Battle-Hymn of the Republic', published 1862. See *Reminiscences* (New York, 1899).

Elizabeth Barrett Browning: see also p. 61 and n. and below, pp. 394–401.

Browning: 'The Battle of Marathon', Preface, *The Poetical Works of Elizabeth Barrett Browning* (Oxford, 1911), 1, 3.

p. 96   Browning, 'The Battle of Marathon', Preface, *Poetical Works*, 4.

Gina Lombroso: *The Soul of Woman: L'Anima della Donna* (London, 1924), 158–9

Browning: 'The Battle of Marathon', Book iv, *Poetical Works*, 25.

p. 97   Margaret Cavendish, Duchess of Newcastle: *Poems and Fancies* (London, 1653); see p. 8 and n.

p. 98   Browning: 'An Essay on Mind', *Poetical Works*, 31.

Browning: 'Stanzas occasioned by a passage in Mr Emerson's journal Which states that, on the mention of Lord Byron's name, Captain Demetrius, an old Roumeliot, burst into tears', *Poetical Works*, 55.

p. 99   Browning: 'Riga's Last Song', *Poetical Works*, 59.

Browning: 'The Tempest', *Poetical Works*, 60–63.

'There is a silence. . .': 'The Past', *Poetical Works*, 56.

Browning: 'A Vision of the Poets', *Poetical Works*, 167, 170.

p. 100   Browning: 'The Runaway Slave at Pilgrim's Point', *Poetical Works*, 228.

Browning: 'To George Sand. A Recognition', *Poetical Works*, 335.

Poems by Acton, Ellis and Currer Bell, i.e. Anne Brontë (1820–49), Emily Brontë (1818–48) and Charlotte Brontë (1816–55), privately printed in 1846.

p. 101   'Vernon Lee' actually Violet Paget (1856–1935): *DNB*.

'Radclyffe Hall': Marguerite Antonia Radcliffe-Hall (1880–1943) published five volumes of poetry and seven novels. The best-known work, *The Well of Loneliness*, was prosecuted and condemned as an obscene libel in 1929. See Una, Lady Troubridge, *The Life of Radclyffe-Hall*.

'Michael Field': pseudonym of Katherine Harris Bradley (1864–1914) and her niece Edith Emma Cooper (1862–1913) who wrote verse tragedies in collaboration, as well as volumes of poetry, *Underneath the Bough* (1893), *Long Ago* (1889), a version of Sappho, and *Sight and Song* (1892).

Elizabeth Bishop (1911–79): Bishop was born in Massachusetts and brought up in Nova Scotia. She became a pupil of Marianne Moore in Boston, and closely associated with Robert Lowell, but later chose to travel widely and ultimately to settle in Brazil.

CHAPTER 4: THE ENIGMA OF SAPPHO

p. 102   The most accessible and comprehensive account of Sappho is given in the Harvard University Press edition for the Loeb Classical Library, *Greek Lyric I: Sappho and Alcaeus* (Cambridge MA and London, 1990), edited and translated by David A. Campbell and printed in parallel Greek and English.

The *Suda*: Campbell, 2–3 (No. 1), cf. 8–9, (Nos. 6 and 5). For the coinage featuring portraits of Sappho, see G. Richter, *Portraits of the Greeks*, i, 70–72.

The Florentine ostracon: Campbell, 56–7 (No. 2); M. Norsa, *La Scrittura letteraria greca dal secolo IV A. C. all'VIII D. C.*, Fig. 5 B.

Hermogenes: Campbell, 57.

Athenaios: Campbell, 58–9 (No. 2).

p. 103   'Psappha' as 'lapis lazuli': David M. Robinson, *Sappho and her Influence* (London, 1926?), 21.

p. 104   Camille Paglia: *Sexual Personae: Art and Decadence from Nefertiti to Emily Dickinson* (London, 1990), 624.

'Hymn to Aphrodite': Campbell, 52–3 (No. 1).

E. Lobel: Sapphois Meli Σαπφοῦς Μέλη: *The Fragments of the Lyrical Poems of Sappho* (Oxford, 1925), xi.

Alexandrian scholar: G. M. Kirkwood, *Early Greek Monody: The History of Poetic Type* (Ithaca NY, 1974), 102–3.

p. 105   pupils three: Campbell, 6–7 (No. 2); Apollonius of Tyana; Campbell, 20–21 (No. 21); Gorgo and Andromeda: *ibid.*

Oxyrhynchus: E. G. Turner, *Greek Papyri: An Introduction* (Oxford, 1968), 27–31.

'Caprice governs': Turner, 30, 67.

'filling up gaps': Lobel, xi.

p. 106   'something formulaic': Turner, 67–8.

'scant mercy': Turner, 69–70.

B. P. Grenfell and A. S. Hunt discovered the papyrus dumps at El Bernesa in 1896–7 and began to publish transcriptions almost immediately as *The Oxyrhynchus Papyri* (London, 1898–).

p. 107   Oxyrhynchus 1, 231: *The Oxyrhynchus Papyri* x, (1914), 22.

Oxyrhynchus 7: *The Oxyrhynchus Papyri* i, 10, Plate 2.

p. 108   Oxyrhynchus 1, 231: *The Oxyrhynchus Papyri* x, Plate 2, 20–50; Lobel's correction from Oxyrhynchus 2, 166 (a), *The Oxyrhynchus Papyri* xxi (1951), 122.

p. 109   'Hymn to Aphrodite': Campbell, 52–5 (No. 1).

Joan DeJean: *Fictions of Sappho 1546–1937* (Chicago and London, 1989), 32.

The selection of translators here is fairly arbitrary; there are literally thousands of versions of the Hymn to Aphrodite; the extraordinary variations in the rendering of 'ποικιλόθρον' would indicate that no one is sure what the word actually means.

A. and W. Barnstone: *A Book of Women Poets: from Antiquity to Now* (New York, 1978).

Mary Barnard: *Sappho: A New Translation* (Berkeley, 1958), No. 38.

Jeffrey Duban: *Ancient and Modern Images of Sappho; Translations and Studies in the Ancient Greek Love Lyric* (Lanham, 1983).

G. Davenport: *Archilochos, Sappho, Alkman: Three Lyric Poets of the Late Bronze Age* (Berkeley, 1990), 79.

'φαίνεταί μοι': Campbell, 78–81 (No. 31).

p. 111   J. M. Edmonds: *Lyra Graeca* (Leipzig, 1928), i.

T. Bergk: *Poetae Lyrici Graeci* (Leipzig, 1882).

J. Sitzler: 'Bibliography on Sappho' in *Jahresbericht über die Fortschritte der klassischen Altertumswissenschaft*, cxxxiii (1907), 104ff., 176ff. and clxxviii (1919), 46ff.

Plutarch: *Progress in Virtue, Moralia* i, 81.

'A papyrus commentary': Campbell, 198–9 (No. 213B); *P. S. I.* (Florence, 1965), 16s; see Eva Marie Voigt, *Sappho et Alcaeus* (Amsterdam, 1971).

p. 112   Apollonius Dyscolos: Campbell, 168–9 (No. 165).

Longinus, *De Sublimitate*: Campbell, 81.

DeJean: 49–50.

p. 115   Paglia on Sappho: *Sexual Personae*, 228, 624.

p. 116   the complexity of Sappho's verse: see Apuleius, *Apology*, Campbell, 42–3.

Oxyrhynchus 1, 800: Campbell, 2–3 (No. 1).

'the poetess': Robinson, 5.

p. 117   Solon: Campbell, 12–13 (No. 10).

Plato: *Phaedrus*, 235b.

Anthologia Palatina: Campbell, 48–9 (No. 60) cf. 26–7 (No. 27), 48–9 (No. 58).

Aristotle: Campbell, 152–3 (No. 137).

Athenaios: Campbell, 8–9 (No. 8).

Cicero: Campbell, 24–5 (No. 24); Constantinople (*ibid.*).

p. 118   Tullius Laurea: Campbell, 28–9 (No. 28).

Horace, *Carmina*: Campbell, 18–19 (No. 18) and 44–5 (No. 51).

Francesco Petrarca (1304–74): *Trionfi d'Amore*, iv. 25 cf. 'docta puella' in the tenth of his Latin eclogues.

p. 119 Plutarch: Campbell, 46–7 (No. 54).

T. G. Tucker: *Sappho* (Melbourne, 1914).

Horace: Campbell, 32–3 (No. 34).

Seneca: Campbell, 22–3 (No. 22).

p. 120 Catullus: 51, *Catullus, Tibullus, Pervigilium Veneris* (Loeb Classical Library, Cambridge MA and London, 1988), 58–61.

p. 121 'plagiarism': e. g. Tucker; 'having taken over Sappho': e.g. DeJean, 35–6.

Catullus's Lesbia poems: 5, 7, 45, 51 58, 62, 69, 83, 87, 92, 107. 'Sapphica musa': 35, 16.

Dionysius of Halicarnassus: Campbell, 36–9 (No. 42).

p. 122 standardization of Greek: A. M. Bowie, *The Poetic Dialect of Sappho and Alcaeus* (New York, 1981), 1–15.

'the female Homer': *Anthologia Palatina* 9. 26. 3f cf. 7. 15, Campbell, 46–7 (No. 57 and n.).

John Tzetzes: Campbell, 50–51 (No. 61).

Anacreon: 376, Euripides Cyclops: 166–7; Ausonius, 8. 24: Campbell, 22–3 (No. 23 and n.).

p. 123 The imagery of Phaon and Adonis is often confused, see Arthur Palmer ed., *Heroides* (Hildesheim, 1967), 419.

Epistula Sapphus (*Heroides* XV): *Ovid I: Heroides and Amores*, trans. Grant Showerman, 2nd ed. revised by G. P. Goold (Harvard University Press for Loeb Classical Library), 182, ll. 15–20.

some sources: e. g. Giomini, but see Palmer's gloss, 427–8.

Politian: *Commento inedito all'epistola ovidiana di Saffo a Faone*, ed. E. Lazzeri (Florence, 1971), 7.

Porphyrio: Campbell, 18–9 (No. 17).

Martial's caricature of Philaenis: *Epigrams* I, Book vii, lxvii.

p. 124 'If nature. . .': *Epistula Sapphus*, ll. 31–4.

'molle meum. . .': *Epistula Sapphus*, ll. 79–84.

p. 125 'non mihi. . .': *Epistula Sapphus*, ll. 198–9.

MS history of *Epistula Sapphus*: Palmer, xxxiii–xliii cf. Howard Jacobson, *Ovid's Heroides* (Princeton, 1974).

p. 126 Giovanni Boccaccio (1313–75): *De Claris Mulieribus: Concerning Famous Women*, trans. G. Guarini (New Brunswick NJ, 1963), 99.

p. 127   Christine de Pisan, *Le Livre de la Cité des Dames: The Book of the City of Ladies*, trans. E. J. Richards (New York, 1982), 67–8. For a less jaundiced view of Christine's strategies see C. Reno, 'Christine de Pizan: Feminism and Irony', in F. Simone et al., eds., *Seconda Miscellanea di Studi e Ricerche Sul Quattrocento Francese* (Chambéry/Turin, 1981); also M. Quilligan, 'Allegory and the Textual Body: Female Authority in Christine de Pizan's Livre de la Cité des Dames', *Romanic Review* 79, No. 1 (1988), 224; S. Delany, 'Rewriting Woman Good: Gender and the Anxiety of Influence in Two Late-Mediaeval Texts', in *Mediaeval Literary Politics: Shapes of Ideology* (Manchester, 1990); R. de Pernoud, *Christine de Pisan* (Paris, 1982); C. C. Willard, *Christine de Pizan: her Life and Loves* (New York, 1984).

p. 128   *The Boke of the Cyte of Ladyes*, trans. B. Anslay (London, 1521).

Politian: Lazzeri, 5–6.

p. 130   George Turbervile (1540?–1610?): *Heroycall Epistles of the Learned Poet, Publius Ovidius Naso* (London, 1567), Epistle XVII, 108. Turbervile's translation, dedicated to Thomas Howard, Viscount Byndon, was not carried out for the benefit of ladies.

John Donne (1572–1631): 'Sappho to Philaenis', *The Complete English Poems*, ed. A. J. Smith, 127–9.

Raffaelle Sanzio – Stanza della Segnatura: G. Comini, *Raffaello nell'Appartamento di Giulio II e Leone X* (Milano, 1993).

Gabriel de Petra: D. *Longini Liber de Sublimitate Latine redditus* (1612).

Gerard Langbaine, the elder (1609–58): *Dionysii Longini Rhetoris Praestantissimi Liber de Grandi Loquentia sive Sublimi dicendi genere, Latine redditus* (Oxford, 1636) – this is actually an unacknowledged printing of De Petra. It was twice reissued, in 1638 and 1650; the first successful edition was that of 1710.

Remi Belleau: 'Je suis un demi-dieu', *Les odes d'Anacréon Teien traduites par remi Belleau. . . Ensemble quelques petits hymnes de son invention* (Paris, 1556).

Antoine De Baïf: *Oeuvres en rime* (Paris, 1573).

Pierre de Ronsard: *Amours* (Paris, 1559).

p. 132   préciosité: see Odette de Mourgues, *Metaphysical, Baroque and Précieux Poetry* (Oxford, 1953).

[John Lyly]: *Sapho and Phao* (London, 1584); see also G. K. Hunter, *John Lyly, Humanist as Courtier* (London, 1962), 166–77.

p. 133   French prose translation: *Les Epistres d'Ovide. Traduites en prose françoise.*

Par les Sieurs Du Perron, des Portes, de la Brosse, de Lingendes, Hedelin et Colletet (Paris, 1621), 356–7.

Wye Saltonstall (fl. 1630–40), *Ovids Heroicall Epistles* (London, 1636), Sig [A4].

p. 134   '[Je] suis si. . .': Du Perron et al., 358.

Saltonstall, Sig [I iiiᵛ].

John Hall (1627–56): *Longinus Of the Height of Eloquence* (London, 1652).

Katherine Philips: *The Collected Works of Katherine Philips, the Matchless Orinda* (Stump Cross, 1989–93), i, *The Poems*, ed. P. Thomas, 23.

p. 135   Abraham Cowley (1618–67): 'On the death of Mrs Katherine Philips', *Philips*, iii, *The Translations*, ed. G. Greer and R. Little, 216.

John Oldham (1653–83): 'Bion', *Works* (London, 1684), 84.

Nicholas Boileau: *Oeuvres diverses du Sieur D*** Avec le traité du sublime* (Paris, 1674). A second edition appeared in the same year, followed by another in 1675, 1677, 1680, 1686, 1688, 1689, 1694, 1695 and three in 1701.

p. 136   Pulteney: *A treatise of the Loftiness or Elegancy of Speech* translated by Mr J[ohn] P[ulteney] (London, 1680).

Anne Le Fèvre, Madame Dacier: *Les Poësies d'Anacréon et de Sapho, traduites de grec en françois avec les remarques par Mademoiselle Le Fevre* (Paris, 1681); see also DeJean, 57–8.

Madeleine de Scudéry: *Les Femmes illustres ou les Harangues héroïques* (Paris, 1642), *Artamène ou le grand Cyrus* (1649–53).

p. 137   Tanneguy Le Fèvre: *Abrégé des vies des poètes grecs* (Saumur, 1664).

Edward Phillips: *Theatrum Poetarum Or a Compleat Collection of the poets of all Ages* (London, 1675), 247–8.

p. 138   John Shirley: *The Illustrious History of Women: or A Compendium of the many virtues that adorn the fair sex* (London, 1686).

John Evelyn: *Numismata* (London, 1697), 265.

Aphra Behn: *Miscellany, Being A Collection of Poems by Several Hands* (London, 1685), 212.

John Adams: 'To the Excellent Madam Behn on her Poems', *The Works of Aphra Behn*, ed. M. Summers (Oxford, 1915) vi, 120.

Aphra Behn: 'Of Trees', ll. 597–9, *The Second and Third Parts of the Works of Mr Abraham Cowley. . .containing his Six Books of Plants. . .Now made English by several hands* (London, 1689), reprinted in *The Uncollected Verse of Aphra Behn*, ed. G. Greer (Stump Cross, 1989), 127.

p. 139   Anne Wharton, 'To Mrs A. Behn, On What she Writ of the Earl of Rochester', first published in *A Collection of Poems by Several Hands* (London, 1693) (*The Surviving Works of Anne Wharton*, ed. G. Greer and S. Hastings, Stump Cross, forthcoming). See *Kissing the Rod*, 251:

> May yours excel the matchless *Sappho's* Name;
> May you have all her Wit, without her Shame:. . .

Ovid's *Epistles Translated by Several Hands* (London, 1680), 1–2, ll. 1–10; 2–3, ll. 19–22.

p. 140   Matthew Stevenson, *The Wits Paraphras'd* (London, 1680).

the Whig satire factory: little has been done to reconstruct the propaganda operations directed by Charles Sackville, Earl of Dorset in the run-up to the Bloodless Revolution of 1688. The chief distributors of Whig satires, Robert Julian and Captain Warcup, were known to be in Dorset's pay. Bodleian Library MS Firth c. 16 is derived from one of the scriptoria that produced anti-Tory lampoons. Dorset's most distinguished protégé was Matthew Prior; Charles Montagu, Robert Gould and Charles Blount were involved as well.

Alexander Radcliffe: *Ovid Travestie, a Burlesque upon Ovid's Epistles*, 1, ll. 1–14, 3, ll. 25–32 (London, 1681).

p. 141   Ephelia as Sappho: These lines from Daniel Kendrick, 'To Mrs B. on her Poems', *Lycidus or The Lover in Fashion* (London, 1688), Summers, vi, 297, are taken to refer to Ephelia:

> Sappho tastes strongly of the sex, is weak and poor,
> At second hand she russet Laurels wore. . .

Delarivier Manley refers to Behn in *Memoirs of Europe* as 'Sapho the younger' (i, 289; ii, 104).

Sara Fyge was praised by S. C., probably Susannah Carrol, Mrs Centlivre, in a commendatory poem in her *Poems on Several Occasions* (London, 1703) as Sappho's heir.

p. 142   John Dunton: *The Athenian Mercury*: 12 January 1691, question 8.

John Dunton: *The Athenian Mercury*, 27 November 1694.

Charles Gildon, ed., *Chorus Poetarum* (London, 1694). The habit of referring to Behn as Sappho was by then well-entrenched; Nahum Tate called her an English Sappho in a commendatory poem for *La Montre* in 1686, an unknown lady called her 'the much-lov'd Sappho of our Isle' in a poem included in *Lysidus* (1688), Robert Gould hailed her ironically as 'chaste Sappho' in *The Play-House* in 1689 and again in a satire of 1691.

p. 143   William Bowles: 'Sapho's Ode out of Longinus', *Poems by Several Hands and on Several Occasions*, ed. Nahum Tate (London, 1685), 85.

Alexander Pope: *Sappho to Phaon* (London, 1712). Pope takes Sappho's name in vain too many times to list here; see the Index to the Twickenham edition.

p. 144   For an early reference of Elizabeth Barrett Browning to Sappho, see p. 99. Mrs Browning also translated a poem thought by some to be by Sappho and quoted by Achilles Tatius in *Clitophon and Leucippe*, as 'Song of the Rose Attributed to Sappho' some time before 1850, *The Poetical Works of Elizabeth Barrett Browning*, (London 1911) 293.

Christina Rossetti: 'Sappho', *The Complete Poems of Christina Rossetti*, ed. R. W. Crump (Baton Rouge and London, 1979–90), iii, 81–2.

Christina Rossetti: 'What Sappho would have said had her leap cured instead of killing her', ll. 65–6, Crump, iii, 168.

Ladies of Llangollen: Lady Eleanor Butler (1739–1829) and Sarah Ponsonby (1755–1831) lived together at Plas Newydd from 1780, where they were visited by all the celebrities of the day.

p. 145   Balzac, *La Fille aux Yeux d'Or*.

Theophile Gautier, *Mademoiselle du Maupin*. See also Alphonse de Lamartine, *Nouvelles Meditations Poetiques* (Paris, 1823).

Baudelaire: 'Lesbos', *Les Fleurs du Mal* (original title 'Les Lesbiennes'); *Sapho* (1845) cf. Arsene Houssaye, *Sapho* (1850), Paul Verlaine, 'Les Amies', and Pierre Louys, *Les Chansons de Bilitis traduites du grec* (1895).

Dante Gabriel Rossetti: S. Reynolds, *The Vision of Simeon Solomon* (Stroud, 1984), 7.

Simeon Solomon: Sappho and Erinna at Mytilene (1864), Tate Gallery, London; the Tate holds a preparatory study of the head of Sappho.

Swinburne paid women to beat him: D. Thomas, *Swinburne: The Poet in his World* (London, 1979), 149–51 and *passim*.

Algernon Swinburne, *The Living Age*, No. 280 (London, 1914), 817–18 cf. 'Posthumous Essays', *The Saturday Review*, 21 February 1914.

CHAPTER 5: THE REWRITING OF
KATHERINE PHILIPS

p. 147   All references to Philips's text are to *The Collected Works of Katherine Philips, the Matchless Orinda*, i, *The Poems* and ii, *The Letters*, ed. P. Thomas; Vol. iii, *The Translations*, ed. G. Greer and R. Little (Stump Cross 1990–93).

Peter Beal: *The Index to English Literary Manuscripts 1450–1700*, ii, 126.

the Tutin MS: National Library of Wales MS 775B.

Two leaves: University of Kentucky W. Hugh Peal Collection, Accession No. 8379. See E. H. Hageman and A. Sununu, 'New Manuscript Texts of Katherine Philips, The "Matchless Orinda"', *English Manuscript Studies*, 4, 1993.

juvenilia: National Library of Wales Orielton MSS, parcel 34.

p. 148   'Rosania to Lucasia': BL MS Harl. 6947, f. 270.

'To the Countess of Carbery': Huntington Library MS EL 8767.

'No blooming youth': Poem 129, *Collected Works*, i, 253–4.

'A married state': Poem 130, *Collected Works*, i, 254.

four manuscript versions: Bodleian MSS Eng. misc. c. 292, f. 110; Firth c. 15, pp. 335–7; University of Nottingham Portland MSS PwV 40, f. 242 and PwV 41, pp. 149–50.

'To the Memory of the most Ingenious and Virtuous Gentleman Mr William Cartwright, my much valued Friend' with variant title 'In memory of Mr Cartwright': Poem 51, *Collected Works*, i, 143.

p. 149   Sir Edward Dering's copy: Humanities Research Center, University of Texas at Austin Pre-1700 MS 151, 2.

Dering letter-book: University of Cincinnati library, Phillipps MS 14392, DA 447f, D4 A3 R.

'To the much honoured Mr Henry Lawes on his Excellent Compositions in Music': with variant title 'To the truly noble Mr Henry Lawes', Poem 15, *Collected Works*, i, 87.

'Friendship's Mysteries': Poem 17, *Collected Works*, i, 90.

p. 150   Orinda's business in Ireland: *Collected Works*, i, 15; see also P. W. Souers, *The Matchless Orinda* (Cambridge MA, 1931).

National Library of Wales: MS 21867B.

p. 151 'No Pompey's Blood': *Collected Works*, iii, 68–9.

Orinda to Poliarchus, 3 June 1663: *Collected Works*, ii, 93.

'I know I gain': *Pompey*, V. v. 31–2, *Collected Works*, iii, 87.

Orinda to Poliarchus, 10 January 1663: *Collected Works*, ii, 70.

Orinda to Poliarchus, 8 April 1663: *Collected Works*, ii, 77–8.

'If heaven': *Pompey*, V. ii. 7–8, *Collected Works*, iii, 78.

'And he who then': *Pompey*, I. i. 51–2, *Collected Works*, iii, 7–8.

p. 153 'Sure love in you': *Pompey*, II. i. 13, *Collected Works*, iii, 23.

'Since too much power': *Pompey*, IV. ii. 18, *Collected Works*, iii, 62.

'By dreadful shrieks': *Pompey*, II. ii. 93–4, *Collected Works*, iii, 23.

p. 154 Orinda to Poliarchus, 11 December 1662: *Collected Works*, iii, 64. The couplet was

> And lending his Despair a kind Effort
> It should the staggering Universe support (*Pompey*, I. i. 27–8).

Orinda to Poliarchus, 8 April 1663: *Collected Works*, ii, 78.

Orinda to Poliarchus, 15 April 1663: *Collected Works*, ii, 79.

The sole surviving copy of *Poems by Several Persons* (Dublin 1663) is in the Folger Library (C6681.5).

Orinda to Poliarchus, 15 May 1663: *Collected Works*, ii, 88.

p. 155 'An Ode upon retirement, made upon occasion of Mr Cowley's on that subject': Poem 77, *Collected Works*, i, 193–5.

'To the Right Honourable, the Lady Mary Butler, at her Marriage to the Lord Cavendish. Octobr. 1662': Poem 125, *Collected Works*, i, 250–51.

'The Irish Greyhound': Poem 78, *Collected Works*, i, 195–6.

p. 156 Orinda to Poliarchus, 29 January 1664: *Collected Works*, ii, 125.

p. 157 Orinda to Poliarchus, 29 January 1664: *Collected Works*, ii, 128–9.

p. 160 Katherine Philips to Dorothy Temple, 22 January 1664: *Collected Works*, ii, 142.

p. 162 'Publication being made': *The Intelligencer*, 18 January 1664.

Worcester College MS 6. 13 agrees with the printed texts more often than with Orinda's autograph. The three accidentals here listed are significant because they do not appear in any printed text after 1664. The misreading of 'beauty' for 'bounty' occurs in line 32 of Poem 14, 'To the Truly Noble Sir Edward Dering' (*Collected Works*, i, 87) and there are dozens of other such shared misreadings. The dropped lines are line 12 of Poem 4, 'On the fair weather at the Coronation' (*Collected Works*, i, 73) and line 25 of Poem 12, 'To the noble Palaemon on his incomparable discourse of Friendship' (*Collected Works*, i, 84).

p. 163 John Aubrey: *Brief Lives*, ed. Andrew Clark (Oxford, 1898), ii, 54.

'the worthy persons': Orinda to Poliarchus, 29 January 1664, *Collected Works*, ii, 130.

the Rosania Manuscript: National Library of Wales MS 776B.

p. 166 'A Sea Voyage from Tenby to Bristol': Poem 16, *Collected Works*, i, 88–90.

'Lucasia, Rosania & Orinda, parting by a fountain': Poem 83, *Collected Works*, i, 200.

'A Farewell to Rosania': Poem 84, *Collected Works*, i, 201.

p. 167 'On Rosania's Apostacy and Lucasia's Friendship': Poem 68, *Collected Works*, i, 176.

'To Mrs M. A., upon Absence': Poem 49, *Collected Works*, i, 141.

'Rosania's Private Marriage': Poem 37, *Collected Works*, i, 122.

Marriott turned over his rights: *Transcript of the Registers of the Worshipful Company of Stationers*, ed. G. E. B. Eyre and C. Rivington, ii, 373.

p. .168 'On the fair weather at the Coronation': Poem 4 , *Collected Works*, i, 73, l. 12.

'La Grandeur d'Esprit': Poem 60, *Collected Works*, i, 157, l. 70.

'On the numerous access of the English': Poem 2, *Collected Works*, i, 70, l. 4.

p. 169 'To the Queen on her arrival at Portsmouth': Poem 5, *Collected Works*, i, 74, ll. 23–4, 33–4.

'In memory of. . .Mrs Mary Lloyd': Poem 31, *Collected Works*, i, 141, ll. 51–2.

The five couplets dropped in 1667 from 'Rosania Shadowed': Poem 34, *Collected Works*, i, 117–20, are ll. 29–30, 43–6, 57–60. The couplet beginning 'She scorns' comprises ll. 65–6.

p. 170 'A Friend': Poem 64, *Collected Works*, i, 168, l. 82.

'Friendship': Poem 57, *Collected Works*, i, 151.

For the text of 'Horace' as Philips left it fully collated with later printings, see *Collected Works*, iii, 119–81.

p. 171 'On the death of my first and dearest child, Hector Philips': Poem 101, *Collected Works*, i, 220, l. 6.

For the letters from Orinda to Berenice see *Collected Works*, ii, 1–12, and Appendix 5.

CHAPTER 6: DID APHRA BEHN EARN A LIVING BY HER PEN?

p. 173 Yvonne Roberts: *The Guardian*, 27 December 1994.

Virginia Woolf: *A Room of One's Own* (London, 1928), 65.

p. 174 Angeline Goreau: *Reconstructing Aphra: A Social Biography of Aphra Behn* (New York, 1980), 173–4.

Bowman on Behn as an actor: Alexander Oldys, MS marginalia in his copy of Langbaine's *Dramatick Poets*; see also 'From MS Adversaria', *Notes and Queries*, 2nd Series. No. 11 (1861), 201.

Rochester: *A letter from Artemiza in the Town to Chloe in the Country*, ll. 189–208, Walker, 88.

p. 175 'a wit uncommon': 'A Letter to Mr Creech at Oxford, Written in the last great Frost', first published in Behn's *Miscellany* of 1685, also in *The Uncollected Verse of Aphra Behn*, 16, ll. 46–7.

gossip of 1687: I am indebted to P. A. Hopkins, of Lancaster University, for the reference in Roger Morrice's entering book, ii, 53, week ending 29 January 1687.

Alexander Radcliffe: *The Ramble: An Anti-Heroick Poem* (London, 1682), *Works* (London, 1696), 6–7.

'Letter to Mr Creech', ll. 44–5.

James Wright: *Humours and Conversations of the Town* (London, 1693), 136.

Delarivier Manley, *Kissing the Rod: An Anthology of Seventeenth-Century Women's Verse*, ed. G. Greer, S. Hastings, J. Medoff and M. Sansone (London, 1988), 396–405. Mrs Manley says herself that she was the mistress of John Tilley, Warden of the Fleet, and gossip had it that earlier she had been the mistress of Sir Thomas Skipwith, manager of the Drury Lane Theatre.

Hoyle's arraignment before the Grand Jury: N. Luttrell, *Diary*, 23–29 March 1687; Corporation Record Office, Guildhall, London Sessions Record, Newgate Gaol Delivery.

Prologue to *The Feign'd Curtezans*: *The Works of Aphra Behn*, ed. M. Summers (Oxford, 1915), v, 308.

p. 177 Nell Gwyn (1650–87): *DNB*.

'a successful courtesan': Thomas Killigrew, 'Thomaso or The Wanderer' Part 1, I. i. *Comedies and Tragedies* (London, 1666), 315.

The *Abraham's Sacrifice* case: J. Fitzmaurice, 'Aphra Behn and the *Abraham's Sacrifice* Case', *Huntington Library Quarterly*, Summer, 1993, 319–26.

p. 178 'It did advance': 'To Mrs. W. On her Excellent Verses (Writ in Praise of some I had made on the Earl of Rochester) Written in a Fit of Sickness', Summers, vi, 172.

disapproval expressed: see Gilbert Burnet's letters to Mrs Wharton in *The Surviving Works of Anne Wharton* (Stump Cross, forthcoming), and p. 235.

Rochester as Alexander Bendo: [Gerald P. Mander], 'Rochester and Dr Bendo', *Times Literary Supplement*, 13 June 1942, 300; V. de Sola Pinto, *The Famous Pathologist, or The Noble Mountebank, by Thomas Alcock, and John Wilmot, Earl of Rochester* (Nottingham, 1961).

'*Strephon*, the Soft': 'To Mr Creech (under the Name of Daphnis) on his Excellent translation of Lucretius', Summers, vi, 169.

Yale MS miscellany: Yale MS Osborn b. 105. For a detailed discussion of this MS see D. M. Vieth, *Attribution in Restoration Poetry* (New Haven, 1963), 93–100.

Poems on Several Occasions by the Right Honourable the E. of R.: published in 1680 with a false imprint 'Printed at Antwerp', with no bookseller's name and very hastily printed, was the most successful piece of poetry publishing of the period, being reprinted at least eleven times. Little more than half the total number of poems included are actually by Rochester.

p. 179 miscellany she collected: *Miscellany, Being A Collection of Poems by several Hands Together with Reflections on Morality, or Seneca Unmasqued* (London, 1685), 43, 'A Song by the Earl of Rochester', which has not been authenticated as by Rochester.

revival of *Valentinian*: see p. 224.

Daniel Defoe: *A Review of the State of the English Nation*, iii, 131, 2 November 1706.

Elizabeth Barry (1658–1713): see also p. 239.

Hester Barry: see p. 243.

Rochester's creditors: see John Cary to Sir Ralph Verney, 2 January 1683, Claydon Papers.

Henry Savile to Lord Rochester: 17 December 1677, *The Rochester–Savile Letters 1671–1680*, ed. J. H. Wilson (Cleveland OH, 1941).

p. 180 Astraea Behn: William Byam to Sir Robert Harley, 14 March, 1664, V. J. Harlow, *Colonizing Expeditions in the West Indies and Guiana, 1623–1667*, Hakluyt Society, 2nd Series, No. 56 (London, 1923), 191; Astraea was the virgin goddess of justice who dwelt on earth in the Golden Age, and then fled to heaven; see also Honoré d'Urfé, *L'Astrée, passim*. Behn is also called 'Astraea' by Langbaine in *Momus Triumphans; Or, the Plagiaries of the English Stage* (London, 1688) and by John Dunton in *The Ladies Dictionary; Being a general Entertainment for the Fair Sex* (London, 1694).

Aphra Behn to Arlington, 22 September 1666: Public Record Office, Chancery Lane, SP 29/182, No. 143.

'Anne Behn': the Verney Collection of broadsides, Cambridge University Library; see also Mary Anne O'Donnell, *Aphra Behn: An Annotated Bibliography of Primary and Secondary Sources* (New York, 1986), 2:

> The name 'Ann' persists in the printing history of Behn's works, not just in Narcissus Luttrell's use of it in his ascription of *The Revenge*. In 1682 the first state of the dedication of *The Roundheads* is signed 'Ann Behn'; in the next state the two *n*'s have been inked out; in the final state the name is corrected to 'A. Behn'.

If Behn was as ill as she says she must have used an amanuensis, who possibly also delivered her work and collected commissions. The most likely candidate would have been a member of her own family, whose name may have been 'Ann' and who may have been thought by some to be the writer herself.

Martial: *Epigrams*, I, c:

> Mammas atque tatas Afra, sed ipsa tatarum
> dici et mammarum maxima mamma potest

The Golden Legend: Aphra or Afra was martyred at Augsburg during the reign of Diocletian, according to the Martyrology of St Jerome. The 'repentant prostitute' version does not make an appearance before the eighth century, and seems to have been a result of her sharing a feast-day with St Venerea (*New Catholic Encyclopedia*).

p. 181 ffyhare: Afra might after all be no more than a rendering of the Dutch 'Juffrow', 'Miss'.

Byam to Harley (undated): H. Platt, 'Astraea and Celadon: an untouched portrait of Aphra Behn', *Proceedings of the Modern Languages Association*, 49 (1934), 544–59.

Maureen Duffy: *The Passionate Shepherdess: Aphra Behn 1640–89* (London, 1977), 44.

Behn hated Byam: *Oroonoko: or, the Royal Slave*, Summers, v, 129–208; 180; 177–8.

George Marten: *Oroonoko*: Summers, v, 177–8.

p. 182 *The Younger Brother: or, the Amorous Jilt*: Summers, iv, 319–99.

Charles Gildon (1665–1724): thought by some to have been Behn's literary executor (e.g. Goreau, 117). By his own account, but not according to the records, he was born a gentleman and trained for a priest at Douai, but returned to England before he could be ordained. He laid claim to personal acquaintance with Behn in 1691 in *The History of the Athenian Society*, penned for John Dunton. He tells his own story and that of his treatment of Behn's play in his rewriting of Langbaine's *Momus Triumphans*, published in 1699 as *The Lives and Characters of the English Dramatick Poets . . . improv'd and continued down to this time, by a careful Hand*.

Surinam history: see *A Discription of Guyana*, Hakluyt Society, 11, lvi; S. Cohen (trans.) *Historical Essay on the Colony of Surinam* (New York, 1974); J. Wolbers, *Geschiedenis van Suriname* (Paramaibo, 1861); L. L. E. Rens, *The Historical Background of Surinam Negro-English* (Amsterdam, 1953); R. J. Van Lier, *Frontier Society: A Social Analysis of the History of Surinam* (1971); J. Rodway and T. Wyatt, *History of the Discovery and Settlement of Guiana 1493–1668* (Georgetown, 1888). The best sources for George Marten are the Loder–Marten letters in the Brotherton Library of the University of Leeds.

R. Sanford: *Surinam Justice in the case of Several persons proscribed by several Usurpers of Power in the Colony* (London, 1662), 8, 11, 34, 36.

commendatory poem: 'To Mr Creech (under the Name of Daphnis) on his Excellent translation of Lucretius', Summers, vi, 168.

annoyed by this presumption: see Behn's undated (c. 1684) letter to Jacob Tonson, Pierpont Morgan Library.

p. 183 flight from Kent: Duffy, 25–6.

Behn's family: in *Oroonoko* the narrator mentions a father (Summers, v, 177), a brother and a maid (184, 185) and a mother and a sister (208): mentions of her brother and her mother can be found in the state papers relating to her spying mission.

p. 184 spying mission: the chief sources for this are letters and memoranda in the Public Record Office, Chancery Lane, SP 29/167, 60; SP 29/169, 38, 39, 117, 118; SP 29/170, 75; SP 29/171, 65, 120; SP29/172, 14, 66, 81; SP 29/173, 3, 4; SP29/177, 42; SP 29/182, 143. See also *Calendar of State Papers Domestic, 1666–7*, 31 August 1666.

Colonel Edward Butler: the identification of this individual is by no means certain, see for example Duffy, 80, 86, 90, 124.

imprisonment: Duffy, 92 and Chapter ix, 'To Prison' *passim*.

six-day run: Downes quoted by Summers, iii, 284.

p. 185 Prologue to *The Forc'd Marriage*: Summers, iii, 285–6.

'At twenty-five': *A New Collection of Poems* (London, 1674).

dedicatory epistle: *The Young King*, Summers, ii, 105.

p. 186 *Philaster:* Buckingham's adaptation of Beaumont and Fletcher's *Philaster* was to have been called 'The Restauration or Right will take Place'. It was first printed in full in the 1715 edition of Buckingham's works, but the prologue and epilogue had appeared in the 1704 *Miscellaneous Works*. According to Christine Phipps, *Buckingham: Public and Private Man. The Prose, Poems and Commonplace Book of George Villiers, second Duke of Buckingham* (New York, 1985) 64, he began working on his adaptation in 1678; on 3 February 1683 a *Philaster* presumed to be Buckingham's was performed by the United Company (W. van Lennep, *The London Stage 1660–1800, A Calendar of Plays . . .*, Carbondale IL, 1965, Pt 1, 319).

1679: Van Lennep, Pt 1, 281; see also Summers, ii, 104.

'On a Copy of Verses': Summers, vi, 174–5.

'Desire: A Pindaric': Summers, vi, 357.

p. 187 William Bowles's paraphrase of Sappho: *Chorus Poetarum*, ed. Charles Gildon (London, 1693), 30; *Poems on Affairs of State Poems, From the Reign of K. James the First to this Present Year 1703* (London, 1703), 'On Madam Behn'; *The Dramatick Works of his Grace George Villiers, late Duke of Buckingham* (London, 1715).

'To the Memory of the most Illustrious Prince, George, Duke of Buckingham' is not by Mrs Behn; see O'Donnell, 310–11, 318.

William Wycherley, 'To the Sappho of the Age': *Miscellany Poems* (London, 1704). Further evidence of Behn's career as a woman of pleasure can be found in a letter of Charles Mordaunt, third Earl of Peterborough, who was thirty when Behn died, to Lady Mary Wortley Montagu (Pope, *Imitations of Horace*, ed. J. Butt, iv, 17).

p. 188 'A letter to a Brother of the Pen in Tribulation': *Poems on Several Occasions* (1684), Summers, vi, 185–6.

'A Session of the Poets': D. M. Vieth, *Attribution in Restoration Poetry* (New Haven, 1963), 309.

p. 189 Behn: 'Of Trees', *The Second and Third Parts of the Works of Mr*

Abraham Cowley . . . containing his Six Books of Plants . . . Now made English by several hands (London, 1689), reprinted in *The Uncollected Verse of Aphra Behn*, ed. G. Greer (Stump Cross, 1989), 127, ll. 593–6.

Epilogue to *The City Heiress*: Summers, ii, 300.

p. 190   commendatory poems: Charles Cotton 'To the Admir'd Astraea'; Nahum Tate, 'To the Incomparable Author'; G[eorge] J[enkins], 'To the Divine Astrea, on her Môntre'; George Jenkins, 'To his admired Friend, the most ingenious Author'; Richard Faerrar, 'To the most ingenious Astrea, upon her book intituled, La Môntre, or the Lover's Watch', *La Montre, or, The Lovers's Watch* (London, 1686), Summers, vi, 6–11; J[ohn] Cooper, 'To Mrs Behn on the publishing her Poems'; J[ohn] C[ooper], 'To Astraea, on her Poems'; J. Adams, 'To the excellent Madam Behn, on her Poems'; T[homas] C[reech], 'To the Author, on her Voyage to the Isle of Love'; J. W., 'To the excellent Astraea'; F. N. W., 'To Madam A. Behn on the publication of her Poems'; H. Watson, 'To Madam Behn, on her Poems', *Poems on Several Occasions, with a Voyage to the Isle of Love*, Summers, vi, 117–37.

Jacob Tonson: 'To the lovely witty Astraea, on Her Excellent Poems', *Poems on Several Occasions*, Summers, vi, 123. Tonson, the publisher of *Poems on Several Occasions*, did not put his own name to this puff in 1684, only acknowledging it as his in a letter to his son, 22 April 1728 (S. L. C. Clapp, *Jacob Tonson in Ten letters by and about him*, Austin TX, 1948).

'A damn'd intrigue': Prologue to *The Amorous Prince*, Summers, iv, 121, 119.

Jeffrey Boys: 'The Diary of Jeffrey Boys of Gray's Inn, 1671', *Notes & Queries*, 27 (December, 1930), 456.

p. 191   Behn's letter to Jacob Tonson: Pierpont Morgan Library.

'A Letter to a Brother of the Pen in Tribulation': *Poems on Several Occasions*, Summers, vi, 185–6.

'Epistle to Julian': British Library MS Harl. 7317, f. 58*.

Robert Gould: *A Satyrical Epistle to the Female Author of a Poem call'd Sylvia's Revenge &c* (London, 1691).

Covent Garden Drollery: O'Donnell, 214. The case for Behn's editorship is made by G. Thorn-Drury in his edition, *Covent Garden Drollery: A Miscellany of 1672* (London, 1928), v–xx.

very rare first issue: Harvard 11445.1.

p. 192   stage history of *The Dutch Lover*: Summers, i, 219–20.

Edward Phillips, *Theatrum Poetarum; Or, A Compleat Collection of the Poets* (London, 1675), 255.

Abdelazar or the Moor's Revenge: Summers, ii, 4–5.

Nell Gwyn at *Abdelazar*: Goreau, 209.

'kept company with court wits': Goreau, 211.

dedication to *The Feign'd Curtezans*: Summers, ii, 305.

Thomas Otway: Summers, iii, 284.

p. 193 'let not poor Nelly starve': John Evelyn, *Diary*, ed. E. S. De Beer (Oxford, 1959), 4 February 1684.

stage history of *The Town Fopp*: Summers, iii, 4.

stage history of *The Rover*: see p. 197.

Sir Patient Fancy, 'To the Reader': Summers, iv, 7.

The Roundheads: Summers, i, 333; *The False Count*: Summers, iii, 97; *The City Heiress*: Summers, ii, 197.

'A Letter to Mr Creech at Oxford, Written in the last great Frost': first published in *Miscellany* (London, 1685), reprinted in *Uncollected Verse*, 15–7, ll. 26–9, 38–40.

p. 194 took Mulgrave's shilling: see *Uncollected Verse*, 174–7.

Behn to Jacob Tonson: Pierpont Morgan Library.

p. 195 Wycherley in prison: Charles Gildon, *The Life of William Wycherley, Esq., ... with a Character of Mr Wycherley and his writings by the Lord Lansdowne*, printed by Curll in 1718, 7, claims that Wycherley was incarcerated in Newgate in 1682; his book so incensed Charles Dennis that he exacted an apology and published it. The Fleet Prison Commitment Book 1a reports Wycherley's commitment as 7 June 1685. James II gave orders for his release, but Wycherley understated the amount he owed and was not finally released until the spring of 1686. See Willard Connely, *Brawny Wycherley: First Master in English Modern Comedy* (London, 1930), 186–204.

Behn to Zachary Baggs: Folger MS.

Behn to Abigail Waller: Pierpont Morgan Library (the enclosed poem is the only known copy of literary work by Behn in her own hand).

Behn, 'On the Death of E. Waller, Esq.': ll. 3–6, first printed in *Poems to the Memory of that Incomparable Poet Edmond Waller Esquire* (London, 1688): Summers, vi, 405–6.

p. 196   Dryden to Elizabeth Thomas: [Edmund Curll, ed.,] *Miscellanea. In Two Volumes . . . Letters from Mr Dryden, to a Lady, in the Year 1699* (London, 1727) ii, 149.

posthumous publications: for a detailed discussion of these see G. Greer, 'Honest Sam Briscoe', *A Genius for Letters*, ed. R. Myers and M. Harris (London, 1995).

CHAPTER 7: APHRA BEHN AS GHOSTWRITER

p. 197   the success of *The Rover*: Summers, i, xxxviii.

Behn, *The Rover*, 'Postcript' (*sic*), Summers, i, 107.

p. 198   Thomas Killigrew (1612–83): *DNB*; see also A. Harbage, *Thomas Killigrew Cavalier Dramatist 1612–83* (Philadelphia, 1930).

For a full discussion of the various states of the various issues of *The Rover*, see O'Donnell, 35–8.

title-page of *Sir Patient Fancy*: O'Donnell, 42.

Prologue to *The Rover*: Summers, i, 7.

success of *The Forc'd Marriage*: J. Downes, *Roscius Anglicanus* (London, 1708), 34; Summers, iii, 284.

success of *The Amorous Prince*: Summers, i, xxxi; iv, 120.

stage history of *The Dutch Lover*: Summers, i, 219–20 cf. Behn's 'Epistle to the Reader', Summers, i, 221–5.

p. 199   stage history of *Abdelazar*: Summers, ii, 4–5.

stage history of *The Town Fop*: Summers, iii, 4.

The Debauchee: Summers, i, xxxvi; M. Duffy, *The Passionate Shepherdess: Aphra Behn 1640–89* (London, 1977) 143.

The Counterfeit Bridegroom: Summers, i, xxxvi–vii; Duffy, 143.

Edward Phillips: *Theatrum Poetarum: or, a Complete Collection of the Poets of All Ages* (London, 1675), 255.

All quotations from 'Thomaso' are taken from *Comedies and Tragedies written by Thomas Killigrew, Gent.* (London, 1664), the only known printing. There are no MSS extant, for reasons that should become apparent.

p. 200   dramatis personae: 'Thomaso', 312.

The Rover, Pt 1, I. i (Summers, i, 12) uses 15 lines from 'Thomaso', Pt 1, III. iv (*Comedies and Tragedies*, 349).

The Rover, Pt 1, I. i (Summers, i, 12–14) also uses 25 lines from 'Thomaso', Pt 2, II. i (*Comedies and Tragedies*, 399–401).

p. 202 *The Rover*, Pt 1, I. ii (Summers, 26) uses 13 lines from 'Thomaso', Pt 1, I. i (*Comedies and Tragedies*, 314) and 25 lines (Summers, i, 25–6) from 'Thomaso', Pt 1, I. v (*Comedies and Tragedies*, 325).

The Rover, Pt 1, II. i (Summers, i, 28–32) uses 83 lines from 'Thomaso', Pt 1, II. ii (*Comedies and Tragedies*, 327–34) and 11 lines (Summers, i, 29) from 'Thomaso', Pt 1, I. iii (*Comedies and Tragedies*, 318).

The Rover, Pt 1, II. i (Summers, i, 30, 31) cf. 'Thomaso', Pt 1, II. i (*Comedies and Tragedies*, 327, 328).

The Rover, Pt 1, II. ii (Summers, i, 36–7) uses 27 lines from 'Thomaso', Pt 1, II. iii (*Comedies and Tragedies*, 336–7) and 80 lines (Summers, i, 38–42) from II. iv (*Comedies and Tragedies*, 337–42).

p. 203 *The Rover*, Pt 1, III. i (Summers, i, 45–6) uses 44 lines from 'Thomaso', Pt 1, III. ii (*Comedies and Tragedies*, 345–6).

The Rover, Pt 1, III. ii (Summers, i, 42–5) uses 4 lines from 'Thomaso', Pt 1, V. v, 2 lines from V. vi, 8 lines from V. vii and 9 lines from V. xi (*Comedies and Tragedies*, 374–80).

p. 204 *The Rover*, Pt 1, III. iii (Summers, i, 45–9) uses 40 lines from 'Thomaso', Pt 1, IV. ii (*Comedies and Tragedies*, 357–8).

The Rover, Pt 1, IV. ii (Summers, i, 69–77) uses 25 lines from 'Thomaso', Pt 2, IV. i (*Comedies and Tragedies*, 428, 430, 431); though the structure of the scene is based on a longer treatment in 'Thomaso', the effect is very different.

The Rover, Pt 1, IV. iii (Summers, i) uses 16 lines from 'Thomaso', Pt 2, I. i (*Comedies and Tragedies*, 386), and 84 lines from Pt 2, II. iv (*Comedies and Tragedies*, 408–11).

Jones De Ritter: 'The Gypsy, *The Rover* and the Wanderer: Aphra Behn's Revision of Thomas Killigrew', *Restoration* (1986).

p. 205 Gerard Langbaine: *An Account of the English Dramatic Poets* (London, 1691), 20–21.

'Thomaso', Pt 1, III. i (*Comedies and Tragedies*, 343).

p. 206 Richard Flecknoe: Richard Flecknoe, in *The Life of Tomaso the Wanderer. An Epitome An Attack upon Thomas Killigrew*, rept from the original of 1667, ed. G. Thorn-Drury, 10.

Harbage: Harbage, 80.

'written in Madrid': this leads Harbage (103, 228–9) to identify the 'Arrigo' of 'Thomaso' as Henry Proger, leader of the assassins of Anthony Ascham, Commonwealth Ambassador to Madrid in 1650. In fact it is Edward Proger, not Henry, whose name figures in Killigrew's ciphers. 'Arrigo' was the coterie name of Killigrew's cousin, Henry, Lord Jermyn, then with Henrietta Maria in France. See Davenant's 'Madagascar', l. 423, also 'Written, When Colonell Goring Was beleev'd to be slaine, at the siege of Breda: His death lamented by Endymion, Arigo' and 'To Henry Jarmin', l. 61 (*Sir William Davenant; The shorter Poems, and Songs from the Plays and Masques*, ed. A. M. Gibbs, Oxford, 1972, 21, 69–73, 77).

p. 207 1650: if Harbage, who says that Killigrew left England in 1643 (75) is right. Killigrew was also wandering round Europe from 1639 to 1641 (A. B. Grosart, ed., *The Lismore Papers*, Second Series, Vol. 5, 112, 190–92, 201–7, 202–3 and J. W. Stoye, 'The Whereabouts of Thomas Killigrew 1639–41', *Review of English Studies*, 25 (1949), 245–8). In the dedication to *Comedies and Tragedies* Killigrew claims that his plays were written during 'twenty years banishment', presumably from 1640 to 1660.

historic meal: 'Thomaso', Pt 2, V. vii (*Comedies and Tragedies*, 456).

fund-raising expedition: see 'On my Lord Crofts and my Journey into Poland, from whence we brought 10000 L. for his majesty by the Decimation of his Scottish Subjects There' and 'On Mr. Tho. Killigrew's return from his Embassie from Venice and Mr. William Murray's from Scotland' in *The Poetical Works of Sir John Denham*, ed. T. H. Banks, Jr. (New Haven, 1928), 107–12.

dating of 'Thomaso': Harbage, 106.

'Gondibert's foes': Banks, 317–24; see also B. O Hehir, *Harmony from Discords: A Life of Sir John Denham* (Berkeley, 1968), 91–7; D. W. Gladish, ed., *Sir William Davenant's Gondibert* (Oxford, 1971) pp. 272–86; A. H. Nethercot, *Sir William D'Avenant, Poet Laureate and Playwright-Manager* (Chicago, 1938) 276–7; A. B. Grosart, ed., *The Lismore Papers*, Second Series, v, 112, 190–92, 201–7, 202–3; and, most recently, T. Raylor, *Cavaliers, Clubs, and Literary Culture: Sir John Mennes, James Smith, and the Order of the Fancy* (Newark, 1994), 198–9.

p. 208 *cortigiane oneste*: Masson, *Courtesans of the Italian Renaissance* (London, 1975), *passim*. Killigrew could have gathered information about courtesans from literary sources like Germini's *Sopra Quaranta Meretrici della Citta di Firenza* (Florence, 1553), or Aretino's *Ragionamenti* (1536), or the *Dialogo di Zoppino Fatto frate e Ludovico Puttaniere*, or Bandello's *Novelle*, Burchard's *Liber Notarum*, Giovio's *Historiae sui Temporis*, *Il Vanto della*

Cortigina Ferrarese, the *Novelle* of Pietro Fortini da Siena, *Il Trionfo della Lussuria* (Venice, 1537) or A. C., *Tutte le cortigiane principali et honoratissime di Vinegia*, if he had ever acquired a word of Italian. Interestingly Flecknoe (*The Life of Tomaso the Wanderer. An Epitome An Attack upon Thomas Killigrew*, rept from the original of 1667, ed. G. Thorn-Drury, 6) accuses Killigrew of having visited Italy to study 'la Puttana Errante' which suggests that he knew of Lorenzo Venier's book, *La Puttana Errante*. Harbage thinks that Killigrew had some French, in which case he could have found prototypes for his courtesans in Brantôme's *La Vie des Dames galantes* and Montaigne's *Journal de Voyage en Italie*. It seems likelier on balance that during his sojourns in Italy in 1636, 1639–41 and 1651–2, Killigrew simply observed the great courtesans, who were spectacular public figures (see 'Thomaso', Pt I, I. i, 314). As a distinguished foreign visitor he may have been invited to festivities at courtesans' houses.

Worcester College copy of *Comedies and Tragedies*: the volume was first noticed by W. Van Lennep, 'Thomas Killigrew prepares his plays for production', *J. Q. Adams Memorial Studies*, ed. J. G. McManaway, G. E. Dawson and E. E. Willoughby (Washington, 1948).

p. 209 *The Prisoners and Claracilla. Two Tragaecomedies*. As they were presented at the *Phoenix* in *Drury-Lane* by her M[tes] Servants (London, 1641).

p. 210 Henry Killigrew: Harbage, 45. Dr Killigrew is mocked once more by his brother in 'Thomaso', Pt I, V. i (*Comedies and Tragedies*, 371). If Epigram 16, in *A Book of New Epigrams* (London, 1695) written by Henry Killigrew (long before the date of publication) applies, the hostility was mutual.

Charles Killigrew: J. P. van der Motten, 'Thomas Killigrew: a Biographical Note', *Revue Belge de Philologie et d'Histoire*, 53 (1973) No. 3, 769.

'thrown from his cradle': 'Thomaso', Pt I, I. ii (*Comedies and Tragedies*, 321). See Stoye, 245–8; van der Motten, 769.

the nuns of Loudun: British Library MS Add. 27,402, f. 70, Bodleian MS Ashmole 800, 3, Magdalene College, Cambridge Pepys MS 2099, 3, Trinity College, Dublin, etc.

p. 211 Flecknoe: 10.

failure as resident: BL Add. MS 20,032 contains copies of Killigrew's warrants, and scribal copies of official dispatches evidently prepared as part of his explanation to the king of the disastrous end to his embassy. Killigrew sat mute in his interviews with the senate, who must have been bemused by some of the nonsense in his dispatches, of which he may actually have been unaware. For his interview with the king he prepared largely illegible memoranda for himself (f. 30), ending as if to reassure his master 'ad noen but my own priiat bisnes was ever sent in my own hade'. Killigrew's ciphers (BL Add. MS 33,596, ff. 23–8) which he devised himself, went some way to conceal his difficulties, for whole words are substituted by figures; even so no cipher in his hand is known.

failure as master of the revels: L. Hotson, *The Commonwealth and Restoration Stage* (London, 1928), 256–8; Lord Chamberlain 5/141, 100, 141, 307; 7/1,4.

delegated direction of his plays: Hotson, 24–5.

never censored a play: A. F. White, 'The Office of the Revels and Dramatic Censorship during the Restoration Period', *Western Reserve Bulletin*, N. S., 34 (1931), 5–115.

p. 212   Behn's letters to Killigrew: Public Record Office, Chancery Lane, SP 29/170, no. 75; SP 29/251, no. 91; see also SP 29/172, no. 81, SP 29/167, no. 160, SP 29/169, nos. 38, 117, 118.

Covent Garden Drollery: O'Donnell, 212–17, see p. 191 and n.

Jeffrey Boys: see p. 190 and n.

p. 213   Killigrew's promiscuity: see for example the caricature of Killigrew engraved in 1642 by Wenceslas Hollar, BL and reproduced by Abraham Bosse in 1664.

hired wench: Pepys, *Diary*, 24 January 1669, Latham and Matthews, ix, 427.

CHAPTER 8: ROCHESTER'S NIECE

p. 214   A fully documented biography of Anne Wharton, her poems, letters and her play are to be found in *The Surviving Works of Anne Wharton* (Stump Cross, 1995 – forthcoming) with full critical apparatus and bibliography.

For a discussion of the perennial best-seller *Poems by the Right Honourable the E. of R.* (1680, and reprinted every year thereafter until superseded by Tonson's edition in 1691) which contains sixty-one poems, only about half of them thought to be by Rochester, see D. M. Vieth, *Attribution in Restoration Poetry* (New Haven, 1963).

p. 215   the Lees of Ditchley Park: E. K. Chambers, *Sir Henry Lee: an Elizabethan Portrait* (Oxford, 1936) *passim*, British Library MS Harley 5808, ff. 144v–147.

his young widow: Anne Danvers, daughter of Sir John Danvers, the regicide, by his second wife. See F. N. McNamara, *Memoirs of the Danvers Family (of Dauntsey and Culworth)* (London, 1895), 296.

no one expected the baby to survive: Claydon Papers, Margaret Sherard to Sir Ralph Verney, Anne's principal trustee, 19 April 1659.

Anne's christening: the Spelsbury register, *The Genealogist*, xiv, 168.

Lady Lee's will: *The Genealogist*, x, 231.

Lady Rochester's expenditure: the rebuilding of Adderbury is thought to have cost £19,000, which is one reason why Lady Rochester continued to live there after her son's marriage. In letters to Sir Ralph Verney (Claydon Papers) Cary frequently lamented her failure even to service her debts at the same time as she insisted on living 'as the top of all'.

the conveying of Cornbury and grant of Danvers estates to the Lee girls: *Calendar of State Papers Domestic, 1661–1662*, 119. See also *Wiltshire, The Topographical Collections of John Aubrey, F. R. S.,* corr. and ed. J. E. Jackson (Devizes, 1862), 226, 297.

The Countess of Rochester's appointment at court: *Angliae Notitia* (London, 1669), 320.

p. 216 A considerable number of letters written by the Countess of Rochester are to be found among the papers of Sir Ralph Verney at Claydon House, among the British Library MSS, at the Public Record Office in Chancery Lane and in the Library of the University of Rochester NY.

Anne's poor penmanship can be seen in autograph letters among the Claydon Papers, British Library MS Add. 4, 162 and the MSS of the Marquis of Lonsdale, now at the Record Office in Carlisle.

Anne Wharton's elegy on her uncle was first published in part as 'Elegy on the Earl of Rochester' in *Poems by Several Hands and on Several Occasions* collected by N[ahum] Tate (1685) and in full as 'Elegy upon the Earl of Rochester' in *Examen Miscellaneum* (1702).

Rochester and his wife penning poems: *Kissing the Rod: An Anthology of Seventeenth-Century Women's Verse*, ed. G. Greer, S. Hastings, J. Medoff and M. Sansone (London, 1988), 230–32.

Rochester poems at Nottingham: University Library, Nottingham, Portland MS PwV. 31, 40, 42, 43, 46, 509, 513.

Rochester's marriage: J. H. Wilson, 'Rochester's Marriage', *Review of English Studies* xix (1943), 399–403.

p. 217 the bedding of the Rochesters: Claydon Papers, Margaret Elmes to Sir Ralph Verney, 31 January 1667.

'How hardly I concealed my tears': first published as 'A Song. By Mrs.

Wharton.' in *A Collection of Poems by Several Hands. Most of them written by Persons of Eminent Quality* (1693).

Rochester: 'An age in her embraces past', Walker, 29; 'Phyllis be gentler', Walker 36; 'By all love's soft yet mighty powers', Walker, 45.

p. 218   'The perfect joy of being well-deceived': Rochester, *A Letter from Artemiza in the Town to Chloe in the Country*, Walker, 86, l. 115.

Thomas Wharton: J. Carswell, *The Old Cause: Three Biographical Studies in Whiggism* (London, 1954); C. Robbins, *The Earl of Wharton and Whig Party Politics 1679–1715* (Lewiston NY, 1991).

Goodwin Wharton, 'Autobiography', British Library Additional MSS 26, 006, 308 (Goodwin's pagination).

Memoirs of Grammont: Anthony Hamilton, *Memoirs of the Comte de Grammont*, trans. P. Quennell (London, 1930), 222–3, 237, 238–9, 241.

Rochester, 'A Song of a Young Lady': Walker, 32.

p. 220   A satirist of 1690: *Poems on Affairs of State* (London, 1704), 'The Converts', ll, 11–15, 19–20.

Anne's first serious illness: Claydon Papers, 30 March 1670, John Cary to Sir Ralph Verney.

Wharton unfaithful: Wharton is known to have had a liaison with Jane Dering, daughter of Katherine Philips's friend, Sir Edward Dering; the Countess of Rochester claimed in letters written after Anne's death that he kept 'a woman' and had children by her. Entries in the Winchendon stud book are thought to relate to his human progeny. His indifference to Anne was certainly well-known long before she died.

p. 221   'The poet's talent is to love and rail': Anne Wharton, 'Love's Martyr', iii, i, 10.

religion went out the door: Robert Bennett reported to Anne's father-in-law Lord Wharton on 1 June 1674 that 'Religion is gone from Winchingdon already. . . they have brought the court into the country' (Bodleian Library MS Rawl. lett. 51, f. 96).

'My Fate': no MS version of this poem is known. It was first printed in the first edition of *A Collection of Poems by Several Hands. Most of them written by Persons of Eminent Quality* (1693) and dropped from subsequent printings.

p. 222   'To the Lady Anne Coke' survives only in a MS collection of Anne Wharton's poems in the possession of the Earl of Leicester at Holkham. Though the Holkham connection would suggest that the MS came directly from Anne to her friend, other aspects of the MS make this unlikely. Lady Anne, daughter of the Lord Treasurer, Thomas Osborne, Earl of Danby was privately married to Robert Coke of Holkham in Norfolk in November 1674. The story that she had been found in bed with Monmouth is to be found in newsletters of early September 1675, e.g. letters of John Verney and William Fall to Sir Ralph Verney, 9 September 1675 (Claydon Papers). On 6 September Matthew Smallwood had begged Lord Danby to persuade his daughter to try the Holkham air as a counteractive to scandalous report (British Library MS Egerton 3385B, f. 8). Danby's biographer A. S. Browning has little to say about his daughter; the best account of her marriage is given in Basil Henning, *The House of Commons 1660–1690* (London, 1983), 'Robert Coke'. Some account of Lady Anne's subsequent life is to be found in W. Rye, *The Later History of the Family of Walpole of Norfolk* (Norwich, 1920).

p. 223 'Ah for what crimes': 'Thoughts occasioned by her Retirement in the Country', Holkham MS, ll. 38–46. Mrs Wharton sent the poem to Gilbert Burnet in December 1682. It was printed without attribution and in a largely rewritten version as 'The Retirement' by Charles Gildon in *A New Miscellany of Original Poems* (1701).

Rochester: 'Of Mankind', Walker, 93, ll. 66–71.

atheist conventicle: Gilbert Burnet, *Some Passages of the Life and Death of John Wilmot, Earl of Rochester*, 478.

'Weep drops of blood': 'Elegy on John Earl of Rochester', ll. 7–12.

p. 224 'How should a finite creature': 'Thoughts occasioned by her Retirement in the Country', ll. 53–4, 79–85.

Burnet and Lady Ranelagh: our knowledge of Mrs Wharton's correspondence with Burnet is derived entirely from surviving letters written to her by Burnet, a selection of which were published in *A General Dictionary, Historical and Critical* (London, 1741) under the heading 'Wharton, Anne'; a slightly different selection was published by J. P. Malcolm, who was apparently unaware of the earlier printing, in *Letters of the Reverend James Granger* (London, 1805). In 1815 some of the letters appeared in various numbers of *The Gentleman's Magazine*. All three sources conflate separate letters into single letters and print them out of sequence. The Stump Cross edition of Anne Wharton will reprint them in the correct sequence.

Rochester's *Valentinian* was printed in 1684 'Sodom': attributed to Rochester, and printed several times in the 1680s, this play survives only in MS; see A. S. G. Edwards, 'Libertine Literature in Restoration MSS: Princeton MS AM 14401', *The Book Collector*, 25 (Autumn, 1976), 354–68.

p. 225 'Doubt not, my Ovid': 'Love's Martyr', British Library MS Add. 28693, I, i, 123–6.

'Artemiza': Rochester, *A Letter from Artemiza in the Town to Chloe in the Country*, Walker, 83, ll. 7–11.

'There is an art': 'Love's Martyr', II, i, 22–5.

p. 226 'I nothing can': 'Love's Martyr', II, i, 364–9.

'Sure you are not': 'Love's Martyr', II, i, 548–54.

Behn, 'Ovid to Julia': *Uncollected Verse*, 18–21.

p. 227 Rochester, 'A Very Heroical Epistle': Walker, 112–14; 'My Lord All-pride', Walker, 116–17.

John Grubham Howe: Henning, 'John Grubham Howe'.

'Jack How. . .': John Mountsteven to Henry Sidney, 2 September 1679, *Diary of the Times of Charles II* by the Honourable Henry Sidney, ed. R. W. Blencowe (London, 1843), i, 100.

Rochester and Howe: Bodleian MS Firth c. 15, 146

> How oft has Howe (by Rochester undone,
> Who soothed him first into opinion
> Of being a Wit) been told that he was none?
> But found that art the surest way to glide
> Not into his heart, but his well-shaped backside?
> Not Nobbs's bum more adoration found,
> Though oft 'twas sung; his was more white and round.

The Essay on Satire: Bodleian MS Rawl. poet. 159, f. 112.

An anonymous satire: 'An answer to the Satire on the Court Ladies', Bodleian MS Firth. c. 15, 86.

p. 228 Rochester's translation of *Amores* 2. 9: 'Oh Love, how cold and slow to take my part', Walker, 49.

'Love, the most generous passion. . .': *A Letter from Artemiza in the Town to Chloe in the Country*, Walker, 84, ll. 40–49.

p.229 'Almighty love': 'Love's Martyr', IV, i, 192–201.

Ben Jonson, *Poetaster*: *The Poetaster: Or, his Arraignment* (London, 1601).

Nathaniel Lee: *Gloriana: or the Court of Augustus Caesar* was produced at the Theatre Royal on 29 January 1676; Wharton's subtitle, 'Wit above crowns', is quoted from II. i. 289–90.

p. 230 'His anger': Wharton, 'To Doctor Burnet upon his Retirement', ll. 30–47.

Rochester on Charles II: Walker, 74 , 122.

The Countess of Rochester and the Duchess of Cleveland: the chief evidence for this is the marriage arranged between the king's favourite child by the Duchess, Charlotte Fitzroy, and the Countess's grandson, Sir Edward Henry Lee, created Earl of Lichfield.

The king's letter: 14 July 1673, quoted by E. Corbett, *A History of Spelsbury including Dean, Taston, Fulwell and Ditchley* (Banbury, 1962), 180. See also Claydon Papers, Lady Gardiner to Sir Ralph Verney, 8 September 1673.

affair with Jack Howe: Goodwin Wharton, 'Autobiography', 308.

a long episode of seizures: Claydon Papers, John Cary to Sir Ralph Verney, 29 April, 11 May, and undated (May) 1680.

p. 231 sent to her uncle: Claydon Papers, John Cary to Sir Ralph Verney, 15 June 1680.

Wharton's elegy: 'Elegy on John Earl of Rochester', ll. 39–43, 54–65, 78–80.

Aphra Behn's elegy: 'On the Death of the late Earl of Rochester', published in her *Miscellany* (1685), Summers, vi, 368–9. Mrs Wharton responded with 'To Mrs A. Behn on what she writ of the Earl of Rochester', published in *A Collection of Poems by Several Hands. Most of them written by Persons of Eminent Quality* (1693). Mrs Behn continued the interchange with 'To Mrs W. On her Excellent Verses (Writ in Praise of some I had made on the Earl of Rochester). Written in a fit of Sickness', which she published in her *Poems on Several Occasions with a Voyage to the Isle of Love* (London, 1684) Summers, vi, 171–3.

Rochester on Isaiah 53: Burnet, *Some Passages in the Life and Death of John Wilmot Earl of Rochester*, 141–2:

> he said to me that as he heard it read, he felt an inward force upon him, which did so enlighten his mind and convince him, that he could resist it no longer: for the words had an authority, which did shoot like rays or beams in his mind; so that he was not only convinced by the reasonings he had about it which satisfied his understanding, but by a power which did so effectually constrain him, that he did ever after as firmly believe in his Saviour, as if he had seen him in the clouds.

p. 232 'Who hath believed': 'A paraphrase on the 53 of Isaiah', 1–4: this poem was never published and can be found only in the Holkham MS.

abscess in her throat: John Cary to Sir Ralph Verney, 25 November and 1 December 1680, Claydon Papers.

storminess of the crossing: Wharton, 'On the Storm between Gravesend and Dieppe; made at that Time', Holkham MS; another copy is to be found among the Waller Family Papers. The poem was printed in *A Collection of Poems by Several Hands. Most of them written by Persons of Eminent Quality* (1693).

Thomas returned: William Taylor to Lord Wharton, 19 March 1681, Bodleian Library MS Rawl. lett. 53, f. 348.

'Forgive me': Anne Wharton to Thomas Wharton, 22 March 1681, British Library MS Add. 4162, f. 232. This letter and the next were published in *A General Dictionary* (1741).

p. 233   'Though I never': Anne Wharton to Thomas Wharton, 29 March 1681, British Library MS Add. 4162, f. 234.

Her next surviving letter: Anne Wharton to Thomas Wharton, 4 April 1681: Lonsdale MSS, Cumbria Record Office, Carlisle.

'I have been': Anne Wharton to Thomas Wharton, 20 April 1681, Lonsdale MSS, Cumbria Record Office, Carlisle.

p. 234   'To begin': Anne Wharton to Thomas Wharton, 1 May 1681, Lonsdale MSS, Cumbria Record Office, Carlisle.

'My grandmother': Anne Wharton to Thomas Wharton, 14 May 1681, Lonsdale MSS, Cumbria Record Office, Carlisle.

wanted to stay in France: Anne Wharton to Thomas Wharton, [June 1681], Lonsdale MSS, Cumbria Record Office, Carlisle.

p. 235   'That wondrous wit': Wharton, 'Elegy on Charles, Earl of Rochester', Holkham MS, ll. 31–4.

Anne's invitation to Burnet: Burnet's first letter dated 14 July 1682 promises that he will 'be hereafter governed by the rules' she set him and deal with the subjects she defined.

Burnet's remonstrations: e.g. the letter begun on 5 December and finished on 8 December 1682 makes clear that Burnet had been advising cancellation of various 'sharp and angry' passages and Mrs Wharton refusing to comply. In his letter of 9 January, he announced that he had struck out of his copy of 'Thoughts of Retirement' two lines about the afterlife:

> Of what we there may do we here may boast,
> But there for aught we know all thought is lost.

'The use of knowledge': Wharton, 'The Despair', ll. 1–27.

p. 236   Rochester, 'Of Mankind', Walker, 94, ll. 13–19, 25–8.

p. 237   Burnet on the merits of *An Essay upon Poetry*: letter of 10 December 1682.

p. 238   *An Essay upon Poetry* (first published as anonymous pamphlet in late 1682), 6.

Burnet responded: letter of 19 December 1682.

Waller: Burnet's letter of 28 December 1682.

Mulgrave revealed as author: Burnet's letter of 9 January 1683.

Mulgrave and Rochester took their seats in the House of Lords on the same day and were rivals ever after. In November 1669 Mulgrave challenged Rochester but the duel, for reasons that remain unclear, was never fought. Mulgrave alleged cowardice, and repeated the allegation long after Rochester was dead. Rochester was antagonized not only by Mulgrave's arrogance but by the coldness with which he seduced the most beautiful women at court for the mere pleasure of humiliating them. Mulgrave had been an effective soldier, a successful courtier and was fast becoming a virtuoso politician, turning every turn of state affairs to his own advantage, while Rochester careered from disaster to disaster. In 1674 when Mulgrave challenged Rochester's friend, Henry Savile, Rochester acted as second. Rochester attacked Mulgrave in 'An Epistolary Essay from M. G. to O. B.' (Walker, 107–9); 'A Very Heroical Epistle in answer to Ephelia' (Walker, 112–14) and 'My Lord All-pride' (Walker, 116–17); Mulgrave revenged himself by vituperative lines in his 'Essay on Satire' and later in *An Essay upon Poetry*.

revival of *Valentinian*: Van Lennep, i, 325–6.

John Howe to Mrs Wharton: no MS of this poem is known. It was published in *Examen Miscellaneum* (London, 1702) after Mrs Wharton's elegy as 'On the forgoing Elegy' (19–20).

Behn, 'Prologue spoken by Mrs Cook': Summers, vi, 401–2.

p. 240   'He taught thee': William Wharton, 'A Familiar Answer to a late familiar Epistle Humbly addrest to the best of poets alias the worst', Bodleian Library MS Firth c. 16, 232.

'Will, a pert youth': [Charles Sackville, Earl of Dorset?] 'The Duel', ll. 23–6.

'To you, this generous task': 'Mrs Wharton to Mr Wolseley. On his Preface to Valentinian', printed by Aphra Behn among the poems appended to *Lycidus, or the Lover in Fashion* (London, 1688). A fair copy may be seen in the Bodleian Library (MS Rawl. poet. 159) and one leaf of a similar copy is preserved in the Folger Library (MS x d 383).

Wolseley replied: see MSS of Mrs Wharton's poem and also University of Nottingham Portland MS PwV 516, and Behn's *Lycidus*.

p. 241   'While soaring high': Wolseley, 'To Mrs Wharton', ll. 1–14, 69–76, 90–99.

p. 242   'Jack Howe': 'Letter to Julian', British Library MSS Harl. 7317, 115; 7319, 339, published in *Poems on Affairs of State* (London, 1705), 338.

p. 243   Wolseley's duel with Wharton: reported in the Gaol Delivery Records, 9 December 1687, Middlesex County Records, ed. J. C. Jeaffreson (London, 1892), iv, 320.

That Anne had broken the entail and given her whole estate bar Hester Barry's £3,000 to her faithless husband became known at her funeral (Claydon Papers, Sir Ralph Verney to John Verney, 15 November 1685). See also John Cary to Lord Lichfield, Buckinghamshire Record Office, Dillon Papers, XVIII, f. 3. The letters of the Countess of Rochester preserved at the University of Rochester NY deal with her fruitless attempts to persuade the Earl of Lichfield and Lord Norries to contest Anne's will. The clearest testimony of the identity of Hester Barry and that she was dead by 1689 is to be found in a vicious lampoon addressed by the player William Mountfort 'To the Most Virtuous and Most Devoted Overkind Notorious Madam Barry' (Ohio State University MS 'A Choyce Collection', 303–5; cf. Princeton MS Restoration 2).

CHAPTER 9: WORDSWORTH AND WINCHILSEA

p. 245   R. A. Brower: 'Lady Winchilsea and the Poetic Tradition of the Seventeenth Century,' *Studies in Philology*, 42 (1945), 62.

'Cherries': Anne Finch, Countess of Winchilsea, 'The Petition for an Absolute retreat', *The Poems of Anne Countess of Winchilsea*, ed. Myra Reynolds (Chicago, 1903), 70, ll. 42–7.

p. 246   'No intruders': Reynolds, 69, ll. 8–9, 12–21.

'Give me there': Reynolds, 72, ll. 104–13.

p. 247   'Good Heav'n': Reynolds, 14.

p. 248   scholars: e.g., Brower, 62–3, 67; Thomas Seccombe, 'Lesser Verse Writers', *The Cambridge History of English Literature*, ed. A. W. Ward and A. R. Waller (New York, 1913), ix, 189; C. A. Moore, *Backgrounds of English Literature, 1700–1760* (Minneapolis, 1953), 74; John F. Sena, 'Melancholy in Anne Finch and Elizabeth Carter: The Ambivalence of an Idea', *Yearbook of English Studies*, 1 (1971), 115.

William Wordsworth: 'Essay, Supplementary to the Preface', *The Prose Works of William Wordsworth*, ed. W. J. B. Owen and Jane Worthington Seymour (Oxford, 1974), iii, 73.

Harold Littledale, ed.: *Poems and Extracts chosen by William Wordsworth for an Album Presented to Lady Mary Lowther Christmas, 1819* (London, 1905), Introduction, ix.

Wordsworth on Dryden: *The Early Letters of William and Dorothy Wordsworth (1787–1805)*, ed. Ernest de Selincourt (Oxford, 1935), 541.

p. 249 'In the Muses' paths': *Poems and Extracts*, 2.

Seccombe: 189.

'Now a Dead Sea': Reynolds, ll. 6–7, 9–10, 40–43, 50–55, 61–63, 74–79.

'The most celebrated': *The Letters of William and Dorothy Wordsworth: The Later Years*, ed. Ernest de Selincourt (Oxford, 1939) i, 475.

'Her style in rhyme': *Later Letters*, i, 478.

p. 253 *Poems by Eminent Ladies*: ed. George Colman and Bonnell Thornton (London, 1755), ii, 287–316.

'British poetesses': *Later Letters*, i, 473.

'of a serious cast': *Poems by Eminent Ladies*, ii, 146.

p. 254 Pope's 'Impromptu': *The Poems of Alexander Pope*, ed. Norman Ault and John Butt (New Haven, 1954), vi, 121.

Swift, Delany and Constantia Grierson: *The Correspondence of Jonathan Swift*, ed. Harold Williams (Oxford, 1965), iv, 192n.

the same advice: *Later Letters*, i, 476.

p. 255 'When scattered glow-worms': Finch, 'A Nocturnal Reverie', Reynolds, 269, ll. 17–20.

p. 256 'Their short-lived jubilee': Finch, 'A Nocturnal Reverie', Reynolds, 270, ll. 37–46.

Poems and Extracts chosen by William Wordsworth, 74–5.

p. 257 'Style and versification': *Later Letters*, i, 478.

CHAPTER 10: SUCCESS AND THE SINGLE POET

p. 260 'We wish very much': Dorothy Wordsworth to Lady Beaumont, 4 May 1805, *The Early Letters of William and Dorothy Wordsworth*, ed. E. de Selincourt (Oxford, 1935), 589.

p. 261   'luckless, transient Sappho': M. Sadleir, *Bulwer: A Panorama. Edward and Rosina 1803–1836* (London, 1931).

kittenish charm: S. C. Hall, *A Book of Memories of the Great Men and Women of the Age from Personal Acquaintance* (London, 1871), 270.

p. 262   Hannah More: see p. xxii and n.

Helen Maria Williams: see p. 57 and n.

Eleanor Anne Franklin (1797?–1825), born Porden, published her first volume of poetry, *The Veils, Or the Triumph of Constancy, a Poem in Six Books* in 1815. After writing a poem on the Arctic expedition, she met the explorer John Franklin whom she married in 1823, after she had published *Coeur de Lion, an Epic Poem in 16 Cantos*. After the birth of her daughter in 1824, her health failed (*DNB*).

Anna Laetitia Barbauld: see p. xix and n.

Hester Lynch Salusbury, Johnson's Mrs Thrale, later Mrs Piozzi (1741–1821), published verse before her first marriage; thereafter she underwent childbirth twelve times; four of her babies survived. Even so her house at Streatham Park was frequented by the most significant literary figures of the day. After her second marriage she went to Italy where she worked seriously on her poetry and contributed to *The Florence Miscellany* (*DNB, Eighteenth-Century Women Poets: An Oxford Anthology*, ed. R. Lonsdale, Oxford, 1989, 389–90).

Ann Radcliffe (1764–1823) included verse in her Gothic novels and after 1802 concentrated on writing poetry published posthumously as volumes iii and iv of her novel *Gaston de Blondeville* in 1826 (Lonsdale, 448–50).

Amelia Opie (1769–1853) born Alderson, as a girl in Norwich sang ballads of her own composition and gave dramatic recitations. Her childhood verse appeared in newspapers and magazines. In London she became a member of the radical circle that included Godwin and Mary Wollstonecraft. Her one novel before her marriage to painter John Opie in 1798 was not a success; her next, *Father and Daughter*, printed with a selection of poems, was to go through more than eleven editions. Mrs Opie became a much celebrated figure in literary circles; a volume of poems published in 1802 was much quoted and reprinted six times. After her husband's death she returned to Norwich where in 1825 she was received into the Society of Friends and gave up writing novels. Her last publication, *Lays for the Dead*, appeared in 1833 (*DNB*).

Joanna Baillie: see p. xix and n.

Margaret Holford (1778–1852) born Wrench: was principally a novelist. Her metrical romance, *Wallace, or the Fight of Falkirk* (London, 1809), was followed by *Poems* (1811), and *The Past &c* (1819) (*DNB* as 'Margaret Hodson').

Mary Russell Mitford (1787–1855): Mitford is known today for her masterpiece, *Our Village*, but she also produced besides essays and plays, *Miscellaneous Poems* (1810), *Christina, the Maid of the South Seas* (1811) and *Narrative Poems in the Female Character* (1813) (*DNB*).

Mary Howitt: see p. xxii and n.

Caroline Anne Bowles (1786–1854) had considerable success with *Ellen Fitzarthur, a Metrical Tale* (1820), *The Widow's Tale with other Poems* (1822), *Tales of the Factories* (1823) and *Solitary Hours* (1826). She began corresponding with Southey in 1819 and married him twenty years later, when he was on the verge of total senility. When he died in 1843 she returned to her cottage near the New Forest. Her greatest achievement is her long poem, *The Birthday* (1836) (*DNB* entry on Southey).

Elizabeth Barrett Browning: see pp. 61–4, 95–100, 394–401 and n.

Felicia Hemans: see pp. 59–61, 91–4 and n.

Maria Abdy (d. 1867): the daughter of Richard Smith by a sister of James and Horace Smith and wife of the Rev. Channing Abdy. She contributed verse to the *New Monthly Magazine* and *Metropolitan Magazine* and the annuals and between 1830 and 1862 printed eight collections of poems for private circulation (*DNB*).

p. 264 Angria: F. E. Ratchford, *The Brontës' Web of Childhood* (New York, 1941). See also *The Hand of the Arch-Sinner: Two Angrian Chronicles of Branwell Brontë* (Oxford, 1993).

Mrs Norton: the Honourable Caroline Norton: see p. xx and n.

Lady Caroline Lamb (1785–1828): daughter of the Earl of Bessborough, married in 1805 to the Honourable William Lamb, later Lord Melbourne; infatuated with Byron she behaved so indiscreetly that he terminated their liaison in 1813, but not in time to prevent a legal separation. Lady Caroline meanwhile portrayed Byron in her novel *Glenarvon* and went on to write several novels with reasonable success (*DNB*).

p. 265 Fuseli: Johann Heinrich Füssli (1741–1825), *DNB*.

Maclise: Daniel Maclise (1806–70); W. Justin Driscoll, *Memoir of Daniel Maclise* (London, 1871); *Daniel Maclise 1806–70* (Exhibition Catalogue, London, 1972).

Richard Dadd (1817–86): P. Allderidge, *The Late Richard Dadd* (London, 1974); D. Greysmith, *Richard Dadd, The Rock and the Castle of Seclusion* (London, 1973).

Wollstonecraft and Godwin's *Memoir*: C. Tomalin, *The Life and Death of Mary Wollstonecraft* (London, 1974), 233–4.

Olympe de Gouges: Oliver Blanc, *Olympe de Gouges: une femme de libertés* (Paris, 1989); *Oeuvres*, ed. B. Groult (Paris, 1989); *The Rights of Woman*, trans. V. Stevenson (London, 1989).

Etta Palme von Aedelers (1743–?): see M. Villiers, *Histoire des Clubs de Femmes et des Legions d'Amazones* (*The Bloomsbury Guide to Women's Literature*, ed. C. Buck, London, 1992).

Théroigne de Méricourt: E. Roudinesco, *Théroigne de Méricourt: a melancholic woman during the French Revolution*, trans. M. Thom (London, 1991).

Claire Lacombe: (1765–?): known as 'Rose', a famous actress and revolutionary, see L. Lacour, 'Rose Lacombe', *Révue Hébdomadaire*, Paris, October 1899, 450, 28a (*International Dictionary of Women's Biography*).

p. 266   Anna Doyle Wheeler: *Lord Beaconsfield's Letters 1830–1852*, ed. R. Disraeli (London, 1887), 71, 73.

L. E. L.'s critical reception: W. S. Ward, comp., *Literary Reviews in British Periodicals 1821–1826: A Bibliography* (New York and London, 131).

p. 267   Edward Lytton Bulwer-Lytton (1803–1873): *The New Monthly Magazine*, 1831, No. 32, 346, quoted by S. Laman Blanchard, *Life and Literary Remains of L. E. L.* (London, 1841), i, 32–33. Blanchard, who was assisted by the poet's brother, the Rev. Whittingdon Landon, is the unacknowledged source of most of the later memoirs.

William Jerdan (1782–1869): *An Autobiography* (London, 1852–3), iii, 174–5.

p. 268   H. F. Chorley: *Autobiography, Memoir and Letters* (London, 1873), i, 107–8.

p. 269   'saying things for "effect"': Hall, 266.

p. 270   L. E. L. on difficulties with *The Improvisatrice*: Alaric Watts, *Miscellaneous Correspondence*, 21, undated letter (of 1824) from L. E. L. to Watts cf. Blanchard, i, 41–2.

p. 271   critical reception of *The Improvisatrice*: Ward, 131.

p. 272   'I like to show...': letter from L. E. L. to Alaric Watts, A. A. Watts, *A Narrative of His Life* (London, 1884), ii, 21.

p. 279   Felicia Hemans, 'Properzia Rossi': *Records of Woman* (London, 1828).

Ouida : pseudonym of Marie Louise de la Ramée (1839–1908), writer of sensational romances. See Y. Ffrench, *Ouida: a study in Ostentation,* and E. Bigland, *The Passionate Victorian.*

Elizabeth Barrett Browning on the struggles of female genius: *Aurora Leigh, passim.*

Mary Russell Mitford (1787–1855): *Poems on the Female Character,* (London, 1813); see also Maria Abdy: 'The Destiny of Genius' in E. A. Sharp, *Women Poets of the Victorian Era.*

p. 281   'If she came home. . .': Blanchard, i, 6–7; 'Grace Wharton' (K. Thomson and J. C. Thomson), *Queens of Society* (London, 1860), 194–5.

'Rollins': Blanchard, i, 9, 10.

'At so early': Blanchard, i, 10.

p. 282   'I have known': L. E. L., 'Francis Beaumont', *Traits and Trials of Early Life,* 187–280.

L. E. L. to Katherine Thomson, Blanchard, i, 56.

'I petitioned': Blanchard, i, 13.

p. 283   'Oh, don't speak': Blanchard, i, 17–18.

'On her days': Blanchard, i, 18.

p. 284   L. E. L., 'The History of a Child', *Traits and Trials of Early Life,* 292, 301–3.

'The embarrassed state': L. E. L. to Mrs Hall, Hall, 267.

p. 286   '. . . it was properly': L. E. L. to Katherine Thomson, Blanchard, i, 49.

reception of *The Troubadour*: Ward, 131–2.

p. 289   'Jerdan has been': *The Wasp A literary salute containing an expose of the most notorious literary or theatrical Quacks of the day* (London 1826), No. 2.

L. E. L. to Rosina Doyle Wheeler (later Lady Lytton), Blanchard, 47–51; as one letter is dated 'about 1825', another, from London, '13 October, 1825' and another, from Aberford, 'October, 1825', the dating can hardly be considered secure.

p. 290   'Thus it befell. . .': Jerdan, *Autobiography,* iii, 170.

'(alias Letitia Languish)': *The Wasp,* No. 3.

'Consultations were held': 'Wharton', i, 205.

L. E. L. to Mrs Thomson: Blanchard, i, 55–7; cf. 'Wharton', 207–8.

p. 292   No tensions: 'Wharton', i, 218.

'I first saw': Hall, 269, quoting his wife, the writer Anna Maria Hall.

p. 293 'After the manner': *Letters of Thomas Hood*, ed. P. F. Morgan (Edinburgh, 1973), 232.

'A most thoughtless girl': Mary Howitt, *An Autobiography* (London, 1889), 187; Howitt thought that L. E. L. was Jerdan's ward.

Bulwer Lytton: *The Life, Letters and Literary Remains of Edward Bulwer, Lord Lytton*, 48, 128.

p. 294 'When I first': Hall, 272, quoting Mrs Hall.

Rosina Wheeler: L. Devey, *The Life of Rosina, Lady Lytton, with numerous extracts from her MS Autobiography and other original Documents* (London, 1887), 41.

p. 295 'The drawing-room': 'Wharton', i, 205.

'who on the strength': Hall, 268, quoting Mrs Hall.

p. 296 Miss Spence: Elizabeth Isabella Spence (1768–1832), author of many novels besides *Sketches of the present Manners, Customs and Scenery of Scotland* (London, 1811) here referred to (*DNB*).

Elizabeth Ogilvy Benger (1778–1827) was sent to a boys' school by her father so that she might learn Latin; her modest London lodgings were the scene of animated literary gatherings (*DNB*).

'Fortunately': Devey, 47.

'I do not feel': Sadleir, 84–5.

p. 297 'Perhaps in not returning': 'Wharton', i, 205. Katherine Thomson, one of the writers under this pseudonym, wrote to Bulwer Lytton alleging that the poet's mother believed Jerdan to be the 'source' of their separation. Letter quoted by J. Burch, in her unpublished Ph.D. dissertation, 'The Literary Life of L. E. L.' (Cambridge University Library), 26.

p. 298 'Her mother, I never saw. . .': 'Wharton', i, 206.

'L. E. L. established': 'Wharton' i, 279.

p. 300 L. E. L. attachment: Sadleir, Appendix ii, 414–16.

Mary Greene: Sadleir, 139.

William Maginn (1793–1842): *DNB*, Miriam M. Thrall, *Rebellious Fraser's: Nol York's Magazine in the Days of Maginn, Thackeray and Carlyle* (New York, 1934) 193–8.

p. 301 'Here, early to bed': Sadleir, 421.

'If she was unrefined. . .': Chorley, i, 246.

p. 302 'Undoubtedly. . .': Hall, 275.

'Certain it is. . .': Edward Kenealy, 'Our Portrait Gallery No. xxxix, William Maginn, LL. D.', *Dublin University Magazine*, xxiii, 74 (January, 1844).

p. 303 K. Thomson: *Recollections of Literary Characters and Celebrated Places* (London, 1854), ii, 81–2.

'In the middle twenties. . .': Sadleir, Appendix iv, 422–6.

p. 304 Norton–Melbourne scandal: see p. xx and n.

Maclise: see note to p. 265, and Driscoll, 57.

p. 305 'Maclise's Portrait Gallery': *A Gallery of Illustrious Literary Characters 1830–1838 Drawn by Daniel Maclise R. A. and accompanied by Notices chiefly written by the late William Maginn* (London, 1873).

p. 306 'ignoble little snub': according to Rosina, Lady Lytton. See Devey, 48.

Wollstonecraft's letters to Fuseli: Tomalin, 90, 112, 118.

p. 307 'Preface', *The Venetian Bracelet, the Lost Pleiad, A History of the Lyre and other poems* (London, 1829), vi–viii.

p. 310 'Was she to go on. . .': Blanchard, i, 276.

p. 311 'The syntax is. . .': Sadleir, 149.

pilloried together: e. g. 'Literary Dialogues No. 1', *The Age*, 25 December 1831, quoted by Sadleir, Appendix ii.

p. 312 'L. E. L. in her *Romance*': William Bates, *The Maclise Portrait Gallery, or Illustrious Literary Characters with Memoirs* (London, 1883), 8.

'I can only say': 'Note', *Romance and Reality* (London, 1831), Sig. [A4–A4ᵛ].

Thackeray and the Annuals: Thackeray reviewed the Annuals for many years for *Fraser's Magazine*: the present author has been unable to verify this precise attribution.

p. 313 'As years went on': Chorley, i, 252.

p. 314 'Walter Maynard': *Ethel Churchill, or, The Two Brides* (London, 1837), i, 156–66; ii, 9–26, 68–9, 150–66; iii, 98–117, 104, 284–322.

'I cannot help'. . .: *Ethel Churchill*, ii, 150–52

p. 316 'In her own little home. . .': Thomson, 84.

p. 317 L. E. L. on proposals 'much talked of but never seen': Devey, 145, Blanchard, i, 50–51.

Rosina Lytton: *Unpublished Letters of Lady Lytton to A. E. Chalon*, ed. S. M. Ellis (London, 1914), 128.

p. 318 Mrs Thomson on John Forster: Thomson, 86–7.

Forster satisfied: Blanchard, i, 129.

p. 319 L. E. L. to John Forster: Blanchard, i, 130–31.

p. 320 L. E. L. to Bulwer Lytton: Sadleir, 425–6.

p. 321 'Called on Forster': *The Diaries of William Charles Macready 1833–1851*, ed. W. Toynbee (London, 1912), i, 262.

p. 322 'You are quite right': Hall, 276.

p. 324 'She then informed me': Berkeley, 68.

p. 325 Grantley Berkeley: The Hon. George Charles Grantley Fitzhardinge Berkeley, *My Life and Recollections* (London, 1865), 66. See also C. Kirby, *The English Country Gentleman: A Study of Nineteenth-Century Types* (London, [1937]).

'All I was enabled': Berkeley.

p. 327 'Mr Grantley Berkeley's statements': Hall, 277.

p. 328 'After the deed': 'Wharton', i, 216.

p. 329 'He had rested': Chorley, i, 253.

p. 330 G. E. Metcalfe, *Maclean of the Gold Coast: The Life and Times of George Maclean, 1801–1847* (London, 1962), 10.

p. 332 'George Maclean': Metcalfe, v–vi.

p. 333 'quelling an insurrection': Thomson, 89.

'When very young. . .': Blanchard, i, 135.

'In her enthusiasm': 'Wharton', i, 219.

p. 335 Mrs Enfield: D. E. Enfield, *L. E. L.: A Mystery of the Thirties* (London, 1928).

'He was a grave': 'Wharton', i, 220.

p. 337 'Everybody makes': Metcalfe, 212.

p. 339 'Since I last': Metcalfe, 213.

p. 340 'At a time': Metcalfe, 238.

'Now after all': Metcalfe, 213.

p. 343 '. . . it was all': Harriet Martineau, *Autobiography* (Boston, 1877), i, 318–19.

p. 345 'The wedding was': 'Wharton', i, 222.

'In fact my marriage': Metcalfe, 215.

p. 346 'The gay': 'Wharton', i, 223.

p. 347 'The last time': Hall, 277–8.

p. 349 4 July: Blanchard, i, 179.

Mrs Bailey: 'Wharton', i, 225.

p. 350 'The Castle': L. E. L. to Mrs Hall: Hall, 279. L. E. L. wrote what was substantially the same letter to various recipients.

p. 352 L. E. L. to Whittingdon Landon, 27 September 1838: Blanchard, i, 206.

p. 354 'We dare not': Blanchard, i, 266.

p. 357 'afterwards poor Blanchard': Toynbee, i, 486. Blanchard, who was evidently convinced of L. E. L.'s suicide despite his fudging of the issue in *The Life and Literary Remains*, was to cut his own throat seven years later.

'The papers': Blanchard, i, 239.

p. 358 'The Secretary of State': Blanchard, i, 242.

CHAPTER 11: THE PERVERSITY OF CHRISTINA ROSSETTI

p. 359 leader of pre-Raphaelites: W. T. Going, '*Goblin Market* and the Pre-Raphaelite Brotherhood', *Pre-Raphaelite Review*, 3, 1979, No. 1. C. Murciaux, 'Christina Rossetti: La Vierge Sage des Préraphaélites', *Revue de Paris*, December 1964, lxxii.

a poet important for feminists: L. Palazzo 'Christina Rossetti: two forgotten sketches', *Notes and Queries*, 37, 1990 No. 1; I. Armstrong, 'Christina Rossetti: diary of a feminist reading', *Women Reading Women's Writing*, ed. S. E. Campbell; 'Of Mothers and merchants: female economics in Christina Rossetti's *Goblin Market*', Roe (Brighton, 1987); *Victorian Studies*, 3 (1990), No. 3; M. Sacian, 'Christina Rossetti's *Goblin Market* and feminist literary criticism' (*PRR* 1979).

considered herself a religious poet: L. M. Packer, *Christina Rossetti* (Cambridge, 1963), 353. See also L. M. Packer, 'Swinburne and Christina

Rossetti: Atheist and Anglican', *University of Toronto Quarterly*, 33 (October, 1963).

verdict of history: not shared by L. Stevenson, *The Pre-Raphaelite Poets* (Berkeley 1972), 118: 'In the religious poems the fervour of her worship and the agony of her supplications for divine mercy have seldom been rivalled by an English poet, and certainly never by a woman. They merit comparison with those of Donne, Crashaw and Herbert . . .' See also D. Rosenblum, *Christina Rossetti: the poetry of endurance* (Chicago, 1986).

'On the flyleaf': Frances Rossetti, quoted by W. M. Rossetti, *The Poetical Works of Christina Rossetti* (London, 1908), 464.

p. 360   *The Complete Poems of Christina Rossetti: A Variorum Edition*, ed. Rebecca M. Crump (Baton Rouge and London, 1979–90), iii, 515: Rossetti's first notebook is among the manuscripts owned by the British Library.

The Sacred Harp as a poetic sampler: G. Battiscombe, *Christina Rossetti: A Divided Life* (London, 1981), 22.

W. M. Rossetti: lii–liii.

'On the edge of the world I lie, I lie': Margaret Oliphant (1828–97, *DNB*) is supposed to have dictated these verses on her deathbed according to Mrs Harry Coghill, *Autobiography and Letters of Mrs Margaret Oliphant* (Edinburgh and London, 1899), 438. An accidental corruption has been emended by the present author.

p. 361   Dante: A. A. De Vitis, '*Goblin Market*: Fairy Tale and Reality' (*JPC* 1968).

John Donne, Holy Sonnet xiv.

'E'en so we met': Francis Quarles: *Emblemes*, Book 5, iii, 'My beloved is mine and I am his; He feedeth among the lilies', ll. 7–12.

George Herbert: see also J. McGann, 'The Religious poetry of Christina Rossetti', *Critical Inquiry*, 10 (1983); D. D'Amico, 'Reading and rereading George Herbert and Christina Rossetti', *John Donne Journal*, 4 (1985), No. 2.

p. 362   St Teresa of Avila (1515–82): founder of the order of Discalced Carmelites, wrote *El Camino de Perfección*, *El Libro de la Vida* and *El Castillo Interior*, all published after her death.

Richard Crashaw: 'The Flaming Heart upon the Book and Picture of the Seraphicall Saint Teresa', ll. 93–108.

p. 363   'the Eternal Smile': 'Unforgotten', l. 20, Crump, iii, 241.

p. 364   Keats: B. Fass, 'Christina Rossetti and St Agnes Eve', *Victorian Poetry*, 1976.

'ripped up her arm': Packer, 10, citing a newspaper article by the poet's niece, Helen Rossetti Angeli, 5 December 1930.

p. 365 W. M. Rossetti, lviii, 'A Medical Comment on Christina Rossetti', James A. Kohl, *Notes and Queries*, November 1968.

p. 366 Gabriele Rossetti: Packer, 43.

Dante Gabriel's guilt and terror: S. Weintraub, *Four Rossettis: A Victorian Biography* (New York, 1977), 157, 161–3; B. and J. Dobbs, *Dante Gabriel Rossetti, An Alien Victorian* (London, 1977), 171.

'One thing': W. M. Rossetti, lxi.

'Tell me not': 'Hope in Grief', Crump, iii, 132 and 410.

p. 367 Maturin: D. R. D'Amico, 'Christina Rossetti: The Maturin Poems' (*Victorian Poetry*, 1981), suggests that Maturin's novels were influential on her work because she recognized herself in his heroines; 'All of Maturin's novels have at least one passionate, independent woman whose very strength sets her at war with herself and . . . at times with her God'.

'Yes, I loved him': 'Eva', Crump, iii, 78, 390.

p. 368 'For though': 'Fair Margaret', Crump, iii, 84, 393.

p. 369 'My youth': 'Divine and Human Pleading', Crump, iii, 88, 395.

'Will these hands ne'er be clean': Crump, iii, 96, 398.

'The Dead Bride': Crump, iii, 101, 400.

'Zara': Crump, iii, 101, 404.

'The Dream': Crump, iii, 104, 401.

Ellen Moers: *Literary Women: The Great Writers* (London, 1976), 101–5.

p. 370 'The Dying Man to his Betrothed': Crump, iii, 106, 402.

p. 371 'Death's Chill Between': Crump, iii, 15, 350.

'Heart's Chill Between': Crump, iii, 16, 351.

'Repining': Crump, iii, 17, 352.

'Isadora': Crump iii, 137, 411.

'Advent Sunday', published in *Feasts and Fasts*: Crump, ii, 211, 413.

'Whitsun Tuesday', Crump, ii, 234, 421.

'Feast of the Annunciation': Crump, ii, 238, 432.

D. G. Rossetti's picture, 'The Childhood of the Virgin', is in the Tate Gallery.

p. 372 'Ecce Ancilla Domini': begun 1849, not finished until 1853, National Gallery.

'The Lowest Room', ll. 65–8, and ll. 77–81, Crump, i, 200.

Dante Gabriel Rossetti, quoted by W. M. Rossetti, 460–61.

p. 373 'The Lowest Room': Crump, iii, 520; for the revisions of the poem see Crump, i, 301.

p. 374 'The Heart Knoweth its own Bitterness': Christina Rossetti wrote two poems with this title. One, written in 1852, has 34 lines beginning 'Weep yet a while' (Crump, iii, 207, 440), and the other, written in 1857, 56, beginning 'When all the over-work of life' (Crump, iii, 265, 464). The first was published in part in *Verses* (1893) and in full in 1896 and 1904; 16 lines of the second were published in *Verses* (1893) with the title 'Whatsoever is right, that shall ye receive' (Crump, ii, 267, 435).

'How can we say enough': 'The Heart Knoweth its own Bitterness', ll. 9–16, 23–32.

p. 375 'The Heart Knoweth its own Bitterness', ll. 33–56.

p. 376 'The Convent Threshold': Crump, i, 61–5, ll. 6, 3, 30–37, 56–7, 106.

p. 378 'A Pause of Thought': Crump, i, 51.

p. 379 Ford Madox Brown: Packer, 99.

Autograph note dated 7 December 1893, in the copy of *Goblin Market* (1893) preserved in the Iowa State Department of History and Archives, Des Moines, Iowa; Crump, i. 234; emendations to the text: Crump, i, 234–7.

p. 382 Blake: 'The Sick Rose', *Songs of Innocence and Experience* (London, 1794).

fit for children: J. Watson '"They sell not such in any town"': Christina Rossetti's Goblin fruit of fairy tale', *Children's Literature*, 12 (1984).

p. 384 G. L. Goldberg, 'Dante Gabriel Rossetti's "revising hand": his illustrations for Christina Rossetti's poems' (*Victorian Poetry*, 1982).

p. 385 Keats: 'The Eve of St Agnes', stanza xxx.

p. 386 anorexic: the suggestion has been made more than once: see for example P. M. Cohen, 'Christina Rossetti's *Goblin Market*: a paradigm for nineteenth-century anorexia nervosa' *University of Hartford Studies in Literature*, 17 (1985), No. 1.

EPILOGUE

p. 390   Jeni Couzyn: *The Bloodaxe Book of Contemporary Women Poets: Eleven British Writers*, ed. Jeni Couzyn (London, 1985) Introduction, 17.

p. 392   Ingrid Jonker, *Selected Poems*, translated from the Afrikaans by Jack Cope and William Plomer (London, 1968), Preface *passim*, 'Pregnant Woman', 18–19.

Jonker, 29, 51, 'I drift in the Wind'.

p. 393   William Cowper: D. Cecil, *The Stricken Deer: The Life of Cowper* (London, 1929), 59–66.

'Verse, Fame, and Beauty': Keats, 'Why did I laugh tonight?', ll. 13–14.

published in 1848: *Life, Letters, and Literary Remains of John Keats*, ed. Richard Monkton Milnes (London, 1848).

Chatterton: Linda Kelly, *The Marvellous Boy: the Life and Myth of Thomas Chatterton* (London, 1971); A. Alvarez, *The Savage God: A Study of Suicide* (London, 1971?).

p. 394   'I love your verses with all my heart. . .': *Robert Browning and Elizabeth Barrett, The Courtship Correspondence*, ed. D. Karlin (Oxford, 1981), 1.

'That was a strange, heavy crown. . .': quoted in J. Richardson, *The Brownings: a biography compiled from contemporary sources* (London, 1986), 116–7; see also F. D. Thomas, *Robert Browning: A Life within a Life*.

self-starvation and opiate abuse: Peter Dally, *Elizabeth Barrett Browning: A Psychological Portrait* (London, 1989), 85–7, 135, 144, 174–5.

p. 395   'never cried out once. . .': Dally, 139.

'a true marriage. . .': *Elizabeth Barrett Browning: Letters to her Sister 1846–1859*, ed. L. Huxley (London, 1929).

p. 396   spiritualism and Pen's clothes: C. De L. Ryals, *The Life of Robert Browning: A Critical Biography* (Oxford, 1993), 108, Dally, 168–9.

Henriette Corkran: Richardson, 145.

poor reception of *Men and Women*: Richardson, 133.

p. 397   'heart walking up and down': Browning, letter to her sister, 13 May 1857, Huxley, 272.

'brooding': Richardson, 163.

Hawthorne: Richardson, 165.

Robert's social life: Richardson, 171.

Isa Blagden: Ryals, 135.

Elizabeth's death: *Letters of Robert Browning*, ed. T. Hood (London, 1933), 62–3.

undoing the damage: Ryals, 140.

p. 399   autobiography in *Aurora Leigh*: M. Reynolds, ed., *Aurora Leigh* (Athens OH, 1992) argues that this element has been greatly exaggerated (7–12).

feminists on *Sonnets*: She is often used as the 'token' woman – the civilizing influence of the gentler sex demure in a corner, and represented appropriately by love poems dedicated to her husband. Jeni Couzyn, Introduction, *The Bloodaxe Book of Contemporary Women Poets: Eleven British Writers*, ed. Jeni Couzyn (London, 1985).

p. 401   Male poets writing in English who killed themselves include Sir John Suckling, Thomas Shadwell, Eustace Budgell, Thomas Lovell Beddoes, John Davidson, Adam Lindsay Gordon, Vachel Lindsay, Hart Crane, and John Berryman. As well Gogol, Esenin and Mayakovsky, Kleist, De Nerval, Pavese and Mishima Yukio ended their own lives.

Charlotte Perkins Gilman was seventy-five when she ended her life in 1930.

p. 402   Karoline von Günderrode (1780–1806) came from an impoverished noble family and was a beguine at the Cronstetten-Hynspergische Evsangelical Sisterhood in Frankfurt when she published her poems in 1804 and 1805 under the pseudonym 'Tian'. She attracted the attentions of Clemens Brentano, Freidrich Karl von Savigny and Friedrich Creuzer, whose affection she passionately returned. She stabbed herself when Creuzer broke off their relationship. In 1840 Bettine von Arnim published a version of their correspondence as *Die Günderode*. Günderrode's *Gesammelte Werke* were published in 1970. See Christa Wolf, *No Place on Earth* (London, 1983).

p. 403   'I am I': Amy Levy, *Xantippe* (Cambridge, 1881), 20.

p. 404   'A creature maimed': *A Minor Poet* (London, 1884) 15, 21–2.

'Deep in the grass': *A London Plane-Tree* (London, 1889), 79.

Diakonova: Elisaveta Aleksandrovna Diákonova (1874–1902) became famous after her suicide, through the publication of her diary (1904) which was reprinted three times before 1912.

Renée or René Vivien (1877–1909) was born Pauline Tarn. She began writing stories at six years old and love poems at nine. From 1899 to 1904 she was the lover of Natalie Barney. Barney and Vivien, whose translation of Sappho was published in 1903, hoped to found a Lesbian community at Mitylene. See Karla Jay, *The Amazon and the Page: Natalie Clifford Barney and Renée Vivien* (Bloomington, 1988), and Paul Lorenz, *Sapho 1900: Renée Vivien* (1977) and Clarissa Cooper, *Women Poets of the Twentieth Century in France* (1943).

p. 405 Charlotte Mew, *Collected Poems* (London, 1953), FB 42–3, 'The Quiet House', 48–9; 'From a Window', 54; 'The trees are Down', 57, 'The Changeling', 70–71, *The Mystery of Charlotte Mew and May Sinclair*, T. E. M. Boll (1980); Penelope Fitzgerald, *Charlotte Mew and her Friends* (London, 1984).

p. 407 Florbela de Alma da Conceiçao Espanca (1894–1930) was married three times, always unhappily. Her first volume of verse was called *Livro dos Magoas* (Book of Woes), her second *Livro de Soror Saudad* (Book of Sister Heartache). Her third was published posthumously. See Agustina Bessa Luis, *A Vida e a Obra de Florbela Espanca* (Lisbon, 1979).

Sara Teasdale, *Collected Poems* (New York, 1966); Jean Gould, *American Women Poets: Pioneers of Modern Poetry* (New York, 1980) 85–121; *Mirror of the Heart: Poems of Sara Teasdale*, ed. with Intro. William Drake (New York and London, 1984); Margaret Carpenter, *Sara Teasdale* (New York, 1960); W. Drake, *Sara Teasdale: Woman and Poet* (New York, 1979).

Antonia Pozzi (1912–38): a volume of verse, *Parole*, and a study of Flaubert, were both published posthumously (*Bloomsbury Guide*).

Alfonsina Storni (1892–1938): her first book of poems, *La inquietud del rosal*, was published in 1916, followed by *Languidez* (1921), *Ocre* (1925) and *Mundo de siete pozos* (1934) (*Bloomsbury Guide*).

Robin Hyde: all citations from *Selected Poems*, ed. Lydia Wevers (Auckland, 1984).

p. 408 Charles Brasch, *Indirections: A Memoir 1909–1947* (Wellington, 1980), 340.

p. 409 Virginia Woolf (1900–41): after a series of mental breakdowns she walked into the Ouse with her pockets weighted down with stones.

Karin Boye (1882–1941): published *Moln* (1922), *Gomda Land* (1924), *Härdarne* (1927) and *För Trädets Skull* (1935) (*Bloomsbury Guide*).

'No one can see': The Russian original is to be found in Tsvetayeva, *Neizdannye Pisma* (Paris, 1972), 630, here quoted the translation by Simon Karlinsky, *Marina Tsvetaeva: The Woman, her World and her Poetry* (Cambridge, 1985), 236. Another version of the same passage can be found in Elaine Feinstein, *A Captive Lion: The Life of Marina Tsvetayeva* (London, 1987), 251.

p. 410   Tsvetaeva as mythomane: Karlinsky, 176.

Tsvetaeva as pariah: Karlinsky, 177–8.

dirt: Feinstein, 194.

Mur's reaction: Karlinsky, 245–6.

one of a thousand women: Feinstein, 193.

p. 411   refusal to wear glasses: Feinstein, 43, 178.

death at seventeen: Karlinsky, 39.

Non-existent qualities: Karlinsky, 120.

Tsvetaeva was most unfair to the two people who loved her most faithfully, her husband, Sergei Efron and her daughter, Ariadna, both of whom were loyal to her to the end. After seven years of hard labour followed by seven years in Siberia, though she keenly resented her mother's treatment of her father, whom she idealized, Ariadna devoted her life to collecting and preserving her mother's work, aided by her mother's sister, Anastasia.

Mandelstam: Feinstein, 70.

Moor: Feinstein, 188–9.

p. 412   One of her contemporaries: i.e. Alexei Remizov, Karlinsky, 223; Another: Ivan Bunin, ditto.

'Now what shall I do': Feinstein, 221.

p. 413   'My heart cries': *Mirror of the Heart: Poems of Sara Teasdale*, ed. with Intro. W. Drake (New York and London, 1989), 37, 'Song Making'.

p. 414   Anna Wickham (1884–1947) was born Edith Alice Mary Harper.

'It is the fourth': *The Writings of Anna Wickham, Free Woman and Poet*, ed. with Intro. R. Smith (London, 1984), 'Fragment of an Autobiography: Prelude to a Spring Clean', 51, 52.

'I feel that': *Writings*, 52–3.

'Lawrence Hope': Adele Florence Nicolson (1865–1904) became famous as Lawrence Hope after the publication in 1901 of *The Garden of Kama and Other Love Lyrics from India* (*Feminist Companion*).

p. 415   'She will be a poet': memoir by R. D. Smith, *Writings*, 5.

epigraph: memoir by R. D. Smith, *Writings*, 1.

p. 416   'It's no good': *Writings*, 296.

'Let us consider': *Writings*, 351.

much-deplored husband: Anna Wickham's most anthologized poem, 'Nervous Prostration', begins

> I married a man of the Croydon class,
> When I was twenty-two.
> And I vex him and he bores me
> Till we don't know what to do!

and ends

> And as I sit in his ordered house
> I feel I must sob or shriek,
> To force a man of the Croydon class
> To live, or to love, or to speak!   (*Writings*, 210)

'As I look back': 'Prelude to a Spring Clean', *Writings*, 157.

p. 417   'Often, very often': Anne Sexton, 'The Barfly Ought to Sing', *The Art of Sylvia Plath*, ed. C. Newman, 178.

See also *Sylvia Plath: A Biography*, Linda Wagner Martin (London, 1988); Paul Alexander, *Rough Magic: A Biography of Sylvia Plath* (London, 1991); Anne Stevenson, *Bitter Fame: A Life of Sylvia Plath* (London, 1989); Linda K. Buntzen, *Plath's Incarnations: Woman and the Creative Process*; David Holbrook, *Sylvia Plath: Poetry and Existence* (1976); Mary Lynn Broe, *Protean Poetic: the Poetry of Sylvia Plath* (Columbia MO, 1980).

p. 418   Elizabeth Hardwick, 'On Sylvia Plath', in Paul Alexander, ed., *Ariel Ascending: Writings about Sylvia Plath* (New York, 1975), 102.

'She has posthumous fame': letter from Aurelia Plath to Judith Kroll, 1. 12, 1978, Smith College Library.

Joyce Carol Oates: 'The Death Throes of Romanticism: The Poetry of Sylvia Plath', in M. Butscher, ed., *Sylvia Plath, The Woman and the Work* (New York, 1977), 219.

p. 419   Plath's journal entry: *The Journals of Sylvia Plath*, ed. F. McCullough and Ted Hughes (New York, 1982), 70.

Anne Sexton: A Biography, Diane Wood Middlebrook (London, 1991), xix.

'I have gone out': 'Her Kind', *The Complete Poems of Anne Sexton* (Boston, 1981), 15–16.

p. 420   Louise Bogan: 'Several Voices out of a Cloud', *The Blue Estuaries: Poems 1923–1968* (New York, 1977).

p. 421   Sexton, 'Sylvia's Death': *Complete Poems*, 126.

Sexton, 'Wanting to Die': *Complete Poems*, 142.

tetchy reviewer: Middlebrook, 264.

George MacBeth: Middlebrook, 280.

Adrienne Rich: 'Anne Sexton: 1928–1974', *On Lies, Secrets, and Silence: Selected Prose 1966–1978* (New York, 1979), 122.

p. 422   Anne Stevenson: 'Making Poetry', *Sixty Women Poets*, ed. L. France (London, 1993), 274.

Anne Stevenson: 'And even then', *Sixty Women Poets*, 275.

p. 423   J. C. Squire: *A Book of Women's Verse* (Oxford, 1921), xiii.

Of the eighteen post-Rossetti poets included by Squire, only Ingelow and Meynell, and perhaps Katherine Tynan Hinkson, Frances Cornford and Mary Elizabeth Coleridge, are still read. In 1949, Clifford Bax and Meum Stewart edited an anthology of women's verse called *The Distaff Muse*, in which 117 of the 192 entries were post-Rossetti. Even so, seven of Squire's poets were dropped, Alice Meynell (inexplicably), Fanny Parnell, Rose Terry Cooke (perhaps because she was American), Violet Jacob, Anna Bunston de Bary, Rose Macaulay and Sylvia Lynd. What is apparent from these disparities is that there is little seriousness or method in the attempt to distinguish which women are worthy of notice. Bax and Stewart are so careless that Ingelow's name is spelt Inglelow throughout. Of the fifty-six poets in the post-Rossetti section, twenty-five are unmentioned even by the *Feminist Companion*.

Jean Ingelow (1820–97) was educated 'at home'; she published her first volume of verse in 1850; the second, which contained her best-known poem, 'High Tide on the Coast of Lincolnshire 1571', went through four editions in 1863 and continued to be reprinted over many years. Her British success was replicated in America, where she sold 200,000 copies (*DNB*).

'Violet Fane' is the pseudonym of Mary Montgomerie Singleton, later Lady Currie (1843–1905), who published her first volume of verse *From Dawn to Noon* under that name in 1872 because her family severely disapproved of her activities as poet and painter. In 1875 she published *Denzil Place: a Story in Verse*, in 1876 *The Queen of the Fairies and other Poems*, in 1877 a drama *Anthony Babington*. In 1880 her *Collected Verses* appeared and in 1892 another collected edition in two volumes. At the same time she was well-known as a society hostess. She travelled to Constantinople with her second husband and there produced two more volumes of verse in 1896 and 1900 (*DNB*).

The Hon. Emily Lawless (1845–1913) is not noticed by the *DNB* though she was a well-known novelist and poet of the turn of the century. She was the daughter of Lord Cloncurry, and educated at home. Her first publications were anonymous; in 1886 she successfully published a novel under her own name. Stopford Brooke encouraged her to publish her poems *With the Wild Geese* in 1902. Her second volume of verse, *The Point of View*, was privately printed for the benefit of Galway fishermen in 1909. Her collected poems were published in 1965 (*Feminist Companion*).

Fanny Parnell (1854–82) was the sister of the Irish political leader and wrote poems in support of the Fenian cause; when her American mother returned to the United States she accompanied her and continued to pour out passionate verses in support of the land league that were published in Boston and in Dublin. Her best-known poem, however, is 'After death', which she wrote in anticipation of her own end (*DNB*, 'Charles Stewart Parnell').

Rose Terry Cooke (1827–92) was born in Connecticut and was educated to be a schoolteacher. A legacy enabled her to concentrate on writing, though obliged to care for her dead sister's children. Her first short story was published in 1845 and her first poem in 1851. She published two collections of poems in 1861 and 1888. In 1873 she married Rollin H. Cooke (*Feminist Companion*).

Violet Jacob (1863–1946) though 'recognised in her own time as a skilled poet and fiction writer. . .has been allowed to slip into relative obscurity' according to the editor of her *Diaries and Letters from India* (Edinburgh, 1990). None of the feminist companions or biographical dictionaries mentions her, though Hugh McDiarmid called her 'the most considerable of contemporary vernacular poets' among whom were numbered Helen Cruickshank and Marion Angus. She was born Violet Kennedy Erskine in Angus and married an army officer in 1894, following him the next year with her new-born son to India. Her first published works were novels; in 1915 *Songs of Angus* appeared, followed by *More Songs of Angus* in 1918.

Anna Bunston de Bary is not mentioned by feminist companions or biographical dictionaries though Lady Margaret Sackville, who included ten of her poems in *A Book of Verse by Living Women*, said of her in 1911:

> The carefully-wrought, deep-hearted work of Anna Bunston stands out among more recent productions as worthy of special consideration. Fine, distinguished verse, the expression rarely falling short of its conception.

Her first publication, *Leaves from a Woman's Manuscript: A Ball of Verses,* was well received in 1904, followed by *Mingled Wine* in 1909 and *The Porch of Paradise* in 1911. In 1912 appeared *Songs of God and Man* followed by *Letters of a School-ma'am* in 1913. In 1923 she brought out *New and Selected Lyrics*, and in 1925 a revised edition of *The Porch of Paradise*. In 1931 she wrote a verse play, *Jephtha's Daughter*, and a year later *Verses* appeared. Her collected poems were published in 1947 and two years later *Love and Loss, or Remembering by Night*. She also wrote novels. As none of her work was included in *The Distaff Muse* it seems that by 1949 she had sunk into obscurity.

Eva Gore-Booth (1870–1926) was the best known female disciple of George Russell who, as 'A. E.', was the principal instigator of the Celtic revival. Her first volume of verse was published in 1898. *The One and the Many* (1904) contains her best-known lyric, 'The Little Waves of Breffny'. Gore-Booth never married, but lived with her friend Esther Roper. She is best known to students of twentieth-century poetry through the patronizing elegy Yeats wrote for her and her elder sister, Constance Markiewicz (*Feminist Companion*).

> I know not what the younger dreams –
> Some vague Utopia – and she seems
> When withered old and skeleton-gaunt,
> An image of such politics.

Katherine Tynan Hinkson: see p. xx and n.

Rose Macaulay (1881–1958) is better known as a novelist; her earliest published works were poems sent to the *Westminster Gazette*. She published two books of poems, *The Two Blind Countries* (1914) and *Three Days* (1919) (*DNB*).

Sylvia Lynd (1888–1952) was born in London, educated at the Slade and RADA and married in 1909. Her first volume of poetry, *The Thrush and the Jay* was published in 1916, in between her two novels. She served as literary editor of the *News Chronicle* for many years and published further volumes of verse in 1928 and 1945 (*FCLE*).

Dora Sigerson: see p. xx and n.

'Moira O'Neill' was the pseudonym adopted by Agnes Skrine, the mother of Molly Keane ('M. J. Farrell'). Under this name she was well known as a poet of the Celtic movement together with Lady Gregory, 'Ethna Carbery' (Anna Johnston), Alice Milligan and Eva Gore-Booth.

Mary Elizabeth Coleridge: see p. xx and n.

Margaret L. Woods: see p. xx and n.

Frances Cornford (1886–1960), granddaughter of Charles Darwin, was privately educated and began writing poetry when she was sixteen. She married the Cambridge classicist Francis Cornford in 1908 and published her first book of poems in 1910. Her *Collected Poems* was the official choice of the Poetry Book Society in 1954 and she won the Queen's medal for poetry in 1959 (*DNB*).

Alice Meynell: see p. xx and n.

INDEX